# K–8 INSTRUCTIONAL METHODS

## A Literacy Perspective

Allan C. Ornstein

*St. John's University*

Richard Sinatra

*St. John's University*

PEARSON

Boston | New York | San Francisco
Mexico City | Montreal | Toronto | London | Madrid | Munich | Paris
Hong Kong | Singapore | Tokyo | Cape Town | Sydney

*Series Editor:*   Traci Mueller
*Series Editorial Assistant:*   Janice Hackenberg
*Senior Marketing Manager:*   Elizabeth Fogarty
*Editorial-Production Service:*   Omegatype Typography, Inc.
*Composition Buyer:*   Linda Cox
*Manufacturing Buyer:*   Andrew Turso
*Cover Administrator:*   Linda Knowles
*Electronic Composition:*   Omegatype Typography, Inc.

For related titles and support materials, visit our online catalog at www.ablongman.com.

Between the time Website information is gathered and published, some sites may have closed. Also, the transcription of URLs can result in typographical errors. The publisher would appreciate notification where these errors occur so that they may be corrected in subsequent editions.

**Library of Congress Cataloging-in-Publication Data**

Ornstein, Allan C.
    K–8 instructional methods : a literary perspective / Allan C. Ornstein, Richard Sinatra.
      p.    cm.
    Includes bibliographical references and index.
    ISBN 0-205-40267-4
    1. Language arts (Elementary)   2. Language arts—Correlation with content subjects.
  3. Content area reading.   I. Sinatra, Richard.   II. Title.

LB1576.O78  2005
372.6—dc22

                                                                        2004044691

Printed in the United States of America

10  9  8  7  6  5  4  3  2  1      09  08  07  06  05  04

## Chapter Three
## Word Acquisition and Understanding          76

## Chapter Six
## Instructional Planning     177

*Chapter Eleven*

Strategies for Understanding Literature and Informational Sources     346

# Chapter Thirteen
## Assessing and Evaluating Students  408

This text, *K–8 Instructional Methods: A Literacy Perspective,* provides a comprehensive overview of content and pedagogy taught in methods courses accenting instruction from the primary to eighth grades. The authors have written the book for students who are preparing for or are engaged in a teaching career and who desire to learn how literacy instruction impacts the entire curriculum. We are of firm conviction that K–8 instructional methods and techniques need to be reconceptualized and revisited to stress the effects of listening, speaking, reading, writing, viewing, and computer skills through all of our students' content coursework. Students' success in school, particularly in these days of vigorous academic standards and high-stakes testing, is related to their abilities to read, comprehend, analyze, and reflect through critical thinking, writing, and computer interactions. In short, students' academic success is based on their abilities to read and think about the content and ideas in their reading books or workbooks, their trade books, textbooks, and World Wide Web informational sources.

We reach out to preservice and inservice education students presenting relevant instructional methods, strategies, and techniques to help them develop an understanding of what it is like to teach. We have organized the material in a realistic and easy-to-read form, assuming that the reader has had limited experience with teaching. We have presented the material from an educator's point of view, with the ideas of integrating theory with practice and of improving the teaching and learning process. We attempt to show that teachers can make a difference with good instructional practices that emphasize reading and related literacy development through the grades and the content subjects.

In addition to the book's generic literacy emphasis, the authors have noted how reading and literacy development have a significant bearing on other themes prevalent in modern education, these being (1) diversity and multiculturalism, (2) special and disabled learners, (3) at-risk, economically disadvantaged students, and (4) technology and computers. The book contains a number of textually appealing, graphic features in efforts to make the reading user friendly. These features are:

- **Focusing Questions** at the beginning of each chapter to whet the reader's mental appetite about the content to follow
- **Headings** that are short and easy to follow and facilitate understanding of main ideas
- **Boxed features** to emphasize and illustrate topic concepts
- **Tables** that graphically illustrate key points and concepts
- **Research findings** that emphasize results of instructional methodologies, curriculum approaches, and teaching and learning practices
- **Tips for Teachers** which highlight teaching strategies and provide practical advice
- **Summaries** at each chapter's end that are sequenced to correspond with the chapter's narrative
- **Things to Do** and **Questions to Consider** at chapters' ends to provide practical, useful suggestions in applying the instructional ideas offered and questions about content
- **Recommended Readings** which offer additional reading sources relevant to each chapter's content and ideas

# ■ ACKNOWLEDGMENTS AND DEDICATION

We wish to thank our colleagues, secretarial staff, and student assistants at St. John's University. They aided us greatly in the production required to complete the book. Special thanks go to Leeanne G. Bowley, who typed some chapters of the book, and to graduate assistant Marie Dolce, who ensured that many of the text references and research citations were in correct format. Two undergraduate students used their computer talents to enhance the text features. Initially Kwok Fan Chow executed most of the chapter figures, tables, and charts and designed them to fit text specifications. Kamille James added many boxed features and continued designing additional figures.

The thoughts and suggestions of the reviewers are acknowledged, namely, Patricia Anders, University of Arizona; Belinda Anderson, Lambuth University; Mary Hamm, San Francisco State University; Marie Lassmann, Texas A & M University; Marc Mahlios, University of Kansas; and Patricia McGee, University of Texas at San Antonio.

Finally, Dr. Ornstein wishes to acknowledge and dedicate the book to his wife Esther, sometimes called Theresa Bear, with love and affection. Then there is always Joel, Stacey, and Jason—lively, optimistic, confident, and steadfast. Dr. Sinatra acknowledges and dedicates the book to his wife, Camille Sinatra, who encouraged and respected his quiet writing time, and to the Department of Human Services and Counseling secretary, Ann DePaulis. Mrs. DePaulis not only typed many of the chapters, but also her meticulous work and steadfast production kept the coauthor in the mental and writing game.

*chapter* **1**

# Theories of Learning

1. Why is the study of learning theories important for the teacher?
2. How would you compare classical conditioning with operant conditioning?
3. In what way does modeling influence performance?
4. How would you compare behaviorism with cognitive psychology?
5. What are the differences and similarities between Piaget's thinking and Bruner's thinking?
6. What are the differences between moral knowledge, moral character, and moral development? How does values clarification foster moral thinking?
7. How can students learn how to learn? What cognitive processes contribute to learning?
8. What is critical thinking? How can teachers teach critical thinking?

Historically, two major theories of learning have been classified: (1) **behaviorism** or association theories, the oldest of which deals with various aspects of stimulus-response and reinforcers, and (2) **cognitive psychology,** which views the learner in relationship to the total environment and considers ways in which learners apply information. When behaviorist theories are discussed separately, learning tends to focus on conditioning, modifying, or shaping behavior through reinforcement and rewards. Many of our ideas about goals, objectives and standards, practice and drill, classroom management, and teacher education programs involve behaviorist theory. When cognitive psychology (or cognitive information) theories are stressed, the learning process focuses on the student's developmental stages, environmental experiences, and problem-solving strategies. Both schools of thought consider phenomenological aspects of learning, which deal with the needs, attitudes, and feelings of the learner—what some educators might call the affective domain of learning (Krathwohl, Bloom, & Masia, 1964).

Both schools are concerned with the teaching and learning process, and teachers need to understand how the theories of each can contribute to this process. Questions of mutual interest to psychologists and teachers include the following: What are the most effective teaching methods for a specific group of students? How do teachers respond as they do to the efforts of students? What is the impact of prior experience on student learning? How do cultural experiences (or differences) influence student learning? How does age (or maturation) affect learning? How should curriculum and instruction be organized to enhance learning?

For John Dewey (1938), psychology was the basis for understanding how the environment (in our case, how the teacher can modify the environment) helps the learner improve his or her reasoning process. The process goes on for life, and the quality of interaction determines the amount and type of learning. Jerome Bruner (1959) linked psychology with modes of thinking that underlie bodies of knowledge comprising specific disciplines. The goal of the teacher was to teach the concepts, principles, and generalizations that form the structure of specific disciplines, especially in math and science.

For the last fifty years, B. F. Skinner has been the most quoted learning psychologist. His basic principle for learning is that the teacher can modify and shape student behavior by consistently and systematically rewarding appropriate behavior and eliminating rewards (sometimes punishing) for inappropriate behavior. The use of proper rewards and punishments forms the basis of learning, as well as manipulating the surface behavior (what we call classroom management in schools) of learners. Parents, teachers, and the clergy are always modifying and shaping the behavior of the young, just as CEOs, spouses, and drill sergeants modify and shape the behavior of adults.

Within the same fifty-year period, Jean Piaget has been the second most quoted learning psychologist. He has influenced the world of environmental and cognitive psychology—the idea that learning can be inhibited or enhanced by experience. During their waking hours, children and youth are always engaged in some form of learning; the teacher needs to shape their environment, to help them learn particular knowledge, concepts, and skills. The central problem is for the teacher to provide proper stimuli (methods, materials, media, etc.) on which to focus students' attention and efforts to enhance learning.

# ■ BEHAVIORISM

The behaviorists, who represent traditional psychology, are rooted in philosophical speculation about the nature of learning—the ideas of Aristotle, Descartes, Locke, and Rousseau. They emphasize conditioning behavior and altering the environment to elicit selected responses from the learner. This theory has dominated much of twentieth-century psychology.

## Classical Conditioning

The **classical conditioning** theory of learning emphasizes that learning consists of eliciting a response by means of previously neutral or inadequate stimuli; some neutral stimulus associated with an unconditioned stimulus at the time of response gradually acquires the ability to elicit the response. The classical conditioning experiment by Ivan Pavlov conducted in 1903 and 1904 is widely known. In this experiment, a dog learned to salivate at the sound of a bell. The bell, a biologically neutral or inadequate stimulus, was being presented simultaneously with food, a biologically nonneutral or inadequate stimulus. So closely were the two stimuli associated by the dog that the bell came to be substituted for the food, and the dog reacted to the bell as he originally had to the food (Pavlov, 1927).

The implications for human learning were important. Some neutral stimulus (bell) associated with an unconditioned stimulus (food) at the same time of the response gradually acquired the association to elicit the response (salivation). The theory has led to a wealth of laboratory investigations about learning and has become a focal point in social and political discussions—for example, Aldous Huxley's futuristic novel *Brave New World* and the movies *The Deer Hunter, Jacob's Ladder,* and *The Silence of the Lambs.*

On the U.S. scene, James Watson (1939) used Pavlov's research as a foundation for building a new science of psychology based on behaviorism. The new science emphasized that learning was based on the science of behavior, what was observable or measurable, and not on cognitive processes. The laws of behavior were derived from animal and then human studies and were expected to have all the objectivity of the laws of science.

For Watson and others, the key to learning was to condition the child in the early years of life, based on the method Pavlov had demonstrated for animals. Thus Watson (1926) once boasted: "Give me a dozen healthy infants, well-informed, and my own specified world to bring them up and I'll guarantee to take anyone at random and train him to be any type of specialist I might select—a doctor, lawyer, artist . . . and yes into beggar man and thief, regardless of his talents . . . abilities, vocations and race" (p. 10).

## Connectionism

One of the first Americans to conduct experimental testing of the learning process was Edward Thorndike, who is considered the founder of behavioral psychology. At Harvard, Thorndike (1911) began his work with animals, a course of experimentation other behaviorists adopted as well. Thorndike focused on testing the relationship between a stimulus and a response (classical conditioning). He defined learning as habit formation—as connecting more and more habits into a complex structure. He defined teaching, then, as arranging the classroom so as to enhance desirable connections into bonds.

Thorndike (1913) developed three major **laws of learning:** (1) the *Law of Readiness*—when a "conduction" unit is ready to conduct, to do so is satisfying and not to do so is annoying; (2) the *Law of Exercise*—a connection is strengthened in proportion to the number of times it occurs, and in proportion to average intensity and duration; and (3) the *Law of Effect*—responses accompanied by discomfort weaken the connection.

The Law of Readiness suggests that when the nervous system is ready to conduct, it leads to a satisfying state of affairs; this has been misinterpreted by some educators as referring to educational readiness, such as readiness to read. The Law of Exercise provides justification for drill, repetition, and review and is best illustrated today by instruction in basic math and foreign language classes and basic skills instructional approaches. Although rewards and punishments were used in schools for centuries prior to Thorndike's formulation of the Law of Effect, his theory did make this system more explicit and furnished justification for what was already being done. B. F. Skinner's operant model of behavior, programmed instruction, military training, and many current ideas based on providing satisfying (and unsatisfying) experiences to the learner, as well as reinforcement in the form of prompt feedback, are rooted in this law.

Thorndike maintained that (1) behavior was more likely influenced by conditions of learning; (2) attitudes and abilities of learners could change (and improve) over time through proper stimuli; (3) instructional experiences could be designed and controlled; and (4) it was important to select appropriate stimuli or learning experiences that were integrated and consistent—and that reinforced one another. For Thorndike (1924), no one subject was more likely than another to improve the mind; rather, learning was a matter of relating new learning to previous learning (an idea that both Dewey and Tyler later adopted). According to Thorndike, the view that one particular subject is better than another subject for "improvement of the mind . . . seems doomed to disappointment." The fact is, "good thinkers" take certain subjects, not that certain subjects result in good thinking. "If the abler pupils should all study physical education and dramatic art, these subjects would seem to make good thinkers" (p. 98).

Thus, Thorndike was critical of the "psychology of mental discipline," the dominant theory of learning at the turn of the twentieth century and advocated by traditional educators of the era. In his approach, there was no hierarchy of subject matter and learning involved constructs between stored knowledge, memories of experience, and new information or stimuli—a schema theory similar to Piaget's and Bruner's notions of knowledge acquisition and comprehension.

But entrenched beliefs die hard. Traditional educators argued that certain subjects such as Latin, classical studies, rhetoric, and mathematics were most valuable for training the mind, that such training was transferable to various mental tasks, and that such subjects (or lack of these subjects) led to "superior" and "inferior" curriculum tracks. This view was criticized not only by Thorndike but also subsequently by John Dewey (1938) and other progressive educators who felt that such a mind-set was rooted in traditionalism and elitism and that the underlying philosophy taught students "docility, receptivity, and obedience" (p. 18).

Although the two most prominent educators of the era (Thorndike and Dewey) objected to the mental discipline approach, these ideas for the next fifty years served as a basis for formulating the standard elementary and secondary curriculum, with the concurrent belief that the right of students to an education should persist only as far as their intellectual capabilities. Little recognition or provision was made for the less able student—well illustrated by the fact that as late as 1950 the high school dropout rate was as high as 40 percent, and only 27 percent of eighteen- to twenty-one-year-olds were enrolled in college (Ornstein & Hunkins, 2004).

The Committee of Fifteen (1895), the prestigious and conservative task force headed by Charles Eliot, then president of Harvard University, solidified this position. It was reported that "grammar, literature, arithmetic, geography and history [were] the subjects in the elementary school with the greatest value for training the mind"(p. 284). This view set the tone for education during the entire twentieth century, especially in the post-Sputnik and cold war era, when the subjects with the greatest value were considered to be math and science. Music, art, and physical education were considered secondary or unimportant, an idea that persists today in many schools in which essentialist philosophy and back-to-basics have been revived under the banner of standards-based education and school reform.

## Operant Conditioning

Perhaps more than any other recent behaviorist, B. F. Skinner attempted to apply his theories to the classroom (see Box 1.1 for a discussion of conditioning taken to excessive lengths). Basing a major part of his theories on experiments with mice and pigeons, Skinner (1953) distinguishes two kinds of response: *elicited,* a response identified with a definite stimulus, and *emitted,* a response that is apparently unrelated to an identifiable stimulus. When a response is elicited, the behavior is termed *respondent.* When it is emitted, the behavior is **operant**—that is, no observable or measurable stimuli explain the appearance of the response. In operant conditioning, the role of the stimuli is less definite; often the emitted behavior cannot be connected to a specific stimulus.

Reinforcers can be classified as primary, secondary, or generalized. A *primary reinforcer* applies to any stimulus that helps satisfy a basic drive, such as those for food, water, or sex. (This reinforcer is also paramount in classical conditioning.) For students, *secondary reinforcers* consist of things such as getting approval from friends or teachers, receiving good grades, or winning school awards. Although secondary reinforcers do not satisfy primary drives, they can be converted into primary reinforcers because of their choice and range, and therefore Skinner refers to them as *generalized reinforcers.* Classroom teachers have a wide variety of secondary reinforcers at their disposal, ranging from words of praise or smiles to words of admonishment or punishment.

Operant behavior will discontinue when it is not followed by reinforcement. Skinner classifies reinforcers as positive or negative. A *positive*

**BOX 1.1**   Hijacking the Mind

Money, for most people, is similar to drugs, food, or sex—or anything a person expects as a reward; cookies and candy have a similar effect on small children. People crave it! Anything that people crave can be used as a vehicle for modifying behavior. Some people crave winning in sports because of the recognition or money and will engage in unethical behavior to get it; others crave power and will steal or kill to maintain it; still others crave martyrdom and will commit suicide for the emperor, the fuhrer, or Allah. Once the mind is hijacked (conditioned), to the point that the person loses a sense of conscious awareness, he or she becomes capable of engaging in group behavior, even fanatic behavior. Once humans lose sight of their individual thoughts or consciences and become part of group or mob behavior, then all forms of atrocities and vile deeds are possible. If the desire is to condition people to commit murder, it is easier if the reward is fixed to some political or religious utopia.

reinforcer is simply the presentation of a reinforcing stimulus. A student receives positive reinforcement when a test paper is returned with a grade of A or a note that says, "Keep up the good work." A *negative* reinforcer is the removal or withdrawal of a stimulus. When a teacher shouts to the class "Keep quiet," and the students quiet down, the students' silence reinforces the teacher's shouting. Punishment, on the other hand, calls for the presentation of unpleasant or harmful stimuli or the withdrawal of a (positive) reinforcer, but it is not always a negative reinforcer (Skinner, 1953, 1970). Although Skinner believes in both positive and negative reinforcement, he rejects punishment because he feels it inhibits learning.

## Acquiring New Operants

Skinner's (1970) approach of selective reinforcement, whereby only desired responses are reinforced, has wide appeal to educators because he has demonstrated its application to the instructional and learning process. An essential principle in the reinforcement interpretation of learning is the variability of human behavior, which makes change possible. Individuals can acquire *new operants*—that is, behavior can be shaped or modified, and complex concepts can be taught to students. The individual's capability for making the desired response is what makes the shaping of behavior or the learning possible. Behavior and learning can be shaped through a series of successive approximations or a sequence of responses that increasingly approximate the desired one. Thus, through a combination of reinforcing and sequencing desired responses, new behavior is shaped; this is what some people today refer to as **behavior modification.**

Although behavior modification approaches vary according to the student and the behavior being sought, they are widely used in conjunction with individualized instructional techniques, programmed and computerized learning, and classroom management techniques. Student activities are specified, structured, paced, reinforced, rewarded, and frequently assessed in terms of learning outcomes or behaviors desired. With this approach, curricula can be defined by Popham and Baker's (1970) definition: "all planned outcomes for which the school is responsible and the desired consequences of instruction" (p. 48; see also Popham, 1999).

## Observational Learning and Modeling

Albert Bandura (1977, 1986) has contributed extensively to what we know today about how aggressive behavior can be learned from viewing human adults acting aggressively in real situations as well as in movies and television; the same children also learned nonaggressive behavior by observing humans of subdued temperaments.

The repeated demonstration that people can learn and have their behavior shaped by observing another person or even a film (obviously, the influence of television is immense) has tremendous implications for modifying tastes and attitudes (e.g., whether we deserve to take a break at McDonalds or Burger King), for determining how we learn and perform, and for deciding whether as a society we want to develop soldiers or artists. For behaviorists, the idea suggests that cognitive factors are unnecessary in explaining learning; through **modeling**, students can learn how to perform at sophisticated levels. They can learn how to ski, participate in democratic citizenry, learn how to use literacy skills and conventions, engage in moral or caring behavior, or become the culprit in a shootout in the school cafeteria. While recognizing the value of reinforcement and reward, the learner needs mainly to attend to and acquire the necessary responses through observation and then to model the behavior later (see Tips for Teachers 1.1).

Bandura (1977, 1986) is also associated with the theories of **vicarious learning.** Although most modeling is reinforced by first observing and then imitating behavior, others learn by seeing other people rewarded or punished for engaging in certain behaviors. We all know that our chances of winning the lottery are perhaps one out of ten million, but seeing or reading about others rewarded makes many of us participate—actually "throw away money." Teachers use the same principle in rewarding certain behaviors in front of the class, providing verbal praise or displaying a student's work on the bulletin board.

*Tips for Teachers* **1.1**

## Behaviorism in Classroom Learning Situations

A wide range of behaviors can be used when applying behavioral theories in the classroom. The following suggestions have meaning for behaviorist teaching and learning situations.

1. Consider that behavior is the result of particular conditions; alter conditions to achieve desired behaviors.
2. Use reinforcement and rewards to strengthen the behavior you wish to encourage.
3. Consider reducing the frequency of undesirable behaviors through punishment.
4. Reduce undesirable behaviors as follows:
   a. Withhold reinforcement or ignore the behavior.
   b. Call attention to rewards that will follow the desired behavior.
   c. Take away a privilege or resort to punishment.
5. When students are learning factual material, provide frequent feedback; for abstract or complex material, provide delayed feedback.
6. Provide practice, drill, and review exercises; monitor learners' progress.
7. Consider workbooks, programmed materials, and computer programs that rely on sequenced approaches.
8. When students struggle with uninteresting material, use special reinforcers and rewards to motivate them.
   a. Select a variety of reinforcers students enjoy (candy bars, bubble gum, baseball cards).
   b. Establish a contract for work to be performed to earn a particular award or grade.
   c. Provide frequent, immediate rewards.
9. Make use of observational learning.
   a. Select the most appropriate model.
   b. Model the behavior clearly and accurately.
   c. Insist that learners attend to what is being modeled.
   d. Provide praise when the desired behavior is exhibited.
   e. Have the learner practice the observed behavior.
   f. Provide corrective feedback during practice.
   g. Repeat demonstrations when necessary.
10. Assess changes in learning and behavior.
    a. Diagnose learning problems.
    b. Establish levels of competency or mastery.
    c. Provide feedback.
    d. Integrate old tasks or skills with new ones.
    e. Reteach, when necessary.

## Behaviorism and Teaching

Behaviorism still exerts a major impact on education. Teachers who are behaviorists use many principles of behaviorism in the classroom and in creating new programs. Although what influences learning differs for different students, teachers can adopt procedures to increase the likelihood that each student will find learning relevant and enjoyable. When new topics or activities are introduced, connections should be built on positive experiences each student has had. Things about which students are likely to have negative feelings should be identified and modified, if possible, to produce positive results.

The behaviorists believe that the curriculum should be organized so students experience success in mastering the subject matter. Of course, all teachers, regardless of their psychological camp, hold this view. The difference is that behaviorists are highly prescriptive and diagnostic in their approach, and they rely on step-by-step, structured methods of teaching; learning is monitored and broken down into small tasks with appropriate sequencing of tasks and reinforcement of desired behaviors.

Behaviorist theories, it should be noted, have been criticized as describing learning too simply and mechanically—and as perhaps reflecting overreliance on classical animal experimentation. Human learning involves complex thinking processes beyond respondent conditioning (or recall and habit) and operant conditioning (or emitted and reinforced behavior). A further concern, according to Robert Travers (1982), is that there is little justification for defining learning in terms of "collection of small bits of behavior each of which has to be learned separately." Although behavior consists of organized sequences, it is not a collection of tiny bits of behavior. The stress on prescribed, lockstep procedures and tasks—and a "belief that a behavioral science should be definable in terms of observable events—[are] hardly justifiable today" (p. 505).

The latter criticism may be an overstatement because many behaviorists today recognize cognitive processes much more than do classical or stimulus-response theorists, and they are flexible enough to admit that learning can occur without the individual's having to act on the environment or exhibit overt behavior. To the extent that traditional behavioral theory can be faulted for having to rely on identifying all behavior, many contemporary behaviorists are willing to consider that cognitive processes partially explain aspects of learning.

But behaviorism is alive and well; it is linked to many current educational practices affecting classrooms and schools. Wrote Robert Glaser (1979) some twenty-five plus years ago:

> Much of the application of psychological theory currently going on in schools represents the earlier behavioristic approach. The concepts of behavioral objectives, and behavior modification, for example, now pervade all levels of education, including special education, elementary school instruction in basic literary skills and personalized systems of instruction (p. 12)

The same statement could be made today; and it would be appropriate to add such behavioral approaches as mastery learning, outcomes-based, and standards-based education. In general, combining behaviorism with learning includes careful analyzing and sequencing of the learner's needs and behaviors. The principles of testing, monitoring, drilling, and feedback are characteristic. The learning conditions needed for successful outcomes are carefully planned through small instructional steps and sequences of responses that increasingly approximate the desired behavior or learning. The teacher emphasizes a carefully planned lesson and clearly stated objectives, coinciding with logically organized materials with emphasis on getting the "correct" answer or achieving clearly defined outcomes. The teacher monitors the progress of students on a regular basis, using individualized materials, tutoring, and small-group projects. These basic principles tend to coincide with today's basic skills training programs in reading and language development, as well as methods of individualized instruction, direct instruction, continuous progress, instructional design, and competency-based education. Although these procedures are predetermined, linear, and planned in advance, some observers might claim they have a cognitive flavor, too.

The contributions of behaviorists to both psychology and education, as well as teaching and learning, were great during the twentieth century, and it is likely that behaviorism will continue to influence the teaching field. However, most behaviorists are aware that as we learn more about learners and learning we cannot adhere to rigid doctrines. Human beings are not pigeons or mice, the subjects of early behaviorists. We are a little more complicated in terms of thinking and behavior. Perspectives that allow for investigations of the mind and psyche have been incorporated into behaviorism. Cognitive developmental theories are being integrated into some behaviorists' approaches to human learning—often called cognitive psychology or cognitive science.

# ■ COGNITIVE LEARNING

Anytime we categorize any phenomenon, we run the risk of misinterpretation. Today, most psychologists classify human growth and development as cognitive, social, psychological, and physical. And though an individual grows and develops along all these fronts, most psychologists agree that learning in school is mainly cognitive in nature. Despite this acknowledgment, some psychologists, known as **developmentalists,** are more concerned with the developmental aspect of human learning; others, known as *cognitive structuralists,* focus more on the ways in which content is structured for learning; and a third major group, the *cognitive scientists,* investigates the various cognitive structures that individuals create in order to generate meaning and ultimately knowledge. **Constructivism,** a fashionable and perhaps overused term, is nothing more than old-fashioned John Dewey, Jean Piaget, L. S. Vygotsky, and Jerome Bruner mixed together with some new vocabulary, in which students acquire learning strategies and integrate (or construct) new information with social experiences to form new knowledge (Glassman, 2001; Prawat, 2000). It represents the learner's awareness of and control over cognitive processes—usually high-order mental processes.

Most, if not all, psychologists would agree that humans and their learning are the sum total of the results of their interactions with their world. However, there is no agreed-on way to determine exactly to what extent an individual's characteristics (cognitive, social, psychological, and physical) are the result of inherited limitations or potential (harmful or favorable circumstances) and of a person's environment. Considerable controversy continues about the extent or role of heredity versus environment in determining cognitive outcomes (that is, IQ scores and achievement scores) in school. As an increasing number of educators view the results of schooling as more than just achievement scores, these debates are likely to intensify. It is essential that teachers be aware of these debates because the issue affects teaching and learning theories.

## Piaget's Cognitive Theory

Most **cognitive theory** is developmental; that is, it supposes that growth and development occur in progressive stages. Jean Piaget represents the most comprehensive view of this theory. The Swiss psychologist's work came to the attention of U.S. educators during the 1950s and 1960s, coinciding with the rising influence of cognitive developmental psychology, environmentalist theories, and the subsequent compensatory education movement.

Like many other investigators today, Piaget (1950) describes cognitive development in terms of stages from birth to maturity. The overall stages can be summarized as follows (Piaget, 1950):

1. *Sensorimotor stage* (birth to age two). The child progresses from reflex operations and undifferentiated surroundings to complex sensorimotor actions in relation to environmental patterns. The child comes to realize that objects have permanence; they can be found again. The child begins to establish simple relations between similar objects.

2. *Preoperational stage* (ages two to seven). In this stage, objects and events begin to take on symbolic meaning. For example, a chair is for sitting; clothing is what we wear. The child shows an increased ability to learn more complex concepts from experience as long as familiar examples are provided from which to extract criteria that define the concept. (For example, oranges, apples, and bananas are fruit; the child should have the chance to touch and eat them.)

3. *Concrete operations stage* (ages seven to eleven). The child begins to organize data into logical relationships and gains facility in manipulating data in problem-solving situations. This learning situation occurs, however, only if concrete objects are available or if actual past experiences can be drawn on. This child is able to make judgments in terms of *reversibility* and reciprocal relations (for example, that the left and right are relative to spatial relations) and *conservation* (that is, a long narrow glass may hold the same amount of water as a short wide one).

4. *Formal operations stage* (age eleven and onward). This stage is characterized by the development of formal and abstract operations. The adolescent is able to analyze ideas and comprehend spatial and temporal relationships. The young person can think logically about abstract data, evaluate data according to acceptable criteria, formulate hypotheses, and deduce possible consequences from them. He or she can construct theories and reach conclusions without having had direct experience in the subject. At this stage (by age fifteen to sixteen), there are few or no limitations on what the adolescent can learn: Learning depends on his or her intellectual potential and environmental experiences. Theoretically, by age sixteen a student should be able to learn any subject, including advanced courses in calculus, physics, statistics, or philosophy. The only possible

barrier, besides the teacher's low expectations of the student, is a lack of the learner's prerequisite content. Theoretically, there is no longer need to postpone "tough" or highly abstract subject matter.

Piaget's cognitive stages presuppose a **maturation process** in the sense that development is a continuation and is based on previous growth. The mental operations are sequential and successive. The stages are hierarchical, and they form an order of increasingly sophisticated and integrated mental operations. Although the succession of stages is constant, stages of attainment vary within certain limits that are a function of heredity and environment. Although hereditary or environmental factors may speed up or slow down cognitive development, they do not change the stages or the sequence.

Environmental experience is the key to Piaget's cognitive theories, as it was also the crux of Dewey's (1938) learning principles. The educator's role involves "the shaping of actual experience by environing conditions" and knowing "what surroundings are conducive to having experiences that lead to growth" (p. 40). Three basic cognitive processes form the basis of the environmental and experiential theories of both Piaget and Dewey.

For Piaget (1932), **assimilation** is the incorporation of new experiences into existing experiences; it represents a coordination of the child's experiences into his or her environment. But assimilation alone does not give the child the capacity to handle new situations and new problems in context with present cognitive structures. The child must organize and develop new cognitive structures in context with existing structures—that is, how he or she thinks. This is **accommodation,** whereby the child's existing structures are modified and adapted in response to his or her environment. **Equilibration** is the process of achieving balance between those things that were previously understood and those yet to be understood; it refers to the dual process of assimilation and accommodation of one's environment.

This coincides with Dewey's (1938) "conceptions of situation and interaction [which] are inseparable from each other" and which form the basis of continuity (p. 43). For Dewey, a *situation* represents the experiences of the environment affecting the child, similar to Piaget's assimilation. *Interaction* is concerned with current or latitudinal transactions taking place between the child and his or her environment, including his or her capacities to establish meaning, similar to Piaget's accommodation. *Continuity* refers to longitudinal learning or to situations and interactions that follow, similar to Piaget's equilibration.

## Bruner: Structure of Subject Matter

The notion of **structure of subject matter** advocated by Jerome Bruner (1959) and Phil Phenix (1964) during the post–World War II era encourages the teacher to teach "deep understanding" of the content, the basic logic or structure of each major discipline—the key relationships, concepts, principles, and research methods. This is what Harry Broudy called "applicable knowledge," what Lee J. Schulman called "procedural knowledge," what E. D. Hirsch called "process," and what some old-fashioned educators, including John Dewey, might call "problem solving" and some more recent educators such as Lauren Resnick and Robert Sternberg might call "critical thinking."

The idea is to go beyond the realm of knowledge to higher-order processes—such as understanding, analysis, and problem solving—by teaching the underlying concepts and principles of a subject. The idea is also to teach learners how to learn on their own, how to inquire and hypothesize, by using the investigative methods of the subject to acquire and assimilate new information. The student who cultivates fluency with this mode of inquiry attains mastery of the content area and is able to continue independently his or her own self-paced learning in the subject area. As Jacques Barzun (1944) said more than half a century ago, a good education produces learners who are capable of, and very much inclined toward, lifelong growth and education.

Age is not a hindrance. The process can start at the primary grade level. All that's needed is for the teacher to teach the concepts and principles of the subject that are relevant and meaningful to the age (and abilities) of the student. So first graders are asked by the teacher to rub their hands together and feel the heat produced—a concept that deals with high school physics but is taught in a manner suitable for the child. For supporters of this approach, students would employ the methods of scientists or mathematicians when learning science or mathematics. When studying history or geography, the students would employ the methods of historians and geographers. The goal is for students to become "little scholars" in their respective fields and for high-achieving students to take more demanding course work.

Subjects such as language arts, social studies, general science, and global studies are not considered real subjects, or what Bruner refers to as "disciplines," because they lack structure and a clear domain of knowledge. These are **broad field subjects,** originally popularized in the 1940s and 1950s and based on an interdisciplinary design in an effort to correct what many educators (including John Dewey and later Ralph Tyler) considered the fragmentation and compartmentalization of subject matter. Whereas the broad fields approach is an attempt to integrate content that appears to fit logically, the notions of "structure" and "disciplined knowledge" represent the content of a "real" field of study (such as English, mathematics, history, science, and foreign languages, as well as music and art), adopted by scholars and leading to "deep meaning" and research inquiry.

Piaget's equilibration forms the basis of Bruner's notion of a **spiral curriculum,** in which previous learning is the basis of subsequent learning, learning should be continuous, and content in a subject field is related to and built and expands on a foundation (from grade to grade). Bruner is also influenced by Dewey, who uses the term *continuity in learning* to explain that what a person has already learned "becomes an instrument of understanding and dealing effectively with the situations that follow." Bruner (1959) also uses the term *continuity,* in the same way as Piaget and Dewey, to describe the spiral curriculum; subject matter and mental operations can be "continually deepened by using them in a progressively more complex form" (p. 13).

## ■ MORAL LEARNING

How a person develops morally is partially, if not predominantly, based on cognitive and social development, on the way he or she interacts with family, schools, and society—more precisely, on the roles and responsibilities he or she learns and deems important based on contact with people who are considered important.

Schools have traditionally been concerned with the moral education of children. In the nineteenth century, moral education became linked to obedience and conformity to rules and regulations. Standards of moral behavior were enforced by rewards and punishments and were translated into grades in what at different times were called morals and manners, citizenship, conduct, or social behavior.

Until the middle of the nineteenth century, public schools typically exhibited a strong, nonsectarian Protestant tone, which was reflected in activities such as Bible readings, prayers, and the content of instructional materials such as the McGuffey readers. By the turn of the twentieth century, the notion of moral education shifted to purely secular activities such as student cooperation in class, extracurricular activities, student councils, flag salutes, assembly rituals, and school service. In short, schools have never ignored moral education, but teachers have often avoided the teaching of morality because of its subjective nature and its potential trappings of or overlap with religious indoctrination.

## Moral Knowledge

Is it possible to give instruction in **moral knowledge** and ethics? We can discuss philosophers such as Socrates, Immanuel Kant, and Jean-Paul Sartre; religious leaders such as Moses, Jesus, Mohammed, and Confucius; and political leaders such as Abraham Lincoln, Mohandas Gandhi, and Martin Luther King Jr. Through the study of the writings and principles of these people generally considered to be moral, students can learn about moral knowledge. For young readers, there are Aesop's fables and "Jack and the Beanstalk." For older children, there are *Sadako, Up from Slavery,* and the *Diary of Anne Frank.* And for adolescents, there are *Of Mice and Men, A Man for All Seasons, Lord of the Flies,* and *Death of a Salesman.* All these books deal with moral and value-laden issues. Whose morality? Whose values? There are agreed-on virtues such as honesty, hard work, integrity, civility, caring, and so forth that represent an American consensus. The consensus is there if we have sufficient moral conviction to find it. See Box 1.2 for an elaboration on a moral curriculum.

According to Philip Phenix (1964), the most important sources of moral knowledge are the laws and customs of society, and they can be taught in courses dealing with law, ethics, and sociology. However, moral conduct cannot be taught; rather, it is learned by "participating in everyday life of society according to recognized standards of society" (pp. 220–221). Although laws and customs and obedience to them are not always morally right, accepted standards do provide guidance for conduct and behavior.

**BOX 1.2**  On Defining Good Reading

Readings in school should have a moral flavor to encourage discussion, thinking, and ultimately the transformation of the learner. Even at the primary grade level, time must not be wasted by assigning *See Spot Run* or *A Sunday Trip to Granny's;* rather, the emphasis should be on folktales and stories such as "Jack and the Beanstalk," "Rumplestiltskin," "Seasons," and "The Mouse and the Wizard"—stories from all parts of the world.

The relationship between history, literary criticism, and philosophy raises many questions about human conditions and civilizations and gives rise to ideas that express the nature of humanity and society, a subject considered by some to be part of the Great Books, Junior Great Books, or Great Ideas program. Call it what you want, these readings deal with moral conscience and historical consciousness, and this is what students should be reading.

The content of moral knowledge, according to Phenix, covers five areas: (1) *human rights,* involving conditions of life that ought to prevail, (2) *ethics,* concerning family relations and sex, (3) *social relationships,* dealing with class, racial, ethnic, and religious groups, (4) *economic life,* involving wealth and poverty, and (5) *political life,* involving justice, equity, and power. The way we translate moral content into moral conduct defines the kind of people we are. It is not our moral knowledge that counts; rather, it is our moral behavior in everyday affairs with people that is important.

## Moral Character

A person can have moral knowledge and obey secular and religious laws but still lack moral character. **Moral character** is difficult to teach because it involves patterns of attitudes and behavior that result from stages of growth, distinctive qualities of personality, and experiences. It involves a coherent philosophy and the will to act in a way consistent with that philosophy; it also means helping people; accepting peoples' weaknesses without exploiting them; seeing the best in people and building on their strengths; acting civilly and courteously in relations with classmates, friends, or colleagues; expressing humility; and acting as an individual even if it means being different from the crowd.

Perhaps the real test of moral character is the ability to cope with crises or setbacks, to deal with adversity, and to be willing to take risks (that is, possible loss of job, even life itself) because of one's convictions. Courage, conviction, and compassion are the ingredients of character. What kind of people do we want to emerge as a result of our efforts as teachers? We can engage in moral education and teach moral knowledge, but can we teach moral character? In general, the morally mature person understands moral principles and accepts responsibility for applying these principles in real-life situations.

The world is full of people who understand the notion of morality but take the expedient way out or follow the crowd. Who among us (including our colleagues) possesses moral character? Who among our students will develop into morally mature individuals? To be sure, moral character cannot be taught by one teacher; it takes a concerted effort by the entire school, cooperation among a critical mass of teachers within the school, and the nurturing of children and youth over many years.

Ted Sizer and Nancy Sizer (1999) ask teachers to confront students with moral questions and moral issues about their own actions or inactions in ways that may be unsettling or difficult. As teachers we need to address things that threaten the self-concept and self-esteem of students. We need to deal with issues of inequity and social injustice while promoting cooperative behaviors and intergroup relations among children and youth.

The Sizers want teachers to "grapple" with ideas, to "dig deep," to ask why things are so, what evidence there is, what thoughts and actions mean. They hope that teachers will stop "bluffing"—that is, taking shortcuts in their preparation or testing/evaluation practices—and they hope that schools will reduce the "sorting" practice in ways that sometimes correspond with social (class or caste) groupings. Although some sorting of students is necessary, it should be flexible enough to respect students' and parents' wishes and to avoid stereotyping. In the end, the Sizers argue, students should not experience hypocrisy in classrooms and schools that claim all students are equal or all students can be what they can be while at the same time discriminating against students based on class, caste, or low ability.

The schools must adopt moral character as a priority or policy that all teachers are expected to follow. One or two teachers by themselves cannot have a real impact—one that is relevant and long term. It takes a school community to implement a program of moral character whereby students are taught that they are responsible for their actions and that values such as honesty, respect, tolerance, compassion, a sense of justice, and so forth are worthwhile and important concepts to learn and adopt as benchmarks in life or calls for action.

## Moral Values

Good moral character requires a clear set of values. The values a person holds depend on many factors, including environment, education, and personality. Teachers and schools are always transmitting values to students, so do the home, church, and media. There was a time, when the authors were attending elementary schools, that the core values were transmitted by the TV program *Father Knows Best.* Today, *Sex in the City* and the likes of Madonna and Michael Jackson dominate the air waves and transmit many values. **Value clarification** (sometimes called values building) is now considered part of the teaching–learning process. Advocates of values clarification have a high regard for creativity, freedom, and self-realization. They prefer that learners explore their own preferences and make their own choices.

Confusion over values can result in apathy, uncertainty, inconsistency, extreme conformity, or extreme dissension. Values clarification is designed to help people overcome values confusion and become more positive, purposeful, and productive, as well as to have better interpersonal relationships.

In a popular text, Louis Raths (1978) and his colleagues outlined the process of valuing in terms of *choosing, prizing,* and *repeating* feelings and beliefs—to what extent students are consistent or inconsistent, and whether students are willing to act upon their feelings and beliefs. They developed various dialogue, writing, discussion, and activity strategies for teaching valuing on a how-to-do basis. In short, the focus is on expressing attitudes, feelings, aspirations, and interests—ideas and behaviors that are not easy to measure or quantify but that shape the student and influence cognition.

It is possible to identify other ways of teaching valuing. The first is *inculcation,* or teaching accepted values with the support of common law. Next is *moral development,* highlighting moral and ethical principles of application. Third is *analysis of issues* and situations involving values. Fourth is the *taxonomy of educational objectives,* the affective domain that deals with feelings, attitudes, and emotions in behavioral form. Finally is *action learning,* or trying and testing values in real life (Doll, 2001; Krathwohl, Bloom, & Masia, 1964). In addition, the approaches used by Abraham Maslow, Carl Rogers, and David Johnson and Roger Johnson may be described as *evocation,* calling forth from the learner's personal values and the ability to make choices and become self-actualizing.

## Moral Development: Piaget and Kohlberg

Although some self-control of behavior may be seen in the preschool years, researchers agree that not until the child is about four years old do moral standards begin to develop at a rapid rate. During the period when the child begins to abandon behavior governed by what he or she wants to do at a particular moment, conscience tends to be erratic, largely confined to prohibitions against specific behaviors and based on external sanctions. Before age five, morality does not exist for children, because they have little or no conception of rules. From about age five to six years, conscience becomes less confined to specific behaviors and begins to incorporate more generalized standards; it becomes determined less by external rewards or punishments and more by internal sanctions (Baker, 1999; Kagan, 2001).

*Piaget's Theory of Moral Development.* Piaget's theory was based on techniques of investigation that included conversing with children and asking them questions about moral dilemmas and events in stories. For example, he might ask a child, "Why shouldn't you cheat in a game?"

As children grow older, they become more flexible and realize that there are exceptions to rules. As they become members of a larger, more varied peer group, rules and moral judgments become less absolute and rigid and more dependent on the needs and desires of the people involved. Wrote Piaget (1965), "For very young children, a rule is a sacred reality because it is traditional; for the older ones it depends upon a mutual agreement." On the basis of numerous studies, Piaget concluded that from ages 5 to 12

> the child's concept of justice passes from a rigid and inflexible notion of right and wrong, learned from his parents, to a sense of equity in moral judgments. Eventually, the concept takes into account the specific situation or circumstances in which behavior occurs. As the child becomes older, he or she becomes more flexible and realizes that there are exceptions to the rule, and there may even be circumstances when it's best to hold back information or even lie. (p 182)

See Box 1.3 for a discussion of morality.

*Kohlberg's Theory of Moral Reasoning.* More recently, Lawrence Kohlberg (1963, 1964) studied the development of children's moral standards and concluded that the way people think about moral issues reflects their culture and their stage of growth. He outlined six developmental stages of moral judgment and grouped three moral levels that correspond roughly to Piaget's three stages of cognitive development:

I. *Preconventional level.* Children have not yet developed a sense of right or wrong. The level comprises two stages: (1) children do as they are told because they fear punishment, and (2) children realize that certain actions bring rewards.

II. *Conventional level.* Children are concerned about what other people think of them, and their behavior is largely other-directed. The

**BOX 1.3** On Morality and Moral Character

Good moral character requires a clear set of values, but someone who has a clear set of values (e.g., Adolf Hitler, Osama bin Laden, or Enron CEO Kenneth Lay) may not be moral. The values a person holds depend on many factors, including historial and social environment, education, and personality. Teachers and schools are always transmitting values to students, both consciously and unconsciously. Sometimes the transmission occurs through what educators call the "hidden curriculum," the unstated meanings conveyed by teachers' attitudes and behavior, class routines, and school policies, as well as through the "formal" or "intended" curriculum.

two stages in this level are (3) children seek their parents' approval by being "nice," and (4) children begin thinking in terms of rules and laws.

III. *Postconventional level.* Morality is based not only on other people's values but also on internalized precepts of ethical principles and authority. This level also includes two stages: (5) children view morality in terms of contractual obligations and democratically accepted laws, and (6) children view morality in terms of individual principles of conscience, as well as in terms of a higher being (our addition).

Unless a reasonable degree of moral development takes place during childhood and adolescence—that is, unless standards of right and wrong are established—the child, and later the adult, is likely to engage in asocial and/or antisocial behavior. On the other hand, if the acceptance of others' standards or the internalization of standards and prohibitions is unduly strong, guilt may develop in association with a wide variety of actions and thoughts. Ideally, individuals work out an adequate sense of morality and at the same time avoid self-condemnation in the context of the culture in which they live.

Kohlberg's theory has been widely criticized on the grounds that moral reasoning does not necessarily conform to development and involves many complex social and psychological factors, that particular moral behaviors are not always associated with the same reasoning (and vise versa), and that his prescriptions are culture-bound and sexist. However, he has made researchers and practitioners aware of moral reasoning and provided a moral theory, along with Piaget's, to guide teaching and learning.

*Beyond Piaget and Kohlberg.* Although Kohlberg found that his theories of moral reasoning have been replicated in various countries and that the development of moral reasoning occurs in the same order and at about the same ages across cultures, he has been criticized because his early research was limited mainly to boys. For example, Carol Gilligan (1982) has maintained that boys and girls use different moral criteria; male morality centers more on individual rights and social justice, whereas female morality focuses on individual responsibilities, self-sacrifice, and caring.

Kohlberg revised his research on the basis of this criticism; however, he failed and others have failed to find any significant differences between males and females in moral reasoning or moral maturity. Although there is no convincing evidence that women are more caring, cooperative or altruistic (Eagley & Crowley, 1986; Smetana, Killen, & Turiel, 1998), as Gilligan has argued, these ideas have been embellished by Nel Noddings (1992, 2002) and by several feminists who advocate the virtue of caring within the family and in educational, social, and medical settings and the need to reduce competitive behavior in schools and society (Martuseweicz, 2001; Tetreault, 2001). Gilligan's ideas also seem to coincide with the everyday folk belief that men are from "Mars" and women are from "Venus," as well as the sentiments expressed in popular Broadway plays such as *I Love You. You're Perfect. Now Change* and *The Caveman.*

The most important limitation to Piaget's and Kohlberg's theories is that they fail to distinguish between moral reasoning and actual behavior. Moral behavior does not conform to simple rules, guidelines, or developmental stages. The social context, an individual's overall personality and perception of reality, and the individual's motivation to behave morally are factors for consideration. (For example, there are always opportunities to cheat or steal; however, there is also the possibility of getting caught.) But what is at stake? A 50-cent candy bar, a $10 CD, or the SAT test questions that may admit you into Harvard or Yale? Although certain aspects of moral reasoning account for moral behavior (you need to understand what you are doing), the correlation can be weak given social and personal variables. According to research, moral reasoning can be predicted much more precisely than moral behavior. The latter is more complex; furthermore, the link between moral reasoning and moral behavior is minimal (Bear & Rys, 1995; Bebeau, Rest, & Narvaez, 1999).

## Moral Freedom

Intellectuals love to generalize about U.S. culture. Are we a democratic and free society, or are we materialistic and morally corrupt? Are we in a culture of victims, disbelief, and consumerism, or are we a hardworking, God-fearing, and thrifty society? Do we still breed rugged individuals, or have we become anxious conformists? Are we shamelessly permissive or tenaciously hanging on to our puritanical values? Many intellectuals would argue there is a cultural and moral war going on in our nation, illustrated by hot debates on welfare, immigration, labor, religion, homosexuality, and family life. Just about every educator, psychologist, sociologist, and journalist has something to say about these issues in context with "traditional," "emerging," and "postmodern" values.

Moral freedom, according to Alan Wolfe (2001), defines the way we live and the type of society we are. Based on in-depth interviews in eight niche communities, all very different, from a small town in Iowa, a black community in Hartford, a middle-class suburb in Ohio, to a gay district in San Francisco and a wealthy area in Silicon Valley, he focuses on changing morality in the United States. His conclusion is that Americans on all sides of the political continuum are engaged in reconciling individual freedom with a common morality. Those on the political left welcome individual self-fulfillment and reduced powers of the police, and those on the right put devotion to God first and insist on law and order and strict penalties for criminal behavior. Moral relativists on the left support smoking bans, organic food, strict environment laws, and hate-crime legislation. Those on the right acknowledge the profit motive that drives industry, see the need to search for oil in Alaska, and acknowledge the importance of patriotism, forgiveness, and redemption—pretty close to the values the McGuffey readers advanced some 150 years ago and to those William Bennett (2001) preaches today on television and in his books.

In general, Americans are moral moderates. We seek high standards of virtuous behavior but not mandates or prescriptive laws. We strive to live the good, virtuous life, but we worry about the divorce rate and its effect on children. Respect for honesty is neutralized by the need to function in what is perceived as a dishonest world. Morality is a form of common sense and law; it is eclectic, like religion in the United States (Kaminer, 2001). It boils down to the individual, who each of us is and how we relate to others. Americans tend to personalize religion, borrowing from traditional scriptures and New Age spiritual movements. U.S. teachers tend to individualize teaching and learning theories that suit their own personality and knowledge base. Likewise, U.S. people tend to personalize moral behavior, drawing from both conservative and liberal thinking, from ideals of godliness, self-discipline, and modern notions of self-fulfillment, sexual freedom, and counterculture ideals. A lot of this moderation stems from the fact that we are not a homogeneous population driven by one religious or political ideal. We are a mixed breed of people with mixed ideas about morality—a mix of traditional and liberal ideas.

Right now, we have a moral vacuum in many public schools. Alfie Kohn (1998) would go one step further and argue that schooling has become extremely competitive, a system in which students are no longer committed to helping one another, and parents (especially from the upper class) have the attitude that only their child counts—they don't want other students performing as well in school if it jeopardizes their child's chance to play five minutes more basketball or limits their child's chance to learn. White middle-class parents have fought to preserve a tracking system that discriminates against children of color by limiting their opportunities to participate in honors and advanced classes.

The goal of schools is to educate, socialize, and help children and youth function in society. Cognitive learning and information-based skills are important but not the be-all and end-all of education; these elements need to be tempered by moral constraints that recognize and distinguish between selfish behavior, inappropriate behavior, and proper behavior. Although most parents want what's best for their children, we need to constrain parents who send "quiet" messages to school administrators and pressure teachers, coaches, and principals to favor their own kids. The goal is to work for the vast majority of students, not a tiny minority whose parents are "connected" or like to complain.

## ■ BRAIN RESEARCH AND LEARNING

The human brain can be compared to a shrink-wrapped Microsoft disk, a program with precisely coded instructions that evolution has written for the operation and maintenance of an individual. The brain can be likened to a computer, possessing about "100 billion nerve cells wired together with 100 billion interconnections" (Wade, 2000, p. 4). There are about one thousand varieties of connections, each with a special subset of instructions, that make us individually prone to exhibit love or hate, obedience or rebellion, intelligence or lack of intelligence.

Recent controversies in brain research include (1) when do synaptic densities and brain connections peak (ranging from age three to puberty); (2) whether early visual and auditory experiences increase synaptic densities or numbers during or after puberty; (3) whether the use of language and what type of language training and education (formal, informal; oral, reading, TV, etc.), or constant and repeated mental operations, increase the efficiency of connections; (4) whether there is a critical age period during which synapses that are developed influence how the brain will be wired or whether the synaptic densities are more susceptible to being eliminated after puberty; (5) what kinds of synapses are pruned when pruning begins and at what rate, and to what extent pruning affects behavior and memory; and (6) whether we can determine for sure whether people with greater synaptic densities or connections are more intelligent (Bruer, 1999; Huttenlocher & Dabholkar, 1997; Shore, 1997).

In general, according to the research, an optimal brain requires that we use as many synapses as possible before puberty or lose them afterward; that brain connections and intelligence have a genetic and environmental component; that connections used to a lesser extent during a critical period (some claim prior to age three, some say prior to age ten or eleven) are more susceptible to being eliminated; and that the brain area undergoes considerable reorganization during puberty and these changes modify how we process information and behave after puberty.

These brain data parallel and give credibility to (1) the "mental discipline" approach to intelligence, developed during the early twentieth century, which holds that exercising the mind as if it were a muscle will improve the mind; (2) the "deprivation theory" of the late twentieth century, which holds that the quality of early environmental stimuli affects intelligence and academic achievement, and that learning gaps increase between those who possess and those who do not possess basic skills; (3) and Benjamin Bloom's longitudinal research on cognitive development, which holds that 50 percent of the child's potential for learning is developed by age four, another 25 percent is developed by age nine, and the remaining 25 percent is developed by the age of seventeen. (This last piece of research implies that the impact of teaching and schooling is limited and dramatically declines with the student's age. Taken literally, it means that teachers are partially off the hook, because preschool conditions and family factors are of greater importance than school conditions and teacher factors, especially in the later grades.) See Box 1.4 for a glimpse into the future of education.

## Learning Styles

According to research, the way we think and learn is associated with different brain functions such as preferences about movement, intake (of foods or liquids), and how we react to sound and light. These brain functions result in areas of "strengths" and "weaknesses," and, in some cases, different **learning styles** (Alexander, 2003; Vacca, 2001). In short, learning differences are not solely tied to ability factors; rather, we all have propensities that influence our thinking and guide our intellect. Just as baseball players have different batting styles, we have different ways of thinking, learning, and processing verbal and nonverbal forms of literacy. Yet most teachers treat their students alike and teach as if they were all the same.

For example, some of us learn best alone and others prefer to learn in small groups and share information. Some students exhibit on-task persistence, whereas others fidget, tap, or doodle while taking notes in class or studying at home. Some learn best through hands-on activities and manipulative materials, and some are better able to digest abstract and verbal infor-

**BOX 1.4   Altering the Learning Environment**

In our schools, about 26 percent of the student population is on Ritalin and other drugs to control hyperactivity and other so-called disruptive behavior. And other drugs are available that can enhance memory and others that make present learning theory outdated and mundane. Drugs, psychological conditioning, and behavior modification, all of which are debated in the profession, have the potential to make George Leonard's vision, as illuminated in *Education and Ecstasy*, a reality. Society has already reached a point that approaches Orwell's *1984* and Huxley's *Brave New World*. All our notions of human equality, human rights, and moral choices are being challenged as we develop new techniques for altering personality, behavior, the quality and growth of intellectual and physical attributes, and even the rate and vision of living.

mation. Some of us display preferences for eating and drinking while reading or studying, and others need little intake. Some of us are night owls and others are morning people, traits that suggest when we are most efficient in performing schoolwork or studying. A good number of students process cognitive information with background music or stretch out on the couch or even on the floor, and others need a quiet place to work and sit upright behind a desk or table. Some students seem to procrastinate and need extra time to warm up, whereas others immediately jump into the assignment and perform meticulously. Hence, teachers need to observe their students in class and make adjustments in instruction to suit the way each student learns. There is no one way for all children to learn.

One of the more popular theories of the brain involves **left–right brain** or hemispheric functioning. Traditionally, teachers have taught students in a "left brain" way—based on verbal symbolism, logic, and analytical thinking. Yet a substantial percentage of students (40 to 75 percent, depending on the research study) are "right brain" oriented; that is, they are more global than analytical, more deductive than inductive, less structured and more dependent on tactile or kinesthetic resources (Abbott & Ryan, 1999; Hardiman, 2001).

According to the prevailing view, the right-brain thinker tends to rely on one or more of the following functions: (1) *visual*—the student "sees" information, doodles while listening to the teacher, draws lots of pictures and arrows when taking notes, and needs a quiet place for studying; (2) *auditory*—the student "hears" information, reads aloud and talks aloud when problem solving or writing, often studies with background music, and says things again and again to memorize information; and (3) *tactile* or *haptic*—the student learns by "moving and doing," doesn't like to listen to or read directions, is antidesk and prefers the floor or couch, needs frequent beaks when doing homework or studying, sometimes procrastinates, and takes notes in class but rarely studies them (Baron, 1994; Bina, 1999; Wagmeister & Shifrin, 2000).

Some caution is needed here. Many students, it would appear, are equally proficient in left and right thinking, and still others rely on both styles although they may have some difficulty in making switches. It is questionable whether auditory preferences always connote right-brain thinking. For example, visual activities such as reading and spelling are in part based on auditory discrimination. Auditory preferences might be more cognitive and related to verbally symbolic and logical thinking than the literature on brain theory suggests.

Related to different kinds of learning styles is the notion of different forms of intelligence, which leads to the theory of multiple intelligences (discussed below) rather than intelligence based solely on tests of verbal and abstract patterns of thought. Similarly, some ways of thinking and learning are culturally bound or, more precisely, associated with ethnic, racial, and immigrant factors. For example, there are cultural differences in attitude toward schoolwork; teacher authority; on-task effort versus social interaction; time orientation (coming early or late to class or meetings and meeting deadlines); present versus future orientation; the value of hard work and studying; abstract versus visual, auditory, or tactile processing; physical space (perceiving the teacher as pushy, when in fact the intent is to foster comfortable interpersonal space or personal relations); touching and kissing in public; role expectations and behavior toward people based on age, gender, job status, and family interactions; group and

**BOX 1.5** TV, Textbooks, and Technology

In the next five to ten years, every home will have the potential to have a "Me" channel—a system by which each member of the family can program from a series of channels an individualized lineup of selections and shows assembled from all but infinite lists of programs pulsing through the digital web. The same digital force will most likely affect magazines and newspapers (even textbooks like this one), causing producers and publishers to narrow their focus and provide multiple options for a wide variety of viewers and readers at the same time. The possibility of assigning specific school programs, homework, and academic enrichment will be immense, but it is questionable whether teachers will make use of this technology or system of "Me" channels. This view is based on how teachers in the past have underutilized television—the most effective mass medium and form of entertainment ever devised.

individual learning situations; and a host of other culturally laden values and behaviors that influence performance in school and how people act.

In short, learning styles differ from culture to culture as well as among individual students, and possibly also on the basis of urban/suburban/rural patterns. Furthermore, many learning modalities are not recognized in classrooms unless schools and teachers are sensitive to and respect diversity. Obviously, teachers need to adapt their instruction to coincide with the learning styles of their students, to capitalize on the students' strengths or preferences, and to accommodate all students. In a classroom of twenty-five or thirty students, the teacher has the daunting task of recognizing individual and group differences based on ability, needs, and interests, as well as cognitive processing and learning styles. See Box 1.5 for a discussion of how technology can accomodate individual learning styles.

## Multiple Intelligences

Howard Gardner (1983) argues for a theory of **multiple intelligences** and contends that there are different mental operations associated with intelligence. But Gardner feels that the search for empirically grounded structures or components of intelligence may be misleading because such a search overlooks many roles and skills valued by human cultures. He maintains that there are many different types of intelligence and that too often (at least in an information society) we emphasize only verbal or linguistic factors. He outlines eight types of intelligence:

1. **Linguistic Intelligence.** This ability consists of using language and literacy forms effectively. For oral language, this skill may be demonstrated by actors, politicians, newscasters, and public speakers, whereas for written language, writers of literary works, poets, journalists, playwrights, or editors would display this intelligence. These people, in short, have a "way with words." They use grammar and structure—the sound and meanings of language—in skillful and creative ways.

2. **Logical–Mathematical Intelligence.** This intelligence has to do with the ability to use numbers and arithmetic operations extremely well, as do mathematicians, statisticians, and accountants. These people also have the ability to reason, hypothesize, and theorize logically, talents exhibited by scientists and engineers, and calculate well, and they are keenly aware of logical patterns and relationships and engage in propositions and abstract thinking.

3. **Spatial Intelligence.** This type of thinking is the capacity to deal with and reconstruct the experimental, nonverbal world. Thus a visual/spatial thinker negotiates

the visible world by reconstructing visions of the visible world; painters, inventors, sculptors, architects, and designers have high degrees of spatial intelligence. These people have the capacity to visualize well, to pictorially or graphically represent visual/spatial ideas, and to orient themselves spatially. Pilots, sailors, architects, builders, and chess players tend to exhibit spatial intelligence.

**4. Bodily–Kinesthetic Intelligence.** This ability is the craft of using one's persona—one's whole bodily self—to handle objects and excel at physical dexterity. This skill is exemplified by dancers, athletes, mimes, surgeons, and artisans. These people use their bodies and physical dexterity to express ideas and feelings and can use their hands to create, transform, and manipulate objects and tools. This ability includes specific physical skills such as coordination, flexibility, speed, tactile dexterity, and strength.

**5. Musical Intelligence.** This ability is bestowed on those who have a strong sensitivity to such aspects as the pitch, melody, rhythm, and tone of a musical piece. Some of these people, such as composers, can create and transform musical forms or "language." Others may be able to express themselves through music, as do instrument performers, or to discriminate and perceive musical features, as do music critics or listeners of music.

**6. Interpersonal Intelligence.** This type of thinking is strongly manifested in those who work with people. People with this capacity understand and interact well with others and include teachers, ministers, counselors, social workers, and (hopefully) politicians. These people are sensitive to the feelings and needs of others, respond well to verbal cues of gestures and facial expressions, sense peoples' mood and motivation, and attempt to influence behavior by proposing positive plans of action.

**7. Intrapersonal Intelligence.** This ability refers to an introspective kind of intelligence. People with this ability have strong self-knowledge and perceptions of themselves, which allows them to skillfully plan and direct their own lives. They know their strengths and weaknesses, their interests and motivations, and their boundaries of self-discipline and work. People with strong intrapersonal intelligence might pursue such disciplines as theology, psychology, and philosophy.

**8. Naturalistic Intelligence.** This is the ability to discriminate features among living things in the plant and animal kingdom and the ability to be sensitive to other conditions of the natural world. A sensitivity to such natural conditions as star constellations, cloud formations, rock configurations, and types of vegetation was highly valued in our past when humans were hunters, gathers, and farmers. The same type of thinking is essential for the natural scientist, biologist, and botanist, as well as for the outdoor adventurist who climbs mountains, backpacks for days or weeks, hunts for bears in remote areas, sails or skis in highly dangerous places. These people have what are called "survival skills," which most "flabby" Americans lack.

*Guilford's Influence on Gardner.* What Gardener has to say about intelligence is not new but rooted in the work of J. P. Guilford (1967) who, in the 1950s and 1960s, formulated a theory of intelligence around a three-dimensional model called the **structure of intellect.** This structure consisted of six *products* (units, classes, relations, systems, transformations, implications), five *operations* (knowledge, memory, divergent thinking, convergent thinking, and evaluation), and four *contents* (figured, symbolic, semantic, and behavioral).

The three dimensions produced a $6 \times 5 \times 4$ model: six products, five operations, and four contents, yielding 120 cells of distinct mental abilities. By 1985, Guilford and his doctoral students had distinguished more than 100 abilities by factor analysis of standardized achievement and aptitude tests. Guilford concluded that the remaining cells indicated uncovered mental abilities. It is possible, however, that our cognitive tests do not measure other mental operations or that such abilities do not exist.

The Guilford model is highly abstract and theoretical and involves administering and grading many extra tests. But rather than recognizing a single index of IQ (or of aptitude), it recognizes and reports several scores. Thus the theoretical issues surrounding intelligence and cognitive operations take on added complexity, much more than do Gardner's theory of intelligence or Binet's and Weschler's idea of reporting one IQ score.

The point is, the idea of multiple intelligences stems from J. P. Guilford's work, and he in turn formulated his theory to challenge Charles Spearman's (1927) idea of **factor of intelligence**—that is, that intelligence is composed of a general factor *g* underlying all mental functions, and a multitude of *s* factors, each related to a specific task. To be smart meant having lots of *g*, because it was an umbrella factor permeating all mental operations. Whereas Gardner feels the search for empirically grounded components of intelligence may be misleading and therefore delineates fewer components (eight in broad areas of life), Guilford maintains that the criteria for intelligence can be quantified and consist of many (120) mental operations or cognitive processes. The idea of 120 different mental operations confounds teachers—and thus remains a theoretical construct. Gardner is more popular with school people because his discussion avoids statistics and is more positive and democratic. He stretches the notion of what is important for human growth and development—more than cognition—fitting the progressive idea of the whole child, expanding the child's full human potential, opening academic and career doors, and encouraging low achievers who might otherwise be shunted aside by schools.

*Beyond Gardner.* Gardner's ideas provide a place in the school curriculum not only for the three Rs and academic core subjects, but also for music, art, dance, drama, sports, and even students with social skills (those who can win friends, influence people, negotiate, and the like). These additional bodies of knowledge and aptitudes have a place in our "other directed" society and foster social and economic achievement and success in adulthood, including in corporate America; the entertainment, artistic, and sports worlds; and the local and civic community. Academic merit is not the only avenue for social and economic mobility—a highly important factor in a democratic society that tries to foster excellence in many endeavors and provides multiple opportunities for people to succeed. Only in a society that requires all the trains to run on time, or when a nation perceives a serious international threat, is academics prized; in these situations, other aptitudes and talents (social, emotional, artistic, etc.) take second or third place.

Subscribing to Gardner's ideas means being not only a cognitivist but also a "positive cognitivist," if we may coin a new term. It means believing people have many opportunities and chances in life. Someone who can paint, dance, sing, act, or accurately hit a golf ball 200 yards can rise to the ranks of a master. If encouraged and given a chance, and if many talents are recognized, then many of our potential school dropouts would not drop out. For those who do, this country allows second, third, and fourth chances to go to school and college.

Those in charge of planning and implementing the curriculum are faced with the task of expanding their vision beyond intellectual and academic pursuits without creating "soft" subjects or a "watered-down" curriculum. Teachers must nurture all types of talents and all types of excellence that contribute to the worth of the individual and society. We must be guided by reason and balance and consider the versatility of children and youth. We need to be aware of students' multiple strengths and abilities and their multiple ways of thinking and learning. Indeed, there are many ways of reaching Rome or finding the end of the rainbow; fixating on one method is restrictive, myopic, and authoritarian. True, the trains may run on time, but a lot of average and less-than-average people will be forced into their place—second place or worse.

What Gardner says has little to do with the traditional concept of intelligence; he is more concerned with aptitude and talent. In the final analysis, intelligence is reflected in the ability to function effectively in one's environment, to support oneself and loved ones, and to prosper and live a full life. In a hunting, fishing, or farming society, verbal skills play a minor role and the importance of muscle power and naturalistic intelligence is key. In a farming society, what counts is the ability to plow the soil and plant, not to read Plato or Kant. Given a technological and information society, however, most jobs and daily routines require a verbal and/or mathematical component for effectively functioning. Less than one-half of one percent of Americans can support themselves as baseball or basketball players, country and western singers, artists, and dancers. People with these special abilities are few in number. Although they should be encouraged as children to maximize their potential in these special areas, the vast majority of children and adults need to be schooled in cognitive bodies of knowledge that deal with verbal and numerical symbols. Why? Because current society requires those skills, and the vast number of employers reward those skills.

## Learning How to Learn

The concept of learning put forward in this text differs from the notion that the learner merely remains passive, reacts to stimuli, and waits for some reward. Here the learner is regarded as active and able to monitor and control cognitive activities. He or she possesses new information through assimilation and integration of previous information. Without this integration, new information is lost to memory and task performance dependent on the information is unsuccessful (Flavell, 1985; Glaser, 1993). Learning new information results in modification of long-term memory. The responsibility for engaging in learning, including control, direction, and focus, belongs to the individual.

This notion that learning is an active, integrative process changed the belief about how reading comprehension occurs. This shift occurred during the later part of the last century and is reflected in a number of landmark studies and reports. The initial *Reading Report Card* indicated that with a conceptual shift in the way researchers and teachers regarded reading, students were believed to have a much more active role in the reading comprehension and learning process. In order to develop higher-level literacy skills, students need to engage in thoughtful and critical elaboration of roles and understandings drawn from text and from what they know (Ehri & Stahl, 2001).

Cognitive structures are searched when students want to identify, categorize, and process new information. If the cognitive structures are disorganized, unclear, or not fully developed (for the person's age), then new information will not be clearly identified, categorized, and assimilated. On the other hand, new learning based on previous learning should be meaningful to students—in context with prior knowledge and real-life experiences, regardless of whether the students are low or high achieving.

High-achieving students have a more expanded prior knowledge base in terms of *in-depth knowledge* and *multiple forms of knowledge* than do low-achieving students (Cobb & Bowers, 1999; Leinhardt, 1992). This mature knowledge base permits learners to integrate important and/or complex information into existing cognitive structures. Similarly, those students who are capable of learning on their own are better able to (1) *narrow*, identify, and place information into preexisting categories, (2) *sharpen* or distinguish prior information from new information to avoid confusion or overlap, (3) *tolerate* or deal with ambiguous and unclear information without getting frustrated, and (4) *assimilate* existing schemata in order to interpret problematic situations (Anderson, Greeno, Reder, & Simon, 2000; Prawat, 1993).

A cognitive framework proposed by Weinstein and Mayer (1986) consists of eight comprehension strategies.

1. *Basic rehearsal strategies*, the ability to remember names or words and the order of things.
2. *Complex rehearsal strategies*, making appropriate choices or selections (such as knowing what to copy when the teacher explains something or what to underline or outline while reading).
3. *Basic elaboration strategies*, relating two or more items (such as nouns and verbs).
4. *Complex elaboration strategies*, analyzing and synthesizing new information with old information.
5. *Basic organizational strategies*, categorizing, grouping, or ordering new information.
6. *Complex organizational strategies*, putting information in hierarchical arrangements (such as in outlining notes or homework).
7. *Comprehension monitoring*, checking progress, recognizing when one is on the proper track or confused, or right or wrong.
8. *Affective strategies*, being relaxed yet alert and attentive during a test situation and when studying.

All of these learning skills combined represent knowledge about and control over cognitive processes, what some educators refer to as metacognition. The specific strategies deal with the identification, categorization, and integration of information.

Of all the specific strategies discussed, **comprehension monitoring** is often considered the most important. This skill permits the student to monitor, modify, and direct (and redirect) his or her cognitive activities. (Such monitoring is sometimes called metacogition and presupposes the ability to understand the basic meaning of a text.) The student remains focused on the task, is aware of whether he or she is getting closer to or further away from an answer, and knows when to choose alternative methods to arrive at the answer (Anderson, 1993). A student with good comprehension monitoring has developed self-correcting cognition processes, including how to determine what part of the problem needs further clarification, how to relate parts of the problem to one another, and how to search out information to solve the problem. In short, the student is able to identify what has to be done, focus attention, and cope with errors.

**Learning to learn skills** are basic thinking skills that are used in all content areas. Although some of these learning skills are generic and can be taught solely as general strategies, without reference to content, it is impossible to avoid a certain amount of subject matter (Andrade, 2000; Crawford & Witte, 1999), especially in the upper (secondary) grades. This assumption seems to make sense—for example, a good mathematical learner may not be as good in English or history. That does not mean there is no transfer of learning skills from one subject to another, although there may be less than we used to think. Bruner may have been right: Different disciplines have their own principles, concepts, and research methods that are distinct from those of other disciplines. Or, as Lauren Resnick (1987) claimed: What is learned in one area is not easily transferable to another area of learning because it is content based.

## Critical Thinking

One of the most important things a teacher can do in the classroom, regardless of subject or grade level, is to make students aware of their own metacognitive processes—to examine what they are thinking about, to make distinctions and comparisons, to see errors in what they are thinking about and how they are thinking about it, and to make self-corrections.

It is now believed that **critical thinking** is a form of intelligence that can be taught. The leading proponents of this school are Matthew Lipman, Robert Sternberg, and Robert Ennis. Lipman's (1984) program was originally designed for elementary school grades but is applicable to all grades. He sought to develop the ability to use (1) concepts, (2) generalizations, (3) cause–effect relationships, (4) logical inferences, (5) consistencies and contradictions, (6) analogies, (7) part–whole and whole–part connections, (8) problem formulations, (9) reversibility of logical statements, and (10) applications of principles to real-life situations.

In Lipman's (1988, 1990) program for teaching critical thinking, children spend a considerable portion of their time thinking about thinking and about ways in which effective thinking differs from ineffective thinking. After reading a series of stories, children engage in classroom discussions and exercises that encourage them to adopt the thinking process depicted in the stories. Lipman's assumptions are that children are by nature interested in such philosophical issues as truth, fairness, and personal identity, and that children can and should learn to explore alternatives to their own viewpoints, to consider evidence, to make distinctions, and to draw conclusions.

Lipman's emphasis on reading and discussing philosophical and moral issues coincides with the objectives and procedures of the Junior Great Books Program for all grade levels (starting at the first grade), originally developed in the 1930s and continuously refined and revised. The emphasis is on good literature, whereby teachers are trained to teach specific *reading* strategies, encouraging students to *think* about and *discuss ideas* and teaching them how to *listen* for different ideas and build on their own and others' ideas, how to reason and *use evidence,* and how to *write* persuasively and creatively. Although the program is based in Chicago, trainers are available for school districts across the country. See Tips for Teachers 1.2.

Lipman (1991) also distinguishes between *ordinary thinking* and *critical thinking.* Ordinary thinking is simple and lacks standards; critical thinking is more complex and is based on standards of objectivity, utility, or consistency. He wants teachers to help students change (1) from guessing to estimating, (2) from preferring to evaluating, (3) from grouping to classifying, (4) from believing to assuming, (5) from simply inferring to logically inferring, (6) from associating concepts to grasping principles, (7) from noting relationships to noting relationships among relationships, (8) from supposing to hypothesizing, (9) from offering opinions without reasons to offering

*Tips for Teachers* **1.2**

## Teaching Critical Thinking Skills

Teachers must understand the cognitive processes that constitute critical thinking; be familiar with the tasks, skills, and situations to which these processes are applied; and employ several classroom activities that develop these processes. Robert Ennis provides a framework for such instruction. He divides critical thinking into four components, each consisting of several skills that can be taught to students.

I. Defining and clarifying
   1. Identifying conclusions
   2. Identifying stated reasons
   3. Identifying unstated reasons
   4. Seeing similarities and differences
   5. Identifying and handling irrelevance
   6. Summarizing
II. Asking appropriate questions to clarify or challenge
   1. Why?
   2. What is the main point?
   3. What does this mean?
   4. What is an example?
   5. What is not an example?
   6. How does this apply to the case?
   7. What difference does it make?
   8. What are the facts?
   9. Is this what is being said?
   10. What more is to be said?
III. Judging the credibility of a source
   1. Expertise
   2. Lack of conflict of interest
   3. Agreement among sources
   4. Reputation
   5. Use of established procedures
   6. Known risk to reputation
   7. Ability to give reasons
   8. Careful habits
IV. Solving problems and drawing conclusions
   1. Deducing and judging validity
   2. Inducing and judging conclusions
   3. Predicting probable consequences

*Source:* Adapted from Robert H. Ennis, "A Logical Basis for Measuring Critical Thinking Skills," *Educational Leadership* (October 1985), pp. 44–48; Robert H. Ennis, "A Taxonomy of Critical Thinking Dispositions and Abilities," in J. Baron and R. J. Sternberg (Eds.), *Teaching Thinking Skills: Theory and Practice* (New York: Freeman, 1987), pp. 9–26; and Robert H. Ennis, *Critical Thinking* (Upper Saddle River: NJ: Prentice-Hall, 1996).

opinions with reasons, and (10) from making judgments without criteria to making judgments with criteria.

Robert Sternberg (1984, 1990) seeks to foster many of the same skills, but in a different way. He points to three categories or components of critical thinking: (1) *meta-components,* high-order mental processes used to plan, monitor, and evaluate what the individual is doing; (2) *performance components,* the actual steps the individual takes; and (3) *knowledge-acquisition components,* processes used to relate old material to new material and to apply new material.

Elsewhere, Sternberg (2001) distinguishes between *creative thinking:* the emphasis on taking risks, the courage of one's convictions and beliefs, and deep-seated personal resources needed to believe in oneself; *intelligent thinking:* the ability to define and refine problems, to think insightfully, to discard irrelevant information and zero in on relevant information; and *ordinary thinking:* whereby one relies on known knowledge and can use this knowledge for basic tasks and highly structured solutions and problems; the person is able to meet minimum standards and general requirements.

Robert Ennis (1989, 1993) identifies thirteen attributes of critical thinkers. They tend to (1) be open minded, (2) take a position (or change position) when the evidence calls for it, (3) take into account the entire situation, (4) seek information, (5) seek precision in information, (6) deal in an orderly manner with parts of a complex whole, (7) look for options, (8) search for reasons, (9) seek a clear statement of the issue, (10) keep the original problem in mind, (11) use credible sources, (12) remain on point, and (13) be sensitive to the feelings and knowledge level of others.

*Promise and Pitfalls of Critical Thinking.* In general, teachers must ask students a great many questions; require students to analyze, apply, and evaluate information; take opposing sides to tease and test students; and require them to support their answers or conclusions. Supplementary materials beyond the workbook and textbook will be needed; it is recommended that teachers work together to develop such materials. By varying instructional activities, ensuring that groups are heterogeneous in abilities and skills, distributing relevant materials, giving instruction in constructing logical arguments, and encouraging students to rely on evidence, teachers can help students learn to think critically in a variety of academic situations.

According to researchers, "giving children a sense of ownership in their classroom can lead to the kind of open and cooperative learning environment that most teachers dream about." This kind of classroom climate is important for developing "confident, active" learners who learn to rely "on their own inner resources" (Zachlod, 1996, pp. 50–51). Children must learn to listen to one another, respect one another's conversation, and thoughtfully respond to what their classmates have to say; there must be room to think, to grow, and to build genuine concern and appreciation for others. These ideas are rooted in Dewey's (1902) notion of group learning and an education involving socialization in the ways of society, including interfacing with others.

Similarly, David Johnson and Roger Johnson point out that students must learn to respect and value one another so they can learn from one another. Students must feel secure enough to challenge one another's ideas and reasoning, and they must be encouraged to engage in controversial discussions, debates, problem-solving activities, and decision-making activities (Johnson, 2003; Johnson & Johnson, 1999). The teacher should promote cooperative learning skills that allow students to join and work together, and reduce competitive learning.

No one teacher can do the job alone; this is a process that takes years to develop. The school administration must establish the professional climate and the need for cooperation and communication among teachers (of all subjects and grade levels) to implement the goal of making students into critical thinkers. The effort will take a critical mass of teachers who agree—and have certain expectations of students—that thinking counts more than facts and that asking "Why?" "How?" and "What if?" is more important than asking "What?" "When?" and "Who?"

One might argue that all this fuss about thinking is nothing more than old-fashioned analysis and problem solving—which good teachers have been infusing into their classroom instruction for years. Moreover, it might be argued that teaching a person to think is like teaching someone to swing a golf club or cook a stew; it requires a holistic approach, not the piecemeal effort suggested by Lipman, Sternberg, and Ennis. Trying to break down thinking skills into discrete units might be helpful for diagnostic proposals, and it might sound like a good theory—suitable for education courses—but it can also be argued that critical thinking is too complex to be broken down into small steps or discrete parts. Rather, as some researchers claim, it involves a wide range of strategic activities such as cause–effect relationships; arguments in the forms of opinions, each supported with multiple forms of evidence; and knowing what one knows and how one knows it (Fischer & Rose, 2001; Krynock & Robb, 1999; Snow, 2001). In short, the whole may be more important than the parts in describing or analyzing a student's mental functioning. See Table 1.1 for a summary of the range of major theories about learning and thinking.

Ultimately, there are no simple answers to the mystery of how we learn and think. Most problems and decisions in real life have social, economic, and psychological implications. They involve interpersonal responsibility and choice. How a person deals with illness, aging, or death or with less momentous events such as starting a new job or meeting new people has little to do with the way a person thinks in class or on critical thinking tests. But such life situations are important matters. In stressing cognitive skills, educators tend to ignore the realities of life. Being an A student in school guarantees little after school or in real life. It certainly has little to do with being a good lover; possessing mental and physical health; being a moral, spiritual, or good person; or earning a lot of money in our society—all of which in the larger scheme of life are more important than being "smart."

There are many other factors associated with the outcomes of life, and many of them have little to do with critical thinking or even intelligence. Thus we need to keep in mind social, psychological, physical, and moral components of learning as well as luck—what some of us might call the unaccounted-for variables in the outcomes of life. Given all the options and factors related to life, luck (good and bad) counts more than "smarts" or intelligence. Do we make our own luck? Type A personalities probably think they make their own luck, but no genius can outwit the macro events of global affairs, the national economy, who gets elected to what political office, or where the next war, terrorist act, or traffic jam will take place. In simple, everyday terms, you cannot determine or control who you will meet at the next party you attend. It could be an idiot or your new lover and future spouse. Anyone with a few ounces of brains mixed with

*Table 1.1*  Overview of Major Learning Theories and Principles

| Psychologist | Major Theory or Principle | Definition or Explanation |
|---|---|---|
| **Behaviorist** | | |
| Thorndike | Law of effect | When a connection between a situation and a response is made, and it is accompanied by a satisfying state of affairs, that connection is strengthened; when accompanied by an annoying state of affairs, the connection is weakened. |
| Pavlov–Watson | Classical conditioning | Whenever a response is closely followed by the reduction of a drive, the tendency is for the stimulus to evoke that reaction on subsequent occasions; association strength of the stimulus-response bond depends on the conditioning of the response and the stimulus. |
| Skinner | Operant conditioning | In contrast to classical conditioning, no specific or identifiable stimulus consistently elicits operant behavior. If an operant response is followed by a reinforcing stimulus, the strength of the response is increased. |
| Bandura | Observational learning | Behavior is best learned through observing and modeling. Emphasis is placed on vicarious, symbolic, and self-regulatory processes. |
| **Cognitive** | | |
| Piaget | Cognitive stages of development | Four cognitive stages form a sequence of progressive mental operations; the stages are hierarchical and increasingly more complex. |
| | Assimilation, accommodation, and equilibration | The incorporation of new experiences, the method of modifying new experiences to derive meaning, and the process of blending new experiences into a systematic whole. |
| Dewey | Problem solving | Being in a situation, sensing a problem, clarifying it with information, working out suggested solutions, and testing the ideas by application. |
| Bruner–Phenix | Structure of a subject | The knowledge, concepts, and principles of a subject; learning how things are related is learning the structure of a subject. |
| Gardner | Multiple intelligences | A cross-cultural, expanded concept of what is intelligence—such areas as linguistics, music, logical–mathematical, spatial, body–kinesthetic, and personal. |
| Lipman– Marzano– Sternberg | Critical thinking | Teaching students how to think, including forming concepts, generalizations, cause–effect relationships, inferences, consistencies and contradictions, assumptions, analogies, and the like. |
| **Humanistic** | | |
| Maslow | Human needs | Six human needs related to survival and psychological well-being; the needs are hierarchical and serve to direct behavior. |
| Rogers | Freedom to learn | Becoming a full person requires freedom to learn; the learner is encouraged to be open, self-trusting, and self-accepting. |

*(continued)*

| | | |
|---|---|---|
| *Table 1.1* **Continued** | | |

| Psychologist | Major Theory or Principle | Definition or Explanation |
|---|---|---|
| **Humanistic** *(continued)* | | |
| Raths | Values clarification | Analysis of personal preferences and moral/social issues to reveal or clarify one's values—that is, beliefs, attitudes, and opinions. |
| Johnson–Slavin | Cooperative learning | Cooperative and group approaches to learning are considered more effective than competitive and individualistic learning situations. |

*Source:* Adapted from Allan C. Ornstein and Francis P. Hunkins, *Curriculum: Foundations, Principles and Issues,* 4th ed. (Boston: Allyn and Bacon, 2004).

old-style wisdom understands that social and personal skills are more important than cognitive skills in the scheme of life, as well as how we get along with people and take advantage of events that affect us.

## Creativity: Looking at Children's Drawings

We move from critical thinking to creativity by looking through the eyes and artwork of fifth graders in a minority school in New Haven, Connecticut. These are kids with imagination, creativity, and a sense of wonder. When asked to draw a day in his life twenty years from now, one student drew his own body shop, painted bright yellow, where for $90 you could get your car fixed. Another student painted two women trading volleys on a tennis court in order to win a trip to the moon. There was Pokemon saving the human race from a host of volcanoes erupting at the same time; and then there was a bare-chested man, surrounded by a half-blue, half-green background, flying to his destiny, with the verbal explanation: "That's my uncle."

One child drew a picture of a minivan full of children, with the verbal explanation: "My mother . . . buys a minivan and she takes us places. This [van] can fly, and only she can drive it. . . . It can go anywhere you want. You just push in the speed like you push in the speed on the treadmill, and it will go. . . . You don't have to drive, you can just tell it your destination and it will take you there." Another student drew a picture of a diploma represented by some wavy lines that were framed, a chair with wheels, a desk, and what appeared to be a computer and a file cabinet. Her explanation: "When I grow up to be a lawyer, I'd like to roll around on my chair and still be able to see the screen. . . . Being a lawyer you can make more friends. You'll help people and they'll remember; 'Yeah, that's the girl that helped me'" (Wilgoren, 2000, p. 17).

How about this last one: a picture of a baby robot and mother robot (no father figure), a balloon, and a small purse or bag. Explanation: "The baby robot is made out of tin, and the mama is made out of copper. They'll probably be just like us; they don't take showers [but] they're be our friends. It's a New Year's Eve party. . . . They're listening to, probably, like sounds of machinery" (Wilgoren, 2000, p. 17).

What will happen to these friendly, imaginative, positive-thinking kids? What goes wrong in the home, school, and community so that many kids from the ghetto are left behind, grow angry, and lose their future? What will happen to these happy, bright, creative fifth-grade students? How important is it that three-quarters of these kids read below grade level? Is reading skill the answer to success or failure? Does it boil down to reading? Surely reading is the strongest link to school success. But what about the other domains of learning?

For every Michael Jordan, Johnny Cash, or Jennifer Lopez who succeeds in sports or entertainment, a hundred thousand or more kids from the ghetto fail school because of limited reading skills and subsequent learning and/or behavioral problems. Other things count, and they will be discussed in other chapters. But, for the time being, we thought it was worthwhile to recapture the world of young, innocent kids who have managed to remain hopeful. They provide us with subtle and simple reminders about our roles and responsibilities as parents and teachers.

## Memory and Brain Expansion

"Who am I?" The question is either the start of a provocative thriller story, an existentialist inquiry, a plot in an artsy-craftsy movie, or a reason to purchase a gift certificate to buy a book on memory exercises or a ticket to a memory fitness class to help our parents or grandparents remember where they left the car in the parking lot. But the appealing notion that our individuality is bound up in our memory runs up against the idea that memory is not reliable and fades as we age.

As one psychologist puts it, what we commonly refer to as memory are "confabulations, artificial constructions of our own design built around . . . retained experience, which we attempt to make live again by influences of imagination" (Wilson, 2000, p. 105). Such a definition leads to all kinds of theories about memory loss, memory boosting, memory manipulation, and memory and imagination. It can lead to the theater of the absurd, a semantic cul-de-sac, or a postmodern conversation: "What?," to which the answer is: "This is what." And "What is this?" "This is what is." "Which is?" "What you want to be." So a fork can temporarily be a knife; good teaching can be defined as a stroll in the park; and for an aspiring art student, one red dot on a large white canvas or a series of Campbell soup cans can be construed as the ultimate in modern art.

Reading about the brain or mind is confusing. We are told that about one trillion neurons are ready to connect in a newborn's brain and that how "the wiring" takes place is dependent on the baby's early experiences (Bruer, 1999; Kulak, 1996). The experiences of childhood determine which neurons are used and how they interconnect in the brain; the connections subsequently determine the potential and limits of cognitive capacity and other domains of learning such as social, moral, psychomotor, and so on. The strategy for optimal brain development is to stimulate and use as many synapses and circuits as possible during childhood, a strategy that corresponds with traditional behaviorist and environmental theorists' ideas: Use it or lose it!

In a somewhat similar viewpoint, two psychologists declare that the brain consists of a "quadrillion connections supported by trillions of nerve fibers," along with branching neurons and "protoplasmic kisses, [whereby a message] vaults across a sliver of space called a synaptic cleft and into the outstretched arm of another neuron" (Tanzi & Parson, 2000, p. 144). In simple terms, we seek all kinds of memory aids, from tests and files to training methods and drugs, in the hope that we will come up with a Viagra pill for the brain. Right now, however, no imagery, no training method, no drug can save us from brain plaque and neurofibrillary tangles. According to researchers, plaque is the "litter" and "rubble" that clogs our memory banks (Tanzi & Parson, 2000), just as plaque forms around our teeth and arteries and leads to gum disease and heart problems. The popular remedy among Indian and Chinese scholars is to sip on warm water to clean out the system of all plaque. And, if you don't believe in warm water (with or without lemon), special chemical drugs, or genetic engineering, there is always the potential for a computer chip. In ten to twenty years, we should have "smarter brains, happier brains, calmer brains, brains that are less forgetful" and less vulnerable to age, disease, and damage (Goode, 2000, p. 27).

There is no question that we will soon have drugs to enhance cognition, drugs that complement the many psychoactive and mood-changing drugs already on the market. We already have treatments for depression, schizophrenia, tangled nerves, and hyperactivity; in fact, we have raised an entire generation of children on Ritalin, which makes it easier for teachers and counselors to modify behavior and control students. We are on the verge of treating Alzheimer's disease and enhancing memory. Soon we will be shaping and expanding intelligence, repairing and improving brain networks, and possibly using computers for a complete brain overhaul. The availability of all these new chemicals (and computer chips) will pose difficult ethical questions—there use by whom and for whom.

One might argue there is nothing wrong in increasing intelligence for kids who have trouble learning or eliminating from their memory a painful or emotional experience such as rape or a parent's death. But, unless you believe in Nazi eugenics, it is part of growth and development to come to terms with loss and emotional injury. The best we can all agree on is the basic need for brains, what the scarecrow in *The Wizard of Oz* wanted. We can also agree on the acceptability of some form of memory improvement through conventional methods such as a two-hour course or ten tips on brain exercise in a magazine or book, as well as some recognition that there are different forms of brain development, intelligence, and styles of learning.

## Global Expansion, Culture, and Human Capital

On a global and much more theoretical level, growth and prosperity among cultures and civilizations can be explained by environment, or by the limits of geographical isolation. Given a make-believe world in which every individual has identical genetic potential, there would still be large differences in education, skills, and related occupations and income among people because of demographic differences, which over centuries shape human behavior and attitudes.

For Thomas Sowell (1998a, 1998b), nothing conflicts with the desire for equality as much as geography; it is the physical setting—reflected by large bodies of water, deserts, mountains, forests, etc.—in which civilizations, nations, races, and ethnic groups have evolved and in turn produced different cultures. Put simply, the people of the Himalayas have not had equal opportunity to acquire seafaring skills, and the Inuit (Eskimos) did not have equal opportunity to learn how to farm or grow oranges. Too often the influence of geography is assessed solely in terms of natural resources that directly influence national wealth. But geography also influences cultural differences by either expanding or limiting the universe of ideas and inventions available to different people.

When geography isolates people, say by mountains, a desert, or a small island, the people have limited contact with the outside world; consequently, technological and innovative advancement is also limited. While the rest of the world trades skills, ideas, and values from a larger cultural pool, isolated peoples are limited by their own resources and what knowledge they have developed on their own. Very few technological advances come from isolated cultures, and those that do are usually modified and improved by people who have learned to assimilate and adopt new ideas from other cultures.

England, France, Portugal, and Spain were tiny countries compared to China, India, and Japan, but the Europeans traveled the navigable waterways of their continent as well as the Atlantic, and they were motiovated by profits and plunder. They came in contact with many countries and civilizations, including South America, Egypt, Turkey, India, China, and Japan, and thus gained from their knowledge. But the older civilizations did not draw on the knowledge of the Europeans or of one another, and eventually those great civilizations (which were once more advanced but isolated) were overtaken and conquered by the smaller countries that had expanded their knowledge base. Once Japan broke from its isolation, it rose to become one of today's economic powers. Similarly, the rise of the United States—in particular through our skills, technology, innovations, and economic advances—is based on the history of immigrants, people who came from all parts of the world, assimilated, and exchanged knowledge and ideas. It is this constant flow of different people from different parts of the globe that helps maintain the American entrepreneurial spirit and sense of innovation and creativity not enjoyed in more static, less dynamic countries.

New knowledge in the United States doubles about every fifteen to twenty years. In many developing countries, the mule and horse is the main mode of transportation, and the local economy is mainly picking berries, dragging banana trees to market, or cleaning out goat intestines that can be turned into leather. This is the real China, India, and Pakistan (Das, 2001; Jian, 2001; Maass, 2001)—the rural hinterland—possibly representative of two-thirds of the world and a lifestyle that U.S. students and teachers cannot fathom. This is not to deny that these countries have a corporate mentality and a class of people that remind us of both old-fashioned industrialists and the new brand of technocrats who are versed in computer software, media, and other high-tech and electronic ventures. What is less clear is the extent to which this new economic and human capital trickles down to the masses who live in poverty, both in the countryside, far away from the "new economy" that deals in the exchange of knowledge and ideas, and in urban squalor, where old and new knowledge, ideas, and values collide: Here in many crowded, filthy third-world cities, East meets West and high tech meets low tech, causing a great cultural rift and the makings of revolution. See Box 1.6 for a discussion of our global ignorance.

For two thousand years, before the invention of railroads, trucks, and airplanes, water was the key for traveling and exploring. Up till the 1850s, it was faster and cheaper to travel by water from San Francisco to China than overland to Chicago. Since the Viking era, the Europeans have understood that geographical isolation can be overcome by the sea or ocean, and given their capitalistic and religious zeal and attitude of superiority, they went out and traded with and also colonized other peoples and cultures; subsequently, they made industrial and technological advances by adopting and modifying the ideas of other civilizations.

**BOX 1.6** Decline of Western Culture and American History Courses

Conservative commentators are concerned that most U.S. students don't know their own history and culture; moreover, many multiculturalists and radical educators from the political left frown on anything that might hint of Western culture—criticized as White, Anglo, male, imperialist, and racist. The outcome is that American history courses are no longer part of the required curriculum in most colleges, and students can satisfy such requirements by taking courses such as Environmental Politics, Global Policy Studies, Urban Life, and others.

Thus, in a Roper 2001 survey among the top 55 colleges in the country, only 40 percent of college seniors knew that the Battle of the Bulge was a World War II event, only 34 percent knew that George Washington commanded the American forces at Yorktown (37 percent thought it was Grant), and only 22 percent could identify that a "government of the people, by the people for the people" came from Lincoln's Gettysburg Address. Remember, these data were compiled from college seniors from the nation's elite colleges!

Anyone familiar with New York City, Chicago, or Los Angeles understands that these cities house people from a vast assortment of countries with different knowledge, ideas, and values. Far from celebrating their particular identities, most urban dwellers have contact with different people and become more hip, sophisticated, or cosmopolitan than their nonurban counterparts. Even kids who come from the backwaters of the world, say from the rice paddies of Vietnam or the mountains of Montenegro, quickly become enculturated into the U.S. environment, especially if they settle in large cities and step out of their parents' cultural and historical isolation. Students who grow up in Iowa, Montana, or Wyoming may score higher on SAT and international tests, but their contact with the outside world is limited. The computer and cell phone may increase our ability to communicate with people from around the world, but without actual contact with different people there is still limited exposure to new thoughts. In short, our thinking is shaped not only by our home environment and community but also by diverse people we come in contact with who reshape and expand our knowledge, ideas, and values; hence, we assimilate more information by coming in contact with more diverse people and cultures.

## ■ SUMMARY ■

1. In classical conditioning, the stimulus-response association depends on the conditioning of the response and stimulus. Pavlov and Watson represent this theory. In contrast to classical conditioning, no specific or identifiable stimulus consistently elicits operant behavior. Operant theory is best represented by the work of B. F. Skinner.

2. People can also learn through observing and modeling; this explanation of behaviorism is associated with Albert Bandura.

3. According to Piaget, four cognitive stages form a sequence of progressive mental operations; the stages are hierarchical and increasingly more complex. Piaget is also noted for his cognitive theory of assimilation, accommodation, and equili-

bration; namely, new experiences are modified and derive new meaning.

4. Moral knowledge can be acquired through academic content, but moral character takes years to develop and reflects the whole person.

5. Whereas Piaget concludes there are three stages of moral development, Kohlberg contends there are six stages to moral reasoning. Both Piaget and Kohlberg view moral development as a socialization process that can be shaped, in part, by schools and society.

6. Students have different learning styles and different ways of thinking, including but not limited to visual, auditory, and tactile responses.

7. Whereas Charles Spearmen viewed intelligence as one general factor, Howard Gardner viewed

intelligence in context with eight broad areas of life, and J. P. Guilford described it in terms of 120 mental operations and/or cognitive processes.

8. Students can be taught learning skills and critical thinking skills. The idea is for the teacher to move from facts and right answers to analysis and problem solving.

9. Our contacts with or lack of exposure to various cultures influence our thinking processes—how we perceive the world and to what extent we make use of universal knowledge.

## ■ DISCUSSION QUESTIONS ■

1. In what ways do behaviorist theory and cognitive psychology differ in terms of how students learn?
2. Why might you think that Piaget's theories of cognitive growth influence elementary teachers more than secondary teachers? What is the difference between assimilation and accommodation of experience?
3. Should teachers be expected to teach moral education? If so, whose morals?
4. How does brain research influence teaching and learning?
5. What teaching methods can be used to improve students' thinking skills?

## ■ THINGS TO DO ■

1. Observe two or three teachers at work. Determine whether they favor behaviorist or cognitive teaching–learning strategies. Explain.
2. Observe the same teachers. Make a list of the instructional patterns that coincide with the descriptions in the chapter.
3. Speak to a local schoolteacher to determine to what extent teachers in the school emphasize behavioral objectives and learning outcomes or broad-based ideas and concepts.
4. Explain to the class the differences between moral education, moral development, and moral values.
5. What learning skills do you personally use in your own homework and class work as a student. Make a list on the chalkboard.

## ■ RECOMMENDED READINGS ■

Darling-Hammond, Linda. *The Right to Learn.* San Francisco: Jossey-Bass, 2001. Ways for improving the teaching–learning process.

Dewey, John. *How We Think,* rev. ed. Boston: Houghton Mifflin, 1998. Originally published in 1918, the book is still relevant and readable today.

Epstein, Joyce, et al. *School, Family, and Community Partnerships,* 2nd ed. Thousand Oaks, CA: Corwin Press, 2002. A research-based guide for teachers and parents to form partnerships and improve school–community relations.

Kohn, Alfie. *What to Look for in a Classroom.* San Francisco: Jossey-Bass, 2000. How teachers can be more effective at helping students learn.

Piaget, Jean. *The Psychology of Intelligence,* rev. ed. London: Broadway, 1950. An overview of Piaget's thinking about how we think and learn; based on environmental stimuli.

Skinner, B. F. *Reflections on Behaviorism and Society.* Englewood Cliffs, NJ: Prentice-Hall, 1978. One of many important books by Skinner, continuing the tenets of behaviorism.

Philip, D. C. *Construction in Education,* 99th Yearbook of the National Society for the Study of Education, Part I. Chicago: NSSE, 2000. Opinions and issues about how knowledge is constructed.

# ■ KEY TERMS ■

accommodation
assimilation
behaviorism
behavior modification
broad field subjects
classical conditioning
cognitive psychology
cognitive theory
comprehension monitoring
connections

constructivism
critical thinking
developmentalists
equilibration
laws of learning
learning skills
learning styles
left–right brain
maturation process
modeling

moral character
moral knowledge
operant behavior
spiral curriculum
structure of intellect
structure of subject matter
values clarification
vicarious learning

# ■ REFERENCES ■

Abbott, J., & Ryan, T. (1999, November). Constructing knowledge, reconstructing schooling. *Educational Leadership,* 66–69.

Alexander, P. A. (2003, November). The development of expertise. *Educational Researcher,* 10–14.

Anderson, J. R. (1993, January). Problem solving and learning. *American Psychologist,* 35–44.

Anderson, J. R., Greeno, J. G., Reder, L. M., & Simon, H. A. (2000, May). Perspectives on learning, thinking, and activity. *Educational Researcher,* 11–13.

Andrade, H. G. (2000, February). Using rubrics to promote thinking and learning. *Educational Leadership,* 13–19.

Baker, B. (1999, Winter). The dangerous and the good? Developmentalism, progress, and public schooling. *American Educational Research Journal,* 797–834.

Bandura, A. (1977). *Social learning theory.* Englewood Cliffs, NJ: Prentice Hall.

Bandura, A. (1986). *Social foundations of thought and action.* Englewood Cliffs, NJ: Prentice Hall.

Baron, S. (1994, January). Chaos, self-organization, and psychology. *American Psychologist,* 5–14.

Barzun, J. (1944). *Teacher in America.* Boston: Little, Brown.

Bear, G. G., & Rys, G. S. (1995, September). Moral reasoning, classroom behavior, and sociometric status among elementary school children. *Developmental Psychology,* 633–638.

Bebeau, M. J., Rest, J. R., & Narvaez, D. (1999, May). Beyond the promise: A perspective on research in moral education. *Educational Researcher,* 18–26.

Bennett, W. (2001). The broken hearth: Revising the moral collapse of the family. New York: Doubleday.

Bina, M. J. (1999, March). Schools for the visually disabled. *Educational Leadership,* 78–82.

Bruer, J. I. (1999, December). Neural connections: Some you use, some you lose. *Phi Delta Kappan,* 264–277.

Bruer, J. T. (1999). *The myth of the first three years.* New York: Free Press.

Bruner, J. S. (1959). *The process of education.* Cambridge, MA: Harvard University Press.

Cobb, P., & Bowers, J. (1999, March). Cognitive and situated learning perspectives in theory and practice. *Educational Researcher,* 4–15.

Committee of Fifteen. (1895, March). Report of the subcommittee on the correlation of studies in elementary education. *Educational Review,* 284.

Crawford, M., & Witte, M. (1999, November). Strategies for mathematics: Teaching in context. *Educational Leadership,* 34–49.

Das, G. (2001). *India unbound.* New York: Knopf.

Dewey, J. (1902). *The child and the curriculum.* Chicago: University of Chicago Press.

Dewey, J. (1938). *Experience and education.* New York: Macmillan.

Doll, R. C. (2001). *Curriculum improvement: Decision making and process* (10th ed.). Boston: Allyn and Bacon.

Eagley, A. H., & Crowley, M. (1986, November). Gender and helping behavior. *Psychological Bulletin*, 283–308.

Ehri, L., & Stahl, S. A. (2001, September). The NPR report on phonics. *Phi Delta Kappan*, 17–27.

Ennis, R. H. (1985, October). A logical basis for measuring critical thinking skills. *Educational Leadership*, 44–48.

Ennis, R. H. (1989, April). Critical thinking and subject specificity. *Educational Researcher*, 4–10.

Ennis, R. H. (1993, Summer). Critical thinking assessment. *Theory into Practice*, 179–186.

Fischer, K., & Rose, T. (2001, November). Web of skill: How students learn. *Educational Leadership*, 6–13.

Flavell, J. (1985). *Cognitive development* (2nd ed.). Englewood Cliffs, NJ: Prentice-Hall.

Gardner, H. (1983). *Frames of mind: The theory of multiple intelligences.* New York: Basic Books.

Gilligan, C. (1982). *In a different voice: Sex differences in the expression of moral judgment.* Cambridge, MA: Harvard University Press.

Glaser, R. (1979, November). Trends and research quotations in psychological research on learning and schooling. *Educational Researcher*, 12.

Glaser, R. (1993). *Advances in instructional psychology* (Vol. 4). Hillsdale, NJ: Erlbaum.

Glassman, M. (2001, May). Dewey and Vygotsky: Society, experience, and inquiry in educational practice. *Educational Researcher*, 3–14.

Goode, E. (2000, January 1). Rx for brain makeovers. *New York Times*, E27.

Guilford, J. P. (1967). *The nature of human intelligence.* New York: McGraw-Hill.

Hardiman, M. M. (2001, November). Connecting brain research with dimensions of learning. *Educational Leadership,* 52–55.

Huttenlocher, P. R., & Dabholkar, A. S. (1997, March). Regional differences in synaptogenesis in human cerebral cortex. *Journal of Comparative Neurology*, 167–178.

Jian, M. (2001). *Red dust: A path through China.* New York: Pantheon.

Johnson, D. (2003). *Reaching out* (8th ed.). Boston: Allyn and Bacon.

Johnson, D., & Johnson, R. T. (1999). *Learning together and alone* (5th ed.). Boston: Allyn and Bacon.

Kagan, S. (2001, October). Teaching for character and community. *Education Leadership*, 50–55.

Kaminer, W. (2001, April 8). Have a nice life. *New York Times Book Review*, 14.

Keller, E. F. (2001). *The century of the gene.* Cambridge, MA: Harvard University Press.

Kohlberg, L. A. (1963). The development of children's orientation toward a moral order, I: Sequence in the development of moral thought. *Vita Humana, 6*, 11–33.

Kohlberg, L. A. (1964). Development of moral character and moral ideology. In M. L. Hoffman & L. W. Hoffman (Eds.), *Review of child development* (Vol. 1, pp. 383–431). New York: Russell Sage Foundation.

Kohn, A. (1998, April). Only for my kid. *Phi Delta Kappan*, 568–577.

Krathwohl, D. R., Bloom, B. S., & Masia, B. B. (1964). *Taxonomy of educational objectives, handbook II: Affective domain.* New York: McKay.

Krynock, K., & Robb, L. (1999, November). Problem solved: How to coach cognition. *Educational Leadership*, 24–35.

Kuhn, D. (1999, March). A developmental model of critical thinking. *Education Researcher*, 16–25.

Kulak, R. (1996). *Inside the brain.* Kansas City, MO: McMeel.

Leinhardt, G. (1992, April). What research on learning tells us about teaching. *Educational Leadership*, 20–25.

Lipman, M. (1984, September). The culturation of reasoning through philosophy. *Educational Leadership*, 54–56.

Lipman, M. (1988). *Philosophy goes to school.* Philadelphia: Temple University Press.

Lipman, M. (1991). *Thinking in education.* New York: Cambridge University, Press.

Lipman, M., et al. (1990). *Philosophy for children* (3rd ed.). Philadelphia: Temple University Press.

Maass, P. (2001, October 21). Emroz Khan is having a bad day. *New York Times Magazine*, 48–51.

Martuseweicz, R. A. (2001). *Seeking passage post structionalism, pedagogy, ethics.* New York: Teachers College Press, Columbia University.

Noddings, N. (1992). *The challenge to care in schools.* New York: Teachers College Press, Columbia University.

Noddings, N. (2002). *Educating moral people.* New York: Teachers College Press, Columbia University.

Ornstein, A. C. (1988, September). The irrelevant curriculum: A review from four perspectives. *NASSP Bulletin,* 14–17.

Ornstein, A. C., & Hunkins, F. P. (2004). *Curriculum: Foundations, principles, and issues* (4th ed.). Boston: Allyn and Bacon.

Pavlov, I. P. (1927). *Conditioned reflexes.* (G. V. Anrep, Trans.). London: Oxford University Press.

Phenix, P. H. (1964). *Realms of meaning.* New York: McGraw-Hill.

Piaget, J. (1932). *The child's conception of physical causality.* New York: Harcourt.

Piaget, J. (1950). *The psychology of intelligence* (Rev. ed.). London: Broadway.

Piaget, J. (1965). *The moral development of the child.* New York: Free Press.

Popham, W. J. (1999). *Classroom assessment* (2nd ed.). Boston: Allyn and Bacon.

Popham, W. J., & Baker, E. I. (1970). *Systematic instruction.* Englewood Cliffs, NJ: Prentice Hall.

Power, C., & Kohlberg, L. (1986, September–October). Moral development: Transforming the hidden curriculum. *Curriculum Review,* 26–32.

Prawat, R. S. (1993, August–September). The Value of ideas. *Educational Researcher,* 5–16.

Prawat, R. (2000, Fall). Dewey meets the "Mozart of psychology." *American Educational Research Journal,* 663–696.

Raths, L. E., Harmin, M., & Simon, S. B. (1978). *Values and teaching* (2nd ed.). Columbus, OH: Merrill.

Resnick, L. (1987). *Education and learning to think.* Washington, DC: National Academy Press.

Shore, R. (1997). *Rethinking the brain: New insights into early development.* New York: Families & Work Institute.

Sizer, T. R., & Sizer, N. F. (1999). *The students are watching: Schools and the moral context.* Boston: Beacon Press.

Skinner, B. F. (1953). *Science and human behavior.* New York: Macmillan.

Skinner, B. F. (1970). *Reflections on behaviorism and society.* Englewood Cliffs, NJ: Prentice Hall.

Smetana, J. G., Killen, M., & Turiel, E. (1998). Children's reasoning about interpersonal and moral conflicts. *Child Development, 68,* 629–644.

Snow, C. (2001, October). Knowing what we know. *Educational Researcher,* 3–9.

Sowell, T. (1998a). *Conquests and cultures: An international history.* New York: Basic Books.

Sowell, T. (1998b, October 5). Race, culture and equality. *Forbes,* 144–149.

Spearman, C. E. (1927). *The abilities of man.* New York: Macmillan.

Sternberg, R. J. (1984, September). How can we teach intelligence? *Educational Leadership,* 38–48.

Sternberg, R. J. (1990, September). "Practical intelligence for success in school," *Educational Leadership,* 35–39.

Sternberg, R. (2001). *Understanding and teaching the intuitive mind.* Mahwah, NJ: Lawrence Erlbaum Associates.

Sternberg, R., & Lubart, T. I. (1999). Creating creative minds. In A. C. Ornstein & L. S. Behar-Hornstein (Eds.), *Contemporary issues in curriculum* (2nd ed., pp. 153–162). Boston: Allyn and Bacon.

Tanzi, R. E., & Parson, A. B. (2000). *Decoding darkness: The search for genetic causes of Alzheimer's disease.* New York: Perseus.

Tetreault, M. K. T. (2001). *The feminist culture* (Rev. ed.). Lanham, MD: Rowman & Littlefield.

Thorndike, E. L. (1911). *Animal intelligence.* New York: Macmillan.

Thorndike, E. L. (1913). *Psychology of learning.* New York: Teachers College Press, Columbia University.

Thorndike, E. L. (1924, February). Mental discipline high school studies. *Journal of Educational Psychology,* 98.

Travers, R. M. (1982). *Essentials of learning* (5th ed.). New York: Macmillan.

Trocco, F. (2000, April). Encouraging students to study weird things. *Phi Delta Kappan,* 628–631.

Vacca, D. M. (2001, November). Confronting the puzzle of nonverbal learning disabilities. *Educational Leadership,* 26–31.

Wade, N. (2000, July 2). The four letter alphabet that spells life. *New York Times,* 4.

Wagmeister, J., & Shifrin, B. (2000, November). Thinking differently, learning differently. *Educational Leadership,* 45–48.

Watson, J. B. (1926). What the nursery has to say about instincts. In C. A. Murchison (Ed.), *Psychologies of 1925* (p. 10). Worchester, MA: Clark University Press.

Watson, J. B. (1939). *Behaviorism.* New York: Norton.

Weinstein, C. E., & Mayer, R. E. (1986). The teaching of learning strategies. In M. C. Wittrock, (Ed.), *Handbook of research on teaching* (3rd ed., pp. 315–327). New York: Macmillan.

Wilgoren, J. (2000, January 1). Through the eyes children. *New York Times*, 17.

Wilson, D. (2000, November 25). As quoted in When memory fails. *Economist*, 105.

Wolfe, A. (2001). *Moral freedom: The impossible idea that defines the way we live now.* New York: Norton.

Zachlod, M. G. (1996, September). Room to grow. *Educational Leadership*, 50–51.

*chapter* 2

# Language and Literacy

*Focusing Questions*

1. What is meant by literacy?
2. Are there different kinds or forms of literacy?
3. Are language and literacy used in the same way, or is literacy an aspect of language acquisition?
4. How are different forms of literacy processed by people to accomplish different ends?
5. What is the connection between different forms of literacy and the concept of multiple intelligences as discussed in Chapter 1?
6. How do computers and the use of electronic/digital technologies redefine our notions of literacy?
7. What are the major issues regarding the effective use of computers in our schools?

This chapter asks the teacher to reflect on language and literacy connections and how these affect learning. Second, we will see how the scope of literacy has broadened to include other ways in which ideas and meaning are communicated. *Language* and *literacy* are terms often used in the same conceptual booklet, prompting educators and the general public to use the words interchangeably. Educators themselves have helped this merger by coining the phase "the language arts." The language arts from a pedagogical position means those aspects of the curriculum that focus on the use and study of four language components—listening, speaking, reading, and writing. Very often such related areas as spelling, handwriting, grammar, and word-attack skills are included as components of language study and appear on children's report cards as aspects of the language arts.

However, there is a major distinction between language and literacy and this has to do with how human beings learn and process language. Listening and speaking are viewed as the primary language systems developed and used by all peoples in their respective cultures. Reading and writing are secondary forms of communication in that a symbol system has to be constructed to represent the oral language structure of the primary system. Thus, whereas listening and speaking are natural learning events, reading and writing are unnatural in that children have to use effort to learn words in some kind of structured way. In learning to read, the beginning reader has to engage in the effortful steps of visual word identification, and this endeavor is an act transplanted onto the natural language system that has evolved (Rayner & Pollatsek, 1994). How children are brought to reading and writing—the domain of literacy—is still a controversial subject today. Should the transfer from the oral language to the printed symbol system be as natural and cushioned as possible, as "whole language" advocates would have it, or should transfer be regulated by a study of the printed language code, as phonics advocates would have it?

Yet there are still others who conceive of a broader definition of literacy that includes myriad meanings and multiple literacies (Piazza, 1999). These multiple literacy forms are composed of the visual arts, music, dance, drama, and film, including video, television, and computer technology. These literacy forms play an important role in the development of learning and learners' lives because they offer communicative choices that go beyond conventional language symbols to offer multiple symbol systems.

The teacher should think of reading and writing as the domain of written literacy, which occurs naturally in a continuum after oral language development. But how do the other literacies fit into the total human whole? Before we provide answers to this question, the reader may wish to consult the literacy explanation chart in Table 2.1. This chart provides a summarized definition of each form of literacy to help clarify for readers what is meant by each literacy. However, these literacies do not often operate independently of one another. They merge in our actions and thoughts to make us what we are. The reader may consider speaking or reading to be independent acts, and they may appear to be so at the moment of occurrence. However, in order to speak, the speaker has had to internalize language through listening (with viewing and movement also playing a large part). In order to obtain meaning while reading, the reader needs to understand the oral language code so that when the printed symbols representing the oral language are recognized, the reader can comprehend the written text.

| *Table 2.1* | Defining the Forms of Literacy |
|---|---|
| Viewing | A basic human function for all seeing people. Through the eyes, the viewer explores, takes in, and responds to information from the environment. Mental images or schemata of past experiences develop based on the interaction of vision and other sensory input, especially motor. |
| Listening | A basic human function for all hearing people. Through the ears, the listener receives sounds and language from people and the environment. Understanding of words and syntax develops to form a repertoire of "receptive oral language" containing a mental dictionary or lexicon of word meanings. |
| Speaking | The ability to express sounds and speech through the organs of the vocal chords and the mouth. Often considered "expressive oral language," speaking or talk allows learners to express their inner thoughts, wishes, and feelings. Talk or oral language is a natural extension of thought, which develops through viewing, listening, and active exploration of the environment. |
| Reading | The ability to decipher and understand printed symbols to obtain meaning. Often referred to as "receptive written language," reading is a secondary symbol system for most cultures in that letters, alphabets, or print symbols have to be invented to represent the features of the oral language. Once the print symbols are mastered, a reader can enlarge his or her vocabulary and learn through continued reading as well as appreciate the world through books. |
| Writing | The ability to use the print symbols of a culture to describe happenings and transmit messages. Often referred to as "expressive written language," writing can express a person's thoughts and feelings by communicating with anyone who can decode or "read" the writer's printed message. |
| Visual (Artistic) Representation | This level of representing experience, meaning, and thought is accomplished mainly through nonverbal means. Young children do this when they draw, shape clay, and fashion blocks independently of verbal language, and artists do this when they paint, sculpt, act, dance, and imagine with the tools and symbolic elements of their craft. The artist reconstructs experience to transcend the ordinary or to make the ordinary appear fresh. |
| Computer Literacy | This was the initial phrase used when computers appeared on the educational scene. The phrase suggests that a separate, unique literacy might occur through computer use. Computer programmers did need to develop special "languages" to allow verbal language to be converted into electronic instructions so that programs and computers would operate. Many of the schools offered course work and programs in computer languages. However, the basic way that computers were used in school settings during the initial period was for computer-assisted instruction and drill and practice to reinforce regular school routines and for word processing, which was another means of writing. |
| Technological/ Electronic/ Digital Literacy | These three terms are often used interchangeably to mean the level of computer use and communication achieved through computers now and in the future. All of the other literacies are achieved and embedded in this computer context. *Technological* means that machines with their accompanying hardware and software formats are used to create and apply information such as through hypertext and hypermedia environments. *Electronic* means that information is being transmitted and received through electrical wires, indicating that any earth locale that has an electrical hookup can support a computer. *Digital* means that the information flowing through the wires is coded in a binary system of electrical impulses with either an off (0) or an on (1). Although the Internet and World Wide Web applications are the present focus of the digital age, this level of literacy also means the ability to use technological savvy efficiently and purposefully and the ability to cope with rapid technological advances to serve self and society. |

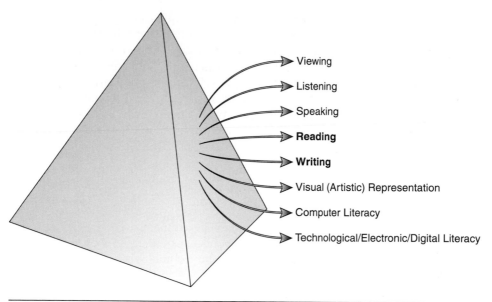

*Figure 2.1* The Language/Literacy Spectrum

The language/literacy spectrum illustrated in Figure 2.1 provides a way to visualize the components of literacy as they occur in a literate society. The reader might think that the bands of literacy are arranged from top to bottom in some kind of developmental way. There is a bit of truth in this as far as the array from "viewing" to "writing." However, very early in life, as soon as children begin pushing wooden blocks to represent trains, children develop nonverbal modes of representation. Also, children today are engaged in electronic literacy formats before or while they are beginning to learn to read and write. Therefore, it is quite helpful for the reader and teacher to group the spectrum bands so that they work in harmony as children develop. We will see how the various aspects of language, literacy, and technology connect and are solidified by one another.

# ■ THE VIEWING, LISTENING, AND SPEAKING CONNECTION

Children are born with sensory, perceptual, and cognitive capacities that allow language to flourish. In a sense, children are wired to listen, to talk, and to learn through talk situations. But there's more to it. There's also the eye traffic reaching the brain. While the neural pathways are being formed that allow understanding of oral language to occur, the young child is also an active viewer and visual explorer of his or her immediate surroundings. For instance, a child hears from his mother when he is looking at a bird on a tree branch, "There's a black bird, a crow." As the bird flies from the tree, the child may have made the **neural connections** of bird-crow-fly (Restak, 2001; Sprenger, 1999). The neural connections refer to the way the neurons or nerve cells interact with one another to communicate messages within the brain. The next time the event occurs—i.e., the child sees a bird on a tree branch—the brain may make the connections again, only this time the connections may occur more rapidly. When neurons practice or "learn" information being transmitted through the neural network, they become more efficient in making connections, thereby making the child a more efficient or fluent learner. Then there's the notion presented in Chapter 1 regarding the critical age periods for learning and how environmental stimulation during these periods may influence neural development.

How does the young child learn? How do vision, listening, talking, and venturing out into the environment shape the young child's perceptual, linguistic, and cognitive life? Children's actions help them construct what they know about the world.

As noted in Chapter 1, Jean Piaget believed that the young child must operate on the immediate environment to bring about change (Piaget, 1963). Children learn by doing, by interacting with their local environment and by formulating **mental schema** of how the natural world operates. Through active participation of their own intelligence, children construct their own rules regarding how the environment is put together.

The immediate environment provides a field of experimentation. Children manipulate materials such as blocks, toys, furniture, utensils, and so forth and get visual/motor feedback about outcomes of their touching behavior. They learn how to adapt and accommodate themselves to environmental changes and mishaps, many of which were self-induced. In essence, children construct mental schemata based on experiences. According to Piaget, a schema is a mental image or pattern of action, and this mental picture becomes a way of representing and organizing all of the child's previous sensorimotor experiences. Thus it is the eye, the basic receptor of a visual literacy, that coordinates with the hand, the feet, the ears, and the talking mouth to continually build nonverbal thinking.

Children's actions are channeled through vision to help them construct their logic, developed through such thinking processes as classifying, ordering, and conserving. For instance, children learn that some things can be grouped and some cannot, and that some things can move when they are pushed, whereas others cannot. Later they learn to see that changes of physical appearance, such as when juice has been poured from the container to the glass, does not mean that a loss of volume has occurred. Or children learn that when a number of pieces of colored clay are merged together to make a rolled-out "snake," there is still the same amount of clay regardless of the constructed creature. Other educators have noted that these insights are independent of language and take the form of images (Norton, 1997). The collection of images becomes a mental filing cabinet of organized knowledge, also known as cognitive structures (Tompkins, 1998). Children's thinking emanates from a nonverbal core, but rather rapidly, usually between the ages of eight to twelve months, this thinking is aided by forthcoming language development.

## Representational Thought

Educators have examined the constructs of **visual literacy** or **visual thinking** in order to study the influence of vision on learning and cognition and to account for a visual shift in our culture and classrooms (Hyerle, 1996). John Debes, credited as the pioneer in the field of visual literacy, pointed out that the disciplines of semantics, linguistics, philosophy, psychology, psycholinguistics, art, science education, and the industrial, vocational, and graphic arts have contributed meaning to the term *visual literacy* (Debes, 1969). In attempt to bring constructive, process-oriented meanings to the two words *visual* and *literacy,* Sinatra saw "visual literacy" operating on two conceptual levels—at a primary level and at a representational level (1986).

At the primary level, the learner is perceiving and interacting with the environment. This is a process of exploring, seeking out, and responding in continual interaction between the viewer and the environment. An outgrowth of this active experimentation and viewing is the formation of nonverbal, representational thought. For young children, **representational thought** is expressed through such forms as body language, play, and art, whereas older people engaging in the physical and mental arts can create works of beauty and grandeur. Nonverbal, representational thought is thinking by analogy, metaphor, and symbol.

Three interrelated areas have contributed to the rapid growth of a highly networked, interactive "seeing" culture (Hyerle, 1996). These three areas are the constructive–cognitive influence, the impact of technology with its visual design tools, and the movement toward increased student-centered control of learning. The rise of visual thinking and the use of visual tools to represent that thinking may bring about a "revolution in representation" in modern classrooms.

Children rapidly enlarge representational thought or mental schemata during their early years, as Piaget has noted. At first they may call all four-footed animals a cat, a dog, or a horse. Then, as the youngster comes into more and more visual and physical contact with each type of animal, the schema for each begins to take on a clearer focus. The youngster has accommodated his or her previous perceptions and adjusted to the more accepted view of each animal. Schemata, therefore, are the collective representations of all of life's experiences and form the bases of the child's conceptual filing system.

It is through such activities as observing and counting objects, sorting toys, modeling with clay, finger painting, building with blocks, playing house, and the hundreds of other visual/motor activities that children engage in that they form mental schemata and learn the cognitive skills of comparing, contrasting, categorizing, sequencing, and so on. Of course, words come along and become attached to all of these aspects of play and activity. Words can be used for objects that appear in the immediate viewing area or for those objects that appear as mental pictures in the child's mind.

Through play and social interaction, children share representational thought. During playtime, one child uses a fluff of cotton to represent a neighbor's kitten because the child visualizes the connectedness of the cotton's whiteness and softness to the kitten. The child can say, "This cotton is kitty" to another child. The connectedness between the real object (cotton ball) and the representational form (the kitten) must be in each child's experience, along with the words *cotton* and *kitten,* to obtain meaning. If the second child says, "Now, this basket can be armadillo," and the other youngster has experienced neither basket nor armadillo in life or words, representational connectedness or meaning will not occur (see Box 2.1).

**BOX 2.1** Why Play Is Important to Literacy Development

Consider life without play. Then consider what the modern world might be doing to young children who experience excessive exposure to media, including television and electronic wizardry. Good old-fashioned play encourages the minds of children to do the "walking" and the "talking." Through play, children become involved in touching and feeling shapes, forms, and properties, and this activity creates the opportunity for words and language to become attached to the play. Then words can be used to express what occurred during aspects of the play as children build a foundation of mental and language experiences.

## The Power of Talk

Language was used in the previous example, and in the second part of the example, one child did not understand the other's use of verbal labels. "What's a basket?" or "What's an armadillo?" the second child might ask. The concrete referents for the words were not in the second child's life experiences. This illustration serves as a caution to the teacher as well. The more that teachers plan to use new words with children who may not have experienced them in early visual literacy or oral language development, the more that teachers need to construct concrete and oral experiences for children to assimilate the new words.

Young children hear language used in actual, immediate contexts, which Frank Smith calls **"situation-dependent spoken language"** (Smith, 1994, p. 37). Initially the object and later the mental picture or schema of the object become referents for the verbal name of the object. A mother is likely to ask, "Do you want some juice?" as a bottle or container is visually displayed before the child. The child sees and hears the connectedness between the object and the words used. This connectedness has to be neurally woven; it has to be fabricated by the individual thinker. Connections have to be processed by the individual thinker even if adults take great pains to point out the connections they themselves have made.

Once connections are made, words, which have been used in specific situational settings, are available to be used by children as a way of imitating their thoughts or making their wishes known in a specific situation. Words become a useful shortcut to acting out a meaning prompted by physical engagement in a concrete situation. Language, then, is both cued by the concrete, visual world and is a cue of what that world holds. Through language, children know and talk of their past, locate themselves in the present, and visualize the future in the form of mental schemata.

Words develop in children's minds from the inside out. In other words, children learn the meaning for words by attaching them to meaningful situations that have become internalized in nonverbal images. Children develop what is called a **deep structure** meaning for words. These deep structure meanings become reflected in their first utterances. Children's first talk is often composed of such phrases as "wan milk," "kitty sleep," "doggie good." Because meaning is learned in wholes, the search for meaning proceeds outward from the child's inner self to become modified according to the language customs of the speaking community. By using language more and more as a tool to describe and achieve satisfaction from the world, the child receives positive reinforcement from parents, guardians, and siblings and becomes motivated to continue with talk. Because of positive reinforcement, the child becomes more and more inclined to talk and interact with the language community of adults and other children.

In the early stages of listening and speaking, children produce grammatical utterances that reflect personalized, meaningful thought. The child has the underlying meaning and basic sentence structure but doesn't know how to connect words and phrases at the **surface level**—or talk level—of language. With time and social interaction with the language community, the child's ability to produce adult talk expands. The child learns to manipulate words and phrases and to transform structures to achieve surface structure "correctness." As children become aware of word and sentence structure, they begin to generalize about the patterns and rules of language. These conventions aren't taught; they are learned. In a sense, they are reconstructed by young children as they experiment with language. Connectedness is established between language and social contexts just as connectedness was established during the nonverbal representation of a basket as an armadillo.

During language situations, the child listens and speaks to obtain meaningful and functional interaction. Youngsters do not learn the rules of oral language production first. The learning of language comes with the use of language and with the increasing understanding of how language structures can be transformed in different ways, on different occasions, and for different people. If the youngster produces a syntactically correct utterance such as "The doggie goed," the child needs to receive feedback about the surface structure appropriateness of the response from significant others such as mom, dad, grandparents, and other siblings. The child's talk is consistent with the grammar of English, indicating that the rules of subject and verb placement in a sentence were internalized. What the child needs now is supportive feedback from the language community to achieve continued surface structure correctness. Bernice Cullinan tells the story of a father who shaped and expanded his three-year-old son's language before the boy jumped into a pool and into his father's arms. Before each jump, they conversed about swimming, made rhymes, and counted off in several languages. The bond of language with experience was nurtured in a highly supportive way by the father acting as a natural teacher (Cullinan, 2000).

## The Social Context

There are additional dimensions to the viewing, listening, and speaking interaction as children develop: (1) an affective, emotional side to language learning; (2) the development of story and story structure; and (3) the book connection. All of these dimensions occur in a social context and strongly influence how children will develop linguistically, socially, and cognitively.

The affective context occurs in natural social situations as children experience language in situational contexts. Children's reactions to the language used during a social situation are also part of the language-learning process. Thus, language and social development are closely intertwined. The writings of the Russian psychologist Lev Vygotsky have contributed to a strong understanding of how language and social interaction enhance each other (1978, 1986). Vygotsky hypothesized a **zone of proximal development** that accounts for the development of children's thinking as a consequence or outcome of their need to communicate with others. Within the zone is a range of activities a child can accomplish with assistance and guidance from others but cannot successfully accomplish on her own. When children are operating within the zone in learning situations, they can perform at their very best. What is needed for optimal performance are support mechanisms by mom, dad, older siblings, grandparents, and other significant caretakers. The support mechanisms are natural parental love, affection from others, and esteem for the child, especially in communicative situations, so that when talking and listening are occurring, there's a shared, bonded interest. This is why conversing with a child and making decisions through conversing are so much more powerful for children's cognitive development than one-directional messages such as commands and orders.

Planning and guiding a learner through successive steps to a successful outcome is called **scaffolding.** Scaffolding occurs when the older sibling, parent, relative, or teacher demonstrates or models what has to be done, guides the learner with actions and talk throughout the activity, points out pitfalls and offers advice, asks questions, and constantly breaks down the larger task into less complex steps so that by successful completion of each "baby step," the larger task can be accomplished (and hopefully internalized).

Can the lesson of scaffolding be transferred to the classroom? Sure it can, but the success of each such staged activity by the teacher takes reflection and understanding of the learning task. Three considerations should guide teachers in mediating student learning within the zone of proximal development (Dixon-Krauss, 1996). First, children's learning should be augmented through social interaction; second, as children are engaged in a learning activity, teachers need to be flexible and provide support based on the children's feedback; and third, according to children's needs, teachers must vary the amount of support from very structured to minimal. In lessons prepared for students, teachers must be mindful of creating optimal conditions for learning (Tompkins, 1998). For instance, when students do not have the background knowledge and schemata for learning new information, teachers need to help students connect and relate what they know about the topic to what they do not know. Also, the new learning needs to be presented in a context that is somewhat familiar to the students so that they can accommodate the new to prior conceptions of the old. Vygotsky's concept of children's conceptual development forms the foundation of many of today's current programs (May, 1998). Elementary school teachers implementing literature-based programs, emergent literacy programs, or the whole language philosophy in their programs should be aware that Vygotsky's ideas form the basis of much of their teaching procedures. (See Box 2.2 on scaffolding a learning task.)

**Representational play,** also called pretend play, is beneficial for the social, affective, and linguistic development of playmates when communication skills are used properly. Pretend play, the thinking of metaphor and representation, occurs when children transform actions, such as pushing a wooden block, into the words "the truck is going fast." By playing and collaborating with others in pretend play, children add more language and story structure to their initially conceived stories. Thus, pretend play lays a foundation for the narrative. Children have objects or characters doing something (the plot) so that something happens (the resolution or outcome).

The structure of the **oral narrative** also develops through talk in the home or in the community. As children and parents talk about experiences they have had, the ability to sequentially order events becomes more and more developed. In some cultures, the structure of the narrative is shaped as traditional stories and tales are told orally to each new generation. In many cases, the development of the narrative or story structure forms more readily when the parent, guardian, or older sibling begins to read to the

**BOX 2.2** Illustrating Adult Guidance in Scaffolding a New Learning Task

Let's observe an illustration of adult guidance in a child's zone of proximal development to see how bonding, language, and cognitive development interact. Five-year-old Ricardo was asked by his grandpa to help him "mend" some broken concrete steps. Wow, what an opportunity for a five-year-old; this was almost as good as playing in the dirt! But grandpa knows that for success to occur for both his apprentice and his concrete steps, he has to arrange the project so that success will be a predictable outcome. Grandpa had to think the project through and plan successive stages of steps in which Ricardo could act and learn in a successful way. An adult should be aware that by giving a five-year-old apprentice dry mortar powder, water, and a mixing pan and telling him to patch some concrete holes without direction and guidance, the procedural steps of learning "how to do it right" will not occur.

Grandpa starts off with a problem (the cracked and broken concrete steps) that he asks his apprentice to help him solve. Ricardo has no awareness of how to help grandpa. Together they talk about how they might fix the steps with the use of products such as concrete patch, water, trowel, and mixing pans. Grandpa reads the directions from the concrete patch container as Ricardo's eyes get big and bright with anticipation. Next, grandpa stages the successive actions so that Ricardo is actively involved in problem solving and is not a passive participant watching someone else accomplish the actions. As grandpa and Ricardo sit on the steps together with shared affection established, the project begins to unfold. Ricardo's jobs are to brush the surfaces of the steps with a small handheld broom to remove loose materials, to shovel the dry concrete powder three scoops at a time into the mixing pan, to add measured amounts of water to the powder, and to stir the powder/water mix into a wet, slurry consistency. Of course, there's the language of the activity going back and forth, such as "Are three scoops enough? Was that enough water, grandpa? Am I mixing the concrete right? Is it ready to trowel?" After praising Ricardo for a nice, wet paste, grandpa does his job of troweling the concrete paste into the cracks and holes. The culminating experience is when Ricardo is shown how to smooth off the paste with the cement trowel to achieve a finished patch job. It may take many such encounters with the concrete patch activity before the mentor can reduce his social and verbal support so that the apprentice can perform the task on his own through independent, internalized knowledge.

child. In this one great act, viewing, listening, speaking, affective engagement, and social bonding come together as the child watches the pages of the storybook turn. As children hear their favorite stories read aloud again and again, their thinking and expectations become those of the story. They hear words, they begin to take note of word shapes, and their attention is guided by the pictures and printed words that are read aloud. They are encouraged to sit in a socially acceptable way so that they can listen attentively and communicate when they want to ask a question or react to a part of the story. They note that parents, grandparents, guardians, and brothers and sisters try to read to them during a "quiet time." Finally, a major by-product of this home reading is that children internalize the structure of the narrative. Much more will be said about the discourse style of narrative and its importance in literacy development in later sections of this book.

The child who reads early is often reared in a language-enriched, emotionally supporting environment. Both David Elkind (1975) and Bernice Cullinan (2000) found that children who succeed with early reading come from homes in which immersion in the oral and written language was rich, in which parents frequently read to their children, and in which social motivation to please adults who model and reward reading was important. Research has pointed out that the great majority of early readers are children born to parents who like to read and write themselves and who share their love of reading and writing with their children (May, 1998). Furthermore, they allow their children's scribble to represent written communication, and they allow children's pretend reading to occur without correcting them needlessly. Frank Smith (1999) adds that when the conditions of print materials and people relationships are right, children will be motivated to read early.

Children, of course, bring their developing language and social and discourse understandings to the classroom. Peers play an important role in language development because they provide opportunities to practice language skills, they role model language appropriateness (or inappropriateness), and they provide feedback (Gallagher, 1993). If the teacher–student and peer–student interaction in the classroom is rich, other positive developments occur. Researchers point out that classrooms rich in social interaction involve children in discourse styles that build on what was learned at home and what the school traditionally offers (Daiute & Griffin, 1993). Peer interaction is a way to link culture and development and allows children to assimilate classroom learning experiences in their own ways.

Although social interaction is the strongest learning force of all time, argues James Moffett (1998), it is scarcely used in the public schools. Outside of school, students learn, for better or worse, a great amount from social experience. In school, with the focus on control and standardization, students are limited in their interaction and from learning what the culture has to offer. Rather than segregating students off by age groups, students should learn from one another and from the broader environment by being allowed to range throughout the classroom to learn from others at work (Moffett, 1998).

## Strengthening Aural–Oral Connections

Young children's speaking/expressive language facility (oral language) and their listening/receptive language facility (aural language) develop and are reinforced by encounters in the home, community, and school. As children learn to speak more and graduate through developmental phases such as single-word utterance to phrases to more complete and complex statements, their fluency increases (Hunsberger, 1994). Fluency, like other language features, is developmental and becomes a real benefit to children early in their lives. Early oral language fluency is a factor in success in later school and public accomplishments. It is a major contributor to success in beginning reading and writing development, and emergent literacy instruction, as we shall soon see, is fundamentally built on the competence of children's oral language. A number of educators and researchers have confirmed that children who have the opportunity to use language in scaffolded interactions with the speaking community and are provided with rich and varied forms of language will develop a greater facility with the forms and functions of language than children who have more limited opportunities (Wishon, Grabtree, & Jones, 1998).

## Language Arts Expansion in Standards

The 1990s revealed a shift in the traditional views of the language arts. The shift undoubtedly reflects the emerging importance of visual literacy and visual thinking in students' lives. To listening, speaking, reading, and writing, major educational associations, some states and large urban school districts such as New York City added viewing and visual representing as separate components of the language arts. This represents a departure from an emphasis on just the four language arts through such tasks as imagining, visualizing, and use of design and graphics often found within the language arts domains of reading and writing.

The domains of the language arts are reflected in the curriculum and performance standards produced by the various cities, states, and professional organizations. Standards are a way of designating the broad content that students are expected to achieve at particular grade levels in each of the separate English language arts. Various groups have added viewing and visually representing to their list of standards. In the twelve English language arts standards published by the joint efforts of the International Reading Association and the National Council of Teachers of English, three standards reflect competency and use of visual language (National Council of Teachers of English, 1999). Standard 4 asks students "to adjust their use of spoken, written, and visual language to communicate effectively with a variety of audiences and for different purposes." Standard 6 requests that students "apply knowledge of language structure, language conventions, media techniques, figurative language, and genre to create, critique, and discuss print and nonprint texts." Standard 12 asks students to "use spoken, written, and visual language to accomplish their own purposes" (p. 3).

One state, New Jersey, has five language arts standards in its expectations for students. Besides standards for listening, speaking, reading, and writing, New Jersey includes a fifth standard: "All students will view, understand, and use non-textual visual information" (New Jersey Department of Education, 1996). An interesting feature of this standard is the way the state connected viewing to comprehension and written production. The standard indicates that effective viewing is essential to understanding and responding to print and electronic media. Furthermore, the standard clarifies that students need to recognize that what they hear, speak, read, and write contributes to the content and quality of their viewing.

Children in New York City schools have to integrate literacies in the Speaking, Listening, and Viewing Standard. The speaking and listening aspects of this standard are organized around a variety of social situations, such as one-to-one interactions, group discussions, and oral presentations (Board of Education of the City of New York, 1997). When preparing and delivering an individual presentation, the child can give an oral research report on a topic of interest to the class, can present plans for a project, or can make a presentation to parents about a science fair project.

As an aspect of the viewing standard, students are asked to make informed judgments about the broadcast media, particularly television, radio, and film productions. The viewing, listening, and speaking connection becomes apparent in the types of activities in which children engage to accomplish this aspect of the standard. Children can do the following: present a report or paper telling why one medium was selected as a choice over another; report on the benefits and information learned from watching media; keep a weekly log on personal viewing habits and analyze information recorded; in an oral or written report, summarize what happens during media viewing; or tell about the appeal of a particular media commercial.

# ■ THE READING AND WRITING CONNECTION

The words *Reading* and *Writing* are bolded in Figure 2.1. This is because in modern technological societies the ability to understand and manipulate the use of printed symbols is often regarded as the major literacy achievement. There's something of a myth in the current "digital divide" controversy regarding who has and who does not have computers and access to the Internet. The issue is not only a matter of having computers and technological hardware but also of what to do with them. It's the "what to do with them" that requires literacy.

Although observing, listening, and speaking are universal features of human life and culture, literacy practices require extensions of the oral language codes. Visible marks have to be produced on a surface to represent sounds (phonemes), words (morphemes), and movement (as in a musical or dance score). A text is produced by a writer. To be read, the writer has to know how to negotiate the symbols—the code—of the printed language. To read and understand, the reader has to decipher the language of the code to approximate the same representational thinking that the writer is writing about. For the writer, the words, sentences, and paragraphs sequenced on a printed page represent a technology. This technology has been with the world for some time and has undergone change as newer ways were discovered to stylize writing. The world has moved from clay tablets and scrolls, to the printing press and mass-produced paper, to a new means of transmitting print—through electronic networking. Whatever the means of technology, the reader and message composer need to be literate in interpretation and use of a printed language code.

Proficiency in reading and writing is considered to be essential by the educational establishment. In fact, it is considered the first or "basic skill" of school success because young children must master reading and writing as they begin the early grades. This initial literacy experience lays the foundation for all subsequent book learning. But what happens when young children experience difficulty at this written literacy level? Does the learning difficulty reside at this level or with lack of experience and/or exposure at the earlier levels of formulating mental representations and oral language proficiency?

## Importance of Prior Knowledge

In the late 1960s and early 1970s, two authors began to challenge current views of the teaching and learning of the language arts. James Moffett and Frank Smith saw a commercially prepared, skills-based approach being used in the nation's language arts classrooms and raised questions about this type of approach. They believed that reading and writing are natural processes and that children learn reading and writing by simply *doing* reading and writing. In his introduction to the fourth edition of *Student Centered Language Arts, K–12* (now coauthored with Betty Jane Wagner), James Moffett noted that when this textbook first appeared, along with its theoretical companion volume *Teaching the Universe of Discourse* (1987), both books were regarded by the educational community as radical and experimental. In these books, Moffett wished to offer alternative views to the current installation of prepackaged curricula, those that mutilated English by containing them in specially prepared books for writing, speaking, spelling, and skill building. He noted that the recommendations and suggestions made years before seemed to be commonplace and current by the time of the fourth edition (Moffett & Wagner, 1992).

Likewise, Frank Smith, in his first edition of *Understanding Reading,* published in 1971 (now in its fifth edition), advocated that readers not be given prepared reading materials so that they have control while reading. Because of factors and knowledge already available to them, readers determine how a text will be handled and how information will be integrated with prior knowledge. Smith's position was far different from that of many others, who believed in putting the text in charge and not the reader's processing skills. When someone else's view of the text controls the reader's ability to interpret text, Smith believed, the focus of reading instruction erroneously shifts to the study of letters and sounds, which in turn hinders fluent reading. Both Moffett and Smith have made major contributions to our understanding of how literacy should be taught. One important contribution is that they remind educators of the critical importance of background information and nonverbal experiences as being at the "core of knowledge" (Smith, 1994).

Also, both authors, along with Piaget and Vygotsky and others noted in Chapter 1, contributed a strong foundation to an intellectual movement that is taking shape in many of our nation's classrooms today. Understandings of how the teaching and learning of literacy occurs, how children's thinking and language are connected, and how social interaction affects literacy have exerted a strong influence on major instructional philosophies and approaches during the last three decades. These authors' combined views can be represented in the word **constructivism,** and their views have been achieved in the **constructivist classroom.** In this classroom environment, when new learning experiences are brought to students, they add on or accommodate the new concepts and information with understandings stored in memory.

This theoretical position on the nature of the communication process maintains that the understanding and writing of texts are acts of construction by readers and writers. Texts are regarded as reservoirs of possible meaning relationships to which the reader brings knowledge and background information that interacts with the text's meaning. This view regarding the reading of texts operates in sharp contrast to prevalent views of reading as obtaining or receiving meaning passively from a text. In the metaphor implicit in constructivism, readers and writers themselves are the constructors, mental meanings are the constructions they make, and prior knowledge is the material in the brain that assists in the constructive process (Spivey, 1994). Proponents view constructivism as a liberating, socially negotiated way to learn, a much more student-oriented process, with learning occurring in environments and activities that go beyond the established strict curriculum offerings (Carr-Chellman & Reigeluth, 2002).

James Moffett and Betty Jane Wagner believe it is erroneous for educators to think of reading and writing as the basic skills. They maintain that the real basic skills are thinking and speaking, with nonverbal thought at the core rather than the "basics," which are construed by many to be word recognition, spelling, and punctuation. They remind educators that reading and writing occur last in the acquisition of coding skills, generally after proficiency in verbal learning and its interaction with nonverbal experience or "raw reality" (Moffett & Wagner, 1992). Schools have ignored the strong interaction between the nonverbal and verbal worlds and have tended instead to concentrate efforts on verbal learning without connecting such learning to raw reality referents.

Moffett and Wagner add that teachers can ask students to compose and comprehend orally, thereby ruling out word recognition and handwriting skills necessary to perform at the print level.

In the same vein, Frank Smith points out that there are two major sources of information during reading. One source of information that the brain receives through the eyes as the eyes see print is called "visual information." The second source reaches the brain "behind the eyes" based on what the reader already knows. This second source of information Smith calls "non-visual information" or "prior knowledge" (1994, 1997). Reading always involves an interaction between the two sources of information or between what is in the reader's brain and the printed text. Smith adds that there is a critical reciprocity in reading. The more nonvisual information a reader has on a particular topic he or she is reading about, the less visual information the reader will need. The less background experience or prior knowledge of the topic the reader has behind the eyes, the more visual information or careful print reading will be required. Providing background-relevant information would help the eyes predict what they will see.

## Oral and Written Language Distinctions

There is a distinction, of course, between the spoken and the written language. The spoken language is meant to be heard, and generally the speaker is looking at someone or a group of someones or is addressing a particular audience via the media. The grammar and vocabulary of the speaker will vary according to the purpose of the talk itself and the relationship between the people interacting with or listening to the talk (Smith, 1994).

The written language, on the other hand, is meant to be read. When a writer writes, the audience ranges from one individual to universal masses. The written language is more complex in its vocabulary, in its grammatical structure, and in genre or text schemes. The writer brings an array of words to the printed page and follows written conventions of spelling, word order, and syntax to arrange words into sentences, paragraphs, and larger units of meaning found in such genres as prose, poetry, and plays.

The importance of the preceding discussion regarding the distinctions between oral and written language can be visualized in Figure 2.2. The figure shows that through oral language, the listener hears the talk of the speech community. For the young child, the speech community is usually composed of the child's immediate caretakers: mom, dad, grandparents, siblings, relatives, and friends. For the older child, the speech community becomes all of those who verbally interact with the child at home, school, the playground, and other meeting and entertainment locales. Peers, and the language of the peer group, become an important factor in the talk used in social encounters. This talk may be limited in its use of varied words (vocabulary) to express meaning and in its grammatical structure, with use of basic sentence patterns and subject-verb-direct object order. The talk of the pop culture transmitted through radio and the visual media may be even more limited in vocabulary and style than that of the child's immediate language community.

The world of the talk community may limit children's ability to absorb more complex vocabulary and syntactic structures that will be unearthed in the world of print. Researchers have indicated that speech is lexically impoverished compared to written language. Astoundingly, the words found in children's books are considerably richer and

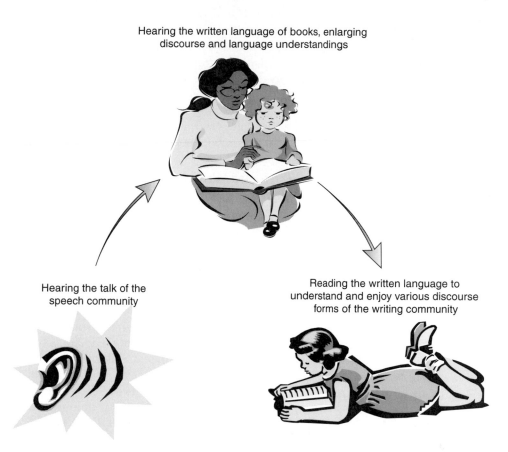

Hearing the written language of books, enlarging
discourse and language understandings

Hearing the talk of the
speech community

Reading the written language to
understand and enjoy various discourse
forms of the writing community

*Figure 2.2* The Importance of Lap Reading

less frequently used in oral language compared to the most frequent English words
used on prime-time adult television (Cunningham & Stanovich, 1998).

Educators and researchers have long acknowledged that home book reading, reading aloud, or "lap reading" is a major contributor to children's language acquisition and
to their anticipated success with schoolbook encounters. **Lap reading** provides opportunities for children and adults to participate in sustained discussion of past, present,
and forthcoming events in a story. Although pictures—visual information—may cue a
lot of the discussion, the discussion proceeds through listening and speaking interchanges. The differing stories children encounter by different authors allow children to
hear new vocabulary and syntactic construction that may not be forthcoming in conversation. Also, as children become more and more familiar with a particular story, they
may question more to gain a fuller or richer meaning.

Thus, lap reading and hearing the written language of books prepares children for
the conventions of written language. Book reading to children may be considered a
bridge between the world of familiar talk and the world of written discourse. Through

storybook listening, children's range of new vocabulary will increase. Children will hear grammatical structures not encountered in the oral language, and they will become more and more immersed in particular genre schemes. Being read to enlarges the child's fund of nonvisual information regarding the structure, conventions, and style of the written language. Children should hear whole units of discourse such as storybooks, children's literature, historical adventures, and articles from magazines and newspapers. In this way, they will hear the language of written communication and enlarge the discourse schema they will bring to their school texts.

## Getting Ready for Reading and Writing

As children approach the world of print, a shift in their language learning occurs. The process of becoming literate with print means a shift from natural, meaningful uses of oral language to an unnatural situation of examining words in order to say or write each word's "name" to obtain meaning. Also, the process of becoming reading literate means that the learner has to rapidly shift from being a word examiner to an examiner of whole sentence chunks, which are efficiently processed by the brain to achieve fluent reading with meaning.

Educators have postulated that there are particular routes or stages a child must undergo in order to be ready for formal reading and writing instruction in the school setting. For many years the concept of "reading readiness" prevailed. This belief focused on a mental age of six and a half years as the ideal time for children to begin reading instruction (Franzen, 1994). Also, prerequisite perceptual and prereading skills needed to be mastered before the reading of words occurred. This caused teachers to focus on training children's auditory and visual perceptual skills and on children learning letters and sounds before attempting whole words. Thus, according to McGill Franzen, instructional materials emphasized a "bottom-up" approach of learning to read, one that focused on helping children master isolated parts of written language, such as the alphabet or letter sounds, before they had enough knowledge to try to learn words.

One comprehensive view of reading levels was a **stage model** proposed by Jeanne Chall in 1983 (reprinted in 1996). A stage model presumes that learners accomplish different tasks at different levels of age or of grade-level development. One advantage of formulating a stage or levels model for reading is that it helps educators focus on the skills and understandings that are necessary at each level. At each of the stages, the reader engages in different mental activities with print, and it is important for readers to "graduate" through each of the stages in order to become critical, efficient lifelong readers. Therefore, a child operating at a higher level in reading will have different skills and understandings about the reading process than a child operating at a lower level or stage (Stahl, Heubach, & Cramond, 1997).

## Emergent Literacy: A New Perspective

Another perspective on how children acquire and develop written language is called "emergent literacy." Marie Clay (1966, 1991) first coined the term and the concept currently has widespread use and acceptance in schools, especially those embracing the constructivist view. Other researchers have traced the theoretical and educational viewpoints of what is meant by emergent literacy. Basically, **emergent literacy** represents a paradigm shift regarding how children become literate. From a concept of "being ready" or developing by age or grade-level-determined stages, the shift is to a belief in children's natural flourishing with literacy. Those bottom-up notions such as letter naming and development of visual and auditory discrimination skills formerly seen as central to reading acquisition are now seen as peripheral, and invented spelling, once regarded as dysfunctional, is now viewed as critical (Lancy, 1994; Smith, 1998; Teale & Sulzby, 1986).

James Moffett (1994) indicates that emergent literacy grew out of standard "folk practices" and represents simply a renaming of long-established learning activities for young children. He does agree, however, that the term legitimizes some unacknowledged and unfavored practices of helping children learn to read and write. He implies that many educators and commercial producers of reading instruction materials have had powerful reasons to deny the naturalness of a concept such as emerging into literacy. This concept, along with that of the whole language philosophy, unsettled many of the educational-industrial complex because their implementation doesn't necessarily require trained professionals. Any literate person can induce the emergence of another person's literacy. All that is needed for successful literacy implementation is people, trade books, and paper—not commercially prepared worksheets and skill-building packages.

William Teale contrasts the concepts of emergent literacy (EL) and reading readiness (RR) in five major ways:

1. EL holds that for almost all children in a literate society, literacy development starts very early in life, whereas RR maintains that learning to read starts after prerequisite perceptual and prereading skills have been mastered.
2. Within EL, reading and writing develop together and are interrelated, whereas for RR, reading is the central area of concern.
3. EL focuses on meaningful/functional uses of reading and writing with the teaching of skills arising out of holistic contexts, whereas RR emphasizes skills isolation and their teaching as separate parts out of a holistic context.
4. EL embraces both the broad and specific areas of language and literacy such as concepts about print, story and informational text structures, and concepts about phonemic awareness and letter–sound relationships, whereas RR stresses skillwork in visual and auditory perception and learning letters and sounds.
5. With EL young children naturally emerge (move into) reading and writing at their own rates and in differing ways, whereas for RR, children scale the same sequence of skill-based hurdles at the same time before reading occurs (Teale, 1994).

The reader can see that the "whole" precedes the "parts" in an emergent literacy framework. Children hear or see a message or story told or written by the teacher. That message has a meaningful context as a whole. The words, letters, and sounds are embedded functionally within that whole context. Children construct their knowledge about words and the letters and sounds that make up words by being curious and actively involved with print (see Tips for Teachers 2.1).

In the emergent literacy view, learning to read is considered a "natural" process, similar to learning to speak and to understand the oral language (see Box 2.3). Also, writing is part of the learning-to-read process; children write words and their own sentences and stories, which are read by other children, the teacher, and parents. In such an

# Characteristics of an Emergent Literacy Classroom

An emergent literacy classroom is a natural extension of children's encounters with print in the home and community environments. The major characteristic of the emergent literacy classroom would extend children's curiosity about reading and writing into ways for them to be successful early on in their classroom experiences.

1. The teacher conducts group storybook reading or lap reading with the whole class, with small groups, or with individuals on a daily basis. Quality children's literature is read and discussion ensues among teacher and children. Reading aloud also reveals that teachers value the reading act and shows that they achieve knowledge and gain enjoyment during reading.

2. Children engage in "pretend reading" of books that have been read to them. They also have access to literature in the classroom-installed library, which is also a place where children can engage in book reading. In a library center, children's writing could be displayed for classmates to read. Some may wish to question the author.

3. A print-rich environment is created to expose the world of print in functional, purposeful ways. Signs and labels are posted on common objects, routines and charts are printed, written notes are exchanged, children's written products are displayed, and tools of writing (pencils, pens, markers, paper, computers) are visibly available. The classroom is a stage of words and children's print.

4. As part of the print-rich setting, an interactive word wall is set up. This is a wall in a section of the room where children can systematically alphabetize words that have been written on index-sized cards. The word wall is not just a major display but a major tool

in building children's sight vocabulary. The words come from any number of sources, such as books read aloud and Big Books produced by children.

5. Children respond to literature readings and discussion by using other literacy forms (found on the literacy spectrum). Besides writing, children engage in artwork, flannel boards, music activities, or a dramatic reenactment of a story read to them. With modern-day software possibilities, children could create a computer-generated retelling of a story if computers are available for young children's use.

6. Writing is part of the daily classroom diet; writing and reading are connected. The teacher can show the process of writing by writing a daily message on the chalkboard or chart paper while reading the message aloud. Then the teacher encourages the children to help her along with the reading as she moves her fingers or hands along the words.

7. Phonemic awareness is fostered through such activities as hearing nursery rhymes, poetry, songs, and oral language games. Children can be asked to focus on particular sounds so that they can discriminate individual sounds that occur in our language.

8. Connected with phonemic awareness is letter association. Through many of the writing and print activities children engage in, they learn the letters of the alphabet and the sounds associated with the letters. One way to achieve the connection is to set up an ABC center. In this center could be magnetic letters and boards, individual chalkboards, and magic markers for children to use when they form letters and words. Old magazines could be cut up to remove letters to make whole words. Manipulating letters and having multisensory experiences about letters and words are key here.

environment, written-literacy learning takes place in a friendly environment in which language serves a function and is used for practical purposes. Teachers need to capitalize on children's intense interest in print by providing consistent and supportive modeling and guidance to help children realize their expectations (Laminack, 2000). In such

**BOX 2.3** Young Children Have Internalized Many Concepts about Literacy before They Begin Kindergarten

Mary Heller enumerates the understandings that young children bring to school:

1. Young children realize that reading and writing are used purposefully to communicate ideas and feelings.
2. Children know many of the forms and functions of environmental print.
3. They know the concept of word and many of the conventions of print; that words progress across the page from left to right; that spaces exist between words and that those words have different lengths and shapes; and that patterns and repetitions occur to make messages meaningful and enjoyable.
4. Their knowledge of sound–symbol relationships assists them in making the transition from oral to written language a smooth one.
5. Children can talk about language terms such as "alphabet, letters, words, sentences," and they know words that have to do with thinking such as "mean," "thought," and "remember."
6. Young readers and writers in an emergent setting expect writing and reading to be interactive and social. Reading and writing are used in numerous literacy events staged in children's homes.
7. These young children enter school quite enthusiastic about accomplishing more writing and reading. They enjoy books and stories and writing about them.

*Source:* Adapted from Mary Heller, *Reading–Writing Connections: From Theory to Practice* (New York: Longman, 1991).

an environment, children learn to read and write naturally by being functionally involved (Stahl, 1999).

The natural connectedness of reading and writing to oral language is demonstrated through the creation of written stories or messages and the retelling by children of those literacy events. When the teacher writes a story or message on chart paper or the chalkboard, he may be writing a piece that children are orally composing with him. He reads the piece several times with the children as he guides his hand and fingers along the words in the sentences. Next, the teacher may have the children retell what the message was by having them write it themselves. Depending on levels of literacy proficiency, some children may write and spell conventionally, some may use invented or "creative" spelling, some may use random letters, and some may scribble or draw. All of these hand–eye–mind activities are degrees of the process of writing, and each child's emergence into the world of print may be separated by degrees of proficiency. To close this literacy event, the teacher should have children read what they wrote to others in order to achieve the oral–written connections of language once again.

## ■ VISUAL AND ARTISTIC REPRESENTATION

Visual and artistic representations are forms of literacy based on humankind's desire to represent meaning in nonverbal, creative, and symbolic ways. We saw earlier that this stage of human development is often an outgrowth of viewing and active experimentation with the environment, processes that give rise to nonverbal, representational thought. Many writers from various disciplines have felt that human learning occurs in a number of different ways or modes of understanding, expression, and communication through which humans interpret and communicate their personal knowledge and experiences (Verriour, 1994). Furthermore, these various modes of thought and experiences cannot be contained within a model of leaning that focuses solely on a logical, sequential approach to describe how thought and language occur. By being attentive to nonverbal modes of learning, teachers can enhance and enrich children's ability to learn and communicate.

## Modes of Knowing and Communication

Vision or sight may be the most important sense for thought because it provides humans with views of direct experience (Arnheim, 1994). Although sight may be the dominant sense for guiding humankind's sense of thought, particularly in regard to visual thinking, other senses, particularly hearing, play a role in the formation of images and thought. First, the mind functions by formulating images of what it is thinking about. Second, the mind attempts to attach meaning to these images so that conceptual understanding occurs. Music, for instance, offers organized shapes that allow musicians to think in the sounds they hear. The senses of touch, smell, and taste can also be regarded as instruments of thought because they are connected to human experience and by extension provide meaningful images. Words acquire meaning only if they are enlivened by the imagery to which they refer (Arnheim, 1994).

Nonverbal thought permeates the world of the arts, the media, and probably designers of computer programs. Nonverbal communication has receptive, expressive, and personally engaging components as well. Visual and/or artistic representation is composed of the receptive processes of imagining or composing, the expressive processes of producing or creating, and the interactive processes of aesthetic engagement and appreciation. The advance of film and later television has made the literacy of visual representation alone a powerful means for influencing human behavior. The old expression rings loudly: A picture is worth a thousand words!

A child's earliest scribbles on paper are pictures that represent meaning. These scribbles later become drawings of simple pictures and stick figures that represent the meaning of a child's thought. A major thinking breakthrough occurs when the child realizes that he or she can make pictures not only of representations in the visual environment but also of ideas represented in the oral language. Furthermore, when young children begin their first writing experiences, their drawings often become the driving force behind their printed messages (Graves, 1979).

A visual composer or artist bypasses the need for verbal language to get at the essence of nonverbal creation. This does not mean that the artist will neglect the use of oral and written language when the artistic piece is discussed. It does mean, however, that the conceptualization of an idea that became, through the process of discovery and creation, the artistic end product was conceived nonverbally and probably as a holistic thought or image. Language will eventually be used to explain the artist's insight, to break the insight down into logical components so that the whole can be discussed and evaluated. In short, the artist had a "big picture" in mind and then proceeded to fill in the pieces. This is an important conceptual process that explains how some learners think when solving a problem.

Although language and written literacy processes may not be necessary during the critical moments of holistic conception, they may be quite important for the visual composer, artist, and aesthetic during the novice or apprenticeship period. The artist listens to and reads about the discoveries and creations of others. This knowledge bank expands the apprentice's landscape and allows the artist to become familiar with both historical influences and technology of craft. The years of school in which the verbal literacies are stressed may not guarantee the future artist his or her skill or craft, but oral and written language are means of learning and outlets for expression and criticism. For the artist and visual composer, the creative outcome rests on the direct exchange between the representational idea or image produced and the implementation of craft to represent that idea.

## Using the Concept of Multiple Intelligences

Howard Gardner, in an initial landmark work titled *Frames of Mind,* proposed that Western cultures had adopted a narrow perspective of the notion of intelligence. He challenged the validity of administering a single intelligence test out of context by removing a person from his or her natural learning environment and having that person do tasks not attempted in normal, practical life situations. In an effort to broaden the view of human capacities beyond the boundaries of a single IQ score based mainly on verbal tasks, he suggested that intelligence has more to do with the individual's potential for solving problems and constructing products in a naturalistic environment (Gardner, 1983, 1997).

Gardner's eight mind frames, already discussed in Chapter 1, reflect the human intellectual condition. He does add that there are subcomponents within each intelligence that enhance the range of abilities. Although creativity and genius can be expressed through all of the intelligences, Gardner believes that most extremely creative people exhibit their creative behavior through one or two frames of mind. Interestingly, Gardner notes that instead of considering a child to be a visual learner, it might be better to say that the child can represent thinking spatially. When teaching children something new, educators should capitalize on the thinking encouraged by spatial representation (Gardner, 1997).

However, it becomes clear that the theory of multiple intelligences is not too far removed from the notion of a literacy spectrum within a culture. Forms of language and literacy that are available to people and the way they use these forms—(1) through oral or written language; (2) through the visual arts, music, or dance; or (3) through the design and production of media events—are expressions of intellectual capital. The more the individual can successfully engage in literacy forms, the more the individual's life will be enriched and allowed to flourish and the more creative and aesthetic the individual's thinking processes. The point is that not all humans will excel in one type of intelligence or frame of mind. Different forms provide opportunities for obtaining comparisons or analogies from different domains as well as ways to capture the key ideas of a topic through different symbol systems (Eisner, 1999; Scherer, 1999). Moreover, human life can be highly enriched by engaging in various forms of literacy. This enrichment allows many kinds of intelligence to be nourished so that one or several can emerge as dominant mind forces in an individual's life.

For instance, Elliot Eisner has identified major outcomes that arts education contributes to a student's overall literacy development and education. First, being in a situation to create art allows a student to get in touch with or to get a feel for the creative process. As students struggle to create formative works, they become involved in the experience of bringing a work to fruition. Such experiences help students recognize the qualities in works of art and the accomplishments of artists. Second, being involved in arts education tunes students' awareness to the aesthetic qualities inherent in life and art. Arts education provides a way to assist students in using an aesthetic frame of reference as they see and hear. This means that students will be sensitized to what to listen for in music and what to look for in the visual arts. When asked about the works they see and hear, students will be able to say something about them with insight, sensitivity, and intelligence. They will not only be able to respond to the work, but they will also know why they respond the way they do and why they have certain preferences (Eisner, 1999). The "why" of knowing how to respond or not to respond is an aspect of metacognition, a level of thinking that is also highly important in skillful reading.

Other educators have put "flesh and bones" on Gardner's theory by devising curriculum frameworks and specific activities to implement the concept of multiple intelligences in the teaching and learning process (Armstrong, 1994; Finders & Hynds, 2000). School and case study reports have described successful implementation of multiple intelligence concepts at all grade levels as indicated by state tests, standardized tests, and anecdotal statements from educators (Campbell & Campbell, 1999; Sweet, 1998).

## Three Perspectives of Multiple Literacies

As noted earlier, one author embraced the concept of multiple literacies. Carolyn Piazza uses the term **multiple literacies** to refer to the rich blend of communication channels, symbols, forms, and meanings found in oral and written language, the arts, and technology (Piazza, 1999). She formulates three perspectives of her concept of multiple literacies to reveal how the blending of the arts and language systems expands their creative potential while demonstrating their connectedness to one another.

One perspective is to view the arts and language as **inquiry.** Inquiry is the process of idea formation through literacy's respective symbol systems. The traditional language arts forms—listening, speaking, reading, and writing—ask the learner to process ideas through the spoken and written language. The visual arts offer a means to question and respond to ideas and feelings in degrees of color, line, movement, texture, and viewpoint. Music and dance offer ways to hear, see, and express ideas through tone, sound, rhythm, distance, and space. Drama, film, and modern technology suggest ways to create and represent meaning through imagery, movement, and point of view.

A second perspective is to consider multiple literacies as a means of **multimodal forms of representation,** or of meaning-making mixtures in which an end product is shaped and presented in different ways. This notion was exemplified by the way a group of students used different intelligences to create scientific end products for a nuclear chemistry unit (Sweet, 1998). Students with strengths in written language wrote a research report; students with strengths in visual–spatial processing produced a poster presentation; the student with a kinesthetic strength built a model from common household products; the student with a strong sense in visualizing spatial relations produced a display out of colored blocks to represent molecular and atomic arrangements. Piazza adds that while each form of communication is unique in the way it conveys messages, there are many possibilities for joining the arts and traditional language forms to create a product that is more than the sum of its parts.

The third perspective is to regard multiple literacies as a display of **conceptual and stylistic elements** for the formation of powerful products and aesthetic messages. This occurs because literacy forms share features with one another. For instance, music and poetry share such features as rhythm, texture, and beat. Picture books and paintings share portraits and word themes. Writers and artists use these conceptual and stylistic elements to engage humans aesthetically through their subjective understandings, personal values and preferences, emotional desires, and ideals of truth and beauty.

This section discussing visual and artistic forms of representation and the concepts of varying intelligences, talents, or multiple literacies is meant to help the practicing teacher deal with the thinking styles of different children in the classroom. By realizing that children have different inclinations or talents in the learning of new content, teachers can modify the literacy perspective in the learning of that content to maximize how each child learns. For instance, if the child likes to draw or is a fairly good artist, the learning of written literacy—writing and reading—could be preceded by the images, pictures, or drawings the child produces. Creating a storyboard sequence of events on a poster board, using a flowchart or cognitive map, or outlining are all spatial ways of organizing thoughts and content before the student switches to verbal delivery through an oral speech or a written report.

# ■ THE ELECTRONIC LITERACY AGE

The reader is certainly aware that modern society along with its schools is engaged in a revolutionary shift in how literacy is engaged and transmitted. This shift, of course, has occurred with the advent of the computer age, which has occurred roughly in the last thirty years in our schools. Even within this time frame, there has been a rapid shift in how computers are implemented in the school setting. Thus, by the time the reader reads this text, new advances and changes will have occurred. Whereas written literacy was bound in a sequential print mode for hundreds of years, technological and electronic media allow readers and writers to create texts and projects in far different ways.

For the schools, the task is not to focus on the technology itself but to ask how technology can be implemented in the classroom. Educators need to ask specific questions about computer use, what options exist for hardware and software, and, most important, how computers can realize their potential to improve the effectiveness of teaching and learning (Milner & Milner, 2003; Picciano, 1998; Roblyer, 2003). They need to ask essential questions such as: "What do we want computers and electronic media to accomplish for our students? What platforms, hardware, interfaces, Internet accesses will help us accomplish these goals for students?" "What specific programs and multimedia packages will assist students in learning and literacy growth?" According to some observers, the ultimate purpose of instructional technology is to support an exciting, quality learning curriculum in three ways: by encouraging students to discover basic data (facts), by helping students integrate and interpret data into information, and by helping them turn that information into action to create knowledge (Maurer & Davidson, 1998). Even beyond improving student achievement, the most important use of computers and the Internet, according to some, is to provide greater equity in literacy learning and to prepare youngsters for the twenty-first-century workforce (Krueger, 2000; Leu, 2002).

## Early Phases of Computer Use

The first stage of the computer era, stretching from about the 1970s to the mid or late 1980s, was centered on the concept of computer literacy and using computers to keep up or modernize the status quo of educational programs. For instance, computer literacy meant the knowledge and competencies involved in how to use computers, such as keyboard skills (Topping, 1999). While computer literacy advocates reveled in the use of the new jargon—the new specialized vocabulary associated with computers—teachers were able to function very well by translating computer terms into familiar processes. For instance, computer-assisted instruction (CAI) could be viewed as an electronic equivalent of workbooks, word processing could be viewed as another way of scribing text, and electronic mail could be seen as a way of networking (Eldred, 1994). National survey results showed that computers were used in three major ways in the early 1980s: to teach about computers, as in computer literacy classes; to teach programming; and to promote rote learning through drill-and-practice programs, tutorials, and integrated learning systems (ILSs). Rarely were computers used to provide students with instruction in core academic subjects (Becker, 1992; Means, 2000).

Computer use focusing on computers as tools appeared in the mid-1980s. This shift coincided with the decrease in mainframe computers controlled by small numbers of technologists and the increase in the use of personal computers and desktop microcomputers by all kinds of workers as productivity tools (Means, 2000). One of the most important tool functions for the educational arena was word processing. Traditional typewriters were discarded. Students didn't need to compose first drafts and revisions by hand; this could all be done at the desktop and saved on a little disk. Educators speculated that because word processing enabled writers to revise more easily, even beginning writers would revise more and revise more effectively. Furthermore, writers might be better able and more willing to share their writing and profit from responses by readers because the texts were more fluid and malleable (Kaplan, 1994). However, as easy and comfortable as word processing may be, it is still an overlay of the writing process itself, still bound by convention. Words are entered according to grammatical conventions, lines are sequenced, and fonts are used to signal important topics, just as on a page from a typewriter or in a book set by movable type. Thought is still captured in the technology of the page.

Soon other innovations appeared in software, such as desktop publishing. This freed the composer from the straight writing of text to integrate clip art and accomplish page layout. Students were now thinking, "Where will I place the artwork on the page? How big should it be? Where should I insert my written text? How do I want each page to appear in my overall project?" Composers now had a bit of freedom to conceptualize the whole rather than attend solely to the sequencing of words in succession. With desktop publishing programs, students could search page layout possibilities and clip art choices to interact with their ideas and writing.

## Electronic Literacy Formats and Environments

Since the 1990s, we have been witnessing the widespread use of personal computers, word processing, electronic networks, and hypermedia systems. Scholars and educators stress the use of computers as facilitators of literacy practices, providing instant communication channels from all parts of the world, rather than as providers of programmed instruction or bodies of knowledge to be explored (Kaplan, 1994).

Now is the time of the electronic literacy environments of hypertext and hypermedia, requiring shifts once again in our notions and definition of literacy. **Hypertext** offers a different way of organizing and linking symbolic (print) information (Topping, 1999). Traditional texts, even word-processed texts, have a page-oriented, linear format. A hypertext, on the other hand, has many segments of linear text that can be accessed by the user in any order through embedded structural electronic links. The user, or reader in this case, chooses segments of the text to scan as a strategic and flexible thinker rather than reading the text in a continuous linear fashion. Writers in this environment are enabled to construct radically different writing spaces with texts that have multiple organizations of their parts (Bolter, 1991). Readers are allowed to actively select sequences of textual elements, and they are able to add their perspectives to the text. In this environment, writers and readers locate materials through electronic search procedures, causing both reader and writer to alter their composing, thinking, and reading strategies as their storage and retrieval of information changes (Kaplan, 1994). Hypertexts can be thought of as a large set of parallel texts with many alternatives for strategic movement among them—a kind of network of possibilities (Topping, 1999).

Reading in a hypertext environment is more like exploring or navigating through a network of possibilities than like reading line by line, page by page to find the information the reader seeks. (Of course, fluent reading in a traditional, linear text works somewhat the same way. The reader has a mind-set or idea of the information he or she wants. Then the reader searches through or navigates the material to find the information that complements the mind-set—the information that suits the reader's own specifications and requirements.) However, hypertext programs contain linkages such as key words or images that when selected by the reader disclose additional information about a topic or lead to a different section of the text (Gerrard, 1994). For instance, a hypertext about *Charlotte's Web* could contain a link to the word *spider*. Readers could cursor to the word *spider* to see a description of the kind of spider Charlotte was, how the web that particular spider makes is fabricated, how this species of spider relates to other members of the spider family, and so on. In short, hypertext reading necessitates more active strategy management by the reader, thereby involving the reader in metacognitive thinking because the reader is making critical choices about "how" to read.

**Hypermedia** is hypertext plus the use of media, such as still and moving pictures, graphics, and sound. A hypermedia document can be enhanced with drawings or photographs, animated graphics, music, or recorded text (Willis, Stephens, & Matthew, 1996). An important comparison between reading in a hypermedia environment and reading a traditional book format should be noted: Hypermedia programs, which are often on CD-ROM, offer faster search and interactive components, many alternative paths to consider from decision points, interactive questioning, and suggestions for future classroom discovery and exploration (Topping, 1999). This multitasking, or jumping from one computer-based activity to another, is teaching students how to learn (Tapscott, 1999). Traditional text reading, on the other hand, necessitates linear sequencing in which print is processed in an ordered way.

## Shifts in Literacy Processing

Digital technology as found in hypermedia systems changes the material format available to writers and alters the literacy skills of document creators and of readers of document processing (Kaplan, 1994). Because electronic technology allows messages to be composed using many forms of media, the messages are partially composed of "lived experience," such as newspaper photos, moving images, and music. This represents another departure from traditional literacy environments, which focus on words, drawings, and photographs in a format that doesn't require the participant to be engaged in the actual experiences. For instance, in a hypermedia document on a Mozart symphony, the user might activate a link connecting a report about the symphony to pictures of the original score or to a picture of the musical passage that activates the music itself (Gerrard, 1994).

Because a composer or creator of a hypermedia document combines print—the traditional area of written literacy—with aspects of raw experience captured in pictures, animation, video, and sound, the boundaries of composing have enlarged to include many facets of verbal and nonverbal interaction. Because electronic technologies are blurring the traditional definitions of literacy, theorists and literacy practitioners have increasingly called for broader and more inclusive definitions of literacy or for the recognition that there are a number of literacies (Kaplan, 1994; Smith, 2002). Some believe that electronic literacy is not just an additional ingredient in the existing definition of literacy but the catalyst to transform the whole definition (Reinking, McKenna, Labbo, & Kieffer, 1998).

The dynamic nature of the **Internet** and the speed of digital processing suggest a future of expanding growth beyond that which exists and can be imagined in the present (Bitter & Pierson, 1999). Someone sitting at a computer anywhere in the world can exchange ideas and information with any other computer user so long as both are linked to the Internet. Any piece of information on any topic can be accessed so long as the information has been created by a person(s) who has entrusted it to the Internet to be read and processed by other people. The Internet is the ultimate interactive learning environment because its technology includes an enormous library of human knowledge, the technological means to manage that knowledge, an amiable way of connecting people, and an exploding array of services and virtual environments to explore (Tapscott, 1999). Yet one author suggests that students can use the Internet more skillfully as a literacy and information tool when they are asked to articulate their intended goal before their surfing and searching begins (Burke, 2002).

## The Myths and Controversy of Computer Use

There is controversy regarding the use and effectiveness of technology in the educational arena just as we saw controversy among the literacy experts regarding how reading and writing should be taught in our nation's schools. The essential question in the technology controversy for school-age children appears to be, "What do educators have to do to ensure that computers are used effectively as learning tools as students join the Internet generation?" Let's examine the tenets of the technological debate.

First, most technology enthusiasts concede that computers are not the be-all and end-all of every learning situation. However, a computer linked to the Internet becomes a powerful tool when used by a talented teacher (Krueger, 2000). This concept of computer as a powerful tool runs counter to the view of computers as an aid to skill work, which is encompassed in such tasks as teaching children how to use the keyboard, how to word process, how to accomplish spreadsheets, how to use e-mail, and how to browse the World Wide Web (Stoll, 1999).

Some corporate and political leaders believe that the culture of schools prevents the full explosion of technology use. This is because schools are wary of allowing children to be in charge of their own learning and because some technological use doesn't fit neatly into the schools' view of educational outcomes (Trotter, 2000).

Finally, we return full circle to the digital divide myth we introduced earlier in this chapter and to the question, "What makes a person, a student, literate?" Most use the term *digital divide* to refer to the "haves" who have ready access to technology compared to the "have nots," who don't have the computers or the Internet access. There are many divides, which can be broken down according to community, ethnic, economic, and age groups (Trotter, 2000). Of course, the politicians and the business community provoke the emotional circuits of these groups because their focus is on access. For them it makes good press, good image building, and good business to sell and install more computers so that everyone has immediate access to information.

Conventional wisdom would have us believe that a wide gap in computer use exists between boys and girls and between Whites and other ethnic groups. Table 2.2 reveals that there is some truth in these gender and ethnic group gaps, but the gaps are not wide enough to justify calling them meaningful "divides." In-school use of computers shows that girls trailed boys in 1984 by 3.5 percent, close to less than 1 percent in 1993, and ended at 2.5 percent in 1997. While all groups have increased their school computer use since 1984, Blacks and Hispanics have consistently trailed Whites, although the gap appears to be closing. In 1997, Blacks were not far behind Whites, whereas Hispanics lagged by almost 10 percent. Blacks also gained a slight lead over the Other ethnic group. An important question is why the Hispanic group is below all other groups, who appear to be reaching a 70 percent use of computers in schools. It is also quite noticeable that while computer use was not reported for grades 1 through 8 until 1993, this group equaled the total computer use in all the grades by 1997.

But some scholars are focusing on the underlying knowledge and literacy base that students need to allow them to take full advantage of the computer as a resource. To be appropriated well by learners, accessible information has to be woven into learners' purposes and motives for desiring particular information. If the data merely wash over users as in mindless browsing, the data are not connected to the user's values and purposes (Burke, 2002; Rud, 1997). The issue is not only one of access but also of ensuring that students have the necessary knowledge—a fund of information internalized in their minds—to allow them to make effective use of the new technological resources.

According to E. D. Hirsch, although the Internet provides a wealth of information in a few keystrokes, the use of that information—the ability to absorb it and add it to one's preexisting schema—requires that the learner already possesses a storehouse of

**Table 2.2** In-School Use of Computers by Gender, Ethnic Group, and Grades 1–8, 1984–1997

|  | 1984 | 1989 | 1993 | 1997 |
|---|---|---|---|---|
| Total | 27.3% | 42.7% | 59.0% | 68.8% |
| Boys | 29.0% | 43.5% | 59.4% | 70.1% |
| Girls | 25.5% | 41.9% | 58.7% | 67.6% |
| White | 30.0% | 45.7% | 61.6% | 71.1% |
| Black | 16.8% | 32.6% | 51.5% | 66.3% |
| Hispanic | 18.6% | 34.9% | 52.3% | 61.5% |
| Other | 28.6% | 42.7% | 59.0% | 65.3% |
| Grades 1–8 | N.R.* | N.R.* | 68.9% | 68.8% |

*Note: N.R. = Not Reported

*Source: Digest of Educational Statistics 1998* (Washington, DC: U.S. Government Printing Office, 1999), Table 428, p. 484.

knowledge. Cognitive psychologists point out that it takes knowledge to gain knowledge. Educators must start as early as preschool to build the pathways of knowledge that will become the bridge over the digital divide (Hirsch, 2000).

How do learners gain this necessary knowledge? They gain it through the use of language and literacy forms as they weave through the various content disciplines in school and learning experiences in the outside world. In short, students bring literacy and knowledge to the world of computers so that they continue the learning situation, rather than being manipulated by information with which they cannot connect. In later chapters, we present ways in which technology can be integrated into students' learning environments to help them achieve in school and develop the habit of lifelong learning.

# ■ SUMMARY ■

1. As children develop, words become attached to aspects of play, activity, and socialization. Words are used for objects, animals, and people that appear in children's immediate viewing areas or for those objects and animate forms that appear as mental pictures or schema in their minds.

2. Scaffolding is when a teacher, parent, or "significant other" plans for and guides a learner through successive steps to a successful outcome. Scaffolding a learning activity suggests that the teacher provides appropriate support mechanisms as the activity unfolds and works within the learner's zone of proximal development, as hypothesized by Lev Vygotsky.

3. Reading to children develops their vocabulary, their sense of syntax, and their understanding of the structure of the narrative. In short, reading to children is a mind-developing strategy.

4. James Moffett and Frank Smith's views on the teaching and learning of literacy and the views of Jean Piaget, Lev Vygotsky, and others regarding the connectedness of children's thinking, language, and social development have exerted a strong influence on current educational philoso-

phies and practices. Most notably, their views are found in the constructivist classroom.

5. According to holistic views of literacy learning, composing and comprehending words, sentences, and paragraphs should be accomplished within the contexts of a complete discourse—a whole unit of language used for a specific purpose. When substructures of sound–symbol relations, words, sentences, or even paragraphs are taught out of context of the larger unit, readers and writers often lose a sense of relevance and the connectedness of the whole meaning.

6. The words found in children's books are richer, more complex, and more varied than the most frequently used words of English on prime-time adult television.

7. The concepts of multiple intelligences, multiple literacies, and arts engagement allow learners to compare, contrast, or form analogies from different mind perspectives and to capture ideas on a topic through different symbol systems.

8. The electronic literacy age is entrenched in our nation's schools, with just under 70 percent of the total school population using computers in 1997. Besides focusing on students' access to the Internet and World Wide Web, educators need to ensure that computers are being used effectively as learning tools.

## ■ QUESTIONS TO CONSIDER ■

1. Why is it important that young children reach out and touch their immediate environment rather than be confined in closed-in spaces with few objects to feel?

2. Why is feedback important as young children begin to talk, and why is conversation with a young child far more powerful for thinking development than giving the child commands and direct statements?

3. How is thinking shaped and enhanced through lap reading and reading to children in the classroom?

4. Why is it doubly important for the teacher to be aware of language-impoverished and language-reluctant children and to engage these children in rich and varied forms of talk, stories, and book reading?

5. How does prior knowledge of a topic influence children's comprehension of that topic?

6. How does the concept of emergent literacy exemplify the constructivist philosophy of learning?

7. How can engagement in the arts enhance children's overall literacy development?

8. How does the use of hypertext and hypermedia redefine our current views of literacy?

9. What are the important uses of computers in the schools?

10. What are the issues of the current digital divide controversy and how does the lack of a preexisting knowledge base serve to widen the divide between the "haves" and the "have nots"?

## ■ THINGS TO DO ■

1. Be sure to continue to read to children in the classroom as parents and "significant others" read to young children at home. Try to approach the conditions of lap reading so that children listen in a socially acceptable way and communicate when they want to ask a question or react to a story part.

2. Set up classroom presentations so that children can integrate the four traditional language arts domains—listening, speaking, reading, and writing—with viewing and visually representing. This can be done when children accomplish a hypermedia computer project on a classroom topic or theme and present the project orally with the computer screen in view.

3. Provide visual and real-object information when children don't have background experience for a topic before they will read about it.

More information "in the head" prior to reading will strengthen reading comprehension.

4. Allow children, particularly those having difficulty learning printed words, to do artwork or draw their stories before they attempt writing them. The artwork/drawings can be accomplished in frames or panels so that children retell their stories in writing accordingly. Provide positive feedback on the early writings and invented spellings of children and show what the correct message should be by writing it on a sticky note to be attached to a child's paper.

5. Show your students how to access the Internet to locate and use information necessary for a report or a project.

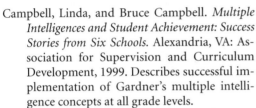

## ■ RECOMMENDED READINGS ■

Campbell, Linda, and Bruce Campbell. *Multiple Intelligences and Student Achievement: Success Stories from Six Schools.* Alexandria, VA: Association for Supervision and Curriculum Development, 1999. Describes successful implementation of Gardner's multiple intelligence concepts at all grade levels.

Dixon-Krauss, Lisbeth. *Vygotsky in the Classroom: Mediated Literacy Instruction and Assessment.* White Plains, NY: Longman, 1996. The ideas of Lev Vygotsky are transferred to the classroom setting, and teachers are shown how to mediate instruction within the zone of proximal development.

Lancy, David (ed.). *Children's Emergent Literacy: From Research to Practice.* Westport, CT: Praeger, 1994. Contains a collection of essays explaining the theoretical and educational viewpoints of emergent literacy.

Moffett, James. *The Universal Schoolhouse: Spiritual Awakening through Education.* Hendon, VA: Calender Islands, 1998. This book reaffirms Moffett's belief that students should create their own learning and collaborate and learn from one another.

Roblyer, M. D. *Integrating Educational Technology into Teaching.* Upper Saddle River, NJ: Merrill/ Prentice Hall, 2003. Explains to teachers why the field of educational technology is open to controversy and change and how software and multi- and hypermedia are integrated into classroom learning situations.

Smith, Frank. *Reading without Nonsense,* 3rd ed. New York: Teachers' College Press, 1997. One of the author's landmark works that explains the nature and wonder of the reading process.

Willis, Jerry, Elizabeth Stevens, and Kathryn Matthew. *Technology, Reading, and Language Arts.* Boston: Allyn and Bacon, 1996. Shows how modern technology and computer tools are integrated into reading and language arts course work.

## ■ KEY TERMS ■

conceptual and stylistic elements
constructivism
constructivist classroom
deep structure
emergent literacy
hypermedia
hypertext
inquiry
Internet

lap reading
mental schema
multimodal forms of
    representation
multiple literacies
neural connections
oral narrative
representational play
representational thought

scaffolding
situation-dependent spoken
    language
stage model of reading
surface level
visual literacy
visual thinking
zone of proximal development

# ■ REFERENCES ■

Armstrong, T. (1994). *Multiple intelligences in the classroom.* Alexanderia, VA: Association for Supervision and Curriculum Development.

Arnheim, R. (1994). Visual thinking. In A. C. Purves (Ed.), *Encyclopedia of English studies and language arts.* (p. 1240). New York: Scholastic/Urbana, IL: National Council of Teachers of English.

Becker, H. J. (1992). Computer-based integrated systems in the elementary and middle grades: A critical review and synthesis of evaluation reports. *Journal of Educational Computing Research, 8,* 1–41.

Bitter, G., & Pierson, M. (1999). *Using technology in the classroom.* Boston: Allyn and Bacon.

Board of Education of the City of New York. (1997). *Performance standards, English language arts, first edition.* New York: Board of Education.

Bolter, J. (1991). *The writing space: The computer, hypertext, and the history of writing.* Hillsdale, NJ: Lawrence Erlbaum.

Burke, J. (2002, November). The Internet reader. *Educational Leadership,* 38–42.

Campbell, L., & Campbell, B. (1999). *Multiple intelligences and student achievement: Success stories from six schools.* Alexandria, VA: Association for Supervision and Curriculum Development.

Carr-Chellman, A., & Reigeluth, C. (2002). Whistling in the dark? Instructional design and technology in the schools. In R. A. Reiser & J. P. Dempsey (Eds.), *Trends and issues in instructional design and technology* (pp. 239–255). Upper Saddle River, NJ: Merrill/Prentice Hall.

Chall, J. (1996). *Stages of reading development* (2nd ed.). New York: Harcourt Brace College.

Clay, M. (1991). *Becoming literate: The construction of inner control.* Portsmouth, NH: Heinemann.

Clay, M. (1966). *Emergent reading behavior.* Unpublished doctoral dissertation, University of Auckland, New Zealand.

Cullinan, B. (2000). *Read to me: Raising kids who love to read.* New York: Scholastic.

Cunningham, A., & Stanovich, K. (1998, Spring/Summer). What reading does for the mind. *American Educator,* 8–15.

Daiute, C., & Griffin, T. (1993). The social construction of written narrative. In C. Daiute (Ed.), *The development of literacy through social interaction.* San Francisco: Jossey Bass.

Debes, J. (1969, October). The loom of visual literacy. *Audio Visual Instruction,* 25–27.

Dixon-Krauss, L. (1996). *Vygotsky in the classroom: Mediated literacy instruction and assessment.* White Plains, NY: Longman.

Eisner, E. (1999, January/February). Does experience in the arts boost academic achievement? *The Clearing House,* 148–149.

Eldred, J. C. (1994). Language and computer literacy. In A. C. Purves (Ed.), *Encyclopedia of English studies and language arts* (pp. 690–691). New York: Scholastic/Urbana, IL: National Council of Teachers of English.

Elkind, D. (1975, November/December). We can teach reading better. *Today's Education,* 34–38.

Finders, M., & Hynds, S. (2000). *Literacy lessons: Teaching and learning with middle school students.* Upper Saddle River, NJ: Merrill/Prentice Hall.

Franzen, A. M. (1994). Reading readiness. In A. C. Purves (Ed.), *Encyclopedia of English studies and language arts* (pp. 1010–1012). New York: Scholastic/Urbana, IL: National Council of Teachers of English.

Gallagher, T. (1993, October). Language skill and development of social competence in school-age children. *Language, Speech, and Hearing Series in Schools,* 199–205.

Gardner, H. (1983). *Frames of mind: The theory of multiple intelligences.* New York: Basic Books.

Gardner, H. (1997, September). The first seven . . . and the eighth: A conversation with Howard Gardner. *Educational Leadership,* 8–13.

Gerrard, L. (1994). Computer aids to writing. In A. C. Purves (Ed.), *Encyclopedia of English studies and language arts* (pp. 243–246). New York: Scholastic/Urbana, IL: National Council of Teachers of English.

Graves, D. (1979). Let children show us how to help them write. *Visible Language, 13,* 16–28.

Heller, M. (1991). *Reading-writing connections: From theory to practice.* New York: Longman.

Hirsch, E. D., Jr. (2000, Spring). "You can always look it up" . . . or can you? *American Educator,* 4–9.

Hunsberger, M. (1994). Language fluency. In A. C. Purves (Ed.), *Encyclopedia of English studies and language arts* (pp. 705–707). New York: Scholastic/Urbana, IL: National Council of Teachers of English.

Hyerle, D. (1996). *Visual tools for constructing knowledge.* Alexandria, VA: Association for Supervision and Curriculum Development.

Kaplan, N. (1994). Literacy and computers. In A. C. Purves (Ed.), *Encyclopedia of English studies and language arts* (pp. 748–752). New York: Scholastic/Urbana, IL: National Council of Teachers of English.

Krueger, K. (2000, March 15). Mostly wrong questions from a high tech heretic. *Education Week,* 46.

Laminack, L. (2000, May). Supporting emergent readers and writers. *Teaching K–8,* 62–63.

Lancy, D. (1994). The conditions that support emergent literacy. In D. Lancy (Ed.), *Children's emergent literacy: From research to practice* (pp. 1–19). Westport, CT: Praeger.

Leu, D., Jr. (2002, February). Internet workshop: Making time for literacy. *The Reading Teacher,* 466–472.

Martorelli, D. (1992, October). The arts take center stage. *Instructor,* 38–39.

Maurer, M., & Davidson, G. S. (1998). *Leadership in instructional technology.* Upper Saddle River, NJ: Prentice Hall.

May, F. (1998). *Reading as communication: To help children write and read* (5th ed.). Upper Saddle River, NJ: Merrill.

Means, B. (2000). Technology in America's schools: Before and after Y2K. In R. Brandt (Ed.), *Education in a new era, ASCD 2000 Yearbook* (pp. 185–210). Alexandria, VA: Association for Supervision and Curriculum Development.

Milner, J. O., & Milner, L. F. M. (2003). *Bridging English* (3rd ed.). Upper Saddle River, NJ: Merrill/Prentice Hall.

Moffett, J. (1987). *Teaching the universe of discourse.* Portsmouth, NH: Boynton/Cook.

Moffett, J. (1994). Foreword. In D. Lancy (Ed.), *Children's emergent literacy: From research to practice* (pp. xv–xix). Westport, CT: Praeger.

Moffett, J. (1998). *The universal schoolhouse: Spiritual awakening through education.* Herndon, VA: Calender Islands.

Moffett, J., & Wagner, B. J. (1992). *Student-centered language arts, K–12* (4th ed.). Portsmouth, NH: Boynton/Cook.

National Council of Teachers of English. (1999). *The List of Standards for the English Language Arts.* Urbana, IL: Author. Retrieved February 19, 1999, from www.ncte.org/about/over/standards/110846.htm.

New Jersey Department of Education. (1996). *New Jersey core curriculum content standards.* Trenton, NJ: New Jersey Department of Education. Retrieved May 1996, from www.state.nj.us/njded/clls/index.html.

Norton, D. (1997). *The effective teaching of language arts* (5th ed.). Upper Saddle River, NJ: Merrill.

Piaget, J. (1963). *The origins of intelligence in children.* New York: Norton.

Piazza, C. (1999). *Multiple forms of literacy: Teaching literacy and the arts.* Upper Saddle River, NJ: Prentice Hall.

Picciano, A. G. (1998). *Educational leadership and planning for technology* (2nd ed.). Columbus, OH: Prentice Hall.

Rayner, K., & Pollatsek, A. (1994). *The psychology of reading.* Mahwah, NJ: Erlbaum.

Reinking, D., McKenna, M., Labbo, L., & Kieffer, R. D. (Eds.). (1998). *Handbook of literacy and technology: Transformations in a post-typographic world.* Mahwah, NJ: Lawrence Erlbaum.

Restak, R. (2001). *The secret life of the brain.* Washington, DC: Joseph Henry Press.

Roblyer, M. D. (2003). *Integrating educational technology into teaching* (3rd ed.). Upper Saddle River, NJ: Merrill/Prentice Hall.

Rud, A., Jr. (1997, October). Musty paper, blinking cursors: Print and digital cultures. *Educational Researcher,* 29–32.

Scherer, M. (1999, November). The understanding pathway: A conversation with Howard Gardner. *Educational Leadership,* 12–16.

Sinatra, R. (1986). *Visual literacy connections to thinking, reading and writing.* Springfield, IL: Charles C. Thomas.

Smith, F. (1994). *Understanding reading: A psycholinguistic analysis of reading and learning to read* (5th ed.). Mahwah, NJ: Erlbaum.

Smith, F. (1997). *Reading without nonsense* (3rd ed.). New York: Teachers College Press.

Smith, F. (1999, November). Why systematic phonics and phonemic awareness instruction constitute an educational hazard. *Language Arts,* 150–155.

Smith, P. (1998). Coming to know one's world: Development as social construction of meaning. In R. Campbell (Ed.), *Facilitating pre-school literacy* (pp. 12–28). Newark, DE: International Reading Association.

Smith, W. S. (2002, April). Weaving the literacy web: Changes in reading from page to screen. *The Reading Teacher,* 662–669.

Spivey, N. N. (1994). Constructivism. In A. C. Purves (Ed.), *Encyclopedia of English studies and language arts* (pp. 284–286). New York: Scholastic/Urbana, IL: National Council of Teachers of English.

Sprenger, M. (1999). *Learning and memory: The brain in action.* Alexandria, VA: Association for Supervision and Curriculum Development.

Stahl, S. (1999, November). Why innovations come & go: The case of whole language. *Educational Researcher,* 13–22.

Stahl, S., Heubach, K., & Cramond, B. (1997, Winter). *Fluency-oriented reading instruction: Reading research report, No. 79.* University of Georgia, Athens, GA: National Reading Research Center.

Stoll, C. (1994). *High tech heretic: Why computers don't belong in the classroom & other reflections by a computer contrarian.* New York: Doubleday.

Sweet, S. (1998, November). A lesson learned about multiple intelligences. *Educational Leadership,* 50–51.

Tapscott, D. (1999, February). Educating the net generation. *Educational Leadership,* 7–11.

Teale, W. (1994). Emergent literacy. In A. C. Purves (Ed.), *Encyclopedia of English studies and language arts* (pp. 424–426). New York: Scholastic/ Urbana, IL: National Council of Teachers of English.

Teale, W. H., & Sulzby, E. (1986). *Emergent literacy: Writing and reading.* Norwood, NJ: Ablex.

Tompkins, G. (1998). *Language arts: Content and teaching strategies* (4th ed.). Upper Saddle River, NJ: Merrill.

Topping, K. (1999, November). Electronic literacy in school and home: A look into the future. *Reading Online.* International Reading Association. Retrieved 1999, from www. readingonline.org.

Trotter, A. (2000, March 15). Top leaders confront the big questions about technology. *Education Week,* 12.

Verriour, P. (1994). Nonverbal leaning. In A. C. Purves (Ed.), *Encyclopedia of English studies and language arts* (pp. 880–882). New York: Scholastic/Urbana, IL: National Council of Teachers of English.

Vygotsky, L. (1978). *Mind in society.* Cambridge, MA: Harvard University Press.

Vygotsky, L. (1986). *Thought and language.* Cambridge, MA: MIT Press.

Willis, J., Stephens, E., & Matthew, K. (1996). *Technology, reading, and language arts.* Boston, MA: Allyn and Bacon.

Wishon, P., Grabtree, K., & Jones, M. (1998). *Curriculum for the primary years: An integrative approach.* Upper Saddle River, NJ: Prentice Hall.

# Word Acquisition and Understanding

chapter 3

## Focusing Questions

1. Why is word learning critically related to understanding?
2. What are the various ways in which words are defined by educators and teachers?
3. What are different viewpoints regarding how words should be learned by beginning readers?
4. How would understanding of text differ for different levels of readers in relation to their fluency with text?
5. Why is it important to understand the nature of the alphabetic principle for beginning reading instruction?
6. What are different ways or system approaches to achieve word identification through sound–symbol associations?
7. Why is the understanding of morphemes important for vocabulary development?

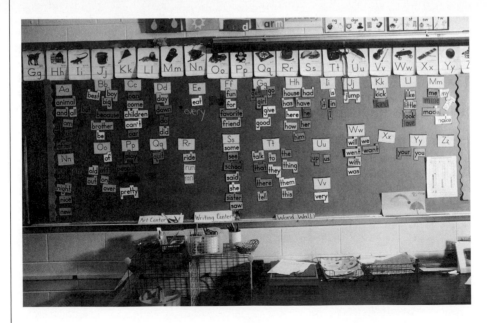

This chapter examines the all-important topic of "words" and their relationship to learning and literacy development. The reader is reminded of the discussion raised in the last chapter regarding the distinction between the oral and the written language systems and how storytelling and early book exposure helps children move from talk to print connections. Lap reading or book reading, we noted, was one bridge between the words of talk language and the words of book language. We also acknowledged that a book recitation extends and enlarges children's knowledge of the world and language meanings and functions while imparting a sense of wonder and joy about real and imaginary happenings of the world.

When the child alone comes to the pages of a book and sees letters and words in initial encounters, what happens has caused parents to hold their breath and wring their hands in anticipation of outcomes and has caused the educational establishment to be engaged in continual controversy for decades. The question boils down to "How do we help children (or those newly acquainted with written English) with their first visual encounters with words?"

# ■ UNDERSTANDING THE WORLD OF WORDS

## What Are Words?

Words are the smallest part of language by which we convey meaning: *Yes* and *no* have absolute meanings and are understood quite early in life. Words are composed of smaller meaningful parts, called **morphemes,** and words are contained in larger meaningful structures called sentences. Sentences shape the meaning of any particular word according to the way the word is used in the sentence. The larger context of the culture, including the classroom, also shapes word meanings and word usage (Cole, 2002–2003; Richgels, 2002). Thus, word meanings are not fixed. Words will change their meaning as word users shift their views of how any particular word is used in particular contexts. Think of the word *web*. When we were young, our perspective of and mental dictionary meaning for the word *web* was that of the silklike network of the spider. Educators' perspective of the word *web* is more apt to be in the context of semantic or cognitive mapping, as in the "webbing" of ideas, or in the context of a network of computers linked by electrical wires in a worldwide system called a "web."

Words, then, act as names or labels for representations of life's experiences. When a learner has a label for a new topic or experience, his or her perception of that experience enlarges and concept understanding becomes enriched. Think of any new experience a young child encounters, such as learning to ski; the first trip to the zoo, aquarium, or planetarium; or the concrete patch activity described in the previous chapter. As youngsters become involved in an activity, and as adults or teachers use the concept words associated with that activity, youngsters acquire new words or labels for objects and happenings.

Words not only contain meaning, but they also have sound and spelling features. Although words appear to be stored in a person's mental dictionary as whole units, they are accessible through two major sets of features (Coady, 1994a). One feature system has to do with the meaning or concept understanding of the word as influenced by its grammatical position in a sentence. The second major system is concerned with sound and spelling features of the word. The sound and spelling features, also known as the phonological and orthographic properties, allow the recognition of one set of features to cue the recognition of other features. This means that when a person needs to "call up" any particular word in the mind to pronounce it, spell it, define it, or use it correctly in a sentence, the person uses the most efficient of the features.

Another type of mental access to words becomes internalized over time and is probably related to reading proficiency. This access is known as the understanding and analysis of word parts or morphemes (Coady, 1994a; Gunning, 2002). These word parts are often called "structural elements," "prefixes," "suffixes," and "roots" in the school setting. Through understanding of word parts, a person makes mental connections to the various structural parts of words that convey meaning so that new words can be understood and even created. For instance, once a person understands the meaning and position of the word part *re,* the person can successfully understand and make new words with *re* in the initial position to mean "to occur or happen again."

These inherent features in words—the meaning–grammar aspect, the spelling-sound associations, and the use of structural parts—have caused educators to weigh the ways in which printed words are introduced and taught to children. The relative importance assigned to each method has given rise to the "never-ending debate," the "interminable controversy," and the "reading wars" about how reading should be taught (Kameenui & Carnine, 1998; Pearson & Raphael, 1999; Smith, 1999).

There is consensus that the most important initial reading act is rapid word identification. Many regard the ability to recognize words as the central activity in the complicated process of reading (Gallas & Smagorinsky, 2002; Stanovich, 1991). One view favored by meaning-emphasis groups stresses the learning of words within meaningful contexts written for and by children, whereas code-emphasis groups would have children learn words out of context by having them focus on the letters and sound properties that make up words (Rayner, Foorman, Perfetti, Pesetsky, & Seidenberg, 2002). Thus, the word takes center stage in the drama of how to teach reading.

## How Words Are Defined

Educators and researchers have used different terms to explain word concepts and give meaning to the world of words. What follows is a discussion of how various word phrases and terms are used by professionals and educators as they emphasize different viewpoints of word learning.

A **familiar word** is a word recognized and understood by a person in either the oral or written language. The person can know the meaning of the word or use the word appropriately in an oral or written context without necessarily being able to explicitly define the word, which is often the case for function words, such as *for, by,* and *but.* Familiar words can be contrasted with unknown words.

**High-frequency words** are words frequently used and needed in the language system to transmit basic meanings and to permit ideas and sentence elements to be joined together. Over the years, researchers have studied the frequency counts of printed words in various types and genres of reading material. By studying word counts, researchers can determine what the most frequently used words are in juvenile and adult reading materials. For instance, we would predict that the words *the* and *a* would be two of the most frequently used words in English because the language system is basically composed of these two articles. All words exist in a continuum from high-frequency words to less frequently used words to rare words.

Word lists were amassed by researchers as they recorded how frequently particular words occurred in written texts. In 1944, Thorndike and Lorge published *The Teacher's Word Book of 30,000 Words,* and this compendium of words became one of the most widely used books for vocabulary research. Soon, computer-based analysis allowed more words to be studied. In 1967, Kucera and Francis accomplished a computational analysis of one million words, and in 1971, Carroll, Davies, and Richman analyzed the frequency count of over five million words. These authors studied the textbooks and recommended readings for students between grades 3 and 9. From the texts of seventeen different subject areas such as mathematics, literature, social science, and music, the authors found highly frequent words such as *receive,* which occurred across most of the content readings, and moderately frequent words such as *reciprocal,* which occurred sixty-seven times in the material studied.

Some very interesting statistics emerged from the Carroll study, which somewhat confirmed and reinforced what educators had known about words. Ten of the words studied occur 24 percent of the time in running text; 100 words occur with 49 percent frequency; 2,000 words occur with 81 percent frequency; 3,000 words occur with 85 percent frequency; 5,000 words occur with 89 percent frequency; and 43,811 words occur with 99 percent frequency in consecutive text. As predicted, the word *the* is the number one ranked word in English word count frequency, whereas the tenth most frequently used word is *it.*

Some educators and researchers analyzed word frequency counts in children's reading materials across age and grade levels to arrive at a "core vocabulary." These published word lists of the core vocabulary became known as **sight-word lists.** Still the most famous of these lists produced from the 1930s to the 1970s is undoubtedly the *220 Basic Sight Word List,* published by Edward Dolch in 1936. It was commonly believed that readers who mastered the Dolch list would be able to meaningfully read approximately 70 percent of the words used in a typical first-grade reader (Robinson & McKenna, 1994). A decade later Dolch published his list of the first 1,000 most frequently used words in children's reading materials (1948). This list included the basic sight words of the previous list plus some of the most common nouns. A list targeted for students experiencing reading difficulties was published in 1975, (Fry) and a more recent list of 240 words, called *Instant Words,* was compiled from over a thousand 500-word samples taken from books covering twelve subject areas between grades 3 and 9 (Fry, Kress, & Fountoukidis, 1993).

An important list that was highly predictive of the readability levels of reading materials from fourth-grade to college level was that compiled by Edgar Dale in 1948. This list of 3,000 words formed the core vocabulary of a widely used readability formula developed by Edgar Dale and Jeanne Chall (1948). The authors maintained that the 3,000-word list contained the most basic and necessary words needed by children in fourth grade. Chall equated mastery of these familiar words with that of a fourth-grade reading level or of being at the beginning of stage 3 of her Stages of Reading Development. Words learned after mastery of the Dale list would be less familiar, more specialized, technical, or literary and would advance the reader into the higher stages of reading as outlined by Chall.

**Function words** are those "little" English words that allow sentence structures to operate and that link meaning-bearing content words to one another. In the sentence preceding this one, the reader will notice four function words: *that, to, and, the.* These words connect sentence ideas with one another; if they were omitted, the sentence meaning would be somewhat incomprehensible. The reader would undoubtedly find many function words in a grammar book in the Parts of Speech section, particularly a section that discussed and listed prepositions, conjunctions, articles, pronouns, and adverbial words of degree (such as *most, yet,* and *still*). Because many of these words are irregular in spelling and pronunciation, they may be difficult for beginning readers to read and conceptualize if taught out of context (Leu & Kinzer, 1999).

Though relatively few in number compared to the vast number of content words, function words are extremely important because they help speakers and writers express specific relationships among ideas. In other words, we wouldn't have understandable sentences without function words (see Box 3.1). We are arriving at a conclusion regarding the labels used by educators for words. The formula looks something like this:

**function words = high-frequency words = words on basic sight word lists**

The reader is asked to acknowledge the various names given to the same class of words and will be asked, later in this chapter, to consider the importance these words have for early and fluent reading success.

**Content words** are those words needed to name, label, or symbolize things, actions, and qualities. The parts of speech to which content words belong are nouns, verbs, adjectives, and some adverbs. A language has many content words to accommodate the richness and character of a language's people as they describe and define themselves and their actions. Whereas function words provide the glue between and among ideas expressed through content words, the latter are constantly evolving. Function words can be described as a "closed class" of words, meaning that only a few hundred exist in our language, but content words can be considered an "open class" of words (Fromkin & Rodman, 1998). This means that meaning-bearing words are not bound or closed and that new ones can be constantly invented (Rayner & Pollatsek, 1994). As a culture advances and words are needed to describe what people do, content words are added to our daily vocabularies. For example, in the past decades when word frequency studies were conducted, most likely the words *Internet, World Wide Web,* and *servers* were either not in use or not used as they are in the digital age. Now if a sentence such as "The Internet and the World Wide Web are supported by servers" is generated, the function words *the, and,* and *by,* prevalent in the language for eons, help the content ideas stick together.

**Sight words** (or an individual reader's sight-word vocabulary) are those words imme-

**BOX 3.1** A Useful Literacy Strategy for English Language Learners

When English language learners master and recognize function words by sight early on, their success with reading increases. First, their rapid efficiency with function words means they are recognizing high-utility words in print, and they can devote energy to the decoding of less frequent words. Second, using function words signals the way to reading understanding, with words such as *first, second, next, now, later, under, most, but,* and so forth.

diately recognized in print. These words are recognized instantaneously and do not require analysis through the activation of word-attack strategies. The time factor for immediate recognition of sight words has been acknowledged to be within one second (Leslie & Caldwell, 2001) and, better yet, in fractions of a second (Rayner & Pollatsek, 1994).

An individual reader's sight words are *not* to be confused with a published list of basic sight words. Many educators, even veteran teachers, make the erroneous assumption that sight words are only those words listed on well-known sight word lists. We know the reason for this assumption. Basic sight word lists contain words of high-frequency use in the printed language, and these self-same words are necessary to join ideas within sentence parts and between sentences. Thus, beginning readers, due to the very nature of the reading materials they are initially offered, would be constantly exposed to high-frequency words. This initial repeated exposure would predispose them to learn to read many words that were found on basic sight word lists.

However, some children do not learn all of their initial words efficiently. For instance, they might read *of* as *from, but* as *by,* and *is* as *so.* If this practice of miscalling basic words persists, these children can experience more confusion and more misnaming of words as additional words are added in classroom offerings. Each individual child should be quite secure and accurate in recognizing the beginning words they are asked to learn before new words are added to their diet.

A number of terms have been used by educators to refer to the process of working out or **sounding out** words that are not immediately recognizable in print. These terms are **word analysis, word-attack skills, word mediation, decoding, breaking the code, phonetic analysis,** and using **sound–symbol relationships.** To these more global terms have been added the specifics of **phonics, phonological** and **phonemic awareness, alphabetic understanding,** and **word families** (Chall, 1992–1993; Johnston, 1999; Kameenui & Carnine, 1998). In the classroom, these words and phrases can be reduced to the teacher's exhortation to "sound it out." What happens in a reader's mind is that the reader has to associate the printed letters of the alphabet with the speech sounds they represent in order to achieve a word's identity in the oral language. Of course, the single word "phonics" is the one that captures the general publics' attention and is a term that has become associated with a method of reading based on using sound/symbol associations to unlock the identity of words.

A **new reading word** is a word that the reader has learned to read and now reads without hesitation and without application of word-attack skills or sounding out behavior. The new word may have been taught through a phonics-oriented approach. Because so many confuse the idea of sight vocabulary with that of basic sight words appearing on high-frequency word lists, we have made a separate distinction for a new reading word. Generally, the word is already familiar to the reader in the oral language, but the reader has not met the word in print. There are two essential conditions here. First, the reader needs to encounter the word in print so that when it is read the match is made with the selfsame word in the spoken language and understanding occurs. Second, the reader needs to have enough encounters with the word so that it is read **instantaneously,** meaning all at a time, and not confused with another word that may look the same. This means that the word has been committed to long-term memory and has become another word added to the reader's sight vocabulary.

A **new meaning** or **vocabulary word** is a word neither familiar in oral language nor printed language for any given learner. This is a difficult, if not befuddling, category for teachers because they can't possibly know the ranges of vocabulary and experience of each child in the classroom. Recall from Chapter 2 that experience and vocabulary development are closely connected. It has been estimated that young children enter school with spoken vocabulary ranges from well under 10,000 to over 20,000 (Fromkin & Rodman, 1998) words and add from 3,000 to 5,000 words a year (Brabham & Villaume, 2002b). Because of the unique partnership of words with experience, the teacher can't know which child had which experiences or, if children had the same experiences, what words were learned during those experiences. As children become fluent readers and read outside of school simply because they enjoy it, reading becomes part of their daily experience. Both theorists and researchers have maintained that the majority of children's vocabulary growth occurs through language exposure (including plain old book reading) rather than through direct teaching (Cunningham & Stanovich, 1998.

A new **concept word** is both a new vocabulary word and a new reading word. Students have little or no background experience with the topic or frame of reference with which this word is associated. For instance, when the topic of photosynthesis is initially encountered, students may not even be aware that green plant leaves make their own food through the action of sunlight, water, and carbon dioxide. As they become familiar with the experience of the photosynthesis cycle by studying figures and charts, focusing on teacher discussion and readings, analyzing a green plant leaf, and viewing slides, filmstrips, and movies, students grow in a conceptual understanding of all the terms and characteristics of the process. Thus, when they hear or read the word *photosynthesis,* they can associate it with the other new words learned and picture its relationship to subcomponents of the process such as chlorophyll, chloroplast, carbon dioxide, oxygen, and so forth.

Thus the concept word embraces all its many parts. Many words, such as *mammals, insects, migration, pioneers,* and *Internet,* belong in this category, so it is a wise strategy for teachers to spend time with such concept words and establish ways for students to use and take ownership of them. One economical and conceptually wise way to do this is to present a **concept map,** which shows the relationship of the concept word to its associated terms (see Tips for Teachers 3.1, with the concept word *mammal* used as the lesson illustration).

**Using the context, context clues,** and **context cues** are phrases used by classroom teachers, when they encourage children to figure out a word's meaning from a particular sentence or contiguous sentences of a larger text. To figure out a new word from context means that the reader has to know how sentences work and how parts of sentences (called phrases and clauses) can be arranged in standard written English to make written communication understandable. This ability is related to an individual's understanding of the rules of grammar or syntax (Barry, 2002). How is this ability learned? Is it learned through the teaching of formal grammar, such as the parts of speech and types of sentence arrangements and rearrangements in English? Are schools still teaching grammar rules in their language arts curricula, or is grammar as a pedagogical subject being covered in the revision stage of the writing process? However grammar is being presented to school-age children in today's classrooms, there is evidence that children

## Mapping a Concept Word to Increase Concept Understandings and Develop Word Learning Proficiency

A map is a visual, graphic array using such figures as boxes, rectangles, and circles to house words and phrases. The figures of the map (with the words therein) are arranged and linked in ways that express a concept to show the relationship of the whole to its parts and the parts to the whole. A logic of organization and meaning is therefore expressed.

1. The teacher writes the concept word such as *mammals* on the chalkboard or large chart paper and boxes it in or circles it.
2. The teacher asks students to tell what they know about mammals, what the word means, and possibly, at this stage, what they're curious about learning regarding mammals. (The skillful teacher can then have another chart ready to record what children *KNOW* and what they're *CURIOUS ABOUT KNOWING*).
3. When different children contribute (often with the teacher's help) such subconcepts as "warm blooded," "babies born alive," "have body hair," "vertebrates," "females give milk to young," "differing habitats," etc., the teacher (or children) link these attribute words to the concept word.

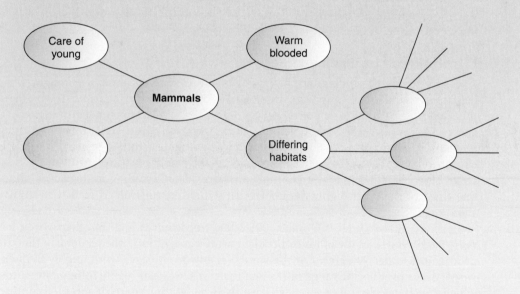

4. The teacher needs to be skillful with such concept map construction. It's not good practice to just place words willy-nilly around the targeted concept word. The teacher needs to think ahead to where he or she is going with this particular concept and what is offered in the textual readings or information resources that add to the children's knowledge base. The teacher wants to arrange the concepts, subconcepts, and related details in the most logical, cohesive way. For instance, one circle is not filled in regarding the map structure above. Why? A logic might be that "have body hair," "vertebrates," and even "warm blooded" are linked to a subconcept, "physical characteristics." Try to engage your students in *how* the map should be constructed. Doing this will involve them in the higher-order thinking processes of categorizing, organizing, and making judgments.

*(continued)*

*Tips for Teachers* **3.1**
*(continued)*

5. More and more words and subparts can be linked by figures to an ever-growing conceptual map. For instance, to "differing habitats" could be linked "tundra, tropical waters, forest." To these words could be linked "musk ox, manatee, and wolf" and all other appropriate animals. In this way, the low-vocabulary-background students see all the words arranged in a conceptual way.

6. It would be a wise move for the teacher to call on such students to provide an oral (or written) recitation of a subtopic to see if such students can use the words appropriately. For instance, point to "differing habitats" and "mammals" and say, "Who can connect these ideas to build a paragraph?" Once a sentence is offered, a new sentence using related concept words would be added and so on. An entire written piece can be reconstructed by the children who used the new words in appropriate contexts as shaped by the teacher. The resulting selection can be read and reread to assist low-vocabulary-performing students in particular.

learn principles of how to use the context, and they learn specific strategies for accessing word meanings (Kuhn & Stahl, 1998).

## Which Words to Teach and Learn

The early frequency studies and the establishment of core vocabularies or sight-word lists have generated four important implications regarding words (Coady, 1994b). First, the reader can determine that on any given page of text a relatively small number of specific words make up a large proportion of all the words on that page. Although we noted that almost 50 percent of all text in written English is made up of 100 words, these words conform to highly regular spelling and sound principles at least two-thirds of the time (May, 1998). This means that if sounding out were the only reading strategy used, about one-third of the most highly frequent words would be difficult to read with understanding, such as the words *the* and *you.*

Second, if the reader is familiar with 5,000 words in reading (in other words, has these 5,000 words solidly in his or her sight-word recognition), the reader can fluently process just under 90 percent of the words on any given page. Third, highly frequent words occur over a wide range of reading materials, whereas highly infrequent words, which are often technical or specialized words, occur within a narrow, specified context. For instance, about 44,000 words constitute 99 percent of the words in any given text. As the reader can note, the gap in number of words frequently recorded in print between 5,000 words at 89 percent frequency and 43,811 words at 99 percent frequency is quite large indeed. Finally, Coady points out that while high-frequency words usually have few syllables, about two-thirds of the low-frequency words found in the English language come from Latin, Greek, or French and are multisyllabic, with identifiable parts (called morphemes) (1994a).

It is time for a reflective pause to take note of the influence on education of the high-frequency word count studies and the resultant lists of sight words or core vocabularies. What developed was a writing style and a word foundation for the materials published for children in the different grades. Textbook authors looked at the words found most often in the vocabularies of children at particular age or grade levels. They subsequently evolved a concept of "controlled vocabulary," which referred to the choice and use of a limited number of words in a printed text to be read by children. Initially begun in the 1930s, the concept of controlled vocabulary has had important implications for reading instruction up to the present day (Robinson & McKenna, 1994). Of course, the most common procedure for word selection of the core vocabulary was to select the most highly frequent words for the first reading book children would read in school, followed by the next group of most frequent words, to the examination of the least frequent words for upper-grade reading materials. These styled books to be used by children became known as **basal readers** and more recently as **leveled texts.** However, according to many sources, leveled texts take into account many variables and criteria for determining the ease of readability of a text other than just vocabulary control (Brabham & Villaume, 2002a; Fry, 2002; Rog & Burton, 2001–2002).

The basal reader and leveled text concepts were grounded in a belief in control—control by authors to write in an altruistic way for children. The rationale was that if children were first exposed to the most frequent words in their early classroom reading material, they would have a strong launch into successful reading occurrences with other materials. Thus, in children's early reading materials published for the classroom, not only were the most frequent words selected first, but also these words were reinforced by continuous exposure in the basal leveled book. The premise here was that the more often the young reader faced a controlled or limited number of new words, the more success the reader would have in adding these words to his or her sight-word vocabulary and the more fluent the reading would be. Another premise was that by reading the most frequently used words in their school texts, the children would also be familiar with these words in the oral language. Therefore, word understanding would not be a difficulty for children, fluency of textual reading would be smooth and unhalting, and comprehension of the written selection would be facilitated if word meaning was known.

## ■ THE WRITTEN LANGUAGE SYSTEM

Although the accent in preceding sections is on providing clarity about word concepts, we know that words (with their phonological, orthographic, and morphological features) are used in their ever-increasing larger contexts of sentences, paragraphs, and literary/textual/informational selections (whole discourses). Also, these larger contexts flavor and shape word meanings. But how do readers process the printed page? Is the visual traffic flowing through the eyes to the brain different for a beginning reader than for a more advanced or **fluent** reader?

The fluent reader (meaning those who can process a text smoothly and efficiently without losing efficiency by employing word-attack skills) is not even aware of how the mind interacts with the mind of the author who has set down readable print on a page. The fluent reader is influenced by the very nature of the author's style in communicating his or her message and by the experiences and concepts the author brings to interface with the reader's schemata (pictures in the head) and conceptual understandings. The reader has to work through the author's sentences and hope that not too many ideas are **embedded** in longer sentences. If the author presents unfamiliar words, the reader hopes that the author has provided some clues within the sentences to help the reader figure out the meanings. If the reader can't guess at a word's meaning from context, he or she may be able to approximate the way the word might sound in oral language by trying to sound it out or by analyzing some of the familiar morphological parts to figure out the meaning of the entire word. The fluent reader can utilize these behaviors because he or she has internalized them over time and through wide and diverse reading. Fluent reading is best described as smooth, effortless reading and an integral component of reading comprehension (Worthy & Broaddus, 2001–2002). But do beginning or emergent readers, who are in varying stages of nonfluency with print, have the same processing behavior?

## Cues Available to Readers While Processing Text

Authors and literacy experts talk about the "clues" available through the printed language that serve as cues to readers to help them process and understand text. These clues also highlight the symbiotic relationship between the writer, who is implicitly using the cues of written language because they are the systematic features that allow writing to happen, and the reader, who is implicitly using the selfsame clues because they are the cues to gain meaning from reading. We can account for five cue systems that are available for readers and writers, although most sources identify the **graphophonic, syntactic,** and **semantic cue systems** as the most important (Deford, 1994; D. Goodman, 1999; Rayner & Pollatsek, 1994). To these we add the **visual cue system** and the **pragmatic/schematic cue system,** which also influence the processing of text (May, 1998). Within word identification alone, three types of specific cues may operate: those of graphemic, orthographic, and grapheme–phoneme correspondence (Rayner & Pollatsek, 1994). Please refer to Table 3.1 for a discussion of the five types of cues and the information potentially transmitted by each one.

It is important for the teacher to understand the nature of the cueing system because the system works differently for readers at different levels of reading proficiency. It is also important for the teacher to note that the spelling–sound or graphophonic system provides just one set of cues—a cue set that readers eventually need to discard to reach high levels of reading fluency. Although readers are influenced by all of these interactive cueing systems, Figure 3.1 shows that a major distinction can be made between readers who are fluent and those who are still learning to read or are nonfluent. Although the chart is a bit of an oversimplification in that readers' reading behavior changes with the complexity of texts, the processing routes through print are mainly influenced by the ability to use the printed language cues to gain efficient understanding.

Thus, beginning/emergent readers (generally anywhere from kindergartners to second graders) or nonfluent readers (all older children, youths, or adults who are struggling with the reading of text and thus are temporarily dysfluent) need to devote analysis time at the visual and graphophonic level to arrive at a word's identity. Yet the grammatical, meaning, and pragmatic understandings are known in the mind.

## *Table 3.1*   The Cue Systems of Written Language

| Cue System | Major Components | Information Transmitted |
|---|---|---|
| Visual | • Word Configuration | • Each word has a visual configuration made up of its length, its shape, its ascending and descending letters, and the arrangement of its internal letters. The word occupies a visible space and is distinct from another word because of a space boundary. |
| | • Paragraph Indentation | • Generally, each new paragraph is indented signaling to the reader that the author is offering a new idea or an addition to a previous idea. Also, the new paragraph signal tips off the skillful, purposeful reader to search for the main idea, which may be explicitly stated in a topic sentence. |
| | • Punctuation | • Punctuation, along with capitalization at the sentence beginning, provides the idea of sentence sense—that the sentence provides a unit of meaning. Different end marks of punctuation (period, question mark, exclamation point) signal meaning. |
| | • Typographical/ Text Features | • Typographical or text features such as page design, font size, boldface, italics, and underlining are used by authors to visually alert readers to ideas of importance. The larger the boldface, the more central the idea. |
| Graphophonic | • Sound–Symbol Associations<br>• Spelling Patterns<br>• Orthographic Cues | • *Grapho* refers to the alphabet letters or strings of letters that the reader initially perceives in the reading of text. *Phonic* refers to the sound or phonemes that readers have to call to mind to match the perceived letters. This system may be called on when a word is not recognized immediately at sight and the reader needs to decode (sound out) the word to obtain meaning. The letters (graphemes) have configurational information as well in that they can transmit rapid visual information while holding the key to the phoneme or spelling-pattern equivalents. |
| Syntactic | • Grammar<br>• Word Order<br>• Sentence Structure<br>• Rules of English<br>• Syntax | • Syntactic information is composed of the grammatical rules and structures readers have come to learn through oral language before reading occurs. Speakers have learned to create sentences and to transform syntactic structures such as phrases and clauses in compliance with the rules of English. Readers will bring these same skills to the printed page. They use word order, function words, morphological structures (often called inflectional endings), and punctuation to both understand and write. |
| Semantic | • Meaning; influenced by experience, concepts, prior knowledge (including rules of English syntax), and vocabulary understanding | • The meaning obtained from a sentence is highly related to the grammar of that sentence—that is, the complexity of the sentence, the order of words within it, and the redundancy of signals (such as pronoun referents) all contribute meaning cues. However, also contributing to comprehension is the information in the mind of the reader. Thus, prior knowledge composed of one's experience, concept understanding, and vocabulary volume all interact with the context as the text is being visually processed. |

*(continued)*

| Table 3.1 | Continued | |
| --- | --- | --- |
| **Cue System** | **Major Components** | **Information Transmitted** |
| Pragmatic | • Social and Cultural Influences<br><br>• Situations and Settings | • Language use is influenced by one's culture and the social considerations of when, where, and how to use particular language styles such as formal, informal, or slang. Situations and settings also influence the language that is appropriate and that one comes to expect at particular times and in particular circumstances. For instance, the language expectation of school, business, and most professional life is that of formal standard English, whereas informal language would be the expectation of a close-knit group of friends. Particular types of settings and groupings in school may influence how reading and writing are accomplished by students. For instance, for some students the pragmatic influence of a school computer lab may engender far more productive writing than an in-class desk setting. |

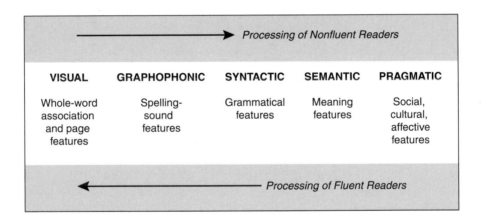

*Figure 3.1* Reading Processing Routes by Different Reading Proficiency Levels

The fluent reader, intent on getting on with it, has knowledge, affective memories, and beliefs shaped by environmental factors and brings these experiences to the printed page (Cole, 2002–2003). The fluent reader picks up visual cues with the eyes, and if these cues confirm words that bring a comfortable sense of meaning that satisfies the reader, the reader reads on. If the fluent reader has to stop to decipher a new or difficult word (as in a Russian novel, perhaps), the fluency process is stalled and the sense of meaning may be disturbed or even temporarily lost. Decoding the graphophonic features of words is a different mental process than reading with meaning. As long as there is no text ambiguity to confuse the reader, the reader can rush purposefully through the text as "the eyes do the walking" and the mind "does the talking." The more that printed words become learned automatically with at-sight visual recognition, the more that the nonfluent reader gains proficiency and enters the more skilled level of fluent reading.

However, anyone who is a fluent reader most of the time can be made nonfluent (or dysfluent, in this case) in an unfamiliar context. Although you handle your favorite authors and periodicals with ease, what happens when you are beckoned to read a lawyer's document or an income tax manual? You now face the same behavior that the emergent, nonfluent reader experiences with new words and new concepts. You bog down in the reading by placing your fingers on particular words as you study them and trace your finger under particular sentences as you try to figure them out. Although the immediate issues facing you are the unfamiliar words in difficult-to-decipher sentences, the real issue here is that you don't have the background semantic knowledge about the topic. Nor do you regularly read laws, legal cases, and tax code manuals, so you don't have the reading experiences of style and vocabulary use to call on either.

So it is with a young emergent reader or an older child, youth, or adult performing as a dysfunctional reader (these latter cases are often labeled "remedial," "at-risk," and "linguistically different") because of mind, text, and word knowledge incompatibilities. Whenever the words get too difficult or the sentences and textual meanings are too far removed from their linguistic and experiential knowledge, these readers will bog down. For the teacher, a major rule is to ensure that new words and sentence structures are practiced in contexts that children and emergent readers can understand.

Depending on the proficiency of the reader, the demands of the text in syntactic and semantic complexity, and the compatibility of cultural/pragmatic influences, the reader samples and uses the printed language cues in the most efficient way. The able reader processes and monitors word chunks based on the incoming visual information while attending to meaning. Less able readers and young children learning to read have not achieved a comfort level of fluency with the intake of words in continuous text. Therefore, the novice reader is compelled to attend to print in a serial order while simultaneously considering what information to attend to in the hierarchy of whole meaning, discourse type, sentence, phrase, word, letter clusters, and individual letters (Deford, 1994).

## Working with the Alphabetic Principle

Let's see if we can capture the essence of what it means to decode or "sound it out" and the principles of language on which this process appears to rest. The English language is based on an alphabetic system or principle, meaning that letters (written symbols or graphemes) represent sounds (phonological representations or phonemes). The strength of the **alphabetic principle** is that a productive writing system is created whereby from a small set of reusable letters an extremely large number of words and morpheme-bearing meanings can be produced (Rayner & Pollatsek, 1994).

Thus the ability to understand that the twenty-six letters of the alphabet make up the visual components of words is an important one for early literacy success (Duffelmeyer, 2002; Kameenui & Carnine, 1998). Also important is visual recognition of the different features that make up the letters (Sipe, 2001). For instance, a vertical line or stroke makes the letter *l*, whereas adding a little horizontal stroke or "hat" makes the letter *t*. Some letters have directionality or spatial orientation features, such as *d* and *b* and *p* and *q*. It is good practice to encourage young children to write (which could look like scribble or created spelling) using the letters so that they engage their visual discrimination skills to study the visual orientation of the letters as they attempt to write them.

The issue appears to be a simple one. There are twenty-six letters in the alphabet. If teachers concentrate their teaching efforts on helping children learn these letters, then children will succeed early on with reading. Common sense and even numerous research studies have shown that knowledge of letter names in kindergarten and first grade has been a strong predictor of early reading achievement (Kameenui & Carnine, 1998; Raymer & Pollatsek, 1994; Snow, Burns, & Griffin, 1998). But the issue with the English language is not that simple. Although there are twenty-six alphabet letters, there are about forty different, distinct sounds or **phonemes** in speech. To represent the sounds in speech with letters of the alphabet would mean the invention of more letters. Furthermore, many letters can represent more than one sound and many sounds are represented by several alphabet letters (Smith, 1994). A further complication arises in establishing a one-to-one letter-sound correspondence in that some sounds are not represented by single alphabet letters but by a combination of letters, such as *oi, oy, ew, ch, th* (Johnston, 2001). These combinations give rise to the concept of "spelling units," which are distinct combinations of letters and sounds. Citing the 1967 and 1970 research of Richard Venezky, Smith notes that in a computer analysis of over 20,000 words, fifty-two major spelling units evolved, thirty-two for consonants and twenty for vowels. So now we have the alphabet clearly doubled in duty.

But wait, there's still more to confound the issue of sound–symbol relationships. Additional research conducted by Berdiansky, Cronnell, and Koehler in 1969 was performed on 6,092 one- and two-syllable words in the understanding vocabularies of children between the ages of six and nine to see if a clear set of phonic rules could be established for the English language (Smith, 1994). Although the researchers found that analysis of their words produced 211 different spelling-sound relationships, they excluded 45 correspondences because they did not occur at least ten times in the 6,000-plus words analyzed. That left 166 sets to which clear sound–symbol rules would apply. Of the 166 spelling-sound correspondences, 60 rules were established for consonants, 73 for the primary, single-letter vowels *(a, e, i o, u, y),* and 33 for complex vowels, meaning a vowel-letter combination that produces its own sound. Thus, in the potential world of phonics instruction alone there are 166 rules of grapheme–phoneme correspondences, suggesting that 166 distinct lessons could be generated to ensure that *all* children were beneficiaries of *all* the rules. In 1963, Theodore Clymer added additional analyses to fuel the fires of phonics teaching utility by concluding that only 45 of 121 phonic generalizations were specific enough to assist readers in word pronunciation (Clymer, 1963/1996).

## The Components of "Sounding It Out"

Implicit in all the terms used for sounding out words is the understanding that visual and auditory components are involved in the process. Although the alphabetic system has produced twenty-six letters that allow us to make an infinite number of words we can understand, the same system can result in difficulties for beginning readers (and those who experience spelling problems throughout their lives) in learning to read many of the words they already understand. One reason for children's difficulty is that the phoneme is an abstraction rather than a natural physical aspect of speech, and the second problem results from the limited number of English vowel letters doing double and triple duty in the generation of vowel sounds (Rayner & Pollatsek, 1994). Phonemes are considered to be abstractions because their sound equivalents don't exist by themselves. Phonemes need sounds before and after to be accurately represented as sounds in speech. For instance, the phoneme /b/ is governed in pronunciation by the vowels and additional sounds that follow it, such as with the words *boy, bat,* and *butter.*

Visual factors related to word identification include those of letter or alphabet recognition (also reinforcing the alphabetic principle); letter discrimination; left to right orientation in word and text order; and an understanding of the word concept in print—that words in print are separated by space boundaries and that each contains its own meaning representation. Have you ever noticed a common behavior when young children and children experiencing reading difficulties are asked to read? Many of these readers will track each word with their finger or mouth each word as they move across the lines. These children have a sense of word and they are analyzing the printed page to ensure that their eyes capture each word in sequence because they are so intent on obtaining meaning.

The most important auditory aspects related to word identification are known as *phonological* or *phonemic awareness.* Whereas many sources seem to use the two terms interchangeably and still others associate phonemic awareness with *phonics* instruction, others note that there are broad differences in the use of the three terms (Armbruster, Lehr, & Osborn, 2001; Richgels, 2001). Figure 3.2 shows that phonemic awareness or the ability to note the distinctive phonemes in spoken words grows out of a larger verbal language and phonological awareness context. Furthermore, the word *phonics* comes into play when the letters of the alphabetic code represent their phoneme equivalents to achieve a sound–symbol correspondence for sounding out words. Although it appears that phonics and phonological or phonemic awareness share some of the same characteristics, researchers and authors point out that they are not the same even though they develop reciprocally in children (Vanderuelden & Siegel, 1995).

Phonemic awareness has been developing in children as they have used oral language in their everyday lives. They come to school with the intuitive, implicit insight that spoken words are composed of smaller elements or parts that adults call syllables and phonemes (May, 1998). Phonemic awareness is the ability to think analytically about words and be able to manipulate the sounds and rhyme schemes of words (Fox, 2000). Phonemic awareness activities focus on playing with the syllables and phonemes that make up spoken words, such as clapping to distinguish syllables; thinking of other words that rhyme with a certain word, such as *cat;* adding a phoneme /d/ in front of a letter cluster like /ad/ to make a familiar word; and raising one's finger or hand when rhyming words are heard. Phonic awareness is a bit more serious for reading and writing development. When children demonstrate their use

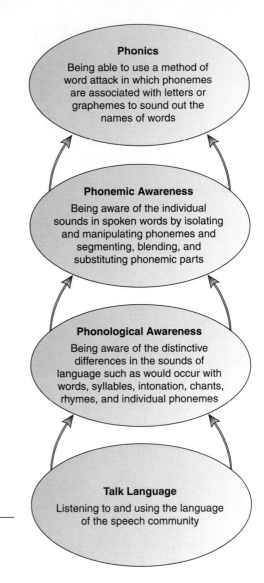

*Figure 3.2* The Relationship of Phonics to Awareness of the Sounds of Language

of phonics, they make letter-sound associations to work out unfamiliar words they encounter during reading or to conjure up the correct spelling during writing. See Box 3.2.

In summary, the sounding it out condition of reading rests on the alphabetic principle. The plus side of having a limited set of alphabet characters is that new words can be added to the written language as long as the letters representing the words can be read by others. The minus aspect of the English alphabetic system is the difficulty and confusion created for beginning readers by the nature of phoneme abstraction and vowel letter-sound correspondences (Rayner & Pollatsek, 1994). The teacher needs to consider

**BOX 3.2** Helpful Literacy Hints for Children at Risk for Potential Reading Delay

Reading research is beginning to show that an important relationship exists between early word reading acquisition and phonological awareness. This relationship appears to be especially true for children attending high-poverty-level schools and children at risk for early reading achievement. By engaging such children in activities that promote phonological and phonemic awareness such as rhyming, chanting, clapping hands to phonemes and syllables, and inserting and blending phonemes into words, children will have a stronger base of phonemic awareness to bring to phonics instruction.

that 166 spelling-sound rules apply with regularity in English, that 45 spelling-sound correspondences were excluded because they didn't reach strict standards, (but they're still there!), and that 106 correspondences in spelling-sound relationships occur with vowels.

## The Importance of Automatic Word Reading

Over the years, a false dichotomy has arisen regarding the teaching of words. This dichotomy centers on the teaching of words "as wholes" as opposed to teaching words through decoding techniques based on the alphabetic principle (often simply referred to as phonics). Basal reading and leveled-text systems, in an effort to control the words introduced to children and to capitalize on the utility of high-frequency words, do offer a limited set of words in each of their series books published for children. Because many of the high-frequency words (also function words) did not have sound–symbol regularities, they were taught as whole words.

However, we have noted in previous sections that it's not a matter of how words are learned but of their becoming committed to an individual's sight vocabulary. Even words that are learned through part-to-whole decoding techniques, requiring increments of time to analyze the word and letter-sound features, need to be read eventually as wholes, immediately and without hesitation. The learning equation that forms when the reader recognizes words as wholes looks something like this:

Rapid whole-word recognition → comprehension → increasing fluency

The comprehension and fluency outcomes of rapid and smooth word recognition could be interchanged, but the two generally go together in skilled reading (Worthy, 2002). Understandably, automatic word recognition does not always equate with adequate comprehension. The factors of cues and clues discussed earlier and found in Table 3.1 remind us that there are written language conventions, author style, and "in the mind" conditions that affect fluent reading with comprehension. Skilled active readers shift their mental processing skills in four ways to achieve meaning: (1) they shift between what the text says and what they know about the topic; (2) they elaborate and make connections to what they have read; (3) they monitor their comprehension to see if what they read makes sense; and (4) they use the influence of the social context to select what is important and meaningful (Walker, 2000). Meaning, however, is highly related to smooth word recognition, making the ability to recognize words rapidly a distinguishing characteristic of the skilled active reader (Juel, 1994).

To obtain meaning during reading, readers need to be able to chunk, or group, words into meaningful syntactic units (Irwin, 1991). This chunking requires that important processes occur between the eye and the brain. First, the eyes remain in location, or fixate, on word parts, a word, or chunk of words as determined by the proficiency of the reader. A **fixation** in reading occurs when the eyes come to rest for milliseconds to allow visual information to enter (Rayner & Pollatsek, 1994). The information obtained during fixation pauses is like viewing a slide show. An initial fixation or "slide" occurs for about a quarter of a second, followed by a brief shift to the next segment of print on a page from which information is extracted in the next fixation slide of a quarter of a second (Rayner & Pollatsek, 1994). Contextual reading thus proceeds until the text is finished.

The mind of the reader is, in effect, in control of the eyes during efficient reading. The reader will direct the eyes to the next chunk, depending on what has been understood. Each subsequent fixation transmits additional meaning about the topic. If the mind of the capable reader has been engaged in understanding what can be expected from the reading context, then this reader will be able to predict meaning by visualizing the words that enter their the field.

The implications for readers who are poor in automatic word recognition become clear. If the reader becomes bogged down in actually figuring out words during contextual reading, the mind and visual processing system have been diverted from making efficient connections to meaning. Because the reader needs to look at the letters and the letter clusters of words (the orthographical properties) to trigger the sounds these letters make (the phonological properties), the mind has shifted from fluent connections to meaning to a process whereby words have to be sounded out to gain access to meaning. Decoding in context and word-by-word reading further limit the development of rich visual images that often accompany the reading of literature and descriptive passages. When faced with a text that is overly challenging, problem readers have difficulty relating the text to their experiential background and elaborating the content (Walker, 2000).

It would be both important and efficient for beginning and problem readers to build a strong sight vocabulary foundation. But each learner is different. Although the visual processing system is available to achieve smooth, fluent word intake, children's memory is a factor, which leads us to believe that each person's mastery of sight words or words immediately recognizable in print is different. And this is correct. This one factor—a person's sight-word vocabulary—is so important to reading success that it basically separates the "haves" from the "have-nots." Think about it for a moment. If every reader of English could master at sight the first 5,000 words in the Carroll, Davies, and Richman frequency count, they would be able to read with about 89 percent accuracy in any given text. If the reader could master the 43,831 words of that same frequency count, they would be able to read any given text with 99 percent accuracy. Thus a major goal of reading instruction should be to assist all learners to add words to their individual basic sight-word vocabularies as rapidly and meaningfully as possible.

This is a statement easy to write, but it's very difficult to do at the same time and at the same pace for all the learners in a classroom. Why? Remember that learning to read is not a matter of seeing the words but rather a matter of retrieving the words from memory to be able to read them automatically. Teachers make statements such as "They knew the words on Monday, but when they came back to their reading groups on Wednesday, many of them had forgotten the words." What's happening is that the children who forgot the words needed more exposure and recall opportunities with the words during the

## BOX 3.3 Assisting Special Needs and At-Risk Students Having Difficulty with Word Reading

Students who have difficulty with the recall of words need to practice looking at, saying, and even tracing the letters of difficult words to anchor them in long-term memory. Students can print difficult words on individual word cards, sticky notes, or small notebooks and then underline syllables or morphemic parts and compose sentences using these words. The words can come from any number of lessons or reading text sources.

Monday afternoon to Tuesday hiatus. The children who learned the words on Monday were able to commit those words to long-term memory, and in most cases word configurations and corresponding word names are secure in the children's safe-deposit boxes of memory. The children who did not learn the printed words were not able to associate the look of the words (the configuration) with the word names to achieve a bond in long-term memory. The answer is, of course, that the children need to practice the words so that they can retrieve them automatically and correctly from long-term memory as soon as they are perceived in print (see Box 3.3).

The teacher can present meaningful activities and contexts so that children can practice and work with words. One way is to use a map structure, as pictured in Tips for Teachers 3.1. The map structure shows words that are connected or associated with one another. The map often appears as a word cluster with the topic written in the center circle and selected words appearing at the end of lines or rays drawn off the center circle (Tompkins, 1998). The teacher should have children connect a few words on the map display to make their own unique sentences.

Naturalness and high motivation in word learning are exemplified through a print-rich environment and use of the word wall strategy (see Tips for Teachers 2.1). The words amassed on the word wall can come from multiple sources: books read or created in class, told experiences of trips or excursions, visitors telling or sharing unusual life stories, and so forth. The word wall also serves as a focal point for the discussion of words and for the building of new vocabulary from topics of study (Brabham & Villaume, 2001). Words are discussed, defined, and used in oral sentences before they are written and placed on the wall. Students can borrow words from the word wall to take to their desks or centers if an opportunity arises for them to use that word in one of their own written stories. Children can then return the words they have borrowed to a manila pocket envelope hanging on the word wall. Because each word has been written on a large index card, the teacher can help an individual child learn the word more securely by tracing the word with the child's fingers and then telling the child to look away and trace the word in the air.

A tried-and-true method of helping children achieve reading fluency is the language experience approach (LEA) often credited to Russell Stauffer (1970, 1975). The reading text produced in this approach is based on the oral language and experiences of one child or of a group of children. Because the language comes from the children themselves, it is an ideal way to connect the oral with the written language while providing a natural context for children to read whole words with immediate understanding. The teacher's role is to elicit information about an experience from the children and write down what the children say in some organized way. Children *want* to read what the teacher has written because they were the authors of the story. Thus, LEA has become a personally meaningful literacy experience.

There are three broad components of LEA. First is a focus on one experience or topic that the children wish to discuss and see in writing on a large piece of chart paper, oaktag, or chalkboard. The second is the written recording of the child's or children's experience in a number of formats. One copy can appear on a large language experience chart, a second copy can be on regular-sized paper for insertion into a binder or notebook, and the third could be on oaktag to be cut up into sentence strips or words. The teacher might need to edit a bit to achieve correct syntax and word choice, but editing should be kept to a minimum. The story should be in the range of four to seven sentences to provide both a meaningful content selection and enough words to transfer to the readers' sight vocabularies. The final component of the LEA approach is providing enough written contexts—charts, individual book pages, sentence strips, flash cards, word banks, journals, cloze selections—so that the children learn to read the words automatically and at sight, allowing them to be efficient with the words in other contexts. A variation of LEA is interactive writing. Here the children and the teacher decide on the message they want to write and share the production of the writing as the teacher assists with spelling and requested information (Sipe, 2001).

Another powerful way to build children's word reading and fluency proficiency is to use the retelling strategy with children's literature as the vehicle of instruction. Retelling is a verbal reconstruction of the selection in the children's own words. When their verbal retellings are written down, the retold stories become the basis of the children's reading experiences. The retelling strategy can work effectively to build sight vocabulary. In Chapter 11, we return to the retelling strategy as a natural way to reinforce children's comprehension of the narrative structure.

Retelling is as effective strategy to use with both emergent and problem readers because having a sense of the whole allows them to predict the words in their own retold stories as well as the retold stories of others. The method of repeated readings coupled with retellings helps readers predict a text's vocabulary. The children's own written context helps them visualize the words that enter the visual field.

All of the new words encountered, practiced, and learned in the activities discussed above (and many others) can be kept in **word banks.** Word banks are simply files of words maintained by one child or a group of children. They play an important role in the development of sight vocabulary and have been identified with the language experience approach and whole language beliefs to literacy instruction (Cramer, 1994). Children write their new words on index cards or in notebooks, often adding definitions to the words when necessary and writing them in sentences to demonstrate the contextual meaning of the words.

# ■ WORD IDENTIFICATION THROUGH SOUND–SYMBOL ASSOCIATIONS

Word identification, also known as word analysis or word-attack skills, refers to one of the cueing strategies used by readers to figure out unknown words. Although word identification can be cued by syntax and semantic information, educators generally acknowledge that the graphophonic system holds a major key to helping emergent readers with the sound–symbol associations necessary to decode or attack words. Of course, in the context of word identification through letter-sound relationships, phonics is the big player.

## How Phonics Instruction Works

With all that's been said about the depth of the alphabetic system and the spelling-sound rules, why are phonics advocates so enthusiastic about the teaching of phonics as a primary system of initial reading? A number of explanations account for the appeal of phonics. First, phonics as a system of instruction is created by adults, who publish books and phonics systems to help teachers make sense of the spelling-sound rules when teaching children. These adults understand the alphabetic system, so they are looking analytically at the sound–symbol regularities that make up words. In other words, familiarity with reading has already been attained, making phonics look "deceptively easy and useful" (Smith, 1999). The wise phonics author would not suggest that the instructor include words such as *have, gone, the,* and *been* in their lessons on long vowels. These words violate the alphabetic principle even though they are high-frequency words in English.

Thus, phonics instruction is made to work because spelling-sound relationships are taught in a regular, patterned way to children. Children have not yet mastered the reading of words and they don't know what to look for in words in order to say them. So when brought to children in a systematic way, phonics *is* deceptively simple. Probably any literate adult can create a systematic phonics program once that person is mindful of the 166 spelling-sound correspondences and is careful to include exceptions to and irregularities in the rules. This way children won't be confused. However, they will likely read with success those materials that follow the instruction of the regular rules but have great difficulty with the written language of award-winning children's authors.

The second reason why phonics works is because it appears to be successful. This statement needs explanation. Author after author has told us that the goals of phonics instruction (or any term associated with word attack) is for students to learn spelling-sound correspondences, which will help them sound out new, unfamiliar words encountered. We might consider this goal to be one of **transfer,** requiring the thinking processes of substitution and blending. For instance, we would hope that the teaching of the /ou/ phoneme, as in the word *out,* would transfer to the sounding out of *flounder* and *boundary.* However, in lesson after lesson of teachers using phonics instruction, it appears that most children can already read all of the words offered in that spelling-sound pattern. Phonics *appears* to be successful because children can already read the words; they're not working out the words though application of the targeted spelling-sound pattern or rule for that lesson. Teachers need to get to the transfer stage to actually determine if children can get to a new word's identity by sounding it out.

Finally, phonics can be made to work successfully in that it can provide children with a large storehouse of words—that is, if the presentation of each phonic element (the grapheme–phoneme correspondence) does not become an end in itself. The goal of each phonic lesson should not be just to practice the spelling-sound correspondence of that lesson, as would occur for the lessons on /ee/ as in *meet,* or /ai/ as in *rain,* or /dr/ as in *drop* (remember, there would be 166-plus such lessons). The goal should also be to practice rapid reading of the words introduced in that lesson, as well as to determine if the phoneme equivalent can be recalled rapidly as the grapheme (letter) features are perceived by the eyes.

Thus, if the teacher plans to plow through the phonic elements in some systematic way, he or she needs to be reminded to sow the field with different levels of words pertaining to each phonic element. First, plant in children visual recognition of the many familiar words they already know in oral language (new reading words). Then present less familiar words so that they can practice and transfer the element to the sounding out of new words. Before moving on, make sure they have that phonic element on the tip of the tongue. In this way, phonics helps children develop a large storehouse of new reading words that are recognized accurately, immediately, and with little or no effort (Ehri, 1997). Or, stated another way, a printed page can be read quickly and easily due to the overlearned knowledge that skillful readers generate regarding letters and spelling patterns (Adams & Bruck, 1995).

There is no consensus regarding the best way to teach phonics and word-attack skills (Snow et al., 1998). Those favoring a code-emphasis instructional focus want to get phonics and decoding done quickly in the early grades so that children can get on to regular reading, whereas the meaning-emphasis group believes that if children attain meaning first, they will, as a consequence of attaining meaning, learn how to associate sounds with letters (Pearson & Raphael, 1999). With phonics done in the early grades, the belief is that children in grade 4 and above will have the letter-sound foundation to focus on the next stage—the multiletter structural features of words, including prefixes, suffixes, root words, contractions, and syllables (Fox, 2000). Those who favor explicit or direct instruction would undoubtedly want a structured phonics and word-attack approach taught by direct instruction in sequenced lessons. The phonics program would be "in charge" and the teacher would implement the program stance.

An implicit curriculum framework would allow for phonics and word-attack strategies to be taught within the context of particular readings, such as might occur through selections in basal anthologies or through types of children's literature. In this regard, teachers often use pattern books and books of rhyme. A pattern book is one in which a pattern of several words (such as a refrain) or even a whole line or sentence is repeated again and again so that the reader predicts the words that are coming. In the implicit approach to word attack or phonics there is a plan of sorts, and a teacher formulates the plan based on striking the right balance between getting the most out of a meaning-oriented, context-driven approach to materials and using a sound–symbol reference system to help them learn words. Because teachers have different views on the "right balance," they place different emphases on the role of phonics in their literacy programs (Freppon & Dahl, 1998). Educators have noted that phonics instruction coupled with whole-word methods that occur through literature-based instruction results in a more powerful way of making reading fun and meaningful than either approach used alone (Rayner et al., 2002).

Quite timely, into a whole-language-versus-phonics-curriculum debate came a research study that investigated how and to what depth phonics was taught in whole language classrooms (Dahl & Scharer, 2000). In eight different urban and suburban classrooms across the United States, involving 178 primarily Caucasian and African American children, the researchers found that nine different whole language teachers covered the concepts of phonological/phonemic awareness and phonemic representation during a full one-third of their instructional time. Phonics instruction became a part of their daily whole language activities, with 45 percent of phonics-documented activities occurring during writing time.

Across the eight classroom environments, the researchers found three common threads:

1. Teachers were able to assess and respond to learners' individual needs during reading and writing conferences. Teachers showed that they had deep knowledge about each student and could provide appropriate individual instruction as needed.
2. Phonics skills were taught within the context of meaningful reading and writing activities. Moreover, students applied phonics concepts and skills in the reading and writing of new words. They appeared to demonstrate a real interest in how words worked and profited from the inquiry procedure in word pattern searches and exploration of letter-sound relationships fostered by their teachers.
3. Phonics instruction was not just a part of the reading curriculum but was featured during writing time when children wrote and discussed their own pieces, surfaced during teacher conferences, and flourished again when children participated in shared writing events (Dahl & Scharer, 2000).

## Constructing the Alphabetic Principle with Invented Spelling

One procedure, which is extremely child centered, is called **invented spelling** or creative spelling. Here the individual child is in control and mentally constructs grapheme–phoneme correspondences to make words (Sipe, 2001). Through the act of writing (not as adults know it, with correct spelling and sentence sense), the child discovers how the alphabetic principle works, and the child's own written products set the stage for reading. Invented spelling is a cornerstone of emergent literacy and whole language constructs because the child is emerging into print to communicate meaningful messages. Like learning to speak, invented spelling and writing in general are developmental. Children have to engage in it, practice it, and receive appropriate feedback regarding the meaning of the message and the risks taken with the spelling. A major concept of invented spelling is that children are not expected to achieve correct spelling and writing right away. Spelling and writing take time. Children need to experiment with printed language and to learn from their mistakes.

Emergent writing and spelling progress through a series of stages (Fox, 2000; Hiebert, 1994). In its earliest form, the writing is pretend in that children initially make random marks or scribbles on a page and then move on to create a representative drawing to communicate a message (Bear, Invernizzi, Templeton, & Johnston, 2000). A bit later children produce a drawing with marks or scribble writing alongside but distinct from the drawing, then produce letterlike words in a linear way across a page, and finally, at the invented spelling stage, produce alphabetic letters that represent sounds in words. In order to invent a spelling such as *DD* for *daddy* or *tr* for *train,* children have developed insights and are attending to sounds in words and the distinct phoneme sounds that make the letters within the words. Children need four skills in order to invent a spelling: (1) they need to know just enough letters of the alphabet and be able to name them; (2) they have to be able to produce the letters they know by writing chunks or segments of letters (the condition of phonemic awareness); (3) they need to understand that the known letters represent sounds (phonemes); and (4) they have to attend to the sounds within syllables and correspond the sounds to get started (Bear et al., 2000). Thus, with emergent writers, we see the condition in which whole words and syllables are represented by one or more letters. Just prior to producing conventional spelling, a transitional stage occurs in which a vowel character appears in every syllable (Hiebert, 1994).

Teachers will sense that they need to be both tolerant and respectful of children's attempts with writing and spelling in the emergent literacy framework. In the developmental process, nonstandard handwriting, spacing, letter formation, and spelling will occur (Leu & Kinzer, 1999). It is through teacher encouragement, modeling, and instruction with continued works-in-progress that variations in nonstandard form will continue to move toward more standard form. In essence, what adults call "mistakes" will be made as children move toward more conventional style. Teachers' attitudes toward children's use of invented spelling need to be ones of discovery, exploration, and risk taking. Children who are engaged in such exploration early on in emergent literacy classrooms are discovering spelling-sound relationships in ways that children who are taught through didactic instruction do not have (Hiebert, 1994). Furthermore, research emphasizes that the association of spelling with sound is a fundamental step in early literacy development (Adams & Bruck, 1995) and that when spelling-sound and speech-sound correspondences are developed concomitantly, phonemic awareness will develop to enhance early writing and reading (Adams, Foorman, Lundberg, & Beeler, 1998).

Whatever approach or technique teachers use to help children decode (read) words and encode (spell) words, they need to remember that these are means to ends. One major end for children is to transfer the words taught through the alphabetic system to sight vocabulary. The second end is to learn the meanings of the words as they appear in different contexts so that, as the child rapidly recognizes the words, understanding occurs as well. The ultimate goal of reading is reading with understanding and enjoyment.

## ■ DEVELOPING WORD MEANING

Vocabulary development is a critical aspect of schooling, especially today, when the words used on prime-time television are less challenging than the words found in most children's books (Cunningham & Stanovich, 1998). Vocabulary not only reflects a person's knowledge (Hirsch, 2000) but also is an excellent predictor of how a person comprehends written text (Kuhn & Stahl, 1998; National Reading Panel, 2000). For many children in the elementary and intermediate grades, a new reading word is also a new vocabulary or new concept word (see Table 3.1). This presents an ever-recurring challenge for the teacher in developing children's meaning and reading vocabularies.

## How Vocabulary Development Works

Here's one way that vocabulary development occurs in the classroom. Fifty percent of the children in your classroom might know the meaning of *tadpole* in the oral language, but they can't yet read it. Another 50 percent may not know what *tadpole* means, and yet they will be facing the word for the first time when it appears in their reading on frogs and toads. These children have to do double duty in that they have to learn the word's meaning as they simultaneously do the word reading. Of course, knowledgeable teachers often discuss the meanings of new words before providing visual encounters in order to establish prior knowledge in the children's minds.

But as far as the teacher is concerned, she or he is presenting the word for the first time in a visual–auditory reading experience to 100 percent of the children. The children are involved with visual recognition of the word, breaking the word into two separate parts, putting the parts back together to reconstruct the whole word, and participating in any other wordplay activities the teacher introduces. The lesson and the reading end. *Tadpole* and all the other new words introduced in the reading and all the other new words with new experiences presented to the children that day are now scattered like unconnected threads across the students' minds as they exit school. Now memory, particularly long-term memory, becomes a factor in learning.

When *tadpole* is exposed to the children on a subsequent day, 25 percent of the children in the group who knew the word's meaning beforehand can read the word at sight, and the other 75 percent are struggling with the word's identity. From the group who didn't know what *tadpole* meant, 85 percent have mastered reading that word. How can this be, the teacher laments? One would think that if the meaning was known, visual recognition of the word would be easy, like matching a visual template to a known concept. But that's the mystery of successful word recognition and vocabulary understanding for particular children at particular times in particular contexts. Children from both groups will need more visual and meaning encounters with *tadpole* before it becomes learned in long-term visual memory.

With another word, the percentage of rapid word identifiers may change. The challenge for the teacher is to help all children acquire new reading words to add to their growing sight vocabularies as efficiently and solidly as possible. To assist this process from a visual and meaning perspective, the teacher should show and have children use the word in written contexts, such as in sentences, paragraphs, letters, and reports.

Acquiring new words enriches children's understanding of each new topic and the concepts associated with that topic. New words open up children's horizons to allow for the attachment of yet more new words (Brabham & Villaume, 2002b). When teachers are about to engage their students in a new topic experience through a textbook reading, as might occur with topics such as amphibians, metamorphosis, the water cycle, or immigration, teachers need to consider the depth of students' prior knowledge with that experience and whether they understand the vocabulary used by the text authors. The

**BOX 3.4**   Why Is It Important to Acquire New Words and Build a Rich Reading Vocabulary?

A rich reading vocabulary supports reading comprehension. Words reflect conceptual understandings, and each new word learned adds additional understanding to a child's prior knowledge bank. Thus, vocabulary acquisition itself supports the intake of new words because prior knowledge word concepts reinforce the learning of new words. New word learning occurs directly and indirectly in and out of school and is best supported by recreational and informational reading.

basic rule is this: Vocabulary represents concepts and information, and the richer a person's vocabulary for a topic, the better chance that person has of success in dealing with that topic.

What happens with children who don't have rich language exposure and enter school with low-vocabulary backgrounds? When provided with the same lesson, the low-vocabulary child will learn less than the high-vocabulary child (Hart & Risley, 1995). This is because the low-vocabulary child is operating on overload. When confronted with so many words he or she can't read efficiently, the low-vocabulary child doesn't integrate well the new concept vocabulary with that previously developed in other topics and subjects. Because vocabulary is a reflection of what someone knows, children need to learn subjects in a cumulative way, thereby attaching new word meanings to their knowledge base while catching up on their vocabulary deficiencies (Hirsch, 2000). The overwhelming message for the teacher is simple: Learning the meanings of and how to read new words is a crucial aspect of schooling. Each new word learned is an incremental step in the comprehension and knowledge process (see Box 3.4).

## Morphemes and Meaning

Now is a good time to return to the discussion of morphemes and the linguistic science of morphology. Educators, teachers, parents, and children conceive of the world of words as "words," whereas many linguists think of the world of words as "morphemes." A *morpheme*, easily defined, is the smallest meaningful unit in the English language. The key concept here is "smallest meaningful unit" (Spencer, 1996). For instance, the word *bird* is a morpheme (unit), but what happens when we say "birds" or "bird's"? In each of these cases, the meaning has changed and meaningful units have been added to the free morpheme *bird*. To the free morpheme have been added two examples of bound morphemes, one of which makes a case for pluralization and one of which indicates grammatical possessiveness.

Linguists use the term *morphology* as they analyze the internal structure of words to determine which parts can result in multiple meanings. Word parts that convey meaning are called "morphemes"; word parts that can also be formed as units of pronunciation and can assist in phonemic awareness but may not have meaning are called "syllables." Sometimes morpheme parts, such as *ed*, and syllables are the same, and many times they are not.

Where does all this heady discussion of morphemes lead, and why is this discussion important for the teacher responsible for students' language and vocabulary development? Recall the information we learned from the word-frequency studies and counts. The Dale list of 3,000 words contained a core vocabulary to sustain children at a fourth-grade reading level, and the Carroll, Davies, and Richman study revealed that 5,000 words occur with 89 percent frequency in texts, while 43,831 words make up 99 percent of all words in running text. What is it about words that some 3,000 to 5,000 are basic to accommodate some measure of reading success, but mastery of another 40,000 words would ensure that the reader has familiarity with 99 percent of the words in all texts? The answer is morphemes.

Earlier in this chapter, we noted that roughly two-thirds of the words less frequently used in English are derived from other languages and are multisyllabic, with identifiable parts or morphemic elements (Coady, 1994b). Knowledge of Greek and Latin root parts is especially effective in building word understanding, and students who can use these parts need less direction from teachers in understanding English words (Fox, 2000). Furthermore, high-frequency words are characterized by few syllables and identifiable parts. The value of understanding morphology and its relationship to vocabulary development should be obvious to teachers, who need to consider spending more classroom time on the systematic learning of morphemes (Arnoff, 1994). Once children have left the early elementary grades, the words they will encounter in school texts and literary readings will have morphological parts joined to familiar words. Readers who have a strong intuitive understanding of morphology are usually able to understand with little effort new words encountered in context. One author indicates that as children learn more words and begin to identify roots and parts inside complex words, they form an analytical mind-set that assists them with new word understandings (Clark, 1998).

Table 3.2 contains many of the common English prefixes and suffixes. Whereas prefixes often change the meaning of the root or base word, suffixes are often added to base words to add both meaning and to achieve syntactic appropriateness. Suffixes change a word's use from one part of speech to another depending on how the base word was used in a sentence. For instance, in the sentence beginning, "Unlikely as it may seem . . . ," the prefix *un* changes the meaning to "not likely," while the suffix *ly* changes the verb *like* to the adverb *likely.* The addition of the two bound morphemes alters the meaning and the way the base word will comply with the grammatical rules of sentence construction.

To conclude, the reflective teacher is the one who weighs the importance of words in children's language and thinking development. The teacher has to use her or his own common sense about how reading and writing work for young, maturing, and problem readers. The teacher has to know a bit about how the English writing system works and what cues are transmitted to readers through the world of print. Regardless of the system, approach, or methodology used by a school, district, or state, the teacher knows that a primary goal of reading instruction is to rapidly increase children's sight vocabularies. Each child's sight vocabulary provides a way for that child to be fluent in reading so that comprehension can proceed smoothly and without halts. Fluency also allows children to maximize the reading energy of known words so that when unknown words or new meaning words are encountered in print, children can devote mental effort to using the context to think. Once children begin thinking about the power of words, they should be encouraged to write using the power they've achieved and to read more to add additional word mastery to their curious minds.

**Table 3.2** Prefix and Suffix Relationships

| Prefixes | | | Suffixes | | |
| --- | --- | --- | --- | --- | --- |
| | *Changes the meaning of the root or base word* | | *Can alter word meaning and changes word usage in sentence from one part of speech to another* | | |
| *Prefix* | *Meaning* | *Example* | *Suffix* | *Meaning and/or Purpose* | *Example* |
| a-, ab-, abs- | away from | absent, abduct | -able, -ible | can be, worthy of | likeable, usable |
| ambi- | more than one | amphibian | | | |
| beni- | good | beneficial | -ence, -ance | state or quality of | absence, resistance |
| co-, con-, cor- | together with | coexist, concord, correlate | -ant, -ent | one who | servant, penitent |
| de- | away from | depart | -ar, -er, -or | one who | liar, teacher, professor |
| dis- | not, opposite | dislike, disapprove | -ful | full of | respectful |
| ex- | out, out from | exit | -ic | having to do with, characterized by | tragic, angelic |
| fore- | ahead of | forefather, foresight | | | |
| im-, in-, il-, ir- | not | immature, inexpensive, illicit, irrational | -ish | like the something named | foolish |
| in- | in, into | inject, invade | -ism | condition or doctrine of | heroism, communism |
| inter- | between | intermission | -less | without | hopeless |
| mal- | bad | malice | -ly | in the way or manner of | rapidly, slowly |
| mis- | wrong, error | mistake, mistrial | -ment | state or quality of | enjoyment |
| multi- | many | multiply | -ness | state or quality of | kindness |
| post- | after | postscript | -ology | study of | biology |
| pre- | before | preview | -ous | having the characteristics of | famous, joyous |
| pro- | forward, before | prospector, proceed | | | |
| re-, retro- | again, back | repay, recede, retrospect | -ship | skill or state of | friendship |
| sub- | under | submarine | -ion, -sion, -tion | state or quality of | tension, attraction |
| super- | above | superior | -ure | state or quality of | failure |
| trans- | across | transport | -y | full of | sleepy, crabby |
| un- | not | unhappy | | | |
| uni- | one | uniform | | | |

# ■ SUMMARY ■

1. Words are the smallest part of language by which meaning is communicated. Words have meaning, sound, and spelling features and are composed of smaller meaningful parts called morphemes, which allow language users to alter meaning and create new words.

2. Words are defined in a number of ways by educators, and understanding the different terms that are used for particular categories of words helps the teacher with conceptual understanding of the complex world of words.

3. The graphophonic, syntactic, semantic, visual, and pragmatic/schematic cue systems are available in the printed language system and serve to transmit information for readers at different proficiency levels.

4. The alphabetic principle provides a productive writing system whereby from a small set of twenty-six reusable letters an extremely large number of words and morpheme-bearing meanings can be produced.

5. A major goal of reading instruction is for learners to achieve automatic word recognition so that comprehension can be enhanced and rich visual images can be produced without halts in the reading of text.

6. The language experience approach to word learning and the retelling strategy used with children's literature are two strong ways to build children's word reading and fluency proficiency.

7. Phonics as a method of instruction becomes successful when it provides students with a means of attacking new words while providing them with a storehouse of learned words.

8. Through invented or creative spelling, children discover how the alphabetic principle works, and children's written products set the stage for reading.

9. Vocabulary development is a critical aspect of schooling, and teachers may wish to devote as much instructional time to analysis and learning of word parts (morphemes) as they do to sound–symbol relationships (phonics).

# ■ QUESTIONS TO CONSIDER ■

1. Why might it be advantageous for the teacher to ensure that his or her students know at sight a core vocabulary as defined by sight-word lists and the Dale/Chall list of 3,000 words?

2. Why is it important to know the distinction between content words and function words?

3. How will learning the structural parts of words, often called prefixes, suffixes, and roots, enlarge students' speaking, reading, and writing vocabularies?

4. How is the mental processing style for fluent reading different from that of nonfluent reading?

5. Does knowledge that there are 166 rules of grapheme–phoneme correspondence help the teacher weigh the way spelling-sound features should be taught?

6. How does phonological or phonemic awareness prepare young children for mastery of phonics and word-attack skills?

7. Why is automatic word reading such an important skill for school and life success?

8. Why is the transfer of phonic elements to the unlocking of new words so critically important in phonics instruction?

9. How is invented or creative spelling a child-centered approach to the learning of the English sound–symbol system?

10. What is the implication of morphemic analysis for increasing word-learning proficiency, and why is vocabulary acquisition so important in the long run?

## ■ THINGS TO DO ■

1. Help young children with phonemic awareness by focusing on rhyme activities and phoneme and syllable manipulation. While rhyming, children can match corresponding sounds, subtract sounds, add other sounds, and blend sound parts together. Children can clap their hands to account for the number of syllables in words.

2. Write children's stories and retellings of books on large paper or the chalkboard so that children can read back these accounts. Read aloud with children several times to achieve fluency and whole meaning understanding; then point to sentences and specific words to be read. Children can copy the written versions as well and add their own written additions.

3. Collect language experience stories as children dictate their experiences, adventures, and knowledge of special events and holidays. Cut up the stories into sentence strips and word cards and

have children read these frequently to gain reading fluency.

4. Lead children into the systematic learning and manipulation of morphemes by having fun with dinosaur names. Because scientists and dinosaur discoverers generally used a combination of two or more Greek or Latin word parts to name a dinosaur, students can learn their meanings and transfer those meanings to many modern-day words. Go to www.enchantedlearning.com/subjects/dinosaurs and www.childrensmuseum.org/dinospherez/index.html to start your morpheme quest for children's word-learning fun.

5. When covering topics or themes, set up a word wall by posting new reading and vocabulary words on large index cards associated with the new learnings. Later, have students group the words into categories and establish a word cluster map.

## ■ RECOMMENDED READINGS ■

Bear, Donald, Marcia Invernizzi, Shane Templeton, and Francine Johnston. *Words Their Way: Word Study for Phonics, Vocabulary, and Spelling Instruction,* 2nd ed. Upper Saddle River, NJ: Merrill, 2000. Provides teachers with a lot of good suggestions for phonics and spelling instruction and how to improve students' vocabularies.

Fox, Barbara. *Word Identification Strategies: Phonics from a New Perspective,* 2nd ed. Upper Saddle River, NJ: Merrill, 2000. Shows teachers other ways besides phonics to present word recognition and identification strategies to students.

Goodman, Kenneth. *Ken Goodman on Reading: A Common Sense Look at the Nature of Language and the Science of Reading.* Portsmouth, NH: Heinemann, 1996. Provides the author's view of reading as a natural process rather than the perspective of reading as a skills-learning process.

Hammond, W. D., and Taffy E. Raphael (eds.). *Early Literacy Instruction for the New Millennium.* Newark, DE: International Reading Association, 1999. A collection of chapters presenting

the most up-to-date concepts and procedures for the teaching of reading instruction to young children.

Raynor, Keith, and Alexander Pollatsek. *The Psychology of Reading.* Mahwah, NJ: Erlbaum, 1994. A book that thoroughly explains how the mind and the senses work during literacy processing and learning.

National Reading Panel. *Teaching Children to Read: An Evidence-Based Assessment of the Scientific Literature on Reading and Its Implications for Reading.* Bethesda, MD: National Institute of Child Health and Human Development, 2000. A landmark report investigating findings and conclusions reached regarding major areas of reading, such as phonics, fluency, comprehension, vocabulary, and computer-related instruction.

Stauffer, Russell. *Directing the Reading–Thinking Process.* New York: Harper & Row, 1975. One of Stauffer's two classic books in which he explains how to accomplish the language experience approach to reading and the stages of the directed reading–thinking activity.

## ■ KEY TERMS ■

alphabetic principle
alphabetic understanding
basal readers
blend
breaking the code
concept map
concept words
content words
context clues
context cues
decoding
embedded
familiar word
fixation
fluent

function words
graphophonic cue system
high-frequency words
instantaneously
invented spelling
leveled texts
morphemes
new meaning word
new reading word
phonemes
phonetic analysis
phonics
phonological and phonemic
    awareness
pragmatic/schematic cue system

semantic cue system
sight-word lists
sight words
sound–symbol relationships
syntactic cue system
transfer
using the context
visual cue system
vocabulary word
word analysis
word-attack skills
word banks
word families
word mediation

## ■ REFERENCES ■

Adams, M. J., & Bruck, M. (1995, Summer). Resolving the "great debate." *American Educator, 7,* 10–22.

Adams, M. J., Foorman, B., Lundberg, I., & Beeler, T. (1998, Spring/Summer). The elusive phoneme. *American Educator,* 18–29.

Armbruster, B., Lehr, F., & Osborn, J. (2001). *Put reading first, kd. through grade 3: The research building blocks for teaching children to read.* Washington, DC: U.S. Department of Education.

Arnoff, M. (1994). Morphology. In A. C. Purvcs (Ed.), *Encyclopedia of English studies and language arts* (pp. 820–821). New York: Scholastic/ Urbana, IL: National Council of Teachers of English.

Barry, A. (2002). *English grammar: Language as human behavior* (2nd ed.). Upper Saddle River, NJ: Prentice Hall.

Bear, D., Invernizzi, M., Templeton, S., & Johnston, F. (2000). *Words their way: Word study for phonics, vocabulary, and spelling instruction* (2nd ed.). Upper Saddle River, NJ: Merrill.

Brabham, E. G., & Villaume, S. K. (2001, April). Building walls of words. *The Reading Teacher,* 700–702.

Brabham, E. G., & Villaume, S. K. (2002a, February). Leveled text: The good news and the bad news. *The Reading Teacher,* 438–441.

Brabham, E. G., & Villaume, S. K. (2002b, November). Vocabulary instruction: Concerns and visions. *The Reading Teacher,* 264–268.

Carroll, J. B., Davies, P., & Richman, B. (1971). *Word frequency book.* Boston: Houghton Mifflin.

Chall, J. (1992–1993, Winter). Research supports direct instructional models: Point/counterpoint, whole language versus direct instruction models. *Reading Today,* 8–10.

Clark, E. (1998). Morphology in language acquisition. In A. Spencer & A. Zwicky (Eds.), *The handbook of morphology* (pp. 374–389). Malden, MA: Blackwell.

Clymer, T. (1996, November). The utility of phonic generalizations in the primary grades. *The Reading Teacher,* 182–185. (Original work published 1963)

Coady, J. (1994a.) Lexicon/vocabulary. In A. C. Purves (Ed.), *Encyclopedia of English studies and language arts* (pp. 736–737). New York: Scholastic/Urbana, IL: National Council of Teachers of English.

Coady, J. (1994b). Word lists. In A. C. Purves (Ed.), *Encyclopedia of English studies and language arts* (pp. 1278–1279). New York: Scholastic/ Urbana, IL: National Council of Teachers of English.

Cole, J. (2002–2003, December/January). What motivates students to read? Four literacy personalities. *The Reading Teacher,* 326–336.

Cramer, R. (1994). Word banks. In A. C. Purves (Ed.), *Encyclopedia of English studies and language arts* (pp. 1275–1277). New York: Scholastic/ Urbana, IL: National Council of Teachers of English.

Cunningham, A., & Stanovich, K. (1998, Spring/ Summer). What reading does for the mind. *American Educator,* 8–15.

Dahl, K., & Scharer, P. (2000, April). Phonics teaching and learning in whole language classrooms: New evidence from research. *The Reading Teacher,* 584–594.

Dale, E., & Chall, J. (1948). A formula for predicting readability. *Educational Research Bulletin,* 27–28, 11–20, 37–54.

Deford, D. (1994). Linguistic and context cues in reading. In A. C. Purves (Ed.), *Encyclopedia of English studies and language arts* (pp. 741– 743). New York: Scholastic/Urbana, IL: National Council of Teachers of English.

Dolch, E. (1936). A basic sight vocabulary. *Elementary School Journal, 36,* 456–460.

Dolch, E. (1948). First thousand words in children's reading. In *Problems in Reading* (Chap. 21). Champaign, IL: Garrard Press.

Duffelmeyer, F. (2002, April). Alphabet activation on the Internet. *The Reading Teacher,* 631–632.

Ehri, L. (1997). Sight word learning in normal readers and dyslexics. In B. Blachman (Ed.), *Foundations of reading acquisition and dyslexia* (pp. 163–189). Mahwah, NJ: Erlbaum.

Fox, B. (2000). *Word identification strategies: Phonics from a new perspective* (2nd ed.). Upper Saddle River, NJ: Merrill.

Freppon, P., & Dahl, K. (1998, April/June). Theory and research into practice: Balanced instruction: Insights and considerations. *Reading Research Quarterly,* 240–251.

Fromkin, V., & Rodman, R. (1998). *An introduction to language* (6th ed.). New York: Harcourt Brace.

Fry, E. (1975, November). Developing a list for remedial reading. *Elementary English, 34,* 456–458.

Fry, E. (2002, November). Readability versus leveling. *The Reading Teacher,* 286–291.

Fry, E., Kress, J., & Fountoukidis, D. L. (1993). *The reading teachers' book of lists* (3rd ed.). West Nyack, NY: The Center for Applied Research in Education.

Gallas, K., & Smagorinsky, P. (2002, September). Approaching texts in school. *The Reading Teacher,* 54–61.

Goodman, D. (1999). *The reading detective club.* Portsmouth, NH: Heinemann.

Gunning, T. (2002). *Assessing and correcting reading and writing difficulties* (2nd ed.). Boston: Allyn and Bacon.

Hart, B., & Risley, T. (1995). *Meaningful differences.* Baltimore, MD: Paul H. Brooks.

Hiebert, E. (1994). Invented spelling. In A. C. Purves (Ed.), *Encyclopedia of English studies and language arts* (pp. 666–668). New York: Scholastic/Urbana, IL: National Council of Teachers of English.

Hirsch, E. D., Jr. (2000, Spring). You can always look it up! . . . Or can you? *American Educator,* 4–9.

Irwin, J. W. (1991). *Teaching reading comprehension processes* (2nd ed.). Englewood Cliffs, NJ: Prentice Hall.

Johnston, F. (1999, September). The timing and teaching of word families. *The Reading Teacher,* 64–75.

Johnston, F. (2001, October). The utility of phonic generalizations: Let's take another look at Clymer's conclusions. *The Reading Teacher,* 132–143.

Juel, C. (1994). Reading fluency. In A. C. Purves (Ed.), *Encyclopedia of English studies and language arts* (pp. 1002–1004). New York: Scholastic/Urbana, IL: National Council of Teachers of English.

Kameenui, E., & Carnine, D. (1998). *Effective teaching strategies that accommodate diverse learners.* Upper Saddle River, NJ: Merrill.

Kucera, H., & Francis, W. N. (1967). *A computational analysis of present day American English.* Providence, RI: Brown University Press.

Kuhn, M., & Stahl, S. (1998, March). Teaching children to learn word meanings from context: A synthesis and some questions. *Journal of Literacy Research,* 119–138.

Leslie, L., & Caldwell, J. A. (2001). *Qualitative reading inventory–II* (3rd ed.). New York: Harper-Collins.

Leu, D., Jr., & Kinzer, C. (1999). *Effective literacy instruction, K–8* (4th ed.). Upper Saddle River, NJ: Merrill.

May, F. B. (1998). *Reading as communication: To help children write and read* (5th ed.). Upper Saddle River, NJ: Merrill.

National Reading Panel. (2000). *Teaching children to read: An evidence-based assessment of the scientific literature on reading and its implications for reading.* Bethesda, MD: National Institute of Child Health and Human Development.

Pearson, P. D., & Raphael, T. E. (1999). Toward a more complex view of balance in the literacy curriculum. In W. D. Hammond & T. E. Raphael (Eds.), *Early literacy instruction for the new millennium* (pp. 1–21). Newark, DE: International Reading Association.

Rayner, K., Foorman, B., Perfetti, C., Pesetsky, D., & Seidenberg, M. (2002, March). How should reading be taught? *Scientific American,* 85–91.

Rayner, K., & Pollatsek, A. (1994). *The psychology of reading.* Mahwah, NJ: Erlbaum.

Richgels, D. (2001, November). Phonemic awareness. *The Reading Teacher,* 274–278.

Richgels, D. (2002, May). Sociocultural perspectives on language and literacy. *The Reading Teacher,* 730–733.

Robinson, R., & McKenna, M. (1994). Controlled vocabulary. In A. C. Purves (Ed.), *Encyclopedia of English studies and language arts* (pp. 297–298). New York: Scholastic/Urbana, IL: National Council of Teachers of English.

Rog, L. J., & Burton, W. (2001–2002, December/January). Matching texts and readers: Leveling early reading materials for assessment and instruction. *The Reading Teacher,* 348–356.

Sipe, L. (2001, November). Invention, convention, and intervention: Invented spelling and the teacher's role. *The Reading Teacher,* 264–273.

Smith, F. (1994). *Understanding reading: A psycholinguistic analysis of reading and learning to read* (5th ed.). Mahwah, NJ: Erlbaum.

Smith, F. (1999, November). Why systematic phonics and phonemic awareness instruction constitute an educational hazard. *Language Arts,* 150–155.

Snow, C., Burns S., & Griffin, P. (1998). *Preventing reading difficulties in young children.* Washington, DC: National Academy Press.

Spencer, A. (1996). *Morphological theory: An introduction to word structure in generative grammar.* Malden, MA: Blackwell.

Stanovich, K. (1991). Word recognition: Changing perspectives. In R. Barr, M. L. Kamil, P. B. Mosenthal, & P. D. Pearson (Eds.), *Handbook of reading research* (Vol. 2, pp. 418–452). New York: Longman.

Stauffer, R. (1970). *The language experience approach to the teaching of reading.* New York: Harper & Row.

Stauffer, R. (1975). *Directing the reading–thinking process.* New York: Harper & Row.

Thorndike, E., & Lorge, I. (1944). *The teacher's word book of 30,000 words.* New York: Teachers College Press.

Tompkins, G. (1998). *Language Arts: Content and teaching strategies* (4th ed.). Upper Saddle River, NJ: Merrill.

Vanderuelden, M., & Siegel, L. (1995, October/December). Phonological recoding and phoneme awareness in early literacy: A developmental approach. *Reading Research Quarterly,* 854–875.

Walker, B. (2000). *Diagnostic teaching of reading* (4th ed.). Upper Saddle River, NJ: Merrill.

Worthy, J. (2002, March). What makes intermediate-grade students want to read? *The Reading Teacher,* 568–569.

Worthy, J., & Broaddus, K. (2001–2002, December/January). Fluency beyond the primary grades: From group performance to silent, independent reading. *The Reading Teacher,* 334–343.

# Instructional Goals, Objectives, and Standards

*Focusing Questions*

1. What should the schools teach?
2. How are aims, goals, and objectives formulated and how do they differ?
3. What are standards? How are they characterized?
4. How would you characterize the approaches to writing objectives by the following: Tyler, Bloom, Gronlund, and Mager?
5. How does each approach differ?
6. How specific should course objectives be? Classroom objectives?
7. How does one connect objectives to standards?

Through the years, educators have used a number of terms to define what they consider the purposes of education to be and what they anticipate or expect of an educational policy on a body of students. They have used such terms as *aims, principles, goals, objectives,* and lately *standards* as a means of identifying what they hope students will gain or achieve after involvement in a district's, a school's, or a classroom's unit of study. The terms have also been used interchangeably. What might be considered an aim or goal to one group of educators might be considered an objective to others. Moreover, what some educators call standards others might call objectives. Today at state and school district levels, the key concept or driving force directing expected student outcomes are standards. At the classroom level, the key concept for the beginning or practicing teacher is that of formulating instructional objectives or outcomes that can be aligned with particular standards.

Naturally, objectives should be consistent with the overriding goals of the school system, the state standards, and the general educational aims of society. Each teacher, when planning for instruction, will contribute to these aims, goals, and standards in a different way. In the new millennium, teachers are finding that the concepts embedded in the terms *aims, goals, principles,* and *instructional objectives* discussed in this chapter have been compressed into the new umbrella term—**standards.** The concept behind standards, as with the earlier terms, is to promote and achieve a high-quality education for all students. We discuss each concept separately to show how each has transitioned into the others.

# ■ AIMS

Historically, the term **aims** has referred to broad statements about the intent of education. Aims are value-laden statements, usually written by panels, commissions, or policymaking groups, that express a philosophy of education and concepts about the social role of schools and the needs of children and youth. In short, they are broad guides for translating the needs of society into educational policy. They are descriptive and often loftily written statements. For example, what does the phrase "Preparing students for democratic citizenship" mean? What do we have in mind when we stress "citizenship preparation"?

Aims provide important statements that guide our schools and give educators direction. Perhaps the most widely accepted list of educational aims in the twentieth century was compiled by the Commission on the Reorganization of Secondary Education in 1918. Its influential bulletin was entitled *Cardinal Principles of Secondary Education.* The seven principles, or aims, designated by the commission focused on (1) health, (2) command of the fundamentals, (3) worthy home membership, (4) vocational education, (5) civic education, (6) worthy use of leisure, and (7) ethical character (Commission on the Reorganization of Secondary Education, 1998).

The commission's work was the first statement of educational aims to address the need to assimilate immigrant children and to educate an industrial workforce, reflecting events in the country during that period. The most important aspect of the document was that it emphasized the need to educate all students for "complete living," not to educate only students headed for college and not to develop only cognitive abilities.

It endorsed the concept of the whole child, meeting the various needs of students, while providing a common ground for teaching and enhancing American ideals and educating all citizens to function in a democratic society. These aims are still relevant for all levels of education and are still found today in one form or another in statements of educational aims.

Some three-quarters of a century later, the Carnegie Foundation proposed a vision of an elementary school that took the educational reform movement back to a focus on the whole child movement while endorsing some of the principles of the earlier commission's work. The elementary school model, called the Basic School, had eight essential building blocks that were its essential aims and goals in schooling a well-educated, well-rounded child (Boyer, 1995; see also Boyer, 1994). The building block concept attempted to overcome the fragmentation of current educational practices by creating a model whereby all eight pieces connected to form a coherent, meaningful whole for each child. The eight building blocks provided the following:

- **A community of learning** in which all of a school's stakeholders under the leadership of the principal share a clear vision of the school's mission.
- **The centrality of language** in which the full range of language symbols from the verbal and written language systems, the arts, and arithmetic are taught and integrated in the curriculum.
- **A coherent curriculum** in which the emphasis is on a core curriculum framework based on integrating eight essential themes called "human commonalities." The learnings from the basic core subjects such as science, history, geography, civics, literature, health, and others support the development of the eight themes so that students learn that peoples across cultures share common life conditions. The eight themes are the life cycle; the use of symbols; the response to aesthetic conditions; a sense of time; the nature of groups and institutions; the nature of producing and consuming; connecting to nature; and the search for meaning.
- **The empowering of students** in which students are nurtured to be active, creative, and cooperative learners. Children are grouped and rearranged in particular ways to achieve different ends, share rich resources, and engage in out-of-school learning activities beyond the school itself.
- **Teachers are viewed as leaders** and "family" team members to assist children in grade-level and across grade-level teams. The principal is viewed as the head or lead teacher.
- **Parents are considered to be partners** and essential teachers of their own children. Teachers report to parents on school and student progress and parents are involved in a wide range of school activities.
- **Services are provided for children** beyond the academic focus. Health professionals, counseling services, and referral procedures to public and private health and social service agencies are made available. The school also responds to changes in family life by offering such options as before- and after-school enrichment programs, Saturday school, and summer enrichment programs.
- Finally, **the school monitors and evaluates each student's progress.** A school-profile index (the school's "report card") is maintained showing how well the school achieved in the eight essential building blocks.

These blocks, along with the Cardinal Principles of Education of 1918, reflected broad ideas and values, a common direction for society, and change as the needs of society change.

# ■ GOALS

Educators needed to translate these broad aims into statements that describe what schools are expected to accomplish (a more focused goal than merely stating the purpose of education). These translations are often called **goals.** Goals make it possible to organize learning experiences in terms of what the state, school district, or school decides to stress on a systemwide basis. In effect, goals are statements that cut across subjects and grade levels and represent the entire school program. Goals provide direction for educators, but they do not specify achievement levels or proficiency levels. Examples of goals are "development of reading skills," "appreciation of art," "understanding of mathematical/scientific concepts," and "competency with computers." Goals are usually written by professional associations, state educational agencies, and local school districts to be published as school and curriculum guidelines for what all students should accomplish over their entire school career.

Goals also tend to reflect the developmental needs of children and youth. According to Peter Oliva (2000), goals "are timeless, in the sense that no time is specified by which the goals must be reached" and at the same time they "are not permanent," in the sense that they "may be modified wherever necessary or desirable." They do not delineate specific items of content or corresponding activities. Goals should be stated broadly enough "to be accepted at any level of the educational enterprise," but specifically enough to lead to desired outcomes (p. 295).

Increasingly, schools are being burdened by the rest of society with roles and responsibilities that other agencies and institutions no longer perform well or want to perform. The schools are seen as ideal agents to solve the problems of the nation, community, and home. Many people and groups, however, refuse to admit their own responsibilities in helping children develop their capabilities and adjustment to society. More and more, schools are being told that they must educate and socialize all children, regardless of the initial input and support from home. Schools may now be attempting to accomplish too many things and therefore not performing many of them effectively (Howe, 1991, Ornstein, 1992). In our high-stress world, increased pressure on schools to achieve higher expectations is resulting in changes in policies regarding homework, recess, retention, and teaching while ignoring research on student learning and motivation (Gratz, 2000).

In preparing his classic on schooling, John Goodlad (1984) surveyed the school goals that had been published by state and local boards of education across the country. From approximately 100 different (school districts') statements of goals, he constructed 12 that represent the spirit of the total list (Table 4.1). He further defined each with subgoals and a rationale statement. The goals summarized what educators were expected to attend to and for what they could be held accountable.

---

*Table 4.1*   Major Goals of U.S. Schools

---

1. *Mastery of basic skills or fundamental processes.* In our technological civilization, an individual's ability to participate in the activities of society depends on mastery of these fundamental processes.

2. *Career or vocational education.* An individual's personal satisfaction in life is significantly related to satisfaction with his or her job. Intelligent career choices require knowledge of personal aptitudes and interests in relation to career possibilities.

3. *Intellectual development.* As civilization has become more complex, people have had to rely more heavily on their rational abilities. Full intellectual development of each member of society is necessary.

4. *Enculturation.* Studies that illuminate our relationship with the past yield insights into our society and its values; furthermore, these strengthen an individual's sense of belonging, identity, and direction for his or her own life.

5. *Interpersonal relations.* Schools should help every child to understand, appreciate, and value persons belonging to social, cultural, and ethnic groups different from the child's and to increase affiliation and decrease alienation toward them.

6. *Autonomy.* Unless schools produce self-directed citizens, they have failed both society and the individual. As society becomes more complex, demands on individuals multiply. Schools help prepare children for a world of rapid change by developing in them the capacity to assume responsibility for their own needs.

7. *Citizenship.* Counteracting the present human ability to destroy humanity and the environment requires citizen involvement in the political and social life of this country. A democracy can survive only with the participation of its members.

8. *Creativity and aesthetic perception.* Abilities for creating new and meaningful things and appreciating the creations of other human beings are essential both for personal self-realization and for the benefit of society.

9. *Self-concept.* The self-concept of an individual serves as a reference point and feedback mechanism for personal goals and aspirations. Factors for a healthy self-concept can be provided by the school environment.

10. *Emotional and physical well-being.* Emotional stability and physical fitness are perceived as necessary conditions for attaining the other goals, but they are also worthy ends in themselves.

11. *Moral and ethical character.* Development of the judgment needed to evaluate events and phenomena as right or wrong and a commitment to truth, moral integrity, moral conduct, and a desire to strengthen the moral fabric of society are the values manifested by this goal.

12. *Self-realization.* Efforts to develop a better self contribute to the development of a better society.

---

*Source:* Adapted from John Goodlad, *What Schools Are For,* 2nd ed. (Bloomington, IN: Phi Delta Kappa, 1994), 44–53. Also see John Goodlad, *A Place Called School* (New York: McGraw-Hill, 1984).

Most schools, however, put more emphasis on cognitive and intellectual goals, especially at the secondary school level, and usually give lip service to moral and ethical considerations. Elementary schools tend to treat the whole child and provide more balance with cognitive, personal, and social growth and development. A number of schools are now becoming increasingly concerned with and formulating goals pertaining to environmental, technical, multicultural, and global understanding.

When we formulate our goals, we might ask the following questions:

- To what extent should our schools emphasize the needs of society and the needs of the individual?
- Should schools emphasize excellence or equality?

- Should we put equal emphasis on academic, vocational, and general education?
- Should we put more emphasis on cognitive learning or humanistic learning?
- Which is more important, national commitment or a higher morality?
- Should we educate students to their own ability level (and for some that might mean only an eighth-grade education) or should we push students beyond their aptitude and achievement level?
- How should we apportion money to be spent on talented and gifted students, average students, and handicapped students?
- How do we compare the payoff to society and the obligations of society in educating different student populations?

These questions are tough and complicated. Not only do educators disagree about them, but educational wars have been fought over them. Indeed, the way we answer these questions both reflects and determines the kind of people we are. Most people in this country readily say they believe in democracy, but how they answer these questions determines what democracy means and how it affects and controls our lives. Trying to resolve these questions, at least in the United States, ideally involves a balancing act—whether our moral and legal restraints overrule our political and economic considerations, and whether needs of the group can be placed in perspective with the rights of the individual.

In this regard, one researcher noted that schools have stood out from other organizations and institutions in the way they have lacked the ability to achieve common goals (Rosenholtz, 1991). The goals of teaching, she added, were often multiple, changing, and quite often in dispute within the organization (school). To achieve success, an organization needs to have a shared sense among its constituents regarding what they are trying to accomplish. Such agreed-on goals and ways to achieve them increase the school's chances to achieve both thoughtful planning and results. Verifying this point, educational reform of the 1980s and 1990s revealed that success in literacy achievement, particularly for high-poverty schools, needed to be initiated at the school level, at which a common mission prevailed among the school stakeholders (Adler & Fisher, 2001).

## From Goals to Standards

In 1983 the report *A Nation at Risk,* compiled by a panel appointed by the U.S. Department of Education, indicated that the well-being of the nation was being eroded by a rising tide of mediocrity. This mediocrity was linked to the foundations of our educational institutions and was spilling over into the workplace and other sectors of society (National Commission on Excellence in Education, 1983). The report sought to upgrade the curriculum (that is, command of the fundamentals) by improving basic skills for young children, improving textbooks, increasing homework, strengthening high school graduation requirements, and raising college admission requirements.

By the 1990s, political, educational, and business leaders in the United States, Canada, the United Kingdom, and Australia began to become seriously concerned with the large learning gaps within segments of student populations in their respective countries. These countries began to initiate attacks on low student standards and to formulate policies of "zero tolerance" of educational failure. These policies called for the establishment of challenging standards that all students were expected to meet. The policies allowed for targets, or defined and measurable goals, to be established so that standards could be met over a designated period of time. They also called for the establishment of national and state assessment policies to see which of the targeted goals were being fulfilled.

In 1997, the U.S. Congress passed legislation called Goals 2000: Educate America Act, which established eight major goals published as The National Education Goals Report (1997). These goals are often simply referred to as Goals 2000 and address such issues as school readiness, high school completion, student achievement, literacy attainments, and drug-free schools.

# ■ STANDARDS

Instructional purposes promoted by national professional organizations and the various state departments of education became known as standards. Thus the term *standards* is the new kid on the block regarding the purposes of education and the way we wish to account for what we expect students to know and accomplish. Accordingly, standards are generally defined in two ways, as content standards or performance standards. **Content standards** define what students through the grades should know in the various disciplines (usually core disciplines). **Performance standards** describe what students should be able to do or accomplish at designated grade levels. Such performance standards represent broad-based objectives established by a state to be accomplished through its school districts for a student to be considered well educated. Educators have noted that the standards movement, which gained more and more momentum in the 1990s, will have a major impact on education in the years to come (Schmoker & Marzano, 1999).

Content and performance standards grew out of the national focus on improving performance in our nation's schools and the national cry to move out of mediocrity to excellence. By 1996 every state had either established its own standards in a number of content areas or had designated their local districts to implement standards for student achievement (Asp, 2000). Moreover, almost all the states had developed state testing programs to measure the success (or nonsuccess) of student achievement with the standards (Editorial Projects in Education, 1999). In the most recent of the "State of the States" report, it was noted that:

- by 2002, 49 states had adopted standards in the core subjects, with 27 states receiving grades of 80 percent or better for their breadth and depth of standards implementation;
- by 2003, 48 states and the District of Columbia required school-level report cards, with 27 states indicating student performance by race, 24 states indicating student performance by poverty, 24 states indicating performance based on English language proficiency, and 29 states indicating performance based on special education placement; and
- by 2003, 28 states and the District of Columbia provided assistance to low-performing schools (Doherty & Skinner, 2003).

## The Standards Approach

One can hardly discuss the standards approach in formulating educational practices without considering the issues of curriculum, testing, and accountability. Curriculum is the way to approach the standards in the classrooms on a daily basis, testing is the procedure of determining if learners achieved a particular standard (an objective), and **accountability** is a plan or method for holding someone or some group responsible for the test outcomes. In Chapter 13, we return to the issues of testing and accountability as we examine the way states and districts are assessing their students and how the results of the assessments force accountability issues on schools at the local level.

The standards approach is decidedly content or discipline oriented. This means that the academic disciplines or traditional core subjects (a conservative approach) provide the curriculum framework. Therefore understanding the concepts, principles, and methods of inquiry of a discipline provide the major goals and objectives in each discipline's course of study through the grades (Glatthorn & Tailall, 2000). Many feel that this content orientation holds promise for U.S. students in helping them achieve high standards in learning. The key appears to be that they be accomplished effectively. Standards and the expectations for students to attain them need to be clear (not confusing) and essential (not overbearing) in quantity (Schmoker & Marzano, 1999).

The reason the standards movement has exerted a major influence on modern education is that it has strong backing from groups that support its success, such as legislators and policymakers, governors, chief school administrators, many teachers, and the general public (Elmore, 1999; Schmoker & Marzano, 1999). The consensus is that standards can provide a focus for schools by establishing clear and defined goals and by representing a positive and possibly historic stage in U.S. education policy in that they attempt to ensure academic knowledge (Sewell, 2000). Because standards inform and shape the work of teachers and educational designers, they can shape both curriculum and assessment with a stronger instructional focus. Some educators argue that teachers are not free to teach any topic they choose, just as an architect or contractor needs to be guided by building codes. Standards guide teachers, allowing them to identify teaching and learning priorities for what students should know and are able to accomplish (Wiggins & McTigue, 1998).

The standards approach is fueled by two primary purposes. The first is based on economics and the second is based on the disparity between high and low achievers (Gratz, 2000). The economic issue is based on the belief that the United States is losing its competitiveness in the world and is falling behind other countries as indicated by international studies of achievement. Thus, the United States needs to push its students and schools harder and faster to be able to compete and keep its economy going. The second purpose, aimed at increasing standards for all students, teachers, and schools, particularly those in urban areas, will improve educational expectations and outcomes for poor and minority students. One report indicates that in some states, less affluent students scored as much as 11 percentile points higher on the state assessment programs than comparable students attending schools in states that had not introduced standard reforms (Grissmer, Flanagan, Kawata, & Williamson, 2000). If education improves for the poor and low achievers, the argument goes, then schools will provide better opportunities to close the income gap between the "haves" and "have nots" within society.

## Translating Standards to School Settings

Standards are derived from three levels of education:

1. National professional organizations representing the major discipline areas. These national organizations have state and local affiliates and membership is made up of teachers, administrators, professors, and sometimes parents who have voices at all levels of membership—national, state, and local.
2. The states, which look to the national organizations for guidance in what is to be taught and then publish their own standards. In the final analysis, the states themselves are responsible for educating the citizenry, as established by the U.S. Constitution.
3. Local districts, particularly those representing large cities, which publish their own standards that may follow or overlap with state standards.

What generally occurs in this layering of standards is a movement from broad aims and goals to more specific targeted objectives. By examining Table 4.2, the reader can note the range of standards promulgated by four professional organizations that represent the traditional core disciplines. Although it is true that within science, mathematics, and social studies there is major emphasis on content knowledge, there is also some process orientation, meaning the thinking required to accomplish the tasks of the discipline. For instance, in content standard 7 of mathematics, we see "recognize reasoning and proof as fundamental to math" and in standard 8, we read "organize and consolidate thinking." The English language arts standards are less content oriented and more concerned with the processing of the language fundamentals of listening, speaking, reading, writing, viewing, and visual representing (as noted in Chapter 2). These four broad bands of national standards set aims and goals for students to be achieved by the time they leave twelfth grade. It's up to the states and local school districts to set their own standards expectations and get more specific as to what instructional outcomes should be accomplished in particular disciplines by particular grade levels.

Let's see how a large school district takes a broad-based aim begun at the national level and "operationalizes" it at the district level to make it achievable by students. Look at the first two statements of the English language arts standards, compiled by the joint effort of the International Reading Association and the National Council of Teachers of English. It would be difficult to find an educator, parent, or community member/taxpayer who did not agree on the importance of achieving such aims through the critical process of reading. The State of New York, in the second standard, called Listening and Reading, of its *English Language Arts Resource Guide,* established similar goals for its elementary and intermediate students. Elementary students will accomplish the following two goals of the six listed:

- Read a variety of literature of different genres: picture books; poems; articles and stories from children's magazines; fables, myths and legends; songs, plays, and media productions; and works of fiction and nonfiction intended for young readers.
- Recognize some features that distinguish the genres and use those features to aid comprehension.

## Table 4.2 Professional Organizations and Their National Standards

| A: English Language Arts | B: Science | C: Mathematics | D: Social Studies |
|---|---|---|---|
| Students should: | 1. Unifying concepts and processes in science: | 1. Numbers and operations: | 1. Culture and cultural diversity: |
| 1. read a wide range of texts (print and nonprint) to build an understanding of themselves and other cultures, acquire information, help society, and for their personal enjoyment. | a) Systems, order, and organization<br>b) Evidence, models, and explanation<br>c) Change, constancy, measurement<br>d) Evolution and equilibrium<br>e) Form and function | a) Understand numbers, ways of representing numbers, relationships between numbers, and number systems<br>b) Understand meaning of operations and how they relate to one another<br>c) Compute fluently and make estimates | Learners should recognize that all humans create, learn, apply, modify, and adapt to their culture. Learners should recognize that culture influences the way we live, interact, and share ideas. Learners should understand that cultural diversity is a fact of life all over the world. |
| 2. read a wide variety of literature of different genres and periods of time to better understand human experiences. | 2. Science as inquiry:<br>a) Understanding scientific concepts and the nature of science<br>b) Appreciating "how we know" what we know<br>c) Attaining independent inquiry skills<br>d) Knowing when to use what skill | 2. Algebra:<br>a) Understand patterns, relations, and functions and analyze change<br>b) Represent and analyze mathematical situations and structures using symbols<br>c) Use math models to represent and understand algebraic relationships | 2. Time, continuity, and change:<br>Learners should understand their roots and locate themselves in time. They should be able to read and reconstruct the past so as to develop historical perspectives. |
| 3. use their prior knowledge and experiences with literature to apply strategies to comprehend, interpret, evaluate, and appreciate texts. | 3. Physical science:<br>a) Properties, changes of property, and structure of matter<br>b) Position, motion and forces of objects<br>c) Light, heat, electricity, magnetism, chemical reactions, and structure of atoms<br>d) Conservation and transfer of energy | 3. Geometry:<br>a) Analyze characteristics and properties of shapes and their relationships<br>b) Specify location and spatial relationships, use spatial reasoning<br>c) Apply transformations and symmetry to mathematical situations<br>d) Use visualization to solve problems | 3. People, places, and environments:<br>Learners should be able to develop spatial and geographic perspectives of the world. Learners should be able to read and interpret maps. Learners should be able to make decisions about relationships between humans and the environment. |
| 4. adjust their written, spoken, and visual language to communicate effectively in different situations. | 4. Life science:<br>a) Characteristics, structures, function, behavior, life cycles, and interdependence of living things<br>b) Populations, ecosystems, and environments<br>c) Diversity, adaptations, matter, energy, and organization of living things<br>d) Reproduction, heredity, and evolution | 4. Measurement:<br>a) Understand measurable attribute of objects and the units and systems of measure<br>b) Apply appropriate techniques, tools, and formulas to determine measurements | 4. Individual development and identity:<br>Learners should recognize that all humans think, learn, act, and develop cognitively, physically, emotionally, personally, and mentally. Learners should understand that all people have multiple concepts and identities as to who they are and should know factors that contribute to who they are. |

(continued)

**Table 4.2** Continued

| A: English Language Arts | B: Science | C: Mathematics | D: Social Studies |
|---|---|---|---|
| 5. recognize the audience for their writing and use the writing process to communicate effectively with them. | 5. **Earth and space science:**<br>a) Properties of Earth materials and the Earth's history<br>b) Structure and changes in the Earth system<br>c) Origin and evolution of the Earth and universe.<br>d) Geochemical cycles and energy in the Earth system<br>e) Objects in the sky and the Earth in the solar system | 5. **Data analysis and probability:**<br>a) Formulate questions that can be addressed by collecting data<br>b) Select and use appropriate statistical methods to analyze data<br>c) Develop and evaluate inferences of data<br>d) Understand and apply basic probability | 5. **Individuals, groups, and institutions:** Learners should recognize the roles of institutions in their lives including schools, churches, families, government agencies, and courts. Learners should recognize the effects of these institutions on their daily lives. |
| 6. apply their knowledge of language, media techniques, figurative language, and genre to create and discuss texts. | 6. **Science and technology:**<br>a) Understanding of science and technology<br>b) Distinguishing between man-made and natural objects<br>c) Abilities of technological design | 6. **Problem solving:**<br>a) Build new knowledge through problem solving and monitor and reflect on it<br>b) Solve problems by applying and adapting strategies | 6. **Power, authority, and governance:** Learners should understand the historical development of power, authority, and governance in our nation and other parts of the world. Using this, students should be able to examine how groups and nations resolve conflicts. |
| 7. conduct research by generating questions, posing problems, gathering and evaluating data, and communicating their ideas effectively to their targeted audience. | 7. **Science in personal and social perspective:**<br>a) Personal and community health<br>b) Natural resources and population characteristics, changes, and growth<br>c) Environment qualities and changes, natural hazards, human-induced hazards<br>d) Local, national, global science, and technology challenges | 7. **Reasoning and proof:**<br>a) Recognize reasoning and proof as fundamental to math<br>b) Make and investigate math conjectures<br>c) Develop and evaluate math arguments and proofs<br>d) Select and use various reasonings and methods of proof | 7. **Production, distribution, and consumption:** Learners should understand that resources are limited and from those limited resources how goods are to be produced and distributed, the problems that arise from unequal distribution of resources, and decisions that need to be made as a result of those problems. |
| 8. use a variety of sources to gather information and share that knowledge effectively. | 8. **History and nature of science:**<br>a) Science as a human endeavor<br>b) Nature of science and scientific knowledge<br>c) History of science and historical perspectives | 8. **Communication:**<br>a) Organize and consolidate thinking<br>b) Communicate math thinking clearly<br>c) Analyze and evaluate strategies of others<br>d) Use mathematical language | 8. **Science, technology, and society:** Learners should understand what technology is and the effects that science and technology have on us today and have had in the past. |

*(continued)*

9. develop an understanding and respect for diversity in language use and dialects across different cultures, regions, ethnic groups, and social roles.

10. use their first language to better their English competency (if ELL students).

11. be knowledgeable, reflective, creative, and critical members of literacy communities.

12. use spoken, written, and visual language for their own purposes in their daily lives.

9. **Connections:**
   a) Recognize and use connections with math ideas
   b) Understand how math ideas interconnect
   c) Recognize and apply math in contexts outside of math

10. **Representation:**
    a) Create and use representations to communicate
    b) Select, apply, and translate math representations to solve problems
    c) Use representations to model and interpret math phenomena

9. **Global connections:**
   Learners should understand the interconnection of our diverse world, analyze tensions between national and global interests, and propose possible solutions to global problems.

10. **Civic ideals and practices:**
    Learners should be able to see discrepancies between current civic ideals and practices and those that our democratic nation is based on and close the gap between the two.

*Sources:*

A. National Council of Teachers of English and International Reading Association, "The English language arts standards," in *Standards for the English Language Arts* (Urbana, IL, and Newark, DE: Authors, 1996);

B. National Academy of Sciences, "Science Content Standards," in *National Science Education Standards* (Landover, MD: Author, 1995);

C. National Council of Teachers of Mathematics, "Standards for School Mathematics," in *Principles and Standards for School Mathematics* (Reston, VA: Author, 2000);

D. Task Force on Social Studies Teacher Education Standards, *National Standards for Social Studies Teachers*, vol. 1 (Washington, DC: National Council of Social Studies Publications, 2000).

Intermediate grade students will accomplish similar goals according to two of the six desired outcomes of the state:

- Read and view texts and performances from a wide range of authors, subjects, and genres.
- Understand and identify the distinguishing features of the major genres and use them to aid their interpretation and discussion of literature (New York State Education Department, 1997).

Next, New York City, with thirty-two local school districts, published its own set of standards for the English language arts. The first two of four parts of the reading standard for elementary and middle school students require the following:

- The student reads at least twenty-five books or book equivalents each year. The quality and complexity of the materials to be read are illustrated in a sample reading list. The materials should include traditional and contemporary literature (both fiction and nonfiction) as well as magazines, newspapers, textbooks, and on-line materials. Such reading should represent a diverse collection of material from at least three different literary forms and from at least five different writers.
- The student reads and comprehends at least four books (or book equivalents) about one issue or subject, or four books by a single writer, or four books in one genre, and produces evidence of reading that:
  - makes and supports warranted and responsible assertions about the texts;
  - supports assertions with elaborated and convincing evidence;
  - draws the texts together to compare and contrast themes, characters, and ideas;
  - makes perceptive and well-developed connections;
  - evaluates writing strategies and elements of the author's craft (Board of Education of the City of New York, 1997).

We hope you can see what transpired as broad aims and goals for student expectations in reading became translated at district and school levels to tasks that could be observed and measured in the classroom. A system of assessing reading achievement can be established by K–8 classroom teachers to measure these targeted objectives established by the city at the central district level. In fact, the school district provides examples of activities that would demonstrate if students achieved the performance objectives of the two standards indicated above (see Box 4.1).

Thus, the standards operate as a sort of guide or road map to achieving common purposes at learning intervals for many kinds of participants. In general, then, the state content standards provide a guide of what content is to be covered at what grade level. Such a guide provides assurances to teachers, parents, and the general public that all students at a given grade level learn the same informative content and

 **BOX 4.1** Literacy Performance Indicators to Complement English Language Arts Standards

To show that a number of literary or informational books were read, students could maintain an annotated list of works read, generate a reading log or journal, or participate in formal or informal book talks. To show that they comprehended some books in depth related to one theme, author, or genre, elementary students could produce a literary response paper, produce an informative report, participate in a book talk, or create an annotated book list, while middle grade students could add the construction of a book review and the production of a research report.

that some students are not denied such learning exposure. Second, the guide discourages teachers from teaching out of context—meaning at an inappropriate time or for an inappropriate grade level—a topical unit that they personally enjoy teaching.

The second type of standard, the performance standard, reveals what students are able to do or accomplish at a particular grade level. When a particular performance is targeted by a state or district for accomplishment at a designated grade level, say for instance at fourth, eighth, or high school levels, this performance is often known as a "benchmark" performance standard. That is, if the student reaches that discipline benchmark reasonably well, that student is well on the way to being promoted or meeting graduation requirements. Such performance standards provide the basis of long-term goals and expectations for students in a given educational system and also provide short-term goals or achievable targets for individual schools and students (Hill & Crevola, 1999). These benchmarks can be likened to "valued performances." A **valued performance** would not focus on meeting each and every individual standard but on "rich" performances, or in-depth learning that occurs over time (Wolf & White, 2000). For example, performances that demonstrate long-term significance would be the writing of a research paper or play, the conducting of a science experiment, or the painting of a mural.

To summarize, Figure 4.1 shows graphically how standards subsume the concepts of aims, goals, and objectives through its two major components of content standards and performance standards. As we noted, content standards refer to the aims and goals the states and school districts want their students to learn in the major disciplines, whereas performance standards refer to those accomplishments they wish students to achieve at designated grade levels. **Benchmarks** are targeted performances established by a state or district to determine if students have achieved competency in performing particular content tasks, such as writing a coherent paper or presenting an oral report.

## Criticisms of Standards

While the standards movement has a lot going for it, namely the compelling influence of state education departments, there are those who raise voices of concern and caution. We can identify five major criticisms of the standards-based movement.

First, the standards structure places more control at the top and takes away from the long-standing practice of community participation and community control of schools by elected school boards. Potential conflict is established in that standards imposed at a state level may not coordinate with the way schools are run at the school district level. Educators at the school level are also caught between explicit standards and the tests that measure them and thereby have to "align" classroom practices with the demands of both (Hoffman, Assaf, & Paris, 2001). Problems may surface between the governor and mayors of large cities and between state educational leaders and local administrators.

Thus, for standards to work effectively, they have to be integrated with practices at the local level (Lieberman & Miller, 2000). Too often, policymakers and educators have responded to change and reform strategies with flip-flop, either/or thinking. What needs to occur is for policies and programs to become merged so that centralization

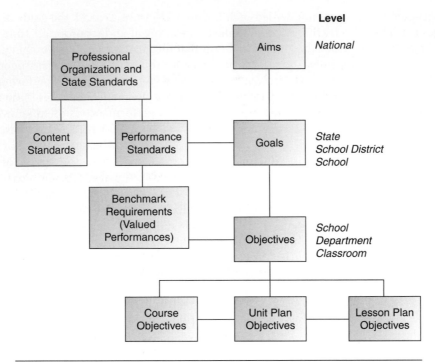

*Figure 4.1* Relationship between Standards and Educational Aims, Goals, and Objectives and the Appropriate Level of Implementation

and control from the top in the form of broad-based standards can be supported by the bottom-up best practices of schools at the local level. What also needs to be avoided, according to two authors, is the schizophrenic relationship imposed on teachers with the product-oriented standards approach on the one hand and process-centered, social, and constructivist approaches on the other (Finders & Hynds, 2003).

A second problem with standards reform is that many states are imposing standards for political rather than educational reasons, with the standards criteria demanded by politicians but not supported by their deeds (Gratz, 2000). Because of lack of follow-through with procedures and staff development practices, many schools may be doomed to failure, and blame will be placed on schools and teachers. This concern is also voiced by Sandra Feldman, president of the American Federation of Teachers. She notes that too many political leaders and school officials have reneged on their promises to provide necessary teacher training, new curricula, and new texts aligned with the standards (Feldman, 2000).

A third criticism is connected to the core disciplines themselves and what focused study of them engenders. Because the standards are formulated on the knowledge of the disciplines, knowledge keeps students rooted in the past and in the status quo (Brady, 2000). The issue boils down to "What's worth knowing?" or "What should students be taught?" One educator feels that the perspectives of the content-area specialists are too narrow and that they argue over details within their separate disciplines rather than investigating what new knowledge should belong in the curriculum and how to integrate knowledge across disciplines (or subjects). He feels that the compelling force of the standards movement is the simplistic and unexamined assumption that what the next crop of students needs to know is what current and former students have been required to learn. This focused or narrow approach maintained by the elders of the various disciplines results in making U.S. subject matter "comfortable" as it replicates itself (Brady, 2000).

Another criticism associated with tougher standards for all is that those students we wish to help and safeguard in the system are the very ones who are bound to suffer and fail standardized tests. The standards often don't allow for individual differences among children and youth (McCabe, 2003). The narrowness and rigidity of the language and translation from standards to disciplines may bruise some children (Sewell, 2000). Because most standards begin with wording such as "All students will be capable of . . . ," the focus is incompatible with personalized learning, with the developmental aspects of learning for children at different age levels, and with those students who operate at the margin of school success (O'Neill & Tell, 1999). The concept of individualized learning emphasizes personal talents in inquiry, deliberation, and intellectual curiosity so that one could frame and follow one's own educational standards. But the standards schools wind up with are usually ones that can be measured easily— at the expense of the more difficult to measure areas of aesthetics, beauty, and art (Eisner, 1992).

This pressure to conform to the narrowness and the "bar levels" of the performance standards has created stress for schools, families, and those students who have difficulty attaining the levels of benchmark achievements. This often leads to negative and/or dysfunctional consequences. Although many schools are creating policies and safeguards to help all students, the policy of retaining low-performing students or requiring that they attend summer school may increase the number of school dropouts, resulting in the opposite outcomes of the stated goal to help the achievement of "failing" students (Seligman, 2000). Instead of asking schools to be excellent in meaningful instruction, these policies will result in schools denying diplomas to those children who can't or won't commit to memory facts that very few adults think are important (O'Neill & Tell, 1999).

Finally, there is concern about the number of standards and the issue of quality. Because of bloated and poorly written standards, teachers will have difficulty teaching and assessing students (Schmoker & Marzano, 1999). In some states, teachers have resisted the implementation of particular standards, more due to the limited view of education that the standards champion than to the way the standards clash with their teaching practices (Edmonson, 2001). To attain a clearer focus and clarity in using standards as instructional objectives, Mike Schmoker and Robert Marzano suggest that teachers within schools develop teams based on grade levels or subjects to align state and district-driven standards with proven methods and practices that have served veteran teachers well over the years. Such successful teacher collaborations are essential and must be encouraged by school principals, who are in the position to set the professional climate and ethos of the school.

# ■ OBJECTIVES

**Objectives** are statements of what should take place at the classroom level. They specify content and sometimes the proficiency level to be attained. Objectives often state specific skills, tasks, content, and attitudes to be taught and learned, and give teachers and students a standard by which to judge whether students have achieved the objectives.

Stated some forty years ago, the words of Hilda Taba remain true today: "The chief function of . . . objectives is to guide the making of . . . decisions on what to cover, what to emphasize, what content to select, and what learning experiences to stress." Because the possibilities of content, learning, and teaching are endless, teachers face the problem of selection: What content is most important? What learning activities are most appropriate? What evaluation plan is most effective? Objectives supply criteria for these decisions, according to Taba. No matter what its nature, the statement of objectives in terms of desired outcomes "sets the scope and limits for what is to be taught and learned" (Taba, 1962, p. 197).

Instructional objectives help the teacher focus on what students should know at the end of a lesson, unit, or course and also help students know what is expected of them. They help the teacher plan and organize instruction by identifying what is to be taught and when it is to be taught. Thus, instructional objectives are often stated in observable and measurable terms (outcomes, proficiencies, or competencies). Their specificity enables the teacher to determine whether what was intended was achieved and to what extent.

## Levels of Objectives

Objectives are formulated on two levels with increasing specificity: course and classroom. Objectives at the classroom level can be further divided into unit plan and lesson objectives. Both are heavily influenced by the impact of the standards. Course objectives are influenced by the standards because they represent the content of the particular disciplines or school subjects. Because classroom objectives are the planning vehicles of teachers as they formulate weekly and daily plans of instruction, teachers need to be mindful of the standards to ascertain the specific content of instruction (Posner & Rudnitsky, 2000).

**Course objectives,** derived originally from school goals, are now mainly influenced by standards. These objectives are formulated at subject (discipline) or departmental level, as well as grade level. They categorize and organize content and sometimes concepts, problems, or behaviors, but they do not specify the exact content to be examined or exact instructional methods and materials to be used. Course objectives are stated in the form of topics, concepts, or general behaviors. Examples of objectives stated as general behaviors (which are not easy to measure or observe) might be phrased, "To develop critical thinking in . . . ," "To increase understanding of . . . ," and "To have experience for . . . "

Course objectives help the teacher organize the content in terms of **scope** (topics, concepts, and behaviors to be covered), **continuity** (recurring and continuing opportunity to learn important content and practice certain skills and tasks), **sequence** (cumulative development or successive treatment of topics, concepts, or behaviors that build on preceding ones), and **integration** (relationships of content in one course to content in another course) (Doll, 1995; Ornstein & Hunkins, 2000).

**Classroom objectives** are usually formulated by the teacher. Classroom objectives divide course objectives into several units. Unit plan objectives usually encompass one to three weeks of instruction, organized in a sequence and corresponding to expectations for the entire class, not for particular individuals or groups. Unit plan objectives are then further divided to create lesson plan objectives, organized ideally around one day of instruction on a particular subject (see Tips for Teachers 4.1).

*Unit Plan Objectives.* **Unit plan objectives** are usually categorized into topics or concepts. For instance, a science unit, written as the concept Science and Method, might be broken down into the following unit plan objectives: "To organize inductive, deductive,

---

*Tips for Teachers* **4.1**

## Stating Classroom Objectives

Theoretically sound and practical recommendations concerning the content and form of objectives are given below. These recommendations should help in the formulation of your own objectives at the unit plan and lesson plan level.

### Content

1. Objectives should be appropriate in terms of difficulty and prior learning experience of students.
2. Objectives should be real in the sense that they describe behaviors the teacher actually intends to act on in the classroom situation.
3. A useful objective will describe both the content and the mental process or behavior required for an appropriate response.
4. The content of the objectives should be responsive to the needs of the individual and society.
5. A variety of behaviors should be stated, since most courses attempt to develop skills other than recall (or simple motor or affective skills).

### Form

1. Objectives should be stated in the form of expected student changes.
2. Objectives should be stated in behavioral or performance terms.
3. Objectives should be stated singly.
4. Objectives should be parsimonious and trimmed of excessive verbiage.
5. Objectives should be grouped logically, so they make sense in determining units of instruction and evaluation.
6. The conditions under which the expected student behavior will be observed should be specified.
7. If possible, the objective should contain criteria for acceptable performance. Criteria might involve time limits or a minimum number or correct responses.

---

*Source:* Adapted from Allan C. Ornstein and Francis P. Hunkins, *Curriculum: Foundations, Principles and Issues,* 4th ed. (Boston: Allyn and Bacon, 2004); David A. Payne, *Measuring and Evaluating Educational Outcomes* (Columbus, OH: Merrill, 1992).

and intuitive methods in answering questions about the (a) biological world, (b) chemical world, and (c) physical world"; "To organize scientific information according to (a) logic, (b) explanations, (c) causal relations, (d) hypotheses, and (e) projections"; "To acquire the methods of (a) inquiry, (b) experimentation, and (c) problem solving"; and "To show interest in scientific hobbies or projects."

Unit plan objectives are sometimes called *general instructional objectives.* They should be specific enough to provide direction for instruction but not so specific that they restrict the teacher's selection of instructional methods, materials, and activities. Almost any appropriate instructional technique—lectures, explanations, discussions, demonstrations, laboratory work, textbook assignments, additional readings—can be used to achieve the unit plan objectives.

*Lesson Plan Objectives.* **Lesson plan objectives,** sometimes called *specific instructional objectives,* further define the unit objectives by providing clear direction for teaching and testing. Instructional objectives at lesson plan level state (1) *expected behaviors,* in terms of specific skills, tasks, or attitudes, and (2) *content.* They may also state (3) *outcomes,* often referred to as *performance standards,* in terms of level of achievement, proficiency, or competency, and (4) *conditions* of mastery. There is currently debate on how detailed these objectives should be and whether too much specificity leads to concern with the trivial.

Lesson plan objectives are more specific than unit plan objectives. Whereas lesson plan objectives may include outcomes and conditions for a specific instructional sequence, unit plan objectives do not. Lesson plan objectives usually include specific methods, materials, or activities; unit plan objectives may or may not, and if they do, they are more general. See Tips for Teachers 4.1 for suggestions on formulating your own classroom objectives at the unit and lesson plan level.

## The Tyler Rationale

Ralph Tyler maintained in his classic text on curriculum and instruction, originally written as a manual for his graduate students at the University of Chicago, that educators need to identify goals by gathering data from three sources: learners, society, and subject specialists. Educators then filter their identified goals through two screens: philosophy and psychology. What results from the screening are more specific and agreed-on objectives, or what he calls **instructional objectives** (Tyler, 1949) (see Figure 4.2).

Even though Tyler uses the term *instructional objectives,* he is not advocating narrow behavioral objectives. For Tyler, objectives cannot be deduced from tiny bits of data or only from objective data. The formulation of objectives involves the intelligence, insight, values, and attitudes of people involved in making decisions. Wise choices cannot be made without the most complete data available, but judgments must still prevail. We now turn to Tyler's three sources from which to select goals and two screens for refining goals into objectives.

1. **Source:** *Studies of the learners.* The responsibility of the school is to help students meet their needs and develop to their fullest potential. Studies that focus on educational needs of students, that distinguish between what the schools do and what other social institutions do, that distinguish between what is done and what should

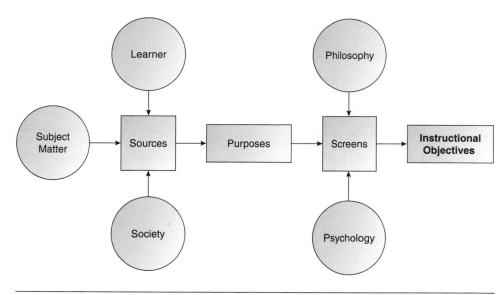

*Figure 4.2* Tyler's Method for Formulating Objectives

*Source:* Adapted from Ralph Tyler, *Basic Principles of Curriculum and Instruction* (Chicago: University of Chicago Press, 1949).

be done, and that identify or differentiate gaps between students of the particular school (or school district) and students elsewhere provide a basis for the selection of goals for the school program. It is possible to identify needs that are common to most students on a national, state, and local basis, as well as other needs that are common to all students in a school or to a certain group of students within a school or school district.

2. *Source: **Studies of contemporary life outside of school.*** Educators must be aware of the tremendous impact of the increasingly rapid rate of change, the explosion of knowledge, and the increasing complexity of technology in our lives today and tomorrow. The trouble is that preparation for the future involves skills and knowledge that we may not fully understand today. As we analyze contemporary life, we need to study life at the community level in terms of needs, resources, and trends, as well as larger societal issues that extend to state, national, and international levels. For example, in preparing students for the world of work, it is necessary to look at local conditions, but some students will move to other states or regions. Further, we live in a "global village," one that is strongly interconnected: State, national, and international conditions eventually affect conditions at the community level.

3. *Source: **Suggestions from subject specialists.*** Every subject area has its professional associations that list goals and important knowledge in its field. What the subject specialists propose, however, is often too technical, too specialized, or inappropriate for goal setting that is concerned with all students. The inadequacy of many of these lists for schools grows out of their misplaced emphasis. What schools need to

ask is not what a specialist in a particular field needs to learn, but what the subject can contribute to the general education of young people who are not going to be specialists in the field.

**4. Screen:** *The use of philosophy.* Once goals have been identified from studies of the learner, society, and subject areas, the educator must review and refine them in light of philosophy and psychology, or as Tyler says, filter them through two screens. The first screen is *philosophy.* As a school tries to outline its educational program, "the educational and social philosophy of the school can serve as the first screen" (Tyler, 1949, p. 34). We should be aware of the values and way of life we are trying to preserve and what aspect of society we wish to improve. Goals should be consistent with the democratic values and ideals of our society, in all aspects of living. In this country, we are educated to live in a democracy, and this overriding philosophy must be reflected in our school goals.

**5.** *Screen: The use of psychology.* Goals must be in conformity with the psychology of learning, that is, the theories, concepts, and specific findings we accept. "A psychology of learning includes a unified formulation of the processes involved, such as how learning takes place, under what conditions, and what mechanisms and variables operate" (Tyler, 1949, p. 41). In formulating goals, teachers need to consider how appropriate the goals are in terms of what is known about learning—whether they can be achieved, how they can be achieved, and what the cost and time will be. Goals that conflict with an acceptable psychological viewpoint about learning should be rejected. Of course, there is more than one psychological viewpoint, and many theories, concepts, and even data are contradictory. However, even opposing theorists of learning can agree on many of the same goals.

Modern-day educators still refer to Tyler as a pioneer in the field of curriculum and instruction. He was one of the first to suggest that educational activities should be evaluated beforehand to assess the values contained in them for learners (Goodlad, 1995). He noted that it was important to identify specific learning outcomes from both teaching and learning perspectives. This focus on establishing and communicating clear objectives not only influenced classroom educational practices but also created an understanding that different content might involve different styles of learning and, therefore, different types of instruction (Marzano, 2000). Some fifty years ago, Tyler formulated a logic of "backward" curriculum design as a way to achieve purposeful educational standards (Wiggins & McTighe, 1998). In backward design, an educator first considers the desired results to be achieved or evaluated (these being the end product, or goals or standards) and second, formulates the curriculum based on how students perform as measured against the goals or standards. Teaching becomes modified to help students perform efficiently and effectively.

## Taxonomy of Educational Objectives

Another way of formulating instructional objectives is to categorize the desired behaviors and outcomes into a system analogous to classification of books in a library, chemical elements in a periodic table, or divisions of the animal kingdom. Through this system, known as a **taxonomy of educational objectives,** standards for classifying objectives have been established, and educators are able to be more precise in their language. The taxonomy is rooted in Tyler's ideas that all words in a scientific system should be defined in terms of observable events and that educational objectives should be defined operationally in terms of performances or outcomes. This method of formulating objectives can be used for writing objectives at the program and course level. By adding specific content, the objectives can be used at the classroom level, including the lesson plan level.

The educational taxonomy calls for the classification of learning into three **domains: cognitive, affective,** and **psychomotor.** The *Taxonomy of Educational Objectives, Handbook I: Cognitive Domain* was developed by a committee of thirty-six researchers from various universities headed by Benjamin Bloom (Bloom, Mesia, & Krathwohl, 1956). The cognitive domain includes objectives that are related to recall or recognition of knowledge and the development of higher intellectual skills and abilities. The *Taxonomy of Educational Objectives, Handbook II: Affective Domain* by David Krathwohl and associates is concerned with aims and objectives related to interests, attitudes, and feelings (Krathwohl, Bloom, & Masia, 1964). The description of the psychomotor domain, dealing with manipulative and motor skills, was never completed by the original group of researchers. A classification of psychomotor objectives by Anita Harrow closely resembles the intent of the original group (1972). The fact that it was published by the same company that published the original two taxonomies adds to the validity of this version of the psychomotor domain. Following is a brief listing of the types of objectives of the three domains of learning.

### COGNITIVE DOMAIN

1. *Knowledge.* This level includes objectives related to (a) knowledge of specifics, such as terminology and facts; (b) knowledge of ways and means of dealing with specifics, such as conventions, trends, and sequences; classifications and categories; criteria; and methodologies; and (c) knowledge of universals and abstractions, such as principles, generations, theories, and structures. *Example:* To identify the capital of France.

2. *Comprehension.* Objectives at this level relate to (a) translation, (b) interpretation, and (c) extrapolation of materials. *Example:* To interpret a table showing the population density of the world.

3. *Application.* Objectives at this level relate to the use of abstractions in particular situations. *Example:* To predict the probable effect of a change in temperature on a chemical.

4. *Analysis.* Objectives relate to breaking a whole into parts and distinguishing (a) elements, (b) relationships, and (c) organizational principles. *Example:* To deduce facts from a hypothesis.

5. *Synthesis.* Objectives relate to putting parts together in a new form such as (a) a unique communication, (b) a plan of operation, and (c) a set of abstract relations. *Example:* To produce an original piece of art.

6. *Evaluation.* This is the highest level of complexity and includes objectives related to judging in terms of (a) internal evidence or logical consistency and (b) external evidence or consistency with facts developed elsewhere. *Example:* To recognize fallacies in an argument.

### AFFECTIVE DOMAIN

1. *Receiving.* These objectives are indicative of the learner's sensitivity to the existence of stimuli and include (a) awareness, (b) willingness to receive, and (c) selective attention. *Example:* To identify musical instruments by their sound.
2. *Responding.* This includes active attention to stimuli, such as (a) acquiescence, (b) willing responses, and (c) feelings of satisfaction. *Example:* To contribute to group discussions by asking questions.
3. *Valuing.* This includes objectives regarding beliefs and evaluations in the form of (a) acceptance, (b) preference, and (c) commitment. *Example:* To argue over an issue involving health care.
4. *Organizing.* This level involves (a) conceptualizing values and (b) organizing a value system. *Example:* To organize a meeting concerning a neighborhood's housing integration plan.
5. *Characterizing.* This is the level of greatest complexity and includes behavior related to (a) a generalized set of values and (b) a characterization or philosophy of life. *Example:* To demonstrate in front of a government building in behalf of a cause or idea.

### PSYCHOMOTOR DOMAIN

1. *Reflex movements.* Objectives relate to (a) segmental reflexes (involving one spinal segment) and (b) intersegmental reflexes (involving more than one spinal segment). *Example:* To contract a muscle.
2. *Fundamental movements.* Objectives relate to (a) walking, (b) running, (c) jumping, (d) pushing, (e) pulling, and (f) manipulating. *Example:* To run a 100-yard dash.
3. *Perceptual abilities.* Objectives relate to (a) kinesthetic, (b) visual, (c) auditory, (d) tactile, and (e) coordination abilities. *Example:* To distinguish distant and close sounds.
4. *Physical abilities.* Objectives relate to (a) endurance, (b) strength, (c) flexibility, (d) agility, (e) reaction-response time, and (f) dexterity. *Example:* To do five sit-ups.
5. *Skilled movements.* Objectives relate to (a) games, (b) sports, (c) dances, and (d) the arts. *Example:* To dance the basic steps of the waltz.
6. *Nondiscursive communication.* Objectives relate to expressive movement through (a) posture, (b) gestures, (c) facial expressions, and (d) creative movements. *Example:* To act a part in a play.

## Guidelines for Applying the Taxonomy of Educational Objectives

The categories of the three taxonomies describe levels of complexity from simple to more advanced. Each level is built on and assumes acquisition of skills at the previous level. When asking questions and formulating instructional objectives according to the cognitive taxonomy, the teacher should keep in mind that the classifications represent a hierarchy. Before students can deal with analysis, they should be able to function at the three previous levels—that is, knowledge, comprehension, and application. The same kinds of questions should be asked when writing objectives in the affective and psychomotor domains. The teacher needs to look at each level within the domain and ask what students are expected to achieve.

Thus, central to the philosophy and framework of Bloom's taxonomy was its cumulative nature. For example, each higher level builds on and incorporates the lower (Furst, 1994). The most significant role of the cognitive domain taxonomy has been to highlight the importance of objectives involving skills and abilities as compared to knowledge gained by memorization. Furthermore, Bloom's taxonomy indicated the possible necessity of learning certain objectives before others while at the same time providing a wider scope of objectives than might otherwise have been considered (Krathwohl, 1994). In the field of education, the cognitive domain taxonomy is undoubtedly the all-time best-seller. Though not without problems and flaws, the taxonomy's greatest legacy is that it offers easily understandable guidelines for the expansion of curriculum and evaluation (Postlethwaite, 1994).

Through the years, teacher educators have used the philosophical construct of the taxonomy to help teachers in four ways: (1) to specify lesson objectives, (2) to prepare tests, (3) to ask questions at different taxonomic levels, and (4) to increase the cognitive levels of activities and tasks teachers ask of students (Anderson, 1994). The notion here is that teachers can be trained and encouraged to follow the cumulative levels of the framework as they ask higher-level questions and as they design learning tasks that require more complex thinking of their students. Some investigators have found that the classifying of questions according to the levels of the taxonomy is not in concordance with its original purpose of classifying the outcomes of instruction (Furst, 1994). Yet others have found it useful as a model for the number of ways in which language can be used to develop curriculum outcomes and also to suggest to curriculum developers types of objectives they might not have previously considered (Sosniak, 1994). The taxonomy may be especially beneficial to new teachers who are examining curriculum goals extending from lower-level to higher-order concerns while they focus their work and set their objective priorities (Zumwalt, 1989) (see Box 4.2).

Lorin Anderson, at first a student of and assistant to Benjamin Bloom and later a professional colleague and friend, noted that although substantial evidence shows that teachers can be trained to formulate questions to cue higher-level thinking in their classrooms, equally compelling evidence shows that teachers continue to use and rely on lower-order questions in the classroom. Elementary students in particular, he noted, were not being taught to raise critical questions in classroom discussions or to think, reason, and defend their points of view (Anderson, 1996).

Some teachers may believe that their students, especially low-achieving students, are not capable of mastering objectives at the higher levels of cognition. Others may feel that they have to cover too much course content in limited time periods and that the most practical way to achieve this is to focus on lower-level objectives and content (knowledge) that will be tested. Still others may shy away from the objectives requiring the thinking skills of analysis, synthesis, and evaluation because students often need reasoning time to think through an answer. Lower-level objectives are easier to handle because they usually have one right or wrong answer that can found in the classroom texts. High-level or critical thinking takes time, involving discussion, point/counterpoint arguments, and thinking. The teaching of knowledge is essential. Bloom asserts that "many teachers . . . prize knowledge . . . because of the simplicity with which it can be taught or learned" (Bloom et al., 1956, p. 34). Tips for Teachers 4.2 indicates some key words that teachers might use to elicit thinking processes at the knowledge level and beyond.

**BOX 4.2** Using Bloom's Taxonomy of Educational Objectives for the Cognitive Domain to Formulate Specific Instructional Objectives

In using the taxonomy to guide what you want your students to learn at particular cognitive levels, you might review the major classifications of the various domains to make sure you are familiar with the thinking required at each level. You might then ask the following questions when formulating objectives:

1. **Knowledge.** What specific facts do you want the students to learn? What trends and sequences should they know? What classifications, categories, and methods are important for them to learn?
2. **Comprehension.** What types of translation will students need to perform? What types of interpretation? What types of extrapolation?
3. **Application.** What will students be required to perform or do to show they can use the information in practical situations (quite similar to performance standards)?
4. **Analysis.** What kinds of elements should students be able to analyze? What relationships? What organizational principles?
5. **Synthesis.** What kind of communication should students be able to synthesize? What kinds of operation? What kinds of abstraction?
6. **Evaluation.** What kinds of evaluation should students be able to perform? Can they use internal evidence? Can they use external evidence?

*Tips for Teachers* **4.2**

## Key Words for the Taxonomy of Educational Objectives: Cognitive Domain

| Taxonomy Classification | Examples of Verb Forms Used to Elicit Level of Thinking |
| --- | --- |
| 1. Knowledge specifics | To define, to distinguish, to acquire, to identify, to recall, to recognize |
| 2. Comprehension | To translate, to transform, to illustrate, to prepare, to read, to represent, to change, to rephrase, to restate, to interpret, to rearrange, to differentiate, to distinguish, to make, to explain, to demonstrate, to estimate, to infer, to conclude, to predict, to determine, to extend, to interpolate |
| 3. Application | To apply, to generalize, to relate, to choose, to develop, to organize, to use, to employ, to transfer, to restructure, to classify |
| 4. Analysis | To distinguish, to detect, to identify, to classify, to discriminate, to recognize, to categorize, to analyze, to contrast, to compare, to deduce |
| 5. Synthesis | To write, to tell, to relate, to produce, to transmit, to originate, to modify, to document, to propose, to plan, to design, to specify, to derive, to develop, to combine, to organize, to synthesize, to classify, to deduce, to develop, to formulate |
| 6. Evaluation | To judge, to argue, to validate, to assess, to decide, to consider, to compare, to contrast, to standardize, to appraise |

*Source:* Adapted from Newton S. Metfessel, William B. Michael, and Donald A. Kirsner, "Instrumentation of Bloom's and Krathwohl's Taxonomies for the Writing of Educational Objectives," *Psychology in the Schools* (July 1969): 227–231.

## General Objectives and Specific Learning Outcomes: The Gronlund Method

Norman Gronlund has developed a flexible way of formulating instructional objectives whereby the teacher moves from a general objective to a series of specific learning outcomes, each related to the general objective. Gronlund's *general objectives* coincide with program- (subject and grade) and course-level objectives, and his *specific learning outcomes* coincide with unit plan and lesson plan objectives. He recommends that teachers start with general objectives because learning is too complex to be described in terms of specific behaviors or specific outcomes and because higher levels of thinking cannot be achieved by one specific behavior or outcome. To illustrate the difference between general objectives and specific learning outcomes, Gronlund has prepared a list of general objectives that can be used for almost any grade, subject, or course:

1. Knows basic terminology
2. Understands concepts and principles
3. Applies principles to new situations
4. Interprets charts and graphs
5. Demonstrates skill in critical thinking
6. Writes a well-organized theme
7. Appreciates artistic aspects of subject matter: poetry, art, literature, dance, etc.
8. Demonstrates scientific attitude
9. Evaluates the adequacy of an experiment (Gronlund, 1994, pp. 47–49; Gronlund & Linn, 1990, pp. 41–42)

Note that the behavior (verb) in each statement is general enough to permit a host of specific learning outcomes. Such outcomes provide useful guides for teachers and students (Gronlund, 1997). There may be six or seven related specific outcomes for each general objective to clarify what students will do to demonstrate achievement of the general objective.

## Guidelines for Applying Gronlund's Objectives

The two examples below illustrate how we move from general objectives to a series of related, intended learning outcomes:

I. Understands the meaning of terms
 1. Defines the terms in own words
 2. Identifies the meaning of a term in context
 3. Differentiates between proper and improper usage of a term
 4. Distinguishes between two similar terms on the basis of meaning
 5. Writes an original sentence using the term
II. Demonstrates skill in critical thinking
 1. Distinguishes between fact and opinion
 2. Distinguishes between relevant and irrelevant information
 3. Identifies fallacious reasoning in written material
 4. Identifies the limitations of given data
 5. Formulates valid conclusions from given data
 6. Identifies the assumptions underlying conclusions (Gronlund, 1994, pp. 47–49; Gronlund & Linn, 1990, pp. 41–42)

The learning outcomes listed above are good examples of content-free objectives that can fit many different grade levels, subjects, and courses. Because Gronlund feels it is important to keep specific learning outcomes content-free, they are not really applicable to the lesson plan level, which should be content oriented.

The teacher can add content to objectives. For example, an objective might be to identify three causes of World War I or to differentiate between a triangle and a rectangle. Gronlund, however, maintains that once a teacher identifies content, there is a risk of writing too many objectives for each general objective or topic. Instead of stating "identifying the causes of World War I" as the objective, as most teachers would do, Gronlund would say the objective is to identify important causes and events. Instead of differentiating between a triangle and a rectangle, the objective, for Gronlund, is to differentiate between shapes. Gronlund's content-free specific outcomes can be used up to the unit plan level that focuses on concepts; only by including content can they be used at the lesson plan level. Table 4.3 highlights Gronlund's steps for setting instructional objectives—both general and specific—and serves as a guide if you wish to adopt this method.

---

### *Table 4.3* Gronlund's Steps for Stating General Objectives and Specific Learning Outcomes

#### Stating General Instructional Objectives

1. State each general objective as an intended learning outcome (i.e., pupils' terminal performance).
2. Begin each general objective with a verb (e.g., *knows, applies, interprets*).
3. State each general objective to include only one general learning outcome (e.g., not "knows and understands").
4. State each general objective at the proper level of generality (e.g., it should encompass a readily definable domain of responses). Eight to twelve general objectives will usually suffice.
5. Keep each general objective sufficiently free of course content so that it can be used with various units of study.
6. State each general objective so that there is minimum overlap with other objectives.

#### Stating Specific Learning Outcomes

1. List beneath each general instructional objective a representative sample of specific learning outcomes that describe the terminal performance pupils are expected to demonstrate.
2. Begin each specific learning outcome with an action verb that specifies observable performance (e.g., *identifies, describes*). Check that each specific learning outcome is relevant to the general objective it describes.
3. Include a sufficient number of specific learning outcomes to describe adequately the performance of pupils who have attained the objective.
4. Keep the specific learning outcomes sufficiently free of course content so that the list can be used with various units of study.
5. Consult reference materials for the specific components of those complex outcomes that are difficult to define (e.g., critical thinking, scientific attitude, creativity).
6. Add a third level of specificity to the list of outcomes, if needed.

*Source:* Adapted from Norman E. Gronlund, *Measurement and Evaluation in Teaching*, 6th ed. (New York: Macmillan, 1989).

## Specific Objectives: The Mager Method

Robert Mager is more precise in his approach to formulating instructional objectives. His objectives have three components:

1. *Behavior,* or performance, which describes what the learner is expected to do. *Example:* To know, to use, to identify.
2. *Condition,* which describes under what circumstances or condition the performance is to occur. *Example:* "Given five sentences with adjectives, . . . "; "Based on the statement . . . "
3. *Proficiency level,* or criterion, which states an acceptable standard, competency, or achievement level. *Example:* 80 percent, 9 out of 10, judged correct by the teacher (Mager, 1997).

Mager is controversial in his approach to writing instructional objectives, and therefore it might be worthwhile to state some of the arguments for and against his approach. Some educators (including Tyler and Gronlund) claim that Mager's method produces an unmanageable number of objectives, leads to trivia, and wastes time. They also contend that the approach leads to teaching that focuses on low levels of cognitive and psychomotor objectives, emphasizes learning of specific bits of information, and does not foster comprehension and whole learning (Haladyna, 1997).

Mager and other educators argue that the approach clarifies what teachers intend, what students are expected to do, and what to test to show evidence of learning (Kibler, Baker, & Miles, 1981; Lyman, 1998). It provides a structured method for arranging sequences of skills, tasks, or content; provides a guide for determining instructional methods and materials; and adds precision for constructing tests. Most teachers prefer a less specific approach, one that corresponds more to the methods of Tyler, Bloom, or Gronlund.

One school district in Florida found that when they were out of compliance with the State Department of Education in providing adequate individualized education plans (IEPs) for special education students, Robert Mager's method gave them a model for writing specific goals and objectives. The school district's special education teachers were not writing short-term objectives that were worded in measurable terms so that learner outcomes could be measured (Jacaruso, 1994).

**BOX 4.3** Planning for Special-Needs Students Receiving Special Education Services

Those students receiving special education services need to have individual education plans (IEPs) to be in compliance with federal law. The IEP needs to show a child's present level of academic performance, long-term or annual goals that can be met to enable the child to progress in the general curriculum, and short-term objectives that will assist the child in reaching the long-term academic goals. Robert Mager's approach provides a way of meeting the specificity required in the spelling out of the short-term objectives.

After training in the writing of measurable behavioral objectives following Mager's method, the district met federal and state compliance guidelines, and special and regular education could communicate more effectively about their shared students. Teachers stated their objectives in measurable terms so that they had clearly defined goals regarding what they wanted their students to do after the instruction was completed. The teachers had to identify by name the behavior they wished their students to attain, identify the condition or setting in which the behavior would happen, and specify what the criteria of acceptable performance would be (as illustrated in the following guidelines) (see Box 4.3).

### Guidelines for Applying Mager's Objectives

Using Mager's approach, a teacher could write hundreds of objectives for each unit, certainly for each course. If we decide on his approach, we would first ask ourselves to identify or describe what the learner will be doing. Next we would identify or describe the conditions under which the behavior is to occur. Finally, we would state the performance criteria or achievement level we expect the learner to meet.

Here are some examples. The behavior, condition, and proficiency level are identified.

1. Given six primary colors, students will be able to identify five. The behavior is to identify, the condition is six primary colors, and the proficiency level is five out of six.
2. From the required list of ten words, students will correctly spell nine of them. The behavior is to spell, the condition is the required list of words, and the proficiency level is 90 percent (9 out of 10).
3. The student will be able to complete a 100-item multiple-choice examination on the topic of pollution, with 80 items answered correctly within sixty minutes. The behavior is to complete an exam, the condition is sixty minutes, and the proficiency level is 80 percent (80 out of 100).

Mager lists eight words or phrases that he considers "fuzzy" and to be avoided in formulating objectives: to know, to understand, to appreciate, to grasp the significance of, to enjoy, to believe, to have faith in, and to internalize. He lists nine words or phrases that are open to fewer interpretations and are more appropriate: to write, to recite, to identify, to sort, to solve, to construct, to build, to compare, and to contrast.

# ■ FORMULATING GOALS, STANDARDS, AND OBJECTIVES

The task of formulating goals and objectives for a school district, school, or course usually falls to district or school committees. These committees are usually composed of district curriculum specialists, administrators, content and grade-level teachers, and parents. Often key committee members have been trained in the scope and sequence of the state's content and performance standards and are mindful of professional association reports, research and articles in the professional literature, and the voices of the community, parents, and students themselves.

Individual classroom teachers are generally responsible for developing unit plans or lesson plans, usually with the goals and objectives of current standards in focus. Teachers need to be particularly mindful of the timing and evaluation criteria of the benchmark performances. Most states require that particular benchmark performance standards be reached by students at designated grade levels. For instance, at grades 3 and

4 in New York State, students have to write a research report on a social studies topic covered in their content standards. The report is evaluated by a scoring rubric that has four levels of achievement—accomplished (4), proficient (3), developing (2), and beginning (1)—and six criteria dimensions—understanding, analysis, idea development, organization, language use, and conventions. The benchmark level of proficiency is generally regarded as proficient (3) or above. Teachers cannot expect students to do the report efficiently without prior content and written literacy work in other content topics. The more facility students have with the procedures of report writing and the more practice they have with feedback from the scoring rubric, the more likely it is they will attain the proficiency level.

The teacher may also wish to consult published lists of goals and objectives and follow through with more intensive study and practice using the models offered in this chapter by Tyler, Bloom and colleagues, Gronlund, or Mager. When using the cognitive taxonomy as a model, teachers might want to consider two options when planning instructional objectives. The first option is based on the discussions presented in Chapter 2 on background knowledge and in Chapter 3 on vocabulary understanding, and on the major roles they play in the comprehension and composing processes. When students have limited vocabularies, lack experiential background knowledge for the topic being presented, and lack the capability to see connections among the content information, the teacher might be wise to order instructional objectives and/or questions beginning at the lower levels and expand them gradually upward to higher cognitive levels. These students may need more experiences in understanding and verifying the cognitive base before they are able to respond to the higher-level cognitive concerns.

The second option might be considered by the teacher when the students have adequate experiential background for the topic and the requisite vocabulary to discuss and think about it. The teacher may then be able to initiate a project that involves the analysis of a problem or focuses on an essential question that gets to the core of the topic under study. An essential question is like an instructional objective but formulated in an inquiry form that also serves as an organizer of many separate activities for students (Jacobs, 1997). For instance, a question such as "How did immigration change the face of America?" would encourage students to study many different periods of history when immigrants came to America and what role they played in changing its state at that time. With this option, the teacher can begin thought processes at higher cognitive levels because students comprehend the content and have the necessary knowledge base.

Following state and school district published lists of standards, teachers can form their own instructional objectives with three considerations in mind. First, consider the state's and school district's benchmark standards (see Figure 4.1). These performances have long-term value and significance for students so that they can reach the aims and goals of education to be competent in professions, careers, and the workforce. Here, the teacher might consider Gronlund's general objectives as valued performances (because they cut across subjects, grade levels, and school locales) and devise ways to move from the general objective to a specific learning outcome that demonstrates mastery of that objective.

A second helpful consideration for teachers is to consult Table 4.2 once again. The teacher will note that while the disciplines of science, mathematics, and social studies are strongly content oriented, the English language arts are process oriented. This means that the student has to use the spoken, written, and visual languages as processing modes to accomplish, understand, apply, or recognize something. Why not take a specific content objective from the three content standards as students read to understand, write to produce, speak to show recognition and insight, and use technology to research and gather a variety of sources on a topic?

For instance, the Nebraska Department of Education asks fourth graders in life science to develop an understanding of the characteristics of living things by describing the differences between plants and animals. In reading, at the same grade level, students are asked to apply the meaning of informational material and provide evidence from texts to support their understandings. Also, for writing, students are supposed to develop plans for writing and write well-organized compositions with a beginning, a middle, and an end (Nebraska Department of Education, 1998). Now, why couldn't all three of these separate listed standards be coordinated to produce one report or project? Students could be asked to take their reading materials on plants and animals and set up a comparison–contrast outline or chart to use as a plan for writing, and then using either conventional writing and art materials or technology, produce a report consisting of a number of paragraphs or screens.

The third consideration is to support those standards that can be adequately assessed. Some educators suggest that teachers focus their initial efforts on those standards that are measured by current state standardized and criterion-referenced testing policies. More is addressed on this topic in Chapter 13.

Control of curriculum is a central issue in how educational aims and objectives will be fulfilled. At the local level, instructional objectives are set by teachers or grade-level teams responsible for the information for which their students will be held accountable. At the other extreme, national or state objectives in the form of standards are formulated by those far removed from the actual implementation of the standards in the classroom. Balancing the two sides is critical (Pearson & Raphael, 1999; Sewell, 2000). On the one hand, educators must agree on those standards that students are accountable for as they move through each grade level. On the other hand, grade-level teachers need to know that particular objectives were met by students entering their classrooms because they are obligated to help students attain their own curriculum content before those students move on to the next grade level.

In conclusion, no matter how carefully you plan your objectives, there are likely to be some unintended outcomes of instruction. These outcomes may be desirable or undesirable, and most are likely to fall into the affective domain of attitudes, feelings, and motivation about learning. Most teachers will be asked to follow their state's or district's published standards as they plan instructional objectives for their students. Teachers will need to take note of the standards for the different content disciplines as they pertain to the teachers' courses or grade levels and the performance tasks students need to accomplish to show that they have acquired the content knowledge skills. However, depending on the district's or school's philosophy and beliefs about the purposes of education, standards objectives may need to be enhanced or tempered by more general or precise instructional objectives.

## ■ SUMMARY ■

1. Aims are broad statements about the intent of education as a whole. Goals are general statements about what schools are expected to accomplish. Objectives specify content and behavior and sometimes a proficiency level to be achieved at some level of instruction. A newer term, *standards,* subsumes many of these concepts by attempting to define the purposes of education and what's expected to be known and accomplished by students.

2. Standards are generally defined in two ways, as content standards and as performance standards. Content standards describe what students should *know* in the various disciplines, whereas performance standards indicate what students should be able *to do* or *accomplish* at particular grade levels. Benchmark performance standards are performances targeted at a particular grade level.

3. Objectives are written at several levels, including grade, subject, course, classroom, unit plan, and lesson plan, and at several degrees of specificity, from broad to precise. As teachers formulate instructional objectives, they will need to make connections to their state or districtwide standards so that there is continuity for students throughout the overall educational system.

4. The most popular approaches to formulating objectives have been based on the work of Tyler, Bloom, Gronlund, and Mager. Tyler identifies purposes and then interprets them in light of philosophical and psychological concerns to arrive at instructional objectives.

5. Bloom's work (the taxonomy of educational objectives) entails three domains of learning: cognitive, affective, and psychomotor. In the field of education, the cognitive domain taxonomy has been hailed as its all-time best-seller.

6. Gronlund distinguishes between general objectives and specific learning outcomes.

7. Mager relies on three major characteristics for writing objectives: behavior, condition, and proficiency level.

## ■ QUESTIONS TO CONSIDER ■

1. In terms of aims and goals, why is the question "What is the purpose of school?" so complex? Also, why is it important for aims and goals to change as society changes?

2. Why is it important for you to be quite cognizant of the content, performance, and benchmark standards for your course or grade level, especially if your school's or district's goal is to improve students' knowledge in content disciplines? Once the benchmark criteria (such as a scoring rubric, checklist, or achievement test) are known, have you apprised your students of the criteria so that they know how they will be judged and evaluated in that performance task?

3. What sources of information does Tyler recommend in formulating his objectives? Which source is most important? Why?

4. Why is Bloom's taxonomy of the cognitive domain still useful as a construct and organizational framework for formulating questions and instructional objectives?

5. How does Gronlund distinguish between general objectives and specific learning outcomes?

6. What are the three components of Mager's objectives?

## ■ THINGS TO DO ■

1. Find a list of school goals in a textbook or curriculum guide and see how they conform to the standards guidelines proposed by the national professional organizations.

2. Arrange the six categories of the cognitive domain into a hierarchy from simple to complex. Give an example of an instructional objective for each category.
3. Arrange the five categories of the affective domain into a hierarchy from simple to complex. Give an example of an instructional objective for each category.
4. Formulate ten unit plan objectives in your area of specialization. Use either Gronlund's or Bloom's method to write these objectives. Give an example of an instructional objective for each category.
5. Look to the performance standards of your state or district so that you can plan instructional objectives to help your students meet the criteria level of competence or mastery for those performance standards.

## ■ RECOMMENDED READINGS ■

Anderson, Lorin, and Lauren A. Sosniak, eds. *Bloom's Taxonomy: A Forty-Year Retrospective.* Chicago: University of Chicago Press, 1994. Looks back on the impact that the *Taxonomy of Educational Objectives: Handbook 1, Cognitive Domain* has had in education.

Gronlund, Norman E. *How to Write and Use Instructional Objectives,* 5th ed. Englewood Cliffs, NJ: Prentice Hall, 1994. Provides a step-by-step procedure for writing and using objectives for instruction and testing.

Kendall, John S., and Robert J. Marzano. *Content Knowledge: A Compendium of Standards and Benchmarks for K–12 Education,* 3rd ed. Alexandria, VA: Association for Supervision and Curriculum Development, 2000. Has comprehensive information on standards-based instruction and benchmarks by grade levels.

Mager, Robert F. *Preparing Instructional Objectives: A Critical Tool in the Development of Effective Instruction,* 3rd ed. Atlanta, GA: Center for Effective Performance, 1997. Describes objectives that specify behavior, condition, and proficiency.

Oliva, Peter F. *Developing the Curriculum,* 5th ed. White Plains, NY: Longman, 2000. Presents a guide for planning and developing the curriculum.

Tucker, Marc S., and Judy B. Codding. *Standards for our Schools: How to Set Them, Measure Them, and Reach Them,* San Francisco: Jossey-Bass, 1998. Shows teachers how to establish and work with standards.

Tyler, Ralph W. *Basic Principles of Curriculum and Instruction.* Chicago: University of Chicago Press, 1949. Is regarded as one of the pioneer texts in the formation of instructional objectives.

## ■ KEY TERMS ■

accountability
affective domain
aims
benchmarks
classroom objectives
cognitive domain
content standards
continuity

course objectives
goals
instructional objectives
integration
lesson plan objectives
objectives
performance standards
psychomotor domain

scope
sequence
standards
taxonomy of educational objectives
unit plan objectives
valued performance

# ■ REFERENCES ■

Adler, M., & Fisher, C. (2001, March). Early reading programs in high-poverty schools: A case study in beating the odds. *The Reading Teacher,* 616–619.

Anderson, L. (1994). Research on teaching and teacher education. In L. W. Anderson & L. A. Sosniak (Eds.), *Bloom's taxonomy: A forty-year retrospective* (pp. 126–145). Chicago: University of Chicago Press.

Anderson, L. (1996, January). If you don't know who wrote it, you won't understand it: Lessons learned from Benjamin S. Bloom. *Peabody Journal of Education,* 77–87.

Asp, E. (2000). Assessment in education: Where have we been? Where are we headed? In R. S. Brandt (Ed.), *Education in a new era, 2000 yearbook* (pp. 123–157). Alexandria, VA: Association for Supervision and Curriculum Development.

Bloom, B. S., Mesia, B. B., & Krathwohl, D. R. (Eds.). (1956). *Taxonomy of educational objectives, handbook I: Cognitive domain.* New York: Longman-McKay.

Board of Education of the City of New York. (1997). *Performance standards, New York City: First edition.* New York: Author.

Boyer, E. L. (1994, January). The basic school: Focusing on the child. *Principal,* 29–32.

Boyer, E. L. (1995). *The basic school: A community for learning.* Menlo Park, CA: Carnegie Foundation for the Advancement of Teaching.

Brady, M. (2000, May). The standards juggernaut. *Phi Delta Kappan,* 649–651.

Commission on the Reorganization of Secondary Education. (1918). *Cardinal principles of secondary education.* Washington, DC: Government Printing Office.

Doherty, K., & Skinner, R. (2003, January 9). State of the states. *Education Week,* 75–101.

Doll, R. C. (1995). *Curriculum improvement: Decision making and process* (9th ed.). Boston: Allyn and Bacon.

Editorial Projects in Education. (1999). *Quality counts: Rewarding results, punishing failure.* Bethesda, MD: Author.

Edmondson, J. (2001, March). Taking a broader look: Reading literacy education. *The Reading Teacher,* 620–629.

Eisner, E. W. (1992, May). The federal reform of schools: Looking for the magic bullet. *Phi Delta Kappan,* 722–723.

Elmore, R. (1999, Winter). Building a new structure for school leadership. *American Educator,* 6–13, 42–44.

Feldman, S. (2000, Fall). Standards are working. *American Educator,* 5–7.

Finders, M., & Hynds, S. (2003). *Literacy lessons: Teaching and learning with middle school students.* Upper Saddle River, NJ: Merrill/Prentice Hall.

Furst, E. (1994). Bloom's taxonomy: Philosophical and educational issues. In L. W. Anderson & L. A. Sosniak (Eds.), *Bloom's taxonomy: A forty-year retrospective* (pp. 28–40). Chicago: University of Chicago Press.

Glatthorn, A., & Tailall, J. (2000). Curriculum for the new millennium. In R. Brandt (Ed.), *Education in a new ERA, ASCD yearbook 2000* (pp. 97–121). Alexandria, VA: Association for Supervision and Curriculum Development.

Goodlad, J. I. (1984). *A place called school.* New York: McGraw-Hill.

Goodlad, J. I. (1995, March). Ralph Tyler: The educator's educator. *Educational Policy,* 75–81.

Gratz, D. B. (2000, May). High standards for whom? *Phi Delta Kappan,* 681–687.

Grissmer, D., Flanagan, A., Kawata, J., & Williamson, S. (2000). *Improving student achievement: What NAEP state test scores tell us.* Santa Monica, CA: Rand.

Gronlund, N. E. (1994). *How to write and use instructional objectives* (5th ed.). Paramus, NJ: Prentice Hall.

Gronlund, N. E. (1997). *Assessment of student achievement* (6th ed.). Boston: Allyn and Bacon.

Gronlund, N., & Linn, R. L. (1990). *Measurement and evaluation in teaching* (6th ed.). New York: Macmillan.

Haladyna, T. M. (1997). *Writing test items to evaluate higher-order thinking.* Boston: Allyn and Bacon.

Harrow, A. J. (1972). *Taxonomy of the psychomotor domain: A guide for developing behavioral objectives.* New York: McKay.

Hill, P., & Crevola, C. (1999). The role of standards in educational reform for the 21st century. In D. D. Marsh (Ed.), *Preparing our schools for the 21st century, 1999 yearbook* (pp. 117–142). Alexandria, VA: Association for Supervision and Curriculum Development.

Hoffman, J., Assaf, L. C., & Paris, S. (2001, February). High-stakes testing in reading: Today in Texas, tomorrow? *The Reading Teacher,* 482–490.

Howe, H., II. (1991, November). America 2000: A bumpy ride on four trains. *Phi Delta Kappan,* 192–203.

Jacaruso, Y. C. *Training special education teachers to write appropriate goals and short term objectives with measurable student outcomes for individualized education plans.* Doctoral dissertation 043, 1994. (ERIC Document Reproduction Service No. ED374597)

Jacobs, H. H. (1997). *Mapping the big picture: Integrating curriculum & assessment K–12.* Alexandria, VA: Association for Supervision and Curriculum Development.

Kibler, R. J., Baker, L. L., & Miles, D. T. (1981). *Behavioral objectives and instruction* (2nd ed.). Boston: Allyn and Bacon.

Krathwohl, D. (1994). Reflections on the taxonomy: It's past, present, and future. In L. W. Anderson & L. A. Sosniak (Eds.), *Bloom's taxonomy: A forty-year retrospective* (pp. 181–202). Chicago: University of Chicago Press.

Krathwohl, D. R., Bloom, B. S., & Masia, B. (Eds.). (1964). *Taxonomy of educational objectives, handbook II: Affective domain.* New York: Longman-McKay.

Lieberman, A., & Miller, L. (2000). Teaching and teacher development: A new synthesis for a new century. In R. S. Brandt (Ed.), *Education in a new ERA, 2000 yearbook* (pp. 47–66). Alexandria, VA: Association for Supervision and Curriculum Development.

Lyman, H. (1998). *Test scores and what they mean* (6th ed.). Boston: Allyn and Bacon.

Mager, R. F. (1997). *Preparing instructional objectives: A critical tool in the development of effective instruction* (3rd ed.). Atlanta, GA: Center for Effective Performance.

Marzano, R. (2000). 20th century advances in instruction. In R. Brandt (Ed.), *Education in a new era, 2000 Yearbook* (pp. 67–95). Alexandria, VA: Association for Supervision and Curriculum Development.

McCabe, P. P. (2003, September). Enhancing self-efficacy for high-stakes reading test. *The Reading Teacher,* 12–20.

National Commission on Excellence in Education. (1983). *A nation at risk: The imperative for reform.* Washington, DC: Government Printing Office.

National Education Goals Panel. (1997). *The national education goals report: Building a nation of learners.* Washington, DC: U.S. Government Printing Office.

Nebraska Department of Education. (1998). *Leading educational achievement through rigorous Nebraska standards.* Omaha, NE: Author.

New York State Education Department. (1997). *English language arts learning standards.* Albany, NY: The State Education Department.

Oliva, P. F. (2000). *Developing the curriculum* (5th ed.). White Plains, NY: Longman.

O'Neill, J., & Tell, C. (1999, September). Why students lose when "tougher standards" win. *Educational Leadership,* 18–22.

Ornstein, A. C. (1992, September). The national reform of education. *NASSP Bulletin,* 89–105.

Ornstein, A. C., & Hunkins, F. P. (1998). *Curriculum: Foundations, principles, and issues* (3rd ed.). Boston: Allyn and Bacon.

Pearson, P. D., & Raphael, T. (1999). Toward a more complex view of balance in the literacy curriculum. In W. D. Hammond & T. E. Raphael (Eds.), *Early literacy instruction for the new millennium* (pp. 1–21). Newark, DE: International Reading Association.

Posner, G. J., & Rudnitsky, A. N. (2000). *Course design: A guide to curriculum development for teachers* (6th ed.). New York: Longman.

Postlethwaite, T. N. (1994). Validity vrs. utility: Personal experiences with the taxonomy. In L. W. Anderson & L. A. Sosniak (Eds.), *Bloom's taxonomy: A forty-year retrospective* (pp. 174–180). Chicago: University of Chicago Press.

Rosenholtz, S. (1991). *Teacher's workplace: The social organization of schools.* New York: Teachers College Press, Columbia University.

Schmoker, M., & Marzano, R. (1999, March). Realizing the promise of standards-based education. *Educational Leadership,* 17–21.

Seligman, D. (2000, November 13). Accountability: The backlash. *Forbes*, 238–240.

Sewell, G. (2000, Summer). Lost in action. *American Educator*, 4–9, 42, 43.

Sosniak, L. (1994). The taxonomy, curriculum, and their relations. In L. W. Anderson & L. A. Sosniak (Eds.), *Bloom's taxonomy: A forty-year retrospective* (pp. 103–125). Chicago: University of Chicago Press.

Taba, H. (1962). *Curriculum development: Theory and research.* New York: Harcourt Brace Jovanovich.

Tyler, R. W. (1949). *Basic principles of curriculum and instruction.* Chicago: University of Chicago Press.

Wiggins, G., & McTighe, J. (1998). *Understanding by design.* Alexandria, VA: Association for Supervision and Curriculum Development.

Wolf, D. P., & White, A. M. (2000, February). Charting the course of student growth. *Educational Leadership*, 6–11.

Zumwalt, K. (1989). Beginning professional teachers: The need for a curricular vision of teaching. In M. C. Reynolds (Ed.), *Knowledge base for the beginning teacher* (pp. 173–184). Oxford, England: Pergammon Press.

chapter 5

# Curriculum Design

**Focusing Questions**

1. What are the four major components of curriculum design?
2. How does one's viewpoint regarding the nature of curriculum influence how one shapes the components of curriculum?
3. Why is it important to attempt to achieve balance between various components of the curriculum plan?
4. How does curriculum integration exhibit similarities with the multisubject/multidisciplinary approach?
5. Why does the design approach of curriculum alignment meet with the approval of the standards proponents?

6. Why might a design approach for diverse learners be important in today's learning environments?

7. How does the unintended or unplanned curriculum influence learning?

Curriculum design sets the tone for instructional planning. That is, teachers plan classroom instruction on the basis of how their district or school expects them to implement planned course work or units of instruction. A **curriculum plan** is a coordinated and articulated plan of instruction (usually in written form) that is designed to result in student achievement of skills and knowledge.

# ■ CURRICULUM FRAMEWORKS

Most curriculum practitioners view curriculum as a broad and dynamic system in which theorists, specialists, and teachers contribute and participate to make an educational system work. An educator's worldview, value system, and knowledge base, which includes an understanding of curriculum foundations and the theories and practical principles of curriculum, influence his or her perspective to favor some curriculum frameworks over others (Ornstein & Hunkins, 2004). Likewise, at the classroom level a guiding framework or set of principles needs to provide the basis of a teacher's actions in establishing instructional activities for lessons (Jalongo, 2000).

Initially coined as "curriculum orientations" by Elliot Eisner (1993), the metaphor of "curriculum streams" is used by Allan Glatthorn and Jerry Jailall (2000) to suggest that five curriculum frameworks or sets of principles have been prevalent in education's past and present. Sometimes they flow together and at other times they are widely separated, with one orientation weak in influence while others gain strength and become prominent because of school or social issues.

The five curriculum frameworks, based on the work of Eisner (1993) and Glatthorn and Jailail (2000), are described as follows:

1. **Cognitive processes.** This framework proposes that the curriculum be focused on a problem-solving format by helping students develop their thinking skills and by showing them how to learn. This orientation, rooted in the works of Jean Piaget and Jerome Bruner, is exemplified in both Howard Gardner's (1997) multiple intelligence theory and in the current belief of constructivists in a literacy learning context. The constructivist viewpoint sees the learner as key in constructing his or her own meaning and literacy development based on prior knowledge and social experiences and regards the teacher as the one who structures and scaffolds the learning environment so that learners can successfully think through problems and engage in meaningful reading and writing activities (Schmidt, Gillen, Zollo, & Stone, 2002). Depth in a curriculum or content topic is emphasized rather than breadth of topic coverage.

2. **Academic rationalism.** This viewpoint is exemplified by the current emphasis on standards. We have noted previously that this orientation strongly favors the learning and study of the academic disciplines as the basis for curriculum planning. To this viewpoint,

we should also add those enthusiasts who favor a skills-based or product-centered approach to learning, particularly in regard to early reading and writing instruction (Baumann, 1991; Flippo, 1999; Smith, 1999). Skills-based learning, such as focusing on bits of knowledge from single academic subjects, encourages students to engage in the learning of discrete skills, and advocates believe that transfer of skill learning will occur in more meaningful contexts. Thus, students might practice using connecting words such as *and, but,* and *however* to join sentences listed on the chalkboard or printed on a ditto sheet. Such practice would provide students with the concepts and thinking to allow them to use connecting words in their own writings. A product-centered or text-centered curriculum focus in written literacy stresses a part-to-whole orientation in which correctness is stressed and learners engage letters before words, words before sentences, and sentences before whole texts (Finders & Hynds, 2003).

3. **Personal relevance.** This orientation begins with the student and is rooted in progressive education. Based on student needs and interest, the purpose of a personal-relevance curriculum is to help students find personal meaning in the works and content they study. The continued interest in whole language approaches to literacy learning is an indication of this curriculum orientation. We could also add those constructivist-based classrooms that engage students in problem solving and relevant, personal learning. This viewpoint is rooted in John Dewey's progressive thought and in ways in which students problem solve (Dewey, 1933). Literacy educators looked to such authors as Nancie Atwell (1998), Lucy Calkins (1994), and Donald Graves (1983), who advocated that teachers provide students with authentic, personal, and meaningful choice in their reading and writing experiences.

4. **Social adaptation and social reconstruction.** Proponents of social adaptation look to the needs of society. Those who favor the view of social adaptation feel that schools should assist students in adapting to the prevalent social order (Dewey, 1933). They propose that schooling should prepare students to fulfill the needs of the workforce and produce the kinds of workers the nation needs to maintain its position and prosperity in the world (an argument also noted in the standards reform movement).

Those who favor social reconstruction, on the other hand, desire a curriculum that allows students to improve society. Established in the early ideas of George Counts and Theodore Bramfeld, this approach attempts to empower students to study and revisit democracy in alternative ways. For instance, students would learn that alternative and worthwhile social arrangements exist (Wood, 1988) or that literacy itself can promote social change by engaging students in readings of race, class, gender, and injustice to discover relevant issues (Finders & Hynds, 2003).

5. **Technological models.** This viewpoint sees curriculum as a technical process with an emphasis on establishing means to accomplish ends. The initial effort is to identify those goals or instructional objectives the curriculum should achieve and then design the curriculum plan to accomplish those stated goals and objectives.

Although computers, along with corresponding use of allied technologies, can be the main feature of a technological curriculum viewpoint, they can also be used with other curriculum orientations. Technology can be used as a tool by students to achieve the philosophical rationales and ends of the other four curriculum orientations. Indeed, the tool uses of technology encourage students to integrate knowledge with forms of literacy while

## BOX 5.1 How Computers May Influence Curriculum

The use of computers may contribute to other curriculum viewpoints and orientations in the following ways:

- They can file and house the curriculum, making it easily accessible to administrators, teachers, parents, and students.
- They can monitor the curriculum through the use of an instructional management system. Teachers can input data, altering or enriching their instructional plans, their instructional objectives, and how they will evaluate student mastery of objectives.
- They can help teachers align the curriculum by adjusting what has been tested with what has been achieved or learned.
- They serve to enrich the curriculum by expanding knowledge sources such as with Internet use and by supplementing text sources with multimedia.

*Source:* Allan Glatthorn and Jerry Jailall, "Curriculum for the New Millennium," in R. S. Brandt, *Education in a New Era: ASCD Yearbook* (Alexandria, VA: Association for Supervision and Curriculum Development, 2000), pp. 97–121.

providing them with the technological and cognitive skills to construct new knowledge (Maslin & Nelson, 2002). The key variables are the teacher's knowledge and the emphasis the school places on computer use. We discussed computer use as a means for achieving greater literacy horizons in Chapter 2, and more is devoted to the promise of technology to inform well-educated youth in Chapter 12 (see also Box 5.1).

# ■ CURRICULUM DESIGN

**Curriculum design** refers to the components and arrangement of the different parts of the curriculum plan. Designs differ because they are influenced by a person's philosophical belief of education, views about learning theory, and the curriculum orientation that supports those beliefs. An educator's philosophical stance and belief in how children learn will affect his or her view of goals, standards, and instructional objectives; influence the curriculum content selected and how it will be organized and sequenced for instruction; affect decisions about how to teach the curriculum content; and guide judgments about how to evaluate the curriculum plan.

## Components of Curriculum Design

Curriculum design is generally composed of four parts. These four parts, also called components or elements of curriculum, are (1) aims, goals, standards, and objectives; (2) subject matter or content; (3) learning experiences or activities; and (4) evaluation approaches (Ornstein & Hunkins, 2004). These parts are grounded in the classic works of Ralph Tyler (see Figure 4.2) and Harry Giles, who was Tyler's student. Giles, in his famous report "The Eight-Year Study," included four curricular components in his design model designated as objectives, subject matter, method and organization, and evaluation. Note that our third component, learning experiences or activities, coincides with Giles's method and organization component, which served as the means for interfacing subject matter or content. In Giles's model, interaction occurs among the four components; decisions made about one component are dependent on decisions made about other components (Giles, McCutchen, & Zechiel, 1942).

The nature of these components and the manner in which they are organized in the curriculum plan constitute what we mean by curriculum design. Although most curriculum plans have these four essential elements, they may not be given equal weight because of the philosophical and psychological perspectives governing the overall design. For instance, if one believes strongly in standards coverage and implementation, thereby embracing a stance of academic rationalism, one would emphasize the subject matter and the evaluation components. On the other hand, if one's philosophical orientation was based more on students' personal development—that is, their cognitive, affective, and psychomotor growth—one would look to the component of learning experiences or activities and the way these learning experiences are orchestrated according to student needs and interests. In essence, one's curriculum orientation or view of the nature and purposes of education and how children learn serves to filter or screen the weight given to the four major components of the curriculum design. This relationship is reflected in Figure 5.1.

## Factors of Curriculum Design

While taking account of the four major components of curriculum design, curriculum specialists need to consider other factors contributing to a particular design's success. These factors have to do with organization, scope, sequence, continuity, integration, articulation, and balance.

*Organization.* There are two basic organizational dimensions in approaching the content component of curriculum design. These are referred to as **horizontal** and **vertical organization**. *Horizontal organization* engages the curriculum specialist in subject-matter relationships within a particular grade level, resulting in side-by-side arrangement of cur-

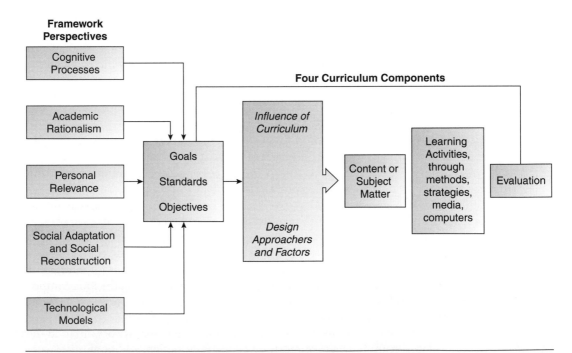

*Figure 5.1* Four Major Curriculum Components Influenced by Both Framework Perspectives and Design Approaches and Factors

**BOX 5.2** Planning for Literacy Experiences Horizontally across the Curriculum

Designing curriculum content horizontally allows the teacher to connect threads of knowledge and learning experiences across the disciplines. When an interesting topic or theme is being studied, the wise teacher finds readings from a number of sources and encourages students to use writing, oral reporting, computer projects, and artwork to connect literary processing modes to their content-area learnings.

riculum elements. One such example is arranging content from one subject such as social studies and relating it to content in another discipline such as the language arts or English. Or, if spiders are the content of study in science class, the mathematics teacher can integrate learning activities by having students note the dimension of the spider's body parts and spiderweb designs. In addition, the language arts teacher can have students read literary selections in which spiders are prominent characters. See Box 5.2.

*Vertical organization* includes longitudinal placement of particular content offerings. This occurs, for instance, when "the family" is a unit of study in the first-grade social studies curriculum, followed by the study of "the community" in the second grade, followed by the study of particular "world communities," such as those found in Europe, Asia, or Africa, in the third grade. The notion here is that as children move up through the grades, their knowledge of the basic family structure can be expanded to include family and community life in different regions and cultures of the world.

Frequently, instruction on learning experiences is organized so that the same general topic is introduced but treated in different ways throughout the grades. The content usually becomes more detailed and difficult. For instance, in mathematics the concept of "set" may be introduced in first grade and reintroduced or mentioned in each succeeding year in the elementary school curriculum.

As another example, kindergartners or first graders are usually introduced to the topic of dinosaurs through literature selections and trade books. They love learning about the different kinds of dinosaurs as their imaginations are stimulated by facts such as size, shape, features, and that they all lived so long ago. Then, in later grades through the disciplines of science or social studies, children may learn about different eras or periods of dinosaur life so that they sharpen their view of the different dinosaurs and when they actually lived. Later in the curriculum, they may learn about climate changes, the relation of plant eaters to meat eaters, the emergence of the mammal family of animals, and why the dinosaurs probably disappeared. These notions correspond with Jerome Bruner's idea of the "spiral curriculum," that is, to reteach subject matter for purposes of reinforcement and expansion of knowledge and ideas (Bruner, 1959). See Box 5.3.

**BOX 5.3** Planning for Literacy Experiences Vertically throughout the Grades

When curriculum content is spiraled throughout the grades, students build on prior knowledge. Prior knowledge provides them with a core vocabulary and some know-how regarding how to address a topic. Students add on and reinforce their preexisting knowledge of a topic by studying it from a new perspective and in greater depth. Additional readings and the accompanying new vocabulary provide additional language fuel for discussing and writing about the topic.

*Scope.* **Scope** refers to the breadth and depth of subject-matter content. Ralph Tyler (1947), in his classic work, likened scope to all of the content, topics, learning experiences, and organizing threads that constitute the educational plan. Others have added that scope refers to the horizontal organization of the substance of the curriculum (Goodlad & Su, 1992).

Scope means not only the depth and range of subject-matter content offered to students, but also all the varieties and types of educational experiences that are designed by teachers to engage students in content learning. One noted American scholar feels that the traditional curriculum subjects of literature, history, math, science, and the arts are essential to the core of subject-matter content because they reveal the conditions of human achievement and inspire us to both practice discipline and open our minds (Barzun, 2002). In its totality, scope refers to cognitive learning, affective learning, and, some would argue, moral and spiritual learning (Goodlad & Su, 1992). Sometimes the scope of the curriculum plan is less broad, encompassing only a simple listing of key topics and activities.

When teachers decide what content and what amount of detail to include with the content, they are considering curriculum scope. In many ways, the twin factors of the current knowledge explosion and the depth of content standards (discussed in the previous chapter) have made dealing with scope a formidable task. Also, the recognized diversity among students places increasing demand on teachers to plan the breadth and depth of scope and its relevant activities to accommodate different student ability levels. In actual day-to-day activity work with students, especially those experiencing difficulty with mastering curriculum content, most teachers would tell us that the most critical factor related to scope is their students' ability to read the material in the first place.

Many teachers realize that the scope of content areas, topics, and standards is just too broad. Some respond to the content overload by ignoring certain content areas or topics, providing minimal coverage of a topic to note that "it was covered in the curriculum," or not including new content topics in their curriculum coverage. Other teachers or teacher teams attempt to relate certain topics to one another by integrating or aligning the knowledge aspects of the topics around a common theme or thread.

One author suggests that curriculum scope can perhaps be maintained at manageable levels if teachers address only a limited number of objectives. These objectives would refer to general clusters of content that would not be allowed to expand to a number beyond effective management (Doll, 1996). The challenge is to achieve consensus with other colleagues that the chosen content categories are indeed of greater educational merit and importance than those not selected. This challenge is even more crucial today with the debate inherent in two major concerns regarding content: What is worth knowing? and Breadth or depth? Furthermore, those teachers dealing with literary instruction are quite aware of the great importance they need to attach to the affective domain by motivating and providing guidance for students to read, write, and improve their literacy skills.

*Sequence.* When curriculum specialists consider **sequence,** they look to the curriculum to provide cumulative and continuous learning, or what is known as the *vertical* relationship within the curriculum plan. In this regard, they must decide how content and learning experiences occur at one grade level and reoccur at others so that students have opportunities to connect and enrich their understandings of the offerings of the full school curriculum (Goodlad & Su, 1992). Hilda Taba, in her classic text *Curriculum Development* (1962), argued that neglecting to pay serious attention to sequence in terms of the cumulative development of intellectual and affective processes resulted in curriculum plans that have achieved less than favorable results (Taba, 1962).

While addressing the issue of sequence, curriculum specialists, teachers, and school administrators are also aware of the issue of children's developmental stages and whether children are cognitively ready to mentally process certain content topics. A long-standing controversy exists regarding whether the sequence of content and learning activities should be based on the logic of the subject matter or on the way learners develop and grow—and are presumed to process knowledge. Those that argue for curriculum sequence based on psychological principles draw on the research and theoretical position on human growth, development, and learning. In this regard, the writings of Jean Piaget (1960) have provided a framework for the sequencing of content and learning activities and experiences as they relate to our expectations of how youngsters function at various cognitive levels. Many schools and districts—as they formulate curriculum objectives, content, and learning activities and experiences by ascending grade levels—consider the stages of students' thinking, as discussed by Piaget, as they likewise consider the implications of the stages of reading development, as discussed by Jeanne Chall (1996).

Arguably, in organizing content into a productive vertical sequence, we cannot totally disregard how individuals develop and learn. But neither can we neglect the content or subject matter itself, the fact that it has, by its very nature, a substantive structure and logic in its understanding components. For example, a way of reasoning is built into the study of atoms and molecules because inherent in the topics themselves are the systems of principles and concepts that make understanding occur. Jerome Bruner (1959) refers to this as the "structure" of subject matter. Nor can we forget the notion that individual learners have particular interests, needs, and propensities to learn particular subject matter well or not so well (some may refer to this as styles of learning). Also, when individuals work in groups, the group interests and needs take on shapes and direction that draw from the collective strength of the individuals. All of these concerns need to be addressed in curriculum sequencing.

Some curriculum specialists have provided us with valuable principles and organizers in the vertical sequencing of content. One set of four organizing principles arranges the vertical sequencing of content knowledge by simple to complex learning, prerequisite learning, whole-to-part learning, and chronological learning.

- *Simple to complex learning* means that subject-matter content is optimally organized in such a way that an understanding of simple subordinate elements builds to an understanding of complex ideas and concepts that have interrelationships among the subordinate elements. This principle notes that optimal learning occurs when students are presented with easy, often concrete, content and then sequentially with more difficult, often abstract, content that has connections to the earlier content.
- *Prerequisite learning* is based on the belief that fundamental information or bits of learning must be grasped before other knowledge bits are offered. When a student has the prerequisite learning(s), the newer information will be easier to comprehend and assimilate. In this connection, it is important for learners to have background information on particular topics so that they can better comprehend text material.

- *Whole-part-whole learning* is supported by cognitive psychologists. They suggest that for optimal learning to occur, particularly of abstract topics or concepts, the whole be presented first in an overview so that the pieces of information can fit together as they are studied. By furnishing students with an overview, a framework, or a visually presented graphic outline of the curriculum content to be studied, the teacher provides the gist of the whole so that the parts can be logically connected as they are read or researched.

- *Chronological learning* is a way to sequence content based on the way it has occurred in history or in world events. Frequently, readings and learnings in social studies, history, and the earth sciences are organized in this manner. This type of organization assists children in their thinking once they have mastered the concepts of time and their associated unfolding of events. Such learning occurs in the usual curriculum presentation of history topics (Ornstein & Hunkins, 2004; Smith, Stanley, & Shores, 1957).

*Continuity.* The factor of **continuity** deals with the vertical repetition and reinforcement of curriculum parts, usually those having to do with subject-matter content and learning activities. It accounts for the reappearance or enhancement of certain knowledge, ideas, or skills of which educators believe students should have over the course of the entire school curriculum. It ensures that students will have the opportunity to revisit and practice crucial content as many times as necessary (Goodlad & Su, 1992).

This notion is particularly evident in the literacy domains of reading and writing and is reinforced by most states in that students have to accomplish benchmark performances at particular grade levels in the ability to read with comprehension and write with proficiency. The skills remain known as "reading" and "writing," but the complexity of the literary tasks increases the higher the grade (see Box 5.4).

**BOX 5.4** Providing for Literacy Experiences throughout the Grades

Like any human activity, the more one reads, writes, and uses computers to succeed in learning and personally fulfilling tasks, the easier the next encounter becomes. Continuity is reinforced by both practice and the increasing complexity of learning and literacy tasks. For instance, at earlier grade levels, children often read personalized narrative accounts that are closer to their style of living and thinking than the informational, expository text accounts read in the middle and upper grades. Also, as children advance through the grades they are shown how to write in different ways and with different tools for different audiences—from personalized stories of firsthand experiences, to reports about places and events, to essays of persuasion exhorting others to believe or act a particular way.

Continuity is most evident in Bruner's notion of the spiral curriculum. Bruner noted that the curriculum should be organized according to the interrelationships between the structures of the basic ideas of each major discipline. For students to grasp these basic ideas and structures, "they should be developed and redeveloped in a spiral fashion" (1959, p. 52) in increasing depth and breadth as the pupils advance through the school program. Furthermore, E. D. Hirsch (2002) maintains that the main reason children fail each year is not due to their lack of abilities or unwillingness to learn but rather to the shortcomings in the continuity of curriculum content. He feels that the failure to build on prior knowledge and to teach children the building blocks of knowledge needed to succeed in the next grade is a major injustice.

*Integration.* **Integration** occurs when educators attempt to link aspects of the curriculum plan, particularly those dealing with content and student learning activities. It is essentially a design factor that brings into close relationship bits and pieces of the curriculum in ways that allow learners to see and comprehend knowledge as unified rather than as isolated fragments (Caulfield, Kidd, & Kotcher, 2000; Goodlad & Su, 1992). It emphasizes horizontal relationships among various topics and themes drawn from the content disciplines.

By emphasizing the integration factor in their school or district, teachers and administrators believe they are providing learners a way to obtain a unified view of knowledge and in-depth meaning of subject-matter content. However, this may not be the case. A number of noted educators have pointed out that, in actuality, learning experiences occur with the learner. While curriculum planners can organize opportunities for learning in ways that integrate the curriculum, it is the learners who actually integrate what they are learning through the various activities, readings, and experiences they are provided (Saylor, Alexander, & Lewis, 1981).

Hilda Taba (1962), long a recognized figure in the field of curriculum, advanced a similar view by noting that integration occurs with an individual, whether or not the curriculum is organized for that purpose. The integrative process occurs when students organize knowledge and experiences, which initially appear to be unrelated, in a meaningful way. However, Taba did not limit integration solely to that which occurred in the student's understanding and belief system. She realized that it was also an attempt by educators to interrelate the content components with learning experiences and activities in ways that would facilitate learning.

Of all the design factors, integration has received the most attention from curriculum theorists and practitioners alike. It has spanned catchwords for plans such as "curriculum integration," "curriculum alignment," "interdisciplinary curriculum," "integrated language arts," "thematic units," and others. Will the trend continue in light of the standards emphasis? Many critics feel that the standards approach makes students focus on the content disciplines themselves, thereby narrowing their perspective of the interrelationships between or connectedness of different subject matter. Critics argue that rather than focus students' attention on details within the separate disciplines, educators should investigate what current and new knowledge belongs in the curriculum and integrate that knowledge across the disciplines (Brady, 2000; Glickman, 2000–2001). In today's schools, many would argue that the curriculum is still arranged in disjointed and uneven ways that prevent students from seeing knowledge as unified and connected. If the study of content becomes a narrow study of just the information within each discipline, as the standards critics foresee, then students may have continued difficulty perceiving interrelationships among concepts and knowledge and becoming literate in the use of different representational forms (Eisner, 2001; Kellaghan, Madaus, & Raczek, 1996).

Although integration as a factor of curriculum design can be operationally defined, there have been a number of interpretations across the curriculum. Educators have attempted to design curriculum parts so that global clusters of content are linked by relational themes or threads. These attempts have been most prevalent in the curriculum area of the English language arts, in which the processes of learning and using language forms are embedded in and connected to learning activities occurring in the language arts and other content disciplines. Students have been encouraged to read authentic children's literature and informational trade books to integrate additional knowledge with social studies and science topics (Rice, 2002; Roser & Keehn, 2002). They became involved in the writing process as they learned to plan, develop, and finalize a coherent essay or report related to a content topic rather than practice writing sentences and paragraphs that were not integrated with topics in the curriculum. Prominent integration movements include Writing Across the Curriculum, Integrating Computers with Content Area Subjects, and Reading Through the Arts, all of which attempted and still attempt to connect ways of knowing with what can be known.

*Articulation.* When various aspects of the curriculum have been connected or interrelated, **articulation** has been achieved. This relation can occur with either vertical or horizontal planning. Vertical articulation refers to the relationships of particular aspects of the curriculum sequence with other lessons, topics, or standards criteria that appear later in a school's or district's curriculum guide. For instance, a team of teachers might introduce the concepts of "nomads," "wanderers," and "immigrants" to children in the primary grades when the topics of local and world communities are often covered in the social studies curriculum. These concepts will become important when children read literary selections pertaining to these types of peoples in their language arts classes in the intermediate grades. When viewed vertically, we can note that teachers formulated a sequencing plan of concept understanding from lower grade to upper grade and from one discipline to another. This vertical articulation effort ensures that students receive information and achieve learnings that serve as prerequisites for later learnings in the curriculum.

Horizontal articulation occurs when associations or connections are made between topics and learnings that are occurring simultaneously in the curriculum. This would occur, for instance, when middle school or junior high school students learn about the history of the Civil War in their social studies classes as they read about the Underground Railroad, and read the biographies of Harriet Tubman and Frederick Douglass and the novel *My Brother Sam Is Dead* in their English classes (Collier, 1997). When student learning experiences are connected across the curriculum, planners and teachers strive to meld the content topics of one part of the curriculum with another's content offerings that have a logical, educational, or conceptual link. Much of the present-day emphasis on integrating the curriculum closely resembles the effort of horizontal articulation.

Although articulation is an easy curriculum factor to describe, it is often difficult to achieve. There are a number of reasons for this. One reason is that it becomes somewhat difficult to determine just what might be the appropriate and meaningful vertical and horizontal interrelationships to make in the curriculum. When curriculum is arranged by subject disciplines, planners pay little attention to connections with any other subject matter. We noted that this was a major criticism of how most standards are organized in the curriculum. Schools and districts have to develop plans and procedures by which meaningful interrelationships within and among subjects are clearly defined for student presentation.

This leads us to the second difficulty in achieving articulation. Because articulation needs to be planned, teachers need planning time. This means that teachers within

**BOX 5.5** A Coherent, Organized Curriculum in the Core Disciplines May Benefit the Poor and Disadvantaged

One forceful argument for the standards approach is that a coherent curriculum is achieved in each of the core subjects across the states and their districts. This centralized focus may benefit poor and minority populations, which often need to relocate. Because our population is becoming increasingly mobile and the poor often have to relocate to find jobs, children move from school to school and from district to district. Students new to a school district sometimes repeat information they covered in their previous school at an earlier grade level. Other times they experience gaps in their learning experiences; that is, they miss a particular concept or topic because it was offered before their arrival at a new district or school.

schools need to have scheduled planning time to achieve articulation and sequencing of curriculum efforts, and teachers within a school district need equal, if not more, time to plan articulation among schools. Very often this planning time is not forthcoming even though school and district leaders know how important the planning time is to achieve curriculum goals. We could also argue, as have standards proponents, that a need exists to achieve articulation between curriculum and teaching and among school districts as well as within school districts. See Box 5.5.

*Balance.*  **Balance** is concerned with the weighting of components in the curriculum design. If one of the four components is stressed more than the others, distortion may occur and schooling practices that should occur do not occur. For example, when a district and school emphasize particular kinds of learning activities, they may not be mindful of the subject matter in which these activities occur and may not have an evaluation strategy to see if the learning activities actually helped students learn. Further, in a balanced curriculum, students should not only be challenged to learn subject matter or content but also have opportunities to use this knowledge in ways that are appropriate for their personal, social, and intellectual goals.

Adding to the difficulty of attaining balance in the curriculum is the consideration that what might be interpreted as balance today could well be unbalance tomorrow. Schools often find themselves in times that are constantly changing with regard to the purposes and aims of schooling. Today is just such a time, with its emphasis on standards-based education and its focus on mastery of subject-matter content and performance assessments to determine if that content was learned. Balance of curriculum components is influenced by the changing currents of society and culture and by how these have an impact on the philosophical views of education's purposes and aims (Glatthorn & Jailall, 2000) (see Figure 5.1). Curriculum specialists and teachers may wish to maintain a balance in the curriculum plan by considering the viewpoints offered by Peter Oliva listed in Box 5.6.

**BOX 5.6** When Considering Balance in the Curriculum, Take Note of Conflicting Viewpoints

1. The child-centered versus the subject-centered curriculum
2. The needs of the individual versus those of society
3. The needs of common education versus those of specialized education
4. Breadth versus depth of curriculum content
5. Traditional content versus innovative content
6. The needs of the unique range of pupils regarding their learning styles
7. Different teaching methods and educational experiences
8. Work versus play
9. The community versus the school as educational forces

*Source:* Adapted from Peter Oliva, *Developing the Curriculum*, 4th ed. (New York: Longman, 1997).

# ■ CURRICULUM DESIGN APPROACHES

In this section, we look at different approaches to curriculum design. We note how curriculum specialists incorporate and balance the various design factors as they establish their particular design frameworks.

## Curriculum Integration

According to James Beane (1997), **curriculum integration** is a type of design whereby students integrate personal and social experiences in a curriculum organized to investigate significant problems and issues that cut across subject area boundaries. There are three main features of this curriculum design: (1) the organizing themes are drawn from life as young people engage in and experience life; (2) the theme generates concepts that are explored through learning experiences and activities without regard for traditional discipline or subject-matter boundaries; and (3) the students become engaged in a collaborative planning process to identify the themes.

Thus, curriculum integration in the classroom involves the application of knowledge to questions, issues, and concerns that have personal and/or social significance. Because personal, socially relevant issues and questions drive the construction of the themes, students use knowledge to pursue or solve the issue or question. The pursuit of knowledge is therefore not confined to the separate subject domains. The curriculum factors of scope and sequence are determined by the questions, issues, and concerns collaboratively activated by students and teachers. In essence, students become engaged in "performing knowledge," in which experiences occur ranging from presentations to actual social action. In theory, because knowledge is actually being put to use, students are driven to accomplish higher standards because they are challenged in their skills and use of content.

The integration aspect of the design is achieved in four ways: (1) integration of experiences, (2) integration of social encounters, (3) integration of knowledge, and (4) integration of the curriculum design (Beane, 1997). Experiences provide a learning resource as students become involved in life as it is lived in and out of the classroom and also a way to reflect on prior experiences. *Integration of experiences* means that the learning of new and the reflection of old become part of the individual to provide highly meaningful learning experiences. These ideas are rooted in Piaget's theory of assimilation and accommodation of prior and new experiences. Such learning generates integration in two ways: first, as new experiences happen and become integrated into one's current schemes of meaning, and second, when one organizes or integrates past experiences to assist in the solution of new problems or issues.

*Social integration* draws on one of the beliefs of schooling in a democratic society; that is, schooling should provide common or shared educational experiences for students from diverse backgrounds and with diverse characteristics. This notion was inherent in the early aims for education compiled in 1918 by the Commission on the Reorganization of Secondary Education and expressed in the works of John Dewey, William Kilpatrick, and other early progressive theorists; in the writings of current cooperative learning theorists such as David Johnson and Peter Johnson and Robert

Slavin; and is a common theme today among those who advocate that diversity in the classroom represents a natural way to enrich student learning (Sapon-Shevin, 2000–2001). Because students are involved in a problem-solving approach to a common theme, they become involved in collaborative work and actively participate in the planning of the curriculum.

*Integration of knowledge* refers to how knowledge is used and organized. In real life, when people are confronted with a problem or an issue to solve they don't stop to consider how mathematics, reading, the arts, history, or science can resolve the situation. Once the problem or issue relative to the theme is selected, students strive to solve the problem or decide the issue using whatever knowledge is pertinent and necessary. Knowledge is not compartmentalized by subject-matter disciplines in such a design, but is sought out, used, and integrated in the context of real problem solving. This idea is rooted in Dewey's and Tyler's ideas of how learning is transferred from one situation to another. Integration, therefore, tears down such long-standing school practices as specific subject classes, specific skills teaching at specific times, and daily and hourly schedules of students moving from one discipline subject to the other.

*Integration of the curriculum* design takes its meaning from the coalescing of the three previously discussed integrations: (1) that the curriculum is planned to deal with problems and concerns that have personal and social significance for the students in the real world; (2) that learning experiences and activities serve to integrate past and present knowledge to achieve the concepts related to the organizing center or central theme; and (3) that knowledge is used to investigate the central theme under current study rather than used for test preparation or grade-level advancement. To these integrating features a fourth aspect is added: (4) that of the active participation of students in the curriculum planning.

How is this type of curriculum framework achieved? To involve students in the collaborative planning process, teachers often begin with two basic questions: "What questions or concerns do you have about yourself?" and "What questions or concerns do you have about the world?" Brainstorming individually, in groups, and then as a whole class takes place. From the lists of Self Questions and World Questions, the group collaboratively tries to connect ideas from both to generate themes that serve as organizing centers for forthcoming investigative projects. Such themes might be Living in the Future, Environmental Problems, Conflict and Violence, or Different Cultures. Once a list of agreed-on themes is produced, the group might vote to determine the order of the themes, which goes first, second, and so on. The first unit begins when all the original relevant questions pertaining to that theme are brought forward once again, become organized around central concepts, and generate activities that allow students to use knowledge and experiences to demonstrate or perform their learnings.

By consulting Figure 5.2, you can see a schematic design of how this type of curriculum integration works. If the theme selected was Conflict and Violence, the related concepts (the interlocking circles around the central theme) might be Gangs, Wars, Abuse, Crime, Political Uses, and so forth. To each of these concepts are webbed specific topics for which project activities and learning experiences are designed. Moreover, the activities and learning experiences help answer the very questions students posed at the

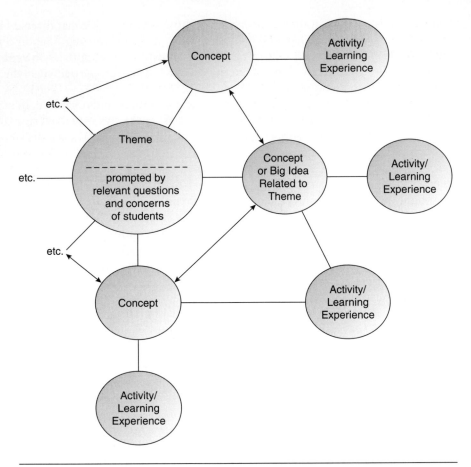

*Figure 5.2* The Plan for Curriculum Integration

*Source:* Based on James A. Beane, *Curriculum Integration: Designing the Core of Democratic Education* (New York: Teacher's College Press, 1997).

outset. Thus, for instance, if one group of students worked on the Wars concept, they might:

- Research some major wars of the past to tell how they influenced history.
- Construct bar graphs of the combatants of the major wars of the twentieth century.
- Do overlapping circle diagrams of world wars and civil wars and tell how they are the same and different.
- Make time lines of America's Revolutionary War or Civil War and highlight the most important events.
- Visit a historical battlefield site and then role-play an attacker or defender in that battle by writing a letter to a loved one.

- Interview a person who either was in an internment camp or visited one, or locate on a world map where such camps exist today.
- Read biographies, autobiographies, or historical novels of people involved in wartime situations.
- Analyze and interpret paintings and other works of art that show the glory and horrors of war.
- Write a newspaper account of what happens when people visit a war memorial.
- Using newspapers, magazines, and the World Wide Web as information sources, place markers or pins on a large-scale world map to show where major conflicts are occurring today (Beane, 1997).

Note that such activities and learning experiences are not fixed by discipline. Because they are problem-centered or project-oriented activities and experiences, students have to use knowledge that may be drawn from different disciplines, in personal and social ways, and through in-school and out-of-school learning experiences. To manage and assess such project work in this type of curriculum integration, teachers and students have a wonderful opportunity to use portfolios. In portfolios, which are collaboratively planned regarding organization, content, and criteria, students can keep a record of their learning experiences and knowledge performances related to each organizing theme.

According to Beane (1997) integration in the design of curriculum integration is quite different from what many other educators consider the term *integration* to mean. What is usually meant by the notion of integration is a multisubject, **multidisciplinary,** interdisciplinary, or thematic unit approach. In this type of curriculum design, although a central or controlling theme is also identified, the major issue becomes, "What can each subject discipline contribute to the development of the theme?" Although the theme acts as a central organizer, each separate subject discipline contributes its own content. Students remain engaged in learning the knowledge and skills of the separate disciplines because a sense of meaningfulness or wholeness is generally the instructional objective of the teachers. By relating content and skills from each of their separate disciplines to the central concept of the theme, teachers feel that the learning will be more relevant, connected, and meaningful for their shared students. A schematic plan for an interdisciplinary or multisubject arrangement to support a central theme is indicated in Figure 5.3.

There are critical differences between the concept of curriculum integration as noted in Figure 5.2 and multidisciplinary arrangements as noted in Figure 5.3. Whereas the former embraces a problem or issue related to a central focus and students engage in learning experiences to satisfy their own issue-seeking questions, the latter looks to the traditional school subjects to contribute knowledge and potential learning activities that enhance the concept of the controlling organizer. However, you should not think that engagement in a multisubject approach is not rewarding for teachers and students.

For instance, a popular thematic unit covered in fourth grade in New York State is the study of Native Americans of early New York. Although many fourth-grade teachers in the same school work collaboratively to plan the unit, they generally each implement the unit separately in their self-contained classes. What teachers do enjoy is seeing

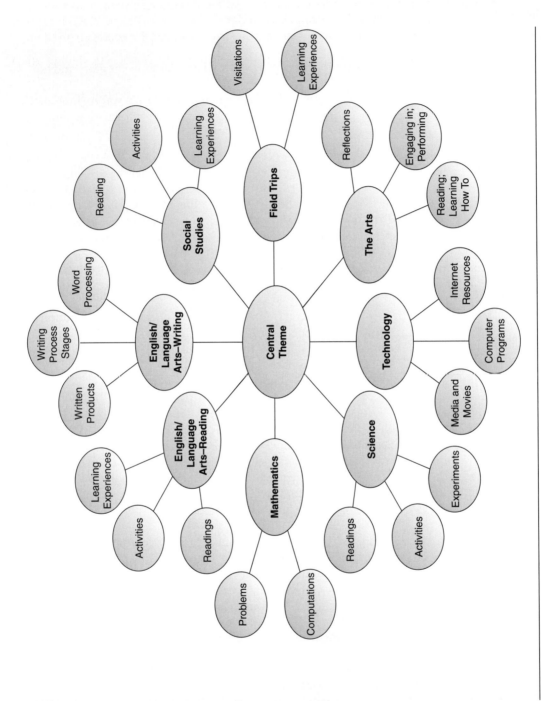

*Figure 5.3* A Plan for an Interdisciplinary or Multisubject Unit Based on a Central Theme

that they can integrate information and activities from different subject domains, allowing students to use such processes as reading, writing, art, and arithmetic across the traditional disciplines. One such unit had the following learning components:

- In social studies, students read about the Algonquin and Iroquois nations that thrived in the region of early New York and compared and contrasted their lifestyles. Some fourth graders were treated to a museum trip in which they saw life-size replicas of the villages and peoples they read about.
- In language arts reading, students read realistic fiction, folktales, and legends generated about the two nations. Such literature included *The Indian in the Cupboard* (Banks, 1999), *The Rough Face Girl* (Martin, 1998), *Glooscap and the Baby,* and *Dancing Stars* (Erdoes, 1997).
- In science, students connected the food chain to the two American Indian nation's lifestyles.
- In the arts, students created an artifact interest center; made masks, dolls, and musical instruments; did drawings; and constructed a three-dimensional village of Algonguin and Iroquois dwellings.
- And in arithmetic, students calculated the area and perimeter of the Algonquin longhouse and quantified the value of a wampum necklace by assigning monetary value to different-colored beads (Sinatra, 1994).

Note that cognitive processes and personal relevance are major philosophical underpinnings in the curriculum integration design offered by Beane (1997). Students engage in problem-solving work, and integration is achieved across academic subjects as students help plan and execute learning activities that focus on solving the problem and answering the questions relative to the central theme.

## Curriculum Mapping

A second approach to curriculum design, called **curriculum mapping,** focuses directly on the disciplines to achieve integration and is based on the work of Heidi Hayes Jacobs (1997). The approach has two major components or goals: (1) to lay out the year's curriculum for a school or district using the school calendar as a time organizer, and (2) to formulate **essential questions,** which serve as conceptual organizers for themes. Both components provide a scope and a sequence of a term or year of a curriculum plan as teachers provide for students' horizontal and vertical integration of learning experiences.

How does this curriculum design evolve? First, each teacher completes a calendar-based map by using a standard calendar as a guide. By using a large sheet of paper, index cards, or a computer screen, individual teachers write down what they actually teach in each of the disciplines by the months of the term or school year. The key here is that teachers record what they actually teach and not what others think they should be teaching. Next, the teachers view and read through one another's maps to see what all teachers in the school building are accomplishing. In this way, they gain horizontal and vertical knowledge of what learning experiences students are afforded in that school or district.

Through small- and large-group review and collaboration, teachers work to achieve consistency in their schoolwide curriculum. They locate repetitions of content, gaps, possible areas where integration of content could occur, mismatches between targeted outcomes (say, in the form of benchmark performance standards) and curriculum, and meaningful and nonmeaningful assessments. By reviewing the curriculum maps, faculty and administration can consider the appropriate steps to take in order to improve the curriculum plan for maximizing student performance.

Two important outcomes emerge from these teacher collaborations with the curriculum maps. First, the opportunity arises to match school district and state standards with the ongoing curriculum offerings in the various disciplines. This helps teachers plan for the yearwide assessments as well. At particular grade levels, the district or state may ask that students perform different tasks to show they have learned content or may require that particular benchmarks or high-stakes testing be accomplished. By noting these assessment schedules on the curriculum map, teachers see the need to plan for them.

The second, and possibly most noteworthy, opportunity that arises out of mapping collaboration is the potential for integration of curriculum offerings. Elementary and middle school teachers use the maps to locate natural connections for interdisciplinary units of study. These units can have a topic focus, a thematic focus, an issue focus, or a problem-based focus (as we saw in the previous discussion of curriculum integration). A topic focus could occur within a separate discipline such as science, social studies, or mathematics. But an integrated unit involving several fields of study could also grow out of a focus on one discipline topic as well. This occurred, for instance, in the earlier example of the fourth-grade unit on the Native Americans of early New York.

When several teachers plan and design a unit to integrate two or more disciplines, the resultant product is often considered to be interdisciplinary, multidisciplinary, multisubject, or thematic. Teachers planning to present a thematic unit to students mutually share traditional curriculum topics and units to be offered at a specified period of the theme. As noted by Jacobs, an "option is to reconfigure when mutually compatible subjects or units are taught so that they run concurrently. . . . In this instance, teachers are not co-writing the unit; they are co-planning for optimum timing" (1997, p. 21).

One might think that teachers would find it easy to formulate essential or key questions once they have decided on a unit that integrates a number of content subjects. However, this is not the case. Essential questions are broad based and conceptual in nature; they set the stage for the unit and pose the crucial question for the entire lesson. They usually are formulated in terms of "how" or "why" in the language arts and social studies, and "what if" in science and math. They ask students to analyze, problem solve, or evaluate. Tips for Teachers 5.1 presents criteria teachers might use in formulating good essential questions.

The curriculum map should include vertical columns based on months of the school term or year and horizontal columns based on content domains or topics. Above the vertical columns would be listed the theme's organizing concept, such as Five Senses, or The Weather, or Feudalism; under that goes the essential question for that theme, followed by notations of the contributions from domains or topics. Along the horizontal domain/content blocks on the map, teachers can indicate different learning activities that would occur during the months.

In the development of one integrated theme based on topics from a number of subject disciplines, teachers often use a graphic organizer to flesh out what they actually

## Criteria for Writing Good Essential Questions

In developing thematic units for and with students, teachers need to develop good essential questions. An essential question serves as a conceptual organizer for a theme and should be broad enough to include inquiry and thinking from several disciplines. Hayes Jacobs suggests the following criteria be followed:

1. Every child needs to understand the meaning of the question. Teachers cannot write the unit-focusing question with the heavy hand of syntax or vocabulary. The question "What is air?" is easy to read but takes inquiry and research to answer.

2. The wording of the question should be written in a broad enough way so that it is distinct and can generate learning experiences and activities for students.

3. The question should reflect the teacher's conceptual priorities. The wording of the question shapes the way students will pursue and examine the unit. Students can participate in the formulation of the question, thereby gaining their commitment to pursue the inquiry.

4. Repetition needs to be avoided when formulating an essential question. Teachers often form a number of tag-on questions related to one conceptual idea. These need to be collapsed so that one essential question can stand on its own.

5. Questions need to be coordinated and sequenced with the period of time planned for a unit or a course of study. Because many teachers allocate from two to eight weeks for an integrated thematic unit, more than one question can be designed. Teachers may wish to have students' input in this decision making and sequencing of the order of the additional questions posed relevant to the theme.

6. Essential questions should be visible in the classroom. This can be done by making a poster or chart showing the question(s) and a schematic map of the theme. Because a number of teachers may be involved in the implementation of one interdisciplinary unit, students see the same essential question(s) as they move from classroom to classroom and see the overall commitment from their teachers.

*Source:* Based on Heidi Hayes-Jacobs, *Mapping the Big Picture: Integrating Curriculum and Assessment K–12* (Alexandria, VA: Association for Supervision and Curriculum Development, 1997).

plan to do. Some of these activities and learning experiences may already be revealed on the curriculum map. However, whereas that map reflects the plan for the entire year, the graphic organizer helps teachers focus on the one theme.

When using this visual organizer, teachers need to decide which of the content headers they want to keep or change. For instance, Figure 5.3 shows that the discipline of the language arts or English is represented in a reading and writing "circle," the arts in another circle, and technology in another. But within the language arts are six domains of processing, those of viewing, speaking, listening, reading, writing, and visually representing; the arts are composed of many forms such as painting, sculpture, dance, music, and photography; and technology is generally used to support learning tasks in disciplines, such as the completion of a report for social studies, the use of a multimedia computer program, or the showing of a film to support content learning within a science topic. Many teachers wish to show writing, art, and technology activities within science, social studies, and field experiences. Therefore these processing means could be embedded within activities that occur in the content disciplines.

In the curriculum mapping approach to curriculum design, the philosophy of academic rationalism is quite strong because the academic disciplines remain the basis for the planning of a unit. However, with the added feature of the essential-question organizer, some of the philosophical notions of cognitive processes and personal relevance are brought into play. The curriculum factors of horizontal and vertical organization, along with the concepts of continuity and sequence, are major elements in achieving an integrated unit of study in the curriculum mapping approach.

## Curriculum Alignment

The design approach of **curriculum alignment** is highly favored by the proponents of standards reform in that alignment of the local curriculum occurs with state and district high-stakes tests (Colby, 1999; Wraga, 1999). Fenwick English (2000) may be considered one of the most prominent curriculum leaders in curriculum alignment design, which can be conceptualized as a triangle with the three key components of teacher, test, and curriculum located at the three angle junctures (see Figure 5.4). The three components connect to or align with one another to ensure that each influences the conduct of the other.

In this design model, we see that because tests are a major component, the teacher has to connect his or her curriculum offerings to the outcomes assessed by the tests being used. Conventional practice has been for teachers, armed with curriculum guides, textbooks, and lesson plans, to begin school in earnest in the fall and institute their own testing and local assessments throughout the year. Through their in-class as-

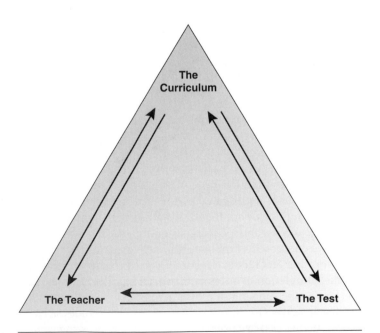

*Figure 5.4* Curriculum Alignment Elements

*Source:* Based on Fenwick W. English, *Deciding What to Teach and Test: Developing, Aligning and Auditing the Curriculum* (Thousand Oaks, CA: Corwin Press, 2000).

sessments they graded students on their content learning performances. When time came to administer the districtwide testing program, teachers took the more centralized testing program in stride and carried out the district plan. Teachers knew that their students might be ranked against others in other districts, cities, states, and at the national level. They waited for the tests to be scored and the results to be sent back through administrative channels so that the results, for better or worse, could be interpreted to parents. Conventional practice, occurring before standards-based reform, revealed that there was little if any congruence between what was taught and what was tested at the district, state, and national levels.

The standards-based movement has introduced a different level of testing or accountability in which the curriculum is connected or aligned with standardized tests or state-developed tests. In this alignment with standards, which now become the driving force behind curriculum, content and performance are bound to change. Achieving the benchmark performances in the district's or state's testing program is now often the critical assessment factor for schools. That is why these tests are called "high-stakes" tests for many stakeholders in the school community (McCabe, 2003).

The importance placed on high-stakes testing does influence the other two components of Fenwick's design. Teachers will tend to teach to the test if important decisions are felt to be related to test outcomes. Because of this emphasis on test results, the curriculum shrinks in content and learning experiences, and testing begins to define the priorities of schooling (Eisner, 2001). Instruction that focuses on test practice results in teaching and learning that operates at low cognitive levels (Kreitzer & Madaus, 1995). Instead of punishing teachers and schools for failing to show good test grades for their students, standards reformers need to ensure that curriculum offerings are aligned fairly with how the school actually implements and formally tests its programs (Gratz, 2000).

A somewhat similar model is a curriculum design called **backward design.** The process has a design sequence of three stages: (1) identifying desired results; (2) determining acceptable evidence; and (3) planning learning experiences and instruction (Wiggins & McTighe, 1998). Rather than enter a curriculum unit with lessons, textbooks, and favored activities, backward design requires that teachers look ahead to the end—the end being the first stage, the identification and achievement of desired results that arise from identified goals or standards. Teachers reflect on what their students should know, understand, and be able to do. They consider their goals, review the content standards established by the state and district, and generally examine curriculum expectations. They establish curriculum priorities by considering three levels of content understandings: (1) those understandings worth being familiar with, (2) important knowledge and skills, and (3) "enduring understandings (Wiggins & McTighe, 1998, p. 10.)" The last refers to those big ideas and important understandings that focus on larger concepts, principles, or processes. **Enduring understandings** are intended to live on in the learner's mind to be applied to and assimilated with future learning.

During stage 2 of the backward-design process, teachers consider what assessment methods they would use to determine if their students have achieved the desired results and standards set out in the first stage. Once teachers have identified the results and enduring understandings they wish to achieve and have charted the assessments they plan to use to demonstrate mastery of results, teachers enter stage 3, the planning of learning experiences and instruction. Here teachers will consider the procedures students need to perform, the activities they will engage in, how they will be taught and mentored, and the materials and resources needed to accomplish the desired results. Note once again that in the backward-design process the specifics of instructional planning—meaning the choices made about the scope and sequencing of lessons and use of resource materials—occurs after the desired results and assessments have been identified and charted.

Because assessment is such a strong feature of both curriculum alignment and backward design, these curriculum strategies include a technical orientation to operationalize testing at the outset of the curriculum process and to closely align the curriculum offerings. The idea is to align the subject-matter content and learning activities with the standards. In fact, the designers of the backward-design model state that their curriculum perspective consists of a specific plan that includes identified lessons derived from content and performance standards (Wiggins & McTighe, 1998).

## A Principles Approach for Diverse Learners

One approach to curriculum is based on a core of six architectural principles for presenting instruction to diverse learners who bring unique characteristics to learning situations. Diverse learners are identified as those who bring instructional, experiential, cultural, socioeconomic, linguistic, and physiological diversity to the classrooms of today. They need different and oftentimes additional requirements to curriculum offerings and instruction (Kameenui & Carine, 1998).

Improved learning can be achieved when accommodating the differing characteristics of diverse learners when instruction brings together and implements the following six principles: Big Ideas, Conspicuous Strategies, Mediated Scaffolding, Strategic Integration, Primed Background Knowledge, and Judicious Review. These six architectural principles can be applied across the core subjects, as well as in reading and writing.

**Big ideas** are those concepts, principles, or design frameworks that present and incorporate a broad band of knowledge. They often reside at the heart of a discipline (subject) or can be integrated through several or a number of disciplines. For instance, consider the writing process. The stages of composing, planning, drafting, reviewing, editing, and proofing are the same whether in the language arts, science, or social studies class. The process is based on the same series and recycling of steps. In whichever class or course of study a paper or report is produced, students follow the big idea of how to write, whether using pen, pencil, or computer.

Regardless of the discipline, there is a "big idea" of how to approach a reading or a book. Most students, when presented with a reading assignment, usually turn to the beginning page and word and start off without a prior thought or plan in their head of what they might be doing or attempting to learn. Teachers and students can reach a common big idea foundation by considering how to approach the reading, whether literature or content based, to maximize the learning experience. A big idea in science is the steps of the scientific process, and a big idea in social studies is that event sequencing and causal relationships account for the unfolding of history. The big idea is akin to an essential question posed by students and teachers to serve as an organizer of integrated themes.

**Conspicuous strategies** are those strategies and learning tools that are made conspicuous to students to help them learn better and well. Such a strategy is not taught and practiced as a one-time shot, as might occur for note taking, underlining, or graphic organizing, but has transfer value and other applications. Students are shown the strategy workings of the good writer, the good reader or the inquisitive scientist so that they can follow similar steps in accomplishing learning tasks. Because two major problems experienced by diverse learners are remembering (poor memory skills) and vocabulary understanding (Kameenui & Carnine, 1998), we suggest that teachers design conspicuous strategies to help these learners organize information and connect new word learnings to existing knowledge, particularly through narrative and content area readings. See Box 5.7.

**Mediated scaffolding** is providing support during learning tasks so that students are guided through the procedures or steps of a learning activity in the most predictably successful way or in ways that allow them to reach goals that may have seemed unattainable (Churton, Cranston-Gingras, & Blair, 1998).

Many diverse learners may not have had rich language exposure to English or the opportunity to use English during their early years and may have limited background experiences to deal with school-related tasks. Teachers need to scaffold the steps of new learning experiences so that the new can be integrated and accommodated with the old. This can occur by initially discussing the series of step so that the language of the steps has been perceived (though possibly not fully understood by students), followed by the careful unfolding of each step with feedback provided by the teacher. Once all the steps have been accomplished with some degree of individual success, the students then practice the steps under the watchful but supportive eye of the teacher. Finally, students apply the strategy on their own and display, through an activity or product, that the steps have been properly internalized and understood. Ownership of the strategy is now proceeding forward.

**Strategic integration** refers to the integration of content and strategies when the "mix" is right, or strategic, for students. When knowledge elements relate naturally within a discipline or across disciplines, teachers should combine or integrate information in ways that help diverse learners see and understand complex relationships. A good example is word problems in the general discipline of mathematics. Most teachers tell us that many diverse learners, especially those with limited vocabularies and English language background, have difficulty performing arithmetic word problems but do well in computational mathematics. This difficulty may be due to the specific vocabulary of the written word problems and the causal relationships students have to comprehend in the wording of the problem.

The idea behind **primed background knowledge** is discussed in some detail in Chapter 2 (see the Importance of Prior Knowledge section).

**BOX 5.7** Assisting Diverse Learners in Curriculum Offerings and Instruction

Diverse learners bring cultural, experiential, linguistic, physiological, and socioeconomic diversity to the classrooms of today. Two major problems they face in learning tasks are poor reading recall and limited vocabulary understanding. By using conspicuous strategies to help these students remember and organize information while using the new vocabulary of the learning experience, teachers would help these students build on their prior knowledge and succeed in new learning tasks.

With diverse learners in particular, when information is presented that is novel or re-moved from students' background experiences and knowledge base, teachers need to prime that background knowledge, fill in gaps, and possibly use means other than ver-bal language to assist in providing background information. This is where introducing films, pictures, and related artifacts before an actual lesson begins helps. By providing background experiences so that students can see as well as listen to the language used for the new concepts and topics, those who might otherwise have difficulty with the reading and the new vocabulary are afforded a greater opportunity to succeed. An adage taught us as beginning teachers still rings true today, especially when instructing diverse learners: "The deeper the concept density of a topic to be read, the more time should be given to readiness in preparing for that topic."

**Judicious review** is the process of aiding recall and memory of taught material so that it can be truly learned. Review needs to be considered judiciously by teachers so that it doesn't become just "drill and practice" of the same material again and again. If well-designed conspicuous strategies were initially used to teach big ideas, teachers have pro-vided a means of organizing information to help students relate major ideas and details so that they can be remembered. By planning other activities and strategies that help students use the same information and concept vocabulary, teachers help students prac-tice the new ideas, thereby aiding memory and fluency. Then, by gradually reducing the scaffolding steps so that students become more personally involved with both the con-cept ideas and the material, teachers increase students' ability to retain and learn new information (Kameenui & Carnine, 1998).

You can see that the six principles above provide the basis for good sound teaching regardless of students' abilities and background experiences. However, because diverse learners often lag behind their classmates in content learning and academic perfor-mance, the six interlocking principles provide a strong conceptual curriculum frame-work for teachers in providing instruction to this ever-growing group of students. Currently, one-third of the elementary school population is made up of children of racial or ethnic minorities, 5 percent of all school-age children speak a language other than English at home, and 20 percent of U.S children come from immigrant families (Sapon-Shevin, 2000–2001). The director of the Center for Demographic Policy notes that in the next two decades about 65 percent of U.S. population growth will occur from "minority" groups, particularly from Hispanic and Asian immigrants (Hodgkinson, 2000–2001).

Because of a number of social, cultural, and economic factors such as the rapid growth of demographic groups, poverty, the changing composition of the traditional family, and the relationship of home experiences to school expectations, diverse learn-ers bring learning characteristics to the classroom that offer instructional challenges to teachers (Churton, Cranston-Gingras, & Blair, 1998; Kameenui & Carnine, 1998; Rasinksi & Podak, 2000). Rather than separate diverse learners into different camps, such as discussing multiculturalism separately from students with disabilities, teachers should be shown how diversity issues are connected and how they can be addressed in an integrated way in the classroom (Sapon-Shevin & Zollers, 1999). Moreover, teachers and schools need to exhibit high expectations and provide appropriate accommoda-tions so that diverse learners and students with disabilities can succeed with the stan-dards (Glickman, 2000–2001; Kearns, Kleinert, & Kennedy, 1999).

# ■ THE PLANNED AND UNPLANNED CURRICULA

The discussion of curriculum design should include other concepts related to curriculum that have a heavy impact on teaching and learning. While every school has a planned, formal, and acknowledged curriculum, it also has an unplanned, less formal, and hidden one that usually involves social–psychological interactions among students and teachers (Doll, 1996). These interactions involve feelings, attitudes, and behaviors that may overshadow the planned effect of the formal curriculum.

Allan Glatthorn (1999) accounts for eight concepts of curriculum, which he presents as those that are recommended, written, supported, tested, taught, hidden, unintended, and learned. One could turn to a blank page or computer screen and place the headers—Planned and Unplanned—on top in order to organize the relationship of the eight concepts in the teaching and learning process.

The **planned curriculum** column would consist of the recommended curriculum, the written curriculum, the supported curriculum, the tested curriculum, and the taught curriculum. According to Glatthorn, the five planned concepts are described in the following way: (1) The *recommended curriculum* is that proposed by experts in the field. (2) The *written curriculum* is usually a document issued by a state education agency, a school system, a particular school, and/or a specific classroom teacher. At the state and district levels, the written plan usually includes a curriculum guide and scope and sequence factors. (3) The *supported curriculum* is those aspects of the approved curriculum that appear in textbooks, software, and multimedia materials. Some states use a state-adopted system for materials approved for school use, whereas in other states, the text and materials selection falls to district and/or school committees. (4) The *tested curriculum* is that curriculum monitored by standardized tests, competency tests, and performance assessments at the state, school system, and teacher levels. (5) The *taught curriculum* is those features and factors of the curriculum that are actually operationalized and taught by teachers. Research indicates that substantial variation occurs in the nature of what is actually taught, despite an aura of uniformity.

In the **hidden,** or unintended **curriculum,** students and teachers learn from one another, from the cultures that are brought into the classroom, and from the school's or district's practices and policies. What some students wear to school, how they look, and how they talk may be more important to many other students than what teachers are trying to do in the planned curriculum. If some students don't have access to computers in schools, the unintended policy message may be that computers aren't important to those students.

The **excluded curriculum** offerings are those that aren't featured; they have been left out either by accident or design. One noted educator believes that the truly important variables in education are not found in our classrooms and schools, but are located outside of schools as students cope with the issues and problems of the larger society (Eisner, 2001). Perhaps some educators and curriculum specialists feel that there is too much to cover in particular content areas or that certain topics are too unpleasant for students to be confronted with at such early ages. When westward expansion is covered, for example, little emphasis is given to the plight of the animals and peoples who inhabited the regions as the newcomers traversed them and settled. Not until an eighth or ninth grader sees the movie *Dances with Wolves* might a different perspective and attitude develop toward the newcomers.

Finally, there's the **learned curriculum,** which Glatthorn (1999) suggests is the "bottom line" or the most important. Under which of the two columns—Planned or Unplanned—would you, the teacher or reader, place the learned curriculum? Your rational mind wants to place it under Planned because this is where all of the professional efforts of the district, school, and classroom have gone. However, your common sense tells you that what was not planned also may have had a great influence on some students. Why, you ask, did some students not do well on the state and district performance assessments, and why did some not achieve well on your locally devised tests to show mastery of curriculum content? Was the curriculum content presented well enough for all? Were enough conspicuous strategies used to capture big, central, or thematic ideas? Did you scaffold and review enough so that students could internalize difficult content and thereby really learn it?

These questions return the teacher, the key figure in the implementation of curriculum, to the planning and delivery of instruction. Figure 5.1 shows that the four major components of curriculum—goals, content, learning activities, and evaluation—are influenced both by one's framework or perspective and by the factors stressed in a particular approach of curriculum design. Thus the various curriculum design approaches and components discussed in this chapter have a bearing on how content and learning activities are structured and offered for instruction. Knowing about the components of curriculum design and the frameworks or perspectives that influence curriculum design will help you be a successful teacher.

## ■ SUMMARY ■

1. An educator's philosophy and view of how student's learn influences how that educator stresses the four major components—objectives, subject matter, learning experiences or activities, and evaluation—of curriculum design.

2. The factors of curriculum design having to do with organization, scope, sequence, continuity, integration, articulation, and balance are weighed by curriculum specialists and teachers as they plan their curriculum offerings.

3. The curriculum integration approach allows students to integrate personal and social experiences as they investigate problems and issues that cut across traditional subject-area boundaries.

4. The curriculum mapping approach shows teachers how to present a thematic unit to students by integrating traditional content topics and units at a specified time.

5. The three major elements of teacher, test, and curriculum align and influence one another in the curriculum alignment approach, an approach highly favored by supporters of standards-based education.

6. The six interlocking principles offered for diverse learners provide a strong curriculum guide for teachers who provide instruction to such learners.

## ■ QUESTIONS TO CONSIDER ■

1. Why is it important to know about the broad perspectives or orientations that influence curriculum approaches?

2. Why might stressing one curriculum factor more than others result in a distortion of good educational practices?

3. How are the curriculum integration and curriculum mapping approaches somewhat similar in approach yet different in how they view the subject-matter disciplines?
4. Why is the curriculum alignment design approach favored by those who believe strongly in standards and accountability?

5. How are curriculum design considerations different from those of instruction?

## ■ THINGS TO DO ■

1. Make a grid or chart showing how you plan for and/or implement the curriculum design factors of organization, scope, sequence, continuity, integration, articulation, and balance.
2. To involve students in the collaborative planning process of curriculum integration, place the basic questions "What questions or concerns do you have about yourself?" and "What questions or concerns do you have about the world?" on the chalkboard and see if students can group and connect ideas to generate themes and concepts for investigative projects.
3. Plan a thematic unit with one or several colleagues, with each teacher constructing a curriculum map based on months of the year and the discipline topics taught each month. See how the group of teachers can reconfigure their content offerings to accomplish an interdisciplinary thematic unit.
4. Take the principles approach for diverse learners to see how you can form "big ideas" of teaching and interrelating content while connecting the remaining five principles to help such learners learn the content.
5. Using children's literature, plan a literature thematic unit for your grade level. You could focus on a particular author, genre, or topic your students find most interesting. After you and your students have identified the theme focus, you could elicit the support of the school or community libraries to place selected books on reserve.

## ■ RECOMMENDED READINGS ■

Beane, James A. *Curriculum Integration: Designing the Core of Democratic Education.* New York: Teachers College Press, 1997. Explains a curriculum design in which students integrate personal and social experiences to investigate problems and issues that cut across subject-area boundaries.

Eisner, Elliot. *The Educational Imagination,* 3rd ed. New York: McMillan, 1993. Provides expansive views of what should be included in curriculum and course offerings.

English, Fenwick W. *Deciding What to Teach and Test: Developing, Aligning and Auditing the Curriculum.* Thousand Oaks, CA: Corwin Press, 2000. A curriculum alignment model based on the three major components of test, teacher, and curriculum.

Glatthorn, Allan, and Jerry Jailall. "Curriculum for the New Millennium," in R. S. Brandt, ed., *Education in a New Era: ASCD Yearbook.* Alexandria, VA: Association for Supervision and Curriculum Development, 2000. Presents five curriculum frameworks that have been prominent in education's past and present and how they merge in influence to produce curriculum streams.

Hayes-Jacobs, Heidi. *Mapping the Big Picture: Integrating Curriculum and Assessment, K–12.* Alexandria, VA: Association for Supervision and Curriculum Development, 1997. Shows how to implement the curriculum mapping approach by integrating the content disciplines to achieve a central theme.

Kameenui, Edward J., and Douglas W. Carnine. *Effective Teaching Strategies That Accommodate Diverse Learners.* Upper Saddle River, NJ: Merrill, 1998. Presents six principles to follow when instructing diverse learners in the core subjects and in reading and writing.

Wiggins, Grant, and Jay McTighe. *Understanding by Design.* Alexandria, VA: Association for Supervision and Curriculum Development, 1998. Explores a backward-design model of curriculum planning that develops in three stages.

## ■ KEY TERMS ■

articulation
backward design
balance
big ideas
conspicuous strategies
continuity
curriculum alignment
curriculum design
curriculum integration

curriculum mapping
curriculum plan
enduring understandings
essential questions
excluded curriculum
hidden curriculum
horizontal organization
integration
judicious review

learned curriculum
mediated scaffolding
multidisciplinary
planned curriculum
primed background knowledge
scope
sequence
strategic integration
vertical organization

## ■ REFERENCES ■

Atwell, N. (1998). *In the middle: A framework for literacy* (2nd ed.). Upper Saddle River, NJ: Prentice Hall.

Banks, L. R. (1999). *The Indian in the cupboard.* New York: Morrow/Avon.

Barzun, J., with Wattenberg, R. (Eds.). (2002, Fall). Curing provincialism: Why we educate the way we do. *American Educator,* 6, 10–11, 42.

Baumann, J. (1991, Spring). Editorial comment: Of rats and pigeons: Skills and whole language. *Reading Psychology,* iii–xiii.

Beane, J. A. (1997). *Curriculum integration: Designing the core of democratic education.* New York: Teachers College Press, Columbia University.

Brady, M. (2000, May). The standards juggernaut. *Phi Delta Kappan,* 649–651.

Bruner, J. S. (1959). *The process of education.* Cambridge, MA: Harvard University Press.

Calkins, L. (1994). *The art of teaching writing* (2nd ed.). Portsmouth, NH: Heinemann.

Caulfield, J., Kidd, S., & Kotcher, T. (2000, November). Brain-based instruction in action. *Educational Leadership,* 62–65.

Chall, J. (1996). *Stages of reading development* (2nd ed.). New York: Harcourt Brace College.

Churton, M., Cranston-Gingras, A., & Blair, T. (1998). *Teaching children with diverse abilities.* Boston: Allyn and Bacon.

Colby, S. (1999, March). Grading in a standards-based system. *Educational Leadership,* 52–55.

Collier, J. (1997). *My brother Sam is dead.* New York: Scholastic.

Commission on the Reorganization of Secondary Education. (1918). *Cardinal principles of secondary education.* Washington, DC: Government Printing Office.

Dewey, J. (1933). *How we think: A restatement of the relation of reflective thinking to the educative process.* New York: D. C. Heath.

Doll, R. C. (1996). *Curriculum improvement: Decision making and process* (9th ed.). Boston: Allyn and Bacon.

Eisner, E. (1993). *The educational imagination* (3rd ed.). New York: Macmillan.

Eisner, E. W. (2001, January). What does it mean to say a school is doing well? *Phi Delta Kappan,* 367–372.

English, F. W. (2000). *Deciding what to teach and test: Developing, aligning and auditing the curriculum.* Thousand Oaks, CA: Corwin Press.

Erdoes, R. (1997). Glooscap and the baby; Dancing stars. *American Indian Myths and Legends*. Magnolia, MA: Peter Smith.

Finders, M., & Hynds, S. (2003). *Literacy lessons: Teaching and learning with middle school students*. Upper Saddle River, NJ: Merrill/Prentice Hall.

Flippo, R. (1999, October). Redefining the reading wars: The war against reading researchers. *Educational Leadership*, 38–41.

Gardner, H. (1997, September). The first seven . . . and the eighth: A conversation with Howard Gardner. *Educational Leadership*, 8–13.

Giles, H. H., McCutchen, S. P., & Zechiel, A. N. (1942). *Exploring the curriculum*. New York: Harper.

Glatthorn, A. A. (1999, Fall). Curriculum alignment revisited. *Journal of Curriculum and Supervision*, 26–34.

Glatthorn, A., & Jailall, J. (2000). Curriculum for the new millennium. In R. S. Brandt (Ed.), *Education in a new era: ASCD yearbook* (pp. 97–121). Alexandria, VA: Association for Supervision and Curriculum Development.

Glickman, C. (2000–2001, December/January). Holding sacred ground: The impact of standardization. *Educational Leadership*, 46–51.

Goodlad, J. I., & Su, Z. (1992). Organization and the curriculum. In P. W. Jackson (Ed.), *Handbook of research on curriculum* (pp. 327–344). New York: Macmillan.

Gratz, D. (2000, May). High standards for whom? *Phi Delta Kappan*, 681–687.

Graves, D. (1983). *Writing: Teachers and children at work*. Portsmouth, NH: Heinemann.

Hayes-Jacobs, H. (1997). *Mapping the big picture: Integrating curriculum & assessment K–12*. Alexandria, VA: Association for Supervision and Curriculum Development.

Hirsch, E. D., Jr. (2002, Summer). The benefit to equity. *American Educator*, 16–17.

Hodgkinson, H. (2000–2001, December/January). Educational demographics: What teachers should know. *Educational Leadership*, 6–11.

Jalongo, M. R. (2000). *Early childhood language arts* (2nd ed.). Boston: Allyn and Bacon.

Kameenui, E. J., & Carnine, D. W. (1998). *Effective teaching strategies that accommodate diverse learners*. Upper Saddle River, NJ: Merrill.

Kearns, J. F., Kleinert, H., & Kennedy, S. (1999, March). We need not exclude anyone. *Educational Leadership*, 33–38.

Kellaghan, T., Madaus, G., & Raczek, A. (1996). *The use of external examinations to improve student motivation*. Washington, DC: American Educational Research Association.

Kreitzer, A., & Madaus, G. (1995). The test-driven curriculum. In D. Tanner & J. W. Keefe (Eds.), *Curriculum issues and the new century* (pp. 23–37). Reston, VA: National Association of Secondary School Principals.

Martin, R. (1998). *The rough face girl*. New York: Putnam.

Maslin, J., & Nelson, M. (2002, April). Peering into the future: Students using technology to create literacy products. *The Reading Teacher*, 628–631.

McCabe, P. (2003, September). Enhancing self-efficacy for high-stakes reading tests. *The Reading Teacher*, 12–20.

Ornstein, A., & Hunkins, F. P. (2004). *Curriculum: Foundations, principles, and issues* (4th ed.). Boston: Allyn and Bacon.

Piaget, J. (1960). *The psychology of intelligence*. Paterson, NJ: Littlefield Adams.

Rasinski, T., & Padak, N. (2000). *Effective reading strategies: Teaching children who find reading difficult* (2nd ed.). Upper Saddle River, NJ: Prentice Hall.

Rice, D. (2002, March). Using trade books in teaching elementary science: Facts and fallacies. *The Reading Teacher*, 552–565.

Roser, N., & Keehn, S. (2002, February). Fostering thought, talk, and inquiry: Linking literature and social studies. *The Reading Teacher*, 416–426.

Sapon-Shevin, M. S., & Zollers, N. (1999, July–September). Multicultural and disability agendas in teacher education: Preparing teachers for diversity. *Leadership in Education*, 165–190.

Sapon-Shevin, M. S. (2000–2001, December/January), Schools fit all. *Educational Leadership*, 34–39.

Saylor, J. G., Alexander, W. M., & Lewis, A. J. (1981). *Planning for better teaching and learning* (4th ed.). New York: Holt, Rinehart.

Schmidt, P. R., Gillen, S., Zollo, T. C., & Stone, R. (2002, March). Literacy learning and scientific inquiry: Children respond. *The Reading Teacher,* 534–548.

Sinatra, R. (1994). A scenario: Using an integrated language arts approach for at-risk students. *ASCD curriculum handbook* (pp. 3.89–3.99). Alexandria, VA: Association for Supervision and Curriculum Development.

Smith, B. O., Stanley, W. O., & Shores, H. J. (1957). *Fundamentals of curriculum development* (Rev. ed.). New York: Hartcourt, Brace.

Smith, F. (1999, November). Why systematic phonics and phonemic awareness instruction constitute an educational hazard. *Language Arts,* 150–155.

Taba, H. (1962). *Curriculum development: Theory and practice.* New York: Harcourt Brace.

Tyler, R. W. (1947). *Basic principles of curriculum and instruction.* Chicago: University of Chicago Press.

Wiggins, G., & McTighe, J. (1998). *Understanding by design.* Alexandria, VA: Association for Supervision and Curriculum Development.

Wood, G. H. (1988). Democracy and the curriculum. In L. E. Beyer & M. W. Apple (Eds.), *The curriculum: Problems, politics, and possibilities* (pp. 166–190). Albany: State University of New York Press.

Wraga, W. (1999, Fall). The educational and political implications of curriculum alignment and standard-based reform. *Journal of Curriculum and Supervision,* 4–25.

## chapter 6

# Instructional Planning

*Focusing Questions*

1. How do teachers plan for instruction? At what levels do they plan?
2. What are the main components of a unit plan?
3. What are the main components of a lesson plan?
4. How do unit and lesson plans facilitate teaching and instruction?
5. How does course mapping help the teacher accomplish unit and lesson planning?
6. Why is it important for teachers to vary instructional methods and combine components of direct and indirect instruction?
7. How do sample daily schedules and lesson plans provide useful ideas for teachers for planning purposes?

In the previous chapters we noted that curriculum is defined and shaped by a number of factors. Chapter 4 showed us that districts and schools are guided by aims, goals, and national, state, and district standards so that their departments and teachers can plan general and specific objectives for course work, units of study, and individual lessons. Chapter 5 presented the four major components of a curriculum plan and particular frameworks and designs that districts, schools, and teachers can consult in implementing their curriculum initiatives. This chapter examines instructional planning, which focuses on the curriculum plan's two primary components—the content or subject matter to be learned and the learning experiences and activities that teachers use to help students learn the content.

# ■ PLANNING FOR INSTRUCTION

Effective instructional planning at the classroom level is based on knowledge of (1) the general goals and curriculum perspectives of the school, (2) the objectives of a course or subject, (3) students' abilities, aptitudes, needs, and interests, (4) content to be included and appropriate units into which the subject can be divided, and (5) techniques of short-range instruction or lesson planning. Authors have likened the role of the teacher in the instructional planning process to that of an architect (Newby, Stepich, Lehman, & Russell, 2000; Wiggins & McTighe, 1998). The architect designs a plan, a blueprint, of what a structure will look like for the population to be served. Similarly, teachers take principles of learning and instruction to their constituents by designing specific plans of how to use instructional materials with particular activities to learn specific context (Smith & Ragan, 1999).

Even though planning for instruction at the school and district level is usually a collaborative effort of administrators, supervisors, and teachers, it is the individual teacher who delivers and implements instruction once the classroom doors are closed. To implement successfully, teachers generate long- and short-term plans to orchestrate learning activities for subject-matter content and to accommodate the different ability levels of students. As instructional experts, teachers plan to select those instructional methods and strategies that meet the needs of all their students in order to fill the gap between students' current and desired levels of skills and knowledge development (Newby et al., 2000). Often teachers modify existing plans or originate their own plans for instruction while remaining cognizant of the state's and district's standards for students and the curriculum design of their school system (see Box 6.1).

**BOX 6.1** When Planning for Instruction, Teachers Consider a Number of Factors and Raise Questions

- How can students become motivated and engaged in learning and how can they be inspired to become lifelong readers?
- What teaching methods and materials can be used to facilitate student learning?
- What literacy strategies will be most effective for different students at different times?
- What resources will be appropriate for a particular lesson indicated in the curriculum plan?
- How should students be arranged or grouped to participate in the learning activities?
- How can technology and computers be integrated to enhance instruction and assist students in the learning process?
- How can standards be implemented successfully in the classroom?

## Levels of Planning

Instructional planning is a form of decision making and occurs through a range of levels from formal planning to informal planning. **Formal planning** is what most educators and researchers recognize as a legitimate and necessary instructional activity. Perhaps it is examined so often simply because it can be prescribed, categorized, and classified. Formal planning is structured and task oriented; it suggests that teaching and instruction can be taught as part of teacher training and staff development. This type of planning would necessarily occur with the various curriculum design approaches presented in Chapter 5.

Formal planning is also the expectation that the educational establishment and individual teachers will confer with professional and community colleagues, especially when planning for standards implementation. Teachers would likewise collaborate with grade-level groups when planning for course, grade, and unit instruction and may engage in formal planning for individual lesson implementation with teacher colleagues, and perhaps students, at a given grade level.

A type of long-range teacher-planning guide is often called a course map or course of study. Such guides in large school districts may be prepared by a committee of experts made up of curriculum specialists and veteran teachers and administrators. They would look, of course, to state guidelines for content and performance standards and the timing of benchmark assessments. Maps can unfold by using the school calendar as a time organizer (Jacobs, 1997), by planning themes in which students are part of the collaborative process (Beane, 1997), or by aligning with the state's testing schedule (English, 2000; Wiggins & McTighe, 1998).

In small school districts, the teachers, working as a group or as individuals, may develop their own map, within limits defined by state standards' documents and district guidelines. As a teacher plans a map, he or she must consider (1) needs assessment data, if available, by the school or district; (2) goals of the school (or school district); (3) preassessment or placement evaluation data of the students, such as reading tests, aptitude tests, self-report inventories, observational reports; and (4) instructional objectives of the course according to district or state standards and guidelines and grade-level or departmental publications (Ornstein, 1990).

**Course mapping** identifies and details the content, concepts, skills, and sometimes values to be taught over the entire course. Performing this task places the teacher in a better position to do unit and lesson planning. The mapping process also helps connect the goals and objectives of the course while aligning standards with specific grade levels, concepts, and course work. It helps teachers view the course as a whole and see existing relationships. Mapping requires that the teacher know, before the term or school year begins, what the important content areas, concepts, and skills of the course are. It also suggests that the content area has a core body of knowledge and skills that can be taught and that the content can be connected to specific standards.

Another type of formal planning occurs during **strategic planning,** when teachers make good use of collaborative or joint planning in preparing unit and lesson plans. One object of strategic planning is to help teachers plan together by sharing their teaching experiences (Nebgen, 1991), and another is to consider those variables within the overall school improvement plan that will improve student performance (Carr & Harris, 2001).

**Informal planning** occurs within the context of formal planning. Informal planning occurs over time with instructional practice and is linked to a teacher's beliefs about the nature and purposes of education. A teacher's belief system is based on the values and understandings the teacher holds about the content and process of teaching and the role the teacher plays in the system in which he or she works. These values and beliefs influence the teacher during decision making and actual teaching and make up what has been called the "culture of teaching" (Richards & Lockhart, 1996).

How do the values and beliefs that teachers hold about teaching arise? A team of authors suggests that they come from at least six sources:

1. Experience as former students and how they were taught by different teachers in different contexts. If a teacher learned something well as a former student, the teacher may pass these successful techniques or strategies on to his or her own students.
2. Experience as to what works best in actual teaching practice. A teacher builds up "pet" strategies over time and uses these rather than others in different class situations.
3. Established practices of their school or district. These practices have worked successfully and teachers buy into what the system has encouraged its staff to use.
4. Connection to the teacher's personal style of teaching and learning. For example, a teacher may enjoy using technology and computers and offers this opportunity to his or her students in many learning contexts.
5. From course work or in-service education a teacher learns of a new approach, classroom organizational pattern, or technique and plans to apply it in the classroom.
6. From a particular philosophy, approach, or method that promotes particular teaching and learning principles that the teacher consistently prefers to use in the classroom. For instance if a teacher believes the principles of whole language and uses a constructivist approach, he or she applies the principles across subject matter domains (Kindsvatter, Wilen, & Isher, 1996).

Planning a course, unit, or individual lesson involves formal and informal decision making in two areas: (1) *subject-matter knowledge,* concerning organization and presentation of content, knowledge of student understanding of content, and knowledge of how to teach the content, and (2) *pedagogical knowledge,* concerning teaching activities such as diagnosing, grouping, managing, and evaluating students and implementing instructional activities and learning experiences (Grossman, 1993; Gudmundsdottir, 1991; Solas, 1992). Both kinds of knowledge are needed for effective instructional planning. Most teachers have initial knowledge of subject matter and then build expertise in various aspects of pedagogical knowledge as they develop classroom instructional experience.

In studies of experienced teachers, research has shown that teachers emphasize subject-matter knowledge or content and instructional activities when planning daily lessons. Of the four major parts of curriculum design, they spend the least amount of time on planning objectives, focusing instead on content, materials, resources, and learning activities (Clark, 1991). Possibly from the teacher's point of view, objectives need not be explicitly stated because they are implicit in the actual content and activities of the lesson. According to one author, a lot of what happens in the classroom cannot be designed in advance because much of teaching is based on impulse and imagination (Eisner, 1993). Yet, according to others, collaborative planning in particular has an important influence on the behavior of beginning teachers in that they tend to consider content and activities, as well as pedagogy, in groups, by themselves, or with mentors. What teachers plan together is associated with classroom instruction and student performance on tests (Lalik & Niles, 1990; Wildman, Magliaro, Niles, & Niles, 1992).

For effective classroom instruction, a valuable aspect of informal teacher planning is the reflective thinking that teachers engage in when they plan lessons or units beforehand and continue to engage in as their lessons develop. Often an exact weekly or daily lesson plan is sketchily outlined. Much of what happens is a reflection of what happened in other years when a similar lesson was taught. The structure develops as the teaching–learning process unfolds and as teachers and students interact in the classroom. Many actions related to planning cannot be predetermined in a classroom of thirty students or more who are rapidly interacting with their teacher and one another.

**Mental planning** is the teacher's spontaneous response to events in the classroom; the teacher considers situations and responds intuitively. Of course, that intuition is often well-grounded in subject-matter and pedagogical knowledge. Mental planning is a part of teaching that is crucial for effectiveness, but it cannot be easily observed, recorded, or detailed. Therefore it often goes unnoticed and unmentioned as part of the planning process. Mental planning suggests that teaching is an art that cannot be planned in advance—that a theory of teaching or a principles (or methods) approach to teaching cannot easily be determined or agreed on. But mental planning is a practical, common, and effective method of instructional planning.

A type of mental planning that occurs while a lesson is unfolding is called a **teachable moment.** Such a moment often occurs when a particular skill, process, or bit of knowledge can be inserted into an unfolding lesson because the timing is right. If the students are inquisitive and curious at that point, then it might be wise to be spontaneous and enlarge their horizons with the added material.

However, the decision to seize the teachable moment, or to let it go because the point of the actual lesson may be interrupted, rests squarely on the shoulders of the teacher. In one instance, a fifth-grade teacher was conducting a science lesson with low-achieving, inner-city fifth graders on the topic of stormy weather conditions. When the textual reading presented the wind velocity during snow blizzards in kilometers instead of miles, the teacher decided at that moment to show students how to make the arithmetic conversion. Such a mental decision, he realized afterwards, was not a wise one. Why? The students were diverted from the "big picture" focus on violent storms and their characteristics to arithmetic calculations of changing kilometers to miles. This diversion took valuable class time, particularly because many students struggled with the arithmetic and the teacher couldn't let their calculations pass until they were all correct.

This section discussed the range of decision making that accompanies the instructional planning process. Much of decision making occurs at a formal planning level. This level of planning is recognized by the educational establishment as a purposeful and necessary instructional activity. Collaboration usually occurs among teachers, administrators, specialists, and others to plan for effective instruction of content to various levels of students in alignment with district and state objectives. Informal planning works in concert with formal planning but is generally the domain of the individual teacher. A teacher activates informal decision making based on his or her educational beliefs, values, and experiences; based on prior success with instructional practices; and based on the reflective thinking that occurs as a lesson is unfolding. Figure 6.1 shows that formal and informal planning activities achieved through efforts pursued by the institution or individual come together in actual, observable teacher plans that become the basis of instruction.

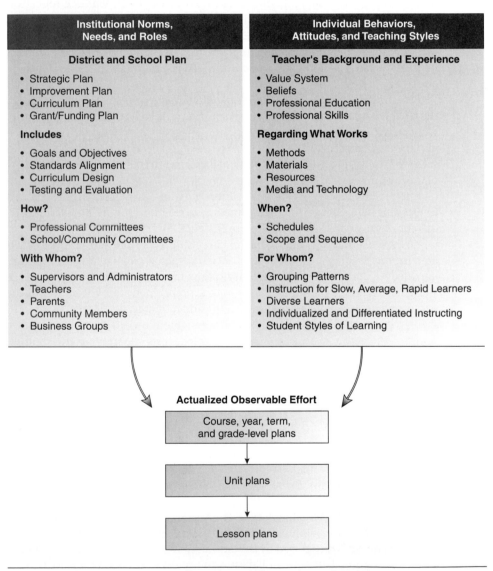

| Institutional Norms, Needs, and Roles | Individual Behaviors, Attitudes, and Teaching Styles |
|---|---|
| **District and School Plan** | **Teacher's Background and Experience** |
| • Strategic Plan<br>• Improvement Plan<br>• Curriculum Plan<br>• Grant/Funding Plan | • Value System<br>• Beliefs<br>• Professional Education<br>• Professional Skills |
| **Includes** | **Regarding What Works** |
| • Goals and Objectives<br>• Standards Alignment<br>• Curriculum Design<br>• Testing and Evaluation | • Methods<br>• Materials<br>• Resources<br>• Media and Technology |
| **How?** | **When?** |
| • Professional Committees<br>• School/Community Committees | • Schedules<br>• Scope and Sequence |
| **With Whom?** | **For Whom?** |
| • Supervisors and Administrators<br>• Teachers<br>• Parents<br>• Community Members<br>• Business Groups | • Grouping Patterns<br>• Instruction for Slow, Average, Rapid Learners<br>• Diverse Learners<br>• Individualized and Differentiated Instructing<br>• Student Styles of Learning |

**Actualized Observable Effort**

Course, year, term, and grade-level plans

Unit plans

Lesson plans

*Figure 6.1* Two Planning Routes for Classroom Instruction

## Planning by Types of Instruction

Teachers engage in five types of planning: yearly, term, unit, weekly, and daily. Planning at each level involves a set of goals, sources of information, forms or outlines, and criteria for judging the effectiveness of planning. Whereas yearly and term planning usually are framed around state and school district standards documents, recommendations, or curriculum guides, unit, weekly, and daily lesson planning permits wider latitude for teachers to develop their own plans. At the elementary school level, the principal or assistant principal is usually considered the instructional leader and is responsible for checking and evaluating teachers' plans. At the junior high school level, the chair of the various subject or academic areas usually performs this professional role and works with teachers to improve instructional planning.

Some research indicates that middle grade teachers rely most heavily on (1) previous successes and failures, (2) district curriculum guides, (3) textbook content, (4) student interest, (5) classroom management factors, (6) school calendar, and (7) prior experience when they plan at the yearly or term levels. At the unit, weekly, and daily levels, they are mostly influenced by (1) availability of materials, (2) student interest, (3) schedule interruptions, (4) school calendar, (5) district curriculum guides, (6) textbook content, (7) classroom management, (8) classroom activity flow, and (9) prior experience (D. S. Brown, 1988; D. Brown, 1993). It seems that during planning, veteran teachers use time-honored instructional routines for monitoring and managing students and for coordinating classroom activities.

But teachers need to consider variety and flexibility in planning, as well as structure and routine, when they consider students' different developmental needs and interests. Some students, especially high achievers, divergent thinkers, and independent learners, learn more in nonstructured and independent situations. Teachers dealing with these students may favor the curriculum integration design proposed by James Beane (1997). Many low achievers, convergent thinkers, and dependent learners prefer highly structured and directed environments. Teachers working with these students and diverse learners experiencing language, socioeconomic, and cultural differences may find the six principles outlined by Kameenui and Carnine (1998) a better approach to follow.

Moreover, many teachers are holistic and intuitive in their planning. They do not use detailed outlines that delineate objectives, content, and activities, but rather use sketchy outlines and last-minute reminders. Some teachers—usually self-confident and experienced ones—prefer not to be limited by prescriptive models. Also, subject matter and grade level may be a factor. Some subjects, as well as the early grade levels, may lend themselves to fewer prescriptive class activities and more exploratory activities.

# ■ UNIT PLAN DEVELOPMENT

A **unit plan** is a blueprint for clarifying what content will be taught by what learning experiences during a specific period. It is a segment of the map, course of study, or integration of concepts (topics) related to a central theme. One reason for developing unit plans is related to the theory that learning by wholes is more effective than piece-by-piece learning. Another reason is the need for teachers to plan experiences in advance to meet the different goals, standards, and objectives instituted by the district or state. Advance planning at the unit plan level requires teachers to survey the entire subject and enables them to be more effective in designing and structuring the instructional and evaluation processes (Finders & Hynds, 2003). The overall view it provides helps teachers anticipate problems that may arise, especially in terms of prerequisite content, concepts, and skills. Especially today, with the accent on standards implementation, unit planning helps teachers integrate content and performance standards into units or courses of study.

## Implementing the Unit Plan

The unit plan consists of six basic components: *objectives, content, skills, activities, resources and materials,* and *evaluation.* All should be considered in planning and implementing a unit, although in many cases all six components do not have to be specified. See Table 6.1 for a listing of unit plan features for each component.

### *Table 6.1* Unit Plan Components

1. **Objectives**
   General objectives and specific objectives
   Behavioral objectives or nonbehavioral objectives
   (topics, problems, questions)

2. **Content**
   Standards-based by discipline
   Knowledge (concepts, problem solving, critical thinking)
   Skills (cognitive, affective, psychomotor)
   Values

3. **Skills**
   Work habits
   Discussion and specific communication skills
   Reading skills
   Writing skills
   Note-taking skills
   Dictionary skills
   Reference skills (table of contents, glossary, index,
   card catalog)
   Library skills
   Reporting and research skills
   Computer skills
   Interpreting skills (maps, charts, tables, graphs, legends)
   Inquiry skills (problem solving, experimenting,
   hypothesizing)
   Social skills (respecting rules, accepting criticism,
   poise and maturity, peer acceptance)
   Cooperative and competitive skills (leadership, self-
   concept, participation in group)

4. **Learning activities**
   Lectures and explanations
   Practice and drill
   Grouping activities (buzz sessions, panels, debates,
   forums)
   Role playing, simulations, dramatizations
   Research, writing projects (stories, biographies, logs)
   Experiments
   Field trips
   Reviews

5. **Resources and materials**
   Written materials (books, pamphlets, magazines,
   newspapers)
   Audiovisual materials (films, records, slides, television,
   videotapes)
   Programmed materials
   Computers and appropriate software programs
   Models, replicas, charts, graphs, specimens

6. **Evaluation procedures**
   Demonstrations, exhibits, debates
   Reviews, summaries
   Quizzes, examinations
   Oral reports
   Scoring of written narratives and reports
   Computer project evaluations
   Reteaching
   Remediation
   Special training

*Objectives.*  Objectives can be behavioral or nonbehavioral (topics, problems, questions). Many teachers today use behavioral objectives (involving content and an action word; students will be required to *identify longitude* and *latitude*—the content is longitude and latitude, the action word is *identify*), partly because of recent emphasis on them in the professional literature. The method you use as the core of your plan will depend on your approach and your school's approach to planning units.

*Content.*  The scope of the content is normally outlined, as is the listing of content standards for each grade level by various subject disciplines. The content often includes three major categories: knowledge, skills, and values. The development of skills is usually more important at the elementary school level and with teachers who emphasize mastery learning, although basic skills are emphasized by many educators. Knowledge becomes more important at the middle and junior high school levels and with teachers who emphasize cognitive or inductive learning. Valuing is more a reflection of the individual teacher and school than the specific grade level.

*Skills.*  A list of cognitive and social skills to be developed is sometimes optional. The skills should be based on the content to be taught but sometimes may be listed as separate from the content. Important basic skills to develop include critical reading, skimming and scanning, understanding graphic materials (maps, diagrams, charts, tables), library skills, composition and reporting skills, note-taking skills, homework skills, study skills, social and interpersonal skills, discussion and speaking skills, cooperative and competitive skills, and leadership skills.

*Learning Activities.*  Learning activities, sometimes called *student activities,* should be based on objectives and students' needs and interests. Only special activities, such as guest speakers, field trips, debates and buzz sessions, research reports, projects, experiments, and summative examinations, need be listed. The recurring or common activities can be shown as part of the daily lesson plan.

*Resources and Materials.*  The purpose of including resources and materials in the plan is to guide the teacher in assembling the reading material, including library and research materials, computer programs, and audiovisual equipment needed to carry out instruction. This list at the unit plan level should include only essential resources and materials. A list of resources is often covered in a listing of learning activities and so is sometimes considered an optional element in a unit plan.

*Evaluation Procedures.*  The major evaluation procedures and culminating activities should be included. Today many of these satisfy district performance standards or indicators. These include formative and summative evaluations: student exhibits and demonstrations; summary debates and discussions; oral reports; quizzes and examinations; evaluations of students' written narratives and reports; reteaching in the form of practice, drill, or review; remedial work; and special tutoring or training. Evaluation can be conducted by students or the teacher or both. The intent is to appraise whether the objectives and content standards have been achieved and to obtain information for improving the unit plan. Chapter 13 explores various types of evaluation procedures in depth.

## Approaches to Unit Planning

The teacher might check with his or her supervisor before planning a unit. Some school districts have a preferred approach for developing units, and others permit teachers more latitude. Some supervisors require teachers to submit units for final approval, whereas other supervisors give more professional autonomy to teachers. Below are three basic approaches to unit planning that teachers may wish to consider.

*Theme Approach.* In Chapter 5, we presented two major designs for accomplishing a **theme approach.** Recall the concept of curriculum integration. Here a teacher collaborates with students to generate a theme that encourages the investigation of a significant problem or issue. To solve this problem or issue, students must draw on content and information from a number of content disciplines. Activities and learning experiences are generated to investigate concepts related to the significant problem, issue, or concern (Beane, 1997). Figure 5.2 presents a schematic diagram or web of how a curriculum integration theme would be organized, and the Curriculum Integration section in Chapter 5 indicates how the components of the unit plan are developed.

The second approach to thematic unit organization was driven by the contribution of the separate subject disciplines to develop the concepts of a theme. This approach toward "wholeness" in generating a theme is also known as multisubject, interdisciplinary, or multidisciplinary and is more teacher directed than the curriculum integration approach to a theme. The central issue in a multisubject theme is the notion of "What can each content discipline contribute to the development of the theme?" Although an essential question or issue acts as an organizer for the theme, each separate discipline, selected by one teacher or a pool of teachers, is investigated to determine what content and learning experiences can support the theme development. Figure 5.3 presents an organizational plan showing how content subjects would contribute to the exploration of a central theme, while the discussion of curriculum mapping in Chapter 5 presents procedures, steps, and tips for developing such a unit plan (Jacobs, 1997).

*Topic Approach.* Table 6.2 illustrates the **topic approach.** The unit plan is organized by topic and objectives. Objectives introduce the lesson, but the topics serve as the major basis for outlining the unit. The objectives coincide with the recommendation that content focus on concept skills and values. Note that the objectives (related to knowledge, skills, and values) do not build on one another (they are somewhat independent), nor are they divided into general and specific. The topics are arranged in the order in which they will be treated, much like a table of contents in a textbook. Indeed, it is appropriate to follow a text, as long as it is well planned and the teacher knows when to modify or supplement the text with related activities and materials. Conspicuous strategies can also be used to develop one topic or a number of related topics.

The topics also represent daily lesson plans. The activities listed are nonrecurring, special activities; repeated activities can be listed at the lesson plan level. The activities are listed in the order in which they will occur, but there is no one particular activity listed for each topic. The evaluation component is separate and includes formative and summative test discussion and feedback. Many junior high school teachers rely on a topic approach to unit planning because they are subject or content oriented.

*Table 6.2* Unit Plan: Topic Approach for Social Studies at Middle School Level

I. Objectives
   A. Knowledge
      1. To recognize that the U.S. Constitution is rooted in English law
      2. To identify the causes and events leading to the forming of the U.S. Constitution
      3. To argue the advantages and limitations of the U.S. Constitution
      4. To illustrate how amendments are enacted

II. Cognitive Skills
   A. To expand vocabulary proficiency
   B. To improve research skills
   C. To improve oral reporting skills
   D. To expand reading habits to include historical events and people
   E. To develop debating techniques
   F. To integrate computers in researching of information and for production of written or multimedia reports

III. Social Skills
   A. To develop an understanding that freedom is based on laws
   B. To recognize the obligations of freedom (among free people)
   C. To appreciate how rights are protected
   D. To develop a more positive attitude toward minorities
   E. To develop a more positive attitude toward classmates

IV. Content Topics
   A. Historical background of the Constitution
      1. English common law
      2. Magna Carta
      3. Mayflower Compact
      4. Colonial freedom
      5. Taxation without representation
      6. Boston Tea Party
      7. First and second Constitutional Congress
      8. Declaration of Independence
   B. Bill of Rights and the Constitution
      1. Constitutional Convention
      2. Framing of the Constitution

   3. Bill of Rights
      a. Reasons
      b. Specific freedoms
   4. Powers reserved to the states
   5. Important amendments
      a. Thirteenth, Fourteenth, Fifteenth (slavery, due process, voting rights)
      b. Nineteenth (women's suffrage)
      c. Twentieth (progressive tax)
      d. Twenty-second (two-term limit to presidency)
      e. Others

V. Evaluation
   A. Short quiz for IV.A
   B. Graded reports with specific feedback for each student; half a lesson
   C. Discussion of students' role as citizens in a free society; compare rights and responsibilities of U.S. citizens with rights and responsibilities of students; a full lesson or one day
   D. Unit test; review IV; II. A–E

VI. Activities
   A. Filmstrip or movie introducing part IV.A
   B. List of major points to be discussed in part IV.A; IV.B.1–5
   C. Homework–reading list for each topic or lesson (IV.A; IV.B.1–5)
   D. Television program on "American Freedom" and discussion after IV.A.8
   E. Field trip to historical museum as culminating activity for IV.A and introduction to IV.B
   F. Topics and reports for outside reading, with two-day discussion of reports after IV.B
   G. Two-day debate (with four teams): "What's wrong with our Constitution?" "What's right with our Constitution?" after IV.B.5
   H. Use of computer program simulating events at Constitutional Congress and use of Internet and World Wide Web to research information for reports and presentations

*Activities Approach.* Table 6.3 illustrates a unit approach that deemphasizes topics and objectives (which most units are based on) and emphasizes various activities. The **activities approach** is often used by teachers when they want their students to practice

---

**Table 6.3** Unit Plan: An Activities Approach for Developing New Word Understandings for a Science Topic

**Objectives**
1. To help students learn new content vocabulary
2. To expand students' thinking development by exposing them to different concept-level activities

**Content** (concepts)
1. Particular words describe behaviors and characteristics of certain groups of animals
2. Particular words name the homes of certain animals

**Activities** (class sessions)
1. Introduction of the first chapter, "Animals and Their Behaviors," from the third-grade science textbook
2. Reading, explanation, and discussion of concepts and ideas found in the chapter
3. Reading and discussion of new words marked by boldface print
4. Practice using new words in different activities arranged according to a taxonomy of concept relations:
   a. Use of a synonym activity; here students look at the "Chapter Word Box" and fill in a word that matches the synonym written below a blank in a listing of sentences (for instance "litter" replaces "group")
   b. Use of an antonym activity; here students have to match a word listed in one column that is the opposite in meaning to a word in a second column (camouflage–show)
   c. Use of an associative activity called "link-a-sentence." Here the teacher arranges three columns of phases; the first column contains the noun or noun phrase, the second column has the verb or verb phrase; and the third, the object. Students have to link words and phrases to make a correct meaning sentence, such as "Camouflage/helps animals blend/into their surroundings" and "Many fish/have the features/of fins and scales."
   d. Use of a classifying activity in which students have to select words from a word box that will fit

one of three categories, "types of movement," "parts of animals," "where animals live." The teacher is wise to note that children can list words in more than one category, if appropriate.
   e. Use of an analogy activity in which students have to complete the analogy relationships using one of their new words (travel is to migrate as sleep is to hibernate)
   f. Use of a multiple meaning activity in which three sentences are provided in a group. Two of the sentences use the new word in the same way, while in the third sentence, the word expresses another meaning. For instance, with the word *litter,* two sentences express the meaning of animal young, whereas the third indicates a meaning whereby a person with a broken leg is carried on a stretcher.
5. Check student work as they engage in independent seatwork to complete activity exercises
6. Review and discuss activity exercises with students. Ensure that they correct inappropriate responses and understand the reason underlying the correct response
7. Chapter test related to new vocabulary understandings

**Materials and Resources**
1. Science text
2. Teacher-constructed activity pages allowing students to use vocabulary in different ways
3. Chalkboard and/or chart paper

**Evaluation**
1. End of chapter vocabulary test
2. Optional: Test to determine if students can use the new words appropriately in the writing of novel sentences

**Review**
Review based on evaluation results

with new content or new learning techniques. A range of activities, usually becoming more complicated and difficult, is prepared for students to engage them in such learning tasks as reading new words, using an arithmetic operation, acquiring new vocabulary, or writing various sentence types. In general, the approach is not detailed and assumes a certain amount of flexibility and fill-in as the teacher progresses through the unit. Elementary school teachers use this approach more often than upper grade teachers in order to help their students learn new concepts and skills and to keep younger students actively involved in their academic work.

Table 6.3 shows such an activity approach to helping students learn new content vocabulary. Let's suppose that a third-grade teacher had completed a theme or topic unit on animals and their behaviors and habits. Within this topic were a number of new meaning and concept words that were important not only for understanding this particular topic but also for promoting understanding of other topics. The teacher decides to use word-level comprehension activities as proposed in a well-known taxonomy that carries students through different thinking levels (Pearson & Johnson, 1978). The types of activities encourage students to use the new content words in thinking exercises involving synonyms, antonyms, classifying, analogies, denotative/connotative relationships, and multiple meanings. Thus, focusing on such new content words as *feature, habitat, migrate, camouflage, predator, prey, dart, hibernate, burrow, litter, talons,* and *trait,* the teacher plans an activity approach to have students use these new words according to the thinking relations.

## Guidelines for Developing Unit Plans

The number of units, the time allotted, and the necessary emphasis for each unit are matters of judgment, though school practitioners tend to recommend about fifteen to thirty units for a year's course and about five to ten lessons per unit. Consideration is usually given to the emphasis suggested by state and school districts in standards implementation, how curriculum guides and textbooks will be used, and the special abilities, needs, and interests of the students. Also, according to test specialists, there is an increasing tendency for teachers to plan units around national, state, and school district testing programs in what is sometimes called "outcome-based" instruction or "high-stakes" evaluation (Mehrens, 1992; Popham, 2001; Willis, 1999). These evaluations are usually aligned with the benchmark performance assessments of the standards (Kohn, 2001).

Having already outlined the basic components of the unit plan, we now provide useful suggestions that deal with some of the daily details.

## ■ THE DAILY LESSON PLAN

A **lesson plan** sets forth the proposed program, or instructional activities, for each day; it is sometimes referred to as a **daily plan.** In general, lesson plans are planned around periods (usually thirty-five to fifty minutes) of the typical school schedule, allowing adequate time for teachers or students to arrive (if they are changing classrooms) and to leave at the end of the period. Shorter blocks of time may be allowed for younger students or for those whose attention span is limited. Longer periods are usually allotted for block instruction, for workshops, and for learning activities accomplished with integrated or multidisciplinary thematic units.

Although special school activities may require shortened or lengthened periods, most lessons should be planned for full periods. Sometimes students need more or less time to finish an activity or assignment, and teachers need to learn how to be flexible in adjusting timing. As teachers develop their planning and pacing skills, they learn to plan better schedules in advance and to plan supplementary activities and materials for use or elimination as the need arises to maintain a good pace. Additional activities might include independent reading, response journal writing, performing a committee function, completing a research project, finishing a workbook assignment, illustrating a composition or report, working on a study activity, looking up information on the Internet, or tutoring another student. Additional materials might include pictures, charts, and models to further demonstrate a major point in the lesson; review exercises for practice and drill; and a list of summary questions to review major points of the lesson.

To avoid omissions or underemphasizing or overemphasizing particular lesson plan components, the teacher needs to consider his or her style of teaching and the students' abilities and interests. The teacher should review the progress of each day's lesson and periodically take notes on student responses to different methods, media, and activities—to reuse with another class or at another time. Inexperienced teachers need to plan the lessons in detail, follow the plan, and refer to it frequently. As they grow in experience and confidence, they become able to plan with less detail and rely more on their spontaneous responses to what happens in the classroom as the teaching–learning process unfolds. Good timing or scheduling is an aid to good instruction and good classroom management.

## ■ LESSON PLAN COMPONENTS

There is no one ideal format to follow for a lesson plan. Teachers should modify the suggestions of methods experts and learning theorists to mesh with their personal teaching style and the suggestions of their school or district. Many school systems often recommend that beginning teachers include the following components in a lesson plan as a way of helping them establish routine procedures:

1. Specific *objectives* of the lesson
2. Appropriate *motivation* to capture the students' interest and maintain it throughout the lesson
3. *Development* or *outline* of a lesson (sometimes referred to as content or activities)
4. Varied *methods,* including strategies, activities, questions, demonstrations, reviews and drills, grouping patterns, and media implementation, designed to keep the lesson on track
5. Varied *materials* and *media* to supplement and clarify content

6. Medial and final *summaries* with student interaction and evaluations
7. Provision for an *assignment* or *homework*

The teacher can vary how much time he or she spends on each component, how much detail is included in each, and which components are included. With experience, the teacher discovers the most useful components to include and the amount of detail needed in the plan as a whole. Because these components provide the essential elements of instruction, they will be covered in some detail.

## Objectives

The first questions a teacher considers when sorting out the content he or she plans to teach are: What do I plan to teach? What do I want the students to learn from the lesson that will be worthwhile? The answers to these questions are the objectives; they form the backbone of the lesson. Motivation, methods, and materials are organized to achieve the objectives. Establishing objectives prevents aimlessness.

Objectives may be phrased as statements or questions. (Most people think they can be written only as statements.) The question form encourages students to think. Regardless of how they are phrased, they should be written on the chalkboard or on a printed handout for students to see. An objective written as a statement for a lesson to follow would be, "To identify how the skin protects the body from diseases." The same objective written as a question would be, "How does the skin protect the human body from diseases?" Recall that with the curriculum integration and curriculum mapping design approaches, questions posed jointly by students and teachers serve as essential organizers for the themes and units of instruction that follow.

## Motivation

Motivational devices or activities arouse and maintain interest in the content to be taught. Fewer motivational devices are needed for students who are intrinsically motivated (that is, motivated to learn to satisfy some inner need or interest) than for students who are extrinsically motivated (that is, require incentives or reinforcers to learn). Lesson planning and instruction must seek to enhance both forms of motivation.

**Intrinsic motivation** involves sustaining or increasing the interest students already have in a topic or task. The teacher selects and organizes the lesson so that it will (a) whet students' appetite at the beginning of the lesson; (b) maintain student curiosity and involvement in the work by using surprise, doubt, or perplexity; novel as well as familiar materials; and interesting and varied methods; (c) provide active and manipulative opportunities; (d) permit student autonomy in organizing time and effort; and (e) provide choices or alternatives to meet requirements of the lesson. Activities and materials that teachers can use to enhance intrinsic motivation are listed in Box 6.2.

**Extrinsic motivation** focuses on cognitive strategies to hold student interest and increase concentration. Activities that enhance success and reduce failure increase motivation. High-achieving students will persist longer than low-achieving students even when experiencing failure, so incentives for learning are more important for average- and low-achieving students. They are important for all students when the subject matter or content is uninteresting or difficult (Stipek, 1993; Covington, 1992). Teachers can

**BOX 6.2** Some Suggestions for Teachers to Use in Planning Activities and Materials to Enhance Students' Intrinsic Motivation

1. *Challenging statements.* It is unnecessary to preserve and save the tropical rain forests.
2. *Pictures and cartoons.* How does this picture illustrate life in a tenement building of cities populated by waves of immigrants?
3. *Personal experiences.* What type of clothing is best to wear during freezing weather? Why do we wear T-shirts and shorts during the summer?
4. *Problems.* Where does sound travel the fastest—in water, through air, or through metal?
5. *Exploratory and creative activities.* I need three volunteers to come to the chalkboard to fill in the blanks of the chart, while the rest of you do it at your seats.
6. *Charts, tables, graphs, maps.* From a study of the chart, what characteristics do all these animals have in common?
7. *Anecdotes and stories.* How does the section I have just read tell about how the main character feels about her school experiences?
8. *Contests and games.* Let's see how well you remember yesterday's homework. We will organize five teams by rows. In your notebooks, list the different kinds of rock related to the three main groups of igneous, sedimentary, and metamorphic. You will have two minutes. We will average the scores. The row with the highest average score will win.

**BOX 6.3** Nine Principles of Extrinsic Motivation

In providing for extrinsic motivation, the teacher may consider these nine basic principles:

1. *Clear directions and expectations.* Students must know exactly what they are expected to do and how they will be evaluated.
2. *Time on task.* Keep students on task. The amount of time allocated to a particular topic or task varies considerably from school to school and from teacher to teacher. Time on task, student motivation, and student achievement are related.
3. *Cognitive match.* Student motivation is highest when work on tasks or problems is appropriate to their achievement levels. When they are confused or when the work is above their abilities, they resist or give up. When it is below their abilities, they seek other interests or move through the lesson as fast as possible.
4. *Prompt feedback.* Feedback on student performance should be constructive and prompt. A long delay between performance behavior and results diminishes the relationship between them.
5. *Relate past learning with present learning.* Use reinforcers to strengthen previously learned content.
6. *Frequent rewards.* No matter how powerful a reward, it may have little impact if it is provided infrequently. Small, frequent rewards are more effective than large, infrequent ones.
7. *Praise.* Verbal praise ("Good," "Great," "Fine work") is a powerful motivating device.
8. *High expectations.* Students who are expected to learn will learn more and be motivated to learn more than students who are not expected to learn.

*(continued)*

 **BOX 6.3** Continued

9. *Value of rewards.* Motivation is partially based on the value an individual places on success, as well as the individual's estimate of the possibility for success. Thus, incentives used for students should have value for them.

*Source:* Adapted from N. L. Gage and David C. Berliner, *Educational Psychology,* 5th ed. (Boston: Houghton Mifflin, 1992); Richard Sprinthall, Norman Sprinthall, and Sharon Oja, *Educational Psychology: A Developmental Approach,* 6th ed. (New York: McGraw-Hill, 1994).

**BOX 6.4** How Can Teachers Motivate Students to Read?

The amount of time students spend in recreational and pleasurable reading is a great contributor to their overall educational success. How can teachers inspire students to read books on their own outside of school? One author found that assessing students' interests, choices, feelings, and opinions was essential to understanding their intrinsic motivations and provided her with the information to help them read more. Another author indicated that students wanted to learn about good books from their teachers and would follow through with the "reading habit" based on their teachers' abilities to show enthusiasm for reading.

*Source:* Adapted from Jill Cole, "What Motivates Students to Read? Four Literacy Personalities," *The Reading Teacher* (December 2002/January 2003), pp. 326–336; Jo Worthy, "What Makes Intermediate Grade Students Want to Read?" *The Reading Teacher* (March 2002), pp. 568–569.

turn to the nine basic principles listed in Box 6.3 to consider ways for enhancing extrinsic motivation. Also see Box 6.4.

## Development

**Development,** sometimes called the lesson *outline,* can be expressed as topics and subtopics, a series of broad or pivotal questions, or a list of activities (methods and materials). Many junior high school teachers rely on topics or questions, whereas elementary teachers often refer to activities.

Emphasis on topics, concepts, or skills indicates a content orientation in a teaching approach. Emphasis on activities has a more sociopsychological orientation; there is more stress on student needs and interests. For example, outlining the problems of the ozone layer on the chalkboard is a content oriented activity. Interviewing someone about the ozone layer is an activity that encompasses a wide range of social stimuli.

Several criteria have been proposed for selecting and organizing appropriate content and experiences in the development section. The following are criteria for *content* developed by Ornstein and Hunkins (2004):

1. *Validity.* The content selected should be verifiable, not misleading or false.
2. *Significance.* The content needs to be constantly reviewed so that worthwhile content—basic ideas, information, principles of the subject—is taught and lessons do not become cluttered by masses of more trivial content now available through the "information explosion."
3. *Balance.* The content should promote macro and micro knowledge; students should experience the broad sweep of content, and they should have the opportunity to dig deep.
4. *Self-sufficiency.* The content should help students learn how to learn; it should help them gain maximum sufficiency in the most economic manner.

5. *Interest.* Content is best learned when it is interesting to the student. Some progressive educators urge that the child be the focus of the teaching and learning process.
6. *Utility.* The content should be useful or practical in some situation outside of the lesson, either to further other learning or in everyday experiences. How usefulness is defined depends on whether a teacher is subject centered or student centered, but most teachers would agree that useful content enhances the human potential of the learner.
7. *Learnability.* It should be within the capacity of the students to learn the content. There should be a cognitive match between the students' aptitudes and the subject (and between their abilities and academic tasks).
8. *Feasibility.* The teacher needs to consider the time needed, resources and materials available, curriculum guides, state and national tests, existing legislation, and the political climate of the community. There are limitations on what can be planned and taught.

## Varied Methods

Although many different procedures and techniques can be emphasized in a lesson, we present here the components of five basic methods of instruction: (1) explanation and discussion, (2) questioning, (3) problem solving, (4) practice, drill, and review, and (5) the scaffolding model. Depending on the type of lesson in the curriculum model followed—as well as the students, the content or subject, and the grade level—these instructional methods will undoubtedly be used to varying degrees. The scaffolding model itself allows for the use and integration of the other instructional methods. These methods will be discussed at length in the next chapter; for now, we present a short synopsis of each one.

*Explanation and Discussion.* Teachers need to use talk to communicate with students. The talk will involve explanation, discussion, and short lecture to explain important points and concepts. Generally, the explanation that accompanies the sequencing of steps necessary to accomplish many activities is very important to learners, and oftentimes these steps need to be repeated.

*Questioning.* Asking questions is one of the teacher's most important tools. Questioning is usually peppered within explanation and discussion as teachers ensure that students' thinking is proceeding in a logical way. Teachers use questions for a number of reasons. Questions provide motivation and whet mental appetites, guide students along successful learning paths, help them think deeply about issues and concerns, and assist them in clarifying concepts.

*Problem Solving.* Problem solving is a way to engage reflective thinking and an inquiry approach to learning. Such learning can occur when students work in an integrated thematic unit and relate content from different disciplines to solve a problem or decide an issue. Also, when students conduct experiments and plan for demonstrations, they usually engage in a discovery method of learning. They may collect data, observe, measure, identify, examine, and reflect on causal relationships.

*Practice, Drill, and Review.* These activities are tried and true methods necessary at all levels of learning. A person doesn't learn a new, complicated computer program all at once; it probably takes practicing the routines and their sequence a few times to achieve some fluency. Learners need to constantly review material in order to retain it and learn it in depth. The methodology of practice, drill, and review, although not considered by many to be highly sophisticated, is quite necessary for learning, particularly for transferring information and ideas from short-term to long-term memory. These activities are also quite important for students who have difficulty remembering, retaining, and integrating information.

*Scaffolding.* Scaffolding is a way of teaching through four successive stages, beginning with explaining and modeling to a conclusion whereby the student takes ownership of the learning activity. It incorporates many of the teaching practices of the other four methods, including discussing and explaining, questioning, demonstrating and showing, working through problems, and practicing and reviewing to be competent at a learning task. The four stages are (1) model/teach/discuss, so students see and hear what they are to do; (2) practice the steps in their proper sequence so that the cumulative effect of the building steps can be realized; (3) apply the strategy as a whole in a similar activity to determine if all the steps have been learned well; and (4) internalize and take ownership of the strategy to apply and transfer it in new contexts and subject disciplines to facilitate learning and memory. The model would be most effective when challenging or difficult content material is taught so that students can be carried through the four stages to a successful conclusion.

*Shifting Instructional Methods.* Relying on the same instructional methods day after day would be boring, even for adults. Different procedures sustain motivation throughout any given lesson. In addition to motivating students and creating interest to learn particular topics in particular subjects by varying instructional methods, educators have witnessed a shift in the teaching–learning paradigm, particularly evident in literacy instruction.

Basically, the paradigm shift in instructional methodology moves from immersing students in prepackaged materials that focus directly on bits and pieces of reading and writing instruction to one that has an interactive reader–writer–text focus in which meaning is both ascertained and created by the students themselves. The teacher is no longer viewed as the fountain of knowledge, from which knowledge flows directly to the students. Instead, the teacher is viewed as the skillful designer and practitioner of instructional methodology through whom students are involved in lessons as learner apprentices, as active participants, and as problem solvers.

The role of the teacher who uses varying instructional methods could be divided into two broad categories. One category would be labeled "direct instruction" and the other "indirect or mediated instruction." The concept of mediated learning comes from Vygotsky, who views adults as helpers or guides of children's learnings in that adults assist, talk, show, and take children through the successive, meaningful steps of an experience (Burns, Roe, & Ross, 1999; May, 2001). Under direct instruction most often would be found instructional procedures such as (1) explanations in which teacher dialogue is prominent; (2) focus on mastery of the direct content being taught; (3) a more formal stance of classroom organization (teacher in front with students seated in rows); (4) textbook bound and driven; (5) and drill and practice to learn particular skills and rules.

With indirect instruction, there's more of a focus on the learner, the process of learning, and how the teacher assists learners with language and thinking development. Thus indirect instruction (1) is more learner centered in that teachers scaffold the steps of a learning experience; (2) focuses on thinking and literacy processes students use to gain subject-matter or content knowledge; (3) shows a less formal stance in classroom organization (teacher may be interacting with groups or individuals throughout the room); (4) achieves more of learning by doing, by involvement with peers, and with a variety of resources; and (5) emphasizes whole, authentic readings and writings from which parts can be analyzed and practiced to gain mastery of a skill.

The distinction between the two broad categories is not an idle one. Taken at their polarized extremes, a direct instruction focus linked to standards content and performance mastery might pose the question: "Is the learner in or out of step with the curriculum?" On the other hand, an indirect instructional climate found in a constructivist classroom or curriculum integration design approach might pose the question: "Is the curriculum meeting the needs of the learner?"

Good instructional methodology comes down to "What is needed to help students learn?" The viewpoint taken by the good, practicing teacher is to use a variety of instructional methods from both the direct and indirect categories to get the job done. At times a teacher may need to use direct explanation for the introduction of a new topic; at other times the teacher may pose questions to mentally pull children into a topic; and at other times, students may need to practice a particular technique so that fluency is achieved.

## Materials and Media

Media and materials, sometimes referred to as instructional resources, facilitate understanding and foster learning by clarifying verbal abstractions and arousing interest in the lesson. Many materials and media are available. The teacher's selection should depend on the objectives and content of the lesson plan; the age, abilities, and interests of the students; the teacher's ability to use the resources; the availability of the materials and equipment; and the classroom time available. The materials and media can be in the form of (1) *visuals* such as posters, slides, graphs, films, and videos; (2) *reading materials* such as pamphlets, magazines, newspapers, reports, and books; (3) *media* such as film, television, and taped recordings; (4) *verbal activities* such as speeches, debates, buzz sessions, forums, role playing, and interviews; (5) *motor activities* such as games, simulations, experiments, exercises, and manipulative materials; (6) *construction activities* such as collages, paintings, logs, maps, graphs, drawings, and models; and (7) *computer programs* that reinforce practice and drill, provide simulations, or allow multimedia projects to be designed.

## Summaries

Teachers cannot assume that learning is taking place in the classroom as a whole (or even with the majority) just because they have presented well-organized explanations

**BOX 6.5** Integrating Reading and Writing Activities with Lesson Summaries

The teacher might:

1. Pose several thought-provoking questions on the chalkboard that ask students to reflect on what they have read.
2. Ask for a comparison of what has already been read or learned with what is being learned.
3. Ask some students to summarize the main ideas of the lesson. Have other students make modifications and additions in writing.
4. Assign review questions (on the chalkboard or in the workbook or from the textbook).
5. Administer a short quiz that need not be graded but that can be used for evaluation purpose.
6. Provide a game-type format in which students might read from cue cards.

and demonstrations or because some students gave correct answers to questions. Some students may have been daydreaming or even confused while a demonstration took place and while other students asked and answered questions and were involved. To ensure understanding of the lesson and to determine whether the objectives of the lesson have been achieved, teachers should include one or more of the following types of summaries.

There should be a short *review* of each lesson in which the lesson as a whole and important or confusing parts are summarized. A short review can take the forms outlined in Box 6.5.

During the lesson, at some point when a major concept or idea has been examined, it is advisable to present a *medial summary*—a series of pivotal questions, a problem, or a series of activities that will bring together the information that has been discussed. Medial summaries slow down the lesson; however, they are important for low-achieving and young students who need more time to comprehend new information and make more links with prior knowledge. A *final summary* is needed to clinch the basic ideas or concepts of the lesson. If you realize that it is impossible to teach all you planned, then end the lesson at some logical point and provide a summary of the content you have covered. Each lesson should be concluded or brought to closure by a summary activity, not by the bell.

## Assignments

The work that students are requested to do at home should furnish them with the content (knowledge, skills, and tasks) needed to participate in the next day's lesson. Following are some characteristics of effective assignments:

1. The homework should be interesting.
2. Attention should be directed to definite concepts or problems.
3. Questions should be framed so as to provide background information necessary to answer the teacher's questions on the following day.
4. Homework should periodically incorporate previously taught content to reinforce learning.
5. The assignment should provide opportunities for students to grow in written (or symbolic) expression, reading, or important skills related to the subject.
6. Provision should be made for individual differences. There should be minimum assignments for all students, with enrichment levels for high-achieving students.
7. Homework should be explained and practice or examples given if necessary. Problems that may arise when doing the homework should be examined briefly in class near the end of the period.

8. Homework should be monitored for completion and accuracy, and students should receive timely, specific, and constructive feedback. When performance is poor, teachers should provide not only feedback and additional time for review but also additional assignments designed to ensure mastery of content.

9. It is important for the school to have a coordinated homework/tutoring program for students who need assistance, and the assistance should be provided on a daily basis, if necessary. Provisions must be made for students who do not understand the daily assignment; otherwise frustration and lack of interest take over and interfere with learning.

You can improve your instruction by observing experienced teachers, conversing with them, and getting feedback about your instruction. Because your supervisor or principal will rarely visit your classroom to observe you and provide feedback unless you are experiencing difficulties with the students, you will need to interpret your own instruction to grow professionally (Bennett & Carre, 1993; Cochran-Smith & Lytle, 1992). Your best barometer is your students. You need to learn to understand your instruction from a student perspective. They are the ones you are teaching and who observe you and interact with you on a daily basis. (The average number of observations per year for teachers involved in special staff development programs ranges from 1.7 to 2.8; it is assumed to be less for teachers not involved in special training programs. See Manderville & Rivers, 1991.)

With experience, good teachers grow less egocentric and more sensitive to student concerns. Such a shift in interest and focus will help you analyze what is happening in the classroom on an ongoing basis. By learning to read your students' verbal and nonverbal behavior, you will improve your instructional planning. As you put yourself in their place, as students, you should become more attuned to them as individuals—with particular needs and abilities—as opposed to viewing them as some amorphous group with generic problems or concerns (Hollingworth, Dybdahl, & Minarek, 1994; Fieman-Nemser & Parker, 1990).

## Guidelines for Implementing Lesson Plans

You will need to consider several factors as you begin to move from planning to performance. Even after you have had some experience, it is wise to review the following factors to ensure your success in the execution of the lesson plan.

1. *Student Differences.* Individual and group differences must be considered as you plan your lesson and then teach it. Teachers need to make provisions for student differences in ability, age, background, and reading level.

2. *Length of Period.* One of the major problems beginning teachers have is planning a lesson that coincides with the time allotted (normally the thirty, forty, or fifty minutes of each period). New teachers must learn to pace themselves, not to plan too much (and have to end abruptly) or too little (and have nothing planned for the last five or ten minutes of a period). If during a lesson a teacher realizes too little has been planned, he or she can:

   a. Pose additional questions to explore various facets of the content.

   **b.** Drill students on the major points of the lesson and have them practice with teacher-made materials to learn the key points.

   **c.** Spend additional time on the new assignment discussing problems that may arise and going over sample questions.

   If during a lesson the teacher realizes too much has been planned, he or she should:

   **a.** Select a major subheading or breakpoint in the development to end the lesson.

   **b.** End the lesson with a brief summary.

   **c.** Conclude the lesson the next day by including in the new lesson the content that was not covered the previous period.

3. *Flexibility.* The teacher must be flexible—that is, prepared to develop a lesson along a path different from the one set down in the plan. Student reactions may make it necessary or desirable to elaborate on something included in the plan or to pursue something unexpected that arises as the lesson proceeds.

4. *Student Participation.* Teachers must encourage the participation of the greatest number of students in each lesson. They should not permit a few students to dominate the lesson and should draw nonvolunteers into the lesson. They should not talk too much or dominate the lesson with teacher-directed activities. They need to encourage student participation, student-to-student interaction, and increased performance among shy students, low-achieving students, and students on the sides and in the rear rows (as opposed to students in the middle or front of the room). This is where different classroom grouping patterns are most useful, and this topic is covered in depth in Chapters 8 and 9.

5. *Student Understanding.* There is often a gap between what students understand and what teachers think they understand. Part of the reason for this gap has to do with the rapidity of the teaching process; so much happens at once that the teacher is unaware of everything that goes on in the classroom. Be sure that students understand the activities, learning experiences, and questions put to them. Students who do not know answers or have trouble understanding the lesson may tend to mumble or speak too quietly to be heard clearly, try to change the subject, or ask another question instead of responding to the original question.

6. *Evaluation.* The lesson plan must be evaluated so that it can be modified and improved. At the end of a lesson, the teacher should have a clear idea of how the students reacted and whether they understood and enjoyed the lesson.

   A good teacher, no matter how experienced, is a critic of his or her lesson and seeks new ways for improving the teaching–learning situation. The teacher takes time for self-reflection and self-analysis. The teacher is aware of what is happening during the lesson and intuitively judges what is worthwhile and what needs to be modified for the next time the lesson plan is used. See Tips for Teachers 6.1.

## ■ SAMPLE SCHEDULES AND LESSON PLANS

A sample weekly lesson plan schedule for the elementary grades and three individual sample lesson plans are included to illustrate how teachers plan for different kinds of

# Organizing and Implementing Lesson Plans

The teacher should always look for ways to improve the lesson plan. Following are twenty-five research-based tips that correlate with student achievement. As many as possible (not necessarily all in one lesson) should be incorporated into portions of the lesson plan. Although most of the statements seem to be based on a mastery approach, the checklist can be used for most types of teaching.

1. Plan lessons by aligning with state standards, school or district objectives, or topics of the unit plan.
2. Require of students an academic focus.
3. Follow the plan. Keep to a schedule, start the lesson on time, and be aware of time.
4. Provide a review of the previous lesson or integrate the previous lesson with the new lesson.
5. Indicate to students the objectives of the lesson or the content standard to be covered. Explain what is to be accomplished.
6. Utilize whole, flexible, and small groups and independent study.
7. Present the lesson with enthusiasm; motivate students.
8. Present the lesson at an appropriate pace, not too slow or too fast.
9. Explain things clearly. Be sure students understand what to do and how to do it.

10. Give students a chance to think about what is being taught.
11. Try to be alert to times when students don't understand.
12. Provide sufficient time for practice.
13. Ask frequent questions; be sure they are challenging and relevant.
14. Answer student questions or have other students answer them.
15. Provide explanations, demonstrations, or experiments.
16. Elaborate on difficult points of the lesson; give details; provide examples.
17. Show how students are to do classwork or individual seatwork.
18. Choose activities that are interesting and promote success.
19. Make smooth transitions between activities.
20. Incorporate supplementary materials and media.
21. Summarize the lesson.
22. Schedule seatwork; monitor and assess student work.
23. Give homework, provide examples of how to do homework, and collect and check homework.
24. Evaluate the lesson plan after teaching.
25. Be open to feedback and modification; listen to students, colleagues, supervisors, and other observers.

instruction. The weekly lesson plan schedule shows how content and activities are planned according to traditional and progressive daily scheduling viewpoints. Explanations accompany each plan to provide some sense of what the teacher is trying to achieve. The weekly lesson plan schedule and the three lesson plans present instruction for learning content in various ways and can be used as guides for students across grade and age levels. Words that appear in italics coincide with the previously discussed components of a lesson plan; they serve to highlight the major ideas of each lesson.

## A Weekly Lesson Plan Schedule

Two types of daily schedules are illustrated in the weekly plan in Table 6.4. The traditional schedule on the left shows that the major content subjects are presented during fixed, scheduled periods during the day. This plan shows the school, the district, the parents, and the community that the major subject disciplines for a grade level are being

*Table 6.4* Sample Weekly Lesson Plan Schedule for Elementary Grades

| Time | Traditional Daily Schedule | Progressive Daily Schedule |
|------|---------------------------|----------------------------|
| 8:40–9:00 | Daily routines: Review day's activities, attendance, announcements, lunch money, etc.; Students do response journal writing. | |
| 9:00–9:20 | Listening, speaking, storytelling, response journal reading, and discussion | Reading workshop minilesson with read-aloud and book discussion |
| 9:20–10:20 | Reading: reading groups, skills and practice, independent seatwork with activity pages | 9:20–9:55 Independent reading and conferences 9:55–10:20 Literature circles |
| 10:20–10:40 | Recess / snacks / independent reading and writing | |
| 10:40–11:30 | Mathematics: whole-class direct instruction; problem solving; drill, practice, and review; independent seatwork | Writing workshop: topic selection, rehearsal, drafting, maintaining writing files, conferences |
| 11:30–12:15 | Science: Topic presentation, demonstrations, experiments, manipulatives | Science, social studies, mathematics, health—reading, research, preparation for project work. |
| 12:15–1:00 | Lunch | |
| 1:00–2:50 | 1:00–1:45 Social studies: Topic presentation, text reading, question and activity work 1:45–2:25 Writing time: art instruction and projects; health; physical education; library visit 2:25–2:50 Independent reading time (USSR, DEAR time) | 1:00–2:30 Thematic unit and project work; center activities and special interest groups 2:30–2:50 Word study, vocabulary and spelling; contribute to next day's response journal prompts |
| 2:50–3:00 | Review homework assignments; prepare for dismissal | |

covered, and this daily plan would also likely correspond to what was being addressed in the district and state standards.

Many teachers at the elementary level implement the traditional daily schedule on a Monday, Wednesday, and Friday basis. The teaching style here would be more direct, with whole-class instruction and grouping by ability levels (see Chapters 8 and 9). The teacher covers topics and skills, and students practice and do independent seatwork to learn the content and the new skills. The lesson plan that follows—the grouping lesson plan (Table 6.5)—could be appropriately implemented during the reading, science, or social studies time blocks.

The progressive daily schedule on the right in Table 6.4 presents instruction in quite a different way. There are allotted time periods during the day, but the length of periods is more flexible. Also, there is far less direct-teaching control by the teacher; the teacher is more of a manager of the students' time, activities, and collaborations. The

*Table 6.5* Grouping Lesson Plan for Vocabulary
and Dictionary Use Development

Lesson Topic: Vocabulary Development
Objective: To learn the meanings of and how to read 10 new words

1. To be able to use context to figure out a word's meaning—a reading comprehension skill
2. To be able to use a dictionary efficiently
3. To be able to read the new words correctly
4. To be able to use the new word correctly in a sentence

Review: Minilesson with oral discussion (7 minutes)

1. Students retell the "Living Things Around Us" topic
2. Questions and probes to elicit more content
3. Use of chalkboard to write new words

Materials: Textbooks, prepared activity sheets, dictionaries, blank flash cards, vocabulary notebooks
Development: Class divided into two groups

| **Group I: Activities** <br> **Direct Instruction and Teams (25 minutes)** | **Group II: Activities** <br> **Individual Seatwork (25 minutes)** |
|---|---|
| 1. Review new words: *predator, conserve, prey, habitat, producer, need, consumer, desert, adapted, shelter.* | 1. Students use "Intelligent Guess" activity page with new words listed on left side: *predator, conserve, prey, habitat, producer, need, consumer, desert, adapted, shelter.* |
| 2. Write words on flash cards and practice reading with teammate. | 2. Students write what they think each word means from science context and the clues that helped them figure out meaning. |
| 3. Find new words in science text and read sentences containing words. | 3. Use dictionaries to confirm word's meaning. |
| 4. Copy sentence with word into notebook on left side of page. | |
| 5. Distribute dictionaries. | |

**Individual Seatwork (15 minutes)**

1. In notebook, students write word meaning as it conforms with usage in science text.

**Medial Summary (15 minutes)**

1. In teams of two, students review activity sheets and agree on word meanings.

**Final Summary (8 minutes)**

To complete "check-up" activity page matching word with meaning.

**Individual Work (8 minutes)**

1. Write words in original sentences that provide clues to readers to figure out meanings.

**Homework: Both Groups**

| | |
|---|---|
| 1. Write sentences using new words appropriately | 1. Finish writing sentences for each new word. |
| 2. Read sentences to parent or family members and get feedback about appropriateness. | 2. Read sentences to others and get feedback. |
| 3. Can write meanings and original sentences on back of flash cards. | 3. Create crossword puzzle using new words for classmates to use (extra credit). |

teaching style here is more indirect and implicit, with a focus on student ownership and empowerment in the content offerings and the methods of instruction. Teachers would need to know how to organize and manage reading and writing workshops, literature circles, and thematic units (see Chapters 5 and 9).

Many teachers like to implement aspects of the progressive daily schedule on a Tuesday and Thursday routine. If they're not comfortable with the literature and writing focus shown in the morning block, they can implement their regular schedule shown on the left and leave the two afternoons for thematic unit, project work, or center activities. Many teachers like some kind of variety in their weekly plan because it allows them to be flexible and keep students interested in different types of projects. Also, by engaging in interdisciplinary or multisubject units, the teacher can help students integrate and apply new learnings and content. The inquiry–discovery lesson plan (Table 6.6) and the creativity lesson plan (Table 6.7) would certainly be appropriate to implement during the Tuesday and Thursday afternoon blocks.

---

### *Table 6.6* Inquiry–Discovery Lesson Plan

| | |
|---|---|
| Lesson topic: | Investigating plant growth |
| Objective: | To grow plants in class and at home<br>To use systematic procedures of scientific investigation |
| Materials: | Empty milk, juice, and/or soup containers; various types of soil and plant seeds |
| Problem: | To investigate the best way to grow plants |

Questions:

1. How long does it take for the seeds to sprout?
2. How deep should the seeds be planted?
3. Can seeds grow downward? (Explain.)
4. Can seeds (a plant) grow without water? Sunlight? How much water? Sunlight?
5. Does it help plant growth to have insects in the soil? Worms?

Medial summary: Depending on the responses of the students

6. Do plants move during the day? Evening?
7. Can a plant grow if a leaf is cut? Why? Why not?
8. Can plants be used to grow new plants? (Explain.)
9. How does music affect plant growth? Smoke? Deodorants?
10. Which plants can we cross to get a hybrid?

Summary: Discuss explanation of above questions—Why? How do we know?

Homework:

1. Students are to grow two of the same kind of plant with different soil and conditions (water, sun, music, etc.).
2. Students are to observe and record growth of the plants on a weekly basis; prepare bar or line graphs of growth.
3. Students are to report conclusions about plant growth and environment.

**Table 6.7** Creativity Lesson Plan

Lesson topic: Creating an island

Objectives:

1. To recognize that all places on earth have special features that distinguish them from other places.
2. To identify landforms and bodies of water.
3. To apply terms for geographical landforms and bodies of water to an original student project.
4. To organize into cooperative groups.

Review/introductory activity (10 minutes)

1. Students use atlases and maps to review land and water terms.
2. Students create a glossary of important geographical land and water terms in the form of a three-column chart giving terms (*basin, bay, canyon, cape, cove, delta, gulf, hill, inlet, island, lake, mountain, peninsula, plateau, river, sea, valley*), definitions, and examples (Florida is a peninsula).

Materials: Atlases, wall maps, textbooks, glossary, large pieces of drawing paper or poster board, felt pens or markers

Development (activities)

1. The class is divided into groups of four or five. Group members are to work cooperatively to plan and draw an imaginary island.
2. Each island should feature at least ten (or fifteen depending on grade level and previous related lessons) of the following geographical forms: basin, bay, canyon, cape, cove, etc.
3. Students are to give all features on the island names of their choice. The names are to be related to one theme, for example, Computer Island, Bytes Bay, and Microchip Mountain, Internet Cove, etc.
4. Students who finish early are to include map features (depending on the grade level) such as latitude, longitude, elevation key, scale.

Summary (10–15 minutes)

1. Each group shows its completed map to the class. Students discuss each group's portrayal of the geographical terms.
2. If time permits, students are to place five fictitious towns on each island and discuss the locations of towns, reasons for their choice, best locations.

Homework

1. Determine the island's climate and natural resources based on latitude and longitude coordinates given by the teacher.
2. Discuss where most of the island's population would most likely live given the island's configuration and natural resources.
3. Discuss possible environmental problems that might develop as a result of using the available resources (suggested for upper grade levels).
4. Discuss possible trade problems that might develop as a result of using available resources (suggested for upper grade levels).

*Source:* Adapted from "Geography Lesson Plan," *National Geographical Society Update* (Fall 1987): 9–10. All the ideas have been restructured to coincide with lesson plan components.

Daily schedule plans have some features in common. It's wise to begin and end the day with a settling *activity.* Many teachers do this by developing a routine of response journal writing and independent reading during either the early morning block or in the late afternoon, dismissal-time period. You'll note that in Table 6.4, we show the teacher conducting the daily routine as students write entries in their response journals, prompting them to begin the school day with a literacy activity.

At the end of the day, we show independent reading time—also known as uninterrupted sustained silent reading (USSR) or drop everything and read (DEAR). This involvement in pleasurable reading at the end of a busy school day may carry over to out-of-school reading time, which also serves as intrinsic motivation to read more (which is the teacher's *objective* for this scheduled routine). Before students leave for the day, the teacher should explicitly review the homework *assignments* and any necessary requirements for the following day's activities.

## A Grouping Lesson Plan for Vocabulary and Dictionary Use Development

1. The *lesson topic* deals with new vocabulary words that came from a unit in science dealing with the topic Living Things Around Us (see Table 6.5).
2. The *primary objective* of the lesson is for students at all ability levels to learn the meaning of ten new words introduced in the science topic. The *secondary objectives* are that the words be read correctly, that dictionaries be used efficiently, and that students use the new words appropriately in their own written work.
3. The teacher begins the lesson with a *review* of the Living Things Around Us topic by asking students to remember and retell what they learned. As the students discuss the topic orally and answer the teacher's questions, the teacher is alert to determine if any of the children use the new words in their oral discourse. She writes the new words on the chalkboard as the words are used.
4. *Materials* specific to the lesson are noted in the lesson plan.
5. The *activities* describe the development or outline of the lesson as it pertains to the work projected for two groups. The lesson focus is directed toward the activities planned for each group as each group works through the plan.
6. The class is divided into *two groups* based on the teacher's knowledge of how students have learned new words in previous lessons. Group I includes those students who will need more direct instruction with practice and reviews, while Group II includes those students who can learn the words independently through the application of good reading strategies.
7. Both groups do *seatwork* that is similar. However, the teacher initially spends more direct instruction time with Group I students to ensure that they can read the words correctly and can understand their usage in the science context. Later in their lesson sequence, they will use dictionaries as their classmates did earlier. Group II students begin work with an "Intelligent Guess" activity page on which they write what the words mean from their contextual use and the context clues that helped them figure out each word's meaning. Group II students are engaged in individual seatwork and use their reading/thinking skills before they turn to

dictionary confirmations of meaning. The teacher is available to monitor the seatwork of all students, and once her initial review of the words is completed, the teacher helps anyone with individual problems.

8. After the initial group, team, and individual work, the two groups accomplish different activities. The teacher now spends more time with Group II in a *medial summary* for feedback, review, and assessment. The teacher reviews the activity pages, discusses the new word meanings, and ensures that all are in agreement about the correct word meanings. Group I students are now engaged in *independent work,* having been provided with the dictionaries and directions to find each word's meaning.

9. Both groups receive the same type of *homework* assignment to write the new words in original sentences and read their sentences to others to get feedback. Group II students are additionally challenged to create a crossword puzzle with the new words for their classmates to enjoy. Group I students are asked to gain additional reinforcement with the words by writing their meanings and original sentences on the back of their flash cards.

## An Inquiry–Discovery Lesson Plan

1. The *lesson topic* is derived from a unit on plant life (see Table 6.6). It will take an extended or double period to complete.

2. The first *objective* is written on the chalkboard to stimulate curiosity and interest; the second objective is only for the teacher or supervisor to see and is a by-product of the first.

3. Because the *materials* are readily found at home, students should be required to bring in their own materials to encourage responsibility and to set the expectation that they are to become less dependent on the teacher and more independent as learners.

4. The *problem* is for the students to investigate, using their own inquiry and discovery techniques. The teacher is to act as a facilitator and to encourage independent thought and activity among the students. They are to do their own work; the teacher may form them into cooperative teams, based on mixed sophistication or abilities of the students, to investigate the problem. If this is their first or second investigation or experiment, then teams would help alleviate some student anxieties.

5. The *questions* should be answered by the students; they should find their own answers and be able to explain why. The teacher can help by suggesting but only if a student (or groups of students) is unsure about how to proceed. The crucial point is to encourage inquiry and discovery. Students need to follow their own ideas and to draw their own conclusions.

6. As a *summary,* all the questions are discussed. Depending on the age and academic sophistication of the students, the teacher may slow down the lesson and incorporate a *medial summary* after five questions or so. This serves as an intermediate check on whether students understand portions of the lesson so they can proceed to the next portion. The time devoted to the summary is hard to determine because it is impossible to preplan what students will understand and how much further ex-

planation will be needed. However, the teacher may want to reteach or at least reemphasize certain concepts that give students trouble.

7. The *homework assignment* (a series of investigative activities) is an extension of the class investigative activities. It requires the students to work on their own; it helps them use discovery techniques and become more independent learners. The homework activity sets the stage for a follow-up set of related problems and questions to be worked out in the near future—perhaps at the end of the unit. Students can report their observations, mathematics and graph calculations, and conclusions about plant growth in their journals. This allows them to transfer their experimental, discovery work into a written literacy form that can serve as a basis for a formal report for others to read and appreciate.

## A Creativity Lesson Plan

1. The *lesson topic* provides an opportunity for students to create or develop their own project, based on key geographical terms they have learned (see Table 6.7).

2. The *objectives* focus on understanding terms that describe and distinguish special features considered essential to geographical education. Students move from understanding geographical concepts to applying them in class. They also learn to work in teams or groups.

3. The *review* component of the lesson may also be considered an introductory activity. The activity provides background information for the main part or development of the lesson.

4. Different *materials* are displayed, available for research, and distributed to students for use.

5. The *development* employs cooperative learning. Rules about working together need to be discussed briefly (see Chapter 9). The number of land and water terms should depend on the students' grade level. The naming of features on the island can be optional based on time considerations, but it provides a way of relating the content of the lesson to the experiences of the students. Activity 4 can be introduced as a bonus.

6. The *summary* component is achieved in part through cooperative learning as students discuss the groups' projects. Provision is made for supplementary discussion and review of hypothetical towns if the lesson is finished with time remaining. This activity can also be assigned as part of the homework.

7. The *homework* is an extension of the class activity. It tests further understanding of the subject and critical thinking. The last two homework problems are geared for advanced students.

In conclusion, unit planning and lesson planning will vary according to the school district and school in which you teach. Some school settings or supervisors will be quite prescriptive and expect you to follow a set method. Your plans may be collected and checked on a regular basis. In other schools and with other supervisors, there will be no prescribed method and very little feedback or concern about your unit and lesson plans. Hence, you will be largely on your own when it comes to instructional planning. For this reason, the suggestions offered in this chapter can help you plan your own units and lessons within your school system.

## ■ SUMMARY ■

1. Teachers plan at five different levels: yearly, term, unit, weekly, and daily, and they engage in formal and mental planning as they prepare and implement lessons.

2. Course mapping takes place at different subject and grade levels; it helps clarify what content, skills, and values you wish to teach.

3. Strategic planning helps teachers plan together, share ideas about unit plans and lesson plans, and reflect on their experiences.

4. The basic components of a unit plan are objectives, content, skills, activities, resources, and evaluation.

5. Types of unit plans make use of thematic, topic, and activity approaches.

6. The basic components of a lesson plan are objectives, motivation, development, methods, materials and media, summaries, and homework.

7. Four lesson plans were discussed: flexible grouping, thinking skills, inquiry–discovery, and creativity, and two types of daily teaching schedules were presented in a weekly plan.

## ■ QUESTIONS TO CONSIDER ■

1. Why do educators advise planning in cooperation with students? Why do many teachers ignore student input when planning?

2. How can course mapping help you in a more formal way to plan a course or unit of study and how might mental planning or strategic planning alter or enhance your implementation of the course map?

3. What are the criteria for a good unit plan?

4. According to what approach do you think a unit for your subject or grade could best be planned? Why?

5. Which are the most essential components to consider when planning a lesson? Why?

## ■ THINGS TO DO ■

1. Prepare a course map or course of study for a unit you plan to teach at your subject and grade level.

2. Speak to an experienced teacher. Ask the teacher to provide you with a series of unit plans for the subject or grade level you plan to teach. Examine the major components together.

3. Plan a unit and list the activities and resources that could be incorporated into it.

4. Plan a lesson in your subject and grade level; then teach it according to the specifications listed. What were the good parts of the lesson? What were the unsatisfactory parts?

5. List some common mistakes in lesson planning. Ask experienced teachers: "What are ways for preventing some of these mistakes?"

## ■ RECOMMENDED READINGS ■

Bennett, Neville, and Clive Carre. *Learning to Teach.* New York: Routledge, 1993. Presents ideas and suggestions to improve the art of teaching.

Carr, Judy, and Douglas Harris. *Succeeding with Standards: Linking Curriculum, Assessment, and Action Planning.* Alexandria, VA: Association for Supervision and Curriculum Development, 2001. Discusses different levels of planning and presents an action plan strategy whereby teachers can help students improve performance in relation to the standards.

Doll, Ronald. *Curriculum Improvement: Decision Making and Process*, 9th ed. Boston: Allyn and Bacon, 1996. Deals with two major parts: that of deciding what the curriculum should be and that of the processes needed to improve the curriculum.

Eisner, Elliot. *The Educational Imagination*, 3rd ed. New York: Macmillan, 1993. Discusses the importance of considering the whole of curriculum context in making educational decisions.

Kindsvatter, Richard, William Wilen, and Margaret Isher. *Dynamics of Effective Teaching*, 3rd ed. New York: Addison Wesley Longman, 1996.

Presents for veteran and beginning teachers a comprehensive review of analysis instruments and techniques for making good and thoughtful decisions.

Newby, Timothy, Donald Stepich, James Lehman, and James Russell. *Instructional Technology for Teaching and Learning: Designing Instruction, Integrating Computers, and Using Media*, 2nd ed. Upper Saddle River, NJ: Merrill, 2000. Shows teachers how to use computers and media effectively by using a "plan, implement, and evaluate" model of instructional integration.

Smith, Patricia, and Tillman Ragan. *Instructional Design*. Upper Saddle River, NJ: Merrill, 1999. Translates the principles of learning and teaching into plans that teachers can follow in using activities and materials in instruction.

## ■ KEY TERMS ■

| | | |
|---|---|---|
| activities approach | formal planning | strategic planning |
| course mapping | informal planning | teachable moment |
| daily plan | intrinsic motivation | theme approach |
| development | lesson plan | topic approach |
| extrinsic motivation | mental planning | unit plan |

## ■ REFERENCES ■

Beane, J. A. (1997). *Curriculum integration: Designing the core of democratic education.* New York: Teachers College Press.

Bennett, N., & Carre, C. (1993). *Learning to teach.* New York: Routledge.

Brown, D. (1993, Spring). Descriptions of two novice secondary teachers' planning. *Curriculum Inquiry*, 34–45.

Brown, D. S. (1988, September). Twelve middle school teachers' planning. *Elementary School Journal*, 69–87.

Burns, P., Roe, B., & Ross, E. (1999). *Teaching reading in today's elementary schools.* Boston: Houghton Mifflin.

Carr, J., & Harris, D. (2001). *Succeeding with standards: Linking curriculum, assessment, and action planning.* Alexandria, VA: Association for Supervision and Curriculum Development.

Clark, C. (1991, September–October). Real lessons from imaginary teachers. *Journal of Curriculum Studies*, 429–434.

Cochran-Smith, M., & Lytle, S. L. (1992). *Inside/outside: Teacher research and knowledge.* New York: Teachers College Press.

Covington, M. V. (1992). *Making the grade: A self-worth perspective on motivation.* New York: Cambridge University Press.

Eisner, E. W. (1993). *The educational imagination* (3rd ed.). New York: Macmillan.

English, F. W. (2000). *Deciding what to teach and test: Developing, aligning and auditing the curriculum.* Thousand Oaks, CA: Corwin Press.

Fieman-Nemser, S., & Parker, M. B. (1990, May–June). Making subject matter part of the conversation in learning to teach. *Journal of Teacher Education*, 32–43.

Finders, M., & Hynds, S. (2003). *Literacy lessons: Teaching and learning with middle school students.* Upper Saddle River, NJ: Merrill.

Grossman, P. G. (1993, Summer). Why models matter. *Review of Educational Research,* 171–180.

Gudmundsdottir, S. (1991, September–October). Ways of seeing are ways of knowing. *Journal of Curriculum Studies,* 409–422.

Hollingworth, S., Dybdahl, M., & Minarek, L. T. (1994, Spring). The importance of relational knowing in learning to teach. *Curriculum Inquiry,* 14–23.

Jacobs, H. H. (1997). *Mapping the big picture: Integrating curriculum & assessment K–12.* Alexandria, VA: Association for Supervision and Curriculum Development.

Kameenui, E. J., & Carnine, D. W. (1998). *Effective teaching strategies that accommodate diverse learners.* Upper Saddle River, NJ: Merrill.

Kindsvatter, R., Wilen, W., & Isher, M. (1996). *Dynamics of effective teaching* (3rd ed.). New York: Addison Wesley Longman.

Kohn, A. (2001, January). Fighting the tests: A practical guide to rescuing our schools. *Phi Delta Kappan,* 348–357.

Lalik, R. V., & Niles, J. A. (1990, January). Collaborative planning by two groups of student teachers. *Elementary School Journal,* 319–336.

Manderville, G. K., & Rivers, J. L. (1991, March). The South Carolina Pet Study. *Elementary School Journal,* 377–407.

May, F. B. (2001). *Reading as communication: To help children write and read* (6th ed.). Upper Saddle River, NJ: Merrill.

Mehrens, W. A. (1992, Spring). Using performance assessment for accountability purposes. *Educational Measurement,* 3–9.

Nebgen, M. (1991, April). The key to success in strategic planning is communication. *Educational Leadership,* 26–28.

Newby, T., Stepich, D., Lehman, J., & Russell, J. (2000). *Instructional technology for teaching and learning.* Upper Saddle River, NJ: Merrill.

Ornstein, A., & Hunkins, F. P. (2004). *Curriculum: Foundations, principles, and issues* (4th ed.). Boston: Allyn and Bacon.

Ornstein, A. C. (1990, Fall). Effective course planning by mapping. *Kappa Delta Pi Record,* 24–26.

Pearson, P. D., & Johnson, D. D. (1978). *Teaching reading comprehension.* New York: Holt, Rinehart, & Winston.

Popham, W. J. (2001, March). Teaching to the test? *Educational Leadership,* 16–20.

Richards, J., & Lockhart, C. (1996). *Reflective teaching in second language classrooms.* New York: Cambridge University Press.

Smith, P. L., & Ragan, T. J. (1999). *Instructional design.* Upper Saddle River, NJ: Merrill.

Solas, J. (1992, Summer). Investing teacher and student thinking about the process of teaching and learning. *Review of Educational Research,* 205–225.

Stipek, D. J. (1993). *Motivation to learn* (2nd ed.). Boston: Allyn & Bacon.

Wiggins, G., & McTighe, J. (1998). *Understanding by design.* Alexandria, VA: Association for Supervision and Curriculum Development.

Wildman, T. M., Magliaro, S. G., Niles, R. A., & Niles, J. A. (1992, May–June). Teacher mentoring: An analysis of roles, activities, and conditions. *Journal of Teacher Education,* 205–213.

Willis, S. (1999, November). The accountability question. *Education Update,* 1, 4–5, 8.

*chapter* **7**

# Instructional Methods

To appreciate instruction, we need to make a distinction between teaching and instruction. *Teaching* is the behavior of the teacher that evolves during the instructional process. *Instruction* is the specific methods and activities by which the teacher influences learning. In this section, we explore basic traditional instructional methods—methods that have been used most of the time by the great majority of teachers: (1) explanation and discussion, (2) questioning, (3) problem solving, and (4) practice, drill, and review. These methods, supported by many years of research and practice, come together in the scaffolding model. To help you better integrate this section, think of a lesson you will be teaching to your class. Which methods will you use? Why? What are the consequences of using these methods? When are these methods most effectively used? How do you make these methods work for your own teaching style?

# ■ EXPLANATION AND DISCUSSION

Teachers often find it necessary to provide explanation, discussion, and short lectures, especially when presenting new subject-matter content. After all, explanations make use of the foremost expressive language mode—that of "talk." We noted in Chapter 2 that talk was an important ingredient for children's cognitive and affective growth and that adults shape and scaffold children's thinking through discussion and conversation.

## The Need to Enrich Explanations

The traditional, historical view of the teacher is probably that of the instructor standing or seated in front of a classroom verbally dispensing information, views, or explanation about a topic. But a lot of talk without accompanying use of demonstrations or visual aids by the teacher may not captivate or enrich many students. This may be especially true for modern youth who grow up immersed in the rapid visual movement of the television and computer screens and may find a lot of formal talk about a topic difficult to attend to and process. Furthermore, a great deal of "telling" in situations in which coaching and interactive involvement should allow students to formulate their own responses may negate children's opportunities to develop their own problem-solving skills and strategies (Taylor, Peterson, Pearson, & Rodriguez, 2002).

However, teachers often use explanation and discussion to emphasize important points, to explain and/or elaborate content presented in a textbook, and to introduce the sequence of steps to follow in accomplishing a learning task, such as the study of a theme or topic. Explanations may require just a one- or two-sentence reminder in the lesson plan, or they may be embedded in the topic to be covered in the lesson plan.

## Discussion and Mental Engagement

**Discussion** is a normal outgrowth or consequence of explanation. A discussion is an oral exchange between or among teacher and students. Discussions permit students to respond to teacher statements, to ask questions, and to clarify ideas. The more involved students are in discussion, the more effective the exchange of ideas is likely to be, because students' thoughts tend to wander as teacher talk increases. Younger and low-achieving students become inattentive more readily than older and high-achieving students. The implication is clear: Teachers should make an effort to maintain student attention by limiting lecture and explanation time and increasing discussion time. This can be done with the skillful integration of questions to maintain student interest in a topic being explained and by establishing a purposeful climate for talk and conversation to encourage thinking.

Researchers have noted that talk is a necessary condition for children's learning during the school day and is essentially beneficial for language arts activities and for academic success in content area mastery. Although quiet classrooms have been historically considered the most conducive to learning, research suggests that talk, discussion, and conversation are essential ingredients for learning (Tompkins, 1998). One group of researchers reported that when students had the opportunity to elaborate their ideas through talk, their learning was facilitated (Pressley et al., 1992). Important considerations in reading instruction should be the ideas that are discussed and savored with students before, during, and after a particular reading (May, 2001).

The spoken language connected with role playing and/or drama has been an excellent tool for allowing students to engage with a problem and understand a situation. Moreover, reading leads naturally to talk, and writing becomes much more fluent and articulate after an individual rehearses or thinks out loud about what he or she is going to write. One author engaged the spoken language of young children in creative and expressive ways to interact with stories (Sipe, 2002). His procedure is illustrated in Box 7.1.

**BOX 7.1** Using Spoken Language to Connect with Children's Literature

One author developed a set of five guiding principles with which to engage young children in highly expressive conversation to help them comprehend stories more deeply. His five types of expressive engagement during story read-alouds are as follows:

1. *Dramatization.* Here the teacher dramatizes the story in verbal and nonverbal ways as the story is unfolding. Children are encouraged to participate by performing the character parts.
2. *Talking Back.* Here the children talk back to events or characters in the story, especially during a critical part when a character faces a situation or conflict. When children are encouraged to spontaneously verbalize about events in a story, they reveal a deep engagement of their understandings and feelings.
3. *Critiquing/Controlling.* The children react to the story by offering suggestions and alternatives to the story plot, settings, and characters' actions. This allows them to participate as authors by conceiving possibilities for a story.
4. *Inserting.* Now the children place themselves or a classmate in the story as one of the characters. This allows children to draw on their background by inserting prior experiences into the story to match what a character is doing.
5. *Taking Over.* When the story is completed, children can mold the text and interpret or react to story parts any way they wish. The story acts as a springboard, allowing them to show creative expression.

*Source:* Lawrence Sipe, "Talking Back and Taking Over: Young Children's Expressive Engagement during Storybook Read Alouds," *The Reading Teacher* (February 2002), pp. 476–483.

According to many researchers, attention span is correlated with age and ability, so the attention span of young and low-achieving students is limited (Bichler & Hudson, 1990; Spaulding, 1992). For such students, it is essential that teacher talk in any form (especially reciting and explaining) be limited to a few minutes' duration at any one time and be intermixed with other instructional activities (audio, visual, and physical). There should be more concrete activities than verbal and abstract presentations.

Lengthy talk can quickly lead to boredom because the audience is passive for a long period. One strategy for helping students learn from talk, and also for engaging them actively, is for the teacher to prepare a series of questions about the content to be covered. For example, "What is the main idea of . . . ?"; How does . . . affect . . . ?"; "Why is . . . important?" (King, 1990). These types of questions help students identify main ideas, organize notes, and engage in critical thinking, as opposed to recording pieces of the lecture and memorizing the information—or, even worse, drifting or losing concentration. Students need to integrate and anchor ideas from the lesson explanation—that is, to become more involved in processing information as opposed to sitting passively. Teachers, as well, need to consider their classroom interaction styles; less accomplished teachers tend to prefer to tell and recite, whereas more accomplished teachers prefer to coach, model, and engage students in discussion and conversation (Taylor, Pearson, Clark, & Walpole, 2000).

One author uses conversation to help students think more critically and reflectively about literature. Through conversation and question probes, students are led away from traditional comprehension questions to consider multiple viewpoints reflected in a story, and their responses are valued. Students are directed to justify and qualify their answers by citing evidence from the reading (Whitin, 2002).

The need to promote conversational involvement while generating intellectual curiosity is also why many teachers use the K-W-L strategy when introducing a new topic or theme. Before they read or engage in the new learning topic, children can discuss or write what they "know" under the K column on a large chart or prepared paper. The question posed by the teacher for the K column is generally worded, "What do I know about this topic [theme]?" Once again prior to reading, children respond to the next question posed in the W column, "What do I want to learn about this topic? (Or, What am I curious about knowing?)" After reading or learning about the topic through explanation or other instructional activities, children discuss or write "What I have learned" in the L column (Ogle, 1989). It is vital that each child have the opportunity to discuss what he or she has learned and whether the "What I want to learn" question was answered (May, 2001).

Others have added a fourth column on the K-W-L chart to continually involve children in discussion with the text and teacher. One author has added an A column for affective responses. Here children can note their feelings, attitudes, appreciation, and values encouraged by the topic (Mandeville, 1994). Another uses the A or fourth column as a means of informal assessment (McAllister, 1994). Here the teacher might make note of the quality of each child's response and interact to achieve elaboration and clarification of a response. We recommend a fourth column with an S heading to indicate, "What am I *still* curious about learning?" to encourage additional discussion, thinking, and curiosity. Children respond to the *still* prompt because the topic engagement has added to their knowledge base. Children now record continuing curiousity gaps in their knowledge and add questions they would still like answered. This allows the teacher to enhance students' intellectual curiosity even further, to provide additional explanation and discussion about the topic, or to elicit the help of students to find the answers to the new questions through library and Internet research (Reutzel & Cooter, 1999).

When dealing with informational topics, one author has suggested adding three more columns to the K-W-L grid to help students deal reflectively with the information explosion on the Internet and other print and media sources. In two columns, students note the sources of their inquiry and their learnings, and in another they state whether their original prior knowledge statements were confirmed. During discussion, students show that they evaluated the information they researched and didn't take one source as confirmation of the validity of an "often-believed fact" (Sampson, 2002).

## When Talk Is Appropriate

Based on a review of several studies of the explanation and lecture method, Gage and Berliner feel that talk is appropriate when (1) the basic purpose is to disseminate information, (2) the information is not available elsewhere, (3) the information needs to be presented in a particular way or adapted to a particular group, (4) interest in a subject needs to be aroused, (5) the information needs to be remembered for a short time, and (6) the purpose is to introduce or explain other learning tasks. They further state that lengthy talk is inappropriate when (1) objectives other than acquisition of information are sought, (2) long-term learning is desired, (3) the information is complex, abstract, or detailed, (4) learner participation is important for achieving the objectives, (5) higher cognitive learning, such as analysis and synthesis, is sought, and (6) students are below average in ability (Gage & Berliner, 1998).

There are administrative and practical reasons for using informal and brief lectures as well as explanations. These methods are well suited to large groups, and few materials and equipment are needed, giving the methods the additional benefit of being economical. The methods are flexible and can be used in regular classrooms, small groups, and large settings. Teachers who travel or change classrooms need only to carry with them their lesson plans or notes. Although good lectures need considerable preparation, their delivery does not require elaborate advanced planning such as having materials ordered or equipment scheduled and moved about. The fact that teachers are not dependent on others to carry out the recitation, explanation, or discussion makes it easy and comfortable for them.

# ■ QUESTIONING

Good teaching involves good questioning, and good questioning stimulates mental engagement, inquiry, and good discussion, especially when large groups of students are being taught (Friedman & Cataldo, 2002; Roser & Keehn, 2002). Skillful questioning can arouse students' curiosity, stimulate their imaginations, and motivate them to search out new knowledge. It can challenge students, make them think, and help clarify concepts and problems related to the lesson. The type and sequence of questions and how students respond to them influence the quality of classroom discussion and the effectiveness of instruction. Good teachers are usually skilled in striking a balance between factual and thought-provoking questions and in selecting questions to emphasize major points and stimulate lively discussion.

## Types of Questions

Questions can be categorized in many ways: (1) according to the thinking process involved, from low level to high level or (according to the cognitive taxonomy) from knowledge to evaluation; (2) according to type of answer required, convergent or divergent; and (3) according to the degree of personal exploration, or valuing. Some educators have also developed descriptive categories of questions, guidelines, or questioning taxonomies to assist students with thinking, problem solving, and reading comprehension or writing processing (Beyer, 1998a, 1998b; Harpaz & Lefstein, 2000).

*Low-Level and High-Level Questions.* **Low-level questions** emphasize memory and information recall. When was the Declaration of Independence signed? Who won the Civil War? Where is the Statue of Liberty? These questions focus on facts and do not test understanding or problem-solving skills. They correspond to lower cognitive processes—what J. P. Guilford calls *information,* Jean Piaget calls *concrete operations,* and Arthur Jensen calls *level-one thinking.*

**High-level questions** go beyond memory and factual information to call for complex and abstract thinking. Low-level questions have their place. They are used to assess readiness for complex and abstract thinking and to see whether students can deal with high-level questions that involve analysis, synthesis, and problem solving. The ideal is to reach a balance between the two types of questions. The trouble is that many teachers do not progress beyond knowledge-oriented questions. In fact, according to researchers, it is not uncommon to find that 70 to 90 percent of the questions teachers ask are low level (Hunkins, 1994; Payne, 1992).

Criticism of the use of low-level questions is complicated by research that indicates that low-level and narrowly defined questions characterize an effective instructional program for inner-city and low-achieving learners (Bereiter & Englemann, 1966; Rosenshine, 1979; Wood, 1992). Teachers who ask high-level questions and encourage student-initiated comments are least effective with these types of students (Doyle, 1985; Medley, 1979; Stallings & Quinn, 1991) because these students lack a knowledge base and need more low-level questions and feedback from teachers before they can move to problem-solving skills and high-level questions. The dilemma such teachers face is that it is easy to become set in the use of low-level questions and thus maintain students at a cognitively second-rate instructional level.

Low-level questions can foster learning, especially with students who lack prerequisite knowledge and who are developing a knowledge base and need to experience simple questions to build their confidence in learning. According to researchers, low-order questioning is effective for such students when it is used for instructional activities involving basic reading and math, or in any subject in which a basic foundation needs to be built and current learning is an extension of prior learning. The new low-order information must be related in a meaningful way to the knowledge and information level the learner already has (P. Peterson, 1988; Schunk, 1991; Solas, 1992). But we would expect teachers to progress to asking as many high-level questions as possible. If we return to the subjects of our three examples of low-level questions, we can ask a series of high-level questions: What were the reasons for signing the Declaration of Independence? What other alternative courses of action were available to the revolutionists? What economic, political, and social events led to the Civil War? Why did the North win the Civil War? How did the results of the war affect black–white relations for the remainder of the nineteenth century? Or this century? What does the Statue of Liberty mean to you? To an immigrant arriving in the United States by ship in 1920? To a Vietnamese or Haitian political refugee today?

These questions are obviously more advanced, more stimulating, and more challenging. In many cases, there are no right or wrong answers. As the questions become more advanced, they involve more abstraction and points of view. Asking high-level questions demands patience and clear thinking on the part of the teacher. Creating appropriate timing, sequencing, and phrasing is no easy task for even the experienced teacher.

Benjamin Bloom's cognitive taxonomy has been a popular vehicle used by teachers to categorize low-level and high-level questions. Low-level questioning corresponds to the knowledge category of the taxonomy—what Bloom calls the "simplest" form of learning and the "most common educational objective" (Bloom, 1956). High-level questioning and problem-solving skills correspond to the next five categories of the taxonomy—comprehension, application, analysis, synthesis, and evaluation. This is shown in Table 7.1.

*Convergent and Divergent Questions.* **Convergent questions** tend to have one correct or best answer. For this reason, they are often mistakenly identified as low-level and knowledge questions, but they can also be formulated to demand the selection of relevant concepts and the working out of problems dealing with steps and structure. Convergent questions can deal with logic and complex data, abstract ideas, analogies, and multiple relationships. According to research, convergent questions can be used when students work on and attempt to solve difficult exercises in math and science, especially those dealing with analysis of equations and word problems (Beyer, 1991; Resnick & Klopfer, 1989). Here the need is to focus on specific exercises and to ensure understanding before progressing to more advanced levels.

**Divergent questions** are often open-ended and usually have many appropriate, different answers. Stating a "right" answer is not always the most important response; rather, how the student arrives at his or her answer is often more important. Teachers should encourage students to state their reasoning and to provide supporting examples and evidence. Divergent questions are associated with high-level thinking processes and can encourage creative thinking and discovery learning. Often, students must first be asked convergent questions to clarify what they know before the teacher advances to asking divergent questions. But the ideal is to ask fewer convergent questions, especially low-level ones, and more divergent questions. The mix of convergent and divergent questions will reflect the students' abilities, the teacher's ability to phrase such questions, and the teacher's comfort in handling varied responses.

## Table 7.1  Categorizing Questions Related to the Cognitive Taxonomy

| Category | Sample Question |
| --- | --- |
| 1.0 Knowledge | |
| 1.1 Knowledge of specifics | Who discovered the Mississippi River? |
| 1.2 Knowledge of ways and means of dealing with specifics | What word does an adjective modify? |
| 1.3 Knowledge of universals and abstractions in a field | What is the best method for calculating the circumference of a circle? |
| 2.0 Comprehension | |
| 2.1 Translation | What does the word *migration* mean? |
| 2.2 Interpretation | Referring to the bar graph, which state has the largest population? |
| 2.3 Extrapolation | Given the extinction rate of sperm whales, what will be their population by the year 2010? |
| 3.0 Application | Can you prepare a travel map to show the route taken by the explorers? Given a pie-shaped lot 120 ft. × 110 ft. × 100 ft., and village setback conditions of 15 ft. in all directions, what is the largest size one-story home you can build on this lot? |
| 4.0 Analysis | Who can distinguish between fact and opinion in the article we read? |
| 4.1 Analysis of elements | How did the Native American tribe we read about organize colors, shapes, and sizes to produce images? |
| 4.2 Analysis of relationships | How does J. K. Rowling in the Harry Potter series depict the concepts of good and evil? |
| 4.3 Analysis of organizational principles | Who can write a simple melodic line? |
| 5.0 Synthesis | |
| 5.1 Production of a unique communication | How would you go about determining the chemical weight of an unknown substance? Can you design a travel brochure of the country we studied using a multimedia computer program? |
| 5.2 Production of a plan or proposed set of operations | How would you go about determining the materials needed to construct a terrarium? |
| 5.3 Derivation of a set of abstract relations | What are the common causes of pollution in the different world environments, such as the sea, land, and air? |
| 6.0 Evaluation | Who can judge what is wrong with the architect's design of the plumbing and electricity? |
| 6.1 Judgment in terms of internal evidence | In this literature selection, what do you think the author was trying to tell us about courage? |
| 6.2 Judgment in terms of external evidence | Even though the giant may have seemed scary and mean, was Jack justified in stealing the giant's golden chicken? |

Convergent questions usually start with *what, who, when,* or *where;* divergent questions usually start with *how* or *why. What* or *who* questions, followed by *whys,* are really divergent questions that are introduced by *what* to get to the *why* aspect of the question. (For example, "Who won the Civil War?" leads to the ultimate question: "Why?") Most teachers ask far more *what, who, when,* and *where* questions than *how* or *why* questions; the ratio is about three or four to one (Dillon, 1984, 1988; Gall, 1984). This is because the convergent questions are simple to phrase and to grade. They help keep students focused on specific data, and they give many students a chance to participate. Convergent questions thus make good questions for practice and review. Divergent questions require more flexibility on the teacher's part. For the student, they require the ability to cope with not being sure about being right and with not always getting approval from the teacher. In general, the pace of questioning is slower. Students have more opportunity to exchange ideas and different opinions. There is also more chance for disagreement among students and between students and teacher—which is often discouraged or viewed as tangential by teachers.

*Right Answers Count.* In most classrooms, teachers ask convergent questions, which entail a "right" answer, and students are expected to give the answer—often resulting in teacher approval. John Holt points out that as students become right-answer oriented, they become *producers,* producing what teachers want, rather than *thinkers.* Only the rare student is willing to play with ideas without caring whether the teacher confirms that an answer is right. But the average child must be right: "She cannot bear to be wrong. When she is wrong . . . the only thing to do is to forget it as quickly as possible" (Holt, 1995). Under these circumstances, divergent questions, which may not have right answers, only prolong the child's agony in the classroom.

Asking questions to which there is only one right answer fosters a highly convergent, even authoritarian mind—one that looks for simple "right" answers and simple solutions to complex problems, one that relies on authority rather than on rational judgment to find the "right" answer. It also breeds a rigid and narrow mind that fails to recognize or is unwilling to admit that facts and figures are screened through a filtering process of personal and social experience and interpretation (Ornstein, 1987; Peverly, 1991).

## Questions for Valuing

A number of educators and psychologists have advocated different ways of enhancing the creative and human potential of students. All these procedures and techniques stress the use of **valuing questions,** a process in which students explore their feelings and attitudes, analyze their experiences, and express their ideas. The emphasis is on the personal development of the learner through clarifying attitudes and aspirations and making choices. The values brought to a reading experience often affect students' intention to read and what they will get out of the reading (Cole, 2002–2003). One author suggests the use of a facts and feelings response diary to help middle school students connect their personal feelings and values to statements of fact in their content area readings (Richards, 2003).

Louis Raths and his colleagues have developed a model for clarifying learners' values. For him, valuing consists of seven components in three levels: *choosing*—(1) choosing freely, (2) choosing from alternatives, (3) choosing after considering the consequences of each alternative; *prizing*—(4) cherishing the choice, (5) affirming the choice to others; *acting*—(6) doing something with the choice, and (7) repeating the action (Raths, Harmin, & Simon, 1978). Raths has also developed several general questions that can be used in any classroom to encourage students to clarify their values by using his model. A sample of these questions is shown in Table 7.2.

---

*Table 7.2*  **Questioning Strategies for the Valuing Process**

---

1. *Choosing freely*
   a. Where do you suppose you first got that idea?
   b. How long have you felt that way?
   c. What would people say if you weren't to do what you say you must do?

2. *Choosing from alternatives*
   a. What else did you consider before you picked this?
   b. How long did you look around before you decided?
   c. Was it a hard decision? What went into the final decision? Who helped? Do you need any further help?

3. *Choosing thoughtfully and reflectively*
   a. What would be the consequences of each alternative available?
   b. Have you thought about this very much? How did your thinking go?
   c. This is what I understand you to say . . . [interpret statement].

4. *Prizing and cherishing*
   a. Are you glad you feel that way?
   b. How long have you wanted it?
   c. What good is it? What purpose does it serve? Why is it important to you?

5. *Affirming*
   a. Would you tell the class the way you feel?
   b. Would you be willing to sign a petition supporting that idea?
   c. Are you saying that you believe . . . [repeat the idea]?

6. *Acting upon choice*
   a. I hear what you are for; now, is there anything you can do about it? Can I help?
   b. What are your first steps, second steps, etc?
   c. Are you willing to put some of your money [energy, time] behind this idea?

7. *Repeating*
   a. Have you felt this way for some time?
   b. Have you done anything already? Do you do this often?
   c. What are your plans for doing more of it?

---

*Source:* Adapted from Louis E. Raths, Merrill Harmin, and Sidney B. Simon, *Values and Teaching,* 2nd ed. (Columbus, OH: Merrill, 1978), 65–66.

## Questioning Guidelines

Other authorities have formulated their own categories and models of questions that correspond to some of the basic types we have just described. For instance, James Gallagher sorts questions into four categories:

1. *Cognitive-memory* questions require students to reproduce facts or remember content through processes such as rote memory or selective recall. For example, "What is the capital of France?"
2. *Convergent* questions require students to recall information that leads to a correct or conventional answer. Given or known information is usually the expected response; novel information is usually considered incorrect. For example, "Summarize the author's major points."
3. *Divergent* questions require students to generate their own data or a new perspective on a given topic. Divergent questions have no right answer; they suggest novel or creative responses. For example, "What might the history of the United States have been if the Nazis had won World War II?"
4. *Evaluative* questions require students to make value judgments about the quality, correctness, or adequacy of information based on some criterion usually set by the student or by some objective standard. For example, "How would you judge the art of Picasso?" or "Why did you think Melissa's story was a good one?"

Gallagher found that in classrooms with gifted students, cognitive-memory questions constituted more than 50 percent of the total questions asked. It is assumed that teachers ask even more cognitive-memory questions with average or low-achieving students. Convergent questions were the second most frequently used category. Few divergent and evaluative questions were asked. Gallagher surmises that teacher–student discussions can operate normally if only the first two categories of questions are used (Gallagher, 1965; Gallagher & Aschner, 1963).

Also, when considering the importance of question types, recall from Chapter 5 that a cornerstone strategy of the curriculum integration and curriculum mapping designs was the use of the guiding or essential question. This type of question is the fundamental query that directs the search for knowledge and understanding in disciplinary and interdisciplinary curricula. Such guiding/essential questions have these characteristics: (1) they are open-ended but focus inquiry on a specific topic; (2) they are nonjudgmental but require high-level thinking to answer; (3) they should contain emotive force and intellectual stimulation to encourage students to probe into national issues, localized concerns, and study of traditional discipline subjects; and (4) they should be brief, pithy, yet full of substance in their asking (Traver, 1998). One author considers the use of such questions that frame learning assignments or lessons to be thoughtful questions (Beyer, 1998a). Others use the term *fertile questions* because they drive the learning to create communities of thinkers and to overcome the narrowness of providing correct answers (Harpaz & Lefstein, 2000).

In most reading comprehension instruction in today's classrooms, questions are a dominant tool. Used by most teachers in many types of reading situations, questions effectively guide the pace of the reading lesson, providing insight to teachers into the level and depth of students' reading comprehension. We showed that the K-W-L-S strategy uses questions as probes to generate interest in and discussion about a topic. Many other valued strategies in guided reading and comprehension instruction, such as the directed reading–thinking activity, the SQ4R method of topic learning and study, the reciprocal teaching strategy, literature circles, and story grammar analysis find their strength through levels and types of questions. We suggest that teachers consult Table 7.3 to note the four major ways that questions are posed in relation to a textual reading: (1) *before reading,* to whet motivation and curiosity while accessing background schema; (2) *during reading,* to monitor, check, and guide comprehension as reading is occurring; (3) *after reading,* to summarize, reflect on, react to, and value aspects of the reading; and (4) *during all phases of the reading,* to be metacognitively involved by knowing where

*Table 7.3* Developing Active Reading Comprehension through Questioning

| Before Reading: Predictive/Motivating Questions | During Reading: Questions to Improve Understanding | After Reading: Summarizing and Thought Questions | Metacognitive Questions |
|---|---|---|---|
| What does the title tell about the selection? | Has what you read made sense so far? | What did you learn from this selection? | Why do you think it was important to read this selection? |
| What type of reading selection is this? | What have you learned so far? | What did you like or not like about this selection? | What was in this selection that could help you and others? |
| What do the pictures (or graphs, diagrams, or artwork) tell us about the meaning? | What did you find most interesting up to this point or what did you like the best? | Can you summarize what the selection was about? | What did you want to gain from this selection? |
| What do you know about this topic? | Did you find parts that were difficult to understand? Can you read those parts to me? | Can you now complete your graphic organizer or map and fill in the information in the most appropriate places? | When something didn't make sense during the reading, were you able to figure out what to do to get the right meaning? |
| What can you contribute? | Did you find some words that were difficult to read? Can you find them for me? | Can you use ideas and information from this selection in another way? | Can you organize the ideas in the reading in another way, such as in a cognitive map, outline, or figures? |
| What else do you want to know about the topic? | What could you do if you didn't understand something? | Was this selection like other materials you have read? | Did you understand why the author may have written this? |
| What do you think the main idea of the reading might be? | Do you think you can begin to make a graphic organizer (a map) of the ideas so far? | What did you tell your friends about this selection? | |
| What do you think you will learn about when you read this selection? | What do you see in your mind about what you've read? | Now that you have finished reading this selection topic, what are you still curious about learning? | |
| Why do you think the author wrote this? | | | |
| What other questions can you ask yourself before you read? | | | |

one is going with the reading, why one wants to know, and how to take action to work through puzzling parts and inconsistencies in the reading.

Some authors call questions that provoke and stimulate effective discussion about text "authentic questions." An authentic question is asked because the range of students' thoughts are unknown and the teacher desires to move students beyond the literal level of text understanding (Rasinski & Padak, 2000). Questions that stimulate thinking also provide for good discussion. Two authors maintain that teacher questions delivered at selected, critical points in a social studies reading encourage students to question the author about unconnected factual information as they read. The teacher queries make students think about why the author presented particular information and what the point of its presentation was (Beck & McKeown, 2002). Good discussion is based both on understanding of the text and on the continuing use of authentic, higher-level questions to keep the discussion going.

In summary, good questioning techniques and stimulating discussions go hand-in-hand in an effective teaching situation. Teachers might include four to six broad questions that serve the dual purpose of stimulating discussion among students and outlining the major topics or parts of the lesson. Teachers who emphasize critical thinking or problem solving also tend to use questions to stimulate the lesson.

## ■ PROBLEM SOLVING

A great deal of the professional literature since the beginning of the twentieth century has focused on problem solving, inquiry-based learning, and thinking skills related to the effective use by students of asking pertinent questions (Owens, Hester, & Teale, 2002; Schmidt, Gillen, Zollo, & Stone, 2002). Educators and psychologists have identified various methods of teaching students how to problem solve since Charles Judd (1918) (at the University of Chicago) and Edward Thorndike (1932) (at Columbia University) showed that learning could be explained in terms of general principles of thinking and methods of attacking problems that can be transferred to different situations.

### Thinking Modes of Problem Solving

John Dewey's process of **reflective thinking** was considered the classic model for problem solving from 1910 until the 1950s, when Piaget's work and other models employing various cognitive and information-processing strategies were introduced. Although Dewey's model is viewed as an oversimplification by cognition theorists, it is still considered practical, especially by science and math teachers. Because Dewey believed that one of the chief functions of school was to improve the reasoning process, he recommended adopting the problem-solving method for all subjects and grade levels. Reflective thinking involves five steps: (1) Become aware of difficulty, (2) identify the problem, (3) assemble and classify data and formulate hypotheses, (4) accept or reject tentative hypotheses, and (5) formulate and evaluate conclusions (Dewey, 1910/1997).

Two authors working with culturally and linguistically diverse at-risk students use some of Dewey's ideas in their four-step reflection and inquiry model. First, the teacher becomes *aware* that communication or ability to perform adequately on a task has not occurred. Second, the teacher *inquires* about the identity of the problem by determining what cultural features in the nature of the lesson may have had a negative impact on students. Third, the teacher *reconceptualizes* the learning problem and forms new hypotheses about the culture of the students, the lesson, the curriculum, and the school culture itself. Finally, the teacher revises and restructures the *lesson* based on new insights and conceptions (Pransky & Bailey, 2002–2003). A similar procedure occurs, as we note shortly, with the teacher's wise use of scaffolding at opportune times so that the old can be accommodated to the new.

A number of educators describe successful problem solving as relying on **heuristic thinking**—that is, engaging in exploratory processes that have value only in that they may lead to the solution of a problem. Physicians often diagnose problems in this manner, for example, doing tests to eliminate what is *not* the problem in order to narrow the possibilities down to a few probable diagnoses of what *is* the problem (Bigge & Shermis, 1998; Good & Brophy, 1990; Mayer, 1992). According to Newell and Simon's method for dealing with a problem, the person first constructs a representation of the problem, called the "problem space," and then works out a solution that involves a search through the problem space. The problem solver may break the problem into components, activate old information from memory, or seek new information. If an exploratory solution proves to be successful, the task ends (Newell & Simon, 1972). If it fails, the person backtracks, sidetracks, or redefines the problem or method used to solve it. This type of problem solving is not linear. The problem solver may jump around, skip, or combine steps.

A heuristic may also be considered a broad-based thinking tool or principle that helps learners discover how to solve problems. For instance, using the steps of the scientific method or designing a flowchart or cognitive map to conceptualize the range of a problem or issue to be investigated is using a heuristic as a way to think through a problem. Thus a heuristic is like a "big idea," a concept, or a principle that can facilitate the most efficient and broadest acquisition of knowledge (Kameenui & Carnine, 1998).

Another way to engage reflective thinking and a problem-solving, inquiry approach to learning is to conduct **experiments** and **demonstrations** in the classroom. Both are ideal for creative and discovery methods of lesson implementation, whereby the teacher and students integrate the subject matter by collecting data, observing, measuring, identifying, and examining causal relationships (see Box 7.2). Young students and low-achieving students may need more instruction and coaching feedback from the teacher. Older and high-achieving students work more independently and participate more in demonstrations and experiments because they are better able to handle quantities of information, reorganize information into new forms, and transfer it to new learning situations (Schutz, 1991; Wentzel, 1991).

There is a consensus today that **metacognitive skills** (or processes) are transferable competencies that play a significant role in problem solving and high-order thinking. Metacognitive skills represent knowledge of how to do something (usually involving a plan, set of steps, or procedures) as well as the ability to evaluate and modify perfor-

**BOX 7.2** Using Demonstrations and Experiments in Inquiry Learning

Consider the following when using demonstrations and experiments in a problem-solving, inquiry approach to learning

1. Plan and prepare for the demonstration (or experiment). Make certain all material is available when you begin. Practice the demonstration (if conducted for the first time) before the lesson to see what problems may arise.
2. Present the demonstration in context with what students have already learned or as a stimulus for searching for new knowledge.
3. Make provisions for students' full participation.
4. Maintain control over the materials or equipment to the extent the students are unable to work on their own.
5. Pose both close-ended and open-ended questions according to students' capacity for deductive and inductive responses. ("What is happening to the object?" is a close-ended question; "What can you generalize from . . . ?" is open-ended.)
6. Encourage students to ask questions as they arise.
7. Encourage students to make observations first and then to make inferences and generalizations. Encourage them to look for and express new information and insights.
8. Allocate sufficient time so that (a) the demonstration can be completed, (b) students can discuss what they have observed, (c) students can reach conclusions and apply principles they have learned, (d) students can take notes or write up the demonstration, and (e) materials can be collected and stored away.

mance. Based on a review of the research, some metacognitive skills that have been found to distinguish successful problem solvers and that can translate into instructional methods are:

1. *Comprehension monitoring.* Knowing when one understands or does not understand something; evaluating one's performance.
2. *Understanding decisions.* Understanding what one is doing and the reason why.
3. *Planning.* Taking time to develop a strategy; considering options; proceeding without impulse.
4. *Estimating task difficulty.* Estimating difficulty and allocating sufficient time for difficult problems.
5. *Task presentation.* Staying with the task; being able to ignore internal and external distractions; maintaining direction in thinking.
6. *Coping strategies.* Staying calm; being able to cope when things are not going easily; not giving up or becoming anxious or frustrated.
7. *Internal cues.* Searching for context clues when confronted with difficult or novel problems.
8. *Retracking.* Looking up definitions; rereading previous information; knowing when to backtrack.
9. *Noting and correcting.* Using logical approaches; double checking; recognizing inconsistencies, contradictions, or gaps in performance.
10. *Flexible approaches.* Willingness to use alternative approaches; knowing when to search for another strategy; trying random approaches that are sensible and

plausible when one's original approach has been unsuccessful (Brophy, 1998; Lohman, 1986; Woodward, 1994).

One implication for teaching is that an increase in knowledge of subject matter does not necessarily produce changes in metacognitive skills. These skills in general reflect high-order thinking processes that cannot be learned or developed overnight or in one subject.

## Problem-Solving Processes

Although most teachers acknowledge that problem solving is important, many need help incorporating it into their lessons. Good and Grouws have identified five **problem-solving processes** for mathematics, but they can be applied to the teaching–learning process in all subjects.

1. *Attending to prerequisites.* Solving new problems is based largely on understanding previously learned skills and concepts of the subject. The teacher should use the skills and concepts mastered by the students as a basis for solving problems.
2. *Attending to relationships.* Subjects comprise a large body of logical and closely related ideas; the teacher should emphasize meaning and interpretation of ideas.
3. *Attending to representation.* The more the student is able to represent a problem in context with concrete or real-world phenomena, the better able the student is to solve the problem.
4. *Generalizing concepts.* Teachers need to explain the general applicability of the idea to students; skills and processes that apply to many settings should be practiced.
5. *Attending to language.* Teachers should use precise terminology of their subject, and students must learn basic terms and concepts of the subject (Good & Grouws, 1987).

Matthew Lipman adds five other processes that cut across situational contexts and subject matter. Problem-solving teaching should take into account:

1. *Exceptional or irregular circumstances.* Certain things may be permissible under certain conditions and not under others.
2. *Special limitations or constraints.* Almost all theories, principles, and concepts have certain limitations or contingencies under which they don't apply or are not valid.
3. *Overall configurations.* A concept or fact may be wrong or objectionable when taken out of context, but valid or proper in context.
4. *Atypical evidence.* Overgeneralizing from a small sample or one experiment is somewhat risky.
5. *Context-specific meanings.* There are terms and concepts for which there are no precise equivalents in other languages or subjects and whose meanings are therefore context-specific (Lipman, 1988).

In general, the improvements made in students' thinking depends on their ability to identify good criteria for their opinions and solutions. The criteria should be based on one or more of the above processes, which can be taught. In this connection, the most characteristic feature of problem solving is that it discovers its own weakness and rectifies what is at fault in its procedures. Thus it is self-correcting, which is metacognitive thinking.

The test for learning to problem solve is the ability to apply or use the strategies that have been learned in new, or at least a variety of, situations. Many times teachers think students have "mastered" relevant facts and procedures. In reality, according to Alan Schoenfeld (1989), they have learned a strategy blindly and can use it only in circumstances similar to those in which they were taught. When given a slightly different version of a problem, or when they must make inferences or leaps in thinking, they are stymied. Similarly, most of the problems found in textbooks, and those we assign for homework, are not problems in the true sense; they are exercises or tasks that reinforce specific, usually rote, procedures for solving a problem. In math, for example, most word problems are solved by students who may rely on a key word without fully understanding the procedures involved. A real problem confronts a student with a difficulty, and the answer cannot be obtained by relying on rote procedures; it calls for relating or rearranging learned concepts or procedures with new ideas generated by the problem. A real problem is not straightforward. A student's understanding of the procedures and the transfer of understanding to new situations are crucial. Most students cannot function in this arena because our instructional methods tend to emphasize rote, mechanical procedures.

## Helping Students Problem Solve

Teachers can help students develop into problem solvers by becoming less content driven and by slowing down the pace of lessons. Class time must incorporate experimental, discovery, and/or reflective processes and activities. An expectation or norm needs to be created in a reflective classroom, in which being right is not as important as how the answer is deduced (see Box 7.3).

This kind of teaching forces the teacher to make tough choices. Open-ended questioning is essential in problem-solving classrooms, but such an approach takes time and thus limits content coverage. For example, it is a very different activity to list the causes of the Civil War or the characteristics of an active volcano than to ask middle-grade students to arrive at such insights themselves. It is one thing to demonstrate to your second-grade students how to fold a paper plane so that it flies; it is a totally different thing, and takes much longer, to encourage students to plan their own solutions: to discover on their own or in small groups how to fold and fly the planes. For the sake of efficiency, the teacher might provide some clues to get them started and then at the

**BOX 7.3** Helping Students Become Problem Solvers

Teachers can help students engage in problem-solving, inquiry-based learning by considering the following suggestions:

- Presenting questions or problems for students to answer rather than giving them answers to copy
- Incorporating students' prior knowledge and then challenging or modifying it
- Having students test and make predictions as in the steps of scientific thinking
- Allowing students to "mess around" and explore rather than limiting them to one way of working or arriving at a solution
- Incorporating students' planning and ideas into the curriculum or lesson plan
- Including a host of hands-on experiences
- Assigning independent projects and readings so that students can develop their own interests and sense of inquiry.

end of the lesson ask students to reach a consensus on the common characteristics of planes that fly the farthest (Casey & Howson, 1993).

Grant Wiggins and Jay McTighe (1998) offer additional principles and guidelines to stimulate student inquiry and self-reliance in achieving deep understandings and insights. They suggest that teachers:

- Resist providing explanations of content all the time using a didactic teaching style; rather, engage students in inquiry learning and discovery work to guide and focus lessons.
- Provide more questions in teaching, asking "big idea" questions while answering the little questions.
- Reverse teacher–student roles by asking innocent questions and requiring students to come forth with explanations and interpretations in their answers.
- Formulate questions that have a number of possible answers so that students consider multiple viewpoints. Follow up with tasks and projects that allow students to look at solving answers from different points of view.
- Mentor students in constructing and performing final projects of high quality, such as through graphic, oral, or computer presentations. In such mentoring, guide students to find information by themselves and to self-monitor themselves in searching out answers of diverse viewpoints (metacognitive thinking).

The difference in approach between giving students answers and having them search for answers themselves can be summed up as *traditional* versus *experimental teaching; direct* or *didactic instruction* versus *inquiry-based, implicit instruction;* or *content-based* versus *process-based learning.* Does the teacher provide knowledge or do the students construct knowledge? The latter choice has more personal meaning for students and equips them to integrate learning into long-term memory more easily because the learners themselves have generated, predicted, and evaluated the content.

A problem-solving approach assumes knowledge of several learning theories. Teachers must consider the students' developmental stages (Piaget, 1963), how students use language (Vygotsky, 1986), how students process information (Ausubel, 1978; Sternberg, 2000), and how students construct meaning (Bruner, 1990; Vygotsky, 1986). These theories are appropriate for all learners of all ages and serve as the basis for problem solving in the classrooms. You cannot design your lesson plans to integrate problem solving unless you have some appreciation for and understanding of how students think.

Students often have problems when they encounter situations to which they must respond but do not know immediately what the response should be. Regardless of the method, students need relevant information to assess the situation and arrive at a response—that is, to solve the problem. Not all successful students will use the same strategy to solve the same problem, and often more than one strategy can be used.

Even with simple addition or subtraction, students use different strategies in solving problems and therefore have a different framework about the relative difficulty of the problems. For example, John has 6 marbles and Sally has 8. How many marbles do they have together? Most students simply add 6 plus 8, in what we might term a *com-*

*mon strategy.* In a *join strategy*, elements are added (6 + 6 = 12, 2 more is 14). With a *separate strategy*, elements are removed (8 + 8 = 16, 2 less is 14). A *part-part-whole strategy* involves undertaking two or more elements ("I tabulated both numbers by adding 1 and 6 and subtracting 1 from 8. That makes 7 + 7, which is 14.") All four student approaches are correct strategies (Cobb, Wood, Yackel, & McNeal, 1992; Peterson & Carpenter, 1989).

Although teachers often stress one specific strategy to solve specific problems, students often use a variety of strategies, especially with more complex problems. In fact, as the problems become more abstract, so do their strategies. The teacher who insists on one strategy and penalizes students who use another appropriate strategy is discouraging their problem-solving potential. In order to teach problem solving according to the way *students* think, teachers need to become aware of how students process information and what strategies students use to solve problems. They can do this by asking questions, listening to responses, and inspecting student work.

New research on cognition shows that successful problem solving correlates with a particular mind-set. According to Robert Marzano (1992), students' attitudes toward school and learning, and their own social concerns and self-concepts, are important dimensions for learning. Students develop "mental habits" that make them more or less efficient as problem solvers. For example, they learn to seek accuracy, test ideas, avoid impulsivity, and persist when answers are not apparent—which in part is based on how they perceive themselves in learning situations.

Being able to translate these ideas into practice is another issue. For teachers, it suggests that we take note of the broad social and psychological dimension of learning. On a cognitive level, it means slowing down the teaching–learning process and studying content in depth. It means using Socratic questions, asking students to clarify and redefine their thinking, as well as discussing, comparing, probing, and debating content—instructional methods that slow down teaching. As a teacher, it means you must be willing to reveal or model your own thought processes—what you are thinking and how you are tackling a problem—and then ask your students to reveal their thinking during problem-solving tasks. It means sometimes discarding the lesson plan and just listening to your students as you pinpoint or focus on a concept, elaborate on one of their statements, or help them clarify an issue or problem.

# ■ PRACTICE, DRILL, AND REVIEW

The mention of practice and drill summons up images of the old-fashioned schoolmaster, the drillmaster, who made learning a repetitive response whereby students either memorized their lessons or experienced the teacher's wrath. However, practice and drill is an instructional method that does serve certain purposes well and can be used to advantage in classrooms on a daily basis. Review occurs across lessons and is practiced to ensure that information and strategies taught have coalesced in students' minds and have transferred to long-term memory.

## Applications of Practice and Drill

**Practice and drill** is a common method used by elementary teachers to teach the fundamentals, especially to young children. Middle school teachers working with students who still lack basic skills or knowledge of academic subject matter also employ this method before asking these students to move on to other tasks or transfer their learning to a new situation.

There is general agreement that students need *practice* exercises to help them transfer new information into long-term memory and integrate new with old learning. Practice problems can come from workbooks, textbooks, and teacher-made materials. Practice, in the form of seatwork, can be helpful for students if it is given for limited periods (no more than ten minutes per class session), the instructions for it are clear, and it is integrated into the lesson (not assigned to fill time or to maintain order). *Drill* can be helpful for basic skills, such as reading, mathematics, and language, and in lower grades with low-achieving students who need more practice to learn new skills or integrate information (Slavin, 1996). A short practice and drill session provides a quick and efficient way for teachers to check on the effectiveness of instruction before moving to the next stage or level in the lesson. It is well suited for mastery and direct methods of lesson planning, especially for low-achieving students (Perrone, 1994; Smith, 1992).

Douglas Carnine, Jerry Silbert, Edward Kameenui, and Sara Tarver (2004) maintain that practice and review should be staples in direct reading instruction. Because learning to read necessitates a lot of practice, many repetitions of the same skill are often necessary for readers to move from struggling to mature levels. Thus, practice needs to occur within lessons and across lessons. They suggest that within lessons a pattern of massed practice or concentrated presentation of examples should occur with each new strategy introduced. This concentrated practice should be followed by review sessions, which occur across lessons, so that the teacher can ascertain if the strategies and information taught have been retained and learned. They also suggest for those reading programs that do not include sufficient practice that teachers provide the supplementary activities to ensure practice and review.

You may recall from Chapter 3 that we noted how important it is for teachers to provide many students with consistent and varied repetitions (practices) so that they can achieve more rapid fluency in word learning and vocabulary understanding. The use of repeated readings is regarded as one highly beneficial practice tool in helping students achieve fluency. Often used with students who have difficulty with word recognition, the repeated reading technique used with a familiar text helps struggling readers achieve greater speed and context accuracy (Worthy & Broaddus, 2001–2002).

Instruction that is arranged in a logical, progressive order and that matches materials and activities to individual needs and abilities is often called **mastery learning.** The basis of mastery learning, and similar forms of teaching such as adaptive instruction and individualized instruction, is making certain that adequate learning and mastery of certain concepts and skills have taken place, usually through practice and drill. Mastery instruction, especially when it is individualized as opposed to group-based instruction, accommodates varying rates of learning among students and can be effective in fostering achievement.

**BOX 7.4** Practice Improves Good Reading and Stronger Writing

How do athletes build and maintain strong bodies, adeptness, and agility? They practice. The more they practice and engage in the activity of their sport, the more they can visualize each segment of ongoing action as it unfolds. Likewise with reading and writing. The more that students do actual reading and writing, the more fluent, agile, and mentally "with it" they become. The more practice gained through oral and silent reading, recreational reading, personal and reflective writing, and computer literacy interactions, the more students can visualize the old and add new words and new sentence combinations to new understandings.

## The Need for Purposeful Review

Low-achieving (and at-risk) students may need more practice, drill, and **review** than high-achieving students before they can move on to subsequent tasks. The teacher may have to reduce the breadth of the work for more depth and reduce the pace and difficulty of the material (Anderson & Pellicer, 1990; Ornstein & Levine, 1990). The teacher will need to monitor the practice and drill closely, providing corrective feedback to help students grasp the material and avoid confusion or frustration (see Box 7.4).

Much of the teaching for low-achieving students will be supportive and corrective in nature. Students who have learning problems often need extra practice and drill and a variety of review experiences that relate new learning to prior learning. They cannot easily keep up with more advanced students and should not be allowed to become embarrassed or defensive. In heterogeneous classrooms, teachers must challenge high-achieving students and let them move on to other content. Practice and drill, and other direct forms of instruction, have limited value for these students. But at the same time, teachers must be sure that slower students learn the basic material thoroughly, in some cases only a limited amount, instead of racing through a large amount of material with little comprehension and retention.

Recall from the presentation in Chapter 5 of a design approach for diverse learners that one of the key principles was called "judicious review." This principle meant that particularly for diverse learners, who traditionally have had difficulty with retention of information, strategies need to be devised to help them with the productive organization of working memory (Kameenui & Carnine, 1998). This can be done by embedding rehearsal and organization techniques within larger strategy lessons. Thus, judicious review is a secondary or tertiary presentation of information, content, and vocabulary through additional activities and strategies to help students recall and organize the major concept ideas. For example, when the major vocabulary of a topic lesson has been taught and read in context, students should maintain a vocabulary notebook, use vocabulary task cards, use a response journal to question others about the new words, and/or write original sentences or paragraphs using the new words in their own original and creative ways.

To summarize, a main goal of practice, drill, and review is to ensure that students understand the content and/or processes of the daily or unit lesson. A high success rate on practice items is important for student learning. Similarly, short practice sessions at one sitting minimize the risk of student boredom or burnout. The amount of time to spend on practice varies with age. Younger students can tolerate less time at practice than older students (Ornstein, 1994; Slavin, 1996). Table 7.4 illustrates the major activities involved in practice, drill, and review.

*Table 7.4* Practice, Drill, and Review Activities

1. Review daily.
   Check previous day's work.
   Check homework.
   Reteach if necessary.

2. Present new content/skills.
   Introduce with concrete examples.
   Proceed in small steps.
   Give detailed instructions and explanations if necessary.
   Gradually phase in material or task.

3. Provide guided practice.
   Provide teacher-led practice.
   Provide varying contexts and exercises for student practice.
   Use prompts, cues, visuals, etc., when appropriate.
   Monitor students' work.
   Continue practice until student responses are firm.
   Aim for 80 percent or higher success rate.

4. Provide feedback.
   Offer teacher-led feedback.
   Provide checklists.
   Correct by simplifying material or task, giving clues, explaining, or reviewing steps.
   Reteach if necessary.

5. Increase student responsibility.
   Diminish prompts, clues, explanations, etc.
   Increase complexity of material or task.
   Ensure student engagement during seatwork.
   Monitor student work.
   Aim for 95 percent or higher success rate.

6. Provide independent practice.
   Encourage students to work on their own.
   Provide extensive practice.
   Facilitate application of new examples.

7. Review weekly and monthly.
   Check for understanding on irregular basis.
   Reteach if necessary.

*Source:* Adapted from Barak V. Rosenshine, "Teaching Functions in Instructional Programs," *Elementary School Journal* (March 1983), p. 338; Barak V. Rosenshine and Carla Meister, "The Use of Scaffolds for Teaching Higher-Level Cognitive Strategies," *Educational Leadership* (April 1992), p. 27.

## Guidelines for Implementing Practice, Drill, and Review

In order to acquire many basic skills, especially in arithmetic, reading, grammar, and foreign languages, certain things need to be learned to the point of automatic response, such as simple rules of grammar and speech, word recognition, and mathematical calculations (adding, subtracting, multiplying). These skills are needed for more advanced learning and are best learned through practice and drill and a variety of reviews. See Tips for Teachers 7.1.

# ■ THE SCAFFOLDING MODEL OF INSTRUCTION

The **scaffolding model** is, quite simply, based on a good commonsense approach to effective teaching. It uses features of the other aforementioned methods of instruction such as discussing and explaining, questioning, demonstrating and showing, creating inquiry, working through problems, and practicing and reviewing. The scaffolding model is therefore a model, or "heuristic," of teaching that can be used again and again during instruction. It would be most effective to use when new, challenging, or

# Improving Practice, Drill, and Review

Research has identified several recommendations for improving practice and drill and other seatwork activities to enhance academic learning.

1. *Have a clear system of rules and procedures for general behavior.* This allows students to deal with personal needs (for example, permission to use the bathroom pass) and procedural routines (sharpening a pencil) without disturbing classmates.

2. *Move around the room to monitor students' seatwork.* Students should feel that the teacher is aware of their behavior and alert to difficulties they may encounter. The extent of monitoring correlates with the students' academic ability and need for teacher attention.

3. *Provide comments, explanations, and feedback.* The more recognition or attention students receive, the more they are willing to pursue seatwork activities. Watch for signs of student confusion and deal with it quickly; this increases students' willingness to persist and helps teachers know how students are doing and how to plan for the next instructional task. Common problems should be explained immediately by interrupting the practice exercise if the problems are serious, or after the practice if students can wait.

4. *Spend more time teaching and reteaching the basic skills.* Elementary and low-achieving youngsters should be exposed to heavy doses of skills learning, which requires practice, drill, and review. When students have difficulty, it is important to instruct in small steps to the point of overlearning.

5. *Use practice and review during and after learning.* Practice and review should be used only sparingly for initiating new learning. They are most effective mixed with other activities as learning progresses, such as demonstrations, explanations, and questions, depending on the students' age and abilities. However, games and simulations for young children and field trips and buzz sessions for older students are not as effective (in terms of use of time) as practice and drill and other paper-and-pencil activities (for review or reteaching).

6. *Provide variety and challenge in practice, drill, and review.* Practice can easily drift into busywork and frustrate or bore students if it is too easy, too difficult, or too monotonous. Remember to present the formal information in a new way. Change the task or activity but focus on the same learning as in judicious review.

7. *Keep students alert and focused on the task.* Teachers need to keep students on task, occasionally questioning them, calling on both volunteers and nonvolunteers, elaborating on incorrect answers, etc.

8. *Maintain a brisk pace.* There should be little confusion about what to do during practice and drill, and activities should not be interrupted by minor disturbances. A snap of the finger, eye contact, or other "signal" procedures should help deal with inattentive or disruptive students without stopping the lesson.

"weighty" content material is to be offered to students or when a new process or strategy is to be learned.

## Why Scaffolding Is Important

We introduced the concept of scaffolding in Chapter 2 and noted that it was based on the work of Vygotsky, who proposed *zones of proximal development* in children's development. Recall that these zones were described as opportune times and conditions for language, cognitive, affective, and social growth for young children. What is needed for the zone to work as the child becomes engaged in any task is for another human being to be present. A parent or grandparent, a sibling, a friend, or a teacher needs to guide and encourage the child with talk and action so that a task is completed successfully. Because a task may be new, cumbersome, or foreign to the child, scaffolding helps the child complete the task that was too difficult for the child to do on his or her own. Talk and conversation are undoubtedly the most important ingredients of the process. The older person, as mediator or helper, gives advice and encouragement, focuses the child's attention on important aspects of the tasks, ensures that the sequence of events is clear, and adds information as necessary for the child to complete a task. Over time, children internalize this talk, which becomes part of their language and thinking and directs their own attention, plans, and activities (McGee & Richgels, 2000).

In Chapter 5, we noted that one of the principles of a design approach for diverse learners was that of *mediated scaffolding* (Kameenui & Carnine, 1998). Because diverse learners may not have had rich English-language exposure, and because they may have had limited background experiences during their early years, teachers need to scaffold the steps of new learning experiences so that the new learning can successfully accommodate to the limitations of the old. This scaffolding may require a lot of talk, discussion, and coaching, particularly with the use of new concept ideas and vocabulary. Through explanation, reading of the new vocabulary words in context, and practice with the new words in similar contexts, diverse students' scaffolded instruction helps them achieve success. Once students begin creating their own oral and written sentences with the new words used appropriately, the teacher can sense that internalization and ownership have occurred and that some degree of mastery has been achieved.

Authors of literacy texts also note that scaffolding steps are important for second language learners faced with English reading and writing tasks. Learning to read in a second language presents students with two major difficulties: (1) comprehension may occur more slowly because of a lack of proficiency with oral English, and (2) background knowledge and experiences related to the cultural aspect of reading in English may be lacking (Boyle & Peregoy, 1990). Teachers of second language learners need to provide competent models of English usage and serve as resources to guide and mentor students through successful reading and writing of English (Reutzel & Cooter, 1999). In one program involving Spanish-speaking students who were learning English as a second language, poetry was used as the vehicle for talk and oral language enjoyment and development. Through a scaffolding approach beginning with the teacher-modeling process, a number of strategies were used to engage students in the words, sounds, story rhythm, and emotional connections afforded through poetry (Hadaway, Vardell, & Young, 2001).

## A Visual Model of Teaching and Learning

In 1983, Pearson and Gallagher introduced a visual model of teaching and learning based on the scaffolding concept (see Figure 7.1). Their model allowed for the gradual release of teacher influence so that students could successfully complete learning tasks (Pearson & Gallagher, 1983). It also proposed three stages of teacher–student interaction, to which we added a fourth, which occurs when students become successful recipients of learning encounters and are able to use new learnings on their own.

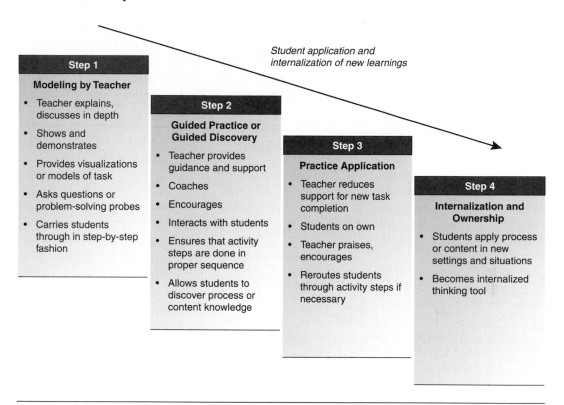

*Figure* 7.1 The Scaffolding Model of Teaching and Learning

*Source:* Adapted from P. David Pearson and Margaret C. Gallagher, "The Instruction of Reading Comprehension," *Contemporary Educational Psychology* (July 1983), pp. 317–344.

During stage 1, the teacher models that which is to be learned. The concept of teaching embedded in the word *model* takes on a different instructional stance than, say, in the term *direct teaching*. We noted this distinction earlier in the presentation of the explanation and discussion instructional delivery approach. Although talk, discussion, and explanation are important in day-to-day classroom instruction, too much teacher talk in the form of direct verbal instruction may prevent students from learning effectively.

Modeling means that the teacher shows or demonstrates what is involved in the learning task. The teacher "talks aloud" to represent his or her "thinking aloud" and tells what the steps, procedures, and/or processes are to accomplish the task. For instance, if the teacher is modeling a study skill strategy, he or she will have a content textbook in hand and say, "This is what I do in the survey part of the study skill. Here's how my mind works. Watch and listen to me and my fingers go to the boldface type, figures, charts, pictures, and other text features. . . ." Students hear and see the teacher involved in the thinking–learning task. This is a far different use of talk from explaining the procedural steps of the study skill as an abstraction removed from the experience of seeing it done. Thus, modeling uses talk, conversation, questioning, and problem-solving probes as the teacher moves through the actual demonstration of thinking and talking aloud.

In stage 2, students engage in the task themselves, either individually, in pairs, or in small groups. Under the watchful eye of the teacher, students practice the activity with the content so that they can "discover" how the process works. It's important that the teacher be actively involved here to provide feedback and monitor student progress. It's best that the teacher not sit at his or her desk waiting until the task is done but circulate through the classroom to coach, answer individual student questions, monitor mistakes, and provide constructive feedback. Teachers also agree that though modeling is a strong way to teach a comprehension strategy, it needs to be followed by the reading of text and the practicing of the strategy under the teacher's guidance (Villaume & Brabham, 2002).

Many teachers know that the sequence of activity events is the key to optimal learning in many mathematics, science, and English grammar lessons, so it's important to guide students through proper sequencing. Teachers may have prepared a chart listing the steps of the activity during the modeling stage. Students should be reminded to consult the chart so that they follow the activity in the proper sequence. Another major factor in this guided practice/guided discovery stage is that students discover the learning and the procedural steps of the learning activity by themselves. Through questioning by the teacher or peers, through explanation and demonstration, and through practice and review of steps, students arrive at the learning by themselves. They are *not* told what to learn through explanation and lecture but are induced to learn by involvement.

In the third stage, students practice or apply the strategy independently. Usually working individually, students accomplish what they did in stage 2, with two major exceptions. The teacher provides new or fresh examples so that students can apply the process or strategy on their own with new learning content. Second, the teacher reduces support, minimizing coaching and question answering so that students can begin to take ownership on their own to become fluent in the process. Students might be rehearsing the steps of the activity in their own minds, but they are on their way to achieving smooth coordination of the activity steps.

The final stage is internalization or ownership of the process, activity, and/or content that accompanied the learning task. The student is able to use the skill, has transferred it comfortably to mind, and can apply it in other settings (classrooms) and situations (content subjects). Here's a good example of how this process works: A teacher likes to use graphic organizers to help her students organize and learn content information. She models the use of a Venn diagram (two circles that overlap) to compare and contrast the features of a moth and a butterfly. In the circle labeled "Moth," children write the characteristics of the moth. In the other circle, labeled "Butterfly," children note the characteristics of the butterfly. In the overlapping part of the adjoining circles, children write the features that are the same for both insects. The teacher has students use the Venn diagram process once again when they study frogs and toads, but this time they practice and apply the process on their own by analyzing the information in their texts.

A bit later one of the students is in social studies class, where the teacher asks the pertinent question, "How is the state of Hawaii like the state of Alaska?" Our student takes a sheet of paper, draws two overlapping circles, and begins to search for the similarities. The student may also jot down features singular to each country so that he or she can visibly see what characteristics the two states have in common. In this case, the student has internalized a thinking tool and has transferred it to help solve a new problem. The student has taken ownership of that which had been taught and now has a thinking heuristic that can be used again and again in the future.

One literacy author maintains that the scaffolding process is highly appropriate for instructional methods that regard highly the students' role in actively constructing knowledge rather than passively receiving it. Therefore, the scaffolding system of teaching and learning would find favor with process-oriented instruction and with constructivist approaches to classroom instruction (Applebee, 1994). Such process-oriented and constructivist-based instruction would be found in the curriculum design approaches of curriculum integration and curriculum mapping, with the principles approach for diverse learners, and with the problem-solving method of instructional delivery.

Applebee (1994) notes that scaffolding offers five major features in the teaching–learning process:

- Students are encouraged to take ownership of the task in that they invest it with personal meaning rather than recite what they've been told or have read.
- Students are allowed to follow a natural sequence of thought and language, thereby allowing new knowledge to be appropriately integrated with the old.
- Students are provided with tasks that are neither too easy to do on their own nor too difficult to complete even with help; tasks are provided at the appropriate level of difficulty so that learning stages can occur with teacher scaffolding of talk and action.
- Students see the teacher as a collaborator and mentor rather than as one who judges whether the task is correct or not (an evaluator).
- Students achieve internalization or inner control of new knowledge that they can transfer to new tasks.

To conclude, this chapter presented five instructional procedures: (1) teachers explain and discuss, (2) teachers question, (3) teachers have students inquire and problem solve, (4) teachers engage students in practices, drills, and reviews, and (5) teachers carry students through a scaffolding model of instruction and learning. We noted that the scaffolding model, by the very nature of the teaching–learning activity during the enfolding of its steps, incorporates many of the other instructional techniques and could be most effectively used when new, challenging content needs to be mastered.

## ■ SUMMARY ■

1. Most instructional activities will occur through one of four instructional methods: practice, drill, and review; questioning; explaining and discussing; and problem solving. These methods are also used in the scaffolding model of instructional delivery.

2. The method of practice, drill, and review has applications for seatwork activities, back-to-basics approaches, behaviorist learning, individualized instruction, and remedial instruction.

3. Questioning is perhaps the most important instructional method used today in whole-group

instruction and is a cornerstone of reading comprehension instruction in whole-group, small-group, and individual settings. Types of questions include low level and high level, convergent and divergent, and valuing.

4. Discussing and explaining are hallmarks of the oldest instructional method. Different types of teacher talks (formal, informal, and brief lectures and explanations) can be effective with different students, but in general the length, complexity,

and frequency of teacher talk should be reduced for younger and slower students.

5. Problem-solving models, strategies, and scaffolding for effective long-term learning also were discussed. There is real need to increase problem solving in our instructional approach; likewise, teachers need to teach their students how to problem solve and master independent learning techniques.

## ■ QUESTIONS TO CONSIDER ■

1. Why is the method of practice, drill, and review used more often in elementary grades than secondary grades?

2. What is the difference between convergent and divergent questions? Why do most teachers rely on convergent questions?

3. When should different types of brief lectures, explanations, and discussion be used?

4. What are the advantages and disadvantages of problem solving as an instructional method?

5. Why is the scaffolding model of instructional delivery beneficial when the objective is transfer of learning?

## ■ THINGS TO DO ■

1. List five recommendations for conducting practice and drill. Indicate any that you feel particularly comfortable or uncomfortable with as a teacher. Based on these preferences, what conclusions can you make about how you will use practice and drill?

2. Outline ten do's and don'ts in asking questions. Discuss each one with your classmates.

3. Teach a shorter lesson to your class by asking questions. Refer to Tips for Teachers 7.1 as a guide to see how well you performed.

4. Develop a checklist for improving your method of explaining and discussing.

5. Identify five characteristics of successful problem solvers. What characteristics coincide with your own problem-solving strategies? What other strategies can be used to enhance your problem-solving instruction?

6. Take a challenging content topic and have students learn a new comprehension or writing strategy by following the steps and procedures of the scaffolding model.

## ■ RECOMMENDED READINGS ■

Beyer, Barry. *Improving Student Thinking: A Comprehensive Approach.* Boston: Allyn and Bacon, 1998. Provides strategies and activities to facilitate student thinking, including scaffolding, posing process-structured questions, and framing lessons around thoughtful questions.

Dillon, J. T. *Questioning and Teaching.* New York: Teachers College Press, 1988. A concise guide to questioning, including when and how to ask questions.

Gage, N. L., and David C. Berliner. *Educational Psychology,* 6th ed. Boston: Houghton Mifflin,

1998. Examination of the research pertaining to practice and drill, lecturing, and problem solving, among other subjects.

Good, Thomas L., and Jere E. Brophy. *Looking into Classrooms,* 8th ed. New York: Addison Wesley Longman, 1999. Examination of the research pertaining to practice and drill, questioning, and problem solving.

Hunkins, Francis P. *Effective Questions, Effective Thinking,* 2nd ed. Needham, MA: Gordon, 1994. A practical approach to the technique of questioning.

Kameenui, Edward J., and Douglas W. Carnine. *Effective Teaching Strategies That Accommodate Diverse Learners.* Upper Saddle River, NJ: Merrill, 1998. Explores ways that mediated scaffolding is applied with diverse learners in the language arts and content subjects.

Raths, Louis E., Merril Harmin, and Sidney B. Simon. *Values and Teaching,* 2nd ed. Columbus, OH: Merrill, 1978. An important book on how to use valuing strategies during lecturing and questioning, among other instructional approaches.

## ■ KEY TERMS ■

convergent questions
demonstrations
discussion
divergent questions
experiments
heuristic thinking

high-level questions
low-level questions
mastery learning
metacognitive skills
practice and drill
problem-solving processes

reflective thinking
review
scaffolding model
valuing questions

## ■ REFERENCES ■

Anderson, L. W., & Pellicer, L. O. (1990, September). Synthesis of research on compensatory and remedial education. *Educational Leadership,* 10–16.

Applebee, A. N. (1994). Scaffolding. In A. C. Purves (Ed.), *Encyclopedia of English studies and language arts* (p. 1054). New York: Scholastic/ Urbana, IL: National Council of Teachers of English.

Ausubel, D. P. (1978, Spring). In defense of advanced organizers. *Review of Educational Research,* 251–259.

Beck, I., & McKeown, M. (2002, November). Questioning the author: Making sense of social studies. *Educational Leadership,* 44–47.

Bennett, N. (1988, January). The search for a theory of pedagogy. *Teaching and Teacher Education,* 19–30.

Bereiter, C., & Englemann, S. (1966). *Teaching disadvantaged children in the preschool.* Englewood Cliffs, NJ: Prentice Hall.

Beyer, B. K. (1991). *Teaching thinking skills.* Boston: Allyn and Bacon.

Beyer, B. (1998a, May–June). Improving student thinking. *The Clearing House,* 262–267.

Beyer, B. (1998b). *Improving student thinking: A comprehensive approach.* Boston: Allyn and Bacon.

Bichler, R. F., & Hudson, L. M. (1990). *Developmental psychology* (4th ed.). Boston: Houghton Mifflin.

Bigge, L. M., & Shermis, S. S. (1998). *Learning theories for teachers* (6th ed.). New York: Addison Wesley Longman.

Bloom, B. (Ed.). (1956). *Taxonomy of educational objectives, handbook I: Cognitive domain.* New York: Longman-McKay.

Boyle, O. F., & Peregoy, S. F. (1990, November). Literacy scaffolds: Strategies for first- and second-language readers and writers. *The Reading Teacher, 44,* 194–200.

Brophy, J. (1988, Summer). Research linking teacher behavior to student achievement. *Educational Psychologist,* 235–286.

Brophy, J. E. (1990, March). Teaching social studies for understanding higher-order applications. *Elementary School Journal,* 351–417.

Bruner, J. S. (1990). *Toward a theory of instruction.* Cambridge, MA: Harvard University Press.

Carnine, D., Silbert, J., Kameenui, E., & Tarver, S. (2004). *Direct reading instruction* (4th ed.). Upper Saddle River, NJ: Prentice Hall.

Casey, M. B., & Howson, P. (1993, November–December). Educating preservice students based on a problem-centered approach to teaching. *Journal of Teacher Education, 361–370.*

Cobb, P., Wood, T., Yackel, E., & McNeal, B. (1992, Fall). Characteristics of classroom mathematics traditions. *American Educational Research Journal, 573–604.*

Cole, J. (2002–2003, December/January). What motivates students to read? Four literacy personalities. *The Reading Teacher, 326–336.*

Dewey, J. (1997). *How we think.* Minneola, NY: Dover. (Original work published 1910)

Dillon, J. T. (1984, November). Research on questioning and discussion. *Educational Leadership, 50–56.*

Dillon, J. T. (1988). *Questioning and teaching.* New York: Teachers College Press.

Doyle, W. (1985, September). Effective teaching and the concept of the master teacher." *Elementary School Journal, 27–38.*

Friedman, A., & Cataldo, C. (2002, October). Characters at crossroads: Reflective decision makers in contemporary Newbery books. *The Reading Teacher, 102–112.*

Gage, N. L., & Berliner, D. C. (1998). *Educational psychology* (6th ed.). Boston: Houghton Mifflin.

Gall, M. (1984, January). Synthesis of research on teachers' questioning. *Educational Leadership, 40–47.*

Gallagher, J. J. (1965). Expressive thought by gifted children in the classroom. *Elementary English, 42,* 559–568.

Gallagher, J. J., & Aschner, M. J. (1963, July). A preliminary report on analyses of classroom interaction. *Merrill Palmer Quarterly, 183–194.*

Good, T. L., & Brophy, J. (1990). *Educational psychology: A realistic approach.* (4th ed.). New York: Longman.

Good, T. L., & Grouws, D. (1987, June). Increasing teachers' understanding of mathematical ideas through in service training. *Phi Delta Kappan, 778–783.*

Good, T. L., Grouws, D. A., & Ebermeier, H. (1983). *Active mathematics teaching.* New York: Longman.

Hadaway, N., Vardell, S., & Young, T. (2001, May). Scaffolding oral language development through poetry for students learning English. *The Reading Teacher, 796–806.*

Harpaz, Y., & Lefstein, A. (2000, November). Communities of thinking. *Educational Leadership, 54–57.*

Holt, J. (1995). *How children fail* (Rev. ed.). New York: Perseus Press.

Hunkins, F. P. (1994). *Effective questions, effective thinking* (2nd ed.). Boston: Gordon.

Judd, C. H. (1918). *Introduction to the scientific study of education.* Boston: Ginn.

Kameenui, E., & Carnine, D. (1998). *Effective teaching strategies that accommodate diverse learners.* Upper Saddle River, NJ: Merrill.

King, A. (1990, November–December). Reciprocal peer-questioning: A strategy for teaching students how to learn from lectures. *The Clearing House, 131–135.*

Lipman, M. (1988, September). Critical thinking—What can it be? *Educational Leadership, 38–43.*

Lohman, D. F. (1986, Summer). Predicting mathathanic effects in the teaching of high-order thinking skills. *Educational Psychologist, 191–208.*

Mandeville, T. (1994, March). KWLA: Linking the affective and cognitive domains. *The Reading Teacher, 679–680.*

Marzano, R. (1992, August). Dimensions of learning. *ASCD Update, 1–3.*

May, F. B. (2001). *Reading as communication: To help children write and read* (6th ed.). Upper Saddle River, NJ: Prentice Hall.

Mayer, R. E. (1992). *Thinking, problem solving and cognition* (2nd ed.). San Francisco: Freeman.

McAllister, P. (1994, May). Using K-W-L for informal assessment. *The Reading Teacher, 510–511.*

McGee, L., & Richgels, D. (2000). *Literacy's beginning: Supporting young readers and writers* (3rd ed.). Boston: Allyn and Bacon.

Medley, D. S. (1979). The effectiveness of teachers. In P. Peterson & H. Walberg (Eds.), *Research in teaching: Concepts, findings, and implications* (pp. 11–27). Berkeley, CA: McCutchan.

Newell, A., & Simon, H. (1972). *Human problem solving.* Englewood Cliffs, NJ: Prentice Hall.

Ogle, D. (1989). The know, want to know, learn strategy. In K. D. Muth (Ed.), *Children's comprehension of text: Research into practice* (pp. 205–223). Newark, DE: International Reading Association.

Ornstein, A. C. (1987, May). Questioning: The essence of good teaching: Part I. *NASSP Bulletin,* 71–79.

Ornstein, A. C. (1994, January). Homework, studying, and notetaking: Essential skills for students. *NASSP Bulletin,* 51–71.

Ornstein, A. C., & Levine, D. U. (1990, November–December). School effectiveness and reform. *The Clearing House,* 115–118.

Owens, R. F., Hester, J. L., & Teale, W. H. (2002). Where do you want to go today? Inquiry-based learning and technology integeration. *The Reading Teacher,* 616–625.

Payne, D. A. (1992). *Measuring and evaluating educational outcomes.* New York: Macmillan-Merrill.

Pearson, P. D., & Gallagher, M. C. (1983, July). The instruction of reading comprehension. *Contemporary Educational Psychology,* 317–344.

Perrone, V. (1994, February). How to engage students in learning. *Educational Leadership,* 11–13.

Peterson, E. F., & Carpenter, T. (1989, December–January). Using knowledge of how students think about mathematics. *Educational Leadership,* 42–46.

Peterson, P. L. (1988, Fall). Making learning meaningful: Lessons from research on cognition and instruction. *Educational Psychologist,* 365–373.

Peverly, S. T. (1991, Spring). Problems with knowledge-based explanation of memory and development. *Review of Educational Research,* 71–93.

Piaget, J. (1963). *The origins of intelligence in children.* New York: Norton.

Pransky, K., & Bailey, F. (2002–2003, December/January). To meet your students where they are, first you have to find them: Working with culturally and linguistically diverse students. *The Reading Teacher,* 370–383.

Pressley, M., Wood, E., Woloshyn, V., Martin, V., King, A., & Menke, D. (1992, Winter). Encouraging mindful use of prior knowledge: Attempting to construct explanatory answers facilitates learning. *Educational Psychologist,* 99–109.

Rasinski, T., & Padak, N. (2000). *Effective reading strategies: Teaching children who find reading difficult* (2nd ed.). Upper Saddle River, NJ: Merrill.

Raths, L. E., Harmin, M., & Simon, S. B. (1978). *Values and teaching* (2nd ed.). Columbus, OH: Merrill.

Resnick, L. B., & Klopfer, L. E. (Eds.). (1989). *Toward the thinking curriculum: Current cognitive research, ASCD yearbook.* Alexandria, VA: Association for Supervision and Curriculum Development.

Reutzel, D. R., & Cooter, R., Jr. (1999). *Balanced reading strategies and practices: Assessing and assisting readers with special needs.* Upper Saddle River, NJ: Merrill.

Richards, J. (2003, January/March). Facts and feelings response diaries: Connecting efferently and aesthetically with informational text. *Reading & Writing Quarterly,* 107–111.

Rosenshine, B. (1979). Content, time, and direct instruction. In P. L. Peterson & H. J. Walberg (Eds.), *Research on teaching: Concepts, findings, and implications* (pp. 28–56). Berkeley, CA: McCutchan.

Roser, N., & Keehn, S. (2002, February). Fostering thought, talk, and inquiry: Linking literature and social studies. *The Reading Teacher,* 416–426.

Sampson, M. B. (2002, March). Confirming a K-W-L: Considering the source. *The Reading Teacher,* 528–532.

Schmidt, P. R., Gillen, S., Zollo, T. C., & Stone, R. (2002, March). Literacy learning and scientific inquiry: Children respond. *The Reading Teacher,* 534–548.

Schoenfeld, A. H. (1989). Teaching mathematical thinking and problem solving. In L. B. Resnick & L. E. Klopfer (Eds.), *Toward the thinking curriculum* (pp. 83–103). Alexandria, VA: Association for Supervision and Curriculum Development.

Schunk, D. H. (1991, Winter). Goal setting and self-efficacy during self-regulated learning. *Educational Psychologist,* 71–86.

Schutz, P. A. (1991, Winter). Goals in self-directed behavior. *Educational Psychologist,* 55–67.

Sipe, L. (2002, February). Talking back and taking over: Young children's expressive engagement during storybook read-aloud. *The Reading Teacher,* 476–483.

Slavin, R. E. (1996). *Educational psychology: Theory into practice* (5th ed.). Boston: Allyn and Bacon.

Smith, F. (1992, February). Learning to read: The never-ending debate. *Phi Delta Kappan,* 432–441.

Solas, J. (1992, Summer). Investigating teacher and student thinking about the process of teaching and learning. *Review of Educational Research,* 205–225.

Spaulding, C. (1992). *Motivation in the classroom.* New York: McGraw-Hill.

Stallings, J. A., & Quinn, L. F. (1991, November). Learning how to teach in the inner city. *Educational Leadership,* 25–27.

Steffe, L., & Woods, T. (1990). *Transforming children's mathematics education.* Hillsdale, NJ: Erlbaum.

Sternberg, R. J. (2000). *In search of the human mind.* San Diego, CA: Harcourt.

Taylor, B., Pearson, P. D., Clark, K., & Walpole, S. (2000, November). Effective schools and accomplished teachers: Lessons about primary grade reading instruction in low-income schools. *Elementary School Journal,* 121–166.

Taylor, B., Peterson, D., Pearson, P. D., & Rodriguez, M. (2002, November). Looking inside classrooms: Reflecting on the "how" as well as the "what" in effective reading instruction. *The Reading Teacher,* 270–279.

Templeton, S. (1991, November). Teaching and learning the English spelling system. *Elementary School Journal,* 185–201.

Thorndike, E. L. (1932). *The fundamentals of learning.* New York: Teachers College Press.

Tompkins, G. E. (1998). *Language arts: Content and teaching strategies* (4th ed.). Upper Saddle River, NJ: Prentice Hall.

Traver, R. (1998, March). What is a good guiding question? *Educational Leadership,* 70–73.

Villaume, S. K., & Brabham, E. G. (2002, April). Comprehension instruction: Beyond strategies. *The Reading Teacher,* 672–675.

Vygotsky, L. (1986). *Thought and language.* Cambridge, MA: MIT Press.

Wentzel, K. R. (1991, Spring). Social competence at school: Relationship between social responsibility and academic achievement. *Review of Educational Research,* 1–24.

Whitin, P. (2002, February). Leading into literature circles through the sketch-to-stretch strategy. *The Reading Teacher,* 444–450.

Wiggins, G., & McTighe, J. (1998). *Understanding by design.* Alexandria, VA: Association for Supervision and Curriculum Development.

Wood, G. H. (1992). *Schools that work.* New York: Dutton.

Woodward, J. (1994, January). Effects of curriculum discourse style on eighth graders' recall and problem solving in Earth science. *Elementary School Journal,* 299–314.

Worthy, J., & Broaddus, K. (2001–2002, December/January). Fluency beyond the primary grades: From group performance to silent, independent reading. *The Reading Teacher,* 334–343.

# Schoolwide Organization for Instruction

chapter **8**

1. Can you think of some major reasons why schools would want or need to provide different organizational patterns for all or some of its students?

2. How does the factor of "time" affect the learner's day?

3. Why might classroom design and student seating patterns influence how students learn?

4. What are some alternative schoolwide procedures by which schools manage time and grouping patterns of students to enhance the common grouping procedure of the self-contained classroom?

5. Why are schools rethinking the pull-out procedure, in which they provided remedial and special education services to students with teacher specialists operating in their own classroom settings?

6. How are inclusion, push-in services, and differentiated instruction aimed at providing instruction for diverse and exceptional learners in their regular classroom settings?

7. What are the pros and cons of heterogeneous and homogeneous grouping?

Schools use different organizational patterns to group students for instruction; however, more often than not, schools attempt to accommodate diverse, at-risk, and exceptional learners by altering features of the typical school day. Schools juggle time, classroom size, teacher assignments, and space to provide the best learning environments and time structures to meet the needs of all students but particularly those who may be at the high or low ends of achievement. A school's particular organizational plan takes into account those matters that affect the school as a whole, such as the master schedule of how periods of instruction are arranged, who is assigned to teach what, and the designated duties of aides or paraprofessionals (Danielson, 2002).

Especially when achievement levels of marginal students have shown a steady decline, schools rush in with reform policies to provide alternative ways to get these students on the right track. Reform strategies that raise the academic capabilities of at-risk and marginal students the most are those both selected and supported by school administrators and faculty (Stringfield, Ross, & Smith, 2002). For instance, when one high-poverty school adopted the use of an early reading program for its students, 50 percent of whom were eligible for free and reduced-cost lunch and 40 percent of whom had high mobility rates, the school consistently outperformed other schools in the state on reading achievement. The key features of the school's success had to do with the staff's strong focus on student learning outcomes in the early grades, strong and committed leadership at the school level, and the use of varied reading programs and small-group configurations to accommodate both achieving and nonachieving students (Adler & Fisher, 2001).

This chapter and the next continue the focus on the major components of curriculum design as we show how subject-matter content and student learning experiences are influenced by school and classroom organizational plans. In this chapter, we present the leading factors that influence both schools and classrooms in organizational decision making, as well as some major configurational patterns at the building level. Chapter 9 deals with the three traditional ways—whole class, groupings, or individualization—in which instruction is offered at the classroom level.

# ■ FACTORS INFLUENCING ORGANIZATIONAL PATTERNS

Four major factors influence schools and teachers as they organize their students for instruction. The first has to do with the district's, the school's, and the individual teacher's educational plan as it affects curriculum and instructional approaches. The second has to do with time allotments and the management of time (Marzano, 2003). Providing for individual differences is the third factor, and organizing students for whole-class activities, group or partner work, and individualized instruction within a classroom setting is the fourth factor. How these factors interact determines how good the instructional practice will be for all students.

## Approaches to Instruction

Particular curriculum design factors and approaches have a significant bearing on how schools and teachers approach instruction in general and how classrooms are organized for instruction. For instance, if a teacher embraces a curriculum integration, curriculum mapping, or problem-solving style of instruction, that teacher would be more disposed to have students work in groups, pairs, and individually for extended periods as they work through the issues and concerns they are investigating. We also noted in the previous chapter that teachers might use different methods of instruction at different times for any curriculum design approach. Teachers can explain and discuss; question; provide problem-solving probes; use practices, drills, and reviews; and follow the scaffolding model of instruction. Thus a major factor in organizing for classroom instruction is applying the *how* of teaching in order to maximize the *learning* of content—the *what* to teach. In this regard, four researchers found that more proficient primary grade teachers used small-group instruction rather than whole-group instruction as a primary mode, preferred to coach and lead students in discussion rather than recite information, generated high levels of student involvement, and used higher-level questions to elicit higher-level thinking during reading (Taylor, Pearson, Clark, & Walpole, 2000).

Given various types of teaching styles, one must consider which classroom pattern of organization—whole group, small group, pairs, or individual—is most advantageous to use in particular contexts. For instance, if students are directly instructed by their teacher to read their textual materials, would the whole-class organizational pattern be the most efficient and utilitarian? Within that pattern, the teacher can still coach by walking down or between the aisles to provide feedback, guidance, and assistance to individual students as they strive to understand the material. However, when researching information for concept or thematic units in an integrated or multisubject design approach, students might be best organized into groups or pairs so that they can discuss and collaborate with one another to present a unified project.

Literacy authors have indicated that because educational practices in reading and writing development have become more holistic, accompanying changes have occurred in classroom organizational patterns and climate (Burns, Roe, & Ross, 1999; Rasinski & Padak, 2000). These more holistic practices involve children in the entire process of reading and writing authentic texts, such as those written by children's authors or found on the Internet. This is in contrast to the reading of "baselized" stories, the vocabulary and sentence complexity of which have been controlled by publishing companies. By engaging children in more holistic reading and writing activities, teachers are encouraging them to operate in more flexible organizational patterns. For instance, instead of establishing reading groups that meet for scheduled time periods, teachers are allowing children to work for longer blocks of time at centers and recreational reading areas (Burns, Roe, & Ross, 1999). One author advocates the use of at least one hour of exploratory time each day so that students become intrinsically motivated, are celebrated for their unique-ness in solving problems using texts and computer resources, and develop a true love of learning (Wolk, 2001).

Some authors maintain that the concepts of "authenticity" and "engagement" are key to how teachers approach literacy instruction in modern-day classrooms. *Authen-tic* means that the materials children read and write are connected to the real world, to other areas of the curriculum, and to the children's interests and lifestyles. *Engaged* means that students are motivated and approach literacy activities eagerly. Instead of being passive about reading and writing, students are engaged in purposeful and plea-surable ways. To accomplish these ends in authentic and engaging classrooms, teachers provide conditions and activities to inspire and motivate students to pursue literacy purposefully. For instance, at the early grade levels, children might play at books to-gether by looking at and telling stories; write their own stories and entries in personal journals; or read individually, with the teacher, with peers, with aides, or with parent vol-unteers. At the intermediate and middle grades, students might engage in workshop ap-proaches to reading and writing. In this type of classroom approach, students self-select their own books and can respond to what they've read through many different writing and artistic modes (Rasinski & Padak, 2000). (See Table 6.4.)

The teacher's viewpoint and instructional stance regarding the nature and purpose of literacy instruction has a great bearing on how students will be organized. In the type of authentic and engaging environments described above, teachers are more like mentors, coaches, and facilitators of constructivist modes of learning rather than direct leaders of groups of students who are reading and responding in their respective groups. Moreover, if the teacher believes that authentic literacy encounters should permeate and be integrated with other discipline subjects, then the classroom organizational plan could proceed along the spectrum of whole-group to individual dimensions throughout a typical school day.

## Utilization of Time

The factor of time can be considered in two ways. One way has to do with the use of time as it pertains to the school day. This becomes the scheduling of time, and educators talk of the school's schedule, the daily schedule, or the student's scheduled periods. The sec-ond consideration has to do with the effectiveness of learning time within the scheduled day and periods. We call this engaged-learning time or **time on task.**

How much **scheduled time** does the teacher devote to particular content subjects and literacy activities on any given day as noted in the daily lesson plan? One answer to this question is provided by the administrative policy on how the typical school day is organized. A traditional schoolwide approach to time is to take the total amount of time children are in school each day (say 8:45 a.m. to 3:00 p.m.); subtract out the arrival and dismissal times, lunch, and any other recess or snack periods; and then segment the rest of the day into "periods," governed by the number of subjects that will be offered each day. Thus the weight given to specific subjects governs the amount of time allotted to particular areas of instruction.

Many elementary school administrators, moreover, believe that children in the pri-mary grades should learn the "basics"—reading, writing, and arithmetic—and often organize their primary-level classrooms into double periods for reading and mathe-matics instruction. For instance, to address the learning needs of its diverse population, the urban school district of Minneapolis established daily schedules of ninety minutes for reading instruction and sixty minutes for mathematics instruction for all of its elementary-level students (Johnson & Taylor, 2001). However, at the junior high level, some schools are mandated by their district or state to include additional subjects, such as AIDS or substance abuse instruction. These subject additions extend the number of periods beyond those of the traditional content disciplines and thereby reduce the amount of time allowed for each period.

At the middle and junior high school levels, as more and more content offerings find their way into the curriculum, extending the periods to seven to nine a day, how does the teacher organize instruction to accommodate for shorter class periods? In some schools, period changes do not allow individuals or groups of students to go to content teachers' classrooms; instead, the content teacher moves to the whole classroom in which the sixth, seventh, or eighth graders remain stable. How can the well-intentioned teacher move rapidly through the building toting books and student assignments, emerge into a classroom, and be expected to accomplish anything more than direct instruction through explanation and discussion, student reading of the course textbook, and practice and review of key content concepts, information, and vocabulary? In short, the time factor and rush between classes works against the teacher's ability to set up diverse instructional resources.

Once inside the elementary, intermediate, or junior high classroom, what do students do with their time? For literacy growth, time engaged in actual reading, writing, and computer activities is critical to success. When students struggle with reading and writing, the teacher can facilitate their progress by providing additional time for engagement in literacy activities (Rasinski & Padak, 2000).

Researchers have pointed out that **engaged time** in literacy activities is not the same as scheduled time. Time spent on actual reading performance yields higher correlation with achievement than any other teacher or learner behavior studied (Carnine, Silbert, & Kameenui, 1997). In one review of engaged-time studies, it was revealed that second graders effectively used only 80 percent of their time allocated to reading, whereas fifth graders were engaged only 75 percent of the time in actual reading during scheduled reading time (Rosenshine & Berliner, 1978). Because literacy engaged time yields success with literacy, teachers need to be effective in using the time of the total school day and also consider integrating literacy activities and reading skills work into the learning of content subjects such as history and science (Hirsch, 2001). For instance, it's not effective to have students waiting to do activities or shift from activity to activity. During the fifteen to twenty minutes of arrival and dismissal times, children can be purposefully engaged in pleasurable reading or response journal writing. The teacher needs to be ever mindful that just as bodybuilders build muscle through physical activity, students build literacy skills through reading and writing (see Box 8.1).

**BOX 8.1** Making Use of Engaged Time in the Classroom

Using the time of the school day in an efficient and productive way is an important variable in learning. Being engaged in learning tasks means that children are not sitting idly or passively during segments of the school day but are actively involved in reading, writing, computer work, or word-learning activities. Research has shown that even reading independently a few minutes a day allows children to face and learn new words and increase their success with future reading. Many a veteran teacher has remarked that when students are motivated to learn and engaged in a purposeful way, they can read and understand materials well beyond their comfortable reading instruction levels.

## Individual Differences

The third factor influencing how teachers organize for instruction is based on the premise of **individual differences** and the background experiences each child brings to each new content topic. We noted in earlier chapters how important it is for each child to have robust sight-word recognition accompanied by an ever-growing storehouse of new meaning words in order to succeed with reading, particularly in content area subjects. Kameenui and Carnine (1998) add that because diverse learners experience major difficulties with memory skills and vocabulary understanding, teachers need to ensure that these learners are shown how to organize information to assist recall and how to connect new word learnings to existing background understandings.

Each and every classroom is essentially alive with **diversity.** Although children are influenced by a variety of developmental and environmental factors that affect the ways they learn, behave, and perform, making each child unique and different, children do exhibit similarities that make them teachable in groups. Teachers must be aware of educational backgrounds and behavioral influences that impinge on learning and encourage children to work together, to assist one another in learning, and to support one anothers' cultural heritages and background (Churton, Cranston-Gingras, & Blair, 1998). Teachers of today are expected to be culturally sensitive and have the skills necessary to teach a wide range of students (Sleeter & Grant, 1999). Furthermore, inner-city, low-income students want teachers to show they care about how and what the students' learn and want their teachers to demand that work be done, that classroom control be maintained, and that varied instructional approaches be used (Corbett & Wilson, 2002).

Each time a learning and literacy event is successfully completed and new knowledge has been added to a child's storehouse of information, the child's background knowledge has been incrementally increased. With increasing background knowledge comes the added learning of skills. A *skill* is defined as a heightened ability, proficiency, or expertise. Thus a skill is a way of knowing or a way of doing and becomes part of one's knowledge base to assist with new learnings.

Let's see how skill utilization works as we consider individual differences with three children. The first child is a fluent reader, a good student, and a high achiever with grades and standardized test scores. Because the child is a good reader, she has learned some strategies for what to do when she meets a new vocabulary word during reading and, more important, she applies these strategies or skills. Depending on her work ethic at the time of reading, she might immediately go to the dictionary to look up the word's meaning, write the word down in her vocabulary notebook to look it up later, try to figure out the word meaning from the surrounding context, or ask a teacher, peer, or parent to help her with the word.

The second child is not a good reader, is a marginal student, and does not achieve well on his standardized test scores in reading comprehension, vocabulary, and decoding skills. He struggles with reading, often reads word by word, and takes a long time to finish assignments. But his motivation to succeed is high. When he encounters a new word, he applies some of the same skills to learn the meaning of the new word that the first student uses. However, one of his major problems is that even after he learns the meaning of the new word, he has difficulty reading it again when it appears in a new context. He has difficulty transferring the visual appearance of the word to long-term memory even though he knows the meaning of the word.

The third student is a weak reader, not a strong student, and does not achieve well in standardized test reading and writing scores. She does not have a great interest in reading and would rather watch television and meet with friends. When she encounters a new word during a textual reading in school, she usually skips the word if she can't immediately recognize it or sound it out. She doesn't apply any other skill or strategy to try to obtain the word's meaning. Because she's omitting words, usually major, meaning-bearing words, her comprehension suffers. With poor understanding during reading tasks, coupled with lack of interest in reading in general, this student falls more and more behind her peers.

Skill development becomes part of a student's background knowledge, and a teacher must monitor every student's progress in developing this knowledge. The range of diversity in any one class in skills use, background experiences, and interests can be quite broad indeed. Adding the remainder of children in a class to these three students makes for a challenging scenario for any teacher who has to provide instruction that considers individual differences in every learning situation. Teachers who succeed with at-risk students generally emphasize reading skills, cultivate higher-order thinking skills through questioning probes, and ensure that at-risk students participate in classroom literacy activities (Bell, 2002–2003). Generally, for literacy instruction the four dimensions of background knowledge, interests, achievement levels, and skills constitute the most important features of individual differences (Leu & Kinzer, 1999). Some authors would add personal tastes, values, and cultural influences to the approach and outcomes of a reading experience (Cole, 2002–2003; Gallas & Smagorinsky, 2002).

## Classroom Design and Organization

The fourth factor influencing the teacher's decision about how to organize for instruction has to do with the physical nature and design of the classroom itself. How space lends itself to different organizational patterns of instruction may affect teachers' decisions regarding the feasibility of using whole-class/whole-group instruction, small-group instruction, and/or individualized instruction. Do the facility and the classrooms within it lend themselves to smooth transition among these three organizational patterns to accommodate different types of learning experiences? Are there rows of desks, or small tables with movable chairs in the classroom? Can desks and tables be moved to create center, activity, and workshop space for groups of students? Is the environment friendly enough to accommodate a recreational reading area with pillows and easy chairs for individual use during pleasure reading? To create space that is efficient, organized, and welcoming, one teacher uses a conference table, plastic crates to house the children's reading and writing folders, plastic bags containing independent reading books, and a small rug area when meeting with groups (Taberski, 2000).

How space is used and organized has a great impact on learning (Hebert, 1998). Effective room arrangements are instrumental in effective literacy learning. The room arrangement for good reading and writing interaction should mirror the concept that learners have ownership of the room and the literacy materials they use and create. Reading centers should have comfortable places to sit, and writing centers should have

**BOX 8.2** Celebrating the Culture of a Print-Rich Environment

A print-rich classroom and school environment are created by the students themselves. Not only is the setting alive and vibrant with the children's work, but also the displays reveal that their work is valued and prized enough to be shown. Showcasing children's work encourages self-esteem and creates the opportunity for literacy work that encourages more literacy engagement as children read one another's work and write additional papers based on what they admire in others' efforts.

materials and computers available for easy access. Library areas should house resource and editing materials, and display areas should both acknowledge and complement children's work while promoting reading and topics of study (Rasinski & Padak, 2000). When students' written efforts adorn the walls, doors, windows, and hallways to celebrate the diversity and range of their work, we call this a "print-rich" environment. Note that the print-rich environment is not based on commercially prepared materials such as posters prepared for teacher use but is based on the culture of literacy learning in authentic contexts by the students themselves. See Box 8.2.

Sadly, unlike elementary school teachers, not many junior high school teachers take advantage of movable furniture and flexibility in seating design. At this level, the traditional classroom design seems firmly entrenched. Students sit in rows behind one another, facing the chalkboard and teacher, just as they did 100 years ago. One possible explanation is that these teachers tend to stress content and ignore socialization and personal relations, which are primary goals of teachers in the lower grades.

Only through experience and time will teachers learn whether a given arrangement suits their teaching style and the needs of their students. It may take several tries and continual revision to achieve a classroom design in which students work efficiently, materials and equipment are used to their best advantage, unnecessary equipment is removed, and the teacher finds it easy to instruct and supervise the students. See Tips for Teachers 8.1.

Teachers who are student centered, indirect, and warm or friendly, as opposed to subject centered, direct, and businesslike, tend to reject the traditional **formal seating pattern** of rows of students directly facing the teacher at the front of the classroom. Formal seating patterns tend to reduce student-to-student eye contact and student interaction and to increase teacher control and student passivity.

In a classic study on the positioning of teachers, Adams and Biddle (1970) found that student participation is restricted by the environment or physical setting in ways that are hidden from both the teacher and the students. It appeared to them that students who sit in the center of the room are the most active learners, or what they called "responders." The verbal interaction is so concentrated in this area of the classroom and in a line directly up the center of the room (where the teacher is in front most of the time), that they coined the term *action zone* to refer to this area (see Figure 8.1).

Student-centered teachers tend to favor **informal seating patterns,** such as forum, circular, and horseshoe (U-shaped) patterns, in which students face one another as well as the teacher (Figure 8.2). One drawback that may result when elementary and middle grade students face one another is that less time is spent on task and more inappropriate behavior is exhibited by students who lack inner control (Axelrod, Hall, & Tamms, 1979; Caproni, 1977; see also Evertson, Worsham, & Emmer, 1996). At higher grade levels, or when being on task requires greater student discussion, the informal patterns are

## Factors to Consider in Arranging Classrooms for Instruction

Classroom design factors will be determined by the size of the room; the number of students in the class; the size and shape of tables and chairs; the amount of movable furniture; the location of fixed features such as doors, windows, closets, and chalkboard; the audiovisual equipment to be used; the school's practice; and the teacher's approach and experience. Eight factors should be considered in arranging classrooms for instruction:

1. *Fixed features.* The teacher cannot change the "givens" of a room and must take into account the location of doors, windows, closets, electric outlets, and so forth. For example, seats should not be too close to doors or closets. Electric equipment needs to be near an outlet, and wires should not run across the center of the room. (If they must, they should be taped to the floor.)

2. *Traffic areas.* High traffic areas, such as supply areas, closets, and space near the pencil sharpener and wastebasket, need to be open and easily accessible. The teacher's desk should be located in a low traffic area.

3. *Work areas.* Work areas and study areas should be private and quiet, preferably placed in the corner or rear of the room, away from traffic lanes and noisy areas.

4. *Furniture and equipment.* The room, furniture, and equipment should be kept clean and in repair so that they can be used. Desks and chairs may be old, but they should be clean and smooth (make the appropriate requisition to the janitorial department or supervisor), and graphics and doodling should be discouraged immediately. The equipment should be stored in a designated space.

5. *Instructional materials.* All materials and equipment should be easily accessible so activities can begin and end promptly and cleanup time can be minimized. Props and equipment that are not stored in closets should be kept in "dead" spaces away from traffic.

6. *Visibility.* The teacher should be able to see all students from any part of the room in order to reduce managerial problems and enhance instructional supervision. Students should be able to see the teacher, chalkboard, projected images, and demonstrations without having to move their desks and without straining their necks.

7. *Flexibility.* The classroom design should be flexible enough so that it can be modified to meet the requirements of different activities and different groupings for instruction.

*Source:* Adapted from Edmund T. Emmer et al., *Classroom Management for Secondary Teachers,* 3rd ed. (Boston: Allyn and Bacon, 1994); Allan C. Ornstein and Francis P. Hunkins, *Curriculum: Foundations, Principles, and Theory,* 4th ed. (Boston: Allyn and Bacon, 2004).

likely to be more effective. However, at all levels there is greater potential for discipline problems with nontraditional seating. Insecure teachers and those who are not good managers may decide to keep to more traditional seating patterns until they gain more experience.

Other classroom designs that accommodate whole-group arrangements are found in Figure 8.2. The traditional seating pattern, as indicated in the lower-left diagram, allows the teacher to have visual and verbal control of the entire class, with the concentration of activity occurring down the center, as noted in Figure 8.1. The forum arrangement (upper right) allows the teacher to move easily down the aisles to provide interaction with individuals and groups of students while allowing groups or pairs of students to work together on various projects and activities. The circular and horseshoe

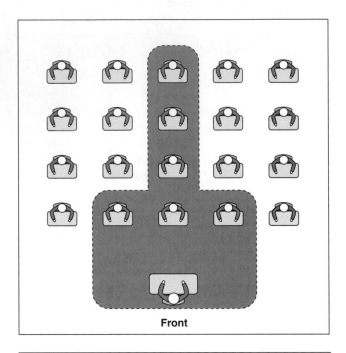

*Figure 8.1* Front-of-the-Room Teacher Positioning and Concentration of Verbal Interaction

or U-shaped patterns allow for strong student interaction in the form of whole-class discussion, forums, or brainstorming sessions that, for instance, begin interdisciplinary or multisubject units. Students using the horseshoe arrangement can turn their desks to the sides so that they have more visual and verbal contact with their follow students.

Because of increased student interaction, discipline problems may arise with these special seating arrangements unless the teacher has good managerial skills. However, all of these designs allow the teacher flexibility in activities. They function for small groups, create feelings of group cohesion and cooperation, and also allow the teacher to present a demonstration, ask the class to brainstorm a problem or debate an issue, or use audiovisual materials.

A popular type of design and room arrangement in today's classrooms is that noted in Figure 8.3. This design has been likened to an **open classroom** seating arrangement; it complements some of the curriculum design approaches discussed in Chapter 5 as well as the authentic and engaged-reading and writing classrooms of holistic literacy learning. The design shows clusters of desks, activity and study tables, work areas, shelves, and computer sites, all of which allow for small-group and individualized instruction. The desk-cluster arrangement and small-group table areas can easily become centers, literature discussion areas, and activity and project areas. The formal rows of fixed desks of the traditional classroom are gone. The desks are arranged in groups or

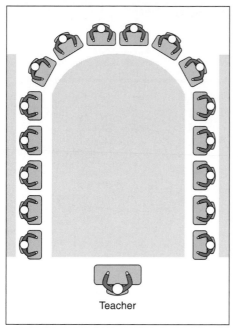

**Horseshoe or U-Shaped Pattern**

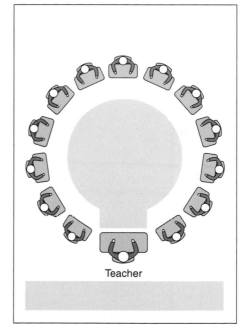

**Forum Pattern**

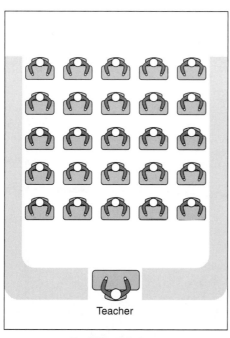

**Traditional Pattern**

**Circular Pattern**

*Figure 8.2* Four Seating Patterns

*Source:* Adapted from Allan C. Ornstein and Tom Lasley, *Strategies for Effective Teaching,* 4th ed. (Boston: McGraw-Hill, 2004), p. 338.

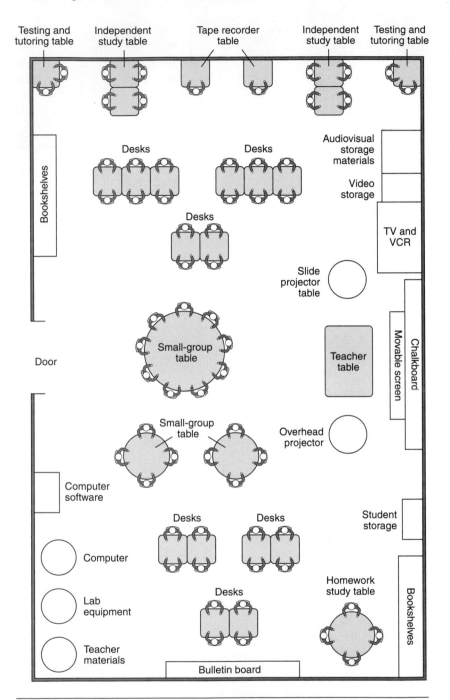

*Figure 8.3* An Open Classroom Seating Pattern

*Source:* Adapted from Allan C. Ornstein and Tom Lasley, *Strategies for Effective Teaching,* 4th ed. (Boston: McGraw-Hill, 2004), p. 340.

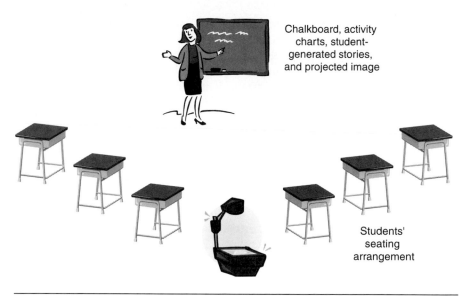

Chalkboard, activity charts, student-generated stories, and projected image

Students' seating arrangement

*Figure 8.4* Small-Group Instructional Model

clusters and can be moved. The open classroom climate increases student interaction and gives students the opportunity to move around and engage in different learning activities in different settings. One teacher reports that in her use of efficient and mobile space, children use trays instead of desks to store their materials (Taberski, 2000).

Within the classroom environment, the teacher often needs to focus instruction with small groups of students at the chalkboard, at an activity chart or at a large poster display to create an experience story, or at the overhead projector to project an image. Figure 8.4 shows how this arrangement might look and suggests that this small-group instructional model could be implemented in many of the other classroom designs alongside one wall.

## ■ SCHOOLWIDE PRACTICES

Districts and schools have also attempted various patterns of organization in order to provide the best educational practices for learners. Usually these patterns attempt to organize groups of students while seeking best practices to accommodate individual differences. Changes in schoolwide patterns of organization occur for a number of reasons. There may be a shift in educational philosophy instituted by the principal or encouraged by a group of teachers. Or there is an overall dissatisfaction with a present grouping pattern and use of time. In this case, based on research findings, positive case reports from other schools and districts reported in journals, or success achieved by an individual teacher who experimented with a different organizational pattern, administrators, teachers, community leaders, and parents meet to achieve an alternative system of organizing students for instruction in their school or district (Delany, Toburen, Hooton, & Dozier, 1997–1998; DiRocco, 1998–1999; Hopping, 2000; Shortt & Thayer, 1998–1999). Following are types of schoolwide patterns of organization that attempt to describe and modify groups between and within classes.

## The Self-Contained Classroom

The most common means of organizing students for instruction is to group twenty-five to thirty students according to age and grade level, and sometimes ability, and assign them to a specific classroom and teacher. When most instruction occurs in this setting, it is called a **self-contained classroom.** At the elementary school level, a teacher is assigned to the class for the entire day and is responsible for most of the content and time allotments for instruction. Students might travel to another class one or two periods a day to receive special instruction (for example, in remedial reading, music, or physical education), or other teachers might visit the class to provide special instruction.

Most self-contained classrooms of today are **heterogeneously grouped.** This means that children who make up the total class mix have been grouped by varying degrees of ability levels. Students are socially motivated and influenced by their peers as well as the teacher, so the rationale behind heterogeneous grouping is that students of varying ability and diversity levels will learn from one another. In particular, it is felt that students of lower ability and with less-developed language facility will benefit from the interaction, and possibly guidance, provided by students of higher ability.

A second type of single-class organization of children is known as **homogeneous grouping.** This occurs when children are grouped by the same ability or achievement level, often defined by the results of the previous year's testing. Thus, if there were five fifth grades in one school and the children were homogeneously grouped by reading level, there would be five classes of ability-level readers ranging from the very capable to struggling readers. What administrators and teachers might collaboratively plan to do in such a schoolwide homogeneous plan would be to assign more children to higher-ability classes and fewer children to the lowest-achieving class. While class 5-1 might have thirty-five children, class 5-5 would contain fifteen to twenty children who have been measured as being the lowest-achieving readers in the fifth grade.

Class 5-1, with more children, is perceived to be more capable, more fluent with reading, and, by extension, more capable of handling challenging content and learning experiences. Thus, even though the whole-class group is large, the teacher might feel that the curriculum integration design approach will motivate and challenge this group of high achievers while providing an organizational system of grouping by concept topics. Class 5-5, on the other hand, might receive more direct instruction and a great deal of teacher support. Direct instruction in reading is intended to make learning to read easier and efficient by having students focus on the component skills of a literacy task and practice those skills with high levels of engagement with structured material (Carnine et al., 1997). With students in class 5-5 working on specific skills with highly structured materials, the teacher has the opportunity to provide focused individualized instruction for each student experiencing difficulty.

**BOX 8.3** Planning for Students from Economically Disadvantaged Situations

When one state reduced class size to fifteen students per teacher to better meet the needs of students who come from economically depressed circumstances, teachers discovered the following:

- Fewer discipline problems
- More time for instruction and individual coaching
- Engagement of students in varied instructional methodologies
- More content covered in greater depth

*Source:* Adapted from Anke Halbach, Karen Ehrle, John Zahorik, and Alex Molner, "Class Size Reduction: From Promise to Practice," *Educational Leadership* (March 2002), pp. 32–35.

In fact, the overall concept of homogeneous grouping is the increased ability of the teacher to provide for individual differences. Because the range of diversity in any given classroom has been reduced, the teacher can modify planned lessons and provide instruction to meet the individual needs of challenged or struggling learners. Class size reduction is another organizational way schools plan for increased achievement, especially for students at risk for literacy or arithmetic success. To increase the academic success of students from economically disadvantaged areas, one state reduced class size to fifteen students from kindergarten to third grade, and teachers felt there were a number of benefits (Halbach, Ehrle, Zahorik, & Molnar, 2001). See Box 8.3.

## Departmentalized Instruction

At the middle school and junior high level, the self-contained classroom is modified by what is commonly called **departmentalization.** Students are assigned to a different teacher for each subject and may have five to seven different teachers each day. Departmentalization may begin at the fifth, sixth, or seventh grade, depending on the school district.

The major rationale behind departmentalized instruction is that students receive instruction in content domains in which the teachers are pedagogically competent; that is, the teachers have studied in some depth the domains they plan to teach and have the content knowledge to pass on to students. Unlike the self-contained classroom, in which the teacher is more of a generalist in content knowledge, the departmentalized classroom provides a content specialist for each whole-class grouping of students. What generally occurs in this type of pattern is that heterogeneous groups of students at the same grade level move from content teacher to content teacher for scheduled periods of instruction.

However, what may also occur is that homogeneously grouped students at a given grade level may remain together throughout the day and travel to each subject area classroom as the same group. For instance, in a large urban school containing enough students to make up a number of sixth-grade homogeneous groups, some content teachers may share the same group of sixth-grade students who are grouped in ranges from the lowest to highest in achievement. In this way, teachers share students at the same ability level and, it is believed, can assist them more effectively because the range of academic diversity has been reduced. Another organizational plan occurs when sixth graders are assigned to heterogeneous classes and then regrouped homogeneously for reading and mathematics instruction. When students of similar achievement or ability levels are assigned to a specific set of courses that are programmed at designated levels such as honors, advanced, basic, and corrective or remedial, the term **tracking** is often used (Scott & Butler, 1994). Thus there may exist particular sections or *tracks* of English 6 or Mathematics 6 to accommodate the various ability levels of students.

Despite widespread criticism of such *between-class ability grouping* (separate classes for students of different abilities), teachers overwhelmingly support the idea because of the ease in teaching a homogeneous group. Parents of high-achieving students perceive tracking to be in their children's best interest. Reality is also a consideration. By the time students are in middle school, the achievement and motivation gaps between the top third and lowest third achievers have grown extremely wide, and the teachers cannot easily accommodate this range of student abilities. Hence, the norms of the school culture resist detracking (Braddock & McPartland, 1990; Oakes & Lipton, 1992).

When all of the social studies teachers in one school implemented a **detracking** plan, they faced three unanticipated and disappointing outcomes. They used many of the practices suggested to make detracking work, such as simulation activities, flexible or block scheduling, small-group activities, projects, thematic instruction, and extra periods for students needing help. Although the teachers were enthused about detracking making their classes more diversified in terms of ethnic makeup and socio-economic levels, they found that (1) the increased variation in ability within a class of students made instruction more difficult to manage in terms of the tasks assigned, the topics covered, the language used, the pace of the lessons, and the standards used to evaluate student achievement; (2) they could not avoid imposing a uniform set of class expectations even while higher-ability students were denied greater challenge and lower-ability and slower students were not able to achieve mastery; and (3) teachers felt they were not doing their job well and often had to apologize to some students about the lack of assignment difficulty or about the apathy and deviance exhibited by others (Rosenbaum, 1999–2000).

The primary criticism of separating students by ability is that it results in low expectations for low-ability students, lowered self-esteem, less instruction time, less homework, and less learning—even worse, it has a compounding and stigmatizing effect on low achievers (Good, 1987; Hastings, 1992). The negative consequences of this practice disproportionately affect minorities and female students, especially in math classrooms. Given our democratic norms and the need to deal with diversity in schools (and society), and given the notion that abilities are multifaceted and developmental (not genetic), many argue that differences in abilities can become assets in classrooms rather than liabilities (Oakes & Lipton, 1992; Wheelock, 1992).

Researchers have found that high-ability students benefit from separate ability groups because the curriculum and instruction are tailored to their abilities, and the classroom work and homework driving the group require extra effort. Fewer competing values curtail the academic ethos and less time has to be devoted to management problems (Gamoran, 1992b; Scott, 1993).

But such arguments tend to run up against our own democratic thinking, the ethos and drive to reduce inequality and differences (including outcomes) that may exist between high- and low-achieving students. Ability-grouping critics contend that the gains made by high achievers do not compensate for the loss of self-esteem and achievement among low achievers, who often find themselves slotted into groups where the instruction is less engaging. It is not clear, however, whether the performance of low-achieving groups suffers because students themselves are less responsive, because of management problems, or because the instruction really is inferior, as critics suggest.

After reviewing sixty years of research on the issue, Slavin claimed that the outcomes of all students (high and low) in ability-grouped classes canceled out or "clustered closely around zero" (1987, p. 112; 1990). In other words, ability grouping rarely adds to overall achievement in a school (although it may for a particular class), but it often contributes to inequality (highs do better, lows do worse).

In addition, studies show that instruction in mixed-ability, untracked classes more closely resembles instruction in high-achieving and middle-track classes than instruction in low-track classes—that is, the mixed-ability grouping tends to benefit low-ability students (Goodlad, 1984; Oakes, 1985). Similarly, average-ability students who are grouped in high-ability math classes achieve significantly higher math grades and higher scores on achievement tests than do their cohorts who are placed in average classes (Gamoran, 1992a; Mason, Schroeter, Combs, & Washington, 1992), perhaps because their teachers have higher expectations for them and the content is more advanced.

## Team Teaching

**Team teaching** or co-teaching generally occurs as a cooperative effort of two or three teachers who pool their instructional talents and methodology for a special purpose. Team teaching, while a less formal arrangement than departmentalization, often has the kind of focus usually associated with homogeneous, ability-grouped students. This pattern of organization most often occurs at the elementary grade levels when a few teachers at the same grade level decide to capitalize on their best instructional talents while relegating their less-favored discipline subjects to another. Teaming also offers a process whereby teachers create a familylike atmosphere because they work together closely to meet the individual needs of their students (Merenbloom, 1996).

Let's see how this pattern of organization works as two third-grade teachers share or team their students. One third-grade teacher prefers to teach the language arts, especially reading and writing, whereas the other third-grade teacher enjoys teaching arithmetic and likes to connect mathematics work with science instruction. The two decide to team teach, allowing all the students of both classes to go to one teacher for language arts and literacy instruction and to the second teacher for arithmetic and science instruction. After each teacher completes his or her first scheduled block of instruction, the two student groups switch classes, and the teacher presents the same content and/or learning experiences to the second group. This two-block arrangement may take the first two scheduled periods of a school day, allowing each teacher to cover the other content subjects in the more traditional way. If another teacher decides to join the team to take responsibility for another content domain such as social studies, the arrangement becomes like the departmentalized instruction of the middle and junior high school.

The teacher team can attempt to provide for individual differences and ability levels by homogeneously grouping students as well. The high-achieving third graders in reading from one classroom would be grouped with the high-achieving readers from the other classroom. Meanwhile, the same system would be used for arithmetic achievement. Thus, high- and low-ability students in both reading and mathematics from both classrooms would be teamed to form homogeneous groups for each teacher. Although the merits of such a parallel team teaching pattern can be defended in terms of ability-level expectations (Rosenbaum, 1999–2000), advocates of democratic and equal education might feel that the "rich get richer and the poor get poorer."

Team teaching has gained strong professional interest in recent years (Welch, Brownell, & Sheridan, 1999), particularly for the way it benefits and shares responsibility for the special-needs students served in general education classrooms. When two teams of general education teachers and special education teachers shared mainstream and special education students at the fourth- and fifth-grade levels, these interesting results emerged: (1) Teachers discovered that because a partner was present, it was easier to deal with unexpected events or interruptions in the class; (2) both special education teachers reported that they broadened their perspective of teaching while forming positive relationships with all students instead of just those who had the special education–mandated individualized education programs (IEPs); and (3) teachers felt that those children who didn't qualify for special education but still had learning and behavior problems received more help (Welch, 2000). See Tips for Teachers 8.2 for organizational ways to co-teach with a colleague.

## Multi-Age Classrooms

The **multi-age classroom** or multi-age teaming organizational pattern attempts to group children at different age or grade levels into cohesive instructional units. Most often the pattern occurs across bordering grade levels, such as multi-age classrooms of children from first to third grade, from fourth and fifth grade (or sixth, depending on the district's organizational plan), and sixth to eighth grade. The leading concept of this organizational plan is that children learn from one another and can cooperate well in shared projects, with the older students acting as surrogate teachers and bringing the younger ones along. A sense of family prevails (Elliott, 1997). Because students of varying ages, life experiences, and ability levels are working together in all or many content disciplines, the curriculum integration or interdisciplinary, thematic unit approaches would both facilitate and encourage these interactions. Because of the wide range of abilities found in a multi-age classroom, a cooperative spirit is engendered, with the lower-grade students learning information from the upper-grade students while older students elaborate and extend their own knowledge by teaching (Wall, 1994).

One middle school comprising students from the sixth to eighth grades adopted a multi-age team model using the following criteria: (1) two teams, with each team composed of four teachers who made a three-year commitment and received special training to work with students of varying ability levels, particularly the gifted; (2) equal numbers of boys and girls assigned to each team; (3) equal numbers of sixth, seventh, and eighth graders who committed to the three-year, multi-age program; (4) equal numbers of high, middle, and low achievers; (5) equal numbers of gifted and special education students; and (6) attention to cultural diversity. A resource teacher joined each team on a daily basis to help with the instruction of the special education students, allowing all students to remain in the same classroom during instructional units. This organizational pattern provided teachers with complete autonomy and flexibility in

# Ways to Accomplish Team or Co-Teaching

Team or co-teaching can take a number of forms. Here are potential ways for two teachers to organize groups of students for diversified instruction.

1. In the *parallel-teaching* pattern, two teachers divide each class into halves, jointly plan their instruction, and take responsibility for working with one-half of each class.

2. Another variety is the use of *station* or *center teaching* whereby specific content is covered in one area of the classroom by one teacher, such as at Station 2. The other teacher works with one group of students with one aspect of the curriculum at a station, and students rotate from station to station.

3. *One teacher teaching and one assisting* is a process in which one teacher takes the lead role in instruction for the whole group while the other moves about the room to assist students.

4. Another technique involves the use of *unbalanced groups.* One teacher takes one larger group, possibly to begin a new lesson with a direct teaching approach, while the second teacher provides instruction to a smaller group, possibly to accomplish drill, practice, and review of necessary skill work.

5. *Taking turns* occurs when two teachers take turns during presentation of a lesson and each shares the discussion and questioning, or the two take turns during demonstration or experimentation activities.

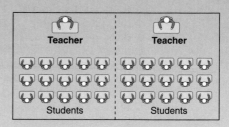

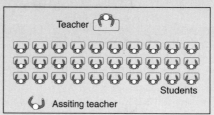

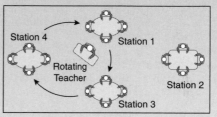

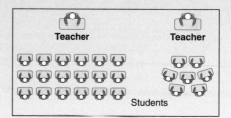

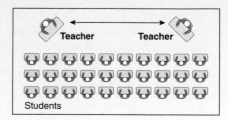

*Source:* Adapted from Lynne Cook and Marilyn Friend, "Co-Teaching: Guidelines for Creating Effective Practices," in E. L. Meyer, G. A. Vergason, and R. J. Whelan, eds., *Strategies for Teaching Children in Inclusive Settings* (Denver: Love, 1995), pp. 155–182.

managing time and developing schedules to engage students in the instructional units (Hopping, 2000).

Within multi-age or grade arrangements, teachers can set up partnerships so that younger and older or higher-ability and lower-ability students benefit from interacting in cooperative learning situations (Burns et al., 1999). Such *cross-grade pairings* may occur during one or more class periods a week. When low-achieving, upper-grade students were partnered with kindergartners in reading, both sets of students made gains in personal growth and achievement (Leland & Fitzpatrick, 1993–1994).

## Block Scheduling

Block scheduling is a way to deal with time during the school day so that greater blocks of time are scheduled for instruction and learning. Two major types of time management configurations are most commonly used in block scheduling. The first is called the **alternating day schedule,** in which classes meet every other day for double-period blocks of time (eighty to ninety minutes) for an entire term or school year. The second is known as **block scheduling,** in which classes meet every day for a double period (eighty to ninety minutes) over one semester (Shortt & Thayer, 1998–1999).

In one middle school, after the seventh-grade teachers implemented a successful alternating day schedule to accommodate an interdisciplinary unit in English and social studies, the eighth-grade teachers were influenced to try the block schedule design. The seventh-grade teachers had instituted a schedule of three academic periods of eighty minutes each on one day and the traditional six periods of forty minutes each on the alternating day. However, in order to provide equitable foreign language instruction for their students, the eighth-grade teachers found it necessary to implement a similar alternating day schedule the following year. The key for both groups of teachers was that they made decisions to use an appropriate instructional design in the best interests of their students (DiRocco, 1998–1999).

One elementary school implemented a parallel block scheduling design in order to raise student achievement in reading and mathematics while reducing the number and severity of student behavior problems. The **parallel block schedule** was managed by teams of teachers from the second- to fifth-grade levels. Each team consisted of three base teachers and one enrichment lab teacher. During a time block, one base teacher instructed a whole class, a second base teacher sent the room's highest achieving half of the class to the enrichment lab, while the third base teacher sent the lowest achieving half of the class to the lab. This block approach allowed two team teachers to teach reading and math to half their class, now homogeneously grouped by ability level. While the remaining base teacher and the enrichment lab teacher had full class groups, these teachers had specific responsibilities in the language arts and in integrating reading and math through science and social studies content (Delany et al., 1997–1998).

Block scheduling is one way to provide more varied and in-depth instruction while increasing students' engaged time in learning activities (Evans, Tokarczyk, Rice, & McCray, 2002). In one review of seven schools using some form of block scheduling, it was found that the longer the periods of concentrated time, the more positive the results for such factors as student academic performance, attendance, discipline, and standardized test scores (Carroll, 1994). Teachers report that longer time blocks allow them to conduct learning experiences more efficiently, plan lessons on the basis of concepts rather than on a textbook chapter, and provide greater flexibility in meeting the needs of at-risk students (Shortt & Thayer, 1998–1999).

Using and managing such scheduling blocks often needs to be a schoolwide effort involving administrators, teachers, parents, and the community. However, the team of teachers participating at a grade level appear to be the key players in that they influence the management of the block schedule and have the ability to alter it to provide appropriate instruction (DiRocco, 1998–1999). Because the team has direct control over the daily schedule, it creates the most optimal learning environment for instruction while increasing the opportunity to provide both integrated instruction and different instructional approaches (Merenbloom, 1996).

# ■ ACCOMMODATIONS FOR STUDENTS WITH SPECIAL NEEDS

Often many children within a school are provided additional resources and specialized periods of instruction. These children can be at either high or low levels of achievement and ability and may have been formally identified as experiencing exceptionality in learning or behavior. Students at the high end of exceptionality have been labeled "gifted" or "talented," whereas those at the low end are often called "remedial," "learning disabled," "at-risk," or "handicapped." The terminology used to describe students at the lower end of ability and the names of the classes they are sent off to attend to receive additional assistance have become a sensitive issue today.

## Who Are the Special-Needs Students?

Who **special-needs learners** are and the associated concerns of *where* and *how* they should be educated have been major concerns in the field of education throughout the latter part of the last century and into this one (McCormick, 2003). As early as 1968, one author questioned the effectiveness of special class placements and the labels used for students diagnosed as mentally retarded and those with mild learning problems (Dunn, 1968). In 1975, Congress intervened and passed the landmark Education of the Handicapped Act (PL 94-142). This act has been the cornerstone of special education policies and programs, has undergone expansion and changes several times, and was renamed the Individuals with Disabilities Education Act (IDEA) in 1990 (Kirk, Gallagher, & Anastasiow, 2003; Lerner, 2000). Then in 1997, when Congress reauthorized IDEA as Public Law (PL) 105-17, it provided the impetus for reform in the field of special education by holding schools accountable for standards-based outcomes for special-needs students (Turnbull, Turnbull, Shank, Smith, & Leal, 2002).

Special education students, students with disabilities, special-needs students, and students with exceptionalities were originally defined by the 1975 act in the following way: as those who are mentally retarded, hard of hearing, deaf, orthopedically impaired, other health impaired, speech impaired, visually handicapped, emotionally disturbed, or learning disabled, and by reason thereof require special education and related services (see Table 8.1 for a listing of handicapping conditions, beginning with 1976–1977 tabulations). Full rights and protection for handicapped children ages three to five was passed in 1986 and implemented in the 1990–1991 school year. Students with disabilities had to be provided with special education and related services at public expense under public supervision and direction. Schools not only had to adopt policies that served all handicapped students, but they also had to conduct searches to locate such students.

One of the major outcomes of identifying the disability areas enumerated in the 1975 act was the terminology that came to be used, and often this terminology became the words or labels used to identify both the students with the disability and the classroom environments they attended. Thus, schools established classroom settings in which students diagnosed as mentally retarded, emotionally disturbed, or learning disabled attended the entire day. Each classroom was staffed by a trained and licensed special education teacher who was often supported by paraprofessionals or teacher aides. Students with such handicapping conditions were then segregated from their school-age peers and perceived to require teaching and learning methodology that was unique to their handicapping condition.

*Table 8.1*  **Numbers of Students Served in Federally Supported Programs for the Disabled, by Type of Disability, 1976–1977 to 1998–1999**

| Type of Disability | 1976–1977 | 1989–1990 | 1998–1999 |
|---|---|---|---|
| Specific Learning Disabilities | 796,000 | 2,047,000 | 2,789,000 |
| Speech or Language Impairments | 1,302,000 | 971,000 | 1,068,000 |
| Mental Retardation | 961,000 | 547,000 | 597,000 |
| Serious Emotional Disturbance | 283,000 | 380,000 | 462,000 |
| Hearing Impairments | 88,000 | 57,000 | 70,000 |
| Orthopedic Impairments | 87,000 | 48,000 | 69,000 |
| Other Health Impairments | 141,000 | 52,000 | 221,000 |
| Visual Impairments | 38,000 | 22,000 | 26,000 |
| Multiple Disabilities | — | 86,000 | 106,000 |
| Deafness-Blindness | — | 2,000 | 2,000 |
| Autism and Traumatic Brain Injury | — | — | 67,000 |
| Developmental Delay | — | — | 12,000 |
| Preschool Disabled | 196,000 | 381,000 | 568,000 |
| Infants and Toddlers | — | 37,000 | — |
| All Disabilities Total | 3,892,000 | 4,630,000 | 6,057,000 |
| Percentage of Public School Enrollment | 8.32 | 11.32 | 13.01 |

*Source:* Office of Special Education and Rehabilitative Services, *Annual Report to Congress in the Implementation of the Individuals with Disabilities Education Act* (Washington, DC: U.S. Dept. of Education, 2001 Edition), Table 53 prepared June 2000.

Students and, of course, parents became aware of these handicapping labels and the associated services offered by their local schools. Parents generally followed three avenues of practice when they learned from their school or district that their child was being considered for a special class placement. Once the child was diagnosed by the school or district as having a particular handicapping condition, the parents agreed with that diagnosis and agreed to have the child placed in the appropriate classroom environment offered by the school or district. Or after diagnosis of the child, parents refused special services or special class placements, preferring to allow the child to remain in his or her regular classroom setting. These parents often agreed to provide extra assistance in the form of tutoring after school, on weekends, or through the summer months.

The third avenue is quite interesting and was probably due to the actual support services offered by the child's district or school. In this instance, the parents received the diagnostic analysis of the child's handicapping condition from the school but didn't agree with the findings. They may not have agreed because they didn't like the labeling associated with the diagnosis (e.g., mental retardation) or because they didn't relish the type of classroom placement their child would receive in their local school. These parents would often "shop around" among other private agencies until they received a diagnosis that presented a more favorable label (e.g., learning disabled) that accounted for their child's difficulty with school-offered learning. Furthermore, using the label "learning different" has become another way to imply the condition of "learning disabled" and the other negative labels used by educators and the public today (Armstrong, 2001).

Table 8.1 shows just three intervals out of a total of sixteen periods when counts of disability conditions were tabulated based on reports from the fifty states and the District of Columbia. The table reveals, from the first tabulation period of 1976 to 1977 (after the passage of the 1975 act) to the most current, the 1998–1999 period, that the number of students counted as having a disability has increased by almost 6.5 percent, or 2 million students. What is most interesting is the dramatic rise of the "Specific Learning Disabilities" category from 21.5 percent to 46.1 percent of all disabilities. Meanwhile, "Speech or Language Impairments" decreased by half in the twenty-two-year period, while "Mental Retardation" decreased from 26 percent to 10 percent of all disability areas (Office of Special Education and Rehabilitative Services, 2001, Table 53). Has the increase in the disability condition of "Specific Learning Disabilities" occurred because students, who may previously have been labeled in the other two categories, are now finding themselves labeled differently?

Now, with the enactment of IDEA in 1997, the mission of special education has shifted even while the assignment to categories of types of specific disabilities continues to change for students served in federal programs. There are two major themes of IDEA legislation; the first has to do with *inclusion*, based on the concept of the **least restrictive environment**, and the second has to do with **collaboration**, particularly of general and special educators as they plan to educate all students in their classes (Turnbull et al., 2002). Thus the intent of IDEA is not to segregate special education or disabled students from their peers but to include them in regular classroom settings to interact with their peers and different teachers (Merritt, 2001).

## Rethinking the Pull-Out Delivery System

Special education students prior to the enactment of IDEA found themselves grouped in a self-contained setting with like students who were classified as learning disabled, emotionally disturbed, or mentally handicapped. If the severity of their disability was not pronounced enough to warrant a special class placement, students with mild handicapping conditions might daily attend a resource room setting in which basic skills were often addressed. This type of special assistance was most often delivered outside of the student's mainstream classroom and is often referred to as "pull out" programming (Welch, Richards, Okada, Richards, & Prescott, 1995) or remedial reading instruction (Carnine et al., 1997). In the latter case, the lowest achieving students in reading were sent on a daily or biweekly basis to a period of instruction with the remedial reading teacher.

There has been a general move in education to rethink the merits of the pull-out system in favor of one in which special-needs students are included in regular education classes and teachers "push in" their specialized services and programs. This shift was prompted by two major concerns, one having to do with fragmentation of the student's day and the second with the use of such labels as *learning disabled, handicapped,* or *remedial* (now considered to be pejorative). A concern connected to the students' marginal academic status as suggested by the label was the locale of the pull-out services. More often than not, students with special needs and their associated peers—language-minority students—met for classwork in school basements, closets, or a modular unit separated from the parent school (Nieto, 2002–2003).

When a student is pulled out of subject-area content delivered to all their classmates to attend another setting for another purpose, it is the student who usually suffers in the long run. The student has missed something that he or she may be held accountable for when test time comes. Some students are pulled out more than once during a school day; the same student could go to remedial reading or remedial math or the resource room. Although it appears that the school and its teachers are providing the best resources they can to move the student out of the remedial situation, the overall result is disconnected, disjointed instruction that the student has to piece together. Because many of these students lack basic skills to begin with, they have difficulty making the necessary connections, especially piecing together the content they missed when they were out of their primary classroom.

Such a situation prompted one middle school to shift to another scheduling arrangement for its students. Its pull-out programs in both special education and gifted education fragmented the school's daily schedule, providing no flexibility in its fifty-minute-period scheduling. Because the school shifted its scheduling approach to accommodate multi-age teams, the accelerated and remedial students benefited (Hopping, 2000).

The pull-out system is also undergoing change to remove the stigmatization that often accompanies the use of specific labels, whether they be given to the students themselves or to a specific class or program. In order to help teachers view children in terms of their learning needs rather than their categorized labels or descriptions, educators are using terminology such as "children with diverse learning abilities" (Churton et al., 1998; Kameenui & Carnine, 1998). This shift encourages teachers to concentrate on the needs and learning abilities of individual students and on the natural diversity in styles of learning while seeking ways to accommodate them in the self-contained classroom (Armstrong, 2001).

## Toward More Inclusive Ways to Service Special-Needs Students

Three other terms are used to describe approaches that accommodate learners with special needs in whole-class settings: (1) push-in or pull-in, (2) inclusion, and (3) differentiated instruction. *Push-in* means that a trained specialist such as a reading, literacy, or language teacher or a paraprofessional goes into a self-contained classroom on a scheduled basis to provide extra or additional reading and writing assistance to students who require such need. The push-in teacher or paraprofessional works cooperatively with the classroom teacher, who may ask that targeted students receive extra help with particular content readings and writing assignments. The push-in teacher works with these specially targeted students in another area of the classroom as the classroom teacher manages instruction for the majority of the class.

**Inclusion,** a program policy generally used for students who have traditionally been in special education pull-out programs, means that those students classified as mildly, moderately, and severely disabled be schooled with their same-age peers in regular school programs (Churton et al., 1998). One author has noted that in the field of special education, the inclusion movement has been the most important outcome arising from school reform and restructuring of special education services (Sailor, 1991). Like the push-in concept, inclusion requires a great deal of cooperation between and among teachers, with the greatest challenge stemming from the necessity to present instruction commensurate with the ability and handicapping conditions of each individual student who is placed or included in a general education classroom. See Box 8.4.

Although increasing numbers of learners with disabilities are being included and accommodated in some general education classes, full inclusion—or the daily placement of special-needs learners and regular education students in the same self-contained classroom—remains an elusive challenge in most school districts (Edmiaston & Fitzgerald, 2000). Also, for full inclusion to occur, children with disabilities need to be included with their mainstream peers in natural proportions (Fuchs & Fuchs, 1994).

One local school board created a position called the "inclusion facilitator" to assist teachers with the transition of having special-needs learners attend regular content classes. When the content teachers had to learn to adjust content, expectations, homework assignments, and assessments on the basis of the included student's ability, a major shift in the teachers' thinking also had to occur because their usual instructional

**BOX 8.4** How Inclusion Works in the Best Interests of Individualized Instruction

Inclusion does not work the same for every special education student, because students' needs are different. For as much of the school day as possible, students' inclusion services should occur in general education classrooms so that special education students receive the same instruction as their peers. Each student's individualized education program (IEP) should take into account the support services needed in the regular classroom to make a student's instruction comparable to that of his or her peers. At other times, a student may leave the classroom to receive specialized support services in another locale by another teacher.

practice was to compare student achievement with course content (Ruder, 2000). A research study looked at students with learning disabilities in three instructional settings, some using inclusion and another using pull-out services, to determine which setting would result in the greatest word reading achievement (Holloway, 2001). These results are presented in Box 8.5.

The early focus of inclusion was to modify, adapt, and add on to existing school practices regarding the interaction between regular and special education teachers, as noted in the programs discussed above. A present focus, called "second-generation inclusion," seeks to place students with special needs in general education classes while accomplishing the restructuring of the school to benefit all students. Such restructuring results in a school climate change in which teaching for diversity becomes the established practice rather than teaching to achievement or ability groups.

Cooperative teaching that involves general and special education teachers working to plan, instruct, and evaluate students in the same general education classroom setting is one approach to accomplishing second-generation inclusion. Such cooperation on a coequal basis reduces the need for pull-out services and maximizes the effectiveness of individualized instruction for students with and without exceptionalities (Pugach, 1995; Turnbull et al., 2002). This very effect was noted in the team teaching study mentioned earlier in which both regular and special education fourth and fifth graders perceived the two teachers in the room as coequals rather than viewing one as a specialist who worked only with a specific group (Welch, 2000).

**Differentiated instruction** is a way to provide for individualized learning in a self-contained classroom. It recognizes the variance among students and encourages teachers to look beyond one teaching strategy for each content subject that is delivered in the same time frame for all. It proclaims that the learner is key, not what the curriculum nor the academic standards set for the teacher to cover. Differentiation necessitates that curriculum and instruction fit the individual, that students have choices about what and how to learn, that they take part in setting learning goals, and that the classroom interfaces with

**BOX 8.5** What Does Research Say about the Effect of Inclusion for Students with Learning Disabilities?

Four different studies examined the effects of inclusion on students with learning disabilities. To draw any valid conclusions about the outcomes of the studies, the researcher had to consider the effective scope and quality of services made available to the students and the ways they were used. In one study, students with learning disabilities received instruction in a mainstream setting from both the regular classroom teacher and a special education teacher; in another, students were instructed in a pull-out situation by a special education teacher in a resource room; the setting in yet another study had features of the other two in that students were instructed in the inclusive setting and supplemented with additional work in the resource room. A fourth study looked at word-learning achievement from the point of view of the different instructional settings. Results in word-reading achievement indicated that students with learning disabilities in the combined model performed significantly better than students in the inclusion-only model or in the pull-out, resource room model.

*Source:* Adapted from John Holloway, "Inclusion and Students with Learning Disabilities," *Educational Leadership* (March 2001), pp. 86–88.

the individual learner's experiences and interests (Brandt, 2001; Tomlinson, 2000). Some teachers use the results of formal and informal assessments to target individual learner needs and to shape instruction (Brimijoin, Marquissae, & Tomlinson, 2003).

You might think that such a discussion should occur under the heading of Individualized Instruction, and well it could. Good and expert teachers have been providing individualized, differentiated instruction in their self-contained classrooms throughout the year and manage it based on *how* they organize for instruction and *how* their students learn. However, when a school or district embraces the concept of differentiated learning, a change occurs in the way *many* teachers approach instruction and the way they provide and manage instruction to accommodate a variety of diverse learners (Pettig, 2000).

Schools and districts provide for teacher in-service and training in ways that help teachers to individualize, encourage peer collaboration, consider ways to detrack, and practice inclusion (Schneider, 2000). When one school district wished to promote equality and reduce discipline problems, it turned to differentiated instruction as the solution to eliminating three tracks of students. The district found that more training was necessary for teachers to learn about differentiation and to develop learning contacts with individual students. They also found that parents, especially those of students at the upper end of ability, wanted the differentiated instructional program to end and a return to the three-tiered tracking system (Brandt, 2001; Fahey, 2000).

The overriding concern in this discussion of how schools organize to provide instruction reveals the ways and means schools accommodate learners at all levels of ability and to provide for their individual differences. This concern is most evident in such patterns as multi-age teaming, block scheduling, and the various combination of ways to accommodate special-needs learners, such as through their own special self-contained classes, pull-out programs, support teachers providing push-in or inclusion services, or differentiated instruction occurring in regular, self-contained classes. Because meeting the individual needs of diverse learners is a major focus of democratic, public schooling, the discussion of patterns of organization continues in the next chapter with ways in which the individual classroom teacher can organize to meet the needs of all students.

## ■ SUMMARY ■

1. To meet the needs of all students and especially those who fall at the high and low ends of academic achievement, schools use different organizational patterns and time arrangements to provide the most opportune learning environments.

2. The four major factors that influence how schools and districts organize for instruction include the educational plan itself, time allotments and the management of time, planning for individual differences, and organizing students in different classroom grouping patterns.

3. Utilization of time during the school day focuses on students' daily schedules or number of periods and the effectiveness of learning time within those periods. Because research has shown that engaged time yields success with literacy, teachers need to be effective in using time during the school day.

4. The design of the classroom and the classroom seating arrangements used have an impact on learning. There are formal and informal seating patterns in traditional classroom settings. The open classroom design allows desks, activity and study tables, work areas, and literacy and

computer centers to be used for individual and small-group work.

5. Departmentalized instruction occurs when students receive instruction in different content domains by teachers who are competent to teach that content.

6. Team teaching or co-teaching occurs with a co-operative effort of two or more teachers who pool their resources and content expertise as they share or team their students.

7. The multi-age teaming or organizational pattern tries to group children at different age or grade levels into cohesive units, with most patterns occurring across bordering grade levels such as a unit of children from first to third grade, from fourth to fifth or sixth grade, and from sixth to eighth grade.

8. The Education of the Handicapped Act, known as Public Law 94-142, and the Individuals with Disabilities Education Act, known as IDEA or Public Law 105-17, are two landmark acts that hold schools accountable for providing disabled, handicapped, and special education students with educational services equal to those of mainstream, regular education students.

9. Besides pulling out special-needs learners to educate them in separate special education settings, three other approaches are currently used to accommodate learners with special needs in whole-class settings. One is to provide push-in services, another is to include these learners in regular school programs with their same-age peers, and the third is to accommodate them with differentiated instruction in the mainstream setting.

## ■ QUESTIONS TO CONSIDER ■

1. Why would the teacher's teaching style influence particular classroom patterns of organization and how time is used?

2. What is meant by "authentic" and "engaged" learning environments and how do these affect the teacher's organizational patterns?

3. How can teachers use the morning's arrival, "warm up" time and the afternoon's dismissal time to provide purposeful, engaged literacy activities?

4. Why would classroom design, the physical arrangement of the classroom itself, and the seating arrangements therein have an impact on student learning?

5. What are the advantages and disadvantages of both homogeneous and heterogeneous grouping patterns?

6. How do middle school and junior high school students and teachers benefit from departmen-

talized instruction? What are some disadvantages of this schoolwide organizational structure?

7. How would team teaching work favorably for two or three teachers at a grade level? Once the teachers have worked out a plan of who teaches which subjects, do the children benefit from this teaching pattern?

8. Would both older and younger students benefit from a multi-age classroom environment? Explain what might be beneficial and if any features of multi-age teaming are not beneficial to students or teachers?

9. Why might some teachers, students, and parents favor a block scheduling arrangement for particular units of instruction?

10. Can you discuss the pros and cons of accommodating special-needs learners through pull-out special services, push-in services, inclusion, and differentiated instruction?

## ■ THINGS TO DO ■

1. Establish class routines during the first ten or fifteen minutes of students' arrival time in the morning and during the last ten to fifteen min-

utes of the school day prior to dismissal. During these times, students can be engaged in reading for pleasure or information acquisition, journal writing, preparing e-mail responses, and other purposeful literacy and learning activities.

2. Review the various types of seating arrangements with your class and determine which types of organizational pattern—such as traditional rows, circular, or horseshoe—they prefer for whole-class management and instruction.

3. Have students bring in tools and artifacts associated with schooling and learning such as books, rulers, scissors, tape, science equipment, computer disks, and so forth, and form the students into groups. With all of the separate artifacts displayed on the floor, ask each group to design the classroom arrangement in which students could best use the tools and artifacts to learn. Have them draw their classroom space on large chart paper and present to the whole class.

4. Ask your students to brainstorm some of their favorite topics or themes. Write four or five of these favorite topics on the chalkboard. Then place on the chalkboard the terms used for different schoolwide organizational patterns, such as the self-contained classroom, departmentalized instruction, team teaching, the multi-age classroom, and block scheduling. Form your students into groups by preferred grade level and ask them how they would teach one favorite topic by the various organizational arrangements.

5. Discuss the various categories and labels that are used for students with special needs. Turn the discussion to the various organizational plans for providing instruction and accommodating students with special needs. List the advantages and disadvantages of pull-out programs for special-needs or special education students; of push-in approaches to serve them in mainstream classes with specialists; of inclusion, where they are placed in groups with their school-age peers; and of differentiated instruction, in which individualized attention is provided in a self-contained classroom.

## ■ RECOMMENDED READINGS ■

Carnine, Douglas, Jerry Silbert, and Edward Kameenui. *Direct Instruction Reading,* 3rd ed. Upper Saddle River, NJ: Prentice Hall, 1997. The authors suggest ways to use structured approaches in reading, especially for those students who need direct instruction to learn in the most effective way.

Churton, Michael, Ann Cranston-Gingras, and Timothy Blair. *Teaching Children with Diverse Abilities.* Boston: Allyn and Bacon, 1998. Presents various approaches and organizational patterns for teaching students with special needs and diverse levels of achievement and abilities.

Evanston, Carolyn, Murray Worsham, and Edmund T. Emmer. *Classroom Management for Elementary Teachers,* 4th ed. Boston: Allyn and Bacon, 1996. Presents management procedures for teachers in the elementary grades and discusses classroom seating arrangements for different kinds of teaching styles.

Oakes, Jeannie A. *Multiplying Inequalities.* Santa Monica, CA: Rand Corporation, 1991. Shows the effects of tracking with regard to race and social class on opportunities to learn.

Sleeter, Christine, and Carl Grant. *Making Choices for Multicultural Education: Five Approaches to Race, Class, and Gender,* 3rd ed. New York: John Wiley and Sons, 1999. Discusses suggestions and strategies useful for teaching a wide range of students.

Turnbull, Rud, Ann Turnbull, Marilyn Shank, Sean Smith, and Dorothy Leal. *Exceptional Lives: Special Education in Today's Schools,* 3rd ed. Upper Saddle River, NJ: Merrill/Prentice Hall, 2002. A comprehensive discussion of the evolution of the public laws that govern the special education field and the accommodations made for special-needs students with different organizational patterns of instruction.

Wheelan, Susan. *Group Processes: A Developmental Perspective.* Boston: Allyn and Bacon, 1994. Various approaches to grouping for instruction are presented along with the advantages and disadvantages of each approach.

# ■ KEY TERMS ■

alternating day schedule
block scheduling
collaboration
departmentalization
detracking
differentiated instruction
diversity
engaged time

formal seating pattern
heterogeneous grouping
homogeneous grouping
inclusion
individual differences
informal seating pattern
least restrictive environment
multi-age classroom

open classroom
parallel block schedule
scheduled time
self-contained classroom
special-needs learners
team teaching
time on task
tracking

# ■ REFERENCES ■

Adams, R. S., & Biddle, B. J. (1970). *Realities of teaching.* New York: Holt, Rinehart and Winston.

Adler, M., & Fisher, C. (2001, March). Early reading programs in high-poverty schools: A case study of beating the odds. *The Reading Teacher,* 616–619.

Armstrong, T. (2001, November). Ikswal: Interesting kids saddled with alienating labels. *Educational Leadership,* 38–41.

Axelrod, S., Hall, R. V., & Tamms, A. (1979, September). Comparison of two common classroom seating arrangements. *Academic Therapy,* 29–36.

Bell, L. (2002–2003, December/January). Strategies that close the gap. *Educational Leadership,* 32–34.

Braddock, J. H., & McPartland, J. M. (1990, April). Alternatives to tracking. *Educational Leadership,* 76–79.

Brandt, R. (2001, October). No best way: The case for differentiated schooling. *Phi Delta Kappan,* 53–156.

Brimijoin, K., Marquissae, E., & Tomlinson, C. A. (2003, February). Using data to differentiate instruction. *Educational Leadership,* 70–73.

Burns, P., Roe, B., & Ross, E. (1999). *Teaching reading in today's elementary schools* (7th ed.). New York: Houghton Mifflin.

Caproni, V. (1977, December). Seating position, instructor's eye contact availability, and student participation. *Journal of Social Psychology,* 315–316.

Carnine, D., Silbert, J., & Kameenui, E. (1997). *Direct instruction reading* (3rd ed.). Upper Saddle River, NJ: Prentice Hall.

Carroll, J. M. (1994). *The Copernican plan evaluated: The evolution of a revolution.* Topsfield, MA: Copernican Associates, Ltd.

Churton, M., Cranston-Gingras, A., & Blair, T. (1998). *Teaching children with diverse abilities.* Boston: Allyn and Bacon.

Cole, J. (2002–2003, December/January). What motivates students to read? Four literacy personalities. *The Reading Teacher,* 326–336.

Corbett, D., & Wilson, B. (2002, September). What urban students say about good teaching. *Educational Leadership,* 18–22.

Danielson, C. (2002). *Enhancing student achievement: A framework for school improvement.* Alexandria, VA: Association for Supervision and Curriculum Development.

Delany, M., Toburen, L., Hooton, B., & Dozier, A. (1997–1998, December/January). Parallel block scheduling spells success. *Educational Leadership,* 61–63.

DiRocco, M. (1998–1999, December/January). How an alternating day schedule empowers teachers. *Educational Leadership,* 82–84.

Dunn, L. M. (1968, September). Special education for the mildly retarded: Is much of it justifiable? *Exceptional Children,* 5–22.

Edmiaston, R., & Fitzgerald, L. M. (2000, September). How reggio familia encourages inclusion. *Educational Leadership,* 66–69.

Elliott, I. (1997, February). Multi-age classroom: Families and flexibility. *Teaching PreK–8,* 45–48.

Evans, W., Tokarczyk, J., Rice, S., & McCray, A. (2002, July/August). Block scheduling. *The Clearing House,* 319–323.

Evertson, C. M., Worsham, M., & Emmer, E. (1996). *Classroom management for elementary teachers* (4th ed.). Boston: Allyn and Bacon.

Fahey, J. (2000, September). Who wants to differentiate instruction? We did . . . *Educational Leadership,* 70–72.

Fuchs, D., & Fuchs, L. (1994, February). Inclusive schools movement and the radicalization of special education reform. *Exceptional Children,* 294–309.

Gallas, K., & Smagorinsky, P. (2002, September). Approaching texts in school. *The Reading Teacher,* 54–61.

Gamoran, A. (1992a, October). Is ability grouping equitable? *Educational Leadership,* 11–17.

Gamoran, A. (1992b). *The variable effects of high school tracking.* Madison, WI: Center on Organization and Restructuring of Schools, University of Wisconsin–Madison.

Good, T. E. (1987, July/August). Two decades of research on teacher expectations. *Journal of Teacher Education,* 32–47.

Goodlad, J. T. (1984). *A place called school: Promise for the future.* New York: McGraw-Hill.

Halbach, A., Ehrle, K., Zahorik, J., & Molnar, A. (2001, March). Class size reduction: From promise to practice. *Educational Leadership,* 32–35.

Hastings, C. (1992, October). Ending ability grouping is a moral imperative. *Educational Leadership,* 14–18.

Hebert, E. (1998, September). Design matters: How school environment affects children. *Educational Leadership,* 69–70.

Hirsch, E. D., Jr. (2001, Summer). Overcoming the language gap: Make better use of the literacy time block. *American Educator,* 4, 6–7.

Holloway, J. (2001, March). Inclusion and students with learning disabilities. *Educational Leadership,* 86–88.

Hopping, L. (2000, December). Multi-age teaming: A real life approach to the middle school. *Phi Delta Kappan,* 270–272, 292.

Johnson, C., & Taylor, R. (2001, March). Excellence for all in Minneapolis. *Educational Leadership,* 55–59.

Kameenui, E., & Carnine, D. (1998). *Effective teaching strategies that accommodate diverse learners.* Upper Saddle River, NJ: Prentice Hall.

Kirk, S. A., Gallagher, J. J., & Anastasiow, N. J. (2003). *Educating exceptional children* (10th ed.). Boston: Houghton Mifflin.

Lerner, J. (2000). *Learning disabilities.* Boston: Houghton Mifflin.

Leland, C., & Fitzpatrick, R. (1993–1994, December/January). Cross-age interaction builds enthusiasm for reading and writing. *The Reading Teacher,* 282–301.

Leu, D., Jr., & Kinzer, C. (1999). *Effective literary instruction, K–8* (4th ed.). Upper Saddle River, NJ: Prentice Hall.

Marzano, R. J. (2003). *What works in schools: Translating research into action.* Alexandria, VA: Association for Supervision and Curriculum Development.

Mason, D. A., Schroeter, D. D., Combs, R. K., & Washington, K. (1992, May). Assigning average-achieving eighth graders to advanced mathematics classes in an urban junior high. *Elementary School Journal,* 587–599.

McCormick, S. (2003). *Instructing students who have literacy problems* (4th ed.). Upper Saddle River, NJ: Merrill/Prentice Hall.

Merenbloom, E. Y. (1996, March). Team teaching: Addressing the learning needs of middle level students. *NASSP Bulletin,* 45–53.

Merritt, S. (2001, November). Clearing the hurdles of inclusion. *Educational Leadership,* 67–70.

Nieto, S. (2002–2003, December/January). Profoundly multicultural questions. *Educational Leadership,* 6–10.

Oakes, J. (1985). *Keeping track: How schools structure inequality.* New Haven, CT: Yale University Press.

Oakes, J., & Lipton, M. (1992, February). Detracking schools: Early lessons from the field. *Phi Delta Kappan,* 448–454.

Office of Special Education and Rehabilitative Services. (2001). *Annual report to Congress in the implementation of the Individuals with Disabilities Education Act.* Washington, DC: U.S. Dept. of Education.

Pettig, K. (2000, September). On the road to differentiated practice. *Educational Leadership,* 14–18.

Pugach, M. (1995, Summer). On the failure of imagination in inclusive schooling. *Journal of Special Education,* 219–229.

Rasinski, T., & Padak, N. (2000). *Effective reading strategies: Teaching children who find reading difficult.* Upper Saddle River, NJ: Prentice Hall.

Rosenbaum, J. (1999–2000, Winter). If tracking is bad, is detracking better? *American Educator,* 24–29, 47.

Rosenshine, B., & Berliner, D. (1978, January). Academic engaged time. *British Journal of Teacher Education,* 3–16.

Ruder, S. (2000, September). We teach all. *Educational Leadership,* 49–51.

Sailor, W. (1991, November/December). Special education in the restructured school. *Remedial and Special Education,* 8–22.

Schneider, E. (2000, September). Shifting into high gear. *Educational Leadership,* 57–60.

Scott, J., & Butler, C. (1994). Grouping, tracking and streaming for instruction. In A. C. Purves (Ed.), *Encyclopedia of English studies and language arts* (pp. 549–552). New York: Scholastic/ Urbana, IL: National Council of Teachers of English.

Scott, R. (1993, October). Untracking advocates make incredible claims. *Educational Leadership,* 79–81.

Shortt, T., & Thayer, Y. (1998–1999, December/January). Block scheduling can enhance school climate. *Educational Leadership,* 76–81.

Slavin, R. (1990, Winter). Achievement effects of ability grouping in secondary schools: A best evidence synthesis. *Review of Educational Research,* 471–499.

Slavin, R. E. (1987, Spring). Grouping for instruction in the elementary school. *Educational Psychologist,* 109–127.

Sleeter, C. E., & Grant, C. A. (1999). *Making choices for multicultural education: Five approaches to race, class, and gender* (3rd ed.). New York: John Wiley and Sons.

Stringfield, S., Ross, S. M., & Smith, L. (1996). *Bold plans for school restructuring: The new American schools design.* Baltimore, MD: Center for Research on the Education of Students Placed At Risk.

Taberski, S. (2000, September). A space that works. *Instructor,* 40–41.

Taylor, B., Pearson, P. D., Clark, K., & Walpole, S. (2000, November). Effective schools and accomplished teachers: Lessons about primary grade reading instruction in low-income schools. *Elementary School Journal,* 121–166.

Tomlinson, C. A. (2000, September). Recognizable differences? Standards-based tracking and differentiation. *Educational Leadership,* 6–11.

Turnbull, R., Turnbull, A., Shank, M., Smith, S., & Leal, D. (2002). *Exceptional lives: Special education in today's schools* (3rd ed.). Upper Saddle River, NJ: Merrill.

Wall, B. (1994, August/September). Managing your multi-age classroom. *Teaching PreK–8,* 68–73.

Welch, M. (2000, November/December). Descriptive analysis of team teaching in two elementary classrooms: A formative experimental approach. *Remedial and Special Education,* 366–376.

Welch, M., Brownell, K., & Sheridan, S. (1999, January/February). What's the score and game plan on teaming in school? A review of the literature on team teaching and school-based problem-solving teams. *Remedial and Special Education,* 36–49.

Welch, M., Richards, G., Okada, T., Richards, J., & Prescott, S. (1995, January). A consultation and paraprofessional pull-in system of service delivery. *Remedial and Special Education,* 16–28.

Wheelock, A. (1992, October). The case for untracking. *Educational Leadership,* 14–18.

Wolk, S. (2001, October). The benefits of exploratory time. *Educational Leadership,* 56–59.

## chapter 9

# Classroom Patterns of Instruction

1. When is it appropriate to use whole-group, small-group, and individual instruction?
2. What are the advantages and disadvantages of large-group instruction?
3. On what basis can students be organized into small groups?
4. What procedures should teachers follow in organizing small groups for instruction?
5. What methods or procedures can be used to provide individualized instruction?
6. What methods are recommended for using adaptive instruction? Mastery instruction?
7. Why would one's approach to instruction influence how one would organize students to receive instruction under that approach?

How does the teacher organize the classroom to obtain optimal environments for learning? Should the teacher use different types of organizational plans and seating arrangements for different subject areas and for different kinds of activities and learning experiences that students encounter? How does the teacher account for individual interests and differences in the classroom organizational plan? Particularly in regard to the different skills and ability levels that students bring to reading, writing, and arithmetic tasks, teachers are faced with the challenge of providing for individual differences while establishing a sense of community within the four walls of their classrooms. These questions and others confront the teacher as he or she considers how to organize the classroom as students engage in the learning of diverse subject matter through different activities and learning encounters every day.

Classrooms can be organized or grouped for instruction in three basic ways: (1) *whole-group instruction,* sometimes called large-group instruction, in which the entire class is taught as a group, (2) *small-group instruction,* in which the large group is broken up into subgroups according to ability, interest, project, or other criterion, and (3) *individualized instruction,* in which the individual student works alone or with another person on a specific task or assignment. Different groupings often require different physical settings so that seating and room arrangements change to accommodate different patterns of instruction (see Figure 8.3).

# ■ WHOLE-GROUP INSTRUCTION

**Whole-group instruction** is the most traditional and common form of classroom organization. Teachers generally gear their teaching to the "mythical" average student on the assumption that this level of presentation will meet the needs of the greatest number of students. A common block of content (in any subject) is taught on the assumption that large-group instruction is the most effective and convenient format for teaching it (Good, McCaslin, & Reys, 1992; Johnson & Johnson, 1999).

### Effectiveness of Whole-Group Instruction

In the large group, the teacher explains and discusses, demonstrates a topic, asks and answers questions in front of the entire class, provides the same practice and drill exercises to the entire class, has students work on the same problems, and employs the same materials. Instruction is directed toward the whole group, but the teacher may ask specific students to answer questions, monitor specific students as they carry out the assigned activities, and work with students on an individual basis.

Whole groups can be an economical and efficient way of teaching. The method is especially convenient for teaching the same skills or subject to the entire class, giving assignments, administering tests, setting group expectations, and making announcements. Bringing members of a class together for certain activities strengthens the feeling of belonging to a large group and can help establish a sense of community and class spirit. The whole group learns to cooperate by working with and sharing available resources, setting up rules and regulations for the learning environment, and exchanging ideas. Finally, this method of grouping students is most effective for managing large numbers of students and for providing direct or explicit instruction. Because teachers face limited amounts of time to teach many reading skills to groups of children with diverse learning abilities, a direct instruction approach is felt to be the most effective (Carnine, Silbert, & Kameenui, 1997). In one study involving twenty-nine third-grade teachers, researchers noted through observations and interviews that teachers used whole-class instruction and the same materials for all students, including those with learning disabilities, during reading instruction. Teachers believed that whole-class instruction conformed to school expectations, in that only one text, a basal or literature-based anthology, was available per class, and they felt that whole-class instruction made planning and classroom management easier (Schumm, Moody, & Vaughn, 2000). Tips for Teachers 9.1 provides some guidelines for implementing direct instruction, and Figure 8.2 shows traditional and less traditional seating patterns for whole-group instruction.

When working with whole groups, teachers usually present new information to the total group while splitting students off into smaller groups for review and practice or enrichment activities. The data are unclear about how small groups should be designed and managed or what the optimal number of groups is. However, too many small groups can create off-task management problems. Interestingly, one study conducted with third graders during mathematics and science lessons revealed that children were more off task during teacher-directed instruction than during small-group and individualized seatwork. The researchers noted that during whole-class, teacher-directed instruction, students were less likely to follow instructions, check their work, and ask for assistance. Although children were observed to be more disorganized

*Tips for Teachers* **9.1**

## Guidelines for Implementing Direct Instruction

Evidence suggests that when teaching low-achieving and at-risk students, teachers find a highly structured approach to be the most effective method. Today this approach is often called "direct" instruction or "explicit" instruction. The major aspects of direct instruction are listed below. (Note, however, that this approach may not be suitable for high-achieving or independent learners who prefer a low-structured and flexible situation so they can use their initiative.)

1. Begin a lesson with a short statement of goals.
2. Begin with a short review of previous, prerequisite learning.
3. Present new material in small steps, with student practice after each step.
4. Give clear and detailed instructions and explanations.
5. Provide a high level of active practice for all students.
6. Guide students during initial practice.
7. Ask many questions, check for student understanding, and obtain responses from all students.
8. Provide systematic feedback and corrections.
9. Obtain a student success rate of 80 percent or higher during initial practice.
10. Provide explicit instruction for seatwork exercises, and, where possible, monitor and help students during seatwork.
11. Provide for spaced review and testing.

*Source:* Adapted from Barak Rosenshine, "Explicit Teaching and Teacher Training," *Journal of Teacher Education* (May–June 1987), p. 34.

during seatwork and small-group instruction, they were more likely to monitor and self-regulate their work and converse about their thinking during these two organizational patterns (Stright & Supplee, 2002).

The critics of whole-group instruction contend that it fails to meet the needs and interests of individual students. Teachers who use this method tend to look on students as a homogeneous group with common abilities, interests, styles of learning, and motivation. Instruction is geared to a hypothetical average student—a concept that fits only a few students in the class—and all students are expected to learn and perform within narrow limits. Students are evaluated, instructional methods and materials are selected, and learning is paced on the basis of the group average (Cuban, 1993; Johnson, 1993; & Posner, 1994). High-achieving students eventually become bored, and low-achieving students eventually become frustrated. The uniqueness of each student is often lost in the large group. Extroverted students tend to monopolize the teacher's time, and passive students usually are not heard from or do not receive necessary attention. Finally, students sometimes act out their behavioral problems in the safety of numbers.

Although a good teacher can compensate for these problems, it is best not to use the whole group as the only grouping pattern for instruction. Different grouping patterns are essential for variety, motivation, and flexibility in teaching and learning.

## Class Size and Achievement

Does class size affect whole-group learning? When it comes to improving student performance, common sense would predict a clear relationship. Surprisingly, smaller class size does not automatically lead to better student performance. In one early review of 152 studies that analyzed smaller classes and student achievement, 82 percent found no significant impact, 9.2 percent reported positive results, and 8.6 percent found negative results (Hanushek, 1989). In a later report, one author noted that according to U.S. Department of Education data, in 1970 there were 22.3 students per teacher, while in 2001 the estimated ratio was 15.1 students per teacher. Yet during the same time interval, the reading and math scores of U.S. students as indicated by the National Assessment of Educational Progress (NAEP) has remained about the same and in decline in some cases (Dianis, 2000).

In yet another review, this of eight studies of low-achieving students, Robert Slavin found that differences in achievement levels of students in larger classes (twenty-two to thirty-seven students) compared to those in small classes (fifteen to twenty students) were insignificant. Across the eight studies, the effect was only +.13—a low figure given that the average class size in the large groups was twenty-seven students compared to sixteen in the small groups (a 40 percent difference) (Slavin, 1989). In another review, Madden and Slavin found that only when class size is reduced to a one-to-one teacher–student ratio, as in tutoring, does size make a difference (Madden & Slavin, 1989; Slavin, 1991).

Although Glass and his colleagues received considerable attention when they concluded that class size below fifteen students had a positive effect on student achievement, the actual impact was only significant in ten out of seventy-seven studies. Learning benefits did not really appear until class size was reduced to three students. The effects of class size and achievement were more positive in elementary grades than in middle

**BOX 9.1** Minority and Inner-City Students May Benefit Most from Small Class Size

Small class size (thirteen to seventeen students) seems to increase academic and literacy success for minority and inner-city youth. Why might this be so? With smaller classes, teacher and students can interact more readily and teachers can be more supportive of students' learning needs. Size alone allows the teacher to work more on an individualized basis and nurture the self-concepts of diverse and special-needs learners.

grades and high school (Glass & Smith, 1978; Glass, 1982).

In the largest single study ever performed in Tennessee, kindergarten students were randomly assigned to classes of fifteen and twenty-five with an aide and twenty-five without an aide. These configurations were retained through grade 3. The study attributed almost zero impact to the presence of aides and only moderate positive effects to the smaller classes when students reached third grade. By the time the students were entering fourth grade, the difference was positive but insignificant (Nye, 1991; Nye, 1992: see also Pool, 2002). However, in a longitudinal review of the data from Tennessee's Project STAR (Student/Teacher Achievement Ratio), it was found that the age of the students mattered. Children who were in small classes (thirteen to seventeen students) during their K–3 years outperformed their peers in all academic tests some twelve years later. Furthermore, inner-city youth and minority students performed two to three times better than Caucasian students when both were taught in small class settings (Elley, 2001). Statewide studies in Indiana and South Carolina at the primary level, however, showed very modest achievement effects when class sizes were reduced (Mueller, Chase, & Walden, 1988; Slavin, Karweit, & Wasik, 1993). See Box 9.1. But when the effects of small class size were reviewed for a number of state initiatives, the results were shown to be impressive for the early grades (Biddle & Berliner, 2002). These beliefs are reported in Box 9.2.

One author team contends that the whole-group or whole-class organizational pattern is an effective way to provide a safety net for emerging or at-risk readers because

**BOX 9.2** What Do Small Classes Provide?

According to two authors who reviewed the effects of small class size in the states of California, Indiana, Tennessee, and Wisconsin, small class size provided the following:

- With careful planning, small classes in the early grades resulted in substantial academic gains, and the gains replicated themselves the longer children remained in the smaller classes.
- Gains appeared to be greatest in the early grades when there were less than twenty students in the class.
- Gains were retained by students who were housed in small classes when they reached larger classes in the middle school and high school.
- Gains appeared to be greatest for those who had been considered disadvantaged in educational settings and practices.
- Gains made in the early grades due to smaller class size seemed to be equal for males and females.

*Source:* Adapted from Bruce Biddle and David Berliner, "Small Class Size and Its Effects," *Educational Leadership* (February 2002), pp. 12–23.

learning to read is a social event and children interact positively when they share their reading experiences. Through such activities as storytelling, story dramatization, sharing of self-written stories, reading and singing aloud of songs, reading of Big Books, and doing silent reading and writing together, at-risk students are socially and linguistically involved with their more competent classmates. Moreover, such whole-class literacy activities negate some of the potentially harsh effects often associated with ability grouping or other labeling of at-risk children, such as "slow learners," "learning disabled," and "resource room students" (Reutzel & Cooter, 1996).

### A Whole-Part-Whole Instructional Framework

A "whole-part-whole" instructional framework or pattern is a way to achieve a balance in literacy instruction, particularly with regard to the weight given to phonics skills instruction and to a whole language or holistic orientation (Fowler, 1998; Strickland, 1998). Recall that literacy has a number of processing and representation modes; the whole-part-whole framework allows the teacher to capitalize on students' active involvement in these modes while providing for various classroom grouping patterns. In the initial "whole," the entire class is together in one group, and they generally participate in a whole reading, listening, discussing, and/or viewing event. During the "part," either individually or in groups, students participate in some directed skill work that has emerged from or is grounded in the context of the whole. With the second "whole," students practice the skill they learned by using another literacy mode such as writing, artwork, or computer representation and share their work with the whole group.

While **whole-part-whole instruction** provides a balanced conceptual framework for planning skills instruction, it addresses learners' needs because it (1) provides for meaningful understanding of whole texts such as literature, basalized stories, information books, poems, and experience stories; (2) allows for in-depth work on language parts through specific skill work; and (3) includes planned practice of the parts of language in meaningful contexts, usually through additional reading and writing activities (Strickland, 1998). One early literacy program consisted of a two-hour literacy teaching block that moved from (a) a teacher-directed, whole-class focus, to (b) small-group, explicit teaching with a few students while the remainder of the class was engaged in independent writing and other self-regulated activities in learning centers, back to (c) whole-class interaction in which students articulated what they had learned and the teacher encouraged the development of the children's oral language skills (Slavin, 1978; Webb, 1985).

Whole-part-whole instruction sets the stage for both effective small-group and individualized instruction. It is a framework that underlies many of the small-group patterns addressed in the next section.

## ■ SMALL-GROUP INSTRUCTION

Dividing students into small groups seems to provide an opportunity for students to become more actively engaged in learning and for teachers to better monitor student progress. Teachers generally group students in order to shift their whole-class grouping arrangement into more manageable and smaller units that make it easier to reach the ultimate goal of individualized, differentiated instruction for all levels of learners. Groups can be between three students to half or an even larger portion of all the students in a given classroom. However, between five and eight students seems to be an optimal number to ensure successful small-group activity. Research indicates that when a group consists of fewer than five students, especially for a discussion, students tend to pair off rather than interact as a group.

## Purposes for Grouping

**Small-group instruction** works best in rooms with movable furniture or no desks at all, but it can also be used in classrooms with fixed furniture (Taberski, 2001). Small groupings can enhance student cooperation and social skills. Appropriate group experiences foster the development of democratic values, cultural pluralism, and appreciation of differences among people. Small-group instruction can provide interesting challenges, permit students to progress at their own pace, provide a psychologically safe situation in which to master the material, and encourage students to contribute to class activities. Learning in groups is also based on the premise that students can learn from one another as well as from the teacher and on their own (Burns, Roe, & Ross, 1999). In the classroom, group processes come together in two ways: (1) in normal interactions of teaching and learning as students and teachers work together and (2) when students learn the dynamics of working together in groups to solve problems or make decisions.

Small groups are typically used in elementary school reading and mathematics. The teacher divides the class into two or three groups, depending on the number of students, their perceived range of abilities, results on informal assessments and standardized tests, and the number of groups the teacher is able to handle (Schumm et al., 2000). The teacher usually works with one group at a time while the other students do seatwork or independent work. The latter may be accomplished at specific centers or stations.

The use of small groups can be extended beyond the typical grouping in elementary reading and mathematics to all grade levels and subjects. There are several other reasons to form small groups, including (1) membership based on *special interests* or *skills* in a particular topic or activity; (2) *ability grouping* or regrouping within a class for specific subjects (reading or mathematics) or specific content (different assignments or exercises), thus reducing the problems of heterogeneity in the classroom; and (3) *integration,* forming groups to enhance racial, ethnic, religious, or gender relations.

## Ability Grouping

Grouping children homogeneously on the basis of ability or achievement, usually from results on standardized or districtwide tests or from general academic or reading competence, is called **ability** or achievement **grouping.** Grouping children according to the level of the reading material they can read with comfort and understanding remains a highly popular practice today.

This practice is heightened by the use of published graded reading series, often called basal readers. Use of such graded books, with accompanying teacher's manuals, skill books, and activity pages, helps classroom teachers form groups based on students' reading competency levels. While the teacher works with one group with a graded book aimed at their level, the remaining students practice skills in their workbooks and activity pages. Because the basal reading series offers a scope and sequence of graded materials in detailed skill development, forming ability-level groups based on reading achievement is common among teachers who favor a specific skill approach to teaching (Leu & Kinzer, 1999). Such grouping means that teachers conform to the levels of instruction rather than modifying the instruction to conform to the needs and interests of the students (Reutzel & Cooter, 1996).

The use of within-class ability groups has both advocates and critics. Some research has shown that students in heterogeneous classes who are regrouped homogeneously based on ability level learn more than students in classes in which such grouping is not used (Oakes, 1992; Scott & Butler, 1994). This appears to be especially the case for reading and mathematics instruction and for students placed in low-achieving groups (Gamoran, 1992; Mason & Good, 1993).

The research data also suggest that a small number of within-class groups (two or three) is better than a large number, permitting more monitoring by and feedback from the teacher and less seatwork and transition time (Heibert, 1983). For example, in a class of three ability groups, students spend approximately two-thirds of the time doing seatwork without direct supervision; but with four groups, they spend three-quarters of the class time doing seatwork without teacher monitoring of their work.

It is generally argued that the formation of within-class ability groups supports the concepts of individualization and meeting the needs of diverse learners. The teacher can teach to the mean or perceived middle level of each group and have students proceed at different paces on different levels of materials. For children in the lowest level group(s), a slower pace helps the teacher provide more individual assistance while assigning more practice, drill, and review to help students master material, particularly new reading and vocabulary words and specific skills or techniques that will assist further reading and writing.

Critics of ability, achievement, and basal reader grouping raise concerns about inequity and social and self-esteem issues (Oakes, 1992; Reutzel & Cooter, 1996; Scott & Butler, 1994). Although such within-class grouping can help to reduce individual differences, it cannot remove them altogether. Children seem to be aware of each group's level even as teachers try to conceal the group's ability-level identity (Burns et al., 1999). Some educators indicate that with low-ability grouped students, teachers use weaker teaching techniques (Brown, Palincsar, & Armbruster, 1994; Wiggins, 1994), and such students usually do not acquire grade-level reading and writing skills (Hall, Prevatte, & Cunningham, 1995). Moreover, those who remain in the low group over the years often form poor self-concepts (Burns et al., 1999).

Two authors have synthesized a body of evidence about the academic task characteristics and social participation of within-class high and low reading groups of elementary school students. When a common three-reading-group system is used, it appears that the low-achieving students fare the worst because they are working with minimum supervision two-thirds of the time. Less capable students do not work well without teacher direction and have difficulty receiving help from their matched colleagues. Overall, students in the lower-achieving groups seem to interact less with the teacher, are not strongly involved in class activities, are asked to read fewer words and engage in more subskills work with their reading selections, are asked more low-level questions, and are interrupted more during their lessons and activities, prompting them to be less engaged and on task (Scott & Butler, 1994).

## Special Interest Groups

One alternative to group formation based on test scores or school achievement is to form **special interest groups.** Such groups are formed based on the personal interests, needs, and friendship patterns of students, thereby shifting the group composition rationale from a teacher-directed to a child-centered purpose. Such a grouping pattern is also much more flexible than the fixed-ability-level or basal reading group pattern, and consequently the teacher can encourage changes in group makeup as learning activities and assignments change.

For instance, teachers might involve students in genre or author studies, in book club or "fishbowl" discussions, or in author circles and have different students in different groups for different purposes. In the genre study, students would read works of the same literary style or type such as realistic fiction, historical fiction, folklore, and so forth and in an author study, students would read different works produced by the same children's author. As the teacher reads off titles and gives a short synopsis of the different books in the collection, the students choose the book they wish to pursue and, by so doing, form an interest group. In this case, reading level is not a major issue because children choose books of personal interest. With a book club discussion, all students who read the same book participate in a thoughtful discussion, whereas in the "fishbowl," one group of students presents a discussion of their book while others watch and listen (Kong & Fitch, 2002–2003). Author circles are formed when small groups of student writers meet to present and discuss their in-process drafts to determine if they are effective in presenting meaning (Villaume & Brabham, 2001). Many veteran teachers also tell us that when students are motivated and interested in pursuing a topic, as in the previous groupings, they can profit from reading materials beyond their usual instructional levels.

Another way in which interest groups form is when topic and thematic units are explored. Recall the curriculum design plan of an integrated or multisubject thematic unit presented in Chapter 5 (see Figures 5.2 and 5.3). The crux of the unit instructional approach is the formation of specific interest groups that explore concepts and topics related to the controlling idea of the theme. These small groups are made up of students of different ability levels. They work together to investigate an issue, a concept, or a body of research about a topic or theme and usually present their combined work to the larger group.

The teacher's role is to make the classroom environment conducive to fluid and flexible grouping patterns (such as that suggested in Figure 8.3), to make resources accessible and bulletin board or display areas available, and to guide each group in taking ownership of their project activity. The classroom teacher may work with the school or community librarian so that resources are readily available. If the teacher has interviewed students beforehand to determine their interests, he or she could ask the librarian to have collections of resources put aside for the interest groups to review and/or use. Teachers can also provide encyclopedias, computer programs and Internet resources, trade books, and arts and crafts materials.

Once the groups' interests and plans are known, some teachers turn to World Wide Web (WWW) locations to find potential web sites that might provide useful information to some of the groups. The teacher makes a list of those web sites that are appropriate and safe for students to use. Then, to guide students through the electronic literacy process, the teacher can take groups of students through the pathway links to reach the same Internet sites of potential interest. One such site that is an excellent source of children's literature, providing information about books, authors' discussions about their books, and links to other sites, is The Children's Literature Web Guide (www.acs.ucalgary.ca/~dkbrown/index.html) (Leu & Kinzer, 1999).

Finally, teachers support the use of interest groups in order to integrate diverse students into mainstream class activities in the spirit of inclusion. For any number of reasons—a child new to the classroom, students of varying ethnic or cultural groups, students with disabilities or handicaps who are joining the classroom—the teacher encourages various types of interest and activity groups so that students merge and cooperate. Classmates play an extremely important role in providing acceptance and support to included children and other special-needs or diverse learners who are mainstreamed in self-contained classes (Burns et al., 1999).

## Cooperative Learning Groups

Cooperative learning is another form of mixed-ability, heterogeneous grouping of from three to six students at the classroom level. **Cooperative learning groups** differ in structure and purpose from the other major grouping patterns discussed in this section. We saw that with ability- or achievement-level grouping students compete for teacher recognition and grades and the same students tend to be "winners" or "losers" over the years. High-achieving students continually receive rewards and are motivated to learn, and low-achieving students continually experience failure (or near failure) and frustration. Reducing competition and increasing cooperation among students may diminish hostility, prejudice, and patterns of failure among many students. Interest-level grouping is one informal way to achieve cooperation and collaboration of different-ability and diversity levels of students in a classroom.

Cooperative learning groups, however, are more formal, structured organizational patterns in that students have roles through which they direct their own learning encounters and are responsible for the learning of their teammates. The key features of cooperative learning groups that make them different from merely being in a group are (1) the positive interdependence among members to succeed in the cooperative task, (2) individual accountability of each member to fulfill his or her task assignment or role, and (3) face-to-face interaction (Scott & Butler, 1994). Thus, students must appropriately apply social skills to enable them to act productively and collaboratively both as individuals and as group members (Burns et al., 1999).

Teachers who take the time to evaluate their students' strengths before forming cooperative groups and who plan the structure of the type of group they wish to form usually achieve good results in terms of both student behavior and academic success (Watson, 1998). A lesson framework using cooperative grouping generally follows a sequence that contains many of the good instructional characteristics noted in the previous chapter.

1. The lesson begins with teacher explanation so the group understands the task. Within this context, there could be discussion, questioning, and modeling by the teacher of a particular way to accomplish the activity.

2. The group works together cooperatively to accomplish the task, activity, or project.
3. Children within the group accomplish their roles and complete their individual assignments related to the task. Each individual needs to be willing to contribute his or her part, and others in the group can collaborate to motivate another to fulfill his or her assigned task. Once again, teachers are reminded that within any classroom will be high-status and low-status students as perceived by their peers. Besides differentiating instructional tasks on the basis of student ability or competence (Schniedewind & Davidson, 2000), the teacher can publicly praise the low-status student when competence on a task has been accomplished. The evaluation praise will be even stronger when the group and class hears that the low-status student used unique abilities or skills in achieving competence (Cohen, 1998).
4. The group shares their completed work with the other groups in the class. This step allows individual group members to become "teachers" in that they talk, explain, and show their accomplishments and findings. The teacher or a designated student from another group could summarize each group's report on chart paper or the chalkboard. If a grading system is used, the teacher may average the individual grades and assign a group grade to each group member (Leu & Kinzer, 1999).

In addition to the instructional aspects and learning experiences of cooperative group activity, there are roles each group member can assume so that the group's work can proceed in a cooperative way and not splinter off into individual, uncooperative efforts. Each time group members meet to accomplish a new or different task, the roles can shift. Teachers need to develop students' awareness of the purpose and responsibilities inherent in each role. Depending on the nature of the task and the number of students in a group, five roles and responsibilities can be assigned; these are described in Box 9.3 (Vacca & Vacca, 2002).

According to reviews of the cooperative group learning literature, such cooperation among participants helps build (1) positive and coherent personal identity,

---

**BOX 9.3** Five Roles and Responsibilities of Cooperative Group Work

Members of a cooperative learning group may rotate among the following roles and responsibilities:

1. The *group leader* keeps the group on its assigned task, may summarize the original directions, and ensure that all individuals know what they need to do to fulfill their part of the task assignment.
2. A *reader* may be assigned to read the material aloud so that all members of the group can understand the information.
3. A *writer/recorder* may take down the responses of the group on paper and prepare a summary of the group's work.
4. A *checker* may assist the group leader by questioning the group members to see if they are on target. The checker may ask group members to explain or summarize material being read or discussed.
5. An *encourager* motivates the members in the group to participate and encourages reluctant or silent ones to contribute.

*Source:* Adapted from Richard Vacca and JoAnne Vacca, *Content Area Reading; Literacy and Learning across the Curriculum,* 7th ed. (Boston: Allyn and Bacon, 2002).

(2) self-actualization and self-esteem, (3) knowledge and trust of others, (4) communication, (5) acceptance and support of others, (6) wholesome intergroup relationships, (7) reduction of conflicts, and (8) increased academic achievement (McManus & Gettinger, 1996). The data also suggest that cooperation and group learning are considerably more effective in fostering these social and interpersonal skills than competitive or individualistic effort (Johnson & F. P. Johnson, 1999; Slavin, 1994). Most important, according to Robert Slavin (1991a), when cooperative learning methods are used, achievement effects are consistently positive compared to those of traditional methods. Those conclusions applied in thirty-seven of forty-four controlled experiments at all grade levels (2–12); in all major subjects (although most of the research deals with grades 3–9 and in reading and mathematics); and in a wide diversity of geographic settings.

In cooperative learning, students divide the work among themselves, help one another (especially the slow members), praise and criticize one another's efforts and contributions, and receive a group performance score. It is not enough to simply tell students to work together. They must have a reason that allows them to relate as a team. The idea is to create some form of interdependence "in such a way that each individual's actions benefit the group and the group's actions benefit the individual" (Meloth & Deering, 1994, p. 139).

Various cooperative learning models have provided learning opportunities across grades, subjects, and ability levels of students. These models are described in Box 9.4

*Literature Circles.* A very popular grouping arrangement that surfaced throughout the 1990s is connected to the use of authentic children's literature in the classroom as a major vehicle for reading and writing instruction. The use of literature circles, also known as literature discussion groups, is based on the concept of the *grand conversation,* the title of a book by R. Peterson and M. Eeds (1990). During grand conversations, participants discuss and reflect on what they have read and gain insights and interpretations from others. The November 2000 issue of *The Reading Teacher* reported that in six of the twelve most recent issues of the journal, an article on the topic of literature circles appeared (Brabham & Villaume, 2000).

Generally, four to six students make up one literature circle group, although the number could be less. The teacher usually has sets of books available related to a particular author, genre, or topic or theme. What is most important is that the books deal with critical issues and experiences that promote reflection, discussion, questioning, and thoughtfulness (Brabham & Villaume, 2000). The talk is student stimulated and generated and is removed from the teacher-directed talk and questioning probes of basal reader–directed talk.

Students' roles and routines during the circle conversations can be informal or more structured. Students can formulate their own questions as they read, jot down ideas on sticky notes and place them in particular book pages, write responses in a journal, or create a graphic organizer or other type of visualization about their thoughts. Or a more formal structural pattern could be followed to help students take responsibility for their own conversation and reflective talk. Roles and responsibilities

**BOX 9.4** Types of Cooperative Learning Models

- **Student Teams-Achievement Divisions (STAD).** Team membership consists of four students, based on heterogeneous abilities. The teacher presents the lesson to the whole group in one or two sessions, and then the class divides into teams for content mastery. Class quizzes are frequent, and student scores are averaged into a team score to ensure cooperation and assistance within groups.

- **Teams-Games-Tournament (TGT).** Like STAD, TGT was developed by Robert Slavin. Instead of quizzes there are weekly "tournament tables" composed of three-member teams, with each member contributing points to the particular team score.

- **Jigsaw.** Originally designed for secondary schools (grades 7–12), jigsaw classroom students work in small groups (4 to 5 members) on specific academic tasks, assignments, or projects. Each team member becomes an "expert" in one area, meets with similar experts from other teams, and then returns to the original group to teach other team members.

- **Learning Together.** Developed by the Johnsons at the University of Minnesota, the method involves students working on assignments in four- to five-member heterogeneous teams. The groups hand in a single product and receive one group score.

- **Team Assisted Individualization (TAI).** This system develops four-member, heterogeneous teams for math, grades 3 to 6. Students are tested and organized into teams by ability. The groups then proceed at their own rates to work on different units and worksheets. Team members help one another and check each other's work. Final unit tests are taken without team help and are scored by student monitors.

- **Cooperative Integrated Reading and Composition (CIRC).** This arrangement was designed to complement traditional reading instruction using graded basal readers and ability-level groups. However, in addition, four-member reading teams are formed, consisting of two pairs from two different reading levels (two fast, two slow readers).

*Sources:* Adapted from Robert Slavin, *Using Student Team Learning,* 3rd ed. (Baltimore: Johns Hopkins University Press, 1986); Robert Slavin, *School and Classroom Organization* (Hillsdale, NJ: Erlbaum, 1988); Robert Slavin, "Synthesis of Research on Cooperative Learning," *Educational Leadership* (February 1991), pp. 71–82; Elliot Aronson et al., *The Jigsaw Classroom* (Beverly Hills, CA: Sage, 1978); David W. Johnson and Roger T. Johnson, *Learning Together and Alone,* 5th ed. (Boston, MA: Allyn and Bacon, 1999); Robert Slavin, Nancy A. Madden, and Marshall B. Leavey, "Effects of Team Assisted Individualization on the Mathematics Achievement of Academically Handicapped and Nonhandicapped Students," *Journal of Educational Psychology* (April 1984), pp. 813–819; Susan A. Wheelan, *Group Processes: A Developmental Perspective* (Boston: Allyn and Bacon, 1994). For an excellent short overview of the six cooperative learning models, see Carol B. Furtwengler, "How to Observe Cooperative Learning Classrooms," *Educational Leadership* (April 1992), pp. 59–62.

that can be assumed and rotated each time the group meets to discuss a different book are as follows:

- **Discussion Director.** The role of the discussion director is to come up with a small set of provocative questions to generate interesting conversation. The questions should be at the high level and deal with opening prompts such as "why," "how," "What do you think," "if," etc.

- **Illustrator.** The illustrator creates some kind of picture or visual representation related to the reading. The picture could be of a scene, a character, or even a feeling obtained from the reading. The group members take turns discussing the meaning of the picture.
- **Vocabulary Enricher.** This group member looks for important meaning-bearing words in the day's reading and also makes note of unfamiliar or puzzling words. The meanings of the words are located through dictionary use or teacher assistance, and the words are presented and discussed when the group meets.
- **Literary Luminary or Passage Picker.** This student finds short sections of the reading to read aloud because he or she thinks these are the most interesting, most important, most revealing, or will provide a good laugh. These passages can be read aloud by group members and discussed as students consider their effectiveness in the overall reading.
- **Summarizer.** The student summarizes the reading and presents the summary to the circle group when it meets.
- **Connector.** The connector's role is to determine what connections can be made between aspects of the reading and life experiences. Connections may be found between the reading and other events, people, places, or a book that has been completed in the past or is currently being read.
- **Quotation Chooser.** If the reading contains speaking characters, the quotation chooser selects dialogue from various characters. The group members then identify the appropriate character when the quotation is read (Burns, 1998; Daniels, 1994, 2001; Schneider, 2000).

Although seven roles have been identified, they can be collapsed and combined to reduce the number of participants in the cooperative circle group. For instance, the role of quotation chooser can also be filled by the literary luminary since specific sections of the reading need to be located. The discussion director can summarize the selection before asking thought-provoking questions. Furthermore, "roll sheets" or assignment pages can be created for each job and serve as supports or scaffolds to help students fulfill the tasks associated with each job. For instance, the discussion director could have a page on which three to five questions are written, and the vocabulary enricher could have a page on which the new words, their location, their definition, and their uniqueness are listed.

However, Harvey Daniels, one of the original creators of such assignment pages, maintains that using the role sheets for too long may actually limit the conversation and ideas generated about a reading. He indicates that in actual work with school-age children he has found that the pages rather than the reading or the literary selection become the center of the students' attention. They view the role sheets as more busywork or seatwork to rush through without much reflection. He suggests instead that the role sheets be placed face down and turned over by students when they need a prompt or suggestion to keep the literary talk going (Daniels, 2000).

## Group Activities

In various kinds of group activities, the teacher's role moves from engineer or director to facilitator or resource person, and many leadership functions transfer from the teacher to the students. Although there is no clear research showing that group activities correlate with student achievement, it is assumed that under appropriate circumstances, instruction in these groups can be as effective as or more effective than relying on the teacher as the major source of learning. It is also assumed that many kinds of group activities (1) help teachers deal with differences among learners, (2) provide opportunities for students to plan and develop special projects on which groups can work together, (3) increase student interaction and socialization while (4) allowing students to engage in individual reflective work to complete their team assignments before returning to dialogue with the group. In short, group activities achieve social, emotional, and individual as well as cognitive purposes.

Using group techniques in flexible and imaginative ways can have important instructional advantages. They give students some control over their own personal adjustment as well as over their cognitive learning. They allow the teacher to plan different lessons to meet the needs and interests of different groups. They permit the teacher to vary instructional methods, to plan interesting and active (as opposed to passive) activities, and to supplement the lecture, questioning, and practice and drill methods.

In a supplementary review of cooperative learning arrangements, the Johnsons point out that each lesson in cooperative learning should include five basic elements: (1) *positive interdependence*—students must feel they are responsible for their own learning and that of other members of the group; (2) *face-to-face interaction*—students must have the opportunity to explain what they are learning to one another; (3) *individual accountability*—each student must be held accountable for mastery of the assigned work; (4) *social skills*—each student must communicate effectively, maintain respect among group members, and work together to resolve conflicts; and (5) *group processing*—groups must be assessed to see how well they are working together and how they can improve (Johnson & Johnson, 1989). Table 9.1 presents fifteen additional ways to group students to achieve various types of products in the spirit of cooperation.

## ■ INDIVIDUALIZED INSTRUCTION

You have undoubtedly noted throughout these past two chapters the consistent references made to individualization of instruction, providing for individual differences, and meeting the individual needs of diverse and special learners regardless of the school or classroom pattern of organization. Indeed, this democratic view of the purpose of education as meeting the individual needs of every child may have begun with John Dewey in 1902. He wrote that the aim of education is the integration of children's individual, real-life experiences with their broader subject-matter course work (Dewey, 1902/1991). Through the decades, advocates of **individualized instruction** have appeared with various theories and methodology and have used such terminology as self-actualization, instructional objectives, programmed learning, the student-centered classroom, outcomes-based education mastery learning, individualized reading, computer-assisted reading instruction, learning centers, and individualized education programs (IEPs) mandated by Public Law 94-142, the Education of the Handicapped Act (Tiedt, 1994).

## *Table 9.1* Group Projects and Activities

Teachers can arrange activities for groups in many ways. Different group arrangements, also called group projects, result in different roles and responsibilities for the students and teacher. Listed on the following chart are fifteen possible group projects.

| | |
|---|---|
| *A committee* | is a small group working together in a common venture for a given period. Using committees succeeds to the extent that members grow socially in the group process and are able to accomplish cognitive tasks apart from close teacher direction. A committee representative may be chosen to report to the entire class. |
| *Brainstorming* | is a technique to elicit large numbers of imaginative ideas or solutions to open-ended problems. Group members are encouraged to expand their thinking beyond the routine sort of suggestions. Everyone's suggestions are accepted without judgment, and only after all the ideas are put before the groups do the members begin to focus on a possible solution. |
| *A buzz session* | provides an open environment in which group members can discuss their opinions without fear of being "wrong" or being ridiculed for holding an unpopular position. Buzz sessions can also clarify a position or bring new information before the group to correct misconceptions. |
| *The debate and panel* | are more structured in format than some of the other small-group activities. In a debate, two positions on a controversial issue are presented formally; each debater is given a certain amount of time to state a position, to respond to questions from others in the group, and to pose questions to the other side. The panel is used to present information on an issue and, if possible, to arrive at group consensus. Several students (three to eight) may sit on a panel. Each panel member may make an opening statement, but there are no debates among panel members. |
| *A symposium* | is not as structured as a debate and not as relaxed as the give-and-take exchange of a panel. The symposium is appropriate for airing topics that divide into clear-cut categories or viewpoints. Participants are expected to represent a particular position and try to convince others, but the method of interaction is more spontaneous and no one is timed, as in a debate. |
| *Role playing and improvisation* | are techniques for stepping outside of one's own role and feelings and placing oneself in another's situation. Role playing also serves as a technique for exploring intergroup attitudes and values. |
| *Fishbowl* | is a technique in which group members give their full attention to what one individual wants to express. The whole group sits in a circle. Two chairs are placed in the center of the circle. A member who wants to express a point of view does so while sitting in one of the chairs. Any other member who wants to discuss the view takes the other chair, and the two converse while the others listen. To get into the discussion, students must wait for one chair to be vacated. |
| *A critiquing session* | is the examination of members' work by the group. The group offers constructive comments and suggestions about ways to improve the work. |

*(continued)*

*Table 9.1*   Continued

| | |
|---|---|
| *Roundtable* | is a quiet, informal group—usually four or five students—who sit around a table conversing either among themselves (similar to a buzz session) or with an audience (similar to a forum). |
| *A forum* | is a panel approach in which members interact with an audience. |
| *Jury trial* | is a technique in which the class simulates a courtroom. It is excellent for evaluating issues. |
| *Majority-rule decision making* | is a technique for arriving at an agreement or selecting an individual for a task when members of the group hold different opinions. It involves discussion, working out compromises, and drawing conclusions or making decisions based on the wishes of the majority. |
| *Consensus decision making* | requires group members to agree. Consensus requires that the views of all members of the group be considered, because the group must arrive at a conclusion or agree on a plan of action. |
| *A composite report* | synthesizes and summarizes the views or information of all members of a group. Rather than a series of reports by individual members, one report is presented in written or oral form to the class or teacher. |
| *An agenda* | is a formal method for organizing a group task. Students or the teacher can plan the agenda, and members of the group must keep to it. |

## Direct Instruction Approaches to Achieve Mastery

Approaches that have been widely used in the public schools are based on the concepts of **mastery learning** or competency-based learning. One such approach is called *outcomes-based education (OBE),* which provides an example of an approach that emphasizes a technological viewpoint of curriculum planning (see Chapter 5). In OBE a team made up of teachers, parents, and students develop personalized learning plans (PLPs) to make expectations about instruction and assessment clear to students. With this approach, both learners and the parents are involved in instructional planning for individualized learning and both are kept informed of personal progress. Moreover, instructional methodology, time, and content are adjusted to meet each student's individual needs, and the student knows how he or she will be assessed for learning (Tiedt, 1994).

*Learning for mastery* often referred to simply as mastery learning, was associated originally with John Carroll and later with James Block and Benjamin Bloom. Their mastery learning ideas have gained supporters, particularly in urban school districts, where there has been a growing need to improve academic performance among inner-city students.

Carroll maintained that if students are normally distributed by ability or aptitude for some academic subjects and are provided appropriate instruction tailored to their individual characteristics, the majority should achieve mastery of the subject and learning should dramatically improve. He also held that if a student does not spend sufficient time learning a task, he or she will not master it. However, students vary in the amount of time they need to complete a task. Nearly all students (assuming no major learning disability) can achieve average outcomes if given sufficient time (Carroll, 1963).

Carroll, and later Robert Slavin, distinguished between time needed to learn (based on student characteristics such as aptitude) and time available for learning (under the teacher's control). High-achieving students need less time than low-achieving students to learn the same material. Group instruction, large or small, rarely accommodates varying learner characteristics or considers the time needed to learn. With mastery instruction, the teacher has the ability to vary instructional time for different individuals or groups of students, especially for low-achieving students who usually need additional time (Carroll, 1989; Slavin, 1987).

A substantial body of data indicates that mastery learning can result in large learning gains for students. One observer, for example, has reviewed more than 100 studies on mastery learning and concludes that the results "indicate that mastery strategies do indeed have moderate to strong effects on student learning when compared to conventional methods of instruction (Burns, 1979, p. 112). Similarly, in a review of more than 25 studies, Block and Burns found that 61 percent of the mastery-taught students scored significantly higher on achievement tests than non-mastery-taught students (Block & Burns, 1976; see also Block, Efthim, & Burns, 1989). In studies of entire school districts, the results show that mastery approaches are successful in teaching basic skills, such as reading and mathematics, that form the basis for later learning; moreover, inner-city students profit more from this approach than from traditional groupings for instruction (Levine, 1987, 1991; Levine & Ornstein, 1993).

**Direct instruction** follows on the heels of mastery learning, and the focus of its curriculum approach is to provide detailed, systematic, and explicit instruction (McKenna & Robinson, 2002). With direct instruction, the teacher assumes a controlling instructional stance and delivers curriculum lessons, generally ordered and arranged by an educational publishing company, in skill sequences for mastery at particular levels (Kozioff, LaNunziata, Cowardin, & Bessellieu, 2000–2001). Its structure most closely resembles that of the curriculum alignment design, with its three major elements of the curriculum, the test, and the teacher, as presented in Chapter 5 (English, 2000). Direct instruction may also be considered to be at odds with the underlying principles of constructivist and inquiry approaches to learning in that the latter ask students to "discover" rules, concepts, and thinking strategies without the use of carefully designed and field-tested sequences of instructional units taught in a direct way by teachers (Kozioff et al., 2000–2001).

A remedial reading intervention program endorsed by the American Federation of Teachers (AFT) takes the name of Direct Instruction (DI). Direct Instruction is a highly structured teaching approach aimed at rapidly improving the reading or spelling performance of at-risk students in low-performing schools. The AFT investigated research-based methods in selecting DI as one of five promising programs for accomplishing remedial reading intervention and raising academic achievement for at-risk students. Each of the programs selected had to demonstrate (1) high standards, (2) effectiveness, (3) replicability, and (4) support structures (American Federation of Teachers, 1999).

Direct Instruction is a highly prescriptive and scripted approach to instruction. It is prescriptive in that each entering student is given a diagnostic assessment, assigned to a performance level, and taught in increments of skills and content. Frequent evaluations are leveled into the skills continuum to ensure that each student has achieved mastery of particular skills and to discover any student who needs to be retaught. Skills are taught in a prescribed lesson sequence through fast-paced, teacher-directed instruction and questioning, interspersed with choral group and individual student responses. Each lesson sequence has been field tested a number of times to determine the most effective way to lead 90 percent of students to mastery of a skill the first time it is taught. Initial lessons in reading begin by focusing on phonemic awareness, followed by lessons on phonics and decoding skills, to later lessons on comprehension and content analysis. After initial whole-group or small-group presentation, guided practice of the new skill follows with frequent checks by the instructor to ensure individual student mastery. The objective of every discrete lesson is for each student to achieve automatic reading behavior of the skill so that it can be transferred to a new learning situation.

The lessons take the form of classroom scripts to ensure that beginning teachers will be successful and that veteran teachers will follow a field-tested route of successful skill development. A group that has been primary in implementing the DI approach at the classroom level and that benefits from the use of fully written out, discrete lessons is the paraprofessional. After paraprofessionals have been trained in the structure and repetitive nature of the DI approach, they work as instructional aides, small-group leaders, and one-on-one tutors under the direction of the certified teacher. Thus, under the management of one corrective or remedial reading teacher, a number of paraprofessionals can serve individuals and small groups, each working on different skills and/or content in different sections of a large classroom, making the Direct Instruction approach quite cost effective.

Moreover, teacher and paraprofessional orientation and training are necessary before and during implementation to ensure that instructional objectives and the sequential, repetitive nature of the approach are understood. In addition, the focus on the teaching of specific skills may require teachers to modify and supplement features of commercial programs their school or district could be using. Thus the orientation of Direct Instruction requires that teachers and their aides stress the teaching of direct skills in the most effective and efficient way possible (Carnine et al., 1997). Tips for Teachers 9.1 presents guidelines for implementing direct, explicit instruction.

## Student Pairs Helping Each Other

Teachers often use two-student arrangements so that students can assist and learn from each other (Finders & Hynds, 2003). Two students working together can also be considered a small cooperative group. Yet, when two students work together—one as the help giver and one as the help seeker—individualized focus and engagement still need to be monitored by the teacher (Webb, Farivar, & Mastergeorge, 2002). Also, the student who becomes the "teacher," as in **peer tutoring**, is also a learner. Any teacher will tell us that through teaching, one learns. Research confirms that when one teacher is a novice, less skilled, or younger, the tutor improves as much or even more than the tutee (May, 1998). Thus we have placed the practice of student pairing, which includes peer tutoring, buddy reading, cross-age tutoring, and partner sharing, under the topic heading of Individualized Instruction.

Assigning students to help each other on a one-to-one basis or in a small-group situation has been generally accomplished in three ways by teachers: (1) students may tutor others *within* the same class; (2) older students may tutor students in lower grades outside of class—this is known as *cross-age tutoring* because students of different ages are involved; or (3) two students may work together and help each other as equal *partners* with learning activities (Foster-Harrison, 1997). The purpose of the first two types is to pair a student who needs assistance with a tutor on a one-to-one basis, although small groups of two or three tutees and one tutor can also be formed. The third type, also called *peer pairing,* is more than tutoring; we discussed earlier that students working together as equals is oftentimes called *cooperative learning.* A fourth type of peer support is also beginning to surface. Mainstreamed, general education students can provide tutoring in a climate of inclusion to "buddies" who are students with disabilities (Hughes, Rung, Wehmeyer, Agran, Copeland & Hwang, 2000).

Of the pairing arrangements, peer tutoring within the same class is the most common in elementary and middle schools. A student who is a high achiever or who has completed a lesson and has shown understanding of the material is paired with a student who needs help. The research suggests that because students are less threatened by peers, they are more willing to ask fellow students questions that they fear the teacher might consider "silly." In addition, they are less afraid that fellow students might criticize them for being unable to understand an idea or problem after a second or third explanation (Slavin & Madden, 1989; Thorkildsen, 1993). It has also been found that a student can sometimes explain a concept in language that another student can grasp. Unfamiliar vocabulary is cut to a minimum, and sometimes a few choice slang terms can make a difficult concept comprehensible. Also, because the faster student has just learned the concept, he or she may be more aware than the teacher of what is giving the slower student difficulty. Peer tutors benefit from the relationship; their own understanding is reinforced by explaining the idea or problem, their social skills are enhanced, and more positive attitudes toward reading develop (Adams, 1990; Foster-Harrison, 1991; Pearson & Fielding, 1991). The teacher benefits by having additional time to work with students who have more severe learning problems. These benefits are reflected in Box 9.5.

## BOX 9.5 Benefits of Peer Tutoring

Peer tutoring provides the following benefits in a win-for-all classroom environment:

1. Peer tutors are often effective in teaching students who do not respond well to adults.
2. Peer tutoring can encourage the development of a bond of friendship between the tutor and the tutee, which is important for integrating slow learners into the group.
3. Peer tutoring allows the teacher to teach a large group of students but still gives slow learners and students with diverse learning needs the individual attention they need.
4. Tutors benefit by learning to teach, a general skill that can be useful in adult society.

*Source:* Adapted from David W. Johnson and Roger T. Johnson, *Learning Together and Alone,* 5th ed. (Boston: Allyn and Bacon, 1999).

## Individualized Reading Approach

The **individualized reading approach** emerged during the 1950s and 1960s as a way to counter the primary instructional practice of using commercially prepared basal reader programs, with their controlled vocabularies, scripted lesson plans in teacher manuals, workbooks, and ditto pages (Veatch, 1994). Individualized reading places literacy development directly in the hands of the teacher and, even more important, ties it directly to the efforts and motivation of students. Undoubtedly, the approach was a precursor to the student-centered movements of whole language and literature-based reading, and the characteristics and procedural steps of individualized reading are found in the workshop and center strategies that are popular today.

From the student's point of view, there are three main characteristics of the approach, those of (1) self-seeking, (2) self-selecting, and (3) self-pacing (Miel, 1958; Parker, 1954; Veatch, 1959). The self-seeking and self-selecting aspects focus on motivating students to read for both learning and enjoyment. Rather than being assigned material to read, students are encouraged to be independent thinkers and choose the trade and literature books they are individually interested in pursuing. Once material is selected, children read at their own pace rather than at the pace of an ability or achievement group.

The individualized reading concept may suggest lack of structure, and for the process to work, the teacher must be especially skillful in managing the process for an entire classroom of students and in providing a framework for each individual. Initially, the teacher provides a large collection of literature, trade books, magazines, and other reading materials that reflect different interest areas and reading levels. Because highly motivated students may read many of the books and materials rather quickly, the teacher needs to continually supplement the in-classroom collection.

While students are engaged in reading their self-selected materials during independent seatwork, the teacher accomplishes another practice of the individualized reading approach, that of individual conferencing. Following a weekly plan, the teacher anticipates which students will be ready to conference during particular days of the week. The teacher maintains individual folders for each child in which the teacher records the date and length of the conference, the materials discussed, the student's expectations for the next pages of the reading, how the student performed in comprehension and oral reading, problems or confusion the student may have faced, and the student's understanding of new words.

Finally, the method necessitates good organizational skills and record keeping. For each child, the teacher maintains files in which he or she notes conference dates, times, and activities accomplished. Some teachers have prepared checklists to assist the conference process, others write narrative statements on a prepared conferencing document, and others use a contracting procedure with students. With contracting the teacher and individual student "contract" or agree to accomplish a certain amount of reading, writing, computer-based research, or project work before the next conference. These agreements are noted on the student's contracting page, and the collection of these pages throughout the course of the individualized method becomes a strong basis of teacher–student–parent documentation and interaction.

It is also important to encourage students to keep well-organized files, folders, or computer disks, and the teacher would be wise to spend time at the outset showing students how this record keeping is done. The better that students maintain and organize their own work, the easier conferencing and instructional assignment times will be for both teacher and students. A separate file cabinet may be necessary to house and organize student folders. If individual folders are kept at the students' desks, students can attach a "log" to the inside cover on which they maintain a record of their own dates, times, and individualized activities in summary form. The rest of the folder (or three-ring binder notebook) will contain the bulk of the student's work separated by dividers.

## Centers

Centers are known by two generic names, **interest centers** or **learning centers.** These are stations or particular classroom work areas at which students engage in activities to learn, practice, or reinforce a skill or concept (Lenski & Nierstheimer, 2004). They may be small enough that only one student at a time can sit and work or large enough for a small group to engage in a project. Small centers can be composed of one student desk partitioned off with cardboard or poster board at the front and sides to create the sense of a unique, private work area, and larger centers can be made by joining two to four desks or using a small table with an appropriate poster board display to announce the name of the center (see Figure 8.3).

Centers are a primary way to provide for individualized activity. Many teachers use centers as a reinforcement tool for students to drill, practice, and review newly taught skills and concepts. Often centers are a useful way to engage those students who finish other lessons or seatwork activities quickly. When finished with the initial assignment, they can go to a center for enrichment and beneficial time-on-task activities such as revising and editing a paper or report.

Thus, while centers can be a useful complement to many instructional frameworks, their strength lies in the potential for enhancing individual learning. As stations for development of a thematic unit, centers are places students can work independently or in groups to research, organize, and present different topics or concepts of a theme. Centers also can provide unique activity areas for students to practice and enhance learning. In this instructional climate, teachers might offer a variety of types of centers, such as a writing center, a reading or literacy center, a science center, an arithmetic center, a social studies center, and so on. After important skills or concepts have been covered in the curriculum, newly named centers can temporarily replace the more traditionally named discipline centers. For instance, a Graphing Center could replace the Arithmetic Center and a Map Center could replace the Social Studies Center.

One author has suggested that learning centers are best suited for the block schedule pattern of organization. With greater engagement and learning time, students can pursue projects to a greater depth, become involved in inductive or higher-order thinking skills, and form cooperative groups (Watson, 1998). Another author conducted a review of empirical research and descriptive accounts to determine the influence of writing centers on writing performance. Concrete evidence did not explicity show the effects of one on the other. However, indirect evidence of peer interaction, which is a cornerstone of most writing center configurations, revealed that both tutor and tutee benefited from the refining of writing and communication skills. What was most interesting was the finding that the best peer tutors (like good teachers) elicited critical thinking about the revising and composing process from the tutee rather than engaging in the telling of information (Jones, 2001).

## Workshops

The word **workshops** suggest that this topic should be covered under group work. Although it could be, according to some of the workshop implementation steps, the intent of the workshop structure is to maximize individual engagement with literacy, particularly with the actual thinking processes necessary for effective reading and writing. There are two kinds of workshop frameworks, the writing workshop and the reading workshop, each with a slightly different but complementary focus. In reading workshop, students often write in response to literature, and in writing workshop, students may read in order to obtain ideas about what to write about or to learn aspects of the writer's craft or of written conventions.

Also, the workshop framework contains features of other instructional procedures discussed earlier in this chapter, such as the whole-part-whole instructional procedure, cooperative learning group work, and the individualized reading approach. Yet a key aspect of both reading and writing workshop is that students take charge of what they do with their time, are able to make choices about what they read and write about, and are encouraged to take risks in their writing. The focus of the workshop structure is on the processes of reading and writing—what readers actually do while reading and reflecting on what they read and what writers actually do to accomplish a publishable, highly readable piece.

The basic elements of the workshop structure are as follows:

- A minilesson that deals with some aspect of the reading or writing process, such as how to start a written piece to grab the interest of the audience (often referred to as a good lead) or the presentation of a particular literary genre and how to show an appreciation for that style of writing.
- An informal check or assessment of each child's progress and intent during the workshop time, often referred to as "a status-of-the-class report." This is accomplished by the teacher recording what each student has done and will be doing as each child's name is called.
- Followed by quiet, individualized reading or writing time, running anywhere from fifteen to thirty minutes, in which students read a literary or informational piece of their choice or write and reflect on a self-selected topic.
- While students are engaged in individualized reading or writing work, the teacher circulates within the group and conducts individual "conferences" with students regarding the status of their work in progress. The teacher can appraise and assist with content, understandings, and suggestions for revision.
- Finally there is whole-group "share time," in which students might tell about what they read, read lines from their book or comments from their response journal, or read excerpts from their in-progress paper in an effort to elicit feedback from the larger group (Atwell, 1998; Ross, 1996; Winship, 1994a, 1994b).

These workshop components tend to reinforce the events that will occur each time. With a writing workshop, a routine is created and students come to know what is required and be able to predict what is expected of them (Piazza, 2003).

Furthermore, teachers need to be flexible and reflective when implementing workshops and to maximize individual student effort during the workshop time, whether the student is a native speaker of English or learning English as a second language (Gee, 1996; Winship, 1994a). Nancie Atwell, in the second edition of her landmark book describing the workshop methodology, cautions that inflexibility and adherence to workshop "rules" can limit student and teacher interaction during the workshop process. Earlier she had suggested that minilessons should run from five to seven minutes but through actual teaching practice found that minilessons can last up to half an hour. This happens, for instance, when the teacher demonstrates to the whole class how he or she operates as a writer, when students critique a written piece, or when computer use is to be integrated into the writing process (Atwell, 1998). Also, there is a trade-off between the teacher acting as expert and the student as apprentice writer. The adult has the wider experience and greater expertise with the range of writing, so the goal is to not "over tell" the ideas and rules of the craft while letting the apprentice writers discover these on their own (Jorgensen, 2001).

Another author suggests that a natural way to approach the writing workshop is to start by using journal writing. When students write for several days on a topic and receive feedback from the teacher regarding high standards and the need for correctness in writing conventions, students sense that writing is an important endeavor. The key, then, for the teacher when using the journal writing procedure to implement the workshop approach is to monitor students' work and progress and to raise their expectations for good, legible writing (Routman, 2000).

## Reading Recovery

**Reading Recovery** is a highly individualized program aimed at one level of student, the beginner who is having difficulty learning how to read and write. Its purpose is to catch children or "recover" them before they fail to achieve success with literacy. The program was introduced in New Zealand during the early 1970s by psychologist and educator Marie Clay with first graders who had received a full year of formal reading instruction in kindergarten.

The practice of implementing the program with first graders took hold in the United States and Canada even while it was acknowledged that many North American children do not receive formal instruction in reading at the kindergarten level (Kepron, 1998; Shanahan & Barr, 1995). It has been used at many sites throughout North America. Its practitioners, called Reading Recovery Trainers, held fast to the original guidelines and practices outlined by its designer (Deford, Lyons, & Pinnell, 1995). In fact, Reading Recovery has been harshly criticized as being too rigid and structured in its intervention approach with struggling first graders (Barnes, 1996–1997), thus receiving the same type of criticism leveled at mastery learning and other direct instruction approaches discussed earlier in this chapter. However, one educator comments that the practice of replicating the design and lesson structure of the original Reading Recovery model was purposeful so that trainers and implementers could maintain program integrity, especially for research applications, at the risk of curtailing teacher individuality (Reutzel, 1999).

Reading Recovery provides individualized daily literacy instruction to those first graders most at risk for reading and writing failure. As in a pull-out model, the young child receives a thirty-minute, routinized session with a trained Reading Recovery teacher. The child remains in the tutoring sessions for a number of weeks and is "discontinued" in the program when he or she attains an average level of reading compared with first-grade peers and is believed to be capable of functioning on an average level in ensuing grades (Pinnell, Lyons, & Jones, 1996). The daily individualized session occurs as a supplement to the child's regular first-grade instruction in reading. The Reading Recovery system has three main features: (1) teacher training in Reading Recovery beliefs and methodology, (2) diagnostics and assessments to gain program eligibility, and (3) the lesson framework carried out according to an established routine.

First-grade children are identified and selected to participate in Reading Recovery through the use of formal (norm-referenced, standardized) and criterion-referenced tests and the judgments of individual teachers. However, Reading Recovery teachers tend to use the assessment criteria originally developed by Marie Clay as part of her total program (Kepron, 1998). The six observational assessments include the following:

1. letter knowledge
2. a word list to be read
3. concept understanding of print
4. the measurement of letter-sound relationships
5. the writing of words
6. the recording of how a child reads an actual text, called a "running record" (Clay, 1985; Spiegel, 1995).

The thirty-minute lesson framework developed by Clay was based on observations made in classrooms and one-to-one clinical settings and tailored to achieve an accelerated, efficient use of instructional time so that the child could interact with reading and writing activities with as much engaged time as possible (Deford et al., 1995). Each lesson had four components that became a daily, predictable routine for the child, allowing the student to know what to expect each day. The lesson components contained many of the good instructional practices used with emergent readers and writers discussed in earlier chapters in this book, such as lap reading so that a bond is established between the adult, the child, and the book; the development of smooth, early fluency in connected reading; and the focus on the features of words to improve word recognition and writing.

The lesson begins with the reading of previously read stories and books, which the child might choose. This allows the child to enjoy a favorite experience and begin the lesson with a high degree of success. The goal, of course, is to practice and achieve fluency in smooth, coordinated reading with full understanding and enjoyment of the reading experience.

The second segment of the lesson repeats the objective of the first, that is, to practice reading previously introduced material. In this case, the child rereads the text of the day before. The teacher now observes how the child reads and records the inaccuracies or "miscues" the child makes. The Reading Recovery teacher asks appropriate questions about the miscued text and may redirect the child to the text in efforts to improve the child's reading proficiency.

After the more global or holistic reading of connected text, the child is directed to focus on parts. Here the child becomes engaged in the writing process in order to focus on the components and features of words. Early on the child may dictate the sentences he or she wishes to be written while the teacher writes these, rereads them for the child, and then possibly asks the child to rewrite them. After connecting the sounds of words with their alphabet letters, the teacher writes the sentence strip and cuts it up into individual words. The child rereads the words and reorders them to make the correct sentence. The child may then take the word cards home for further practice and reinforcement (DeFord et al., 1995; Pinnell, 1994; Rasinski & Padak, 2000). Note that this third component of the Reading Recovery lesson framework also contains many of the good instructional practices for emergent readers and writers discussed in Chapters 2 and 3, such as inventive or creative spelling and the language experience approach.

The lesson concludes with the introduction of a new book or reading selection that is predicted to be just a bit more difficult than the preceding reading selections. The teacher guides and assists the child through the reading. Initially the teacher may discuss the book and engage the child in a "picture walk" through the book. As the child examines and discusses the pictures, he or she uses oral language to become engaged with the characters and plot events. Through talk and the shared viewed/reading interaction, the teacher may capitalize on the language used by the child. For instance, the child may say a word to describe a happening in a picture, but the author may have used a different word. The teacher can reinforce the child's talk by introducing the author's word or words as an alternative, seeking acknowledgment from the child. Therefore, when the child actually reads the book during the day's lesson and the following day during the second segment of that lesson, the child can predict the words actually written by the author.

Supporters of the Reading Recovery intervention approach for first graders are keen on the process and methodology. Overall research on Reading Recovery indicates that it is a more effective program in advancing children to average reading levels than other programs seeking to correct reading difficulties (Pinnell, 1994; Rasinski & Padak, 2000). We must note, however, that Reading Recovery is an expensive proposition for a school or district. Consider how many children can be served by one Reading Recovery teacher in thirty-minute intervals in a day, a semester, or a year. One successful Reading Recovery teacher believed that the training alone cost her district $12,000 (Elliot, 2000). Critics are also wary that Reading Recovery programs, at least those reported in the literature, are not serving the most needy, at-risk first graders; by serving children of higher ability levels, success is easier to achieve (Center, Wheldall, Freeman, Outhred, & McNaught, 1995; Shanahan & Barr, 1995).

On the other hand, is the "recovery" from possible literacy failure of some first graders in a school system worth it in the long run? Once a child begins to experience literacy failure, how many more years of corrective programs, with their concomitant expenses, does to it take to rectify the child's situation? Furthermore, the success achieved by Reading Recovery teachers with low-achieving first graders has rubbed off on other teachers. Schools and districts have initiated programs using some of the best practices of Reading Recovery in conjunction with all its first-grade teachers and the children's parents (Kinnucan-Welsch, Magill, & Dean, 1999; Yates, Nagel, & Libutti, 1997). We might consider, then, that the financial support required of a Reading Recovery program is money well spent.

## ■ SUMMARY ■

1. Instruction may take place in whole-group, small-group, and individual settings. The teacher is responsible for varying these three groupings according to the needs of the students and the objectives of a lesson.

2. A whole-part-whole instructional framework is a way to achieve a balance in classroom organizational structure. In the initial "whole," the entire class participates in the lesson planned by the teacher. During the "part," either as individuals or in small groups, students engage in strategy implementation, skill work, or practice activities that are grounded in the lesson plan. With the second "whole," students apply their learnings by using another literacy mode such as writing, artwork, or computer representation and share their work with the whole group.

3. There are several methods for organizing students in small groups, including grouping by interest, by ability, for peer tutoring, for cooperative learning, and to engage in group activities. Small-group activities are best achieved when group size is limited to five to eight students per group.

4. A type of cooperative grouping arrangement is known as a "literature circle." During literature circles, students discuss and reflect on one book they have collectively read. Roles that may be assumed and rotated each time the group meets to discuss a different book are discussion director, illustrator, vocabulary enricher, passage picker, summarizer, and connector.

5. Individualized instruction permits the student to work alone at his or her own pace and level over short or long periods of time. Individualized instruction permits the teacher to adapt instruction to the abilities, needs, and interests of the learner.

6. Individual instruction can occur in such contexts as direct instruction approaches that focus on mastery of discrete skills, when student pairs assist one another, in the individualized reading approach, within centers and workshops, and in a beginning reading approach called Reading Recovery.

## ■ QUESTIONS TO CONSIDER ■

1. What are the advantages of whole-group instruction?

2. Do you think the number of students in a class affects the quality of learning they receive? Explain why or why not.

3. How might the whole-part-whole instructional pattern allow the teacher to make the best use of different grouping arrangements?

4. Which of the small-group instructional patterns do you prefer to use for different purposes and at different times? Are some of the groups formed on the basis of ability or achievement, on interest, or on cooperative learning beliefs?

5. What are the features of cooperative learning groups that foster social and interpersonal skills while benefiting students' learning achievement?

6. How does the individualization of instruction reflect a democratic view of the purpose of education?

7. Do you think a structured teaching approach such as direct instruction or mastery learning meets the needs of most learners, or is the approach best used with low-performing, at-risk students in chiefly urban schools?

8. What are the learning advantages when student pairs assist each other, as in peer or cross-age tutoring?

9.  What features of the individualized reading approach make it attractive to implement with students who have good reading vocabularies?

10. How does the use of centers and workshops allow the teacher to use different grouping patterns to maximize learning effort?

## ■ THINGS TO DO ■

1.  Have your class focus on the teaching of a topic, a theme, a concept, or a principle. Form them into groups and have each group come up with a plan of how they would organize students to teach one particular lesson sequence. See if they can integrate different classroom patterns of instruction, as presented in this chapter, into their plan.

2.  Form your class into groups once again. Have them plan how they would implement a writing or reading workshop approach by following the procedures outlined in the chapter. Have your students show how they accomplished a whole-part-whole instructional framework, or cooperative learning, or individualized reading approach within their workshop plan.

3.  Defend or criticize the nature of competitive and cooperative classroom organizational patterns.

Be sure to describe the advantages of each, whatever your overall preference.

4.  Have your students form literature circles. They should be formed into groups of five or six, each be assigned a role, and each have read the same literary piece prior to working in the group circle. After they role-play the literature circle roles, have them discuss the merits (or demerits) of using this structure with their own students.

5.  Pass out poster or chart paper to your class groups. Have them design and label a classroom with interest centers. Have each group present to the class how the interest centers would be used and how they would fit in with the ongoing curriculum.

## ■ RECOMMENDED READINGS ■

American Federation of Teachers. *Building on the Best: Learning from What Works.* Washington, DC: American Federation of Teachers, 1999. Presents five successful programs that have raised academic achievement for at-risk students.

Atwell, Nancie. *In the Middle: New Understanding about Writing, Reading, and Learning,* 2nd ed. Norwood, MA: Christopher-Gordon, 1996. A book describing how one author implements the writing/reading workshop approach.

Daniels, Harvey. *Literature Circles: Voice and Choice in Book Clubs and Reading Groups.* York, ME: Stenhouse, 2001. The author describes the format and structure of literature circles, a student grouping pattern that encourages students to discuss and reflect on literary works.

Deford, Dianne, Carol Lyons, and Gay Su Pinnell, eds. *Bridges to Literacy: Learning from Reading Recovery.* Portsmouth, NH: Heinemann, 1995. An edited book with chapters devoted to the guidelines, practices, and merits of the Reading Recovery program.

Foster-Harrison, Elizabeth. *Peer Tutoring for K–12 Success.* Bloomington, IN: Phi Delta Kappa Educational Foundation, 1997. Presents ways in which students can tutor or assist one another in different kinds of grade- and age-level arrangements.

Johnson, David W., and Roger T. Johnson. *Learning Together and Alone,* 5th ed. Boston: Allyn and Bacon, 1999. A basic book on ways to achieve and structure cooperative learning groups and on the merits of individualized learning.

Slavin, Robert E. *Cooperative Learning: Theory, Research, and Practice,* 2nd ed. Boston: Allyn and Bacon, 1994. Shows ways to promote teamwork and group effort through cooperative learning.

# ■ KEY TERMS ■

ability grouping
cooperative learning groups
direct instruction
individualized instruction
individualized reading approach

interest centers
learning centers
mastery learning
peer tutoring
small-group instruction

Reading Recovery
special interest groups
whole-group instruction
whole-part-whole instruction
workshops

# ■ REFERENCES ■

Adams, M. J. (1990). *Beginning to read.* Cambridge, MA: MIT Press.

American Federation of Teachers. (1999). *Building on the best: Learning from what works.* Washington, DC: American Federation of Teachers.

Atwell, N. (1998). *In the middle: New understanding about writing, reading, and learning* (2nd ed.). Portsmouth, NH: Heinemann.

Barnes, B. (1996–1997, December). But teacher you went right on: A perspective on reading recovery. *The Reading Teacher,* 284–292.

Biddle, B., & Berliner, D. (2002, February). Small class size and its effects. *Educational Leadership,* 12–23.

Block, J., & Burns, R. (1976). Mastery learning. In L. S. Shulman (Ed.), *Review of research in education, Vol. 4,* (pp. 118–46). Itasca, IL: Peacock.

Block, J. H. (1971). *Mastery learning: Theory and practice.* New York: Holt, Rinehart and Winston.

Block, R., Efthim, H., & Burns, R. (1989). *Building effective mastery learning schools.* New York: Longman.

Brabham, E. G., & Villaume, S. K. (2000, November). Questions and answers: Continuing conversations about literature circles. *The Reading Teacher,* 278–280.

Brown, A., Palincsar, A., & Armbruster, B. (1994). Instructing comprehension. In R. Ruddell, M. Rapp Ruddell, & H. Singer (Eds.), *Theoretical models and processes* (4th ed., pp. 757–787). Newark, DE: International Reading Association.

Burns, B. (1998, October). Changing the classroom climate with literature circles. *Journal of Adolescent and Adult Literacy,* 124–129.

Burns, P., Roe, B., & Ross, E. (1999). *Teaching reading in today's elementary schools* (7th ed.). Boston: Houghton Mifflin.

Burns, R. B. (1979, November). Mastery learning: Does it work? *Educational Leadership,* 112.

Carnine, D., Silbert, J., Kameenui, E., & Tarver, S. (2004). *Direct instruction reading* (4th ed.). Upper Saddle River, NJ: Merrill.

Carroll, J. B. (1963, May). A model of school learning. *Teacher's College Record,* 723–773.

Carroll, J. B. (1989, January/February). The Carroll model: A 25-year retrospective and prospective view. *Educational Researcher,* 26–31

Center, Y., Wheldall, K., Freeman, L., Outhred, L., & McNaught, M. (1995, April/June). An evaluation of reading recovery. *Reading Research Quarterly,* 240–263.

Clay, M. M. (1985). *The early detection of reading difficulties* (3rd ed.). Portsmouth, NH: Heinemann.

Cohen, E. (1998, September). Making cooperative learning equitable. *Educational Leadership,* 18–21.

Cuban, L. (1993). *How teachers taught.* New York: Teachers College Press.

Daniels, H. (1994). *Literature circles: Voice and choice in the student-centered classroom.* York, ME: Stenhouse.

Daniels, H. (2000). *The prescription for role sheets: Not re-fillable!* Retrieved January 26, 2004, from www.literaturecircles.com.

Daniels, H. (2001). *Literature circles: Voice and choice in book clubs and reading groups.* York, ME: Stenhouse.

DeFord, D., Lyons, C., & Pinnell, G. S. (Eds.). (1995). *Bridges to literacy: Learning from reading recovery.* Portsmouth, NH: Heinneman.

Dewey, J. (1902/1991). *The school and society: The child and the curriculum.* Philip Jackson (Ed.), Chicago: University of Chicago Press.

Dianis, L. (2000, November). Size really doesn't matter. *District Administrator,* 14.

Elley, N. (2001, November/December). Big benefits in small classes. *Psychology Today,* 28.

Elliot, I. (2000, February). A neighborhood school that's big on reading. *Teaching PreK–8,* 40–43.

English, F. (2000). *Deciding what to teach and test: Developing, aligning and auditing the curriculum.* Thousand Oaks, CA: Corwin Press.

Finders, M. J., & Hynds, S. (2003). *Literacy lessons: Teaching and learning with middle school students.* Upper Saddle River, N.J.: Merrill/Prentice Hall.

Foster-Harrison, E. (1997). *Peer tutoring for K–12 success.* Bloomington, IN: Phi Delta Kappa Educational Foundation.

Fowler, D. (1998, March). Balanced reading instruction in practice. *Educational Leadership,* 11–12.

Gamoran, A. (1992, October). Synthesis of research: Is ability grouping equitable? *Educational Leadership,* 11–13.

Gee, R. (1996, Spring). Reading/writing workshops for the ESL classroom. *TESOL Journal,* 4–9.

Glass, G. V. (1982). *School class size: Research and policy.* Beverly Hills, CA: Sage.

Glass, G. M., & Smith, M. L. (1978). *Meta-analysis of research on the relationship of class size and achievement.* San Francisco: Far West Laboratory for Educational Research and Development.

Good, T., McCaslin, M., & Reys, B. (1992). Investigating work groups to promote problem solving in mathematics. In J. E. Brophy (Ed.), *Advances in research on teaching, Vol. 3,* (pp. 115–60). Greenwich, CT: JAI Press.

Hall, D., Prevatte, C., & Cunningham, P. (1995). Eliminating ability grouping and reducing failure in the primary grades. In R. Allington & S. Walmsley (Eds.), *No quick fix* (pp. 1–15). Newark, DE: International Reading Association.

Hanushek, E. A. (1989, May). The impact of differential expenditures on school performance. *Educational Research,* 45–51.

Hiebert, E. (1983, Winter). An examination of ability grouping in reading instruction. *Reading Research Quarterly,* 231–255.

Hughes, C., Rung, L., Wehmeyer, M., Agran, M., Copeland, S., & Hwang, B. (2000, Fall). Self-prompted communication book to increase social interaction among high school students. *Journal of the Association for Persons with Severe Handicaps,* 153–166.

Johnson, D. W. (1993). *Reading out: Interpersonal effectiveness and self-actualization* (5th ed.). Boston: Allyn and Bacon.

Johnson, D. W., & Johnson, F. P. (1999). *Joining together: Group therapy and group skills* (7th ed.). Boston: Allyn and Bacon.

Johnson, D. W., & Johnson, R. T. (1989, April). Toward a cooperative effort: A response to Slavin. *Educational Leadership,* 80–81.

Johnson, D. W., & Johnson, R. T. (1999). *Learning together and alone* (5th ed.). Boston: Allyn and Bacon.

Jones, C. (2001, Fall). The relationship between writing centers and improvement in writing ability: An assessment of the literature. *Education,* 3–20.

Jorgensen, K. (2001). *The whole story: Crafting fiction in the upper grades.* Portsmouth, NH: Heinemann.

Kepron, J. (1998, Winter). Reading recovery: Response from the field. *McGill Journal of Education,* 85–99.

Kinnucan-Welsch, K., Magill, D., & Dean, M. (1999, September/October). Strategic teaching and strategic learning in first-grade classrooms. *Reading Horizons,* 3–21.

Kong, A., & Fitch, E. (2002–2003, December/January). Using book club to engage culturally and linguistically diverse learners in reading, writing, and talking about books. *The Reading Teacher,* 353–362.

Kozioff, M., LaNunziata, L., Cowardin, J., & Besselieu, F. (2000–2001, December/January). Direct instruction: Its contributions to high school achievement. *High School Journal,* 54–71.

Lenski, S. D., & Nierstheimer, S. L. (2004). *Becoming a teacher of reading: A developmental approach.* Upper Saddle River, N.J.: Pearson.

Leu, D., Jr., & Kinzer, C. (1999). *Effective literacy instruction K–8* (4th ed.). Upper Saddle River, NJ: Merrill.

Levine, D. (1991, January). Creating effective schools. *Phi Delta Kappan,* 394–397.

Levine, D. U. (1987, March). Achievement gains in self-contained chapter I classes in Kansas City. *Educational Leadership,* 22–23.

Levine, D. U., & Ornstein, A. (1993, June). Reforms that can work. *American School Board Journal,* 31–34.

Madden, N. A., & Slavin, R. (1989). Effective pull-out programs for students at risk. In R. E. Slavin, N. L. Karweit, & N. A. Madden (Eds.), *Effective programs for students at risk* (pp. 16–32). Boston: Allyn and Bacon.

Mason, D., & Good, T. (1993, September). Effects of two-group and whole-class teaching on re-grouped elementary students' mathematics achievement. *American Educational Research Journal,* 328–60.

May, F. (1998). *Reading as communication: To help children write and read* (5th ed.). Upper Saddle River, NJ: Merrill.

McKenna, M. C., & Robinson, R. D. (2002). *Teaching through text: Reading and writing in the content areas* (3rd ed.). Boston: Allyn and Bacon.

McManus, S., & Gettinger, M. (1996, September/October). Teacher and student evaluations of cooperative learning and observed interactive behaviors. *Journal of Educational Research,* 13–25.

Meloth, M. S., & Deering, P. D. (1994, Spring). Task talk and task awareness under different cooperative learning conditions. *American Educational Research Journal,* 139.

Miel, A. (1958). *Practical suggestions for teaching.* New York: Teachers College Press.

Mueller, D. J., Chase, C. I., & Walden, J. D. (1988, February). Effects of reduced class size in primary classes. *Educational Leadership,* 48–50.

Nye, B. (1992, May). Smaller classes really are better. *American School Board Journal,* 31–33.

Nye, B. A. (1991). *The lasting benefit study: A continuing analysis of the effect of small class size in kindergarten through third grade.* Nashville: Tennessee State University.

Oakes, J. (1992, May). Can tracking research inform practice? *Educational Researcher,* 12–21.

Parker, D. (1954). *Individualized reading.* Chicago: Science Research Association.

Pearson, P. D., & Fielding, L. (1991). Comprehension instruction. In R. Barr, M. Kamil, P. Mosenthal, & P. D. Pearson (Eds.), *Handbook of reading research, Vol. II* (pp. 815–860). New York: Longman.

Petersen, R., & Eeds, M. (1990). *Grand conversation: Literature groups in action.* New York. Scholastic.

Piazza, C. (2003). *Journeys: The teaching of writing in elementary classrooms.* Upper Saddle River, NJ: Merrill/Prentice Hall.

Pinnell, G. S. (1994). Reading recovery. In A. C. Purves (Ed.), *Encyclopedia of English studies and language arts.* (pp. 1012–1014). New York: Scholastic/Urbana, IL: National Council of Teachers of English.

Pinnell, G. S., Lyons, C., & Jones, N. (1996, October). Response to Hiebert: What difference does reading recovery make? *Educational Researcher, 25,* 23–25.

Pool, C. (2002, February). Class size, school size. *Educational Leadership,* 104.

Posner, G. J. (1994). *Analyzing the curriculum* (2nd ed.). New York: McGraw-Hill.

Rasinski, T., & Padak, N. (2000). *Effective reading strategies: Teaching children who find reading difficult* (2nd ed.). Upper Saddle River, NJ: Merrill.

Reutzel, D. R. (1999, October). On Welna's sacred cows: Where's the beef? *The Reading Teacher,* 96–99.

Reutzel, D. R., & Cooter, R., Jr. (1996). *Teaching children to read from basal to books* (2nd ed.). Englewood Cliffs, NJ: Prentice Hall.

Ross, E. (1996). *The workshop approach: A framework for literacy.* Norwood, MA: Christopher-Gordon.

Routman, R. (2000). *Conversations: Strategies for teaching, learning, and evaluating.* Portsmouth, NH: Heinemann.

Schneider, E. (2000, September). Shifting into high gear. *Educational Leadership,* 57–60.

Schniedewind, N., & Davidson, E. (2000, September). Differentiating cooperative learning. *Educational Leadership,* 24–27.

Schumm, J. S., Moody, S., & Vaughn, S. (2000, September/October). Grouping for reading instruction: Does one size fit all? *Journal of Learning Disabilities,* 477–488.

Scott, J., & Butler, C. (1994). Grouping, tracking, and streaming for instruction. In A. C. Purves (Ed.), *Encyclopedia of english studies and language arts.* (pp. 549–552). New York:

Scholastic/Urbana, IL: National Council of Teachers of English.

Shanahan, T., & Barr, R. (1995, October/December). Reading recovery: An independent evaluation of the effects of an early instructional intervention for at-risk learners. *Reading Research Quarterly,* 958–996.

Slavin, R. E. (1978, August). Student teams and comparison among equals: Effects on academic performance and student attitudes. *Journal of Educational Psychology,* 532–538.

Slavin, R. E. (1987, Summer). Mastery learning reconsidered. *Review of Educational Research,* 175–214.

Slavin, R. E. (1989, Winter). Class size and student achievement: Small effects of small classes. *Educational Psychologist,* 99–110.

Slavin, R. E. (1991, April). Chapter 1: A vision for the next quarter century. *Phi Delta Kappan,* 586–89.

Slavin, R. E. (1994). *Cooperative learning: Theory, research, and practice* (2nd ed.). Boston: Allyn and Bacon.

Slavin, R. E., Karweit, N. L., & Wasik, B. A. (1993, December/January). Preventing early school failure: What works? *Educational Leadership,* 10–17.

Slavin, R. E., & Madden, N. A. (1989, September). What works for students at risk. *Educational Leadership,* 4–13.

Spiegel, D. L. (1995, October). Reading recovery: An independent evaluation of the effects of an early instructional intervention for at-risk learners. *The Reading Teacher, 49,* 86–96.

Strickland, D. (1998, March). What's basic in beginning reading? Finding common ground. *Educational Leadership,* 6–10.

Stright, A. D., & Supplee, L. (2002, March/April). Children's self-regulatory behaviors during teacher-directed, seatwork, and small-group instructional contexts. *Journal of Educational Research,* 235–245.

Taberski, S. (2001, September). A space that works. *Instructor,* 40–41.

Thorkildsen, T. A. (1993, March). Those who can, tutor. *Journal of Educational Psychology,* 82–190.

Tiedt, I. M. (1994). Individualization of instruction. In A. C. Purves (Ed.), *Encyclopedia of English studies and language arts* (pp. 618–621). New York: Scholastic/Urbana, IL: National Council of Teachers of English.

Vacca, R., & Vacca, J. (2002). *Content area reading: Literacy and learning across the curriculum* (7th ed.). Boston: Allyn and Bacon.

Veatch, J. (Ed.). (1959). *Individualizing your reading program.* New York: Putnam.

Veatch, J. (1994). Individualized reading. In A. C. Purves (Ed.), *Encyclopedia of English studies and language arts* (pp. 621–622). NY: Scholastic/Urbana, IL: National Council of Teachers of English.

Villaume, S. K., & Brabham, E. G. (2001, February). Conversations among writers in authors circles. *The Reading Teacher,* 494–496.

Watson, C. (1998, Spring). Instructional ideas for teaching in block schedules. *Kappa Delta Pi Record,* 94–98.

Webb, N., Farivar, S., & Mastergeorge, A. (2002, Winter). Productive helping in cooperative groups. *Theory into Practice,* 13–20.

Webb, N. M. (1985, Winter). Verbal interaction and learning in peer-directed groups. *Theory into Teaching,* 32–39.

Wiggins, R. (1994, March). Large group lesson/small group follow-up: Flexible grouping in a basal reading program. *The Reading Teacher,* 450–460.

Winship, M. (1994a). Reading workshop. In A. C. Purves ( Ed.), *Encyclopedia of English studies and language arts* (p. 1017). New York: Scholastic/Urbana, IL: National Council of Teachers of English.

Winship, M. (1994b). Writing workshop. In A. C. Purves (Ed.), *Encyclopedia of English studies and language arts* (pp. 1317–1318). New York: Scholastic/Urbana, IL: National Council of Teachers of English.

Yates, S., Nagel, S., & Libutti, D. (1997, February/March). How do we know Johnny can read? *Thrust for Educational Leadership,* 22–24.

# Improving Teaching

In this chapter, we briefly examine whether teaching is an art or a science; this is an issue that has gained attention among teacher educators in the last twenty or twenty-five years. (Most of the research on teaching, until recently, has emphasized the scientific component of teaching, although we also emphasize the artistic component.) Next, we present an overview of the research on effective teaching and five components of teaching that can be analyzed: teacher styles, teacher interactions, teacher characteristics, teacher effects, and teacher contexts.

In the early stages of research, up to the mid-1970s, the theorists were concerned with *teacher processes*—that is, what the teacher was doing while teaching. They attempted to define and explain good teaching by focusing on teacher styles, teacher interactions, and teacher characteristics. From about 1975 to 1990, researchers shifted their attention to *teacher products*—that is, student outcomes—and the assessment focused on teacher effects and teacher productivity. As we move further into the twenty-first century, theorists are attempting to analyze teacher culture, language, and thoughts; combine (rather than separate) teaching and learning processes; and use qualitative methods to assess what they call *teacher contexts*. We end with a discussion on humanistic teaching from an advocate of reconceptualizing the nature of teaching.

## ■ THE SCIENCE VERSUS THE ART OF TEACHING

Those involved in the preparation of teachers cannot agree on whether teaching is a science or an art. Some readers may say this is a hopeless dichotomy, similar to that of theory versus practice, because the real world rarely consists of neat packages and either/or situations. Gage (1978) uses this distinction between **teaching as a science** and **teaching as an art** to describe the elements of predictability in teaching and what constitutes "good" teaching. A science of teaching is a valid position, he contends, because it "implies that good teaching will some day be attainable by closely following vigorous laws that yield high predictability and control." Teaching is more than a science, he observes, because it also involves "artistic judgment about the best ways to teach." When teaching leaves the laboratory or textbook and goes face to face with students, "the opportunity for artistry expands enormously"(pp. 15, 17). No science can prescribe successfully all the twists and turns as teaching unfolds or as teachers respond with judgment, insight, or sensitivity to promote learning. These are expressions of art that depart from the rules and principles of science.

Is such a limited scientific basis of teaching even worth considering? Yes, but the practitioner must learn as a teacher to draw not only from his or her professional knowledge (which is grounded in scientific principles) but also from a set of personal experiences and resources (sometimes called craft knowledge) that are uniquely defined and exhibited by the teacher's own personality and gut reaction to classroom events that unfold (which form the basis of the art of teaching). For Philip Jackson (1990), the hunches, judgments, and insights of the teacher, as he or she responds spontaneously to events in the classroom, are as important as, and perhaps even more important than, the science of teaching. The routine activities of the classroom, the social patterns and dynamics among students, and the accommodations and compromises between students and teachers are much more important than any theory about teaching because it is the everyday routines and relationships that determine the process and outcomes of teaching (see Box 10.1).

To some extent, the act of teaching must be considered intuitive and interactive, not prescriptive or predictable. According to Elliot Eisner (1993), teaching is based primarily on feelings and artistry, not scientific rules. In an age of science and technology, there is a special need to consider teaching as an art and craft. Eisner condemns the scientific movement in psychology, especially behaviorism, and the scientific movement in education, especially school management, as reducing the teaching act to trivial specifications. He regards teaching as a "poetic metaphor," more suited to satisfying the soul than informing the head, more concerned with the whole process than with a set of discrete skills or stimuli. Our role as teachers, he claims, should not be that of a "puppeteer," an "engineer," or a manager; rather, it is "to orchestrate the dialogue [as the conductor of a symphony] moving from one side of the room to the other"(p. 8; see also Eisner, 1998). The idea is to perceive patterns in motion, to improvise within the classroom, and to avoid mechanical or prescribed rules. Teachers need to act human, to display feelings, to affirm and value their students. A good teacher is able to smile, clap, and laugh with students, even if it means sometimes deemphasizing facts, principles, and propositions.

Louis Rubin (1985) has a similar view of teaching—that effectiveness and artistry go hand in hand. The interplay of students and teacher is crucial and cannot be predetermined with carefully devised strategies. Confronted with everyday problems that cannot be easily predicted, the teacher must rely on intuition and on "insight acquired through long experience"(p. 61). Rubin uses such terms as "with-it-ness," "instructional judgments," "quick cognitive leaps," and "informal guesses" to explain the difference between the effective teacher and the ineffective teacher. Recognizing the limits to rationality, he claims that for the artistic teacher a "feel for what is right often is more productive than prolonged analysis." In the final analysis, Rubin compares the teacher's pedagogy with the "artist's colors, poet's words, sculptor's clay, and musicians notes"(pp. 60, 69), in all of which a certain amount of artistic judgment is needed to get the right mix, medium, or blend.

## BOX 10.1  On Observing Teachers

The observation of teacher behavior is costly and time consuming because it takes a significant amount of time (depending on the observer's purpose and expertise) to obtain a true sense of what is happening in the classroom. The high number of interpersonal interchanges between the teacher and students limits the person who is attempting to describe the context of the teacher's behavior. Moreover, the observations often do not coincide with the rhythm, pace, or verbal messages of the teacher–student exchanges. The observer is limited by human overload, without guarantee that the perceptions of these swift and complex interchanges are accurate. Does a five-minute, ten-minute, or even thirty-minute observation of a teacher on one, two, or three occasions translate into reality? Does the observation instrument—checking or circling on a list some indicators, behaviors, or coded sentences or interactions—coincide with what is really occurring in the classroom? Often the observer, or the observation instrument being used to code the behaviors, does not capture the full flavor of the teacher's and students' behaviors, the interaction effects, or the classroom climate.

Other researchers are more extreme in their analysis of teaching solely as an art, providing romantic accounts and tales of successful teaching and teaching strategies described in language that could hardly be taken for social science research. They consider the act of teaching akin to drama, an aesthetic and kinesthetic endeavor, and feel that those who wish to teach should audition in a teaching studio and be trained as performing artists. Good teaching is likened to good theater and a good teacher is likened to a good actor (Cohen, 1999; Fried, 1995, 2001). Good teaching is also considered a lifelong love and a journey that guides teachers to give their heart to it and help their audience acquire a lifelong love of learning (Barth, 2001; Palmer, 2003).

Seymour Sarason (1999) describes the teacher as a *performing artist*. Like an actor, conductor, or artist, the teacher attempts to *instruct* and *move* the audience. More significant, this author maintains that the actor, artist, or teacher attempts to *transform* the audience in terms of thinking and instilling new ideas (1999). By transforming the audience, we alter the peoples' outlook toward objects or ideas; we encourage them to think—and to ask "Why?" and "What if?" Revolutionary thought, in fact, is built on poetry, music, art, movies, and speeches. And ultimately, it is aesthetics, ideas, and values (the art, music, food, customs, laws, and thoughts) that define who we are. Hence, it is the teacher in the broadest sense, including actors, artists, poets, writers, and, of course, parents who make us think and who make a difference in society.

Given the metaphor of the performing artist, a certain amount of talent or innate ability is needed to be effective, along with sufficient rehearsal and caring behavior. But knowledge or understanding of the audience is also needed. The film *Mr. Holland's Opus* makes the point. The teacher is unsuccessful in the beginning of the movie, despite his knowledge of music, his compassion, and his desire to give the students his "all." In the second half of the movie, however, through some "magic" awakening, he redefines his methods (science of teaching) and acting (art of teaching), with the result that the audience (students) becomes interested and learns to appreciate good music. Mr. Holland originally believes the problem is in the minds of his students. Not until he realizes it is the other way around is he successful (Ornstein & Lasley, 2004; Sarason, 1999).

In *The King and I,* the British teacher is successful from the outset of the movie despite cultural differences and gender inequalities of Siam society. Not only is she caring and compassionate, but she also understands her students. She is able to adapt to their needs, interests, and abilities—and affirm their individuality. The song "Getting to Know You" helps us understand the point—that is, the teacher's ability to connect with her students.

Both movies underscore the need for teachers to understand students and that good teaching is about making *connections* with the audience: Either through previous learning (pedagogical knowledge) or practical experience (craft knowledge), the teacher must know how students think and feel. A certain amount of training helps teachers develop this understanding, but training is only a starting point. A successful teacher first understands and accepts himself or herself and then understands and accepts others. Arthur Jersild (1955) summed it up some fifty years ago: "self-understanding requires something quite different from the methods . . . and skills of know-how . . . emphasized in education [courses]." Planning pedogogical methods and techniques is helpful, what we call scientific principles, but what is also needed "is a more personal kind of searching which will enable the teacher to identify his own concerns and to share the concerns of his students."(p. 3). Almost fifty years later, another educator pointed to the need for teachers to first be able "to maintain their own health and energy levels," to know themselves, so they will have the ability to take care of and be concerned with their students. (Houghton, 2001). Thus, teaching is not just an academic or cognitive enterprise; it involves people and an affective (feelings, attitudes, emotions, and energy) or artistic component that has little to do with pedagogical or scientific knowledge. It also involves being true to yourself, knowing your own weaknesses and strengths, having the ability to look honestly in the mirror, and knowing what is important to yourself and your students—and making appropriate adjustments.

The more we consider teaching as an art, packed with emotions, feelings, and excitement, the more difficult it is to derive from it rules or generalizations. If teaching is more an art than a science, then principles and practices cannot be easily codified or developed in the classroom or easily learned by others. Hence, there is little reason to offer instructional methods courses in education. If, however, teaching is more of a science, or at least partly a science, then pedagogy is predictable to that extent; it can be observed and measured with some accuracy, and educational theory and research can be applied to the practice of teaching (as a physician applies scientific knowledge to the practice of medicine) and also learned in a college classroom or on the job. See Tips for Teachers 10.1.

But a word of caution is needed. The more we rely on artistic interpretations or on old stories and accounts about teachers, the more we fall victim to fantasy, wit, and romantic rhetoric, and the more we depend on hearsay and conjecture rather than on social science or objective data in evaluating teacher competency. On the other hand, the more we rely on the scientific interpretations of teaching, the more we overlook those commonsense and spontaneous processes of teaching and the sounds, smells, and visual flavor of the classroom. The more scientific we are in our approach to teaching, the more we ignore what we cannot accommodate to our empirical assumptions or principles. What sometimes occurs, according to Eisner, is that the educationally significant but difficult to measure or observe is replaced by what is insignificant but comparatively easy to measure or observe (Eisner, 1997).

It is necessary to blend artistic impressions and relevant stories about teaching, because good teaching involves emotions and feelings, with the objectivity of observations and measurements and the precision of language. There is nothing wrong with considering good teaching to be an art, but we must also consider that it lends itself to a prescriptive science or practice. If it does not, then there is little assurance that prospective teachers can be trained to be teachers—told what to do, how to instruct students, how to manage students, and so forth—and educators will be extremely vulnerable to public criticism and to people outside the profession telling them how and what to teach.

True knowledge of teaching is achieved by practice and experience in the classroom. According to some observers, the beliefs, values, and norms—that is, the knowledge teachers come to have the most faith in and use most frequently to guide their teaching—are those consistent with traditions that have "worked" in the classroom. Although it seems to be more everyday and commonsensical than highly specialized and

## Observing Other Teachers to Improve Teaching Practices

Beginning teachers (even student teachers) can supplement their pedagogical knowledge and practice by observing experienced teachers organize their classrooms and instruct students. Following is a list of questions that beginning teachers (as well as student teachers) can consider when observing other teachers.

### Student–Teacher Interaction

- What evidence was there that the teacher understood the needs of the students?
- What techniques were used to encourage students' respect for one another's turn to talk?
- What student behaviors in class were acceptable and which were unacceptable?
- How did the teacher motivate students?
- How did the teacher encourage student discussion?
- In what way did the teacher see things from students' points of view?
- What evidence was there that the teacher responded to students' affective development?

### Teacher–Learning Processes

- Which instructional methods interested the students?
- How did the teacher provide for transitions between instructional activities?

- What practical life experiences (or activities) did the teacher use to integrate concepts being learned?
- How did the teacher minimize student frustration or confusion concerning the skills or concepts being taught?
- In what ways did the teacher encourage creative, imaginative work from students?
- What instructional methods were used to make students think about skills, ideas, or answers?
- How did the teacher arrange the classroom group? What social factors were evident within groups?
- How did the teacher integrate the subject matter with other subjects?

### Classroom Environment

- How did the teacher use classroom space and equipment effectively?
- What did you like and dislike about the physical environment of the classroom?

*Source:* Adapted from Allan C. Ornstein, "Analyzing and Improving Teaching," in H. C. Waxman and H. J. Walberg, eds., *New Directions for Teaching Practice and Research* (Berkeley, CA: McCutchan, 1999), p. 23.

theoretical, the process still includes the receiving and using of data that can be partially planned and scientifically analyzed (Bolster, 1983; Kohn, 1998; Lehrer & Schauble, 2002). But we assume there are still professional and technical skills that can be taught to teachers and that can be designed and developed in advance with underlying scientific principles and research-based data. Some of us would refer to this as "pedagogical knowledge" or "craft knowledge" as opposed to subject-matter or content-based knowledge.

Indeed, the real value of scientific procedures may not be realized in terms of research or theoretical generalizations that can be translated into practice. Research and pedagogical knowledge may have limited potential for teachers, but it can help them become aware of the problems and needs of students. Scientific generalizations and theories may not always be applicable to specific teaching situations, but such propositions can help in the formulation of a reliable and valid base for teaching in classrooms. Scientific ideas can serve as a starting point for discussion and analysis of the art of teaching. The science of psychology can also help us define who we are and understand the teacher within ourselves.

# ■ REVIEW OF THE RESEARCH ON TEACHING

Over the years, thousands of studies have been conducted to identify the behaviors of successful teachers and of unsuccessful teachers. However, teaching is a complex act; what works in some situations with some students may not work in different school settings with different subjects, students, and goals. There will always be teachers who break many of the rules, procedures, and methods and yet are profoundly successful. Likewise, there will always be teachers who enroll in a host of education courses, follow all the rules, and still are unsuccessful.

Biddle and Ellena (1964) maintain that we cannot distinguish between "good" and "poor" or "effective" and "ineffective" teachers, that no one knows for sure or agrees on what the competent teacher is, and that few authorities can "define, prepare for, or measure teacher competence"(p. 3). They point out that disagreement over terms, problems in measurement, and the complexity of the teaching act are major reasons for the negligible findings in judging teacher behavior. As a result, many of the data have been confusing, contradictory, or confirmations of common sense (a democratic teacher is a good teacher), and so-called acceptable findings have often not been repudiated (Ornstein, 1993; Putnam & Borko, 2000; Wiggins, 1998).

The more complex or unpredictable we view teaching as being, the more we are compelled to conclude that it is difficult to agree on generalizations about successful teaching. Because we are unable to agree on or precisely define what a good teacher is, we can use almost any definition (or a list of characteristics, behaviors, or methods) so long as it makes sense, seems logical, and can be tested and validated. Other researchers assert that appropriate teaching behaviors can be defined (and learned by teachers), that good or effective teachers can be distinguished from poor or ineffective teachers, and that the magnitude of the effect of these differences on students can be observed and measured (Borich, 2003; Good & Brophy, 1997; Jacobsen, Eggen, & Kauchak, 2002). They conclude that the kinds of questions teachers ask, the way they respond to students, their expectations of and attitudes toward students, their classroom management techniques, their teaching methods, and their general teaching behaviors (sometimes referred to as "classroom climate") all make a difference.

However, in some cases the positive effects of teachers on student performance may be masked or undone by the relative negative effects of other teachers in the same school; hence, it is difficult to separate or control for the effects of other teachers in the same school, and it is more difficult to separate or control for the effects of secondary school teachers on students (because many teachers have an impact on these students) than for elementary school teachers, who generally work with one class for almost the entire day and school year. The teacher may not be the only variable, or even the major one, in the teaching–learning equation (home environment is more important), but he or she can make a difference, and this difference can be positive or negative. It should be noted that negative teacher influences have a greater impact than positive ones in that students can be turned into nonlearners and experience loss of self-esteem, composure, and academic focusing ability in a matter of weeks as a result of a hostile or intimidating teacher. Similarly, negative stimuli (loss of sleep, food, or water) can have major effects on humans in a very short period compared to positive stimuli (proper sleep, food, or water), which have positive effects over long periods of time.

If teachers do not make a difference, then the profession has problems. For example, if teachers do not make a difference, the notions of teacher evaluation, teacher accountability, and teacher performance are unworkable. Sound educational policy cannot be formulated, and there is little hope for many education students and little value in trying to learn how to teach. However, even if we are convinced that teachers have an effect, it is still true that we are unable to assess with confidence the influence of a particular teacher on student performance because the learning variables are numerous and the teaching interactions are complex, swift, and multidimensional.

# ■ TEACHER STYLES

**Teacher style** is a broad dimension or personality type that encompasses teacher stance, a pattern of behavior or performance, and an attitude toward self and others. Penelope Peterson (1979) defines teacher style as how teachers use space in the classroom, their choice of instructional activities and materials, and their method of student grouping. Still others describe teacher style as an *expressive aspect* of teaching (characterizing the emotional relationship between students and teachers, such as warm, caring, or businesslike) and as an *instrumental aspect* (how teachers carry out the task of instruction, organize learning, and set classroom standards) (Scherer, 2001; Tell, 2001).

Regardless of which definition of teacher style you prefer, the notions of stability and pattern are central. Certain behaviors and methods are stable over time, even with different students and different classroom situations. There is also a purpose or rationale—a predictable teacher pattern even in different classroom contexts. Aspects of teaching style dictated by personality can be modified by early experiences and by appropriate training as a beginning teacher. As years pass, a teacher's style becomes more ingrained, and it takes a more powerful set of stimuli and more intense feedback to make changes. To be sure, it *is* hard to "teach an old dog new tricks," and it is hard (but not impossible) to modify the behavior of a veteran teacher who is used to doing things his or her way. If you watch teachers at work, including teachers in your school, you can sense that each one has a personal style of teaching: namely, structuring the classroom, delivering the lesson, and interacting with students.

## Research on Teaching Style

Lippitt and White (1943, 1958) laid the groundwork for a more formal classification of what a teacher does in the classroom. Initially, they developed an instrument for describing the "social atmosphere" of children's clubs and for quantifying the effects of group and individual behaviors. The results have been generalized in numerous research studies and textbooks on teaching. The classic study used the classification of authoritarian, democratic, and laissez-faire styles.

The authoritarian teacher directs all the activities of the program. This style shares some characteristics with what is now called the *direct teacher*—what some researchers today consider effective behaviors with at-risk students and students who need practice, drill, and monitoring of classroom activities. The democratic teacher encourages group participation and is willing to let students share in the decision-making process. This behavior is typical of what is now called the *indirect teacher*. The laissez-faire teacher (often considered to be an unorganized or ineffective teacher) provides no (or few) goals and directions for group or individual behavior.

One of the most ambitious research studies on teacher style was conducted by Ned Flanders (1965, 1970) between 1954 and 1970. Flanders focused on developing an instrument for quantifying verbal communication in the classroom. Every three seconds, observers sorted *teacher talk* into one of four categories of indirect behavior or one of three categories of direct behavior. *Student talk*, consisting of two categories, was categorized as response or initiation, and there was a final category representing *silence* or when the observer could not determine who was talking. See Table 10.1.

Flanders's indirect teacher tended to overlap with Lippitt and White's democratic teacher, and the direct teacher tended to exhibit behaviors similar to their authoritarian teacher. Flanders found that students in the indirect classrooms learned more and exhibited more constructive and independent attitudes and that students in all types of subject classes learned more with the indirect (more flexible) teachers.

The data obtained from this system do not show when, why, or in what context teacher–student interaction occurs, only how often particular types of interaction occur. For example, low-performing students or students who lack inner control (and often have academic problems) may cause teachers to adopt direct behaviors, and high-performing students may cause teachers to adopt indirect behaviors. Although the correlation of direct teacher and low student achievement was clearly established, the cause–effect relationship was not established; that is, low-achieving students, especially those who also lack inner control, may prompt direct teacher behaviors. Nonetheless, the observation system is considered useful for making teachers aware of their interaction behaviors in the classroom—and of the fact that teachers often talk too much.

The Flanders system can be used to examine teacher–student verbal behaviors in any classroom, regardless of grade level or subject. Someone can observe the verbal behavior of a prospective, beginning, or even experienced teacher and show how direct or indirect the teacher is (Amidon & Flanders, 1971; see also McNergey & Carrier, 1991). (Most student teachers and beginning teachers tend to exhibit direct behavior because they talk too much. Professors also usually lecture and thus exhibit many direct behaviors while teaching.) In fact, education students and student teachers often associate good teaching with some form of lecturing because most of their recent teaching models are professors who often do a lot of talking—the wrong method for younger students who lack the maturity, attentiveness, and focus to cope with a passive learning situation for any length of time. Beginning teachers, therefore, must often unlearn what they have learned through their experiences with their own professors. (See Tips for Teacher 10.1.)

| *Table 10.1* Flanders's Classroom Interaction Analysis Scale |
| --- |

I. Teacher Talk

   A. Indirect Influence

      1. *Accepts Feelings.* Accepting and clarifying the tone of students' feelings in an unthreatening manner. Feelings may be positive or negative. Predicting or recalling feelings is included.

      2. *Praises or Encourages.* Praising or encouraging student action or behavior. Jokes that release tension (but not at the expense of another individual), nodding the head, or saying "um," "yes," or "go on," are included.

      3. *Accepts or Uses Ideas of Student.* Clarifying, building on, or developing ideas suggested by a student. As the teacher brings more of his own ideas into play, shift to category 5.

      4. *Asks Questions.* Asking a question about content or procedure, expressing her own ideas, asking rhetorical questions.

   B. Direct Influence

      5. *Lectures.* Giving facts or opinions about content or procedure, expressing his own ideas, asking rhetorical questions.

      6. *Gives Directions.* Giving directions, commands, or orders that students are expected to comply with.

      7. *Criticizes or Justifies Authority.* Making statements intended to change student behavior from unacceptable to acceptable patter; bawling someone out; stating why the teacher is doing what she is doing; extreme self-reference.

II. Student Talk

      8. *Student Talk-Response.* Talking by students in response to teacher; teacher initiates the contact or solicits student statement.

      9. *Student Talk-Initiation.* Talking initiated by students. If "calling on" student is only to indicate who may talk next, observer must decide whether student wanted to talk.

III. Silence

      10. *Silence or Confusion.* Pausing, short periods of silence, and periods of confusion in which communication cannot be understood by observer.

*Source:* Adapted from Ned A. Flanders, *Teacher Influence, Pupil Attitudes, and Achievement* (Washington, DC: U.S. Government Printing Office, 1965), p. 20.

# ■ TEACHER-STUDENT INTERACTION

One approach to the study of teacher behavior is based on systematic observation of **teacher–student interaction** in the classroom as, for example, in the work of Flanders, which we have already described. The analysis of interaction often deals with a specific teacher behavior and a series of these behaviors constituting a larger behavior, described and recorded by an abstract unit of measurement that may vary in size and time (for example, every three seconds a recording is made). See Box 10.2.

## Verbal Communication

In a classic study of teacher–student interaction, Arno Bellack and colleagues analyzed the linguistic behavior of teachers and students in the classroom. Most classroom ac-

**BOX 10.2** Measuring Teacher Behavior

Rating scales are probably the most common technique used for measuring teacher behavior. A large number of rating instruments have been used, ranging from high to low reliability and validity, and are usually based on policy or custom. On a typical form, the students, other teachers, supervisors or administrators, and sometimes parents or consultants are asked to rate a teacher's abilities or performance. However, different groups markedly disagree in their efforts to identify good teachers. This is not surprising in view of the fact that such judges are human and handicapped by their personal biases and beliefs of what is or should be a good teacher. Often they lack firsthand information concerning the classroom situation (unless they are students) and sufficient knowledge or understanding of teaching or of the subject field to make sound judgments.

tivities are carried out by verbal interactions between students and teachers; few classroom activities can be carried out without the use of language. The research, therefore, focused on language as the main instrument of communication in teaching (Bellack, Kliebard, Hyman, & Smith, 1966).

1. *Structuring moves* focus attention on subject matter or classroom procedures and begin interaction between students and teachers. They set the context for subsequent behavior. For example, beginning a class by announcing the topic to be discussed is a structuring move.
2. *Soliciting moves* are designed to elicit a verbal or physical response. For example, the teacher asks a question about the topic or content with the hope of encouraging a response from the students.
3. *Responding moves* occur in relation to and after the soliciting behaviors. Their ideal function is to fulfill the expectations of the soliciting behaviors. For example, students usually respond to a teacher's soliciting moves.
4. *Reacting moves* are sometimes occasioned by one or more of the preceding behaviors but are not directly elicited by them. Reacting behaviors modify, clarify, or judge the structuring, soliciting, or responding behavior.

According to Bellack, these pedagogical moves occur in combinations he called "teaching cycles." A cycle usually begins and ends with the teacher. The investigators' analysis of the classroom also produced several insights.

1. Teachers dominate verbal activities. The teacher–student ratio in words spoken is 3:1. (This evidence corresponds with Flanders's finding that teacher talk is 80 percent of classroom activity.)
2. Teacher and student moves are clearly defined. The teacher engages in structuring, soliciting, and reacting behaviors, whereas the students are usually limited to responding. (This also corresponds with Flanders's finding that most teachers dominate classrooms in a way that makes students dependent.)
3. Teachers initiate about 85 percent of the cycles (again indicating that teachers talk too much). The basic unit of verbal interaction is the soliciting–responding pattern. Verbal interchanges occur at a rate of slightly less than two cycles per minute.

4. In approximately two-thirds of the behaviors and three-fourths of the verbal interplay, talk is content-oriented.
5. About 60 percent of the total discourse is fact oriented.

In summary, the data suggest that the classroom is teacher dominated, subject centered, and fact oriented. The students' primary responsibility seems to be to respond to the teacher's soliciting behaviors. As a teacher, you need to break this cycle and encourage more student discussion and student-to-student interaction.

## Nonverbal Communication

According to one observer, **nonverbal behavior** in the classroom serves five teacher functions: (1) providing information or elaborating on a verbal statement; (2) regulating interactions, such as pointing to someone; (3) expressing intimacy or liking, such as smiling or touching a student on the shoulder; (4) exercising social control, such as reinforcing a classroom rule, by proximity or distance; and (5) facilitating goals, as when demonstrating a skill that requires motor activity or gesturing (Patterson, 1983). These categories are not mutually exclusive; there is some overlap, and nonverbal cues may serve more than one function depending on how they are used.

Although the teaching–learning process is ordinarily associated with verbal interaction, nonverbal communication operates as a silent language that influences the process. What makes the study of nonverbal communication so important and fascinating is that it comprises so much of the informal evaluation process (nods and gestures of the teacher) and the social meaning of the classroom communication system. As the old saying goes, "Actions speak louder than words."

In another study of 225 teachers (and school principals) in forty-five schools, researchers observed ten specific nonverbal behaviors: (1) smiles or frowns, (2) eye contact, (3) head nods, (4) gestures, (5) dress, (6) interaction distance, (7) touch, (8) body movement, (9) posture, and (10) seating arrangements (Stephens & Valentine, 1986). In general, the first four behaviors are easily interpreted by the observer; some smiles, eye contact, head nods, and gestures are expected, but too many make students suspicious or uneasy. Dress is a matter of professional code and expectations. Distance, touch, body movement, posture, and seating are open to interpretation, are likely to have personal meaning between communicators, and can be taken as indications of the degree of formality in the relationship between the communicators (from intimate and personal to social and public).

Teachers should maintain a social or public relationship—that is, a formal relationship—with their students. Behaviors that are inappropriate, or could be interpreted as indicating intimate and personal relations, must be avoided. It is difficult to define the point in a student–teacher relationship at which friendliness can be misconstrued. To some extent, that point differs for different students and teachers: age, gender, and culture are factors. It is fine to be warm, friendly, and caring, but too much warmth or friendliness in your interaction (distance, touch, body movement, posture) can get you in trouble as a teacher. Teachers need to be aware of the messages they are sending to students, especially if teachers are young and inexperienced.

According to Charles Galloway (1968, 1984), when the teacher's verbal and nonverbal cues contradict each other, the students tend to read the nonverbal cues as a true reflection of the teacher's feelings. Galloway developed global guidelines for observing teachers' nonverbal communication, which he referred to as the "silent behavior of space, time, and body."

1. *Space.* A teacher's use of space conveys meaning to students. For example, teachers who spend most of their time by the chalkboard or at their desk may convey insecurity or a reluctance to venture into student territory.
2. *Time.* How teachers use classroom time is an indication of how they value certain instructional activities. The elementary teacher who devotes a great deal of time to reading but little to mathematics is conveying a message to the students and parents.
3. *Body Maneuvers.* Teachers use nonverbal cues to control students. The raised eyebrow, the pointed finger, the silent stare all communicate meaning.

Galloway suggests that various teacher behaviors can be viewed as encouraging or restricting. By their facial expressions, gestures, and body movements, teachers affect student participation and performance in the classroom. Whether or not you realize it, these nonverbal behaviors—ranging from highly focused to minimal eye contact, a pat on the back to a frown, a supporting to an angry look—all add up and suggest approval and support or irritability and discouragement. In sum, these nonverbal behaviors influence teacher–student interactions. What teachers should do, in both their personal and professional pursuits, is be aware of how their mannerisms influence their communication and relations with others.

# ■ TEACHER CHARACTERISTICS

Of the reams of research published on teacher behavior, the greatest amount concerns **teacher characteristics.** The problem is that researchers disagree on which teacher characteristics constitute successful teaching, on how to categorize characteristics, and on how to define them. In addition, researchers use a variety of terms to name what they are trying to describe, such as teacher traits, teacher personality, teacher performance, or teacher outcomes. Descriptors or characteristics have different meanings to different people. "Warm" behavior for one investigator often means something different for another, just as the effects of such behavior may be seen differently. For example, it can be assumed that a warm teacher would have a different effect on students depending on age, sex, achievement level, socioeconomic class, ethnic group, subject, and classroom context (Ornstein, 1985, 1990; Sawyer, 2001).

Such differences tend to operate for every teacher characteristic and to affect studies on teacher behavior. Although a list of teacher characteristics may be suitable for a particular study, the characteristics (as well as the results) cannot always be compared with those in another study. The problem is that a theory of successful or effective teacher characteristics (or methods) is built from studies that are often misleading because of different definitions and contexts.

As Lee Shulman (1986, 1991) points out, teacher behavior researchers often disregard factors such as the time of day, school year, and content, and combine data from an early observation with data from a later occasion. Data from the early part of the term may be combined with data from the latter part of the term; data from one unit of content (which may require different teacher behaviors or techniques) are combined with those from other units of content. All these aggregations assume that instances of teaching over time can be added up to make meaningful sums of information, which is rarely the case. The accuracy issue is further clouded when such studies are compared, integrated, and built on one another to form a theory or viewpoint about which teacher characteristics (or methods) are most effective.

Despite such cautions, many researchers feel that certain teacher characteristics can be defined, validated, and generalized from one study to another. In turn, recommendations can be made from such generalizations for use in a practical way in the classroom and elsewhere; if this is not the case, then we have folk theory posing as scientific objectivity. If, however, we are unable to generalize among teacher behaviors, then the uncertainty of the classroom becomes so great that it is nearly impossible to plan or predict how a lesson will proceed, how long it will take, and whether concrete strategies and methods can be made relevant to teachers.

## Research on Teacher Characteristics

Although researchers have named literally hundreds of teacher characteristics over the years, A. S. Barr (1959) (the most influential researcher on teacher behavior from the 1930s to 1950s) organized recommended behaviors into a manageable list. Reviewing some fifty years of research, he listed and defined twelve successful characteristics, including resourcefulness, emotional stability, considerateness, objectivity, and drive or energy. Other authorities have made other summaries of teacher characteristics, but Barr's work is considered the most comprehensive of the first half of the twentieth century.

While Barr presented an overview of hundreds of studies of teacher characteristics, the single most comprehensive study was conducted by David Ryans (1960). More than 6,000 teachers in 1,700 schools were involved in the study over a six-year period. The objective was to identify through observations and self-ratings the most desirable teacher characteristics. Ryans developed a *bipolar* list of eighteen teacher characteristics (for example, original versus conventional, patient versus impatient, hostile versus warm). Respondents were asked to identify the approximate position of successful teachers for each pair of characteristics on a seven-point scale. (A seven-point scale makes it easier for raters to avoid midpoint responses and neutral positions.)

The eighteen teacher characteristics were defined in detail and further grouped in three "patterns" of successful versus unsuccessful teachers:

1. **Pattern X:** understanding, friendly, and responsive versus aloof and egocentric.
2. **Pattern Y:** responsible, businesslike, and systematic versus evading, unplanned, and slipshod.
3. **Pattern Z:** stimulating, imaginative, and original versus dull and routine.

These three primary teacher patterns (similar to what we have previously termed *teacher style*) were the major qualities singled out for further attention. Elementary teachers scored higher than secondary teachers on the scales of understanding and friendly classroom behavior (Pattern X). Differences between female and male teachers were insignificant in the elementary schools, but in the secondary schools women consistently scored higher in Pattern X and stimulating and imaginative classroom behaviors (Pattern Z), and men tended to exhibit businesslike and systematic behaviors (Pattern Y). Younger teachers (under age forty-five) scored higher than older teachers in Patterns X and Z; older teachers scored higher in Pattern Y.

A similar but more recent list of teacher characteristics was compiled by Bruce Tuckman (1986, 1995), who has developed a feedback system for stimulating change in teacher behavior. His instrument originally contained twenty-eight bipolar items and was extended to thirty items (for example, creative versus routinized; cautious versus outspoken; assertive versus passive; quiet versus bubbly) on which teachers were also rated on a seven-point scale.

# ■ TEACHER EFFECTS

Teacher behavior research has shown that teacher behaviors, as well as specific teaching principles and methods—all of which influence **teacher effects** on students—make a difference with regard to student achievement. Rosenshine and Furst analyzed some forty-two correlation studies in their often-quoted review of process–product research. They concluded that there are eleven teacher *processes* (behaviors or variables) strongly and consistently related to *products* (outcomes or student achievement). The first five teacher processes show the strongest correlation to positive outcomes:

1. *Clarity* of teacher's presentation and ability to organize classroom activities.
2. *Variability* of media, materials, and activities used by the teacher.
3. *Enthusiasm,* defined in terms of the teacher's movement, voice inflection, and the like.
4. *Task orientation,* or businesslike teacher behaviors, structured routines, and an academic focus.
5. *Student opportunity to learn,* that is, the teacher's coverage of the material or content in class on which students are later tested (Rosenshine & Furst, 1971, 1973).

The six remaining processes were classified as promising: use of student ideas, justified criticism, use of structuring comments, appropriate questions in terms of lower and higher cognitive level, probing or encouraging student elaboration, and challenging instructional material.

Rosenshine (1979) himself later reviewed his conclusions; his subsequent analysis showed that only two behaviors or processes consistently correlated with student achievement: task orientation (later referred to as direct instruction) and opportunity to learn (later referred to as academic time, academic engaged time, or content covered). On a third behavior, clarity, he wavered, pointing out that it seemed to be a correlate of achievement for students above the fifth grade. The other eight processes appeared to be less important and varied in importance not only according to grade level but also according to subject matter, instructional groups and activities, and students' social class and abilities. Nevertheless, the original review remains a valuable study on how teacher processes relate to student products.

## The Gage Model

Nate Gage (1978) analyzed forty-nine process–product studies. He identified four clusters of behaviors that show a strong relationship to student outcomes: (1) *teacher indirectness,* the willingness to accept student ideas and feelings and the ability to provide a healthy emotional climate; (2) *teacher praise,* support, and encouragement; use of humor to release tension (but not at the expense of others); and attention to students' needs; (3) *teacher acceptance,* clarifying, building, and developing students' ideas; and (4) *teacher criticism,* reprimanding students and justifying authority. The relationship between the last cluster and outcome was negative—where criticism occurred, student achievement was low (Gage, 1978). In effect, the four clusters suggest the benefit of the traditional notion of a democratic or warm teacher—a model emphasized for several decades.

From the evidence on teacher effects on student achievement in reading and mathematics in the elementary grades, Gage presented successful teaching principles and methods that seem relevant for other grades as well. These strategies are summarized below. Bear in mind that they are commonsense strategies. They apply to many grade levels, and most experienced teachers are familiar with them. Nonetheless, they provide guidelines for education students or beginning teachers who say, "Just tell me how to teach."

1. Teachers should have a system of rules that allows students to attend to their personal and procedural needs without having to check with the teacher.
2. A teacher should move around the room, monitoring students' seatwork and communicating an awareness of their behavior while also attending to their academic needs.
3. To ensure productive independent work by students, teachers should be sure that the assignments are interesting and worthwhile yet still easy enough to be completed by each student without teacher direction.
4. Teachers should keep to a minimum such activities as giving directions and organizing the class for instruction. Teachers can do this by writing the daily schedule on the board and establishing general procedures so students know where to go and what to do.
5. In selecting students to respond to questions, teachers should call on volunteers and nonvolunteers by name before asking questions to give all students a chance to answer and to alert the students being called on.
6. Teachers should always aim at getting less academically oriented students to give some kind of response to a question. Rephrasing, giving cues, or asking leading questions can be useful techniques for eliciting some answer from a silent student, one who says, "I don't know," or one who answers incorrectly.
7. During reading group instruction, teachers should give a maximum amount of brief feedback and provide fast-paced activities of the drill type (Gage, 1978).

## The Good and Brophy Model

Over the last twenty-five years, Good and Brophy (1986, 2003) have identified several factors related to effective teaching and student learning. They focus on basic principles of teaching but not on teacher behaviors or characteristics, because both researchers contend that teachers today are looking more for principles of teaching than for prescriptions.

1. *Clarity* about instructional goals (objectives).
2. Knowledge about *content* and ways of teaching it.
3. *Variety* in the use of teaching methods and media.
4. *"With-it-ness,"* or awareness of what is going on, alertness in monitoring classroom activities.
5. *Overlapping,* or sustaining an activity while doing something else at the same time.
6. *Smoothness,* or sustaining proper lesson pacing and group momentum, not dwelling on minor points or wasting time dealing with individuals, and focusing on all the students.
7. *Seatwork* instructions and management that initiate and focus on productive task engagement.
8. Holding students *accountable* for learning; accepting responsibility for student learning.
9. *Realistic expectations* in line with student abilities and behaviors.
10. *Realistic praise,* not praise for its own sake.
11. *Flexibility* in planning and adapting classroom activities.
12. *Task orientation* and businesslike behavior from the teacher.
13. *Monitoring* of students' understanding: providing appropriate feedback, giving praise, asking questions.
14. Providing student *opportunity* to learn what is to be tested.
15. Making comments that help *structure learning* of knowledge and concepts for students; helping students learn how to learn.

The fact that many of these behaviors are classroom management techniques and structured learning strategies suggests that good discipline is a prerequisite for good teaching. Although most of Good and Brophy's research was at the elementary school level and with low-achieving students, the argument has been made that their principles are generic—geared for teachers of all grade levels and students.

## The Master Teacher

The national interest in education reform and excellence in teaching has focused considerable attention on teachers and the notion of the **master teacher.** The direct behaviors suggested by Rosenshine and by the Good and Brophy models correspond with Walter Doyle's (1985) task-oriented and businesslike description of a master teacher. Such teachers

> focus on academic goals, are careful and explicit in structuring activities, . . . promote high levels of student academic involvement and content coverage, furnish opportunities for controlled practice with feedback, hold students accountable for work, . . . have expectations that they will be successful in helping students learn, [and are] active in explaining concepts and procedures, promoting meaning and purpose for academic work, and monitoring comprehension (p. 30; see also Doyle, 1992).

When 641 elementary teachers were asked to "rate criteria for recognition of the master teacher," they listed in rank order (1) has knowledge of subject matter, (2) encourages student achievement through positive reinforcement, (3) uses a variety of strategies and materials to meet the needs of all students, (4) maintains an organized and disciplined classroom, (5) stimulates students' active participation in classroom activities, (6) maximizes student instruction time, (7) has high expectations of student performance, and (8) frequently monitors student progress and provides feedback regarding performance (Azumi & Lerman, 1987).

Although the sample of teachers was predominantly female (71 percent), so that it can be argued that the recommended behaviors reflect female norms, it must be noted that the teaching profession is predominantly female (67 percent, according to NEA survey data). Most important, the teachers surveyed were experienced (77 percent had been teaching for at least eleven years) and the rank order list of criteria corresponds closely to Doyle's notion of a master teacher.

Based on a study of several hundred teachers who teach in multiracial and multilingual schools, Martin Haberman's (1992, 1995) portrait of what he termed *star* urban teachers revealed a host of behaviors and attitudes that describe what many educators say makes a master or effective teacher (1992, 1995). **Star teachers** develop an ideology—that is, a pervasive way of believing and acting. These teachers do not use theory to guide their practice; they do not necessarily refer to the theories or principles of Piaget, Skinner, or the like. Star teachers do not consider the research on teaching effectiveness or school effectiveness. They are generally oblivious to and unconcerned with how researchers or experts in various subjects organize the content in their disciplines. Rather, they have internalized their own view of teaching, their own organization of subject matter, and their own practices through experience and self-discovery. Their behaviors and methods are not pieces of knowledge learned in university courses. "Almost everything star teachers do that they regard as important," according to Haberman and Post (1998) "is something they believe they learned on the job after they started teaching"(p. 99). Star teachers reflect on what they are doing and the best way to do it. These teachers are also guided by the belief that inner-city and poor children can learn, think, and reflect.

To the casual observer, it may seem that teachers generally perform the same way. Going beyond the data, the inference is that star teachers or master teachers are different from the average; they have a well-thought-out ideology that gives their performance a different meaning. They have their own identity, and some appear to be mavericks (or at least atypical) and confident in the way they organize and operate their classrooms. They are sensitive to their students and teach in ways that make sense to their students, not necessarily according to what researchers or administrators and colleagues have to say about teaching. These teachers seem to be driven by their own convictions about what is right and not by how others interpret the teacher's role or teacher pedagogy.

The Gallup organization's research uses the terms *outstanding, talented,* and *best* and claims that such teachers can be identified and do make a difference. Yet many school districts take an unsystematic and unorganized approach to defining, identifying, and rewarding such teachers. Gallup argues that "great teachers . . . cannot be taught, trained, or coerced. The qualities . . . are somewhat intangible and come from within the person" (Gordon, 1999, p. 304). The Gallup position suggests that good teaching is more art than science.

## Cautions and Criticisms

Although the notions of teacher competencies and effectiveness are often identified as something new in research efforts to identify good teaching, they are nothing more than a combination of teaching principles and methods that good teachers have been using for many years prior to this recent wave of research. What these product-oriented researchers have accomplished is to summarize what we have known for a long time and confirm the basic principles and methods of experienced teachers. They give credibility to teaching practice by correlating teacher behaviors or methods (processes) with student achievement (products). Product-oriented researchers also dispel the notion that teachers have little or no measurable effect on student achievement; they provide reformers with an arsenal of information on how instruction and the classroom can be altered to improve student outcomes.

However, there is some danger in this product-oriented research. The conclusions overwhelmingly portray the effective teacher as task oriented, organized, and structured (nothing more than Ryans's Pattern Y teacher and Doyle's master teacher). But many teacher competency and teacher effectiveness models tend to overlook the friendly, warm, and democratic teacher; the creative teacher who is stimulating and imaginative; the dramatic teacher who bubbles with energy and enthusiasm; the philosophical teacher who encourages students to play with ideas and concepts; and the problem-solving teacher who requires that students think out the answers. In the product-oriented researchers' desire to identify and prescribe behaviors or methods that are measurable and quantifiable, they overlook the emotional, qualitative, and interpretive descriptions of classrooms—the spirit, joy, and love of teaching. Most of their research has been conducted at the elementary grade levels, where one would expect more social, psychological, and humanistic factors to be observed, recorded, and recommended as effective. A good portion of their work also deals with low achievers and at-risk students; perhaps this is the reason many of their generalizations or principles coincide with techniques of classroom management, structure, control, task orientation, and monitoring behaviors.

The teacher effectiveness models also fail to consider that a good deal of effective teaching might not directly correlate with student achievement. For one famous philosopher of education, Maxine Greene, good teaching and learning involve values, experiences, insight, imagination, and appreciation—the "stuff" that cannot be easily observed or categorized. For her, teaching and learning are an existential encounter, a philosophical process involving ideas, imagination, and creative inquiries that cannot be readily quantified (1998, 2000). See Box 10.3.

Much of teaching involves behavior that is caring, nurturing, and valuing—attributes that are not easily shown or measured through evaluation instruments. Elliot Eisner (2002),

**BOX 10.3** Remembering the Past

The writer, poet, musician, and teacher must remember the people who lived and died. As teachers, we must capture the agony and lessons of history, the myths as well as the goodness of humanity, through our philosophy, history, literature, music, and art. We must retain the vestiges of the lost world, where people died terrible deaths as victims of war, famine, poverty, nationalism, racism, or religious fanaticism, and try to make sense of all the senseless crimes people have committed and are still capable of committing.

an educator who emphasizes the artful elements of teaching, is concerned that what is not measurable goes unnoticed in a product-oriented teaching model. By breaking down the teaching act into dimensions, competencies, and criteria that can be defined operationally and quantified, educators overlook the hard-to-measure aspects of teaching, such as the personal, the humanistic, and the playful. To be sure, to say that excellence in teaching requires measurable behaviors and outcomes is to miss a substantial part of teaching, what some educators refer to as artistry, drama, tones, and flavor.

Academic outcomes alone represent an incomplete, hollow picture of teaching. The new and popular teacher competency and teacher effectiveness models lock us into a narrow mold that misses many nuances of teaching. Many of these prescriptions (which the researchers call principles) are old ideas bottled under new labels such as "with-it-ness," "smoothness," and "clarity." They seem to confirm what effective teachers have been doing for many years, but the confirmation is needed so that beginning teachers have a better yardstick or starting point.

Teaching is a people industry, and people (especially young people) perform best in places where they feel wanted and respected. To be sure, it is possible for a teacher to "disengage" or "disinvite" students by belittling them, ignoring them, undercutting them, comparing them to their siblings or other students, or even "yessing" them (failing to hold them accountable for the right answer) and still perform well on evaluation instruments—on discrete competencies or behaviors associated with the teacher as a technician ("The teacher came to class on time"; "The teacher checked homework on a regular basis"; "The teacher was clear about objectives of the course"; "The teacher graded quizzes on a timely basis," etc.). Such competency-based models, checklists, or behaviorist approaches are common as we search for a research-based model of what a "good" teacher is. But they ignore the ways in which teaching means being part of a helping or caring profession, being a kind and generous teacher, or working with students so that they develop their own uniqueness and identity. (See Tips for Teachers 10.2.)

# ■ TEACHER CONTEXTS: NEW RESEARCH, NEW PARADIGMS

For the last fifty years or more, research on teacher behavior has been linear and category based, focused on specific teacher styles, interactions, characteristics, or effects. It focused on either the *process* of teaching (how the teacher was behaving in the classroom) or the *products* of teaching (that is, student outcomes). As the 1990s unfolded, the research on teaching examined the multifaceted nature and *context* of teaching; this research on **teacher contexts** examined the relationship between teaching and learning, the teacher's subject-matter knowledge, how knowledge was taught, and how it related to pedagogy.

The new emphasis on teaching goes beyond what the teacher does in the classroom to explore teacher thinking from the perspective of teachers themselves, thus

# Helping Teachers Resolve Problems

Effective teachers are able to cope with frustrations and problems that arise on the job. Regardless of the amount of satisfaction they obtain from teaching, there are dissatisfying aspects of the job. What follows is a list of mental health strategies in the form of questions that are a mix of common sense and psychology for self-understanding. They are presented to help teachers deal with problems or dissatisfactions that may arise on the job—to become satisfied and self-actualized as a teacher.

1. *Are you aware of your strengths and weaknesses?* The ability to make realistic self-estimates is crucial, given that your students and colleagues will observe and make judgments about your behavior, attitude, and abilities. Learn to see yourself as others see you and to compensate for or modify areas that need to be improved.

2. *Do you make use of resources?* As a teacher you will come across many different textbooks, workbooks, tests, and materials. You will need to make judgments about their value and how to best utilize these resources for our growth.

3. *Are you aware of your social and personal skills?* You will need to understand the attitudes and feelings of your students and parents, as well as colleagues and supervisors—and how to adapt to work cooperatively with them.

4. *Can you function in a bureaucratic setting?* Schools are bureaucracies, and you must learn the rules and regulations, as well as the norms and behaviors of the school. As a teacher, you are an employee of an organization that has certain expectations of you and your colleagues.

5. *Do you take out our frustrations in class?* Don't vent your problems or dissatisfactions on your students. It solves nothing and adds to your own teaching problems.

6. *Do you make wise choices?* You will need to understand and apply the decision-making process purposefully and logically. Learn to be consistent and rational when making a choice. Think about the impact your decisions have on others in the school.

7. *Do you understand your roles as a teacher?* The teacher's role goes far beyond teaching a group of students in class. Teaching occurs in a particular social context, and much of what you do and are expected to do is influenced by this context. Different students, supervisors, administrators, parents, and community members expect you to perform varied roles depending on the realities, demand, and expectations of a school's culture.

8. *Do you expose yourself to new professional experiences?* Broaden your professional experiences. Volunteer for workshops and exchange teaching. Devote time to study and travel.

9. *Can you cope with school forms and records?* Schools expect teachers to complete a host of forms, reports, and records accurately and on time. The quicker you become familiar with this work, the smoother it will be for you.

10. *Can you study and learn from someone else with similar problems?* It helps to talk to or observe colleagues with similar problems to see what they are doing wrong so as to avoid making the same mistake, or what they are doing right so as to learn what to do.

11. *Do you look for help on specific questions?* Often teacher dissatisfaction pertains to a specific problem, for example, the inability to maintain discipline. Consulting with an experienced colleague or supervisor sometimes helps.

12. *Do you participate in group discussions?* Because many problems of teachers are similar, pool ideas and experience. Even the gripe session in the teachers' lounge has benefits in venting or expressing one's dissatisfaction and learning that others have similar problems.

13. *Are you able to organize your time?* There are only so many hours in a day, and many demands and expectations are imposed on you as a person and professional. You will need to make good use of time, to set priorities, to plan, and to get your work done.

14. *Can you separate your job from your personal life?* Never let the teaching job (or any job) overwhelm

*(continued)*

you to the point that it interferes with your personal life. There are times when you may have to spend a few extra hours in school helping students or working with parents or colleagues. Also there are times when you will have to spend extra hours grading papers and tests, preparing lessons, and performing clerical tasks, but for your own mental health be sure you have time left for your private, family, and social life.

15. *Have you developed a professional identity?* Professional identity involves an understanding of the relation between your professional roles, knowledge of yourself and how others perceive you, and an understanding of your teaching style and relationship with colleagues.

looking at teaching from the "inside." It focuses on the personal and practical knowledge of teachers, the culture of teaching, and the language and thoughts of teachers. It also elevates their status and role as "practitioner-researchers," and thus enhances their professional role and professional development. The teacher is depicted as one who copes with a complex environment and simplifies it, mainly through experience, by attending to a small number of tasks and synthesizing various kinds of information that continually evolve. Professional knowledge (that is, both subject-matter and pedagogical knowledge—knowing what you know and how well you know it) is now considered important for defining how teachers and students construct meaning for their respective academic roles and perform tasks related to those roles (Ornstein, 1995a, 1995c).

An alternative model has evolved for understanding the nature of teaching—one that combines teaching and learning processes, incorporates holistic practices, and goes beyond what teachers and students appear to be doing to inquire about what they are thinking. This model relies on language and dialogue, not mathematical or statistical symbols nor observational instruments or rating scales (now criticized as "technocratic" and "male-dominated" research techniques), to provide the conceptual categories and organize the data. It uses the approaches that reformers, critical pedagogists, feminists, reconceptualists, and postliberal theoreticians have advocated: metaphors, stories, biographies and autobiographies, conversations (with experts), voices (or narratives), and reflective practices (Cochran-smith & Lytle, 1999; Ornstein, 1995a). The following sections discuss some of these approaches.

### Metaphors

Teachers' knowledge, including the ways they speak about teaching, not only exists in propositional form but also includes figurative language, including metaphors. Teachers' thinking consists of personal experiences, images, and jargon, and therefore figurative language is central to the expression and understanding of the teachers' knowledge of pedagogy (Carter, 1993; Clark, 1991; Dooley, 1998).

**Metaphors** of space and time figure in teachers' descriptions of their work ("pacing a lesson," "covering the content," "moving on to the next part of the lesson"). The studies on teacher style use terminology about teachers that can be considered metaphors: the teacher as a "boss," "coach," "comedian," or "maverick." The notions of a "master" teacher, "lead" teacher, "star" teacher, "talented" teacher, or "expert" teacher are also metaphors or descriptors used by researchers to describe outstanding or effective teachers.

Metaphors explain or interpret reality. In traditional literature, this process of understanding evolves through experience and study, without the influence of researchers' personal or cultural biases. But the use of metaphors can also be conceptualized in the literature of sociology to include ideas, values, and behaviors that derive in part from a person's knowledge and life experiences, all which can be described in terms of political, social, cultural, and ideological metaphors (Apple, 1996; Banks, 1997; Grant & Lei, 2001).

Using metaphors, however, is somewhat problematic because traditional researchers and professors consider such language "loosey-goosey" or vague; others consider it biased or tainted, especially when it is used to describe schools in a political or social context. Many have adapted the language to be current but continue to teach what they know, the old conventional wisdom, and still use traditional research models. Hence, there is a gap between our espoused theories and theories in actual use as well as a gap between what is intellectually interesting and provocative for readers and what is realistic and relevant for teachers—which leads to a gap between the academic or theoretical discourse in college and what is acceptable or practical in schools.

The extreme use of metaphors that have a political, social, cultural, or ideological meaning is carried out by educators who are intelligent and accomplished but who have a natural aptitude to push the envelope and stretch reality. Henry Giroux, for instance, advocates a "theory of radical pedagogy" based on an ideological construct that promotes resistance and opposition of subordinate groups to dominant groups. He seeks to shift the explanation for school failure among minority groups and at-risk students from a psychological and educational analysis to a political and cultural analysis. Although his ideas are stimulating, his writing comes perilously close to incoherence. At best, his view of reality gets interrupted by a series of asides and thrusts into tangled prose and little backwaters.

Ivan Illich's (1971) metaphor is about the "deschooling of society." He completely rejects school as a viable agency: If schools were eliminated, education could be open to all (through peer matching, skill centers, and community networks) and could become a genuine instrument of "human liberation." Learners would no longer have an obligatory curriculum imposed on them; they would be liberated from institutional and "capitalistic indoctrination."

Peter McLaren (1995) is perhaps more politically extreme, and his writing is engulfed in verbal asides and ripostes. He states that U.S. schooling promotes a perverse social order in that "it strives through its curriculum to create a culture of desire"—not to nurture a communal consensus but rather to hide from students and the general public the gaps in our society. "Unfortunately, we still mistake the disease (capitalism) for the cure (democracy)" (pp. 91–92). Given the global reaches of capitalism and its agents, whom he calls "global carpetbaggers" who profit from human suffering and short-term profits at the expense of the planet's resources and ecological health, he urges a Marxian end to capitalism, which he calls a "Frakensteinian" monster.

All of these metaphors are academically interesting and provoke discussion in class, but to what extent they are relevant to schoolteachers is another question. It is hard to imagine that well-intentioned and dedicated teachers, intent on reading and teaching the children in their classrooms, are perverse, act as prison guards, and/or are political lackeys, as these critics would have us believe. Actually, the metaphors and accompanying analyses these critical pedagogists and neo-Marxists generate originally surfaced in the 1930s when George Counts (1932) asked progressive educators to consider the social and economic problems of the era and use the schools to help reform society.

## Stories

Increasingly, researchers are telling stories about teachers—about their work and how they teach—and teachers are telling stories about their own teaching experiences. Most **stories** are narrative and descriptive in nature; and both those by and about teachers make a point about teaching that would otherwise be difficult to convey through traditional research methods. The stories told are rich in meaning and reflect the belief that there is much to learn from "authentic" teachers who tell their stories about experiences they might otherwise keep to themselves or fail to convey to others (Elbaz, 1991; Ornstein, 1995b; Page, 2001).

Stories have important social or psychological meaning. Stories of teachers allow us to see connections between the practice of teaching and the human side of teaching. The stories of individual teachers allow us to see their knowledge and skills enacted in the real world of classrooms and lead us to appreciate their emotional and moral encounters with the lives of the people they teach. There are three types of stories.

Stories by novelists, playwrights, and filmmakers entertain us; they may be based on a true account of a teacher (e.g., Jaime Escalante in *Stand and Deliver*), or they may be completely fictional, such as the teachers in *Blackboard Jungle, Mr. Novack, Room 222,* or more recently *Dangerous Minds* and *Dead Poets Society*. Although such stories capture the life of a teacher in a given time and place, they are fictionalized and idealized; they are, in the words of two commentators, "romantic versions of teachers and classrooms in [which problems] are resolved artificially." They help us "capture some truths" about teaching in a "poignant way"(Ornstein & Lasley, 2004, p. 6). Note that there are other stories, not directly related to teaching, that can also help us understand children and youth and the need for teacher–student connections. These stories include classics such as *Grease, West Side Story,* and *Back to the Future*, and, more recently, *A Walk to Remember.* The stories are emotionally engaging, and they serve as excellent advertising and recruiting material for the teaching profession. Such stories help illustrate the *art* of teaching.

Stories by teachers such as Bel Kaufman, Herbert Kohl, Jonathan Kozol, and Sylvia Ashton-Warner have become best-sellers because of their rich and thick descriptions and personal narratives and the way they describe the nuances of teaching. These stories are aesthetic and visual landscapes of teaching and learning and would be missed or ignored by clinically based and traditional researchers. Some criticize such personal teacher stories for lacking scholarly reliability and validity, flaws they see as grounded in personal egotism or exaggeration. In short, the story is told from one viewpoint; there is one world, one context, one interpretation. Truth and accuracy are dependent on the history and social lens of one person—the storyteller, who sometimes exhibits a selective and cloudy memory.

Stories of teachers by researchers are less descriptive, less emotional, and less well known. Nevertheless, they are personal and interesting encounters of teachers, and they provide us with teachers' knowledge and experiences not quite on their own terms but in a deep way that helps us understand what teaching is all about. These stories provide unusual opportunities to get to know and respect teachers as persons on an emotional as well as intellectual level. Most important, these stories represent an important shift in the way researchers are willing to convey teachers' pedagogy and understanding of teaching. However, some researchers point out that field-based observers and authors construct different realities, so that different storytellers can write different versions of the same teacher (Bullough & Pinnegar, 2001; Errante, 2000; Shulman, 1991). But the author is only one variable. Subject matter, students, and school settings can also lead to a striking contrast in different storytellers' portrayals and interpretations of the same teacher or school.

We need to ask whether interviewees (say teachers) can actually recall their experiences, which in some cases occurred many months or years ago. Are the stories being filtered through a biased lens? What is being omitted? Embellished? Did the researcher change the stories in selecting and editing the interviews? Did the researcher lead the interviewee in a way that slants the story to fit the interviewer's message? (Coulter, 1999; Errante, 2000; Rymes, 2001). Can researchers faithfully and objectively tell someone else's story? How does the researcher's politics or lack of experience affect the outcomes? When transcribing the story from tape to print, what part of the story is omitted, modified, or actually altered? What is the difference between telling a story and writing (and editing) it? How much of the actual context or history is absent? Is one story or a series of stories from five or ten subjects as valuable as the results of research involving one thousand subjects in ten or twenty-five schools? These are serious questions that traditional or technocratic researchers raise when confronted with field-based or qualitative research.

## Biographies and Autobiographies

Stories written by researchers about teachers tend to be *biographical* and stories written by teachers about themselves tend to be *autobiographical*. Both **biography** and **autobiography** encompass a "whole story" and represent the full depth and breadth of a person's experiences as opposed to mere commentary or fragments of experience. Unity and wholeness emerge as a person brings past experiences to make present action meaningful and understandable in terms of what a person has undergone (Ayers, 2001; Hillocks, 1999; Popkewitz, 1998).

The essence of an autobiography is that it provides an opportunity for people to convey what they know and have been doing for years and what is inside their heads, unshaped by others. Whereas biography is ultimately filtered through and interpreted by a second party, autobiography permits the author (in this case, the teacher) to present the information in a personal way on his or her own terms.

As human beings, we all have stories to tell. Each person has a distinctive biography or autobiography that is shaped by a host of experiences and practices and a particular viewpoint or way of looking at the world (in our case, classrooms and schools). For teachers, this suggests a particular set of teaching experiences and practices, as well as a particular style of teaching and pedagogy.

A biography or autobiography of a teacher may be described as the life story of one teacher who is the central character based in a classroom or school and of the classroom dynamics and school drama that unfold around the individual. These types of stories are concerned with limited longitudinal aspects of personal and professional experiences and can provide the reader with much detailed and insightful information. They help us reconstruct teachers' and students' experiences that would not be available to us in typical professional literature on teaching; they describe the human dimension of teaching.

The accounts in biographies and autobiographies suggest that the author is in a position of authority with respect to the particular segment of the life being described; hence, the thoughts and experiences of the author take on a sense of reality and objectivity not always assumed in other stories (Coulter, 2000; Horton, Kohl, & Kohl, 1998; Neumann & Peterson, 1997). However, when teachers write an autobiography (as opposed to someone else writing the story in biography form), they run the risk of being considered partial or of having written self-serving descriptions of their teaching process; in fact, the stories by Herbert Kohl and Johnathan Kozol illustrate this danger only too well, because their colleagues are written off as indifferent, incompetent, and/or racist (while they are the "knights in shining armor" teachers).

Thus, Madeline Grumet (1987) suggests that researchers publish multiple accounts of a teacher's knowledge and pedagogy instead of a single narrative. The problem is that this approach suggests taking stories out of the hands of teachers. Joint publications between teachers and researchers may be appropriate in some situations and a method for resolving this problem (Carter, 1993; Kagan & Timmons, 1995; Ornstein, 1995b).

## Voice

The notion of **voice** sums up the new linguistic tools for describing what teachers do, how they do it, and what they think when they are teaching. Voice corresponds with such terms as the teacher's *perspective,* the teacher's *frame of reference,* or *getting into the teacher's head.* The concern with voice permeates teacher empowerment and the work of researchers who collaborate with teachers in teacher research projects. The idea of voice should be considered against the backdrop of previous teacher silence and impotence in deciding issues and practices that affect their lives as professionals. The fact that researchers are now willing to give credit to teachers' knowledge, teachers' practices, and teachers' experiences helps redress an imbalance that in the past gave little recognition to teachers. Now teachers have a right and a role in speaking for themselves and about teaching (Elbaz, 1991; Hargreaves, 1996; Willis, 2002).

Although there have been some serious attempts to include teachers' voices, the key issue is to what extent these new methods permit teachers' "authentic" expression to influence the field of teacher effectiveness research and teacher preparation programs. In the past, it has been difficult for teachers to establish a voice, especially one that commands respect and authority, in the professional literature. The reason is simple: The researchers and theoreticians have dominated the field of inquiry and decided what should be published.

With the exception of autobiographies and stories written by teachers, the voices of teachers generally are filtered through and categorized by researchers' writing and publications. For decades, firsthand expressions of teacher experiences and wisdom (sometimes conveyed in the form of advice or recommendations) were considered nothing more than "recipes" or lists of dos and don'ts—irrelevant to the world of research on teaching. Recently, however, under umbrella terms such as *teacher thinking, teacher processes, teacher cognition,* or *teacher practices,* it has become acceptable and even fashionable to take what teachers have to say, adapt it, and turn it into *professional knowledge, pedagogical knowledge, teacher knowledge,* or *craft knowledge.* Although researchers are now collaborating with practitioners, taking teacher views seriously and accepting teachers on equal terms as part of teacher training programs, teachers still do not always receive credit where it is due. Whereas in scholarly publications, researchers and professors are named as coauthors, practitioners may be acknowledged only by pseudonyms such as "Nancy" or "Thomas." The culture of schools and universities, and of teachers and professors, should be compatible enough to bridge this gap in the near future.

Many of the new voices embody a critique of prevailing institutions (such as schools and schools of education) and relationships of power and inequality (including relationships between students and teachers, teachers and administrators, men and women, etc.). There is a tendency to analyze relationships through dominant and subordinate forms that serve particular interest groups (Burdell & Swadener, 1999; Grumet & Stone, 2000). The words *critical, radical, feminist, postliberal, neo-Marxist, transcendentalist,* and *spiritual* can be added to the narratives and voices to signify this new ethnographic trend. Some of the new voices merely deal with personal testimony and conversations of the political left—their biographies, ideological tracts, and ethnographic practices. Still others want to "decolonialize" traditional researcher-practitioner relationships, as well as dethrone clinical and empirical authority while elevating the notions of subjectivity and ideology (Anderson & Herr, 1999; Burdell & Swadener, 1999).

Some of these new researchers see themselves as "border crossers," that is, they teach in several departments within the educational field, draw on several social sciences as their sources of knowledge, and sometimes bounce around (often isolated in their respective institutions) from university to university until they feel accepted. Their voices are based on poststructural, postcolonial, postcritical, and postmodern theories—a collection of heightened consciousness, theoretical and political discourse, phenomenological and qualitative methods, and race and gender politics as the basis of their knowledge, constructs, and paradigms (Grant, 1999; Pinar, 1999; Sears, 2003). Right now they seek to reframe, redefine, and reconceptualize their respective fields in education (and other social sciences). In doing so, they threaten some colleagues on a professional and personal level—partially because of political ideology (and the way they perceive the world) and partially because of personality differences; thus they often remain isolated in their departments and universities. Many of these people can be considered crusaders, driven type A personalities, and some have made impressive contributions to our field, and we are richer for it. But often they mix politics with their professional relations and have trouble getting along with their colleagues who perceive the world from another perspective—one more traditional, conservative, and/or empirical.

## Reconceptualizing Teaching

To argue that good teaching boils down to a set of prescriptive behaviors, methods, or proficiency levels, that teachers must follow a "new" research-based teaching plan or evaluation system, or that decisions about teacher accountability can be assessed in terms of students passing some standardized or multiple-choice test is to miss the human aspect of teaching—the "essence" of teaching.

Stress on assessment and evaluation systems today illustrates that behaviorism has won at the expense of humanistic psychology. Put in different terms, the ideas of Thorndike and Watson have prevailed over the ideas of Dewey and Kilpatrick. It also suggests that school administrators, policymakers, and researchers would rather focus on the *science* of teaching—behaviors and outcomes that can be observed, counted, or measured—than on the *art* of teaching with its humanistic and hard-to-measure variables.

Robert Linn contends that assessment of teachers and students can be easily mandated, implemented, and reported and thus have wide appeal under the guise of "reform." Although these assessment systems are supposed to improve education, they don't necessarily do so (Linn, 2000). Real reform is complex and costly (for example, reducing class size, raising teacher salaries, introducing special reading and tutoring programs, extending the school day and year), and it takes time before the results are evident. People who seem to be leading this latest wave of educational reform, such as politicians and business leaders, want a quick, easy, and cheap fix. Therefore they will always opt for assessment because it is simple and inexpensive to implement. It creates heightened media visibility, the feeling that something is being done, and the "Hawthorne effect," which is that novelty tends to elevate short-term gains. This assessment focus (which is a form of behaviorism) also provides a rationale for teacher education programs because it suggests we can separate the effects of teachers from other variables and identify good teaching. Yet it is questionable, given our current knowledge of teaching and teacher education and the human factor that goes along with teaching and learning, whether new teachers can be properly prepared in both academic rigor and practical reality.

Those in the business of preparing teachers need to provide a research base and rationale showing that teachers who enroll in and complete a teacher education program are more likely to be effective teachers than those who lack such training. The fact that there are several alternative certification programs for teachers in more than forty states, through which nearly 5 percent (as high as 16 percent in Texas and 22 percent in New Jersey) of the nationwide teaching force entered the profession (Goodnough, 2000) makes teacher educators (professors of education) attempt to demonstrate that their teacher preparation programs work and that they can prepare effective teachers. Indeed, the profession needs to identify teacher behaviors and methods that work under certain conditions, which leads many educators to favor behaviorism (or prescriptive ideas and specific tasks) and assessment systems (closed-ended, tiny, measurable variables) that correlate teaching behaviors (or methods) with learning outcomes.

The reason for all this worry and effort is that there is a growing body of literature informing us that traditional certification programs and education courses make little difference in teacher effectiveness; therefore, these tradtional paths to the teaching profession should be curtailed to allow alternative certification programs to expand. For the time being, Linda Darling-Hammond assures us, the bulk of the research suggests that teachers who are versed in both pedagogical knowledge and subject knowledge are more successful in the classroom than teachers who are versed only in subject matter. It is also true that teachers who hold standard certificates are more successful than teachers who hold emergency licenses or who attend "crash" programs in the summer and then are temporarily licensed (Darling-Hammond, 2001; Darling-Hammond, Berry, & Thoreson, 2001).

Being able to describe detailed methods of teaching and how and why teachers do what they do should improve the performance of teachers. But all the new research hardly tells the whole story of teaching—what leads to teacher effectiveness and student learning. Being able to describe teachers' thinking or decision making and analyzing their stories and reflective practices suggest that we understand and can improve teaching. The new research on teaching—with its stories, biographies, voices, reflective practices, and qualitative methods—provides a platform and publication outlet for researchers. It promotes their expertise (which in turn continues to separate them from practitioners) and permits them to continue to subordinate teaching to research. It also provides a new paradigm for analyzing teaching because the older models (teacher styles, teacher personality, teacher characteristics, teacher effectiveness, etc.) have become exhausted and repetitive. The issues and questions related to the new paradigm create new educational wars and controversy between traditional and nontraditional researchers, between quantitative and qualitative advocates. It is questionable, however, whether this new knowledge base about teaching really improves teaching and learning or leads to substantial and sustained improvement.

## The Need for Humanistic Teaching

The focus of teacher research should be on the learner, not the teacher; on the feelings and attitudes of the student, not on knowledge and information (because feelings and attitudes will eventually determine what knowledge and information are sought and acquired); and on long-term development and growth of the students, not on short-term objectives or specific teacher tasks. But if teachers spend more time dealing with learners' feelings and attitudes, as well as on social and personal growth, teachers may be penalized when cognitive student outcomes (little pieces of information) are correlated with their behaviors and methods in class.

Students need to be encouraged and nurtured by their teachers, especially when they are young. They are too dependent on approval from significant adults—first their parents, then their teachers. Parents and teachers need to help young children and adolescents establish a source of self-esteem by focusing on their strengths, supporting them, discouraging negative self-talk, and helping them take control of their lives in context with their own culture and values.

People (including children) with high self-esteem achieve at high levels, and the more people achieve, the better they feel about themselves. The opposite is also true: Students who fail to master the subject matter get down on themselves and eventually give up. Students with low self-esteem give up quickly. In short, student self-esteem and achievement are directly related. If we can nurture students' self-esteem, almost everything else will fall into place, including achievement scores and academic outcomes. Regardless of how smart or talented a child, if he or she has personal problems, then cognition will be detrimentally affected.

This builds a strong argument for creating successful experiences for students to help them feel good about themselves. The long-term benefits are obvious: The more students learn to like themselves, the more they will achieve; and the more they achieve, the more they will like themselves. But that takes time, involves a lot of nurturing, and does not show up on standardized tests within a semester or school year; moreover, it doesn't help the teacher who is being evaluated by a content- or test-driven school administrator who is looking for results now. It certainly does not benefit the teacher who is being evaluated based on behaviorist instruments such as how many times he or she attended departmental meetings, whether the shades in the classroom were even, whether his or her instructional objectives were clearly stated, or whether homework was assigned or the computer was used on a regular basis.

Clearly, certain teacher behaviors contribute to good teaching. The trouble is that there is little agreement on exactly what behaviors or methods are most important. Some teachers who gain theoretical knowledge of "what works" are unable to put the ideas into practice. Some teachers with similar preparation act effortlessly in the classroom, and others consider teaching a chore. All this suggests that teaching cannot be described in terms of the checklist of a precise model. It also suggests that teaching is a humanistic activity that deals with people (not tiny behaviors or competencies) and how people (teachers and students) behave in a variety of classroom and school settings.

Although the research on teacher effectiveness provides a vocabulary and system for improving our insight into good teaching, there is a danger that may lead to some of us becoming too rigid in our view of teaching: Following only one teacher model or evaluation system can lead to too much emphasis on specific behaviors that can be easily measured or prescribed in advance—at the expense of encouraging humanistic behaviors that cannot be easily measured or prescribed in advance, such as aesthetic appreciation, emotions, values, and moral responsibility.

Although some educators recognize that humanistic factors influence teaching, we continue to define most teacher behaviors in terms of behaviorist and cognitive factors. Most teacher evaluation instruments tend to de-emphasize the human side of teaching because it is difficult to observe or measure. In an attempt to be scientific, to predict and control behavior, we sometimes lose sight of the attitudes and feelings of teachers and their relations with students. As Maxine Greene (2001) asserts, good teaching and learning involve creative inquiries and connections between people—an existential and philosophical encounter—that cannot be readily quantified. By overlooking hard-to-measure aspects of teaching, we miss a substantial part of teaching, what Greene calls the "stuff" of teaching, what Eisner (2002) calls the "artful elements" of teaching, what Palmer (2003) and Perrone (1998) call the "heart" of teaching, and what others refer to as drama, tones, or flavor.

Teacher behaviors that correlate with measurable outcomes often lead to rote learning, to learning "bits" and not the whole picture, and to memorization and automatic responses, not to higher-order learning. These evaluation models seem to miss moral and ethical outcomes, as well as social, personal, and self-actualizing factors related to learning and life—in effect, the affective domain of learning and the psychology of being human. In their attempt to observe and measure what teachers do and detail whether students improve their performance on reading or math tests, these models ignore learners' imagination, fantasy, and intuitive thinking, their dreams, hopes, and aspirations, and how teachers have an impact on these hard-to-define and hard-to-measure but very important aspects of students' lives. Learning experiences that deal with caring, character, philosophy, morality, and spiritual outlook are absent in these models, too.

In providing feedback and evaluation for teachers, many factors need to be considered so that the advice or information does not fall on deaf ears. Teachers appreciate feedback processes that allow them to improve their teaching as long as the processes are honest and professionally planned and administered, as long as teachers are permitted to make mistakes, and as long as more than one model of effectiveness is considered so that they can adopt recommended behaviors and methods to fit their own personality and philosophy of teaching (Ornstein, 1995d, 2003).

## Humanistic Teaching—Examples

In traditional terms, humanism is rooted in the fourteenth- and fifteenth-century Renaissance period of Europe, when a revival of classical humanism evoked the ancient Greek and Latin cultures. The philosophers and educators of the Renaissance, like the medieval Scholastics before them (who were governed and protected by the Catholic Church), found wisdom in the past and revered classical manuscripts. Unlike the Scholastics, however, they were often independent of the church and were concerned with the experiences of *humans* and not God-like or religious issues. (The religious scholar of the medieval period, versed in scripture and theological logic, was no longer the preferred model of the ideal man. The ideal was now the courtier—a man of style, wit, and elegance who was liberally educated, perhaps a diplomat, politician, or successful merchant. See Baldesar Castiglione, *The Book of the Courtier*, rev. ed. [Garden City, NY: Doubleday, 1959]. Machiavelli's *The Prince*, through the format of advice to a young man, describes in perfect detail the philosophy and behavior that permeated the Renaissance.)

In the early twentieth century, humanistic principles of teaching and learning were envisioned in the theories of progressive education: in the *child-centered* lab school directed by John Dewey at the University of Chicago from 1896 to 1904; in the *play-centered* methods and materials introduced by Maria Montessori that were designed to develop the practical, sensory, and formal skills of the prekindergarten and kindergarten slum children of Italy starting in 1908; and in the *activity-centered* practices of William Kilpatrick, who in the 1920s and 1930s urged that elementary teachers organize classrooms around social activities, group enterprises, and group projects and allow children to say what they think and feel.

All of these progressive theories were highly humanistic and stressed the child's interests, individuality, and creativity; in short, they emphasized the child's freedom to develop naturally, freedom to develop without teacher domination, and freedom from the weight of rote learning. But progressivism failed because, in the view of Lawrence Cremin, there weren't enough good teachers to implement progressive thought in classrooms and schools (1961). To be sure, it is much easier to stress knowledge, rote learning, and right answers than it is to teach about ideas, to consider the interests and needs of students, and to give them freedom to explore and interact with one another without teacher constraints.

By the end of the twentieth century, the humanistic teacher was embodied in William Glasser's (1969, 1990) "positive" and "supportive" teacher who could manage students without coercion and teach without failure. The humanistic teacher was also illustrated in Robert Fried's "passionate" teacher, Robert Nash's "ethical" teacher, and Vito Perrone's "teacher with a heart"—teachers who live to teach young children and refuse to submit to apathy or criticism that may infect the school in which they work. These teachers are dedicated and involved, they actively engage students in their classrooms, and they affirm their identities. The students do not have to ask whether their teacher is interested in them, thinks of them, or knows their interests or concerns. The answer is definitely "yes."

The humanistic teacher is also portrayed by Ted Sizer's (1985) mythical teacher called "Horace," who is dedicated and enjoys teaching, treats learning as a humane enterprise, inspires his students to learn, and encourages them to develop their powers of thought, taste, and character. Yet the system forces Horace to make a number of compromises in planning, teaching, and grading—compromises he knows he would not make if we lived in an ideal world (with more than twenty-four hours in a day). Horace is a trouper; he hides his frustration. Critics of teachers don't really want to hear him or face facts; they don't even know what it is like to teach. Sizer simply states: "Most jobs in the real world have a gap between what would be nice and what is possible. One adjusts" (p. 20). Hence, most caring, dedicated teachers are forced to make some compromises, take some shortcuts, and make some accommodations. As long as no one gets upset and no one complains, the system does not try to bridge the chasm between rhetoric (the rosy picture) and reality (slow burnout).

There is also the humanistic element in Nel Noddings's (1992) ideal teacher who focuses on the nurturing of "competent, caring, loving, and lovable persons." Noddings describes teaching as a caring profession in which the teachers should convey to students the caring way to think about one's self, siblings, strangers, animals, plants, and physical environment. She stresses the affective aspect of teaching: the need to focus on the child's strengths and interests and the need for an individualized curriculum built around the child's abilities and needs. Caring, according to Noddings (2001), cannot be achieved by a formula or checklist. It calls for different behaviors for different situations—from tenderness to tough love. Good teaching, like good parenting, requires continuous effort, trusting relationships, and continuity of purpose, the purpose of caring, appreciating human connections, and respecting people and ideas from a historical, multicultural, and diverse perspective. See Box 10.4.

Actually, the humanistic teacher is someone who highlights the personal and social dimensions of teaching and learning as opposed to the behavioral, scientific, or technological aspects. We might argue that everything the teacher does is "human" and that the expression "humanistic teaching" is a cliché. However, we also use the term in a loose sense to describe the teacher who emphasizes the arts as opposed to the sciences and people instead of numbers. Although the teacher understands the value of many subjects, including the sciences and social sciences, he or she feels that students need to understand certain *ideas* and *values*, some rooted in 3,000 years of philosophy, literature, art, music, theater, and so forth. Without certain agreed-on content, what Arthur Bestor and Allan Bloom would call the "liberal arts,"

**BOX 10.4** Teaching the Next Generation

We have thirty or thirty-five years as teachers to make an imprint on the next generation, to pass on our thoughts and deeds to the next generation. As teachers, the necessity of our work requires that we understand what is at stake—improving and enriching society by making the next generation better than ours—and motivate students to accomplish great things that exhibit the good side of what is human. In simple terms, today's youth will determine our future and the type of society we become.

**BOX 10.5** The Role of the Teacher

Teachers must play an active role if we are to be a more compassionate, caring, and just society. They need to encourage open debate concerning the thorniest issues of the present and past, hold discussions free of attacks or stereotyping, and build a sense of community (what the French call *civisme*) and character. We must flee from our comfortable classroom niches, go beyond facts, raise thoughtful questions that stem from meaningful readings, and transcend the cognitive domain to dwell in the social, personal, and moral universe. We must promote this type of teaching at all grade levels.

what E. D. Hirsh and Diane Ravitch would call "essential knowledge," and what Robert Hutchins and Mortimer Adler would call the "Great Books," our heritage would crumble and we would be at the mercy of chance and ignorance; moreover, our educational enterprise would be subject to the whim and fancy of local fringe groups. See Box 10.5.

Humanistic education, according to Jacques Barzun (1972), the elegant and eloquent writer of history and humanism, leads to a form of knowledge that helps us deal with the nature of life, but it does not guarantee us a more gracious or noble life. "The humanities will not sort out the world's evils and were never meant to cure [our] troubles. . . . They will not heal diseased minds or broken hearts any more than they will foster political democracy or settle international disputes." The so-called humanities (and if we may add, the humanistic teacher) "have meaning," according to Barzun, "because of the inhumanity of life; what they depict is strife and disaster" (p. 44). And, by example, they help us deal with the human condition and provide guidelines for moral behavior, good taste, and the improvement of civilization.

On a schoolwide level, we would argue, humanism means that we eliminate the notion that everyone should go to college, because it creates frustration, anger, and unrealistic expectations among large numbers of children and youth. According to Paul Goodman (1964), schoolwide humanism requires that society find viable occupational options for noncollege graduates and jobs that have decent salaries, respect, and social status. It suggests, according to John Gardner (1962), that we recognize various forms of excellence—the excellent teacher, the excellent artist, the excellent plumber, the excellent bus driver—otherwise we create a myopic view of talent and subsequent tension that threatens a democratic society. It also means that we appreciate and nurture different student abilities, aptitudes, and skills, what Howard Gardner calls "multiple intelligences" (1983). Both Gardners have a point, but what really matters is that teachers strive to lift the barriers for their students and to educate them to their fullest potential—not just in the cognititve realm but also in the realm of the whole child, the whole person—and thus to become more humane.

## ■ SUMMARY ■

1. Research on teaching has considered teacher styles, teacher–student interactions, teacher characteristics, teacher effects, and teacher contexts.
2. Although much remains to be learned about successful teaching, research has identified some

   teacher behaviors that seem to be effective and influence student performance.
3. Recent research on effective teaching has shifted from the *processes* of teaching to the *products* of teaching and now to the *context* of teaching.

4. The classic, important research on teaching before the 1970s was the work of A. S. Barr, Arno Bellack, Ned Flanders, and David Ryans. These researchers focused on teacher styles, teacher–student interactions, and teacher characteristics—that is, the process, or what was happening in the classroom or the behavior of the teacher.

5. In the 1970s and 1980s, the research on teaching was primarily based on the work of Jere Brophy, Walter Doyle, N. L. Gage, Thomas Good, and Barak Rosenshine. Their research tends to focus on teacher effectiveness and on the products or results of teaching.

6. During the 1990s and beyond, two basic trends influenced research on teaching. One was the nature of expertise in teaching and how expert and novice teachers differed in approach and in perceiving and analyzing classroom events. The second trend promoted different forms of investigating teaching based on language and dialogue: metaphors, stories, biographies, autobiographies, expert opinions, voice, and reflection. All these methods tend to dismiss traditional quantitative and empirical methods of research.

7. We need to promote caring, supporting and empathetic teachers who are willing to allow students to develop their natural curiosity and talents. We should avoid plans, methods, and evaluation systems that lock us into prescriptive or predetermined behaviors. We might think of teaching as a human endeavor involving human relationships between students and teachers.

## ■ QUESTIONS TO CONSIDER ■

1. How would you use the Flanders interaction analysis scale to provide feedback to a beginning teacher?

2. What teacher characteristics and competencies described in this chapter seem important for effective teaching in your school district? Why?

3. What behaviors listed by Gage or Good and Brophy coincide with the ideal teacher behavior in your school?

4. What makes a master teacher or star teacher? How would you compare your behaviors with a master or star teacher?

5. How would you compare behaviorist teachers with humanist teachers?

## ■ THINGS TO DO ■

1. Discuss in class: To what extent is teaching a science or an art?

2. Volunteer to teach a lesson in class for about ten minutes. Use a simplified version of the Flanders interaction analysis scale (direct versus indirect) or Bellack's verbal behaviors (structuring, soliciting, responding, reacting). Note whether there is agreement among class members in categorizing your teacher behavior.

3. Recall three or four of your favorite teachers. Compare their teacher characteristics, as you remember them, with the list of successful characteristics compiled by Barr. Which characteristics on Barr's list do you think they possess?

4. Interview several experienced teachers about the recommended teacher principles and methods of Rosenshine, Gage, and Brophy. Do the teachers support or reject the recommendations? What reservations do teachers bring up? What do they like about the recommendations?

5. Observe two or three teachers (or professors) while they teach. Categorize them as novice, beginning, advanced, competent, proficient, or expert. Defend your reasoning.

# ■ RECOMMENDED READINGS ■

Darling-Hammond, Linda. *The Right to Learn.* San Francisco: Jossey-Bass, 2001. A discussion concerning how to improve teacher education and staff development.

Good, Thomas L., and Jere E. Brophy. *Looking into Classrooms,* 9th ed. Upper Saddle River, NJ: Pearson, 2003. An important book that helped move the field from the study of teacher processes to teacher products and a convincing argument that teachers do make a difference.

Goodlad, John I. *Teachers for Our Nation's Schools.* San Francisco: Jossey-Bass, 1994. As many as twenty-nine teacher training institutions are examined and nineteen postulates are set forth for reforming teacher education.

Joyce, Bruce, and Marsha Weil. *Models of Teaching,* 6th ed. Boston: Allyn and Bacon, 2000. A book that combines theory with practice and examines various cognitive and behavioral teaching models.

Lieberman, Ann, and Lynne Miller. *Teachers—Transforming Their World and Their Work.* New York: Teachers College Press, 1999. How to improve teaching and institutional changes within schools and school districts.

Ornstein, Allan C. *Teaching and Schooling in America: Pre- and Post-September 11.* Boston: Allyn and Bacon, 2003. A discussion concerning major social issues related to education, including good and evil, morality and immorality, justice and injustice, equality and inequality.

Perone, Vito. *Lessons for New Teachers.* Boston: McGraw-Hill, 2000. A historical analysis of teaching, including the challenges of today's classrooms.

# ■ KEY TERMS ■

autobiography
biography
master teacher
metaphors
nonverbal behavior

star teachers
stories
teacher–student interactions
teacher characteristics
teacher contexts

teacher effects
teacher styles
teaching as an art
teaching as a science
voice

# ■ REFERENCES ■

Amidon, E. J., & Flanders, N. A. (1971). *The role of the teacher in the classroom.* St. Paul, MN: Amidon & Associates.

Anderson, G. L., & Herr, K. (1999, June–July). The new paradigm wars. *Educational Researcher,* 12–21.

Apple, M. W. (1996). *Cultural politics and education.* New York: Teachers College Press.

Ayers, W. (2001). *To teach: The journey of a teacher.* New York: Teachers College Press.

Azumi, J. E., & Lerman, J. L. (1987, November). Selecting and rewarding master teachers. *Elementary School Journal,* 197.

Banks, J. A. (1997). *Cultural diversity and education* (4th ed.). Boston: Allyn and Bacon.

Barr, A. S. (1959, March). Characteristics of successful teachers. *Phi Delta Kappan,* 282–284.

Barth, R. S. (2001). *Learning by heart.* San Francisco: Jossey-Bass.

Barzun, J. (1972). *Teachers in America* (Rev. ed.). Lanham, MD: University Press of America.

Bellack, A. A., Kliebard, H. M., Hyman, R. T., & Smith, F. L. (1966). *The language of the classroom.* New York: Teachers College Press.

Biddle, B. J., & Ellena, W. J. (1964). *Contemporary research on teacher effectiveness.* New York: Holt, Rinehart, & Winston.

Bolster, A. (1983, April). Toward a more effective model of research on teaching. *Harvard Educational Review,* 294–308.

Borich, G. D. (2003). *Observation skills for effective teachers* (4th ed.). Columbus, OH: Merrill.

Brophy, J. E. (1998). *Motivating students to learn.* Boston: McGraw-Hill.

Bullough, R. V., & Pinnegar, S. (2001, April). Guidelines for quality in autobiographical forms of self-study. *Educational Researcher,* 12–22.

Burdell, P., & Swadener, B. B. (1999, August–September). Critical narrative and autoethnography in education. *Educational Researcher,* 21–26.

Carter, K. L. (1993, January). The place of story in the study of teaching. *Educational Researcher,* 5–12.

Castiglione, B. (1959). *The book of the courtier* (Rev. ed.). Garden City, NY: Doubleday. (Original work published 1528)

Clark, C. (1991, September–October). Real lessons from imaginary teachers. *Journal of Curriculum Studies,* 429–434.

Cochran-Smith, M., & Lytle, S. L. (1999, October). The teacher research movement: A decade later. *Educational Researcher,* 1–25.

Cohen, J. (1999). *Educating minds and hearts.* New York: Teachers College Press.

Coulter, D. (1999, April). The epic and the novel: Dialogism and teacher research. *Educational Researcher,* 4–13.

Coulter, D. (2000). Teaching as communicative action. In V. Richardson (Ed.), *The handbook of research teaching* (4th ed., pp. 48–69). Washington, DC: American Educational Research Association.

Counts, G. S. (1932). *Dare the schools build a new social order?* New York: Day.

Cremin, L. A. (1961). *The transformation of the school.* New York: Random House.

Darling-Hammond, L. (2001, May). The challenge of staffing our schools. *Educational Leadership,* 12–17.

Darling-Hammond, L., Berry, B., & Thoreson, A. (2001, Spring). Does teacher certification matter? *Education Evaluation and Policy Analysis,* 57–77.

Dooley, C. (1998, March–April). Teaching as a two-way street: Discontinues among metaphors, images, and classroom realities. *Journal of Teacher Education,* 97–107.

Doyle, W. (1985, September). Effective teaching and concept of master teacher. *Elementary School Journal,* 30.

Doyle, W. (1992). Curriculum and pedagogy. In P. W. Jackson (Ed.), *Handbook of research on curriculum* (pp. 486–516). New York: Macmillan.

Eisner, E. W. (1993, April). The art and craft of teachers. *Educational Researcher,* 8.

Eisner, E. W. (1997, August–September). The promise and perils of alternative forms of data representation. *Educational Researcher,* 4–11.

Eisner, E. W. (1998). *The kind of schools we need.* Portsmouth, NH: Heinemann.

Eisner, E. W. (2002). *The educational imagination* (3rd ed.). Columbus, OH: Merrill.

Elbaz, F. (1991, January–February). Research on teacher's knowledge: The evolution of discourse. *Journal of Curriculum Studies,* 1–19.

Errante, A. (2000, March). But sometimes you're not part of the story. *Educational Researcher,* 16–27.

Flanders, N. A. (1965). *Teacher influence, pupil attitudes, and achievement.* Washington, DC: U.S. Government Printing Office.

Flanders, N. A. (1970). *Analyzing teacher behavior.* Reading, MA: Addison-Wesley.

Fried, R. (1995). *The passionate teacher.* Boston: Beacon Press.

Fried, R. (2001). *The passionate learner.* Boston: Beacon Press.

Gage N. L. (1978). *The scientific basis of the art of teaching.* New York: Teachers College Press.

Galloway, C. M. (1968, December). Nonverbal communication. *Theory into Practice,* 172–175.

Galloway, C. M. (1984). Nonverbal behavior and teaching student relationships: An intercultural perspective. In A. Wolgang (Ed.), *Nonverbal behavior* (pp. 411–430). Toronto: Hogrefe.

Gardner, H. (1983). *Frames of mind: The theory of multiple intelligences.* New York: Basic Books.

Gardner, J. (1962). *Excellence: Can we be equal and excellent too?* New York: Harper & Row.

Giroux, H. A. (1983). *Theory and resistance in education.* Westport, CT: Bergin & Garvey.

Glasser, W. (1969). *Schools without failure.* New York: Harper & Row.

Glasser, W. (1990). *The quality school.* New York: HarperCollins.

Good, T. L., & Brophy, J. E. (1986). Teacher behavior and student achievement. In M. C. Wittrock (Ed.), *Handbook of research on teaching* (3rd ed., pp. 328–375). New York: Macmillan.

Good, T. L., & Brophy, J. E. (2003). *Looking in classrooms* (9th ed.). Boston: Addison-Wesley.

Goodman, P. (1964). *Compulsory mis-education.* New York: Horizon Press.

Goodnough, A. (2000, July 15). Regents create a new path to teaching. *New York Times,* B4, 7.

Gordon, G. L. (1999, December). Teacher talent and urban schools. *Phi Delta Kappan,* 304.

Grant, C. (1999). *Multicultural research: A reflective engagement with race, class, gender, and sexual orientation.* Philadelphia: Falmer Press.

Grant, C. A., & Lei, J. L. (2001). *Global constructions of multicultural education.* Mahwah, NJ: Erlbaum.

Greene, M. (1998). *The dialectic of teaching.* New York: Teachers College Press.

Greene, M. (2000, March–April). Imagining futures: Public school and possibility. *Journal of Curriculum Studies,* 267–280.

Greene, M. (2001). *Variations on a blue guitar.* New York: Teachers College Press.

Grumet, M. R. (1987, Fall). The politics of personal knowledge. *Curriculum Inquiry,* 319–329.

Grumet, M. R., & Stone, L. (2000, March–April). Feminism and culture: Getting our act together. *Journal of Curriculum Studies,* 189–197.

Haberman, M. (1991, December). The pedagogy of poverty versus good teaching. *Phi Delta Kappan,* 290–294.

Haberman, M. (1992, Spring). The ideology of star teachers of children of poverty. *Education Horizons,* 125–129.

Haberman, M. (1995, Winter). The dimensions of excellence. *Peabody Journal of Education,* 24–43.

Haberman, M., & Post, L. (1998, Winter). Teachers for multicultural settings: The power of selection. *Theory Into Practice,* 99.

Hargreaves, A. (1996, January–February). Revisiting voice. *Educational Researcher,* 12–19.

Hillocks, G. (1999). *Ways of thinking, ways of teaching.* New York: Teachers College Press.

Horton, M., Kohl, J., & Kohl, H. (1998). *The long overhaul: An autobiography.* New York: Teachers College Press.

Houghton, P. (2001, May). Finding allies. *Phi Delta Kappan,* 706.

Illich, I. (1971). *Deschooling Society.* New York: Harper & Row.

Jackson, P. W. (1990). *Life in classrooms* (2nd ed.). New York: Teachers College Press.

Jacobsen, D. A., Eggen, P., & Kauchak, D. P. (2002). *Methods for teaching* (6th ed.). Columbus, OH: Merrill.

Jersild, A. (1955). *When teachers face themselves.* New York: Teachers College Press.

Kagan, D., & Timmins, D. J. (1995, Winter). The genesis of a school–university partnership. *Educational Forum,* 48–62.

Kohn, A. (1998). *What to look for in a classroom.* San Francisco: Jossey-Bass.

Lehrer, R., & Schauble, L. (2002). *Investigating real data in the classroom.* New York: Teachers College Press.

Linn, R. L. (2000, March). Assessment and accountability. *Educational Researcher,* 4–15.

Lippitt, R., & White, R. K. (1943). The social climate of children's groups. In R. G. Barker, J. S. Kounin, & H. F. Wright (Eds.), *Child behavior and development* (pp. 485–508). New York: McGraw-Hill.

Lippitt, R., & White, R. K. (1958). An experimental study of leadership and group life. In E. F. Harley (Ed.), *Readings in social psychology* (3rd ed.). New York: Holt, Rinehart, & Winston.

McLaren, P. (1995). Critical pedagogy and the pragmatics of justice. In M. Peters (Ed.), *Education and the postmodern condition* (pp. 91–92). Westport, CT: Bergin & Garvey.

McLaren, P., & Farahmandpur, R. (2000, April). Reconsidering Marx in post-Marxist times: A review for postmodernism? *Educational Researcher,* 25.

McNergey, R. F., & Carrier, C. A. (1991). *Teacher development* (2nd ed.). New York: Macmillan.

Neumann, A., & Peterson, P. L. (1997). *Learning from our lives: Women research and autobiography in education.* New York: Teachers College Press.

Noddings, N. (1992). *The challenge to care in schools.* New York: Teachers College Press.

Noddings, N. (2001). *Educating moral people.* New York: Teachers College Press.

Ornstein, A. C. (1985, November–December). Research on teaching: Issues and trends. *Journal of Teacher Education,* 27–31.

Ornstein, A. C. (1990, October). A look at teacher effectiveness research. *NASSP Bulletin*, 78–88.

Ornstein, A. C. (1993, January). Successful teachers: Who they are. *American School Board Journal*, 24–27.

Ornstein, A. C. (1995a, Winter). Beyond effective teaching. *Peabody Journal of Education*, 2–23.

Ornstein, A. C. (1995b). Beyond effective teaching. In A. C. Ornstein (Ed.), *Teaching: Theory into practice* (pp. 273–291). Boston: Allyn and Bacon.

Ornstein, A. C. (1995c, Winter). The new paradigm in research on teaching. *Educational Forum*, 124–129.

Ornstein, A. C. (Ed.). (1995d). *Teaching: Theory into practice*. Boston: Allyn and Bacon.

Ornstein, A. C. (2003). *Teaching and schooling in America: Pre- and post-September 11*. Boston: Allyn and Bacon.

Ornstein, A. C., & Lasley, T. J. (2004). *Strategies for effective teaching* (4th ed.). Boston: McGraw-Hill.

Page, R. N. (2001, September–October). Common sense: A form of teacher knowledge. *Journal of Curriculum Studies*, 525–533.

Palmer, P. J. (2003). The heart of a teacher. In A. C. Ornstein, L. S. Behar-Horenstein, & E. F. Pajak (Eds.), *Contemporary issues in curriculum* (3rd ed., pp. 66–76). Boston: Allyn and Bacon.

Patterson, M. L. (1983). *Nonverbal behavior: A functional perspective*. New York: Springer.

Perrone, V. (1998). *Teacher with a heart*. New York: Teachers College Press.

Peterson, P. L. (1979). Direct instruction reconsidered. In P. L. Peterson & H. J. Walberg (Eds.), *Research on teaching: Concepts, findings, and implications* (pp. 57–69). Berkeley, CA: McCutchan.

Pinar, W. F. (1999). *Contemporary curriculum discourses*. New York: Peter Lang.

Popkewitz, T. S. (1998). *Struggling for the soul*. New York: Teachers College Press.

Putnam, R. T., & Borko, H. (2000, January–February). What do new views of knowledge . . . say about research on teaching? *Educational Researcher*, 4–16.

Rosenshine, B. V. (1979). Content, time and direct instruction. In P. L. Peterson & H. J. Walberg (Eds.), *Research on teaching: Concepts, findings, and implications* (pp. 28–56). Berkeley, CA: McCutchan.

Rosenshine, B. V., & Furst, N. F. (1971). Research in teacher performance criteria. In B. O. Smith (Ed.), *Research on teacher education* (pp. 37–42). Englewood Cliffs, NJ: Prentice-Hall.

Rosenshine, B. V., & Furst, N. F. (1973). The use of direct observation to study teaching. In R. M. Travers (Ed.), *Second handbook of research on teaching* (pp. 122–183). Chicago: Rand McNally.

Rubin, L. J. (1985). *Artistry of teaching*. New York: Random House.

Ryans, D. G. (1960). *Characteristics of teachers*. Washington, DC: American Council of Education.

Rymes, B. (2001). *Conversational borderlands*. New York: Teachers College Press.

Sarason, S. B. (1999). *Teaching as a performing art*. New York: Teachers College Press.

Sawyer, L. (2001, February). Revamping a teacher evaluation system. *Educational Leadership*, 44–47.

Scherer, M. (2001, May). Improving the quality of the teaching force: A conversation with David C. Berliner. *Educational Leadership*, 6–11.

Sears, J. T. (2003). Challenges for educators: Lesbian, gay, and bisexual families. In A. C. Ornstein, L. Behar-Horenstein, & E. F. Pajak (Eds.), *Contemporary issues in curriculum* (3rd ed., pp. 362–381). Boston: Allyn and Bacon.

Shulman, L. S. (1986). Paradigms and research programs in the study of teaching. In M. C. Wittrock (Ed.), *Handbook of research on teaching* (3rd ed., pp. 3–36). New York: Macmillan.

Shulman, L. S. (1991, September–October). Ways of seeing, ways of knowing, ways of teaching, ways of learning about teaching. *Journal of Curriculum Studies*, 393–396.

Sizer, T. R. (1985). *Horace's compromise*. Boston: Houghton Mifflin.

Stephens, P., & Valentine, J. (1986, Winter). Assessing principal nonverbal communication. *Educational Research Quarterly*, 60–68.

Tell, C. (2001, February). Approaching good teaching: A conversation with Lee Schulman. *Educational Leadership*, 6–11.

Tuckman, B. W. (1986, Janurary). Feedback and the change process. *Phi Delta Kappan,* 341–344.

Tuckman, B. W. (1995, Winter). The interpersonal teacher model. *Educational Forum,* 177–185.

Wiggins, G. (1998). *Educative assessment.* San Francisco: Jossey-Bass.

Willis, S. (2002, March). Creating a knowledge base for teaching. *Educational Leadership,* 6–11.

# Strategies for Understanding Literature and Informational Sources

## chapter 11

Focusing Questions

1. Why is the concept of "experience language" important for considering the building of new vocabulary and new concept ideas?

2. Why is reading comprehension dependent on both reader- or knowledge-based factors and text-based factors?

3. What does the reading of good literature offer students?

4. Why is the expository or informational style of writing more difficult for most students to process than the narrative style?

5. Can you think of some major instructional strategies that can be used with story or literature readings and what particular strength each strategy brings to the reading comprehension process?

**6.** How can teachers help students plan for, understand, and write about the many topics found in content area subjects with so much information found in textbooks, information books, and the World Wide Web?

**7.** Why is it important to develop students' metacognitive thinking abilities about strategies?

This chapter presents major concepts regarding teacher and student use of learning strategies. After examining the underlying features of comprehension in general and why experience is a significant factor in the understanding process, we look at the nature of literature and of expository, informational sources to see what each contributes to the learning and understanding processes. Also, the chapter focuses on the strategies and instructional tasks teachers use to help students gain proficiency in understanding while using both literary and informational sources.

Using scaffolding procedures, teachers initially model or demonstrate how to engage in a strategy, then allow students to practice and apply the strategy as apprentice learners, and then encourage students to take ownership of the learning strategy to apply on their own in ever-changing content situations. Other teachers systematically introduce comprehension strategies in a logical way, allow the strategies to take root in students' minds over time, and monitor students' progress to determine what they can do and what they still need (Villaume & Brabham, 2002). Whereas this chapter looks at what teachers and students do to learn and enjoy textual readings, the next chapter examines the rich and varied world of text presentation—how literary and informational sources are arranged and made available for students.

## ■ EXPERIENCE AS A PRIME CONCEPT RESOURCE

Oral language fluency and life experiences contribute to the reading understanding process. In Chapter 2, we discussed the interactive relationship between the preexisting information in the reader's head and the information that meets the reader's eyes during the act of reading. The less information a reader has about a topic, the more critical reading is needed to gain the information. The more information and experience the reader has about the topic, the less actual reading of words in serial order need occur; the reader can sample, select, and predict what chunk of words to read.

Thus, children's experiences with oral language, with stories in verbal and in print form, with other people, and with life activities provide the naturalness that allows them to move into a written language environment. Ken Goodman, a well-known literacy author, suggests that direct instruction in word-attack skills, phonemic awareness, phonics, and even reading comprehension is probably unnecessary because proficiency with oral language provides the reader with a meaning-based structure for the analysis and recognition of unfamiliar words (K. Goodman, 1996). This notion is supported by Lucy Calkins, who notes that the foundation for reading is not to be found in the phoneme–grapheme association code, but in children's play, in their talk, and in sharing time when they listen to adults read (Calkins, 1997).

Although we agree that real-life experiences provide the most direct kind of learning, we also realize that they are difficult to achieve in the traditional classroom setting. Most experiential learning in the classroom occurs through the secondary layer of spoken and written words. Even though talk and print are easier modes for the teacher to supply, they may not be enough to allow students to conceptualize the underlying concrete experiences they represent. When teachers use and provide language sources, students think and conceptualize in the abstract. Through firsthand experience, the impact of learning is immediate and concrete.

When the language experience approach is used, as discussed in Chapter 3, the text that is produced comes from the children themselves as they dictate to the teacher an event or experience. The strategy behind language experience is to provide a natural, smooth way for children to learn to read. They read the words in the sentences they themselves have produced. They fully understand what they read, and no unknown vocabulary words hinder their understanding of content.

Now suppose that the premise of the strategy is reversed. Suppose that we wish to place *experience* before *language* so that the world of natural experiences provides new insights and new ways to use language. With the concept of **experience language,** the teacher provides a new or enriching experience with the explicit purpose of associating new vocabulary with that experience so that students can make experiential and language gains. Parents do this in a natural way when they involve their children in life's wonderful experiences. They take their children shopping, to museums, to zoos, and to other points of interest; they help their children with arts and athletic activities; and they take them on trips to near and far destinations. Each of these life experiences involves a unique vocabulary, and parents and other adults naturally use the words of their experiences as they are unfolding. This learning context is that of the natural environment.

During the regular school year, with its scheduled periods of instruction occurring at fixed intervals during the school day to cover state- and district-mandated subjects, schools have a difficult time involving students in such natural learning contexts. They do this best when they offer after-school programs and send their students off-campus for summer and weekend educational programs, field trips, and cultural events. For instance, in one such program, seven outdoor activities provided the natural context for the introduction and learning of 175 vocabulary words (Sinatra, 1991). In the one activity of field mathematics, inner-city children demonstrated "pace," "pivot," the three-foot "stride," "intervals," and so forth in order to "calculate" distance between buildings. Based on the students' calculations, they could do "area" and "perimeter" calculation work and use the new words in their reading and writing activities.

Teachers do provide experiential, hands-on learning situations when they involve their students in science experiments, computer-generated projects, and math problem-solving activities, such as measuring, weighing, and calculating. The key for teachers is to structure a learning situation in which children are involved in action while the teacher uses the words of the experience and weaves them into the learning activity. Think of the ways in which action-oriented activities occur in school settings, such as in the rapidly disappearing school "subjects" of gym, music, shop, home economics, health, and the visual, graphic, and fine arts. A recurring "shame on you" attitude preva-

*Table 11.1*   Content Lessons Initiated through Activities Having an Experiential Base

| Discipline and Grade Level | Concept Topic | Concrete Activity Materials and/or Settings | New Vocabulary |
|---|---|---|---|
| Science—Primary | How a seed grows | Potting soil, seeds, containers or plastic bag, paper towels, and water placed near sunlight | *Seed, stem, sprout, soil, roots, stalk, flowers, sunlight, growth, mineral, air, gases* |
| Science—Intermediate | Effects of oil spill in ocean | Low-depth basin half-filled with water and sand layered on one side. Beach effect is created with rocks, shells, driftwood, etc. Latex gloves for students when pouring heavy-duty motor oil. | *Crude oil, oil spill, components, prevention, environment, protection, destruction, inhabitants, predict, disaster* |
| Social Studies—Intermediate | How the archeologist and anthropologist work | A large tank or basin filled with soil or sand. Different-colored soil would indicate strata. Into soil are placed artifacts such as coins, pottery pieces, jewels, bones, etc. Children have brushes, spoons, tweezers, strainers, and magnifying glasses. | *Anthropologist, archeologist, artifacts, primitive, excavate, hypothesis, civilized, strata, composition, conclusions* |

lent in education today is doing away with these opportunities to enhance childrens' thinking and literacy skills (because they're considered frills). Instead, teachers are doubling up on periods of the so-called basics, which are often presented in an abstract way without concrete referents.

In Table 11.1, some selected concept topics are presented by discipline area and general grade-level range. The activity materials and settings needed to provide the experiential base to activate the lesson are indicated. Finally, the new vocabulary words introduced through the lesson are indicated in the last column. Do you agree that these words are appropriate for students to learn at these grade levels and for these topics, and that the strategy of using experientially based learning can assist learners with new concepts and vocabulary development?

# ■ INSTRUCTIONAL TASKS AND STUDENT UNDERSTANDING

Instructional tasks are at the core of decisions that affect the classroom setting and establish how students approach and process literacy events. Most teachers maintain control over instructional tasks by choosing what is to be taught, what materials and methods are to be used, and how much students can interact. Some teachers, however,

**BOX 11.1** Instructional Tasks Can Ensure Academic Success for At-Risk, Poor, and Minority Students

One author has observed that teachers across districts and grade levels favor the following instructional tasks and strategies when attempting to close the achievement gap between minority and nonminority students:

- They emphasize reading skills.
- They teach higher-order thinking skills to at-risk students through good questioning and response techniques.
- They routinely reteach to make sure students "got it."
- They use "Fishbowl" and other grouping techniques to ensure that at-risk students participate.
- They motivate students by getting them emotionally and affectively involved.
- They show patience and care.

*Source:* Adapted from Larry Bell, "Strategies That Close the Gap," *Educational Leadership* (December 2002–January 2003), pp. 32–34.

do permit student input in planning content and activities, as we noted in the discussion of cooperative group activities in Chapter 9. The key variable, of course, is the teacher and not the grade level. When the teacher has complete control over instruction, it is likely that most students, if not all, will be engaged in a single classroom task and work toward the same goal with the same content. According to four authors, an important principle of the direct instruction model is that students *can* learn what is being taught. The factors of family history, race, and social class are not considered an explanation for poor achievement. If the teacher follows the exact procedures of the curriculum strands of a direct instruction approach and has control of students' progress though mastery checkup tests, students will, according to the theory, consistently achieve mastery of content (Kozioff, LaNunziata, Cowardin, & Bressellieu, 2000–2001). Conversely, when students have input, they will probably work on different classroom tasks (Peverly, 1991). Box 11.1 indicates some major instructional tasks and strategies that teachers have found useful for at-risk learners.

## ■ UNDERSTANDING TEXT

Throughout this book, we refer to some of the basic processes readers must use to understand the texts they read. Just as printed words are at the center of the reading act itself, reading comprehension is at the core of reading (Durkin, 1992). There's a lot more to reading understanding than simply reading the words correctly. Nor are life experiences or having many experiences with different kinds of texts enough to guarantee full and rich reading comprehension. While reading, the reader has to think in various ways, and we label these ways using terms such as *making predictions* or *hypothesis testing, confirming predictions and hypotheses, interpreting and analyzing text, synthesizing ideas, accommodating text to prior experiences,* and so on. In essence, a reader has to ask, "Am I getting it? Is what I'm reading in this story or this informational text making sense to me?" Furthermore, as we noted in earlier chapters, students' cultures, the culture of the classroom and school, and the popular culture have an impact on how particular students approach and sustain the reading act (Finders & Hynds, 2003; Pransky & Bailey, 2002–2003).

Making sense of a text involves the processes of bringing both cognitive and affective information from the mind to printed words and organizational patterns of writing. Many authors refer to this dual processing as being both reader or knowledge based and text based (Burns, Roe, & Ross, 1999; Leu & Kinzer, 1999). What a reader brings to a text is based on stored knowledge of the reading process itself, on expectations of what is to be gained from reading a particular text, and on prior knowledge related to the topic. The text bears a collection of meanings that the reader must insightfully puzzle out to gain meaning. The expression "learning from texts" is better construed as "learning with texts," because readers have a great deal to contribute to the learning of information from texts as they mentally interact to gain meaning and construct knowledge (Vacca & Vacca, 2002). In its detailed review of 451 studies published since 1970 on the issue of text understanding, the National Reading Panel (2000) noted that when readers actively associate print ideas with their own knowledge and experiences, allowing them to construct representations in their minds, their reading comprehension is strengthened. The panel also noted that rather than teaching specific skills or even strategies, teachers need to help students see reading as a problem-solving task that requires the activation of strategic thinking.

## ■ HOW TEXT IS ORGANIZED

With all of the preceding factors related to the understanding of text, how does the teacher help students achieve reading comprehension, from basic comprehension levels to higher-level interpretive thinking, creativity, and application? First, we need to look at the two basic ways prose text is organized. Historically, prose has been categorized into literary or fiction writing and expository or informational writing. Literary and fiction writing is generally called literature, stories, or narration. In recent years, a large amount of research has been done on the nature of story organization, and this focus has nicely coincided with or been sparked by great interest in the whole language philosophy and the use of children's literature as a major vehicle for reading instruction. Two authors comment that for over a decade a "quiet revolution" has taken place in our elementary schools as teachers have used children's literature both in reading instruction and in support of all other areas of the curriculum (Freeman & Person, 1998).

We have commented on the importance of early and sustained book reading to and with children—a process we call lap reading—and how reading aloud prepares children for the language and structural organization of the narrative. The use of children's literature is a common practice in the school setting and is reinforced with basal readers and anthology collections. Indeed, by the mid-1980s, authorities believed that basal readers contained up to 95 percent narrative text format (S. Ryan, 1986). Soon after, another author commented that the materials children read in elementary school are 90 percent of the narrative type (Trabassor, 1994), and in 2000, it was pointed out that literacy instruction in today's classroom focuses almost exclusively on fiction and the appreciation of literature (Venezky, 2000). The strength of using literature as a major vehicle for reading instruction is that it promotes great interest in reading, furthers language development, and encourages the ability to write (Galda & Cullinan, 1991).

## What Art Thou, Literature?

Most of us would agree that the narrative format is a primary condition of human thinking. We think in sequence and causality as the mind works to plan our everyday lives. We plan this and arrange that; because of how we planned, we anticipate that particular outcomes will occur; when they don't happen the way we wished them to happen, we experience tension (I'm really angry); acquiescence (It was fate); or fortitude (I'll try again). This notion that narrative is essential to human thought and experience prevails in the research and study of children's development with literacy; scholars and researchers have emphasized the value of story in children's oral language, reading, and writing development (Freeman & Person, 1998).

When humankind writes down its natural order of thinking to relate to others and sprinkles the prose with a lot of imagination, the story—a.k.a. literature—is born. Stories not only help us make sense of our lives and help us think with mental pictures but they also reveal a desire to do and be good (Kilpatrick, 1993). Because the compelling feature of all good stories is mystery or dilemma, solving the mystery through problem-based inquiry can be incorporated in such disciplines as mathematics, chemistry, and even abstract calculus (Wiggins & McTighe, 1998). To be sure, stories are an excellent medium for presenting young minds with the strategy of scientific thinking because science can be told as an intriguing and informing story (Wilson, 2002). One writer of historical information books notes that when students read original source materials left behind by the peoples of a specific period, they come to see how their own lives connect with chains of generations (Metzer, 1993).

Many have acknowledged the importance of immersing children, youth, and adults in the reading of stories and literature as a way to provide a sound basis for humanistic education. Literature shows humans at their best. They strive for something against adversity. These strivings are often called "conflicts" (or troubles), and resolving the conflicts is the classical basis for plot. Thus we can have conflicts such as humans against nature, humans against humans, or a human against himself or herself. As young people read and sense the struggle of their kind to overcome and forbear, they can learn to appreciate and emulate the human condition. Because the main characters in contemporary award-winning children's books are about the same age as middle school students, from ten to fifteen years old, the literary characters face emotional and moral dilemmas and decisions similar to those of young readers today (Friedman & Cataldo, 2002). Through the study of literature, students can be shown how to understand the human qualities revealed in stories, how to enhance and broaden their perspectives of others, how characters interact with the institution of society to resolve or not resolve conflicts, and how to become more tolerant of and empathetic with both the fictional characters and the real people they meet (Barzun, 2002; Emery, 1996). William Kilpatrick adds that through stories caring parents and thoughtful teachers can help children identify with models of courage and virtue in ways that problem-solving exercises and classroom discussion don't encourage (Kilpatrick, 1993).

Through literature, young children's understanding of the human experience enlarges as they partake of the folk and cultural stories passed down through generations of peoples. Through mulitcultural literature, children can develop a true understanding of people from other cultures and get beneath the surface differences of color, ethnicity, and culture to discover that all people have universal qualities of worth and kindness (Dowd, 1992). Multicultural literature is one way to support diversity in the curriculum while teaching children about cultural issues that are rarely covered in schools and that require students to question traditional, prevailing views about people of color and other cultures (Boyd, 2002; Perini, 2002).

Becoming engaged in a story requires desire and mental energy. A literary reading can be likened to a problem-solving process, note three authors (Barone, Eeds, & Mason, 1995). As readers are pulled into a good story through the dilemmas of its characters, the story invites vicarious participation so that readers invest their mental energy in the dilemma. This immersion in the fictional world can encourage inquiry and elicit questions about the reader's own life. Literature, then, offers readers unique opportunities to take part in life experiences that might otherwise not be attainable.

Another teacher of literature asserts that many students labeled "poor readers" are actually lazy or reluctant readers. They don't interact mentally with the literary work. Reacting passively to the text, they eyeball pages assigned and expect the print to transmit information to the brain (Jago, 2000). At the other extreme, those designated as "academically gifted" students don't always "get it" either even if they read automatically and accurately and have good reading fluency. Careful, thoughtful reading of sophisticated literature takes dynamic comprehension work in which students gain metacognitive control of thinking and reading strategies (Cunningham & Wall, 1994).

## The Matter of Informational Text Sources

Students run into the informational or expository style of writing in all course work except in those reading, language arts, or English classes in which the narrative is the primary genre. Often, informational reading is called **content area reading** because the content is related to the traditional school subjects of social studies, science, health, mathematics, history, and so forth. These reading materials often introduce information concepts and terms, are written in a style different from the narrative, and require students to use the readings in particular ways, such as to remember great quantities of information or complete projects or experiments (Readence & Moore, 1994).

As children approach the fourth grade, they begin to do more and more of their reading in content textbooks, and it is at this grade level that students may begin to experience reading difficulties (Freeman & Person, 1998). These difficulties may begin to emerge because of the shift away from the familiar narrative focus to a text style that requires a great deal of information intake. Students in general have more difficulty understanding the expository text structure than the narrative structure because of insufficient prior knowledge of the many content topics, poor reading ability, lack of interest and motivation to learn about particular topics, and lack of sensitivity to how texts are organized (Wright & Rosenberg, 1993). The emphasis on the reading of expository structure found in content area textbooks and most Internet web sites increases with grade level. As students advance through the upper elementary and junior high grade levels, especially if they are segmented into departmentalized instruction by content domains, they are increasingly expected to read and understand their text materials (Vallecorsa, 1997).

The teacher cannot assume that students understand the organizational structure of expository text in particular and how authors use text features and typographical cues (such as boldface headings and italicized print) to signal ordering and importance of ideas. Later in this chapter, we discuss how teachers can help students use text features to understand more fully and use expository patterns of writing to follow the author's organizational plan.

## The Structure of Narrative and Expository Texts

Teachers use story schema, **story grammar analysis,** story maps, and even storyboarding to help students interpret the structure of childrens literature. These variations all refer to the same generic construct of the features of stories such as character, setting, problem or conflict, precipitating or initiating event, and plot, with attempts, outcomes, consequences, and resolution. Christine Gordon and Carl Braun initially postulated an ideal representation of story structure based on four essential features; setting, theme, plot, and resolution (Gordon & Braun, 1983). Paul van den Broek reviewed a number of story structures and found that the common "rules" for combining story events into coherent sequences were the setting in which the action took place, the initiating event, the internal response of the protagonist to the initiating event, the goal of the protagonist to motivate action leading to an outcome, and a conclusion containing the protagonist's reaction (van den Broek, 1989). David Lodge reduced the drama of stories to two essential questions—"Who did it?" and "What will happen next?"—and these in turn deal with issues of causality and temporality (Lodge, 1994). Jerome Bruner adds that what makes the story worth telling is Trouble with a capital *T.* The trouble arises out of misfits among those who act, the acts themselves, the goals pursued, and the means used to achieve ends (Bruner, 1997).

Grant Wiggins and Jay McTighe add two more dimensions to the structure of stories. First, they note that the storyteller usually doesn't present a straight-out, ordered sequence of events. The storyteller desires to raise questions about some mystery or dilemma and holds readers off before answering them. Along the way to answering the unanswered, the writer teaches the reader about people, situations, and ideas. Second, they believe that a curriculum based on the structure of stories offers teachers and students greater engagement and deeper understandings than content instruction based on the logic of explanation (Wiggins & McTighe, 1998).

Whatever the genre and whatever the specific literacy piece, story structure elements exist to some greater or lesser degree and provide a motif for teachers to help students unlock the meaning of a piece as it is being read. By being aware of the structural elements of stories, students have a mental road map to help them navigate through the features of any one particular story. Furthermore, it is likely that with repeated exposure to a familiar organizational pattern, students will develop a schema or cognitive framework that consistently helps them construct meaning from narrative texts.

Unlike narrative, expository text structure doesn't have a generic set of features; rather, **expository text structure** is characterized by a number of organizational patterns. Although authors are not in full agreement about categories or names for expository organizational patterns, there is some overlap. For instance, Judy Irwin identifies the five patterns of spatial description, temporal sequence, explanation, comparison–contrast, and definition–example (1991); Jean Gillat and Charles Temple also discuss five patterns: chronological, cause–effect, comparison–contrast, direction sequences, and expository–explanatory (2000); and Shirley Dickson's review includes the reportive, explanatory, persuasive, and comparison–contrast patterns (1999). Katherine Rowan indicates that whereas some define expository text by its purpose in that it seeks to inform or explain, others define it by the organizational structures of its writing style, such as exemplification, causal analysis, comparison, and contrast (1994).

A key concept of expository text structure is the way ideas and concepts are logically arranged. Those ideas and concepts more central to the understanding of the text are often called the main idea, the central thesis, or the macroselection level (Irwin, 1991). Such top-level structures in expository writing were presented more than twenty-five years ago in Bonnie Meyer's taxonomy of expository structure types (1975). She represented all the information from an informational reading in a detailed outline or "tree" structure (1984). The tree structure illustrates that some content ideas are superordinate to other ideas and that some ideas are subordinate to the top-level ideas. Specific details, which provide additional information to the ideas above them, are found at the bottom of the tree. The importance the author gives to aspects of the text's content is directly related to the way that content is arranged in the organizational plan for the reader to follow.

## What Research Says about Teaching Text Structure

Do students naturally perceive these narrative and expository text plans or do students have to be acculturated to these plans? Most sources agree that students need to be shown how top-level and subordinate structures coordinate in written texts. Direct instruction in narrative and expository organizational patterns helps children gain new knowledge of how writers organize stories, ideas, and concepts. With this prior knowledge, children can form plans or mind-sets of how texts are organized to assist their future comprehension and composing processes. These mental plans, known as text schemata, help guide children in formulating meaning as they read and write. When stories are stored as idealized mental representations, children's comprehension is strengthened (Fitzgerald, 1989). Therefore, a major goal of reading instruction should be to ensure that children learn how to achieve a rich, highly interconnected representation of their reading texts (van den Broeck, 1989; van den Broek, Linzie, Fletcher, & Marsolek, 2000).

Research in the teaching of text structure and organization has reported that such teaching has a positive effect on reading and writing instruction. Elementary and junior high school students who have learned how to identify and use an author's organizational structure comprehend more effectively than readers who do not possess this ability. During reading comprehension instruction, when text structure is intentionally taught before, during, and after the reading of a text, understanding, particularly of the most important information, improves (Mosenthal, 1994). Many educators and researchers use cognitive or semantic maps to teach students how text is organized.

When first graders were shown how to use simplified story mapping to improve comprehension of important narrative elements in unfamiliar stories, their comprehension was stronger than that of children who were engaged in a guided reading, less interactive procedure (Baumann & Bergeron, 1993). Likewise, third graders who were shown how to use mapping to guide their discussion and story construction outperformed matched controls, who followed a guided reading format similar to that of the first graders, in literal and inferential comprehension (Davis, 1994). In another study, middle school students with mild learning disabilities from an urban school district were divided into an experimental and a control group of fifteen students each. Both groups read the same passages and were administered the same pre- and posttests. However, the experimental group was taught how to use a mapping strategy that self-guided students step-by-step in how to construct the map while reading. The researcher found that the experimental students who were taught to create maps during the actual reading of text showed substantial gains in reading comprehension with below-grade-level reading passages as well as with on-grade-level reading passages when compared with the matched control group (Boyle, 1996). Low-achieving, inner-city seventh graders also significantly improved their understanding of science content, related to a study of the circulatory system, when they used a "tree map" or classification system to organize major and minor concept ideas (Guastello, Beasley, & Sinatra, 2000).

Teaching students about how their textbook ideas are organized or providing them with models of text organization has had a positive influence on both content reading comprehension and report writing (Englert, Raphael, Anderson, Anthony, & Stevens, 1991). Text organization instruction helps give writers a framework for producing, organizing, and editing their own compositions (Wong, 1997). When eighth graders took a state written essay examination before they had the opportunity to engage in text organization and accompanying mapping instruction, 1 percent scored in the inadequate category, 21 percent scored below average, and 79 percent scored in the average to excellent levels of writing. The following year, after students had text organization instruction in content area subjects, the eighth graders scored 88 percent in the average to excellent range and 12 percent in the below-average category (Cronin, Sinatra, & Barkley, 1992).

# ■ LITERATURE-BASED STRATEGIES

In this section, we present three broad-based strategies that can be used repeatedly with various literary readings to help readers enjoy, understand, and process what they read. However, in keeping with the general theme of the book to interject literacy principles and perspectives within the larger landscape of instructional practices throughout grades K–8, we have presented many strategies and techniques for helping children with literary understandings within other topics in the various chapters. To review the more obvious sections, in Chapter 2 we discussed how the social context is important in storytelling and story reading encounters and how visual and artistic representations strengthen children's understanding of the narrative. In Chapter 5, we discussed how literature and readings from content subjects are integrated within curriculum design approaches. In the different patterns of classroom grouping discussed in Chapter 9, we presented many modern-day approaches to literature-based learning. We showed that literature circles are a form of cooperative learning, that the individualized reading approach can be a highly successful way to engage children in literary and informational readings of their own choice, that reading and writing workshops assume their structural focus through identity with a literary piece or writing style, and that Reading Recovery uses children's stories to help children gain reading fluency and competency.

The strategies that follow present high-utility ways to help children enjoy and learn from literature without the skills focus that often accompanies direct instruction and teacher control over instructional tasks. Although these strategies are versatile enough to use with informational readings as well, we present a similar functional menu to use with that organizational style. Furthermore, the type of instruction inherent in these strategies supports the findings of the National Reading Panel (2000), which notes that there is a solid scientific base to the claim that story mapping in the form of semantic organizers, question answering, story structure analysis, and summarizing improves reading comprehension. Writing is connected to these strategies to make students even more active participants in the learning process.

## The Retelling Strategy

The **retelling strategy** is a highly motivational and versatile way to help children comprehend text at both literal and interpretive levels. In Chapter 3, we discussed how this strategy can be implemented to build the word reading skills of students at all levels. Retelling is versatile because the language of instruction comes from both authors and readers. Children's literature and sometimes informational books are the vehicles of instruction. Retelling is a more child-oriented way to say "reconstructing." Retellings, therefore, become verbal, artistic, and written reconstructions of author's stories in the children's own words and imagery. When a child or a group of children verbally retell an author's story, they reconstruct the story in their minds using their own language as well as the language of the author. Thus, teachers derive insight into how children constructed the text in their minds, allowing the teacher to witness and analyze comprehension as it occurs (Richek, Caldwell, Jennings, & Lerner, 2002).

As these retold stories are written down, they become a part of the children's reading and writing experiences. But they can also be expressed through the use of felt boards (storyboarding), puppet shows, and role playing (Walker, 2000). One author uses a technique of story reenactment, supported with simple costumes and/or small props, to enhance and demonstrate the events of a story (Herrell, 2000). A "live" reenactment requires that students use or create verbal interactions that make the characters come alive as students sequence the developing action.

Because the volume of children's literary and informational selections is extensive today, connected to all ages and grade levels as well as to the themes and topics children cover in school, retellings can be integrated nicely into the language arts curriculum while providing a fun way for students to read and write. Moreover, when teachers connect the sheer volume of children's literature to the number of ways to accomplish retellings, the literacy possibilities become enormous. It's best to begin the strategy use with a simple story map, as discussed below (and in Tips for Teachers 3.2), to elicit the written language and artistic plan of the first retelling draft. After teacher and/or peer interaction with the initial draft, students can transfer their initial and revised efforts to a retold "book." The book can be cast in the shape of a story character (a shape book), presented in an accordion format, or made to come alive with "pop-up" characters (as in pop-up books). Sequencing events is a natural, intrinsic part of the retelling process.

The teacher could prepare a basic story map by taking sheets of copy paper, either the 8½" × 11" or the 8½" × 14" size, and dividing them down the middle (see also the Story Maps section later in this chapter). The teacher will need to leave room on top of the page for children's names, the title and author of the book they are retelling, and any other information required. With two or three inches used on top for the author's information, students have the rest of the paper on which to make picture and writing panels. With a ruler, they measure off about four sections down the page and draw lines across. They then have a page layout with four panels to the left of the line drawn down the page and four panels to the right side—eight panels in all.

One side of four panels is for children's artwork and the other side is for their written retellings. Students draw key episodes of the story plot by revisualizing the story or by looking at the artist's illustrations. The number of picture panels a student produces depends on the richness of the student's imagination, his or her ability to draw, and the teacher's purpose in having the students re-create the story in depth. For each picture panel generated, there should be an accompanying text. The writing panels are prepared on the other side of the divided page. Each student retells the story in writing by matching the ideas reflected in the picture panels. Some teachers create a graphic figure or icon to represent the selection the children will retell. For instance, one teacher represented the story of Johnny Appleseed by placing an icon of an apple in both the left and right columns of a story map.

But the best of instructional tasks and strategic learning is yet to come. The teacher can exploit the fun students have in completing the story map procedure by considering the product just produced as a first draft. Use the story maps, run off on a copy machine, to collect the students' first-draft efforts. Then downplay the energy and creativity that children often put into their artwork; tell them to make simple planning drawings using stick figures and just a little coloring. Although children can make retold books in many different shapes, patterns, and styles, a simple but high-utility book that even junior high students enjoy is the fold-a-book, illustrated in Tips for Teachers 11.1. By using just one sheet of standard 8½" × 11" paper, students at all grade levels can make little fold-a-books to retell their stories or to summarize content in other courses.

The retelling procedure encourages strategic literacy development through narrative structure in three major ways. First, children naturally create their own **print-rich environment.** When the story maps and various child-constructed books are displayed around the classroom, an observer has a sense that the environment is alive with the written words and illustrations of children.

Second, children are immersed without formal teaching in the writing process while developing the structure of the narrative. The children are authors in apprentice. Thus the concept of retelling and **retold books** is an important one. The "retold by" written on the title page means that a child was engaged in the process of telling a story.

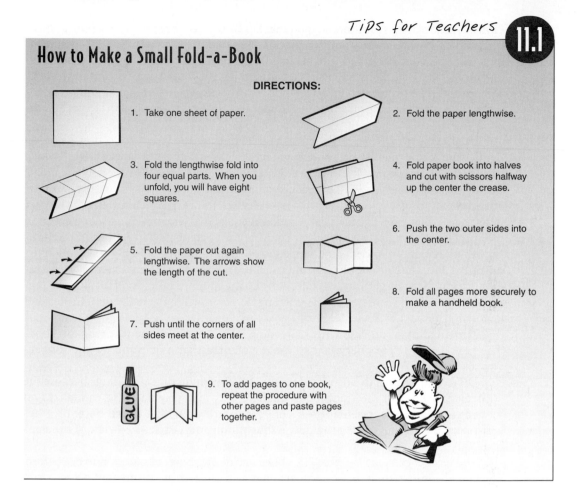

## How to Make a Small Fold-a-Book

**DIRECTIONS:**

1. Take one sheet of paper.

2. Fold the paper lengthwise.

3. Fold the lengthwise fold into four equal parts. When you unfold, you will have eight squares.

4. Fold paper book into halves and cut with scissors halfway up the center the crease.

5. Fold the paper out again lengthwise. The arrows show the length of the cut.

6. Push the two outer sides into the center.

7. Push until the corners of all sides meet at the center.

8. Fold all pages more securely to make a handheld book.

9. To add pages to one book, repeat the procedure with other pages and paste pages together.

The third major benefit derived from the production of retold books is that teachers collect a natural children's library of the narrative writing style. Children truly enjoy reading one another's books. So not only does the print-rich environment visually display the children's literacy efforts to the larger school community but also the books themselves are a source of the children's independent reading materials.

### The Directed Reading–Thinking Activity (DRTA)

The **directed reading-thinking activity (DRTA)** is a guided reading strategy in which the teacher establishes an instructional plan for moving or guiding children through a reading in incremental steps. The teacher sets the plan of reading and directs the plan but does not engage in direct teaching of the piece. The teacher's goal is to engage children in deep, meaningful reading by stimulating thinking through the liberal use of questions and subsequent discussion. Credited to Russell Stauffer, DRTA is a way to direct the reading–thinking process to capitalize on children's curiosity and desire to inquire

(1969). Although most authors suggest that DRTA be used for stories in published basal or anthology reading series and trade books and with expository, informational readings (Burns et al., 1999; Vacca & Vacca, 2002), we suggest this strategy be used with narrative-based selections because the nature of the flow of activity moves in waves of understanding and curiosity just like those that occur when parent and child read together at home. The naturalism of DRTA makes it refreshing to use with stories and literary selections.

Here's how the DRTA works. After the teacher reads the literary selection, he or she divides the reading into appropriate segments. The key concept is "appropriate," which may not be governed by the number of pages in each segment. Generally, segments break down by plot episodes. The teacher could determine when the initiating event occurs, as determined by something the main character does. From this event, the teacher determines what happens next and whether there is another consequence or resolution of a previous event. Or a natural halt could occur at characters' reactions to events as they think about or ponder what happened or what to do next. On it goes through the narrative until the story resolution and conclusion is reached. The teacher may have selected from three (beginning, middle, end) to any number of logical halt stops to segment the reading. There's no right or wrong decision making here to cause the teacher anxiety.

The dividing of the segments of reading is one aspect of the teacher's direction. The next is how the teacher plans to use the segments with questioning and interactive discussion.

DRTA can be a highly successful teaching tool with literature readings because the strategy brings all of the traditional language arts into play and also capitalizes on viewing and visual representation if children follow up with a retold book or other artistic creation. Figure 11.1 provides an illustration and a capsulized view of the steps of DRTA.

The teacher can turn to Table 7.3 when considering types of question to use before, after, or during reading, or the teacher may wish to use questions that access story grammar elements. The teacher could then use the questioning guide in Table 11.2. These questions can be used in the context of the DRTA procedure or used with the story mapping procedures discussed next.

## Story Maps

**Story maps** can be used to graphically represent the structure of stories as story grammar elements are being portrayed. Using story maps supports two of the National Reading Panel's recommendations to improve reading comprehension: (1) by making graphic representations of the material being read and (2) by learning the structure of stories as a means of remembering story content (2000). When using maps or **visual organizers** to represent the structure of the narrative, the teacher needs to consider adhering to the "glue" of plot structure: chronology (sequencing) and causality. We noted earlier that a character acts and this action causes a series of events to unfold. To be sure, the setting element of place often has a great bearing on the development and outcome of many stories. But it is the unfolding of time, sometimes cast backwards, that sets the plot in motion and carries the characters along with it as they cause twists and turns

| **Initiating Procedures** | | **Reading Act Procedures** |
|---|---|---|
| Teacher presents story or children's literature selection and motivates students to read. A "picture walk" could be taken and discussion and predictions generated about the story. | *Storybook walk and talk*<br> | Teacher presents story or children's literature selection and motivates students to read. A "picture walk" could be taken, discussion, and predictions generated about the story. |
| Teacher asks prediction and curiosity questions about first story segment (see before-reading questions in Table 7.3). | *First Segment*<br> | After reading first segment, teacher asks questions about the story in general and about characters, beginning events, and influence of setting and confirms children's earlier predictions. New vocabulary and concepts are discussed in context (see during-reading questions in Table 7.3). |
| Teacher asks prediction and curiosity questions about next story segment. | *Next Segment*<br> | After reading second segment, teacher asks interpretive, classifying, and retrospective questions. Earlier predictions are again discussed and students' reactions to story up to this point are encouraged. |
| Teacher asks prediction and curiosity questions about final story segment. Students tell about how they think story will end and what resolution will be. | *Final Segment*<br> | After final segment, teacher again asks clarifying, interpretive, reactive, and retrospective questions about story content and meaning. Students can also retell, summarize, tell feelings, and write reactions (see after-reading questions in Table 7.3). |

*Figure 11.1* The Directed Reading–Thinking Activity (DRTA): Strategy Steps for a Story Reading

*Table 11.2*  **Teacher Questioning Prompts to Elicit Story Grammar Elements**

| Story Element | Sample Questions |
|---|---|
| Characters | • Who are the main characters?<br>• Why do you think so?<br>• How do the minor characters support the story?<br>• Why does the main character want to start the story action?<br>• Do you identify with any of the characters? |
| Setting (time) | • When does the story occur?<br>• Does the time period change though the story? In what way? |
| Setting (place/locale) | • Where does the story take place?<br>• Does the locale (place) change through the story?<br>• What changes in the setting features of time or place affect the story?<br>• How does where the story takes place influence the characters? |
| The problem or goal | • Did the main character face a problem in the story? What was it?<br>• Or did the main character wish to achieve something, gain something, or learn something? If yes, what was this character's goal or objective in the story? |
| Starter action or precipitating event | • What was the event or incident that made the story begin?<br>• Why did the character allow this event to happen? |
| The plot sequence of events | • What were the main events or episodes that occurred after the starter action?<br>• Why did these events occur in the order they happened?<br>• Did the setting change when the plot events took place? If yes, did the change of setting influence what occurred in the action?<br>• What event occurred whereby the main character solved the problem or achieved the goal?<br>• Did this story have a main event that all of the action leads up to? What was that event? What happened after this main event or turning point? How did the event change the story? |
| Outcomes or attempts | • What were the outcomes of the major events?<br>• How did these outcomes make the characters react or feel?<br>• How did the characters show their thoughts or feelings?<br>• What attempts did characters make to solve problems that arose?<br>• How did a character feel when (a particular event) occurred? |
| Resolution or final outcome | • How did the story turn out once the main character solved the problem or achieved the goal?<br>• How did the character feel about the final outcome? Did he or she achieve what was wanted?<br>• Did the major problem get solved? In what way?<br>• How did you feel about the story conclusion? |
| Moral or theme | • Was the author trying to teach us something in the story? What was it?<br>• Did the main character act in a correct manner to solve the problem or achieve the goal?<br>• What lesson is learned from this story?<br>• Would a reader become a better person after reading this story? |

along the way. Furthermore, if students understand that stories have predictable patterns such as an introduction (a beginning), a stage of events (the middle), and a resolution (an end), their ability to understand and write stories following predictable patterns is greatly enhanced (Tompkins, 2003).

While many researchers, literacy authors, and the National Reading Panel feel that story mapping is highly beneficial for students' reading comprehension, several authors point out that these maps can mislead in meaning or not go deep enough with inferential comprehension. One author suggests that after students list the story grammar features on a type of story map, they go back and engage in an analysis and discussion of the characters' perspectives and motives in regard to the problem, the story events, and the resolution (Emery, 1996). Students can accomplish this analysis by writing main characters' perspectives of the story elements in columns on either side of the story map. Such character perspective charting goes beyond the basic understanding of what's in the text to an interpretation and a wondering about what was meant as it helps students use structural information as a basis of interpretation (Shanahan & Shanahan, 1997).

A generic story map that captures some degree of inferential and deep understanding is illustrated in Figure 11.2. The map features most of the elements of story grammar and allows for student interpretation as well.

## ■ INFORMATIONAL SOURCE STRATEGIES

Informational sources include those readings that are expository or nonfictional in nature. Informational readings are not solely those found in students' content area textbooks. Probably most of the sources that users of all age levels find on the Internet are expository; therefore, the more study and research students do for projects, themes, and topics using computers, the more likely they are to engage in and need to know how to process the various types of expository styles. Fortunately, many informational books today present material to children in a more appealing, user-friendly way than Internet sources, which are generally written by adults for adults. Because reading provides knowledge power, even primary grade children should be shown how to "read to learn" through content area readings and not be deprived of such text because the prevailing mentality is that they first have to "learn how to read" (Guillaume, 1998).

We noted earlier that sometime after the fourth grade and well into the middle, junior high, and high school years, many students experience difficulty with their school texts. One set of authors has called this phenomenon the "quiet crisis," in which students have attained some literacy capability but not enough to help them meet the challenges of gaining full understanding of many content area and informational readings (Schoenbach, Greenleaf, Cziko, & Hurwitz, 1999). Furthermore, the timing of young adolescence coincides with the beginnings of a downturn in academic success (Ryan & Patrick, 2001). For reluctant readers, students from economically disadvantaged backgrounds, and minority students, the trend toward failure with texts is especially likely if they are not engaged in readings that are interesting and relevant to them (Newman & Celano, 2002; Worthy, 2002).

**CHARACTERS:** _____

**SETTING:**     Time: _____

            Place: _____

            Influence of setting on character(s') action: _____

| What does the main character wish to do or achieve? | What problem does the main character have to solve in the story? |

_____

_____

_____

_____

Why?_____

What are the plot actions to achieve the goal or solve the problem?

_____

_____

_____

_____

_____

_____

**Relate the major events in order and why characters reacted the way they did**

First,

Second,

Third,

**Write about what finally happened and what you think.**

The story ended by

The lesson I learned from this story is that

My feeling about the characters and this story is

*Figure* **11.2** Mapping and Reacting to Stories

We know that most readers find expository text more demanding than narrative because of its format, its unique content-specific vocabulary, and its topic unfamiliarity. Commenting on the 1998 Nation's Report Card in Reading published by the National Assessment of Educational Progress (NAEP), in which 26 percent of eighth graders in U.S. schools were performing below the basic level of reading, one author noted that poor reading comprehension was identified as the major handicap of most struggling readers in the nation's middle schools. This means that basic comprehension or the ability to gain meaning from what was read is weak, probably due to lack of reading fluency, limited vocabulary, lack of background information or knowledge, and lack of motivation to gain information from the material (Allen, 2000).

One factor influencing student comprehension of expository texts is the instructional style of the various content area teachers whom students face each day, as well as teachers' perceptions of students' literacy capabilities. These teachers concentrate on the delivery of the content information of their disciplines. According to one literacy author, if the content area teacher notes that students are gaining little information from their readings, the teacher teaches around the text, becoming an "enabler" (Gunning, 2002). Thus the teacher might summarize or explain the content, have students copy notes or even distribute a page of teacher-prepared notes, show a film that touches on aspects of the reading, or use other audiovisual means to address the ideas of the topic. Such a procedure encourages students to minimize or even stop reading and let the teacher do the necessary deep-processing work.

Other authors note that content area teachers believe that reading has been adequately mastered by students in the elementary grades (Guthrie & Davis, 2003). Therefore, when content area teachers teach topic subjects through textual readings without providing explicit instruction on *how* to understand the content material, students experience comprehension problems. Learning the content becomes intimidating due to the combination of lack of experience with many topics, the inability to read with adequate comprehension, and the absence of teacher-provided strategies for helping students understand the content through reading. The problems of adequate reading comprehension are even more pronounced for middle and junior high school struggling readers, who are trapped in a dilemma. Because they avoid reading, they minimize the practice that would help them become fluent and more efficient readers (Dreher, 2003). Being poor readers, they sense that they lack the competence to succeed in challenging content area reading assignments. As noted by two authors, these students need to be motivated to contribute effort to school reading tasks, and they need teacher support and teacher belief that they can gain competence (R. Ryan & Deci, 2000).

One way to assist struggling middle school students is to connect their feelings and emotions to expository text as it is being read. Students record facts of an informational reading on one column of a response diary, and in the second column they tell about their feelings related to the listed facts. Richards (2003) suggests that the response diary helps middle school students achieve more effective reading of content material.

## The Directed Reading Activity (DRA)

The **directed reading activity** (DRA) was probably one of the first structured reading strategies that focused on students' comprehension of text, and it has enjoyed a long and lasting history in the field of reading instruction (Gunning, 2002). Credited to Emmett Betts in 1946, the activity supports the comprehension process by attending to students' background knowledge of a topic, engaging readers' interest before reading, setting a purpose for reading, and monitoring students' understanding of the selection (Hammond, 1994). DRA provided the underlying framework for basal reading selections until Russell Stauffer modified the more direct teaching approach of DRA into the more implicit teaching strategy of DRTA.

Because we began our teaching careers when basal readers were the main staple of the language arts curriculum, we learned the **guided reading** steps of DRA quite well. For us then and for teachers now, especially those beginning their classroom careers, this strategy, along with DRTA, should be one the teacher can readily implement. However, with the advent and implementation through the years of many other reading activities and suggestions that assist the reading comprehension process, we recommend that you employ DRA with informational, content area readings and use DRTA with literature-based readings. This is a suggestion only, and of course the teacher can borrow a step or a subprocedure from one strategy to use with the other. Part of the skill of teaching is learning to integrate various effective reading activities within the larger framework of a specific approach, as we did with levels and kinds of questions for the DRTA discussion.

As formatted by Betts and modified by many current authors, DRA has five major steps:

1. Readiness and preparation to read
2. Reading either silently, orally, or both
3. Discussion with some oral rereading with a purpose
4. Skills building or strategy-level development related to specific content within the reading that has transfer value
5. Individual or group follow-up enrichment and extension activities related in some literal, interpretive, or applied (creative) way to the reading (Burns et al., 1999)

Box 11.2 presents the lesson flow of the directed reading activity.

## The SQ4R Strategy

The **SQ4R strategy** has its roots and tradition in a long history of literacy methodology. Originally conceived as SQ3R by Francis P. Robinson in 1941 (revised in 1961) as a reading-study procedure for junior high and high school students, the procedure is found in almost every literacy textbook, bound in its original format of S (survey), Q (question), R (read), R (recite), and R (review) (Burns et al., 1999; Leu & Kinzer, 1999). In 1972 the procedure was altered by two authors to SQ4R, with the letters meaning survey, question, read, reflect, recite, and review (Thomas & Robinson, 1982). Although the addition of the reflect stage after a word-by-word reading was meant to encourage students to try to make sense of the content material by relating it to their prior experience, we believe that the overall approach to this potentially powerful strategy still isn't truly effective. It isn't effective because the focus appears to be on the first R (read word by word), which means students are basically doing the same thing they do every day in every content area subject in which they read.

**BOX 11.2** Instructional Tasks Accomplished during the Five Guided Reading Steps of the Directed Reading Activity

**Readiness:** In the **readiness/preparation** to read segment, there are four broad instructional tasks that require varying amounts of time, depending on the anticipated difficulty of the topic. The teacher needs to (1) engage students by relating the topic to their background experiences; (2) develop and clarify the predominant concepts underlying the piece; (3) introduce and visually portray the new vocabulary; and (4) set the purpose and motivate students to read.

**Read:** After the teacher establishes the major purpose question that provides a holistic mind-set for students, they read the selection. It might be wise for the teacher to write the purpose question on the chalkboard because it will act as a focus and reminder for students and help start the discussion after silent reading. Sources call this stage "guided silent reading," "directed reading (either silent or oral)," or just "guided reading."

**Discussion and Interaction:** Once the reading is complete, the teacher could begin the discussion stage by returning students to the purpose question. Because the purpose question is generally related to the whole meaning or main idea of the selection, students can begin with the central concept and then connect related, subordinate ideas and information.

**Skills Development:** Skills development refers to ways of working with information presented in the reading. Because some comprehension-level work was accomplished in the discussion stage, the teacher might plan to focus on one strategic skill that has transfer value, such as formulating main ideas or summarizing.

Skill work should be in tune with what the text offers. For example, if social studies readings focus on the exploration and colonization of the Americas, the rise of inventions during the industrial age, or even westward expansion, the skill of sequential organization would be a key strategy for joining the events and chronologically ordering topics.

**Enrichment, Extensions, and Follow-Ups:** This stage of DRA can support and extend any of the concept ideas, content, strategies, or skill work developed through the lesson. This extension can take many forms, engage some or many domains of the language arts, and involve individual or group work. This may be the stage at which real deep learning of a concept idea takes place because students are actively engaged in a project and/or additional work they themselves have selected.

We believe that a new shift in the SQ4R procedure is necessary to make it a highly effective, strategic learning, and text-processing strategy. Like others, we believe that the strategy is powerful because it merges a number of comprehension processes—spanning the before-, during-, and after-reading acts (Herrell & Jordan, 2000)—and because it provides a kind of guided support that allows students to work with difficult content topics in meaningful ways (Vacca & Vacca, 2002). Our procedure for implementing the steps of SQ4R follows.

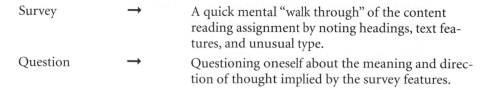

Survey  →  A quick mental "walk through" of the content reading assignment by noting headings, text features, and unusual type.

Question  →  Questioning oneself about the meaning and direction of thought implied by the survey features.

Recite One (R[1]) → Reciting one's understanding of the "whole," the gist that was gained from the survey and mental questioning activity.

Read → Now read word by word to comprehend the whole topic more thoroughly and to fill in the information and detailed knowledge implied by and inferred from the Recite One step.

Recite Two (R[2]) → Be able to understand the content selection, be able to relate supporting details and information to main ideas, and be able to perceive relationships and make connections to one's prior experiences.

Review → Be able to review the material to fill in the gaps left after one's recitation steps above and be able to successfully review before one is assessed on knowledge of the topic.

Here is what teachers need to realize about these SQ4R steps and about how the implementation of the procedure differs quite dramatically from that found in other language arts and content textbooks. First, the teacher needs to divide the strategy work in the SQ4R lesson into two segments, because there are two types of reading–thinking activities going on, and to have each type flourish properly, it's wise for the teacher to create two separate lessons. This could occur with a short break in between or on two successive days, but not too much time should elapse between the breaks.

The first lesson focuses on the SQR[1] steps only and the second on the RR[2]R portion. The SQR[1] steps are the most insightful part of the strategy and the type of strategic reading–thinking behavior that the teacher wants students to transfer. In fact, as soon as primary grade and intermediate grade children achieve fluency in reading, teachers should instigate the SQR[1] steps with informational reading selections. The reading accomplished here is extremely active and goal directed and should not consume a great deal of time.

With the traditional Read stage, students accomplish what they have been conditioned to do during informational readings. They pursue more deliberate word-by-word, sentence-by-sentence reading at their normal fluency rates. With the original segment of the SQR[1] in students' heads, the detailed information contained in the text should allow them to make more meaningful connections.

For those students with deep-rooted comprehension or concentration problems, the Read stage can be strengthened through the use of the **study guide** technique. Here is where the teacher divides the page with the word *Question* heading the left column and *Answer* above the right column. The student takes a deliberate, slow path to answer the questions prompted by boldfaced headers and reads effectively to answer the question posed. Thus this question-and-answer process moves piecemeal through the topic selection, and its intent is to encourage students to be more exacting, deliberate comprehenders. Because students are writing the answers to self-posed questions, the teacher has visible evidence that students are engaged and tracking through a text selection.

## Concept Maps

Concept maps are to informational, expository text what story maps are to narrative literature. Such maps belong to a class of design structures known as graphic organizers, and the term *graphic,* as generally used in the English language arts, relates to *nonlinear* constructs whose purpose is to organize or generate ideas (Claggett, 1994). **Concept maps,** also known as cognitive maps, semantic maps, semantic networks, and visual/ graphic displays, make use of figures, lines, arrows, and spatial configurations to show how content ideas and concepts are related and organized. The concept map, in particular, visually represents a unit of knowledge and portrays the critical concepts, vocabulary, ideas, generalizations, events, and/or facts of that unit (Carnine, Silbert, Kameenui, & Tarver, 1997). Some authors have noted that other graphic organizers such as timelines and continuums, Venn diagrams, H-maps, flowcharts and flow diagrams, graphs, and charts present ways to organize concepts graphically as aids to the reading comprehension process (Hadaway & Young, 1991; Tang, 1994).

When we attended public school, we were shown another strategy for planning for and restructuring text—that of outlining. The conventional structure for outlining is a *linear,* hierarchical ordering of ideas at different levels of meaning relationships and subordination. Roman numerals indicate the superordinate concepts; uppercase letters symbolize the supporting or coordinate concepts; Arabic numbers represent the subordinate details; and lowercase letters signal the sub-subordinate details (McNeil, 1992). Because outlining is a linear way to plan for and/or organize text, the one conventional structure portrays all kinds of prose text. But maps and other graphic organizers allow thinkers, readers, and writers to show superordinate to detailed information in visual, more concrete ways. These users translate or restructure ideas and concepts into a visual, graphic array, creating a "blueprint" plan of their thoughts regarding the organization of a reading assignment or a forthcoming essay, report, or computer project.

Sinatra has long advocated that concept maps can become "idealized" graphic representations of text structure patterns (Sinatra, 2000; Sinatra, Stahl-Gemake, & Berg, 1984). Such idealized plans would help students form mental constructs or schemata of how texts are organized and would assist teachers in designing instructional formats that help students acquire and comprehend knowledge. Not only can concept maps portray model plans of text organization for individual topic tasks but they can also help teachers and students generate strategic ways of thinking to organize and reflect on text.

We noted earlier in this chapter, in the discussion of expository text structure, that different authors use different terms for informational text structure patterns. Based on those authors' descriptions, Bonnie Meyer's categorization system of expository structure, and John McNeil's system of subordination in outlining, we present six major text structure patterns that can be represented by unique visual/graphic concept maps. The use of different graphic representations for different text patterns supports the idea that students should use strategic thinking as they plan for writing or as they unlock the layering of ideas in a content reading selection. Box 11.3 shows the type of thinking and the organizational pattern of ideas for each of the six text structure patterns. These six patterns—sequence, topic development, classification, comparison–contrast (same/different), cause and effect, and persuasion—can be represented by different graphic map configurations (Sinatra, 2000).

**BOX 11.3** Types of Thinking Represented by Use of Different Concept Maps

**Sequence**—The sequential style of organization is also known as temporal, chronological, or steps-in-a-process. The major organizational factor is the unfolding of events and incidents in chronological order, such as would occur in historical accounts and realistic biographies.

**Topic Development**—The topic development structure has many conceptual names such as spatial description, expository–explanatory, exemplification, and arrays. Probably the most popular, generic name is the "spider map." The key thinking here is that of visualizing the components of a topic idea and describing the components in words, which in turn portray the richness of the author's description.

**Classification**—The classification style is a dominant pattern in science writing, and it also appears quite regularly in social studies, arithmetic, and health. The system is arranged in a tree structure pattern with a hierarchical layering of concepts from top level to lower level.

**Comparison–Contrast**—Information about two or more topics is compared and contrasted with this text pattern. Many authors suggest use of the Venn diagram; others use an H-map (a map in the form of a large letter *H* in block form; the sides contain the features of each topic, and the middle connector contains the features common to both.)

**Cause and Effect**—The cause and effect writing pattern addresses the dual aspects of causality and sequence of events. Something happens as a result of something else, or because something happened (an effect) other happenings occur.

**Persuasion**—The writing of persuasion or argumentation is not solely confined to informational writing. This organizational style presents a belief or a thesis position on a topic in a convincing way. To do this kind of writing, the author has to know how to present a logical argument in writing in a believable way. Presenting reasons for one's belief or thesis position develops a persuasive argument, as in an opinion paper or an editorial. These reasons are supported by information, factual evidence, and data; by examples; and by what others have said or written about this topic.

When teachers teach one extended lesson based on the study of one content topic, they can use a concept map to portray the organizational plan of that topic. Furthermore, teachers achieve an interdisciplinary, integrated effect through concept mapping in a whole-group delivery method because viewing, listening, speaking, reading, writing, and visual representation are processing modes naturally used by students as they comprehend and write about one content topic.

In the next chapter, we look at the range of instructional contexts in which teachers apply many of the instructional strategies discussed in this chapter.

##  SUMMARY

1. Reading comprehension involves juxtaposing former knowledge of a topic with the current textual rendition of the ideas and information written about that topic.

2. The writing of prose is generally categorized into literary or fiction writing and expository or informational writing.

3. Stories and literature have a generic set of features called story grammar elements that are generally composed of characters, settings, goals, plots, problems or conflicts, resolutions, and themes.

4. Informational or expository text does not have a generic set of features but is characterized by a number of organizational text patterns such as

occurs for the writing of sequence, description, classification, comparison–contrast, causation, and persuasion.

5. The retelling strategy, the directed reading–thinking activity (DRTA), and the use of story maps to portray the structure of the narrative are three high-utility and strategic ways to help students enjoy and learn from literature.

6. According to the National Reading Panel, the use of story maps can improve reading comprehension in two ways: (1) children make graphic representations of content being read, and (2) they learn the structure of stories as a means of remembering story content.

7. Because expository or informational text is more demanding for most readers due to its text format, unique context-specific vocabulary, and topic unfamiliarity, the three strategies of directed reading activity (DRA), SQ4R, and concept maps are good ones to use with content area readings.

8. Using concept or cognitive maps with a content area selection in an extended lesson sequence provides students with a strategic way to comprehend and write about expository text.

## ■ QUESTIONS TO CONSIDER ■

1. Why is connecting concrete experience to reading and writing a powerful way to teach and apply literacy learnings in meaningful ways?

2. What is within the fabric of literature that makes it an excellent medium for teaching young people about ethical, virtuous, and moral issues?

3. Why is the teaching of narrative and expository text organization beneficial to students?

4. How is the construction of retold books by children an important strategy in teaching the writing process as well as reading comprehension?

5. How does following the guided reading steps of the directed reading–thinking activity (DRTA) engage students in deep understanding of a literary selection?

6. Why does story mapping help children comprehend?

7. What is involved in the guided reading steps of the directed reading activity (DRA) that may make it more beneficial to use with concept-laden, informational text?

8. How does altering the traditional SQ3R or SQ4R techniques into two segments of SQR[1] and RR$_2$R with two different levels of reciting make it much more of a strategic thinking and metacognitive learning activity for students?

9. How do concept or cognitive maps help students with both comprehension and writing?

## ■ THINGS TO DO ■

1. When taking children on a trip, excursion, or "walk about," or when conducting a hands-on lesson, be sure to use new concept vocabulary in the context of the activity as children are experiencing it. Later in the classroom, write the words on the chalkboard or word wall as you discuss them again. Then try to have children use the new words in a written retelling or writing assignment.

2. After children read a compelling selection of children's literature, ask them to translate their reading understanding into some art form such as visual art, poetry, drama, puppetry, or sculpture. Then they can present their "revisualized"

work to the class group, sharing their expressive and aesthetic feelings.

3. Experiment with the tree structure or classification concept map design when presenting a topic, focusing on "categories of," "groups of," or "kinds/types of." Have students establish the top-level idea, then the next most important subordinate ideas (which are coordinate to one another), and then the specific details or factual information that is found at the bottom of the tree design.

4. Accomplish a directed reading–thinking activity with a literary selection with a group of students. Plan predictive, during-reading, retrospective,

and summative questions as you break the selection into appropriate reading segments. See how your questions work as children give you feedback with their answers. (Note Figure 11.1.)

5. Try the SQ4R strategy by following the two-segment approach. After teaching what to look for in a survey to students, accomplish Survey, Question, and Recite[1] with a subchapter of a social studies or science book. Prepare some global activities to check for main idea knowledge for R[1]. Then have students divide a notebook page and have them write their questions in a left column and their answers in the right column during the Read portion of the strategy.

## ■ RECOMMENDED READINGS ■

Burns Paul, Betty Roe, and Elinor Ross. *Teaching Reading in Today's Elementary Schools,* 7th ed. Upper Saddle River, NJ: Merrill, 1999. This book familiarizes teachers with many important aspects of elementary reading instruction and presents many practical suggestions for teaching reading.

Calkins, Lucy. *Raising Lifelong Learners: A Parent's Guide.* Reading, MA: Addison-Wesley, 1997. Presents the author's view on natural ways to involve children in learning how to read and write.

Freeman, Evelyn, and Diane Goetz Person. *Connecting Informational Children's Books with Content Area Learning.* Boston: Allyn and Bacon, 1998. Explains different types of informational trade books and how these can assist children with learnings from content area topics.

Glazer, Joan. *Literature for Young Children,* 4th ed. Upper Saddle River, NJ: Prentice-Hall, 2000. Explains the various genres of children's literature and how to engage young children in appreciating and learning from literature.

Tompkins, Gail. *Literacy for the 21st Century,* 3rd ed. Upper Saddle River, NJ: Merrill/Prentice Hall, 2003. The book fuses four modern theories of literacy learning—constructivist, sociolinguistic, interactive, and reader response—to show teachers how to implement a balanced literacy program.

Vacca, Richard, and JoAnne Vacca. *Content Area Reading: Literacy and Learning Across the Curriculum.* Boston: Allyn and Bacon, 2002. Focuses on the abilities to use talking, listening, reading, and writing with conventional text and electronic resources to learn content material across subject areas.

Walker, Barbara. *Diagnostic Teaching of Reading: Techniques for Instruction and Assessment,* 4th ed. Upper Saddle River, NJ: Merrill, 2000. Presents a good array of strategies for reading instruction with steps on how to implement them.

## ■ KEY TERMS ■

| | | |
|---|---|---|
| concept maps | expository text structure | SQ4R strategy |
| content area reading | guided reading | story grammar analysis |
| directed reading activity (DRA) | print-rich environment | study guide |
| directed reading–thinking activity (DRTA) | readiness/preparation | visual organizers |
| experience language | retelling strategy | |
| | retold books | |

## ■ REFERENCES ■

Allen, R. (2000, Summer). Before it's too late: Giving reading a last chance. *Curriculum Update,* 1–3, 6–8.

Barone, T., Eeds, M. A., & Mason, K. (1995, January). Literature, the diciplines, and the lives of elementary school children. *Language Arts,* 30–38.

Barzun, J. (with Wattenberg, R., Eds.). (2002, Fall). Curing provincialism: A conversation with Jacques Barzun. *American Educator, 6*, 10–11.

Baumann, J., & Bergeron, B. (1993, December). Story map construction using children's literature: Effects on first graders' comprehension of central narrative elements. *Journal of Reading Behavior,* 407–437.

Boyd, F. (2002, Fall). Conditions, concessions, and the many tender mercies of learning through multicultural literature. *Reading Research and Instruction,* 58–92.

Boyle, J. (1996, Spring). The effects of a cognitive mapping strategy on the literal and inferential comprehension of students with mild disabilities. *Learning Disability Quarterly,* 86–98.

Bruner, J. (1997). *The culture of education* (2nd ed.). Cambridge, MA: Harvard University Press.

Burns, P., Roe, B., & Ross, E. (1999). *Teaching reading in today's elementary schools* (7th ed.). New York: Houghton Mifflin.

Calkins, L. (1997). *Raising lifelong learners: A parent's guide.* Reading, MA: Addison-Wesley.

Carnine, D., Silbert, J., Kameenui, E., & Tarver, S. (2004). *Direct instruction reading* (4th ed.). Upper Saddle River, NJ: Merrill.

Claggett, F. (1994). Graphics as a learning tool. In A. C. Purves (Ed.) *Encyclopedia of English studies and language arts* (pp. 544–545). New York: Scholastic/Urbana, IL: National Council of Teachers of English.

Cronin, H., Sinatra, R., & Barkley, W. (1992, March). Combining writing with text organization in content instruction. *The NASSP Bulletin,* 34–45.

Cunningham, J., & Wall, L. (1994, March). Teaching good readers to comprehend better. *Journal of Reading,* 480–486.

Davis, Z. (1994, July–August). Effects of prereading story mapping on elementary readers' comprehension. *Journal of Educational Research,* 353–359.

Dickson, S. (1999, January). Integrating reading and writing to teach compare–contrast text structure: A research-based methodology. *Reading & Writing Quarterly,* 49–79.

Dowd, F. S. (1992, Summer). Evaluating children's books portraying Native American and Asian cultures. *Childhood Education, 68,* 219–224.

Dreher, M. (2003, January–March). Motivating struggling readers by tapping the potential of information books. *Reading & Writing Quarterly,* 25–38.

Durkin, D. (1992). *Teaching them to read* (6th ed.). Boston: Allyn and Bacon.

Emery, D. (1996, April). Helping readers comprehend stories from the characters' perspectives. *The Reading Teacher,* 534–541.

Englert, C., Raphael, T., Anderson, L., Anthony, H., & Stevens, D. (1991, Summer). Making strategies and self-talk visible: Writing instruction in regular and special education classrooms. *American Educational Research Journal,* 372–387.

Finders, M., & Hynds, S. (2003). *Literacy lessons: Teaching and learning with middle school students.* Upper Saddle River, NJ: Merrill/ Prentice Hall.

Fitzgerald, J. (1989). Research on stories: Implications for teachers. In K. D. Muth (Ed.), *Children's comprehension of text* (pp. 2–36). Newark, DE: International Reading Association.

Freeman, E., & Person, D. G. (1998). *Connecting informational children's books with content area learning.* Boston: Allyn and Bacon.

Friedman, A., & Cataldo, C. (2002, October). Characters at crossroads: Reflective decision makers in contemporary Newbery books. *The Reading Teacher,* 102–112.

Galda, L., & Cullinan, B. (1991). Literature for literacy: What research says about the benefits of using trade books in the classroom. In J. Flood, J. M. Jensen, D. Lapp, & J. R. Squire (Eds.), *Handbook of research on teaching the English language arts* (pp. 529–535). New York: Macmillan.

Gillat, J., & Temple, C. (2000). *Understanding reading problems: Assessing and instructing* (5th ed.). New York: Longman.

Goodman, K. (1996). *Ken Goodman on reading: A common sense look at the nature of language and the science of reading.* Portmouth, NH: Heinemann.

Gordon, C., & Braun, C. (1983, November). Using story schema as an aid to reading and writing. *The Reading Teacher,* 116–121.

Guastello, E. F., Beasley, T. M., & Sinatra, R. (2000, November–December). Concept mapping effects on science content comprehension of low-achieving, inner-city seventh graders. *Remedial and Special Education,* 356–365.

Guillaume, A. (1998, March). Learning with text in the primary grades. *The Reading Teacher,* 476–486.

Gunning, T. (2002). *Assessing and correcting reading and writing difficulties* (2nd ed.). Boston: Allyn and Bacon.

Guthrie, J., & Davis, M. (2003, January–March). Motivating struggling readers in middle school through an engagement model of classroom practice. *Reading & Writing Quarterly,* 54–85.

Hadaway, N., & Young, T. (1991, April). Content literacy and language learning: Instructional decisions. *The Reading Teacher,* 522–527.

Hammond, W. D. (1994). Directed reading activities. In A. C. Purves (Ed.), *Encyclopedia of English studies and language arts* (pp. 378–380). New York: Scholastic/Urbana, IL: National Council of Teachers of English.

Herrell, A. & Jordan, M. (2000). *Fifty strategies for teaching English language learners.* Upper Saddle River, NJ: Merrill/Prentice Hall.

Irwin, J. W. (1991). *Teaching reading comprehension processes* (2nd ed.). Upper Saddle River, NJ: Prentice Hall.

Jago, C. (2000, Winter). Don't discard the classics. *American Educator,* 20–23, 44–46.

Kilpatrick, W. (1993, Summer). The moral power of good stories. *American Educator,* 24–35.

Kozioff, M., LaNunziata, L., Cowardin, J., & Bressellieu, F. (2000–2001, December/January). Direct instruction: Its contributions to high school achievement. *High School Journal,* 54–71.

Leu, D. Jr., & Kinzer, C. (1999). *Effective literacy instruction, K–8.* (4th ed.). Upper Saddle River, NJ: Merrill.

Lodge, D. (1994). *The art of fiction.* New York: Viking.

McNeil, J. (1992). *Reading comprehension: New directions for classroom practice* (3rd ed.). Glenview, IL: Scott, Foresman.

Metzer, M. (1993). Voices from the past. In M. O. Tunnell & R. Ammon (Eds.), *The story of ourselves: Teaching history through children's literature* (pp. 27–30). Portsmouth, NH: Heinemann.

Meyer, B. (1975). *The organization of prose and its effect on memory.* Amsterdam: North-Holland.

Meyer, B. (1984). Organizational aspects of text: Effects on reading comprehension and applications for the classroom. In J. Flood (Ed.), *Promoting reading comprehension* (pp. 113–138). Newark, DE: International Reading Association.

Mosenthal, J. (1994). Text structure. In A. C. Purves (Ed.), *Encyclopedia of English studies and language arts* (pp. 1201–1203). New York: Scholastic/Urbana, IL: National Council of Teachers of English.

National Reading Panel. (2000). *Teaching children to read: An evidence-based assessment of the scientific literature on reading and its implications for reading.* Bethesda, MD: National Institute of Child Health and Human Development (NIH).

Newman, S., & Celano, D. (2002). Access to print in low-income and middle-income communities: An ecological study of four neighborhoods. *Reading Research Quarterly, 36,* 8–26.

Perini, R. (2002, February). The pearl in the shell: Author's notes in multicultural children's literature. *The Reading Teacher,* 428–435.

Peverly, S. T. (1991, Spring). Problems with the knowledge-based explanation of memory and development. *Review of Educational Research,* 71–93.

Pransky, K., & Bailey, F. (2002–2003, December/January). To meet your students where they are, first you have to find them: Working with culturally and linguistically diverse at-risk students. *The Reading Teacher,* 370–383.

Readence, J., & Moore, D. (1994). Content area reading. In A. C. Purves (Ed.), *Encyclopedia of English studies and language arts* (pp. 287–290). New York: Scholastic/Urbana, IL: National Council of Teachers of English.

Richards, J. (2003, January–March). Facts and feelings response diaries: Connecting efferently and aesthetically with informational text. *Reading & Writing Quarterly,* 107–111.

Richek, M., Caldwell, J. A., Jennings, J., & Lerner, J. (2002). *Reading problems: Assessment and teaching strategies* (4th ed.). Boston: Allyn and Bacon.

Rowan, K. (1994). Expository writing. In A. C. Purves (Ed.), *Encyclopedia of English studies and language arts* (pp. 474–477). New York: Scholastic/Urbana, IL: National Council of Teachers of English.

Ryan, A., & Patrick, H. (2001, Summer). The classroom environment and changes in adolescents' motivation and engagement during middle school. *American Educational Research Journal,* 437–460.

Ryan, R., & Deci, E. (2000, January). Intrinsic and extrinsic motivations: Classic definitions and new directions. *Contemporary Educational Psychology,* 54–67.

Ryan, S. (1986, March). Do prose models really teach writing? *Language Arts,* 284–289.

Schoenbach, R., Greenleaf, C., Cziko, C., & Hurwitz, L. (1999). *Reading for understanding.* San Francisco: Jossey-Bass.

Shanahan, T., & Shanahan, S. (1997, May). Character perspective charting: Helping children develop a more complete conception of story. *The Reading Teacher,* 668–677.

Sinatra, R. (1991, March). Integrating whole language with the learning of text structure. *Journal of Reading,* 424–433.

Sinatra, R. (2000, May–June). Teaching learners to think, read, and write more effectively in content subjects. *The Clearing House,* 266–273.

Sinatra, R., Stahl-Gemake, J., & Berg, D. (1984, October). Improving reading comprehension of disabled readers through semantic mapping. *Reading Teacher,* 22–29.

Stauffer, R. (1969). *Teaching reading as a thinking process.* New York: Harper & Row.

Tang, G. (1994). Graphic organizer. In A. C. Purves, (Ed.), *Encyclopedia of English studies and language arts* (pp. 542–543). New York: Scholastic/Urbana, IL: National Council of Teachers of English.

Thomas, E. L., & Robinson, H. A. (1982). *Improving reading in every class: A source book for teachers* (3rd ed.). Boston: Allyn and Bacon.

Tompkins, G. (2003). *Literacy for the 21st century* (3rd ed.). Upper Saddle River, NJ: Merrill/Prentice Hall.

Trabasso, T. (1994). The power of the narrative. In F. Lehrand & J. Osborn (Eds.), *Reading, language, and literacy: Instruction for the twenty-first century* (pp. 187–200). Hillsdale, NJ: Erlbaum.

Vacca, R., & Vacca, J. (2002). *Content area reading: Literacy and learning across the curriculum* (7th ed.). Boston: Allyn and Bacon.

Vallecorsa, A. (1997, May). Using a mapping procedure to teach reading and writing skills to middle grade students with learning disabilities. *Education and Treatment of Children,* 173–188.

van den Broek, P. (1989). The effects of causal structure on the comprehension of narratives: Implications for education. *Reading Psychology, 10,* 19–44.

van den Broek, P., Linzie, B., Fletcher, C., & Marsolek, C. (2000, July). The role of causal discourse structure in narrative writing. *Memory and Cognition,* 711–721.

Venezky, R. (2000, Fall). The origins of the present-day chasms between adult literacy needs and school literacy instruction. *Scientific Studies of Reading,* 19–39.

Villaume, S. K., & Brabham, E. G. (2002, April). Comprehension instruction: Beyond strategies. *The Reading Teacher,* 672–675.

Walker, B. (2000). *Diagnostic teaching of reading: Techniques for instruction and assessment* (4th ed.). Upper Saddle River, NJ: Merrill.

Wiggins, G., & McTighe, J. (1998). *Understanding by design.* Alexandria, VA: Association for Supervision and Curriculum Development.

Wilson, E. (2002, Spring). The power of story. *American Educator,* 8–11.

Wong, B. (1997, Spring). Research on genre-specific strategies for enhancing writing in adolescents with learning disabilities. *Learning Disability Quarterly,* 140–159.

Worthy, J. (2002, March). What makes intermediate-grade students want to read? *The Reading Teacher,* 568–569.

Wright, R. E., & Rosenberg, S. (1993, March). Knowledge of text coherence and expository writing: A developmental study. *Journal of Educational Psychology,* 152–158.

# The Selection and Use of Instructional Resources

*Focusing Questions*

1. Why do you think the basal reader system was a dominant reading resource in the language arts curriculum throughout the twentieth century?

2. Why might student workbooks be appealing to the average teacher?

3. Can you think of some advantages and some disadvantages of teaching course work through the singular resource of textbooks and how trade book use might assist the learning of some textbook units?

4. What are forms of instructional media that can assist teachers in enlivening their delivery of various content and help diverse learners in learning the content?

5. How does electronic access through computers alter print learning and make print engagement different from that offered through traditional book resources?

6. Why are electronic media—particularly television, video, and film—winning the battle over print resources?
7. How can the Internet be a prime educational resource?

Whereas the last chapter examined some major strategies teachers use with literary and informational texts to aid students' comprehending and composing processes, this chapter presents the range of instructional resources teachers have at their disposal. We explore three kinds of instructional resources: (1) traditional book and print sources; (2) instructional aids; and (3) electronic texts. Each has its place in the classroom and teachers often modify other resources or develop their own materials to fit a particular curriculum objective.

# ■ SELECTING INSTRUCTIONAL RESOURCES AND MATERIALS

Selecting appropriate commercial materials, especially textbooks, is the responsibility of teachers and administrators, sometimes acting in small professional groups (at the district, school, department, or grade level), in professional lay groups that include parents and community members, or as individuals.

Although committees make decisions about the purchase or adaptation of materials on a schoolwide or districtwide basis, the teacher still needs to make professional judgments about the appropriateness and value of the materials, as he or she is closest to the students and should know their needs, interests, and abilities. Both teachers and committees also need to look at their state and local content standards to ensure that materials and resources selected for use are compatible with published standards by curriculum areas and grade levels. The evaluator (committee or individual) should examine as many available resources and materials as possible. The following general questions should be considered:

1. Do the materials fit the objectives and the standards? Materials should fit the curriculum objectives, the standards, and projected unit and lesson plans. Given the general nature of published materials, some may fit only partially, or it may not be possible to find materials to cover all the objectives. In such cases, teachers need to create all or some of their own materials.
2. Are the materials well organized? Good instructional materials will relate information on a few basic ideas or concepts in a logical manner.
3. Do the materials prepare the students for presentations? The materials should include instructional objectives or advance organizers.
4. Are the materials well designed? The materials should be attractive; the size should be appropriate for the intended use; and print should be readable, with adequate margins, legible typeface, and comfortable type size.

5. Have the materials been presented in a technically appropriate manner? The materials should not be overpresented, with too much emphasis on design, elaborate presentation for its own sake, decorative but uninformative illustrations, or unnecessary type elements. Nor should it be underpresented so that it lacks useful guides to its organization and content. Visual presentations, side notes in margins, appropriate headings, graphics, and color should be incorporated into the material.

6. Do the materials provide sufficient repetition through examples, illustrations, questions, and summaries to enhance understanding of content? Young students and low-achieving students need more repetition, overviews, and internal summaries, but for all students the material should be paced properly, and students should have sufficient time to digest and reflect on it.

7. Are the resources and materials suitable to the reading level of the students? Many teachers can make this type of judgment intuitively by reading or browsing through the material, and others can make the judgment after students experience the materials. When students use computers as instructional resources, are the software programs selected for them to use with topics and themes and the Internet web sites they visit to obtain information within their reading levels?

8. Does the difficulty of the materials match the abilities of the students at high and low levels of achievement?

# ■ TRADITIONAL PRINT AND BOOK SOURCES

What would schools and classrooms be like without books? Although computers provide immediate access to electronic texts when children are in school and at home, modern school-age children are not burdened with computers in their backpacks when they leave school each day. Books, especially textbooks, are still the "golden rule" of primary resources that children use in school. This section addresses the flourishing world of books and how traditional print materials are categorized and made accessible for children.

Books are divided into two main camps by the publishing industry. Books that are generally published in large sets for commercial or educational use such as textbooks, dictionaries, encyclopedias, research publications, and government documents are known as "outside the trade." Such books are published for a particular audience and are not usually made available in retail bookstores (Scharer, 1994). Those books made available in retail stores and through book dealers and accessible to the general buying public are known as "trade books." Even with the rapid explosion of electronic media within the last twenty years, there has been an almost equal proliferation in the availability and use of trade books at home and in schools.

## School Reading Series

Commercially prepared print materials for state, district, and school use can be further categorized into two main categories, those of textbooks and basal reader/anthology resources, the latter often referred to as the school-published reading program or series.

The publishing companies have shifted the focus of the reading selections in their commercially prepared reading series. For many years, the published reading series were known as basal readers. However, the trend has been to more literature-based and language-integrated readers as the publishers take note of the criticisms of the traditional basal philosophy and take into account the current beliefs and research regarding the reading process (Burns, Roe, & Ross, 1999). Thus, although all commercially prepared books used in school are technically textbooks, almost all educators refer to the textbooks used in their reading program as either basals or anthologies. The term *textbooks* refers more to those books used in content area courses such as science, social studies, and arithmetic.

*Basal Readers.* The **basal reading system** has been a dominant literacy force in the elementary and middle school language arts curriculum throughout the twentieth century and will probably continue to be so well into the future (Reutzel & Cooter, 1999). By the mid-1900s, a basal reading series augmented with student workbooks provided the resources for the reading curriculum (May, 2001). A series generally comprises grade-level readers ranging from kindergarten to sixth or eighth grade, a teacher's manual for each level, student workbooks or skill books for each level, ditto masters, and very often accompanying "checkup" tests. The checkup tests let teachers, students, and parents know how children are faring with each graded book.

The basic controlling focus of the traditional basal reader was on the words that made up a book's content. The lower the level of the reader, the more that high-frequency words and words in regular spelling patterns were the main reading diet of the child at that grade level. The words were practiced again in the skill books and appeared liberally on the checkup tests. There were usually two readers produced for each half-year up to the fourth-grade level. From fourth grade to sixth or eighth grade, there was generally one reader for the entire year, but it was enhanced by all the other aides that accompanied each reader. By the early 1990s, however, a shift occurred from teaching the words of commercially prepared and controlled reading resources to the real language used by original authors.

*Literature-Based Readers.* Most, if not all, of the major publishing companies of basal reading series now focus on authentic (as opposed to expurgated and controlled) children's literature and other genres such as poems, plays, and informational readings as the basis for children's reading. Some people think of the modern readers as **literature anthologies** in which whole selections or excerpts from high-quality children's literature are found (Burns et al., 1999; May, 2001). For instance, one vignette from A. A. Milne's collection of stories on Winnie-the-Pooh may find its way into a new literature-based basal as a complete story.

The publishing companies are still in control of the reading series market, although the consensus is that they're doing a better job of it with the infusion of literature (Burns et al., 1999; May, 2001). They are still producing the teacher's manuals, which are especially useful to beginning teachers because they provide suggestions and economize preparation time. Individual student workbooks remain, sometimes called "practice books," as well as the checkup procedures of informal assessments such as checklists, tests, and suggestions for portfolio collections. However, the more

**BOX 12.1** School Reading Programs Reduce Teachers' Decision Making about Reading Material in Three Ways

1. Because published reading programs contain a large array and variety of instructional resources, they reduce the time teachers need to select materials for instruction.
2. Within the organizational structure of the reading series is a systematic plan for grade-level instruction, sequence of skills, and use of thematic units.
3. The teacher's manuals published for each series level provide elaborate lesson planning information, thereby reducing time needed for decision making and planning.

*Source:* Adapted from Donald Leu Jr. and Charles Kinzer, *Effective Literacy Instruction, K–8* (Upper Saddle River, NJ: Prentice Hall, 1999).

recent resource enhancements, such as the focus on thematic units, usually five to seven per reader; the inclusion of trade books related to the theme; the availability of manipulatives, audiotapes, and even multimedia software; are appealing to the average grade-level teacher.

**Strengths and Weaknesses of the Published Reading Programs.** Two authors suggest that a strength of published school reading programs is that they reduce the complexity of teacher decision making about reading materials (Leu & Kinzer, 1999). Box 12.1 shows the three ways this is done. Other authors note that because the new basals are more literature driven and less skills and word-attack driven, teachers can leave out some of the readings if they feel they are not appropriate for their students, and teachers can choose among the various suggestions that will best fit student levels and interest to accommodate their special needs (Burns et al., 1999; May, 2001). This also means that because the word learning activities aren't as controlled and cumulatively organized as in the traditional basals, the teacher has to be more skillful in helping children learn new words and commit those words to sight vocabulary.

The particular factors of **sequencing** and **balancing** of material presentation are well managed and structured in a commercially prepared reading series. Because most series have been planned with literacy and language arts consultants working in conjunction with a publishing staff, a scope and sequence of readers and other ancillary materials are laid out that generally express the philosophical viewpoint of literacy instruction held by the collective team. Thus, when a published reading system is used within a school or district, teachers have a clear notion of what students have been taught (or should have been taught) in previous years (Wiggins, 1994).

## Textbooks

Textbooks receive as many positive and negative comments from the educational community and its stakeholders as do the commercially prepared basal reader and anthology series. But **textbooks** remain the main ingredient in students' information diet beyond the primary grades. The textbook, along with the workbook format, provides the material resource for most of what is taught (Eisner, 1987). By 1997 the consensus was that textbooks were used as the sole instructional resource in 75 to 90 percent of U.S. classrooms (Palmer, 1997). In terms of cost, textbooks used in the content area courses and reading series used in the language arts programs are only equaled or bettered by the cost of expensive hardware such as computers, copy machines, and other media materials.

In conventional classrooms in which content area teaching is occurring, reading assignments are based almost exclusively on textbooks, making the textbook the primary source of students' information (Vacca & Vacca, 2002). In both reading and arithmetic classes, there appears to be an excessive dependence on text material (Woodward & Elliott, 1992; Fairbanks, 1994). This reliance on conventional print-bound material may be due to the way teachers themselves were educated. By and large, teachers are capable and fluent readers. Textbooks worked for them, and they're just passing on what worked.

Generally, teachers use textbooks in two ways, either as the sole text for the course or as a source book. As the sole course resource, the textbook becomes the scope and sequence of the curriculum, whereas as a source book the text is used more flexibly by the teacher, who selects readings in particular order to suit the needs of students (Fitzgerald, 1994). When textbooks are used as the sole instructional resource, they become the only point of view in a course. In effect, the course is based on the theories and biases of the author of the text. Even though the author may try to maintain objectivity, what is selected, what is omitted, and how the discussion is slanted reflect the author's views.

The narrow viewpoint isn't the only drawback to using a textbook as the sole instructional resource. In order to have wide application, and to increase potential sales, textbooks tend to be general, noncontroversial, and bland. They are usually written for a national audience, so they do not consider local issues or community problems. Because they are geared for the greatest number of "average" students, they may not meet the needs and interests of any particular group of students. Moreover, issues, topics, and data that might upset potential audiences or interest groups are omitted (Bernstein, 1988; DelFattore, 1992).

Textbooks summarize large quantities of data and in so doing may become general and superficial and may discourage conceptual thinking, critical analysis, and evaluation. With the exception of those on mathematics, most textbooks quickly become outdated because of the rapid change of events. However, because they are costly, they are often used long after they should be replaced.

Textbook authors and publishers disregard a basic maxim of reading success—that is, the more redundancy, the easier to read with understanding. Textbooks do not treat content topics with the breadth and depth necessary for students to develop a full and rich understanding of the concept ideas (Vacca & Vacca, 2002). Most textbook authors provide only the minimum requirements for understanding knowledge basic to a topic before they introduce another topic. In this way, a lot of content knowledge can be crammed into one textual source to increase marketability. Some textbook critics have noted that because social studies textbooks fail to make explicit connections between facts and ideas presented, students should question the text author as they read to better understand why the author presented particular information (Beck & McKeown, 2002).

Considering these criticisms, you might ask why teachers, when they have access to other instructional materials, rely so heavily on textbooks. The answer is, of course, that textbooks do have many advantages, and these are listed in Box 12.2 (Cherryholmes, 1993; Ornstein, 1992).

**BOX 12.2** Textbooks Can Provide a Number of Advantages in Content Learning

A textbook (1) provides an outline that the teacher can use in planning courses, units, and lessons; (2) summarizes a great deal of pertinent information; (3) enables the students to take home in convenient form most of the material they need to learn for the course; (4) provides a common resource for all students to follow; (5) provides the teacher with ideas for the organization of information and activities; (6) includes pictures, graphs, maps, and other illustrative material that facilitate understanding; (7) includes other teaching aids, such as summaries and review questions; and (8) relieves the teacher of the chore of preparing material for the course, thus providing more time to prepare lessons and integrate other sources.

*Source:* Adapted from Cleo H. Cherryholmes, "Readers Research," *Journal of Curriculum Studies* (January/February 1993), pp. 1–32; Allan Ornstein, "The Textbook Curriculum," *Educational Horizons* (Summer 1992), pp. 167–169.

## Trade Books

Along with the rapid use of electronic text, **trade books** have experienced a widespread use in schools and at home in recent years. Probably encouraged by the interest in using authentic children's literature in the language arts curriculum, authors today write about all conceivable topics so that children and adolescents can listen to and read stories and informational books to support content presented in traditional textbooks. Research has indicated that the addition of trade books in the classroom helps in the development of oral language and reading ability, assists in vocabulary acquisition, and increases children's motivation to read in school and at home (Galda & Cullinan, 1991). Furthermore, publishers are increasingly using trade books or adapting trade book selections for inclusion in basal reader anthologies that are marketed as literature based (Scharer, 1994).

Trade books can be grouped into three broad categories: (1) stories and children's literature, (2) information, and (3) pictures. **Picture books** are those that contain many photographs and illustrations with relatively little text. The words that are used and the artwork support each other's meaning (Cullinan & Galda, 1998). Picture books lean more toward informational knowledge, and one author suggests that they can be used as a means for helping young and elementary grade students understand the expository text structure patterns of sequence, description, compare–contrast, and cause–effect (Hancock, 1999). One author comments that some modern-day picture books have new stylistic characteristics in that they don't follow traditional, linear story structure and so allow the reader's eyes and thought process to jump around the page, much like surfing through TV channels and Internet web sites (Goldstone, 2001–2002).

Teachers use trade books strategically as they augment topic and theme units in their curriculum offerings. In the language arts, teachers use high-quality trade books to present literature-focused units that may examine the work of one children's author or one genre, generally categorized into folklore, fantasy, and realism (Tompkins, 2003). With knowledge of curriculum topics and good planning, the teacher could profitably run a meaningful literacy program with just the use of trade books—profitable from a learning perspective given the amount of reading children would engage in and profitable from a cost perspective because the basal reader/anthology program would not be necessary. Based on a topic or theme covered at the grade level, teachers would have each child read a **core book.** A core book is like the child's personal reader for that topic or theme, is used for whole-class reading, and is ordered in class sets (Burns et al., 1999).

Besides the variety in reading and relevance they offer, **informational trade books** provide learners with a more comprehensive perspective on a topic or theme because they develop concepts and ideas in greater depth than the textbook (Vacca & Vacca, 2002). One author notes that informational books can be a valuable learning resource even for kindergartners and a way to increase their vocabulary development and concept knowledge (Richgels, 2002). Another indicates there is a rising popularity in the use of informational books in the teaching of elementary science. She notes that not only do they provide a more focused and in-depth perspective on a science concept, but they also can be used to accommodate students with different reading abilities, they are crafted to be more interesting and less confusing than science textbooks, and they present a positive view of women and minorities at work in the sciences (Rice, 2002). Box 12.3 suggests that informational trade books can assist curriculum offerings in five ways (Freeman & Person, 1998).

## Junior Great Books

**Junior Great Books** is an established program of the Great Books Foundation, which publishes collections of classic and modern literature to promote reading and discussion programs for children and adults. The premise of the Great Books Foundation is that reading interpretively is a complex mental activity that needs to be cultivated over time. To accomplish interpretive reading, students read challenging literature, and through a method of inquiry and discussion, students construct meaning, draw inferences, weigh evidence, and make comparisons and conclusions (Great Books Foundation, 1999).

**BOX 12.3** How Informational Trade Books Support Children's Intersubject Learning

Informational trade books can support children's learning across the curriculum in five major ways, according to two authors:

1. Informational books are a means of satisfying the natural curiosity of children as they wish to know about and explore topics of interest.
2. Such books assist children in understanding connections and interrelationships among concepts and content topics.
3. As children compare and contrast readings from books on the same topic, their critical thinking and problem-solving skills are enhanced.
4. Children learn of distant places, past times, different animals and peoples, and intriguing ideas.
5. Such books help children inquire, think critically, and problem solve as they investigate a topic.

*Source:* Adapted from Evelyn Freeman and Diane Person, *Connecting Informational Children's Books with Content Area Learning* (Boston: Allyn and Bacon, 1998).

Because the foundation publishes great children's literature as the focus of collections for grades kindergarten to 9, the resource material is in the form of anthologies. Each student anthology from grades 2 through 8 contains twelve selections, which include folktales and classic and modern fiction. Because two anthologies are available, one for each semester of the year, students read a minimum of twenty-four literary selections a year. Thus, for instance, in third grade, students would be exposed to Russian, Japanese, Canadian, Nigerian, German, English, Ethiopian, and Georgian folktales as well as classics by Hans Christian Andersen, Charles Perrault, and Kenneth Grahame. Each anthology, costing about the same as one hard cover children's trade book, is supported by a teacher's edition, a student activity book (if desired), and audiotapes (if desired).

The foundation suggests that before using Great Books resource materials, teachers participate in the foundation's professional development training program called "The Basic Leader Training Course." Here teachers learn how to use the shared inquiry discussion method and to follow up interpretive and writing activities with the Junior Great Book materials. In the shared inquiry approach to interpretive reading of literature, children are led through questioning to search for more than one answer suggested by the reading. The teacher leader guides students with a series of "why?" and "how?" questions to help them reach their own interpretations instead of providing them with his or her own opinion for an answer. Students use writing as part of the interpretive inquiry process by writing responses and original questions, personal reactions to story ideas, and reflection on divergent ideas.

Junior Great Books has been recognized as an exemplary program in improving achievement for mainstream, highly capable, and at-risk student populations. The program brought success in Title I settings by improving the academic achievement of minority and less capable readers (Northwest Regional Laboratory, 1998) and was noted as being one of seven recent promising reading programs for raising student achievement in reading (American Federation of Teachers, 1998). In three of Chicago's inner-city schools, teachers redefined their beliefs about direct instructional approaches for their students and expressed surprise when the real literature and inquiry process worked even with children with severe learning disabilities (Wheelock, 1999). The foundation has made an effort to connect its inquiry-based language arts program to the many state language arts standards, such as those for New Jersey, New York, Texas, and the District of Columbia. Additional information can be found at The Great Books Foundation's web site at www.greatbooks.org.

## Text-Based Aids

Text-based aids—also known as textbook aids, reader aids, graphic aids, and textbook elements—are designed by authors and publishers to enhance student understanding of text content and to facilitate learning. A key feature of the SQ4R strategy, discussed in Chapter 11, was training the reader to mentally note the information transmitted through such text aids to achieve a global understanding of a text's content. **Text-based aids** should not be confused with other teaching aids often referred to as audiovisual aids, instructional aids, and pedagogical aids. These aids are not contained in a single text but act as supplements to the teaching process or to the book itself.

Text-based aids can appear at a number of places in any given book. Aids that appear at the beginning of a chapter include overviews, instructional objectives, and focusing questions (prequestions). Aids that occur throughout the chapter include headings, key terms in special type, marginal notes (trigger items), overview tables, outlines, and discussions (point–counterpoint, pro–con) and illustrations such as graphs, charts, and pictures. Aids that come at the end of the chapter include summaries, discussion questions (postquestions), case studies, problems, review exercises, sample test questions, suggested activities, suggested readings, and glossaries.

Those aids used before students start to read the chapter acquaint them with the general approach and the information and concepts to be learned. The aids used while students are reading the chapter focus on organization of the content, provide examples, supply supplementary information, and repeat objectives. Those used after the chapter reinforce learning through summaries and exercises and encourage critical thinking through problems and activities. Also see Tips for Teachers 12.1 for an array of text-based aids and questions that can be generated during the SQ4R procedure.

Textbook aids in particular can facilitate the development of cognitive processes. Table 12.1 lists four stages of cognitive processes and corresponding cognitive operations, reader activities, and their relationship to various textbook aids. In theory, the cognitive processes, operations, and reader activities form an untested hierarchy in which one level is prerequisite to the next. The aids are not hierarchical but overlap—and one aid can facilitate learning at more than one level of the hierarchy.

# ■ TECHNOLOGICAL AIDS AND INSTRUCTIONAL MEDIA

This section discusses those aids and tools that teachers use in the classroom to enhance their presentation of content, to provide background information for students, or to supplement the use of verbal language. These aids and tools differ from the text-based aids and may be thought of as more traditional, conventional resources before the current widespread use of computers and electronic literacy formats. Authors have many names for these aids and tools such as *audiovisual aids, instructional media, educational technology, technology-based education,* and *informational technology* (Tang, 1994). According to one author, the view of technology as media grew out of the concept of audiovisual instruction in which slides and film were believed to be capable of delivering information in more concrete and effective ways (Roblyer, 2003a).

Technological instruction refers to the use of specialized materials and equipment to supplement the conventional process of instruction. The special materials and equipment make it possible for learners to experience stimuli that might otherwise be impossible or impractical to bring to the classroom or school. Places, objects, and events can be seen and heard in the classroom.

Just what technology teachers use will depend on their knowledge, the teaching assignment, and the capability of the equipment and its availability. Turning on a movie projector or showing a computer slide show is not quite as simple as opening a book,

# Student Use of Textbook Aids

Textbook aids (textbook elements) have continued to grow as publishers and authors respond to the growing needs of teachers and textbook selection committee criteria for selecting texts. Below is a list of features now commonly found in textbooks, along with questions to ask the students to help them understand how to use these tools. Don't forget that these are many of the same features that transmit important information during the Survey part of the SQ4R procedure.

*Contents*
1. How do you use the table of contents?
2. What is the difference between major and minor headings?
3. In what chapters would you find information about _____?

*Index*
1. What information do you find in an index?
2. On what pages would you find the following information _____?
3. Why is the subject on _____ cross-referenced?

*Opening material* (overview, objectives, focusing questions, outline)
1. What are the main points or topics of the chapter? How do we know?
2. Do the objectives correspond with the outline of the chapter?
3. In what section can we expect to find a discussion of _____?

*Graphic material* (charts, graphs, diagrams) *and tabular material*
1. How does the legend at the bottom of the chart explain the meaning of the data?
2. Based on the lines of the graph, what happened in the year 2000? What do the dotted lines represent?
3. Where in the narrative does the author explain the table?

*Pictures*
1. Are the pictures relevant? Up to date?
2. What is the author trying to convey in this picture?
3. How do the pictures reveal the author's biases?

*Headings*
1. What main ideas can you derive from the headings? Subheadings?
2. How are the subheadings related to the headings?
3. On what page would you find a discussion of _____?

*Information sources* (footnotes, references)
1. Where did the author get the information for the chapter?
2. Are the footnotes important? Up to date?
3. What references might you use to supplement those at the end of the chapter?

*Key terms in text*
1. Which are the important terms on this page?
2. Why are some terms in bold print? Why are other terms in italics?
3. Where can you find the meaning of these terms in the text?

*Marginal notes* (or trigger items)
1. Do the marginal notes catch your eye?
2. Why are these terms or phrases noted in the margin?
3. Quickly find a discussion of the following topics: _____.

*Supplementary discussion* (point–counterpoint tables, lists of suggestions, case studies)
1. Why are the point–counterpoint discussions interesting? Which side do you take?
2. What are the important issues on this topic?
3. Which tips make sense to you? Why?

*(continued)*

*Tips for Teachers*
*(continued)*   **12.1**

*Summaries*

1. If you could read only one page to find out what the chapter is about, what page would you read? Why?
2. Where can we find a summary of the main ideas of the chapter?
3. Does the summary correspond to the major headings?

*End-of-chapter material* (review exercises, questions, activities, sample test items)

1. Are the exercises meaningful? Do they tie into the text?

2. Which discussion questions seem controversial? Why?
3. Why should we do the activities?
4. Take a practice test. Answer the sample test questions to see what we need to study.

but guidelines governing their effective use are not unlike the steps recommended for all other instructional materials. Before examining the technological aids and materials you are most likely to encounter, it is important to understand the influence media have on learning.

## Technology and Learning

Technology has a number of instructional capabilities: (1) It can deliver *symbol systems* (words, picture components, graphs, etc.) when text narrative alone is insufficient. Symbols can be used to specify relationships in almost any subject or field of study, but certain symbol systems are better than others in representing certain tasks or describing information to certain learners. For example, novice learners or slow learners often need visual aids to help them understand complex linguistic information (e.g., the concept of the "human skeleton") or tasks (e.g., how a volcano is made); (2) technology can provide *processing operations* to help learners perform difficult tasks or tasks that otherwise would take an inordinate amount of time to perform (such as computing complex statistical data), or to help learners learn content by engaging other senses such as seeing, listening, or manipulating; (3) technology can also *motivate learners* and *increase the attention span* to help learners focus on specific content; and (4) it can provide students with *independent control* of the learning they will experience through their own manipulation of the controls.

There are, however, opposing views on the influence of technology on learning. First, some believe that technology is a vehicle for delivering instruction but one that has minimal influence on student learning; that is, learning from any technical tool or medium has little to do with the medium itself. What counts are such factors as the teacher's instructional strategies or lesson plan design. Many educators believe that the teacher is key to how technology will be used in the classroom and in literary instruction (Burns et al., 1999). Whatever the selected instructional medium, be it a videotape,

*Table 12.1* How Text-Based Aids Support Cognitive Operations and Reader Activities

| Cognitive Process | Textbook Aids | Cognitive Operations | Reader Activities |
|---|---|---|---|
| Identifying | • Overviews<br>• Instructional objects<br>• Prequestions<br>• Key words or terms<br>• Marginal notes<br>• Summaries<br>• Review exercises | • Focusing on selective information<br>• Sequencing selective information | • Copying<br>• Underlining<br>• Simple note taking or discussion |
| Conceptualizing | • Headings, subheadings<br>• Marginal notes<br>• Point–counterpoint discussions<br>• Summaries<br>• Postquestions<br>• Problems<br>• Review exercises | • Classifying main ideas of text<br>• Comparing main ideas of text | • Logical or structured note taking or discussion<br>• Distinguishing relevant information<br>• Relating points to one another |
| Integrating | • Headings, subheadings<br>• Graphs, tables<br>• Models, paradigms<br>• Postquestions<br>• Case studies<br>• Problems<br>• Activities | • Analyzing main ideas of text<br>• Modifying ideas of text into variations or new ideas<br>• Deducing main ideas of text<br>• Expanding main ideas of text<br>• Applying main ideas of text to problems | • Elaborate note taking or discussion<br>• Making generalizations<br>• Hierarchical ordering of items<br>• Drawing inferences from text information |
| Transferring | • Graphs, tables<br>• Models, paradigms<br>• Simulations<br>• Case studies<br>• Problems<br>• Activities | • Evaluating text information<br>• Verifying text information<br>• Going beyond text information<br>• Predicting from text information | • Elaborate note taking or discussion<br>• Evaluating, problem solving, and inferring based on text information<br>• Using text information to create new information |

*Source:* Adapted from Allan C. Ornstein, "Textbook Instruction: Processes and Strategies," *NASSP Bulletin* (December 1989), p. 109.

an audiotape, a slide show, or an overhead projector, its job is to connect learners with the teacher's intent and the purpose of the instruction (Newby, Stepich, Lehman, & Russell, 2000). Research has long confirmed the critical role the instructor plays in effective use of instructional media (Heinich, Molenda, Russell, & Smaldino, 2002).

Some maintain that though technology may influence the way in which instruction is delivered, the technological medium itself is unlikely to modify the cognitive processes involved in learning (R. Clark, 1983; Snider, 1992).

Another view is that technological media present images or information with which the learner constructs new knowledge. Learning is viewed as an active, constructive process through which new information is extracted from the environment (media) and integrated with prior knowledge (Cuban, 1993; Kozma, 1991; Lewis, 1991). Although constructivist thinking was included as one of six examples of instructional design and technology initiatives of recent decades, two authors felt that the impact of technological design on teaching and learning using constructivist principles is still emerging and yet unstudied and unreported in the educational literature (Carr-Chellman & Reigeluth, 2002).

Conventional print sources of books, textbooks, and trade books—the most common medium used for school learning—and technology have unique strengths and weaknesses as instructional vehicles. Although both employ symbol systems such as words or pictures, text symbols have a limited impact because they are stable. Learning with technological media such as films, television, and videos draws on symbols that are transient and depict motion. On the other hand, texts have advantages in that readers can progress at their own rate of comprehension, whereas the pace of technological presentations (audio and visual elements per unit of time) must coincide with the cognitive level of the viewer. If a presentation is out of sync with the viewer's capabilities or interests (too fast or too slow), then the viewer tends to tune out or not comprehend the information. Put in a different way, technological media forge ahead whether or not comprehension is achieved; unless there are playback features, the learner misses the information. With a textbook, the learner can always reread the material, and the reading can be sped up or slowed down depending on the cognitive abilities of the learner (expert or novice, high or low achiever) and the sophistication of the material.

In a nutshell, the modes of presentation of the emerging technologies are fascinating and multiple, with the potential to combine sound, still or motion pictures, text, graphics, animation, and computer-generated sound and voice. But these capabilities may inadvertently be dysfunctional for the intended learning because the modes of presentation are cognitively simple (Hooper & Hannafin, 1991; Miller & Olson, 1994). They usually entertain rather than expect the individual to think, apply, or problem solve. Viewing images or listening to simple audio or visual messages involves little mental effort, which results in simple cognitive processing. Computers, however, can be quite useful in managing and processing information, and this usefulness is shown in Box 12.4.

The fact is that **electronic media** (especially television and videos) are winning the battle with books and turning our children and youth into a generation of nonreaders. As one observer asserted: "Most students learn how to read, but many do not choose to read." Why should they? Their schools, homes, and communities are bursting with new and exciting television programs, videotapes, movies, and computer games, while a majority of the books in their school library may be obsolete and unattractive. Best estimates are that nearly 90 percent of the books in a typical school library were published before the landing of a man on the moon (Humphrey, 1992). Considering that many youth have "wired bedrooms," furnished with radios, stereos, televisions, telephones,

**BOX 12.4** How Computers Benefit the Thinking and Learning of Information

Computers have the capacity to store, retrieve, and process information, which is vital for careers in our information society. Computers can also transform one symbol system (e.g., words) to another (e.g., speech) or vice versa. The computer can tally numerical values or equations and transform them into tables, graphs, and other pictorial representations. Computers can also be used to construct relationships between symbol domains (e.g., words and pictures) and real-world phenomena. According to one author, such relationships could show what will happen under certain conditions, how interpretations of specific laws or principles operate in the real world, and demonstrate problem-solving sequences.

*Source:* Adapted from Decker Walker, "Technology and Literacy, Rasing the Bar," *Educational Leadership* (October 1998), pp. 18–21.

VCRs, and computers, the pull of the printed medium in the form of books is waning even among middle-class students. Because students are immersed in these electronic images, teachers must learn how to integrate teaching and learning into this new electronic culture—or run the risk of becoming irrelevant to their audience (Ornstein, 1991). Furthermore, reports indicate that young males are becoming more at-risk for print failure than young females (Allen, 2001).

## A Rationale for Instructional Technology

Advocates of instructional technology point out that traditional methods of instruction, which rely on an oral discourse and verbal comprehension, have proved ineffective for a large percentage of students and are not cost effective (Branson, 1991; Semb & Ellis, 1994). Not only is traditional instruction based on faulty assumptions (e.g., students naturally absorb teacher talk, read and enjoy textbooks, come to class prepared, learn best when placed in organized rows and hardback chairs, and learn at the same rate or pace), but also the method no longer coincides with or meets the modern technological needs or nuances of the society in which we live.

Instructional technology is based on using modern electronic communication devices—such as VCRs, audiotapes, closed-circuit television, cable systems, CD-ROMs, computers, compact discs and laser disc players, and electronic bulletin boards—many of which rely on multisensory learning and in-depth ways of gaining knowledge. These represent a new resource that makes instruction come alive, and they offer a multimedia dimension to learning that may be more suitable for nonverbal learners. The assumptions with instructional technology are that (a) information in school can be independently learned from electronic media and data sources other than the teacher or text; (b) students are capable of assuming responsibility for their own learning, especially if the material presented is visually and aurally stimulating; (c) students learn best when they control their rate of learning; and (d) teachers can be trained in the delivery of technology-based instruction. The latest technological pedagogical tools permit teachers to customize instruction to the needs and pace of individual students, and all students do not have to be available or present at the same time in order for instruction to take place (Hooper & Rieber, 1995; Newby et al., 2000).

## Chalkboards and Display Boards

Chalkboards and display boards certainly do not represent advanced technology, but they are definitely visual aids. The chalkboard is perhaps the oldest and most traditional piece of equipment found in the classroom. Next to the traditional book, it is the most widely used instructional aid. Two educators note that the chalkboard commands such a presence in the classroom that many of us fail to think of it as a visual aid at all; however, most teachers would not be pleased if they had no chalkboards available (Clark & Starr, 1995).

The **chalkboard** is popular because it allows for spontaneity, speed, and change. The chalkboard can fit the tempo of any lesson in any subject. It can be used for displaying pictures and important clippings; drawing sketches, maps, and diagrams to help illustrate points of a lesson; projecting films and other materials; listing suggestions or items as they are offered; writing outlines, summaries, and assignments; and working out problems and evaluating procedures and answers. The chalkboard is particularly valuable for emphasizing the major points of a lesson and working out problems for the whole class to see.

**Display boards** are used for displaying student projects and progress; displaying current items of interest related to a lesson or unit; posting announcements, memos, and routine assignments; and decorating the room. Display boards come in many types: bulletin board, pegboard, flannel board, magnetic board. The boards stimulate student creativity and interest, promote student participation in the learning activity, and make the room more cheerful, print rich, and student oriented. If there are no display boards in the room, a portion of the chalkboard can be reserved for this purpose. Especially in the elementary grades, portions of the classroom walls often house multiple display boards to exhibit and showcase the students print-rich work.

## The Overhead Projector and Transparency Use

The **overhead projector** projects images of prepared or developing instructional transparencies on a screen, wall, or chalkboard. The **transparency** is placed on the glass on top of the projector. Because the room does not need to be dark, students can take notes. Because the overhead projector is so convenient to use, it remains standard equipment in many classrooms and is often used in conjunction with the chalkboard to present unfolding information. There are three reasons why the overhead projector remains popular as a classroom instructional resource: (1) teachers are able to face their students and can adjust and monitor instruction according to their needs, (2) teachers can disclose information progressively as they engage students attention, and (3) transparencies can be created quickly and efficiently by busy teachers (Hooper & Reinartz, 2002). A highly positive aspect of writing on blank transparencies while presenting new material is the fact that the teacher maintains control of the class with the face-to-face exchange (Burns et al., 1999).

## Film Resources and Videotapes

Other than television, **film** (or movies) is perhaps the most influential and seductive educational medium for transmitting ideas and persuading an audience to a point of view. Because of the vivid, often larger-than-life images it presents, the motion picture has a dramatic impact on its audience. Films both interest and motivate students. Thousands of good films have been made expressly for educational purposes. They can be divided into the following categories: (1) historical, (2) dramatic, (3) special topic, (4) "slice of life," and (5) animated (Heinich, Molenda, & Russell, 1992; Naylor & Diem, 1987). The movie is particularly useful for showing processes in which motion is involved or in which slow motion can be used.

Some authors maintain that **videotapes** have completely replaced films and filmstrips in most schools. This is because they are easy to use with videotape recorders and students can rewind to view a segment again. Furthermore, movies that are based on children's books or topics in textbooks abound, and these visual tales give less proficient readers and those lacking relevant experiential background additional information (Burns et al., 1999).

In one program that ran for a full year with inner-city students from grades K–8, videotaping was used as a means of improving students' oral presentation skills to meet the state standards for delivering an oral recitation. Students were videotaped three times during the year either reciting poems, reading orally, delivering speeches, or giving an oral report of a book they had read. The students, their teachers, and their parents all had the opportunity to view the videotape for evaluation purposes (Guastello & Sinatra, 2001). The benefits of using videotaping to assist in the development of oral communication skills include (1) evaluating for improvement, (2) analyzing content robustness, (3) identifying distracting mannerisms, such as gestures, long pauses, and lack of eye content, and (4) gaining a sense of oneself in a literary event.

Other authors suggest that students use a **collaborative listening–viewing guide** so that they are not passive during the viewing of a videotape, movie, science experiment, or even field trip. The guide is outlined on a single sheet of paper on which a student individually writes his or her notes of the viewing event in the left column and records the group's notes, which enhance and enrich the individual notes, in a right column. Cooperatively, they record what they learned and what they will research further on the bottom section of the guide (Flood & Wood, 1998).

## Television and Its Influence

Recent evidence makes it clear that **television** has become a "second school system." Children under ten years of age watch television an average of 30 to 35 hours a week, or about one-fifth of their waking hours. By the time a child graduates from high school, he or she will have spent 15,000 to 20,000 hours in front of the screen compared to 11,000 to 12,000 hours in school (Buckingham, 1992; Dorr, 1986). With the average home tuned into television an average of seven hours a day (Chen, 1994), it is no wonder that children spend more time watching television than in any other activity, with the exception of sleeping. This may also suggest that television becomes an important socializing agent and competes with time spent with family, friends, school acquaintances, and other socializing groups.

Rather than viewing television as a second school system, Neil Postman views it and other mass media (radio, comic books, movies) as the "first curriculum" because they appear to be affecting the way children develop learning skills and acquire knowledge and understanding (1979; see also Oskamp, 1987). According to Postman and others,

Teaching students how to "deconstruct" television shows such as news reports, commentaries, and political campaigns gives them an important media-viewing skill. Students can be taught to consider questions such as (1) Who made this show? (2) Why do I think it was made? (3) What techniques are being used to gain viewing attention? (4) Who profits from this message? (5) What is not being presented? and (6) What beliefs and value systems are embedded in the visual/text message?

*Source:* Adapted from Larry Mann, "The Aha! of Media Literacy," *Education Update* (November 1999), pp. 1, 6, and 7.

television's curriculum is designed largely to maintain interest, whereas the school's curriculum is supposed to have other purposes, such as mastery of thinking skills. In addition, watching television requires little effort and few skills; children do not have to think about or solve problems. Rather, they become accustomed to rapidly changing stimuli, quick answers, and "escapist" fantasies, not to mention overdoses of violent and sexual behavior on the screen. See Tips for Teachers 12.2.

Table 12.2 reveals where nine- and thirteen-year-olds spend most of their out-of-school time. The table shows, between 1984 and 1999, the percentage of time the two age groups watched three or more hours of television daily, how much time was devoted to homework, and the time spent on enjoyable reading. Notice that by 1999, the nine-year-olds were devoting a bit more daily time to reading for fun than to watching three or more hours of television, whereas the thirteen-year-olds read less for fun in ratio to their television viewing. However, thirteen-year-olds did get more homework and spent twice as much time as nine-year-olds in getting it done, from one to two hours daily. Box 12.5 suggests ways teachers can help students interpret television and visual messages.

# ■ ELECTRONIC TEXT RESOURCES

You should be aware of four significant aspects of **electronic text resources**. First, in Chapter 2, we discussed computers and electronic text in the context of literacy modes. We explained how user capability through the electronic means of "links" and "shifting about" text and nonverbal materials alters the traditional view of literacy. Second, the audiovisual and other technologies discussed in the previous section of this chapter have to a large degree been rendered obsolete by contemporary multimedia presentation systems, particularly those found in slide shows, web pages, and kiosks (Hooper & Reinartz, 2002). Third, electronic media, as with other forms of media that carry information between a source and a receiver, can be used in two ways: (1) to supplement "live" classroom instruction in which media is used selectively and effectively by the teacher to enhance learning and (2) for small-group or independent work with "packaged" or programmed materials to be used without teacher presence (Heinich, Molenda, Russell et al., 2002). Finally, some contemporary authors writing about computer technology applications point out how rapidly changes are occurring, how a lack of consensus prevails regarding the way to categorize the uses of instructional technology, and how the applications they discuss in their books may not be relevant or useful by the time readers read their texts (Milner & Milner, 2003).

# Using Television at School and at Home

Teachers need to use the resource of television judiciously in the classroom because TV viewing is associated more with pleasure than with learning by most youngsters. Teachers also need to remind parents that too much time in front of the television is harmful for their children. Research suggests that excessive TV viewing interferes with reading, studying, and academic performance in general. Here are some tips for teachers to consider in their classroom uses of television and for teachers to communicate to parents about their children's TV viewing.

## For Classroom Use by Teachers

1. Select programs to coincide with the learners' level of interest and maturity and with instructional objectives. Consider the educational significance, quality, content, writing, and production.
2. Make sure the classroom or media center is suitable for viewing the program. Check the lights and shades, acoustic arrangements, seating facilities, and placement of the television.
3. Lights should be left on if students are to take notes. If they are not expected to take notes, the lights may be dimmed somewhat for improved viewing.
4. Before a program is viewed, give students any necessary background data and tell them what to expect. You may want to hand out question sheets that focus on major points. These are especially helpful if students are assigned to watch a program at home.
5. Avoid using television as a lecturing device or as a substitute for instruction. Integrate it into the lesson and discussion.
6. Keep questions and comments during the program to a minimum, or ask students to save them until the end of the program.
7. After the program, hold a discussion to analyze the main points.
8. The ideal program lasts no longer than two-thirds of the subject period so that there is time for introduction and summary.
9. Videotaped programs can fit into the daily class schedule. If a school system operates a network, it can play programs to fit class schedules. (However, be certain that such rebroadcasting and videotaping comply with federal copyright laws.)
10. When assigning programs for homework, make sure all students have access to a television set. Arrangements (such as a buddy system) should be made for those who do not.

## Suggestions to Parents for TV Viewing

1. Decide if children can watch television on school days and, if so, for how long.
2. Determine how much television can be watched on weekends.
3. Be clear about the amount of time a child can watch television. Don't let children feel TV time can be saved up.
4. Establish rules about finishing homework, reading, or doing chores before watching.
5. Remind children that they have control over the television. When a show is too scary or has inappropriate content, they can turn it off.
6. Keep in mind that specials may arise and some shows offer good educational content. Such additional shows might take precedence over others.
7. Watch for children being captivated by habit-forming soap operas or serialized shows. There is little value in children keeping a daily appointment with such shows.

*(continued)*

8. Observe whether children watch television even when they have friends over. Offer them something to do instead.
9. Ask yourself if television watching could be taking the place of activities that the family might do together. If the television is on during breakfast and dinner, this suggests it is more important than conversation.
10. Consider reading aloud to children for fifteen minutes each day or establish quiet reading times. Some studies have shown that time spent each day reading aloud to children inspires them to turn off the television.

*Table 12.2* Percentage of Time Nine- and Thirteen-Year-Olds Devote Daily to Three or More Hours of Television Viewing, Working on Homework, and Reading for Fun between 1984 and 1999

| *Watched television 3 or more hours daily* | *Time on Homework* | | | | | *Read daily for fun* |
| | *Had homework assigned* | *Had homework assigned, not done* | *Less than 1 hour* | *1 to 2 hours* | *More than 2 hours* | |
|---|---|---|---|---|---|---|
| **Age 9** | | | | | | |
| 1984    66.7 | 64.4 | 4.1 | 41.5 | 12.7 | 6.1 | 53.3 |
| 1999    51.1 | 74.2 | 3.8 | 53.1 | 12.4 | 4.9 | 54.1 |
| **Age 13** | | | | | | |
| 1984    63.4 | 77.4 | 3.7 | 35.9 | 29.2 | 8.6 | 35.1 |
| 1999    45.9 | 75.9 | 4.5 | 37.2 | 26.3 | 7.9 | 28.2 |

*Source: The Condition of Education 2001* (Washington, DC: U.S. Dept. of Education, Office of Educational Research and Improvement, 2001), p. 42.

## How Electronic Text Is Used

Current **electronic technology**—and related video and telecommunication technology—has greater potential for enhancing the instructional and learning processes today than did the computer technology of the past several decades. Unlike initial computer uses, the new technology can supplement complex interactions between learners and the information base.

We are in the midst of an "information explosion" stemming from the generation and availability of an ever-increasing quantity of information through the use of the computer. As educators, we should aim at making our students computer literate at an early age and view computer literacy as "a fourth R" or a fundamental skill (Dooling,

2000; Todd, 1999; Walker, 1999). Furthermore, once teachers begin using the new computer technologies, they need to realize that these technologies prompt changes in the daily classroom routine and learning experiences of the students (Carr-Chellman & Reigeluth, 2002).

## Computer Software

Instructional software offerings have gradually improved in quality and variety and are available for all subjects and grade levels. No longer do they cover only isolated topics or provide practice in one or two skills. Current software presents entire units and courses of instruction. The most common explanation for the poor ratings of the early stage or first generation of software was that material was written either by persons with expertise in computers but not in education or by persons with expertise in educational theory but not in computers.

Probably the most frequent criticism of early educational software in general was the predominance of drill and tutorial programs. This is changing as more simulation and interactive systems are being introduced (Hooper & Reinartz, 2002). Whereas the early software consisted of sequenced questions with specific answers, the new software permits a variety of student responses with branching to appropriate levels of instruction based on the student's response. If the student fails to master the task or concept, the new drill and tutorial software breaks down the concept using analogies, examples, and suggestions rather than merely presenting a sequenced repetition of the subject matter.

Amid the array of information systems available through computer software—CD-ROMs, electronic bulletin boards, external databases, and mobile/electronic wide-area networks—teachers will find the CD-ROM to have particular educational potential. Its capacity is enormous and educators are just beginning to understand it. For example, an entire encyclopedia can be put on one CD-ROM through which the user experiences a world of data via a combination of audio, visual, and kinesthetic stimuli.

Whereas most school learning relies on aural stimuli (listening to the teacher) and is based on linear sequencing, the CD-ROM permits students to select from diverse topics and mediums, entering and exiting by a sequence of easy commands. The CD-ROM software brings life to learning through audio tracks such as music, speeches, and voices of actual people; visual tracks such as printed text, graphs, pictures, news clippings, and films; and physical motion.

Not only do the graphics and sound presentations enhance the overall appeal of contemporary educational software, but the new **computer simulations** also permit students to vicariously experience real-life situations. Students can conduct experiments and experience past events, current trends, or future possibilities—and encounter "what if" dilemmas—all through simulations. Through the learner's interactive participation, software can promote logical thinking, hypothesizing, and problem-solving strategies. There are two types of simulations: (1) those that try to teach, as when students manipulate objects or events shown on the screen or "iterate" a process again and again so that they can study the effects of a process, or (2) those that show "how to" by explaining the steps of a process or procedure and those that present a hypothetical problem situation and students provide reactions, such as when playing the stock market (Alessi & Trollop, 2000).

## Computerized Books

One commercial electronic literacy format that is becoming increasingly popular in our schools is known as "talking books." **Talking books** are electronic versions of traditional books. Through computerized story line screens, the talking books present stories that contain the traditional elements of the narrative, such as characters, setting, goal, events, character development, resolution, and theme. However, after each screen's presentation, the reader (or user) can access multimedia features to interact with the story (Hales & Russel, 1995). The screen becomes interactive by clicking the mouse, and children can hear how words are pronounced, reread passages, view animated illustrations, and witness special effects that elicit visual or auditory responses (Labbo, 2000). These **computerized books,** usually on CD-ROM, are designed as reading support programs for schools and often assist particular populations within the school setting.

With talking books, the unique capabilities of electronic technology allow computers to go beyond conventional materials while addressing a problematic area of literacy for some students, particularly struggling readers, who could benefit from a new approach (Labbo, Reinking, & McKenna, 1999; Meyerson & Kulesza, 2002). Computerized books offer four thinking–literacy strategies to different levels of learners. First, in addition to the overall benefits of story listening, they can support the reader by providing pronunciation of words. Such support has been called "electronic scaffolding" (McKenna, 1998). When the reader encounters an unknown word, he or she can easily overcome the obstacle by accessing the stored pronunciation and moving on in the text (McKenna, Reinking, & Labbo, 1997). Second, they allow beginning readers to read and enjoy books at or even above their listening levels because unfamiliar words can be pronounced on demand with minimal interruption. Third, they offer other motivating features such as animation, sound effects, and gamelike formats. Finally, such books invite users to be interactive with writing and artwork, thereby inviting other instructional connections to the original printed version.

## Connecting the Internet to Learning Experiences

A contemporary educational goal is to prepare students for our rapidly changing, complex, information-based society. To do this, schools have access to the Internet and worldwide multimedia resources such as articles, maps, photographs, and film clips. The **Internet** allows students and teachers to access up-to-the-minute information for information and research purposes. One author points out that research on the Internet has severed the spatial connection inherent in library resources (Elkind, 2001). Others see it not only as a new medium that can offer levels of implementation in school environments, but also as a cultural phenomenon because school's have the infrastructure to make web-based instruction a pervasive aspect of the educational climate (Jones, Harmon, & Lowther, 2002).

At the beginning of the 1990s, the World Wide Web was nonexistent, so the subsequent use of the Internet and World Wide Web as tools for communication and education has been so meteoric that few realize how recent this development has occurred. In 1990, fewer than 10 percent of the nation's schools had Internet connections and Internet access within regular classrooms. By 1994 this figure was 35 percent, and in 1997 it had reached 75 percent (Means, 2000). In 1999, 95 percent of our nation's schools had

Internet access, with the average public school housing 100 computers (Heinich et al., 2002).

The **World Wide Web (WWW)** provides a way to use a standardized system for creating electronic pages on the Internet. While the "net" may be thought of as the communications link, the "web" sets up the way—the language, the protocol, and the procedures—to link documents to other documents that can be housed on the computers connected to the Internet. The documents are established as **web pages,** and each collection of web pages becomes a **web site** (U.S. Department of Education, 2001). Web pages involve multimedia and hypermedia (Willis, Stephens, & Matthew, 1996). Because web pages may contain text with high-resolution color graphics, voice, and video, they are multimedia, and because the student (or user) can quickly move from one location to the next through links, the pages are also hypermedia. Take the example of researching a Mozart symphony. Suppose a student was doing a report or presentation on the World's Great Composers. The student might be able to go to a home page web site that enumerates the great composers. The student clicks on "Mozart" and is transported to that document. The site that generated the Mozart document could inform the searcher of other sites around the world that have information on Mozart. The student (or searcher) moves from site to site to locate and absorb the information necessary to fulfill the requirements of the search.

As few as two computers linked together in a classroom make up a **network.** A number of computers linked together in a school or a computer laboratory is known as a local area network (LAN). For a very large network like the Internet to occur, all of the smaller networks that connect computers in various locales around the word are linked together. Information is transmitted through electrical power over the Internet, allowing students in school and at home to have access to a wide breadth of information as long as they have access to a computer and an electrical plug. A student's access to Internet links on the World Wide Web provides a fertile means for learning, with electronic text on every subject imaginable (Vacca & Vacca, 2002).

However, access to the web is one thing; knowing how to use it well to gain information and do research is another. Todd (1999) suggests that obtaining the best information to satisfy a personal need or a school-imposed requirement requires some knowledge about how to use **search engines.** For students, this would mean knowing what search engines work best to provide information about a given topic, what levels of information the search engines look into, and how to question various databases using search terms. Search engines are simply searching programs that companies have developed to help electronic text users navigate the Internet efficiently to find information on a given topic (Roblyer, 2003b). Common search engine sites used by teachers and students are Lycos, Yahoo!, and Google.

## The Promise of Technology for Literacy Shifts

Tapscott (1999) feels that the ultimate interactive learning environment is the Internet because its technology includes the large library of human knowledge, the technological means to manage this knowledge, an amiable way to connect people, and an exploding array of services and virtual environments to explore. As outlined in Box 12.6, he maintains that eight shifts are occurring in teaching and learning that also have an impact on learners' literacy development.

**BOX 12.6** The Eight Shifts in Teaching–Learning Environments

Eight shifts are occurring in teaching–learning environments in the following ways:

- From linear to hypermedia learning in the processing of information.
- From instruction to construction and discovery with a shift away from traditional formats of teaching to the formation of learning partnerships in which students plan, help design, and accomplish or "do."
- From teacher-centered to learner-centered education in that the new technologies focus learning experiences on the learner rather than on the senders. Learning-centered environments are also highly active with students discussing, arguing, researching, and collaborating on projects with one another and with the teacher.
- From taking information and memorizing to learning how to navigate and how to learn through the increased necessity to use the thinking of synthesis. Because students are engaged in accessing information sources and people on the Internet, they construct higher-level thinking structures and form mental images.
- From classroom settings to lifelong learning because Internet youth are continuously reinventing their school-introduced knowledge base.
- From one approach to learning something for all to customized learning, because the digital technologies treat each student as an individual. The flexibility of digital media use allows each learner to find his or her own personal way to learn to succeed and produce.
- From learning as something to be avoided in the enclosed school setting to learning as fun.
- From the teacher as transmitter of facts and information to the teacher as facilitator and technical consultant on ways to use the digital media for optimal learning.

*Source:* Adapted from Dan Tapscott, "Educating the Net Generation," *Educational Leadership* (February 1999), pp. 7–11.

Furthermore, in an age in which students are creating their own web sites, students are thinking and communicating as designers and artists, which requires understanding the use of art to communicate. Students integrate pictures, video, graphics, and animation into their presentations, moving them away from text-centered and traditional word-oriented ways of communicating and presenting projects (Ohler, 2000). *The National Educational Technology Standards for Students,* published by the International Society for Technology in Education (2000), includes these concepts of multimedia resources and artistic creation in its elaboration of six broad categories of standards (see Table 12.3).

However, a number of educators have urged caution in promoting computers as the answer to educational and social reform. Although they believe that digital information technology is important, it is still incomplete because schools, homes, and the workplace function separately and don't share a common purpose and plan of collaborative action. Digital technologies must connect schools, homes, workplaces, libraries, museums, and social services in order to weave education into the fabric of the community (Kozma & Shank, 1998). For instance, an Internet connection between school and home will allow students to extend the academic day, enable teachers to use students' daily experiences to enrich their lives at home, and allow parents to become more involved in their children's education while finding educational insights and opportunities for themselves. Internet

## *Table 12.3* The National Educational Technology Standards for Students

The technology standards for students are categorized into six broad areas. These standards, with accompanying student applications, are to be used as guidelines for planning activities using technology in school and life-learning tasks.

| Standard Category | Student Applications |
|---|---|
| Basic Operations and Concepts | • Students demonstrate a sound understanding of the nature and operation of technology systems.<br>• Students are proficient in the use of technology. |
| Social, Ethical, and Human Issues | • Students understand the ethical, cultural, and societal issues related to technology.<br>• Students practice responsible use of technology systems, information, and software.<br>• Students develop positive attitudes toward technology uses that support lifelong learning, collaboration, personal pursuits, and productivity. |
| Technology Productivity Tools | • Students use technology tools to enhance learning, increase productivity, and promote creativity.<br>• Students use productivity tools to collaborate in constructing technology-enhanced models, preparing publications, and producing other creative works. |
| Technology Communications Tools | • Students use telecommunications to collaborate, publish, and interact with peers, experts, and other audiences.<br>• Students use a variety of media and formats to communicate information and ideas effectively to multiple audiences. |
| Technology Research Tools | • Students use technology to locate, evaluate, and collect information from a variety of sources.<br>• Students use technology tools to process data and report results.<br>• Students evaluate and select new information resources and technological innovations based on the appropriateness to specific tasks. |
| Technology Problem-Solving and Decision-Making Tools | • Students use technology resources for solving problems and making informed decisions.<br>• Students employ technology in the development of strategies for solving problems in the real world. |

*Source:* International Society for Technology in Education (ITSE), *National Educational Technology Standards for Students* (Eugene, OR: Author, 2000).

connections between school, the workplace, and worldwide communities will foster learning in real-life situations and allow teachers and students to connect with other teachers, other students, professionals, and technical and business experts as resources.

Another argument is that although great technological increases have occurred in our nation's schools, the United States still hasn't provided a convenient, robust, and reliable technology support structure for its teachers and students. Common uses of the Internet and the desktop computer do not approximate an educational ideal. The modern World Wide Web is disorganized, of uneven quality, and overburdened with advertising. In far too many cases, students and teachers are either not using the technology available to them or they are using technology to accomplish tasks that could be done offline in a quicker way (Means, 2000). Teachers also need to realize that uses of technology mirror and even magnify many of society's problems and trends, such as those related to societal, cultural, equity, educational, and technical issues (Roblyer, 2003a). Teachers have to help students use the resource of the World Wide Web in critical and constructive ways by showing students how to sort out reliable information from the misinformation, inappropriate information, and meaningless information that is found on the ambiguous world of the Web (Todd, 1999). By 1999 the majority of our nation's teachers (53 percent) reported they felt "somewhat prepared" and 13 percent reported they were "not at all prepared" to use computers and the Internet for instructional purposes. This is in contrast to the 10 percent who felt they were "very well prepared" and the 23 percent who believed they were "well prepared." Figure 12.1 shows the total respondents and the number of years of teaching experience.

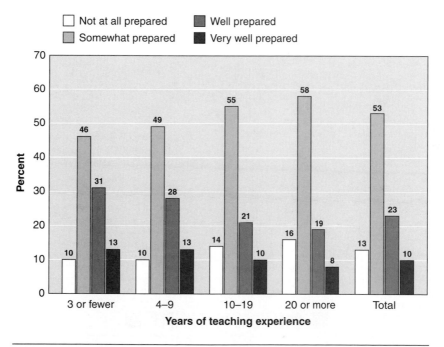

*Figure 12.1* Public School Teachers in 1999 Reporting How Well They Felt Prepared to Use Computers and the Internet for Classroom Instruction by Years of Teaching Experience

*Source: The Condition of Education 2001* (Washington, DC: U.S. Department of Education, Office of Educational Research and Improvement, 2001), p. 66.

Interestingly, in its review of studies of electronic technology related to reading, the National Reading Panel (2000) found a striking absence of studies relating Internet applications to reading instruction. It did note that (1) hypertext use presents an instructional advantage in that it creates links to definitions and supporting reading material, (2) word processing is useful in that reading instruction becomes effective when combined with writing instruction, and (3) electronic technology cannot be studied alone, or apart from its relationship to instructional content; that is, technology is a resource and not an instructional method. Summing up this last notion is one author's belief that computers don't drive curriculum content (Bjorklund, 2000). We know that good teaching, connected to print and electronic resource materials, makes the educational difference for most students.

## ■ SUMMARY ■

1. Instructional resources can be categorized into those that are traditional book and print sources, instructional aids and media, computers and electronic texts, and teacher-made or -modified instructional materials.

2. Types of print instructional resources include school reading series; textbooks and workbooks; trade books; journals, magazines, newspapers; and reference sources. Textbooks and workbooks tend to dominate as the major instructional material in many classrooms.

3. There are significant differences between textbook aids, designed to facilitate student comprehension, and technological/instructional aids, designed to facilitate the teacher's instruction.

4. Basic guidelines related to using instructional technology include (a) selecting equipment suitable to curriculum and standards-based objectives, (b) previewing the materials, and (c) using the technology meaningfully in lessons.

5. Visual images increase effectiveness of presentation of materials. Visual images can be incorporated into a presentation through the use of chalkboards and display boards; films, filmstrips, and film slides; and overhead projectors.

6. Television has to be used judiciously in the classroom because it is primarily an entertainment medium. Two types of TV programming for use in schools are educational television (informative programs produced by commercial and public television stations) and instructional television (programs produced by educators for specific teaching purposes).

7. The quality and variety of computer software have improved in recent years. The most challenging and interesting uses of computer-based instruction are in the growing number of simulations and interactive systems. The World Wide Web and Internet can be a great resource but students have to be shown how to use them as an informational resource.

## ■ QUESTIONS TO CONSIDER ■

1. Why is it wise to have committee input into the selection and purchase of resources for classroom and school use?

2. What is the main purpose of using instructional materials?

3. Which textbook aids are most important? Why?

4. What are important factors to consider when supplementing the textbook with trade books or workbooks?

5. Is there a danger in using too many materials in a class? Explain.

6. Do you agree that the chalkboard and overhead are still valuable instructional aids? Explain.
7. Some educators feel that computers are revolutionizing education. Do you agree? Explain.
8. How can teachers encourage students to change their television and video habits from movies to documentaries, from entertainment to education?
9. What can you do to make the Internet an instructional and meaningful resource when students do assignments and homework?

## ■ THINGS TO DO ■

1. Discuss in class ten questions to consider when evaluating instructional materials. Which questions or concepts are the most important? Why?
2. In class prepare up to three checklists, one for evaluating textbooks, one for evaluating a school reading series, and one for trade books. You could have groups of students engaged in these and checklists for other resources and present their group work to the class.
3. Select one of the instructional or technological aids discussed in this chapter. Do an oral report on its advantages and disadvantages.
4. Compose a visual story and project it through a filmstrip, a film slide, or computer images on a screen or wall. Ask students to write the story they see unfolding in images. Find out if they sense that writing from a visually composed story will enhance and motivate their K–8 students to write more and more coherently.
5. Based on a topic or theme, have students access the World Wide Web to locate informational sources. You may suggest search engines or web sites that students could turn to initially as they begin their search.

## ■ RECOMMENDED READINGS ■

Brandt, Ronald S., ed. *Education in a New Era; ASCD Yearbook 2000*. Alexandria, VA: Association for Supervision and Curriculum Development, 2000. Authors, chosen for the experience they bring to their fields, write about events and developments foreseen in the twenty-first century and how resources will be used.

The Great Books Foundation. *An Introduction to Shared Inquiry*, 4th ed. Chicago: Author, 1999. Presents the procedures for teacher leaders of Junior Great Books to follow and reveals the process of inquiry to implement with active reading of the literary sources.

Heinich, Robert, Michael Molenda, James Russell, and Sharon Smaldino. *Instructional Media and Technologies for Learning*, 7th ed. Upper Saddle River, NJ: Merrill/Prentice Hall, 2002. Shows how teachers play the critical role in the effective use of instructional media, computers, and electronic networks.

Kelly, M. G., et al. *National Education Technology Standards for Students: Connecting Curriculum and Technology*. Eugene, OR: International Society for Technology in Education and U.S. Department of Education, 2000. Presents a comprehensive list of the technology standards for students, practical applications of how to implement them, and actual plans created by teachers for classroom lessons.

##  KEY TERMS

balancing
basal reading system
chalkboards

collaborative listening–viewing guide
computerized books

computer simulations
core book
display boards

electronic media
electronic technology
electronic text resources
film
informational trade books
Internet
Junior Great Books
literature anthologies

network
overhead projector
picture books
search engines
sequencing
talking books
television
text-based aids

textbooks
trade books
transparency
videotapes
web pages
web site
World Wide Web

# ■ REFERENCES ■

Alessi, S., & Trollop, S. (2000). *Multimedia for learning: Methods and development* (3rd ed.). Boston: Allyn and Bacon.

Allen, R. (2001, Summer). English teachers fight back: Connecting literature in an image-driven world. *Curriculum Update of ASCD,* 1–3, 6–9.

American Federation of Teachers. (1998). *Building on the best, learning from what works: Seven promising reading and English language arts programs.* Washington, DC: Author.

Beck, I., & McKeown, M. (2002, November). Questioning the author: Making sense of social studies. *Educational Leadership,* 44–47.

Bernstein, H. T. (1988). *America's textbook fiasco: A conspiracy of good intentions.* Washington, DC: Council for Basic Education.

Bjorklund, A. (2000, November). One more tool for the toolbox. *English Journal,* 42–46.

Branson, R. K. (1991). Why the schools can't improve. In J. E. Bowgher (Ed.), *Why and how to restructure educational systems* (pp. 1–13). Warrenton, VA: Society for Applied Learning Technology.

Buckingham, D. (1992). *Television literacy: Talk, text, and context.* New York: Palmer Press.

Burns, P., Roe, B., & Ross, E. (1999). *Teaching reading in today's elementary schools* (7th ed.). Boston: Houghton Mifflin.

Carnine, D., Silbert, J., Kameenui, E., & Tarver, S. (2004). *Direct instruction reading* (4th ed.). Upper Saddle River, NJ: Merrill.

Carr-Chellman, A., & Reigeluth, C. (2002). Whistling in the dark? Instructional design and technology in the school. In R. A. Reiser & J. P. Dempsey (Eds.), *Trends and issues in instructional design and technology* (pp. 239–255). Upper Saddle River, NJ: Merrill/Prentice Hall.

Chen, M. (1994). *The smart parent's guide to kids' TV.* San Francisco: KQED Books.

Cherryholmes, C. H. (1993, January/February). Readers research. *Journal of Curriculum Studies,* 1–32.

Clark, L. H., & Starr, I. S. (1995). *Secondary and middle school teaching methods* (6th ed.). Upper Saddle River, NJ: Prentice Hall.

Clark, R. E. (1983, Winter). Reconsidering research on learning from media. *Review of Educational Research,* 445–459.

Cuban, L. (1993, Winter). Computers meet classrooms. *Teachers College Record,* 185–210.

Cullinan, B., & Galda, L. (1998). *Literature and the child.* Ft. Worth, TX: Harcourt Brace.

DelFattore, J. (1992). *What Johnny shouldn't read: Textbook censorship in America.* New Haven, CT: Yale University Press.

Dooling, J. O. (2000, October). What students want to learn about computers. *Education Leadership,* 20–24.

Dorr, A. (1986). *Television and children.* Newbury Park, CA: Sage.

Eisner, E. W. (1987, January/February). Why the textbook influences curriculum. *Curriculum Review,* 11–13.

Elkind, D. (2001, December/January). The cosmopolitan school. *Educational Leadership,* 12–17.

Fairbanks, C. (1994, Winter). Teaching and learning beyond the text. *Journal of Curriculum Supervision,* 155–173.

Fitzgerald, S. (1994). Textbooks, design and use. In A. C. Purves (Ed.), *Encyclopedia of English studies and language arts* (pp. 1204–1206). New York: Scholastic/Urbana, IL: National Council of Teachers of English.

Flood, J., & Wood, K. (1998, November). Viewing: The neglected communication process or "When what you see isn't what you get." *The Reading Teacher*, 300–304.

Freeman, E., & Person, D. (1998). *Connecting informational children's books with content area learning*. Boston: Allyn and Bacon.

Galda, L., & Cullinan, B. (1991). Literature for literacy: What research says about the benefits of using trade books in the classroom. In J. Flood, J. Jensen, D. Lapp, & J. Squire (Eds.), *Handbook of research on teaching the English language arts* (pp. 529–535). New York: Macmillan.

Goldstone, B. (2001–2002, December/January). Whaz up with our books? Changing picture book codes and teaching implications. *The Reading Teacher*, 362–370.

Goodman, K. S., Shannon, P., Freeman, Y. S., & Murphy, S. (1988). *Report card on basal readers*. Katonah, NY: Richard C. Owen.

Great Books Foundation. (1999). *An introduction to shared inquiry* (4th ed.). Chicago: Author.

Guastello, E. F., & Sinatra, R. (2001, Spring). Improving students' oral presentation skills through the use of technology and multimedia. *The Language and Literacy Spectrum*, 5–17.

Hales, K., & Russel, S. (1995). *Text, images and sounds equals multimedia*. In J. Griffin & L. Bash (Eds.), *Computers in the primary school* (pp. 70–80). London: Cassell.

Hancock, M. (1999). *A celebration of literature and response*. Upper Saddle River, NJ: Prentice Hall.

Heinich, R., Molenda, M., & Russell, J. D. (1992). *Instructional media and the new technologies* (4th ed.). Upper Saddle River, NJ: Prentice Hall.

Heinich, R., Molenda, M., Russell, J., & Smaldino, S. (2002). *Instructional media and technologies for learning* (7th ed.). Upper Saddle River, NJ: Merrill/Prentice Hall.

Hooper, S., & Hannafin, M. J. (1991, Winter). Psychological perspectives on emerging instructional technologies: A critical analysis. *Educational Psychologist*, 69–95.

Hooper, S., & Reinartz, T. J. (2002). Educational multimedia. In R. A. Reiser & J. V. Dempsey (Eds.), *Trends and issues in instructional design and technology* (pp. 307–318). Upper Saddle River, NJ: Merrill/Prentice Hall.

Hooper, S., & Rieber, L. P. (1995). Teaching with technology. In A. C. Ornstein (Ed.), *Teaching: Theory and practice* (pp. 155–170). Boston: Allyn and Bacon.

Humphrey, J. W. (1992, March). The glitzy labyrinth of nonprint media is winning the battle with books. *Phi Delta Kappan*, 538.

International Society for Technology in Education. (2000). *National education technology standards for students: Connecting curriculum and technology*. Eugene, OR: International Society for Technology in Education/U.S. Dept. of Education.

Jones, M., Harmon, S., & Lowther, D. (2002). Integrating Web-based learning in an educational system: A framework for implementaion. In R. A. Reiser & J. V. Dempsey (Eds.), *Trends and issues in instructional design and technology* (pp. 295–306). Upper Saddle River, NJ: Merrill/Prentice Hall.

Kozma, R., & Shank, P. (1998). Connecting with the 21st century: Technology in support of educational reform. In C. Dede (Ed.), *Learning with technology: 1998 ASCD yearbook* (pp. 3–27). Alexandria, VA: Association for Supervision and Curriculum Development.

Kozma, R. B. (1991, Summer). Learning with media. *Review of Educational Research*, 179–212.

Labbo, L. (2000, April). 12 things young children can do with a talking book in a classroom computer center. *The Reading Teacher*, 542–546.

Labbo, L., Reinking, D., & McKenna, M. (1999). The use of technology in literacy programs. In L. B. Gambrell, L. M. Morrow, S. B. Neuman, & M. Pressley (Eds.), *Best practices in literacy instruction* (pp. 311–327). New York: Guilford Press.

Leu, D. Jr., & Kinzer, C. (1999). *Effective literacy instruction, K–8*. Upper Saddle River, NJ: Prentice Hall.

Lewis, T. (1991, March–April). Introducing technology into school curricula. *Journal of Curriculum Studies*, 141–154.

May, F. B. (2001). *Reading as communication: To help children write and read* (6th ed.). Upper Saddle River, NJ: Prentice Hall.

McKenna, M. (1998). Electronic texts and the transformation of beginning reading. In D. Reinking, M. C. McKenna, L. D. Labbo, & R. D. Keiffer (Eds.), *Handbook of literacy and technology: Transformations in a post-typographic world* (pp. 45–59). Mahwah, NJ: Erlbaum.

McKenna, M., Reinking, D., & Labbo, L. (1997, April/June). Using talking books with reading disabled students. *Reading & Writing Quarterly: Overcoming Learning Difficulties,* 185–190.

Means, B. (2000). Technology in America's schools: Before and after Y2K. In R. Brandt (Ed.), *Education in a new era, ASCD 2000 yearbook* (pp. 185–210). Alexandria, VA: Association for Supervision and Curriculum Development.

Meyerson, M., & Kulesza, D. (2002). *Strategies for struggling readers: Step by step.* Upper Saddle River, NJ: Merrill/Prentice Hall.

Miller, L., & Olson, J. (1994, March/April). Putting the computer in its place: A study of teaching with technology. *Journal of Curriculum Studies,* 121–142.

Milner, J. O., & Milner, L. M. (2003). *Bridging English* (3rd ed.). Upper Saddle River, NJ: Merrill/Prentice Hall.

National Reading Panel. (2000). *Teaching children to read: An evidence-based assessment of the scientific literature on reading and its implications for reading.* Bethesda, MD: National Institute of Child Health and Human Development.

Naylor D. F., & Diem, R. (1987). *Elementary and middle school social studies.* New York: Random House.

Newby, T., Stepich, D., Lehman, J., & Russell, J. (2000). *Instructional technology for teaching and learning: Designing instruction, integrating computers, and using media* (2nd ed.). Upper Saddle River, NJ: Merrill/Prentice Hall.

Northwest Regional Laboratory. (1998). *Catalog of school reform models: Electronic edition.* Portland, OR: Author.

Ohler, J. (2000, October). Art becomes the fourth R. *Educational Leadership,* 16–19.

Olson, D. R., & Astigton, J. W. (1993, Winter). Thinking about thinking. *Educational Psychologist,* 7–24.

Ornstein, A. C. (1991, May). Video technology and urban curriculum. *Education and the Urban Society,* 335.

Ornstein, A. C. (1992, Summer). The textbook curriculum. *Educational Horizons,* 167–169.

Oskamp, S. (1987). *Television as a social issue.* Newbury Park, CA: Sage.

Palmer, R. (1997, May). Nonfiction trade books in content-area instruction: Realities and potential. *Journal of Adolescent and Adult Literacy,* 630–641.

Postman, Neil. (1979). *Teaching as a conserving activity.* New York: Delacorte.

Reutzel, D. R., & Cooter, R. B., Jr. (1999). *Balanced reading strategies and practices: Assessing and assisting readers with special needs.* Upper Saddle River, NJ: Merrill.

Rice, D. (2002, March). Using trade books in teaching elementary science: Facts and fallacies. *The Reading Teacher,* 552–565.

Richgels, D. (2002, March). Informational texts in kindergarten. *The Reading Teacher,* 586–595.

Roblyer, M. D. (2003a). *Integrating educational technology into teaching* (3rd ed.). Upper Saddle River, NJ: Merrill/Prentice Hall.

Roblyer, M. D. (2003b). *Starting out on the Internet: A learning journey for teachers* (2nd ed.). Upper Saddle River, NJ: Merrill/Prentice Hall.

Scharer, P. (1994). Trade books. In A. C. Purves (Ed.), *Encyclopedia of English studies and language arts* (pp. 1231–1233). New York: Scholastic/Urbana, IL: National Council of Teachers of English.

Semb, G. B., & Ellis, J. A. (1994, Summer). Knowledge taught in school: What is remembered? *Review of Educational Research,* 253–286.

Snider, R. C. (1992, December). The machine in the classroom. *Phi Delta Kappan,* 316–323.

Tang, G. (1994). Audiovisual instruction. In A. C. Purves (Ed.), *Encyclopedia of English studies and language arts* (pp. 102–104). New York: Scholastic/Urbana, IL: National Council of Teachers of English.

Tapscott, D. (1999, February). Educating the net generation. *Educational Leadership,* 7–11.

Todd, R. (1999, March). Transformational leadership and transformational learning: Information literacy and the World Wide Web. *NASSP Bulletin,* 4–12.

Tompkins, G. (2003). *Literacy for the 21st century* (3rd ed.). Upper Saddle River, NJ: Merrill/Prentice Hall.

U.S. Department of Education. (2001). *Digest of education statistics.* Washington, DC: National Center for Education Statistics.

Vacca, R., & Vacca, J. A. (2002). *Content area reading: Literacy and learning across the curriculum* (7th ed.). Boston: Allyn and Bacon.

Walker, D. (1999, October). Technology and literacy: Raising the bar. *Educational Leadership,* 18–21.

Wheelock, A. (1999, October). Junior Great Books: Reading for meaning in urban schools. *Educational Leadership,* 48–50.

Wiggins, R. (1994, March). Large group lesson/small group follow-up: Flexible grouping in a basal reading program. *The Reading Teacher,* 450–460.

Willis, J., Stephens, E., & Matthew, K. (1996). *Technology, reading, and language arts.* Boston: Allyn and Bacon.

Woodward, A. (1986, Spring). Over-programmed materials: Taking the teacher out of teaching. *American Educator,* 26–31.

Woodward, A., & Elliott, D. L. (1992, Summer). School reform and textbooks. *Educational Horizons,* 176–180.

# Assessing and Evaluating Students

chapter 13

## Focusing Questions

1. Why should students be assessed and evaluated, and what do teachers, schools, districts, parents, and the students themselves wish to gain from assessment procedures?

2. Can standardized tests help teachers make classroom instructional decisions?

3. What are the basic differences between norm-referenced and criterion-referenced assessments?

4. Why are states and districts leaning toward the use of performance-based or "authentic" assessments as a way to measure students' mastery of standards?

5. How do teacher-constructed and/or performance-based tests differ from high-stakes tests?

6. What are the controversial aspects of high-stakes testing plans?

7. Why is it important to communicate with parents about their children's work and progress? Why is it highly important to maintain good communication with parents?

Evaluation of students involves a two-stage process. Evaluation means that we are assigning a worth to something or placing a value on some kind of behavior or performance. To evaluate properly, then, we need to initially assess students' performances on specific types of tasks. Once the assessment is complete and the information of that assessment is analyzed, we form inferences and make judgments about each student's achievement with that task.

The first stage of the process involves assessment, testing, or measurement. Such assessment is usually expressed in a quantitive way. Something is described in terms of specific numbers, percentages, or grade-level equivalents. For example, a student scores 65 on a test. This score is a measurement. However, the number does not indicate whether the score should be judged good or poor, high or low. If most students score over 65, we may decide that the score is low and indicates poor performance. If most students score in the 60s, we may decide that the score is not so low. Measurement provides us with test data (numbers and percentages); judgment interprets the numbers and turns them into evaluations. Thus, once the measurement has been made, judgments are made about the adequacy of the performance, usually in the context of instructional objectives.

Problems with test content, sampling (norming), and procedures can result in errors in measurement, and all evaluations are subject to error because human judgment is involved. The best we can hope for is to reduce the chance for and margin of error by careful measurement and evaluation procedures. In this chapter, we focus on different types of assessments, the information gained from each type, and how evaluations of student performance differ based on the criteria of the assessment procedures and protocols.

# ■ STANDARDIZED TESTS

**Standardized tests** are primarily designed by testing experts to objectively measure the amount of knowledge that a student has gained or learned over a given period (Wineberg, 1997). They are also a form of **formal assessment.** Because of the objectivity factor and because these tests were not produced by teachers themselves in the context of lesson, unit, or course plans, classroom teachers have very little if any use for the results obtained by these tests in making classroom and curriculum planning decisions (Rothman, 1996). Basically, standardized tests do not support classroom instruction; on the other hand, they are used to evaluate the effectiveness of educational programs (Taylor & Walton, 1997).

Standardized tests are also known as **norm-referenced tests,** meaning that the performance of sample populations on particular tasks has occurred and norms of achievement have been established. These norms serve as a basis for interpreting one student's relative test performance against those of his or her peers in the normative group. Thus a norm-referenced assessment allows teachers to compare one student with another student within the same grade- or age-level grouping (Gage & Berliner, 1998). The talented people who write standardized tests are attempting to create an assessment instrument that will allow others to make a valid inference about the knowledge and/or skills one student has gained in a particular subject area (Popham, 1999).

Norm-referenced, standardized tests are assessment instruments that contain sets of items that need to be administered and measured according to uniform scoring procedures. Such tests were developed with extremely structured and specific directions for administration, scoring, and interpretation that need to be adhered to as indicated in the testing manual (Overton, 2003). This strict adherence is necessary so that the teacher, school, or district using the standardized test can make sound judgments and evaluation comparisons with the same age and grade-level students who were in the normative group. If procedures set forth in the testing manual are violated, users cannot make sound and fair judgments about a student's performance.

Standardized, norm-referenced tests have been pilot tested and administered to representative populations of similar individuals to obtain the normative data. The scores obtained from norm-referenced tests may be:

- the actual **raw score** or number correct;
- the **percentile rank** or where the student's score fell relative to a ranking of percentages from 1 to 99;
- the **grade-equivalent score** or the score equivalent to other students at the grade level;
- the **scaled score,** which is a continuous ranking score usually from the range 000 to 999 in the same series of norm-referenced tests from kindergarden/first grade to high school; or
- the **stanine,** which is a score expressed in a scale of 1 to 9 with 1–3 being below average, 4–6 being average, and 7–9 being above average.

These scores for norm-referenced tests are based on the central concept of the **normal curve** (Gunning, 2002). The logic expressed by this concept is that when a number of students take this test in the future, roughly two-thirds of them should achieve on the average range; one-third would predictably fall below average, while another third would perform above average.

Most standardized tests are published by testing and well-known publishing companies. They can be grouped into major types: **aptitude tests,** which are given to predict how well students will perform in a future academic endeavor, and **achievement tests,** which tell how well students have performed in academic areas such as reading, spelling, social studies, science, and arithmetic (Popham, 1999). Popham indicates that on a national basis, five major tests are being used: the California Achievement Test (CAT), the

Comprehensive Test of Basic Skills, (CTBS), the Iowa Test of Basic Skills (ITBS), the Metropolitan Achievement Test (MAT), and the Stanford Achievement Test (SAT).

## Test Criteria

*Reliability* and *validity* are two major criteria that should be used in the selection of tests. The third is *usability.*

*Reliability.* By **reliability** we mean that the test yields similar results when it is repeated over a short period of time or when a different form is used. A reliable test can be viewed as consistent, dependable, and stable. Test reliability can be expressed numerically. A coefficient of .80 or higher indicates high reliability, .40 to .79 fair reliability, and less than .40 low reliability. Many standardized tests comprise several subtests or scales and thus have coefficients to correspond with each of the subtests as well as the entire test. For example, reliability for a reading test might be reported as .86 for comprehension, .77 for vocabulary, .91 for analogies, and .85 for the test as a whole.

*Validity.* By **validity** we mean that the test measures what it is represented as measuring. An invalid test does not measure what it should. For example, a pen-and-pencil test is not suitable for measuring athletic abilities. Basically, we try to determine whether we are measuring what we think we are measuring.

Validity also refers to the appropriateness and meaningfulness of the inferences drawn from the assessment results that can be transferred to some intended use (Gronlund, 1998). For instance, suppose we wished to make a valid inference about a student's ability to write coherently. Would we make a more valid judgment based on writing samples on different topics provided by the student or by judging the student's ability to identify correct punctuation and capitalization conventions in a series of test items?

Within the testing manual, a comparison is made to other students, and the teacher assesses his or her student only on the basis of a predetermined standard. Scores can demonstrate progress (or minimal progress) in learning over time and can be useful to both parents and teachers in noting different areas of achievement (Popham, 1999). Suppose, for example, that a fifth-grade student reveals achievement scores at the following percentiles: reading, 93rd; writing, 96th; science, 82nd; social studies, 76th; and arithmetic, 25th. Both parents and teachers(s) know that this student is strong in the language arts and that his or her reading and writing abilities might carry over to success in science and social studies. This child is relatively weak, however, in arithmetic, which may pose later problems when the student takes the Scholastic Aptitude Tests (SATs) for college entrance. Robert Slavin (2003) adds that the entire field of education has not examined valid research well enough. Although innovative programs and untested, widely embraced programs come and go, he feels that valid research occurs only when meaningful measures of achievement are examined between schools that used a given program approach and carefully matched control schools that did not use that approach.

*Usability.*  A third criterion for selecting a test is **usability.** A test should be easy for students to understand, easy to administer and score, within budget limitations if it has to be purchased, suitable to the test conditions (for example, time available), and appropriate in degree of difficulty (Gronlund & Linn, 1990; Kubiszyn & Borich, 1999).

A test may be valid in content, but the questions may be so ambiguous or the directions so difficult to follow that a student who understands the material may give the wrong answer. Or the questions might be phrased in such a way that a student who does not understand the material could give the right answer. For example, students expect a true/false or multiple-choice item containing the word *always* or *never* to be false or an inappropriate choice. They sometimes answer such an item correctly when they are ignorant of the facts. By the same token, the vocabulary of the test should not be too difficult for students taking the test or the test will no longer be measuring only content but also reading comprehension. Placing too many difficult items in the front of the test will cause students to spend too much time on them at the expense of reaching items at the end that they could have easily answered. Finally, if a test is too short, representative content will not be adequately tested, resulting in lower test validity (Gronlund & Linn, 1990; Thorndike, 1996).

# ■ CRITERION-REFERENCED TESTS

Suppose a teacher, a school, a district, or a state didn't want to compare and sort students with one another, but wished to find out what students know or have achieved in relation to curriculum goals. Thus, in a specific content domain or learning task, a *criterion* or a standard is established to determine if a student has achieved learning mastery of a body of knowledge or a skill. In a **criterion-referenced test,** the student is evaluated in a "go" or "no go" construct, meaning that the student has reached the standard criterion or has not. Almost all adults have experienced this model with their state driving tests. There are two possible outcomes: one either passes the driving test or doesn't (but in this case, the adult has an opportunity to try again).

Because teachers use an instructional construct in which they identify goals, objectives, and standards and teach to help learners achieve these outcomes, one author feels that the criterion-referenced design is highly suited to providing the kind of assessment information teachers need (Brookhart, 2002). As such, these tests are closely related to expressing achievement in instruction or can give information that can be used to plan for instruction (Gunning, 2002). Criteria scores for particular skills that need to be mastered are established, and student results are reported usually as simple numerical scores, such as the number correctly achieved, the percentage correct, or a letter grade (Gronlund, 1998; Spinelli, 2002). They are also practical for the teacher when assessing achievement in acquiring specific knowledge (for example, the Civil War in social studies, the planets in science, and division applications in arithmetic). Much of criterion-referenced design is also used for assessment purposes in special programs and for special-needs students who may be involved in individually prescribed instruction, mastery learning, and differentiated instruction. Most informal reading inventories use criteria such as 70 or 75 percent needed for comprehension on specific paragraphs at designated grade levels with 90 to 95 percent needed on word accuracy, with the oral reading of the same passage to be placed at the appropriate instructional reading level. On other literacy measures such as alphabet knowledge or sounds of initial consonants, the criteria might be established at 100 percent (Gunning, 2002).

One author indicates that the current term **benchmark** is a form of criterion assessment in that the benchmark is a major task that students are expected to perform (Gunning, 2002). For example, in New York State fourth- and eighth-grade students are expected to write coherent, well-organized papers using the standard conventions of written English. If they do not meet the state scoring guidelines that indicate successful writing competency, they face the possibility of grade repetition in order to reach that benchmark standard.

## Distinctions between Norm-Referenced and Criterion-Referenced Tests

The norm-referenced test measures a student's level of achievement at a given time compared to other students elsewhere. Scores from a criterion-referenced test do not indicate a relative level or ranking of achievement because no comparisons are made. The test indicates how proficient a student is in terms of a specific body of learning. It can measure changes in learning over time, but it cannot produce meaningful comparisons or standards among students. Norm-referenced tests usually have better overall reliability and validity because they have been constructed by test experts and tested on larger sample populations (Ornstein & Gilman, 1991; Popham, 1992). However, the criterion-referenced tests allow the teacher to judge students' proficiency in specific content areas, and therefore they usually have better curricular validity than norm-referenced tests.

According to researchers, the norm-referenced test is valuable for measuring higher and abstract levels of the cognitive domain, whereas the criterion-referenced test is valuable for measuring lower and concrete levels of learning. The norm reference is valuable for heterogeneous groups in which the range of abilities is wide and when the test is intended to measure a wide range of performance. The criterion test is more useful in homogeneous groups in which the range of abilities is narrow and a test is intended to measure a limited or predetermined range of objectives and outcomes. With norm-referenced tests, external standards can be used to make judgments about a student's performance, whereas criterion-referenced tests lack uniform standards, and the interpretation of the scores is only as good as the process used to set the proficiency levels (Hambleton, Swaminathan, Algina, & Coulson, 1988; Linn, 1986; Wiggins, 1992). Also, this means that criterion-referenced interpretation is aided when a large number of test items per task are included and a detailed description of intended student performance is indicated (Gronlund, 1998). In short, norm-referenced assessments compare performance, whereas criterion-referenced measures are intended to describe performance (Richek, Caldwell, Hennings, & Lerner, 2000). Table 13.1 shows the characteristics of norm-referenced and criterion-referenced tests.

*Table 13.1* Comparison of Norm-Referenced and Criterion-Referenced Tests

| Characteristic | Norm-Referenced Test | Criterion-Referenced Test |
|---|---|---|
| 1. Major emphasis | Measures individual's achievement (or performance) in relation to a similar group at a specific time; aptitude test, survey test, achievement test | Measures individual's change in achievement (or performance) over an extended period of time; mastery test, performance test |
| 2. Reliability | High reliability; usually test items and scales are .90 or better. | Usually unknown reliability; when test items are estimated, they are about .50 and .70. |
| 3. Validity | Content, construct, and criterion validity usually high | Content and curricular validity usually high if appropriate procedures are used |
| 4. Usability | For diagnosing student difficulties; estimating student performance in a broad area; classifying students; and making decisions on how much a student has learned compared to others; administration procedures are standardized and consistent from class to class.<br><br>Large-group testing | For diagnosing student difficulties; estimating student performance in a specific area; certifying competency; and measuring what a student has learned over time; administration procedures usually vary among teachers or schools.<br><br>Small-group, individual testing |
| 5. Content covered | Usually covers a broad area of content or skills; school (or teacher) has no control over content being tested.<br>Linked to expert opinion | Typically emphasizes a limited area of content or skills; school (or teacher) has opportunity to select content.<br>Linked to local curriculum |
| 6. Quality of test items | Generally high; test items written by experts, pilot tested, and revised prior to distribution; poor items omitted before test is used | Varies, based on ability of test writer; test items written by teachers (or publishers); test items rarely pilot tested; poor items omitted after test has been used |
| 7. Item selection | Test items discriminate among individuals to obtain variability of scores; easy and confusing items usually omitted | Includes all items needed to assess performance; little or no attempt to deal with item difficulty; easy or confusing items rarely omitted |
| 8. Student preparation | Studying rarely helps student obtain a better score, although familiarity with the test seems to improve scores; students unable to obtain information from teachers about content covered | Studying will help student obtain a better score; students able to obtain information from teachers about content covered |
| 9. Standards | Norms used to establish a standard or to classify students; intended outcomes are general, relative to performance of others; score determined by a ranking, average, or stanine | Performance levels used to establish students' ability; intended outcomes are specific, relative to a specified level; score determined by an absolute number, e.g., 83 percent right |

*Source:* Adapted from Allan C. Ornstein, "Norm-Referenced and Criterion-Referenced Tests," *NASSP Bulletin* (October 1993), pp. 28–40.

# ■ AUTHENTIC ASSESSMENT

**Authentic assessment,** both the concept and the implementation methodology, can go by many other names and can have different shades of meaning for various users. Most sources agree that authentic assessment is a form of **informal assessment.** But it can also be termed *classroom-based assessment, curriculum-based assessment, performance assessment, alternative assessment,* and even *portfolio assessment,* and although some differences may exist among these categories of assessments, there is more similarity than difference (Venn, 2000). The underlying basis of agreement among all these terms is that such assessment is accomplished through actual tasks or performances students do in the classrooms as they are observed by teachers so that teachers can make sound professional judgments about each student's progress.

Initially standardized tests and the more recent measurement model of criterion-referenced assessment were designed to test large numbers of students inexpensively while at the same time permitting prompt and almost error-free scoring in hopes that teachers could use the information to maximize each student's individual development (Stiggins, 2002). In addition, items were screened and piloted to increase validity and reliability of these large-scale tests. But the price for this efficiency is that the measurement is indirect and one dimensional; it does not measure direct performance or "real life" contexts (Cizek & Rachor, 1994; Steinberg, 1990). The contexts for authentic assessment include the students' natural school environments such as the classroom, the science and technology labs, the playground, and the gymnasium, and the assessments occur during the day's typical routine happenings such as in learning centers, during group activities, during social interactions, and in connection with academic and art-related subjects (Spinelli, 2002).

Educators, who had long protested the misuse of standardized tests and often criticized teacher-made tests as even more unreliable than published ones, welcomed the trend of **performance assessment**—that is, the testing of actual performance. Perhaps more than any other form of testing, performance assessment allows students to integrate learning and apply problem-solving skills to broad and specific course content. Other than essay writing (which is a good example of performance assessment), most teacher-made and standardized tests have relied on short-answer responses to knowledge-based questions that assess skills broken down into discrete parts. Critics contend that by encouraging teachers for years to break down learning into "factoids" and then to test those factoids (Herman, Aschbacher, & Winters, 1992; O'Neil, 1992), the result was to de-emphasize teaching or assessment aimed at high-order thinking.

One author believes that authentic assessment differs from performance assessment in the following way: During authentic assessment, students must show that they can apply knowledge in a real-world setting by using techniques that are consistent with the field of study in which the student is being evaluated. In this setting, the student may use a variety of resources and materials (Chapter 12) and may collaborate with other students. Taking its cue from the U.S. Office of Technology Assessment (1992), performance assessment focuses on the student's ability to produce an answer or product that demonstrates knowledge or skills. In this context, the student actively constructs knowledge to produce something (Overton, 2003). Among other criteria, Alan Glatthorn

(1998) asks that the performance tasks (1) appear real and purposeful while connected to a meaningful context, (2) require higher-order and creative thinking processes, (3) require the activation of prior knowledge to accomplish the task, and (4) connect closely with the standards and benchmarks that are being assessed.

Other authors note that performance assessment gained the considerable interest of educators during the last decades of the twentieth century because of the increased attention given to discovery approaches to learning, hands-on engagement, and higher-order, problem-solving thinking processes (Hymes, Chafin, & Gondes, 1991). Still others use the term *authentic* within the context of performance assessment by suggesting that performances can be authentic or contrived. Whereas authentic assessment requires that students reveal their knowledge of a topic and/or process in an actual situation such as during a science experiment or an oral report, contrived assessment occurs when students respond during simulated or artificial conditions such as when they write essays based on prompts provided by others (Bartz, Anderson-Robinson, & Hillman, 1994). See Box 13.1.

## The Criteria of Authentic Assessment

Features of both authentic and performance assessment can be likened to assessment as **inquiry,** notes Serafini (2000–2001). This viewpoint is based in part on constructivist concepts of knowledge acquisition, on student-centered learning, and on the process of inquiry in which teachers gain a deeper and richer understanding of each individual student engaged in specific learning contexts. Moreover, the audience promoting the assessment has shifted from external authorities to student, parent, and teacher, all of whom reflect on actual work accomplished in the classroom.

The learning tasks being evaluated through authentic assessment are contextualized and involve complex thought processes, not atomized tasks or isolated bits of information. The students are evaluated in reference to a performance standard or expectation, not on a curve or absolute standard. The scoring system is often multifaceted instead of one aggregate grade, and self-assessment is often part of the assessment process. Instead of having students uninvolved in the assessment process (Bushweller, 1997), students

---

**BOX 13.1** Authentic Works Necessitate Two Types of Authentic Assessments

Norman Gronlund adds another useful concept to the evaluation of performance tasks. He suggests that some may be considered *restrictive* and others *extended,* with the overall deciding factor between the two involving their *comprehensiveness.* Restricted tasks do involve student performance but they are limited in scope and amount of allotted time and tend to be highly structured (as contrived), as when students are evaluated on a one- or two-minute speech on a topic or need to write a one-page or 150-word report, read aloud a particular selection, or construct a graph from data provided. Extended performance tasks allow students to integrate a number of skills and psychomotor processes to produce a high-quality product. These extended performances might include the design, construction, and reporting of a project for social studies or the writing of a story or poem, with a rewriting accomplished after teacher or peer feedback.

*Source:* Adapted from Norman Gronlund, *Assessment of Student Achievement,* 6th ed. (Boston: Allyn and Bacon, 1998).

## BOX 13.2 What Authentic Assessments Accomplish for Learners

Authentic assessments such as essays, research projects, group projects, scientific experiments, oral presentations, exhibits, and portfolios maintained in various subject areas monitor students' know-how with knowledge and ideas required in our complex world. Authentic assessment techniques encourage learners to stretch their capacities, undertake independent assignments, and generate new ideas and projects. Teachers are expected to act as facilitators and coaches during the assignment process, engage learners in a dialogue, and ask them to defend their ideas during the assessment process.

may, for instance, become intimately connected such as when they are asked to formulate their own report cards in a negotiated way with teachers and parents (Serafini, 2000–2001). Even young children can self-regulate and evaluate their work when shown how to do it with, say, a choice card. When five- to seven-year-old children with multiple disabilities were shown how to set goals, make choices about their classroom work, and then evaluate their own progress, they accomplished more work and more correct responses than when prompted by the teacher (Mithaug, 2002). The performance assessment provides room for various student learning styles, aptitudes, and interests, and comparisons among students are minimized. See Box 13.2.

### Types of Performance and Authentic Assessments

Student performance and progress can be measured through a variety of methods other than pencil-and-paper tests, although classroom testing is the most common source of data and should be included as part of the total evaluation.

Although performance assessments appear in many different modes, the majority of them occur when students accomplish:

- ways to solve real problems, such as how to clean up polluted water;
- use of oral or psychomotor skills even when a product is not produced, such as presenting a speech or formal talk, fixing an engine, or using a microscope; and
- use of writing and psychomotor skills when a product is forthcoming, such as in the writing of an essay or report, preparing a multimedia slide show presentation, word processing a letter, and constructing a model or replica of something (Gronlund, 1998).

These modes appear in many of the informal assessments discussed next. See also Tips for Teachers 13.1 for help in constructing a variety of assessment tests.

*Observation of Student Work.* The teacher has the opportunity to watch students perform various tasks on a daily basis, under various conditions, alone and with different students. The teacher sees students more or less continually simply by virtue of being in the classroom, but he or she needs to know what to look for and to have some self-consistent system for collecting and assessing data, such as checklists or anecdotal reporting.

Although the teacher should observe all students, individuals who exhibit atypical behavior or learning outcomes are often singled out for special study. The keys to good observation are objectivity and documentation. Teachers cannot depend on memory or vague statements such as "Johnny misbehaves in class." They must keep accurate, specific written records. If observations are free from bias and tempered with common

# Constructing Classroom, Performance-Based, and Criterion-Referenced Tests

Although the specific purposes of tests and intended use of outcomes vary among teachers and schools, tests play an important part in the life of students and teachers. One of your goals as a teacher should be to consider your use of tests and how they connect with your curriculum and standards objectives. Below is a checklist to consider using when constructing your criterion-referenced tests and performance-based assessments.

I. Is my test appropriate?
   1. Does it fit my objectives and is it helpful in assessing learning of content standards?
   2. Do the test items reflect a wide representation of the content and skills of the subject?
   3. Does the test have credible and worthwhile items to anchor the scoring system?
   4. Does it consider reality: the conditions of the classroom, school, and community?

II. Is my test valid?
   5. Does it discriminate between performance levels?
   6. Does it fit external and agreed-on standards?
   7. Will my colleagues in the subject or at the grade level agree that all necessary items are included?

8. Does the test measure actual performance rather than the students' reading levels or simple recall of information?

III. Is my test reliable?
   9. Are all test items clear and understandable?
   10. Are the items consistent with test performance?
   11. Are there at least two items per objective, and do students who get one item of a pair correct get the other item correct?
   12. Are there sufficient test items to measure important content and skills?

IV. Is my test usable?
   13. Is my test short enough to avoid being tedious?
   14. Does it have sufficient breadth and depth to allow for generalizations about student performance?
   15. Are there clear and standard procedures for administration of the test?
   16. Is it authentic: Does it measure worthwhile behaviors and tasks rather than what is easy to score?

sense, this informal, nonstandardized evaluation method can provide more insightful information about a student than test scores alone.

*Group Evaluation Activities.* Teachers can set aside a time to allow students to participate in establishing instructional objectives, evaluate their strengths and limitations, and evaluate their own progress in learning. Students can evaluate themselves or their classmates on study habits and homework, class participation, quizzes, workbook or textbook activities, and other activities. They can keep anecdotal reports or logs about their own work in which successes and difficulties are recorded and then discussed in class. They can check off assignments they complete and evaluate their work in group discussions. Evaluation techniques such as these make it possible for teachers to diagnose and measure student progress in a quick and efficient way.

*Class Discussions and Recitations.* Many teachers consider a student's participation in class discussion an essential source of data for evaluation. Teachers are impressed by students who volunteer, develop thoughts logically, and discuss relevant facts and relationships. Answering the teacher's questions frequently and carrying out assignments in class are considered evidence of progress. The inability to answer questions and the inability to perform assignments in class are taken as indications of learning problems or lack of motivation.

*Homework.* The teacher can learn much about students' achievements and attitudes by checking homework carefully. A good rule is not to assign homework unless it is going to be checked in some way, preferably by the teacher and in some cases by another student or by the student himself or herself. The idea is to provide prompt feedback to the student, preferably emphasizing the positive aspects of the work while making one or two major recommendations for improvement. As Herbert Walberg and others point out, student achievement increases significantly when teachers assign homework on a regular basis, students conscientiously do it, and comments and feedback are provided when the work is completed (Sikorski, Niemiec, & Walberg, 1994; Walberg, 1985).

*Reports, Essays, and Research Papers.* Written work serves as an excellent way to assess students' ability to organize thoughts, research topics, and develop new ideas. In evaluating written projects, the teacher should look to see how well students have developed their thoughts in terms of explanations, logic, and relationship of ideas; whether ideas are expressed clearly; whether facts are documented or distinguished from opinion; and what conclusions or recommendations are evidenced. Spelling and grammar should not be the key to evaluating students; rather, emphasis should be on the students' thinking processes, the use of interesting language, and the ability to keep to the topic and develop it logically.

Interestingly, when the National Council of Teachers of English teamed with the International Reading Association to formulate the twelve national English language arts standards (1996), at least five asked students to communicate effectively through writing—by creating, researching, and discussing texts and by using a variety of sources to gather and share information. Written work such as essays provides students with a way to show their knowledge of content information while applying that information in ways that reveal higher-order thinking skills (Bartz et al., 1994). In assessing and evaluating students' written work, many contemporary programs and educational agencies are using a process of **holistic scoring.** With holistic scoring, the teacher or evaluator doesn't focus on only one aspect of the written piece, such as mechanics or written conventions, but assesses the student's essay or composition on the basis of the overall quality of the written work (Gunning, 2002). Generally, the qualities of topic focus or meaning, organization, development, content, sentence structure, language use or word choice, and mechanics make up the holistic impression of how to judge a written paper.

To evaluate a piece of writing holistically, a popular device is the **rubric.** Used by teachers, evaluators, and students themselves, the rubric is a written scoring scale that provides descriptive guidelines for each of the qualities of writing found on the scale. Usually expressed in a numerical rating system of 1 to 4 or 1 to 6 or a verbal rating system of good (high), average (middle), or poor (low), the evaluator of the written work judges each quality of writing—such as organization—in relation to the rating system (Farr & Tone, 1997; O'Neill, 2000). Although the formats of rubrics can be different, all rubrics have two main features in common; they show and describe the criteria or "what counts" in a written project, and the rating scale or system acknowledges a graduation in the quality of writing (Andrade, 2000).

Rubrics assist teachers in two ways: (1) by making the rating process more consistent and objective and (2) by making the analysis of sets of student exhibits, such as those in their portfolios, easier to evaluate (Reutzel & Cooter, 2003). Popham (2000) adds the notion that well-designed rubrics themselves can make an impact on instructional quality because they show the key features that should appear in a top-quality paper. Likewise, Andrade (2000) believes that rubrics serve learning as well as evaluation and accountability. She notes that like other authentic means of assessment, such as portfolios and exhibitions, rubrics erase the distinction between instruction and assessment and should be called "instructional rubrics."

*Oral Reporting.* Evaluating oral work is less reliable than evaluating written samples, but oral work may reveal creative and critical thinking that cannot be measured through other methods. David Johnson and Roger Johnson (1999) and others point out that when students freely discuss topics of interest to them, their thinking is based on many skills, insights, and experiences not evidenced in a one-hour written test. The idea is to involve students and for them to discover, in front of their peers, that they can succeed (Guastello & Sinatra, 2001). Because they are in front of their peers, it is essential that no humiliation, no sarcasm, and no negativism be introduced into the discussion or evaluation process.

*Peer Evaluators.* Developing a "community of learners" enhances student interaction and cooperation and enables students to learn from one another. It also enhances group spirit and contributes to student empowerment. Research suggests, too, that when students provide and receive feedback from peers about their academic work, social responsibility and student achievement are enhanced (Bonty & Everts-Danielson, 1992; Ornstein, 1994). Students can serve as peer evaluators for quizzes or peer editors for written projects. Ideally, a set of criteria should be provided to enable students to evaluate others.

*Student Journals.* Students can record their ideas about what they are reading, relate content to their own experiences, make comparisons, or develop thoughts, plots, or projects. They can also keep logs about articles or books they are reading. These journals can serve as a basis for student–teacher conferences or group discussions. Also, the journals serve as a basis for fusing writing and reading activities across the curriculum, as well as providing samples of student work that exemplify some task or project for assessment.

*Student Portfolios.* Student **portfolios** can be used to demonstrate a sample of the students' work—to show a range of performance or the "best" pieces of work. Although portfolios have been generally used as a way to assess writing, they also can be used to measure performance in reading and content area subjects (Gunning, 2002). According to the 1998 National Assessment of Educational Progress (NAEP) results in writing, 81 percent of fourth graders and 79 percent of eighth graders self-reported that their written work was saved in portfolios or folders, and this group indicated higher writing scores than those students who did not maintain a portfolio/folder system (Greenwald, Persky, Campbell, & Mazzeo, 1999).

The portfolio makes it possible to document instruction and learning over time and is an excellent resource as teacher, parents, and student discuss overall school performance and progress. Portfolios portray a wide and rich array of what students know or can do. In effect, they capture multiple dimensions of learning, not just right answers or cognitive dimensions. Allowing students to select the contents of the portfolio also enables them to take an active role in their own instruction and assessment. Portfolios become a means to encourage student reflection and self-evaluation (Tierney, 1998). They illuminate the process by which students solve problems, produce work, or perform in real-life contexts—the "authentic" assessment climate. Portfolios also help students integrate instruction (Arter & Spandel, 1992; Sperling, 1993). As a tool for developing habits of reflection, they can lead to greater student confidence in their own learning (Frazier & Paulson, 1992; Herbert, 1992). See Box 13.3.

Defining selection and assessment criteria becomes crucial. The work assigned to students for the portfolio should match the behavior the teacher is trying to elicit and the content the teacher is trying to cover. For example, we cannot conclude that the writing sample or research project in the portfolio is "typical" work for the student if the student has selected only his or her "best" sample. The significance or value of the portfolio product also changes with the teacher analyzing it. Teacher bias and subjectivity in grading are much harder to control with this assessment system than in a short-answer test or when grading is based on right answers with a prescribed answer key.

One author indicates that artifacts or products in the portfolio are not generally scored but rather serve the purpose of allowing students to reflect on their contents as a way to document their academic and literacy growth (Serafina, 2000–2001). Yet another author maintains that portfolios should be assessed using some form of rubric so that both students and teacher can use the assessment results to plan accommodating instructional activities (Popham, 2000). Portfolio conferences could be held at least quarterly but more frequently with low achievers and small class groups (Farr & Farr, 1990). Instead of scoring papers or using a rubric to assess the portfolio products, the teacher may wish to use a narrative, anecdotal procedure. The left portion of Figure 13.1 indicates what students could reveal about their products as they are chosen for portfolio entry, and the right portion suggests what students could write about at the end of a unit or course of study if portfolio evaluation is part of the overall assessment procedure.

---

**BOX 13.3**  How Portfolios Help Students and Teachers

Portfolios have become increasingly popular because they are considered an excellent way for the teacher to get to know the student. They help students see the "big" picture about themselves, heightening their awareness of their own learning. With most portfolios, students are expected to show a variety of skills and the ability to improve performance. Portfolios tell an in-depth story, especially if they are maintained for the entire year and cut across domains or subjects. They may consist of a written autobiography; a statement about the quality of a work; an essay on a particular subject or a series of essays; a special project, paper, or experiment; a series of photographs, drawings, or plans; artwork; a multimedia computer-generated project; or even a video, computer printout, or software developed by the student.

---

### Ongoing Evaluation of Portfolio Products

Student Name: _____ Date: _____

Type of Product: _____

Student Statements

I have chosen this product for my portfolio because




I made this product because




Something special about this product is




This product helped me learn




Teacher Comments






Student's Signature _____

Teacher's Signature _____

---

*Figure* 13.1 Evaluating Portfolios

Evaluation of Portfolio Products at Completion of Theme, Project, Unit, or Term

Student Name: _____ Date: _____

<u>Student Statements</u>

My products for this _____ are special because

My products reveal what I have learned in that

One way my products have changed is

I think my greatest progress has been

With this _____, I tried my best to

For next _____, I will try to

<u>Teacher Comments</u>

Student's Signature _____

Teacher's Signature _____

---

*Figure* 13.1 Continued

# ■ HIGH-STAKES TESTING

**High-stakes tests** are not another form of testing instrument bearing its own criteria. High-stakes tests can appear in the guise of any of the major test procedures presented earlier in this chapter—as norm-referenced, as criterion-referenced, or as performance-based. What makes a high-stakes test unique and what provides the basis of its name is the test consequences. These tests result in outcomes that have significant consequences in the way of rewards or punishments and sanctions for those who take and administer the tests (Gratz, 2000). Students may repeat a grade or not graduate, schools may have funding sources cut off and lose their accreditation, and those who wish to be licensed to teach may not be able to based on the test results. Districts and states have come under increasing pressure from the public to measure student and school **accountability,** and students need to demonstrate that they are achieving academic standards for their grade levels (Overton, 2003).

## The Status of High-Stakes Tests

During the 1990s, the stakes were increased. School districts began to use such tests as the California Achievement Test (CAT) in the lower grades and the Scholastic Aptitude Test (SAT) in the upper grades, as well as other statewide achievement tests, to compare schools and hold teachers and school administrators accountable for the outcomes. State assessments also increased in number and complexity, and an incentive system was tied into the process. Most school districts were either rewarded for improvement with increased allocation of funds and bonuses for teacher salaries or penalized for continuous failure by reductions in funding and even loss of accreditation (Raivetz, 1992; Wilson, 1991). By the year 2000, at least twenty-six states were using state assessment results to ascertain which of their students could graduate, and six states were using the assessments to determine promotion to the next grade (U.S. Department of Education, 2000). Also during 2000, thirteen states had not only linked testing in elementary school with grade promotion but had also instituted options for students to obtain extra instruction in after-school classes or summer school or for retaking the tests (Thernstom, 2000).

To be sure, high-stakes tests are partnered with the states' standards, allowing centralized control to be achieved (Hoffman, Assaf, & Paris, 2001). Although clear and sound standards can reflect high achievement for our nation's youth, they need to be aligned with appropriate assessments (Schmoker & Marzano, 1997). Because the type of assessment plans are left up to the separate states, they can use various types of testing procedures, and one has to look closely at the type of construct being used to determine how students are assessed. For instance, a keynote presenter at a National Association for Supervision and Curriculum Development conference noted that almost all of the states are testing writing not by having students fill in the blanks but by actually asking them to perform by writing, thus getting beyond relying only on multiple-choice formats (Schwartz, 2002). While many states have attempted to use performance-based assessments in their statewide testing programs, due to problems with cost, instructional time, technical quality, problems with connecting large-scale applications to the classroom, and political uneasiness, many states are reverting to using norm-referenced test components (Asp, 2000; Borko & Elliot, 1999). In addition, much of the current performance-based and alternative assessments envisioned in the professional literature have been shown to be unproved and lacking in sound technical standards (Eisner, 1993; Kean, 1992).

The Individuals with Disabilities Education Act (IDEA) was amended in 1997 to allow for the inclusion of students with special needs in statewide testing programs. However, most states weren't able to accommodate such students with special testing procedures (Thurlow, Elliott, & Ysseldyke, 1998). The amendments asked educators to include in the individual educational program (IEP) which students would sit for the statewide tests, which students would need **accommodations** during testing, and which students might need an alternative mode of assessment (Overton, 2003). The Office of Special Education and Rehabilitative Services (2000) notes that the accommodations cannot change the intent of the test (that is, change what the test is seeking to measure). Accommodations can occur in the scheduling, setting, and format of the test and in the way a student responds to the test items. Likewise, for English language learners, accommodations can be made to offset their limited English proficiency. However, for some speakers of other languages learning English (ESOL students), accommodation needs to be tempered by the interpretation of the formal testing and assessment instruments. In some cases, the formal testing often required for students referred for special education services can lead to erroneous conclusions about academic interventions if the student is also a speaker of another language and from another culture (Abrams, Ferguson, & Land, 2001).

## The Controversy of High-Stakes Tests

Promoting a student who cannot read or do math probably does the child no favor in the long run, especially because learning gaps tend to widen over the years. However, critics of high-stakes testing maintain that such testing blames the victim, or that the tests contain a cultural or racial bias, because a disproportionate number of poor and minority students fail these statewide, "gatekeeping" tests. This might be more true if performance assessments are used in state- and districtwide testing programs. Because performance assessments tend to reflect what a district or state wishes to test in a particular context, as in a reading or writing situation, such assessment programs may increase ethnic and gender score differences and be construed as less fair (Herman, 1998).

State and national tests are being used as school "report cards" with the results sent to parents, published in local newspapers, and used to determine school district funding and sometimes for teachers' and administrators' jobs. For instance, Susan Brookhart reports that in her state, Pennsylvania, the major outcome of publishing the schools' achievement scores in reading and math at grades 5, 8, and 11 is the ranking of schools. The ranking, using standards-based scores achieved from a state-developed test, is a norm-referenced function. Thus, in a Sunday edition of the *Pittsburgh Tribune-Review* was the headline "How Your Kids' School Stacks Up" (Brookhart, 2002). In a neighboring state, the *Daily News* headline of July 11, 2002, rang with "60% Fail Math, Reading; City Pupils Flunk Big State Tests" (Williams, 2002). Then the edition published the scores school by school so that readers could see the rankings in each neighborhood of the city, along with a graph of fourth and eighth graders' passing/failing percentages during the four years of the state testing program.

Because the public often concludes from these news reports that high-scoring districts are better than low-scoring districts, it is not surprising that educators and policymakers take serious note of these results. Schools have been caught excluding low-performing students from test taking (possibly labeling them with "special needs" student status), teaching to the test, extending the testing time beyond the limits, and even altering test scores to improve their school's ranking. It is true, however, that according to law, students with special needs have to be accommodated for their specific disabilities during high-stakes assessment.

Local, state, and national testing programs have taken on such importance that high-stakes tests now drive the curriculum, affect the school culture, and become the way the public grades the effectiveness of its schools (Linn, 2000). The current high-stakes testing climate can give way to dysfunctional instruction such as teaching to the tests and emphasizing recall of information and right answers found on standardized tests. The tests are, in essence, becoming the curriculum and in many cases dictating how instruction in literacy occurs (Gunning, 2002; Reutzel & Cooter, 2003). Besides the reduction of curriculum offerings, Popham (2001) notes, the behavior of many test-oppressed teachers is to "drill and kill." This means that teachers relentlessly drill their students on the types of items and tasks found on the high-stakes tests.

What suffers in a "drill and kill" instructional climate are those aspects of the curriculum not tested, such as critical thinking and creativity, as well as written and oral expression (Darling-Hammond, 1991). Two educators note that a favorite assumption of high-stakes testing is that the rewards and punishments attached to the testing results will encourage the unmotivated—usually identified as students from low socioeconomic circumstances in urban schools—to learn and achieve. Yet, they point out, researchers have found that when such rewards and punishments are attached to tests, students actually become less intrinsically motivated to succeed and less likely to think critically about topics that interest them. Furthermore, because control is an issue, teachers firmly take the reins of the instructional tasks and learning experiences, denying students the opportunity to become engaged in their own lifelong learning in school and beyond (Amrein & Berliner, 2003).

The high-stakes testing climate has raised a number of concerns about issues of fairness, loss of instructional time, reliability, and validity. The International Reading Association (1999) notes that it is important to recognize ethical and unethical practices when practicing test-taking skills. Familiarizing students with the test format so that they are familiar with the types of questions and the kinds of responses needed is ethical. Devoting a great deal of instructional time teaching to the test and working with those students who would predictably be most at risk for obtaining low scores while ignoring other students is not ethical.

Two highly respected authors in the field of testing and accountability are vitriolic in their condemnation of high-stakes tests and what they are doing to the teaching–learning process. W. James Popham (2001) feels that unsound high-stakes testing programs are "doing serious educational harm to children" in that children are being immersed in ineffective educational programs (p. 1). Richard Elmore (2002) denounces the school accountability provision announced in the reauthorization of the Elementary and Secondary Education Act of January 2002. The act requires not only annual testing at each grade level but also the breakdown of test scores by students' socioeconomic and racial identities. The federal government additionally identifies a single means—the standardized test—as the way to measure the accountability of schools and its students and requires schools to show progress each year in order to avoid sanctions. Elmore notes that these provisions negate the earlier expansive views of performance-based assessment and constitute "the single largest—and possibly most destructive—federal intrusion into America's public schools" (p. 35).

# TEACHER-MADE TESTS

Teachers are expected to write their own classroom tests. Most of these tests will be subject related, focus on a specific domain of learning, assess whether a subject has been mastered, and indicate when it is time to move on to a new content area. In this context, classroom tests are criterion-referenced measurements, and when they are connected to the curriculum implementation plan they become curriculum-based assessments (Overton, 2003).

Teacher-made tests given at the end of units of instruction are very often a primary way in which students are evaluated in different subject domains. But quizzes are often given as well. Frequent and systematic monitoring of students' work and progress through short quizzes helps teachers improve instruction and learning. Errors serve as early warning signals of learning problems that then can be corrected before they worsen. According to researchers, student effort and achievement improve when teachers provide frequent evaluation and prompt feedback on quizzes (Kubiszyn & Borich, 1999; Wittrock & Baker, 1991). Although quizzes are easy to develop, administer, and grade, thus providing an avenue for multiple and prompt evaluation, they may not provide a deep and rich evaluation of student work.

In spite of limitations, classroom tests still serve important and useful purposes. They provide information related to (1) formulating and refining objectives for each student, (2) deciding on curriculum content, (3) evaluating and refining instructional techniques, and (4) evaluating the degree to which learning outcomes have been achieved.

## Short-Answer and Essay Tests

Most classroom tests fall into two categories: **short-answer tests** (multiple choice, matching, completion, and true/false), sometimes called objective tests, and **essay** (or discussion) **tests.** Short-answer tests require the student to supply a specific and brief answer, usually one or two words; essay tests require the student to organize and express an answer in his or her own words and do not restrict the student to a list of responses. An essay test usually consists of a few questions, each requiring a lengthy answer. A short-answer test consists of many questions, each taking little time to answer. Content sampling and reliability are likely to be superior in short-answer tests. Essay tests provide an opportunity for high-level thinking, including analysis, synthesis, and evaluation. Most short-answer items emphasize low-level thinking or memorization, not advanced cognitive operations.

The quality (reliability, validity, usability) of an objective test depends primarily on the skill of the test constructor, whereas the quality of the essay test depends mainly on the skill of the person grading the test. Short-answer tests take longer to prepare but are easier to grade. Essay tests may be easier to prepare but are difficult to grade. Short-answer items tend to be explicit, with only one correct answer. Essays permit the student to be individualistic and subjective; the answer is open to interpretation, and there is more than one right answer. Short-answer tests are susceptible to guessing and cheating; essay tests are susceptible to bluffing (writing "around" the answer) (Ebel & Frisbie, 1991; Thorndike, 1996).

Short-answer tests include multiple choice, matching, completion, and true/false items. Regardless of the type of objective test, the writing of the test questions or items by the teacher generally involves finding the most appropriate manner in which to pose problems to students. The test questions or items often involve the recall of information, exemplified by knowledge of facts, terms, names, or rules, but they can also involve higher-order cognitive abilities. A number of suggestions should be considered when preparing and writing both short-answer and essay tests, and these are reflected in Tips for Teachers 13.2. See also Box 13.4.

Short-answer questions, no matter how well formulated, cannot measure divergent thinking or subjective or imaginative thought. To learn how a student thinks, attacks a problem, writes, and uses cognitive resources, something beyond the short-answer test is needed. Essay questions, especially when there is no specific right answer, produce evaluation data of considerable value. One test expert, in fact, considers the essay to be "the most authentic type of testing" for middle school students on up through college, and is perhaps the best one for "measuring higher mental processes" (Tuckman, 1991, p. 299).

An entire test composed of essay questions can cover only limited content because only a few questions can be answered in a given period. The essay answer is affected by the student's ability to organize written responses. Many students can comprehend and deal with abstract data but have problems writing or showing that they understand the material in an essay examination. Students may freeze and write only short responses, write in a disjointed fashion, or express only low-level knowledge. One way of helping to alleviate this problem is to discuss in detail how to write an answer to an essay question. Sadly, few teachers take the time to teach students how to write essay exams, often expecting English teachers to perform this task.

On the other hand, some students write well but haven't learned the course content. Their writing ability may conceal their lack of specific knowledge. It is important for the teacher to be able to distinguish irrelevant facts and ideas from relevant information. Even though essay questions appear to be easy to write, careful construction is necessary to test students' cognitive abilities—that is, to write valid questions. See Tips for Teachers 13.2 to consider the advantages and disadvantages of the various types of teacher-made tests.

 **BOX 13.4** The Positive Effect of Short Quizzes and Checkup Tests

Quizzes and "checkup" tests provide an excellent basis for monitoring homework and for evaluating students' progress. Some teachers give unannounced quizzes (or "pop" quizzes) at irregular intervals, especially quizzes related to specific assignments. Others give regular, scheduled quizzes to assess learning over a short period, say a week or two. Quizzes encourage students to keep up with the assignments and demonstrate their strengths and weaknesses in learning. Thus, they provide a means of ongoing assessment to check on the effectiveness of instruction and learning.

# Advantages and Disadvantages of Short-Answer and Essay Questions

Following are the various types of questions you would use for classroom tests and quizzes of content material. You may find the discussion of advantages, disadvantages, and precautions helpful when you plan your question types.

| Question Type | Advantages | Disadvantages | Precautions |
|---|---|---|---|
| Multiple choice | 1. Flexibility in measuring objectives or content.<br>2. Well-constructed items have potential to measure high-level thinking.<br>3. Guessing can be minimized by a built-in penalty.<br>4. Easy to score; little interpretation to count correct responses.<br>5. Requires knowledge of test construction and depends on constructing plausible incorrect answers. | 1. The stem or alternatives are sometimes too long, confusing, or vague.<br>2. A correct answer can sometimes be determined without knowledge of content.<br>3. Susceptible to guessing and eliminating incorrect choices.<br>4. Time consuming to write.<br>5. Sometimes there is more than one possible correct answer. | 1. Write short, parallel stems and alternatives.<br>2. Avoid clues based on longer or shorter alternatives or incorrect grammar.<br>3. Use plausible choices or alternatives.<br>4. Avoid textbook language or direct phrases.<br>5. Be sure there is only one correct answer. |
| Matching | 1. Relatively easy to write and easy to score.<br>2. Well suited to measure associations.<br>3. Amenable to testing a large body of content; many options available.<br>4. Fun for students to take, especially for those who enjoy puzzles.<br>5. Guessing can be minimized by a built-in penalty. | 1. Necessary to use single words or short phrases.<br>2. Cannot be used to assess all types of thinking; lists or individual pieces of information can mainly assess limited situations.<br>3. Directions are sometimes confusing; students are not always told clearly how to respond.<br>4. Harder to write than other short-answer items because all items must fit together and be distinguishable from one another.<br>5. By eliminating choices, last few questions are susceptible to guessing. | 1. Avoid trivia information; avoid textbook language.<br>2. Be sure the choices are parallel; avoid clues within items; avoid additional or modifying words.<br>3. Attend to complete directions and mechanical arrangement of choices.<br>4. Provide consistency in classification of items for each set; place all test items and choices on the same page.<br>5. Provide extra choices, say 6 or 7 per 5 test items; avoid too many choices because of confusion. |

*(continued)*

| Question Type | Advantages | Disadvantages | Precautions |
|---|---|---|---|
| Completion | 1. Easy to write test items.<br>2. Minimal guessing; clues are not given in choices or alternatives.<br>3. Amenable to what, how, where, and how many.<br>4. No distracters, options, or choices to worry about. | 1. Difficult to score.<br>2. Some answers are subjective or open to interpretation.<br>3. Usually measures simple recall or factual information.<br>4. Test items are sometimes confusing or ambiguous; constrained by grammar. | 1. Consider scoring convenience; require short wording.<br>2. Be sure there is only one correct answer.<br>3. Avoid too many blanks, or long sentences, to prevent confusion.<br>4. Keep test items brief; avoid instances in which grammar helps in answering question. |
| True/false | 1. Easiest test items to write; easy to score.<br>2. Comprehensive sampling of objectives or content.<br>3. Guessing can be minimized by a built-in penalty.<br>4. No distracters to worry about; highly reliable and valid items. | 1. Sometimes ambiguous or too broad.<br>2. Simplicity in cognitive demands; measures low-level thinking.<br>3. Susceptible to guessing.<br>4. Dependence on absolute judgments, right or wrong. | 1. Ensure a single correct answer, true or false; avoid "trap" or tricky items.<br>2. Avoid long sentence structure, double negatives or "not," in order to avoid confusion.<br>3. Avoid clues such as absolute terms (*always, never, all*).<br>4. True items are easier to construct than false items; use approximately equal true and false items. |
| Essay | 1. Can show how well students organize thoughts about a topic, support a point of view, and engage in analyzing and hypothesizing ideas.<br>2. Usually easy to write and construct in short amount of time.<br>3. Can use rubric scoring system to provide consistent evaluation criteria. | 1. Takes considerable time to read and evaluate answers.<br>2. Very subjective in scoring.<br>3. Quality of answers is influenced by student's ability to write with appropriate conventions and spellings of written English.<br>4. Limited sampling of content. | 1. With wording such as "explain," "discuss," and "examine," students can tell their thoughts about a topic. Using "why," "how," and "what consequences" wording allows students to show knowledge and concepts of subject matter but also requires analysis, inferences, and showing cause-and-effect relations. |

*(continued)*

| Question Type | Advantages | Disadvantages | Precautions |
|---|---|---|---|
| Essay | 4. Can provide a choice of questions so that students choose to write those essay answers that best show their knowledge of the whole. | 5. Students may need extended time to complete answers. | 2. The more specific and restricted the questions, the less ambiguous the answer, allowing for less subjectivity in scoring.<br>3. May need to spend time showing students how to formulate essay answer, e.g., use of topic sentence, elaborating with content, etc. |

# ■ COMMUNICATING TEST RESULTS

One way to improve test-taking skills is to review tests promptly after they have been administered and scored. In this way, evaluation of test results helps to enhance future test-wiseness. As the papers are returned, the teacher should make some general comments to the class about the group effort, level of achievement, and general problems or specific areas of the test that gave students trouble.

Each question on the test should be discussed in class, with particular detail given to questions that many students missed. If the missed test items are fundamental for mastery, then the teacher should take extra time to explain the material and provide similar but different exercises for students to review. Some teachers call on volunteers to redo and explain parts of the test that were missed, although this method may not always be the most profitable use of time.

## Keeping Parents Informed

Keeping parents informed of their children's progress and ability to perform well on district and state assessments is a vital aspect of schooling today. Parents are major **stakeholders** in their children's benchmark performances at particular grade levels because those children who fall below the established state criteria for language arts, mathematics, or content subject mastery usually need to do something extra to catch up with their peers. This means that these children may need to repeat a grade, attend summer school, or receive early morning, after-school, or weekend tutorial help. All of these extras may affect a family's lifestyle because accommodations may need to be made with the schedules of other siblings or the wage earner(s). Although most parents welcome the extra support and consideration for their children who are achieving below state standards, just as many parents would prefer to keep their children up to standards in the first place and may wish to intervene earlier if they know their child needs extra help.

The importance of parent involvement in their children's education and literacy development is well documented (Smith & Elish-Piper, 2002). How the teacher can help parents improve their children's academic work and behavior is often a major concern among parents and teachers alike. According to Joyce Epstein (1986; Epstein & Dauber, 1991), more than 85 percent of parents spend fifteen minutes or more a day helping their child at home when asked to do so by the teacher. Parents claim they can spend more time, forty minutes on the average, if they are told specifically how to help. Yet fewer than 25 percent receive systematic requests and directions from teachers to assist their children with specific skills and subjects. Epstein (1987, 1988) further notes that parents become involved most often with reading activities at the lower grades: reading to the child or listening to the child read, taking the child to the library, and helping with teaching materials brought home from school for practice at home. Parents of older students (grade 4 and above) become more involved with specific homework and subject-related activities. Based on a review of research regarding the kinds of recommendations made to parents of struggling readers, one author indicates that parents who have the greatest impact are those who provide enjoyable, flexible, and relaxed experiences with reading sources rather than those who provide tightly directed tutoring with an excessive focus on skills development (Baker, 2003).

Parental involvement in school matters is considerable at the elementary school level, less at the middle school or junior high level, and least at the high school level. Research also shows that children have an advantage in school when their parents support, participate, and communicate on a regular basis with school officials (Comer & Haynes, 1991; Henderson, 1988; Vandegrift & Greene, 1992). In one school with low high-stakes test scores, teachers showed parents how to use practice sheets at home to improve their children's test-taking skills. Over a three-year period, third graders improved from 77 percent reaching the state criterion level (known as the State Reference Point) to 95 percent scoring above that point (Berendt & Koski, 1999).

# ■ USING TESTS TO INFORM INSTRUCTIONAL DECISIONS

Throughout this book, we have examined and supported the principles of sound curriculum design. A sound design calls for one in which assessment and student evaluation coordinate with the instructional objectives or content standards of a school, district, or state. It's what Judy Carr and Douglas Harris (2001) mean when they say that assessment has to be an integral aspect of instruction and that standards-based assessment has to inform teaching and improve learning. Other authors have urged teachers and schools to focus on the "big ideas with judicious review" (Kameenui & Carnine, 1998), on "valued performances" (Wolf & White, 2000), or on "enduring understandings" (Wiggins & McTighe, 1998) when evaluating students to ascertain what they have mastered and learned.

Popham (2001) offers the notion of "properly constructed" tests that significantly highlight the instructional decisions teachers have to make. He urges that teachers create tests that will improve and not denigrate instructional quality and make use of testing procedures that assess learning of great significance. He presents the following four rules for educators at all levels of the teaching profession to consider when planning for classroom assessments:

- Use a modest number of tests, and tests that assess learner outcomes of great importance.
- Use different types of classroom assessments to gain a clear idea of what students can do and the outcomes they can achieve.
- Use the feedback gained from classroom assessments to influence instructional decisions such as if students need additional help.
- Besides testing of content mastery, regularly assess students' affect. This means assessing student interests and attitudes regarding what and how they learn through the various content disciplines and their confidence in their ability to use the major literary skills related to written and oral communication.

As an educator, the overriding reasons for using tests should be to integrate your instruction and assessment, measure and determine whether the important knowledge and skills of the subject you are teaching have been learned, and promote the development of human talent. Tests should be used as a tool, not as a weapon. Test content should not be taught; rather, it is considered appropriate to make students test wise and to take small amounts of time teaching students how to respond to sample test items.

Test reporting to consumers—both students and parents—is expected. Providing appropriate information about what the scores mean and how to interpret the scores should be part of the reporting process. Parents should also receive information about how they can help their children improve their skills and study habits for test taking. The future of students—including whether they graduate or go on to institutes of higher learning—should not hinge on a single test but on a host of information. Decisions about test scores should be made in the context of multiple sources of information. In addition to weighing all these factors, it helps as a teacher to remember your own days as a student, your own test anxieties, and the ways test scores were used to make decisions about you. With those experiences in mind, you are likely to exercise a little more compassion and caution as you assess your own students.

## ■ SUMMARY ■

1. There are two major types of published formal tests: norm referenced and criterion referenced. Norm-referenced tests measure how a student performs relative to other students. Criterion-referenced tests measure a student's progress and appraise his or her ability relative to a specific criterion.

2. For general appraisal of an individual's performance or behavior, the standardized (norm-referenced) test is an excellent instrument. There are two basic types of standardized tests used by educators: aptitude tests, which are given to predict how students will perform in the future, and achievement tests, which tell how well students have performed in academic areas.

3. Authentic assessment is an informal type of assessment that is given to determine how students actually perform or process information during a real (authentic) or contrived learning experience.

4. Authentic or performance-based assessments can occur as teachers use observations, checklists, anecdotal notes, and rubrics or scoring scales. These informal assessments can be used with students' oral presentations, research and group projects, essays or reports, scientific experiments, exhibits, journals, or portfolios.

5. High-stakes tests are administered by states and districts to measure student and school accountability. The results of these tests present "high stakes" to the various school community stakeholders, the major ones being the administrators, the teachers, the students, and the parents.

6. Teacher-made tests may be short-answer tests or essay tests. Short-answer questions include multiple choice, matching, completion, and true/false. Essay or free-response questions also include discussion questions.

7. Proper test administration reduces confusion, curtails student anxieties, and motivates and helps them do as well as possible. Important test-taking skills can be taught to students, and one way to improve their skills is to review tests promptly after they have been scored and evaluated by the teacher.

8. Sources of information for evaluation in addition to teacher-made tests and quizzes include classroom discussion and activity, homework, notebooks, reports, research papers, student journals, peer evaluations, and portfolios.

## ■ QUESTIONS TO CONSIDER ■

1. Why is it necessary for the test administrator of a standardized test to adhere strictly to the specific directions for administration, scoring, and interpretation as indicated in the testing manual?

2. What are the advantages and disadvantages associated with standardized, norm-referenced tests?

3. How would you use the test criteria of reliability, validity, and usability in your selection of a standardized test?

4. In what way did the emergence of the criterion-referenced test herald a new way of assessing and evaluating students? How is the criterion-referenced construct different from that of the norm-referenced construct?

5. What is the underlying basis of authentic assessment and why is this form of assessment useful to the teacher?

6. Can you describe some types of authentic assessments? How would feedback from the teacher after the student has been evaluated on his or her performance assist the student in learning?

7. Why are high-stakes tests important to all members of the educational community?

8. What does it mean when we say that a student needs accommodation during state or district high-stakes assessment?

9. What are the various types of teacher-made tests and what are the advantages and disadvantages of each type?

10. Why is it so important to communicate test results to both students and parents?

## ■ THINGS TO DO ■

1. Display the two sets of terms—*formal tests* and *informal tests*. Form your class into groups and have them list the kinds and features of both kinds of tests. Turn the discussion to the advantages, disadvantages, and reasons for using each type.

2. Either as a whole class or in groups, ask your students to devise performance assessments for authentic or contrived learning experiences. Students could list under experiences the types of learning encounters they wished to assess, such as written reports, oral recitations, understanding of topics or themes, etc. Then under a second column entitled "Type of Assessment," students would relate the kind of authentic or performance-based tool they would use to as-

sess the learning. Under a third column, they could tell how that assessment tool best manages to test a student's proficiency with that learning experience.

3. Using a rubric such as the one discussed in this chapter, show your students how to evaluate school-age children's written papers. You could do this by having samples of children's written work brought into class, copied onto transparency paper, and projected via the overhead. All of your students would need to have a copy of the rubric in front of them as they read and evaluate a child's paper. In the discussion that follows of why a particular rating or numerical score was given for a quality of writing, your students will achieve greater understanding of the qualities of writing and how to evaluate them equitably.

4. Have your class discuss the products that students could choose to include in their portfolios and then the ways that teachers could evaluate these products and the portfolio itself.

5. Form your class into groups of three for role-playing purposes. One student will assume the role of teacher, one of parent, and one of a school-age student. They all have to react to the scenario that the child failed or fell below acceptable criteria on the states high-stakes testing program. Have them role-play what this situation has brought to each of their lives and how each could contribute to make the child succeed the next time.

## ■ RECOMMENDED READINGS ■

Carr, Judy, and Douglas Harris. *Succeeding with Standards: Linking Curriculum Assessment and Action Planning.* Alexandria, VA: Association for Supervision and Curriculum Development, 2001. A book showing how assessment has been linked to instruction and state standards.

Gage, N. L., and David C. Berliner. *Educational Psychology,* 6th ed. Boston: Houghton Mifflin, 1998. A long-standing book describing measurement practices and the constructs of various types of tests.

Gronlund, Norman. *Assessment of Student Achievement,* 6th ed. Boston: Allyn and Bacon, 1998. A clear discussion of the advantages and disadvantages of various tests and evaluation procedures.

Gunning, Thomas. *Assessing and Correcting Reading and Writing Difficulties,* 2nd ed. Boston: Allyn and Bacon, 2002. Presents many informal procedures to use in reading and writing assessments.

Lissitz, Robert W., and William D. Schafer, eds. *Assessment in Educational Reform: Both Means and Ends.* Boston: Allyn and Bacon, 2002. An edited book with good chapters on the state of assessment at the beginning of the twenty-first century and the problems the states and the public are encountering with high-stakes testing.

Overton, Terry. *Assessing Learners with Special Needs: An Applied Approach,* 4th ed. Upper Saddle River, NJ: Merrill/Prentice Hall, 2003. Presents a thorough discussion of the ways to assess and the problems to overcome when testing learners with special needs.

Popham, W. James. *The Truth about Testing: An Educator's Call to Action.* Alexandria, VA: Association for Supervision and Curriculum Development, 2001. With years of accumulated wisdom, the author urges educators at all levels to understand the pitfalls of high-stakes testing and presents four thoughtful guidelines to test makers and to teachers when constructing, using, and evaluating results from tests.

## ■ KEY TERMS ■

accommodations
accountability

achievement tests
aptitude tests

authentic assessment
benchmark

criterion-referenced tests
essay tests
formal assessment
grade-equivalent score
high-stakes test
holistic scoring
informal assessment
inquiry

normal curve
norm-referenced tests
percentile rank
performance assessment
portfolio
raw score
reliability
rubric

scaled score
short-answer tests
stakeholders
standardized tests
stanine
usability
validity

## ■ REFERENCES ■

Abrams, J., Ferguson, J., & Laud, L. (2001, November). Assessing ESOL students. *Educational Leadership,* 62–65.

Amrein, A., & Berliner, D. (2003, February). A research report: The effects of high-stakes testing on student motivation and learning. *Educational Leadership,* 32–38.

Andrade, H. G. (2000, February). Using rubrics to promote thinking and learning. *Educational Leadership,* 13–18.

Arter, J. A., & Spandel, V. (1992, Spring). Using portfolios of student work in instruction and assessment. *Educational Measurement,* 36–44.

Asp, E. (2000). Assessment in education: Where have we been? Where are we headed? In R. S. Brandt (Ed.), *Education in a new era: ASCD yearbook 2000* (pp. 123–157). Alexandria, VA: Association for Supervision and Curriculum Development.

Baker, L. (2003, January/February). The role of parents in motivating struggling readers. *Reading & Writing Quarterly,* 87–106.

Bartz, D., Anderson-Robinson, S., & Hillman, L. (1994, January). Performance assessment: Make them show what they know. *Principal,* 11–14.

Berendt, P., & Koski, B. (1999, March). No shortcuts to success. *Educational Leadership,* 45–47.

Bonty, J. L., & Everts-Danielson, K. (1992, January/February). Alternative assessment and feedback in methods courses. *Clearing House,* 186–190.

Borko, H., & Elliot, R. (1999, June). Hands-on pedagogy versus hands-off accountability: Completing commitments for exemplary math teachers in Kentucky. *Phi Delta Kappan,* 394–400.

Brookhart, S. (2002). What will teachers know about assessment, and how will that improve instruction? In R. W. Lissitz & W. D. Schafer (Eds.), *Assessment in educational reform: Both means and ends* (pp. 2–17). Boston: Allyn and Bacon.

Bushweller, K. (1997, September). Teach to the test. *The American School Board Journal,* 20–25.

Carr, J., & Harris, D. (2001). *Succeeding with standards: Linking curriculum assessment and action planning.* Alexandria, VA: Association for Supervision and Curriculum Development.

Cizek, G. J., & Rachor, R. E. (1994, March). The real testing bias. *NASSP Bulletin,* 83–92.

Comer, J. P., & Haynes, N. M. (1991, January). Parent involvement in schools. *Elementary School Journal,* 271–277.

Darling-Hammond, L. D. (1991, November). The implications of testing policy for quality and equality. *Phi Delta Kappan,* 220–225.

Ebel, R. L., & Frisbie, D. A. (1991). *Essentials of educational measurement* (5th ed.). Boston: Allyn and Bacon.

Eisner, E. W. (1993, February). Why standards may not improve schools. *Educational Leadership,* 22–23.

Elmore, R. (2002, September/October). Testing trap. *Harvard Magazine,* 35–41.

Epstein, J. (1987, February). Parent involvement: What research says to administrators. *Education and Urban Society,* 119–136.

Epstein, J. (1988, Winter). How do we improve programs for parent involvement? *Educational Horizons,* 58–59.

Epstein, J. L. (1986, January). Parents' reactions to teacher practices of parent involvement. *Elementary School Journal,* 277–294.

Epstein, J., & Dauber, S. L. (1991, January). School programs and teacher practices of parent involvement in inner-city elementary and middle schools. *Elementary School Journal,* 289–305.

Farr, R., & Farr, B. (1990). *Integrated assessment system.* San Antonio, TX: Psychological Corporation.

Farr, R., & Tone, B. (1997). *Portfolio and performance assessments.* Fort Worth, TX: Harcourt Brace.

Frazier, D. M., & Paulson, F. L. (1992, May). How portfolios motivate reluctant workers. *Educational Leadership,* 62–65.

Gage, N. L., & Berliner, D. C. (1998). *Educational psychology* (6th ed.) Boston: Houghton Mifflin.

Glatthorn, A. (1998). *Performance assessment and standards-based curricula: The achievement cycle.* Larchmont, NY: Eye on Education.

Gratz, D. (2000, May). High standards for whom? *Phi Delta Kappan,* 681–687.

Greenwald, E. A., Persky, H. R., Campbell, J. R., & Mazzeo, J. (1999). *NAEP 1998 writing report card for the nation and the states.* Washington, DC: U.S. Department of Education.

Gronlund, N. (1998). *Assessment of student achievement* (6th ed.). Boston: Allyn and Bacon.

Gronlund, N. E., & Linn, R. L. (1990). *Measurement and evaluation in teaching* (6th ed.). New York: Macmillan.

Guastello, E. F., & Sinatra, R. (2001, Spring). Improving students' oral presentation skills through the use of technology and multimedia. *The Language and Literacy Spectrum,* 5–17.

Gunning, T. (2002). *Assessing and correcting reading and writing difficulties* (2nd ed.). Boston: Allyn and Bacon.

Hambleton, R. K., Swaminathan, H., Algina, J., & Coulson, D. B. (1988, Winter). Criterion-referenced testing and measurement: A review of technical issues and developments. *Review of Educational Research,* 1–47.

Henderson, A. T. (1988, Winter). An ecologically balanced approach to academic improvement. *Educational Horizons,* 60–62.

Herbert, E. A. (1992, May). Portfolios invite reflection from students and staff. *Educational Leadership,* 58–61.

Herman, J. L. (1998, December). The state of performance assessments. *The School Administrator,* 17–22.

Herman, J. L., Aschbacher, P. R., & Winters, L. (1992). *A practical guide to alternative assessment.* Alexandria, VA: Association for Supervision and Curriculum Development.

Hoffman, J., Assaf, L. C., & Paris, S. (2001, February). High-stakes testing in reading: Today in Texas, tomorrow? *The Reading Teacher,* 482–492.

Hymes, D. L., Chafin, A. E., & Gondes, P. (1991). *The changing face of testing and assessment.* Arlington, VA: American Association of School Administrators.

International Reading Association. (1999). *High stakes assessments in reading: A position statement of the International Reading Association.* Newark, DE: Author.

Johnson, D. W., & Johnson, R. J. (1999). *Learning together and alone* (5th ed.). Boston: Allyn and Bacon.

Kameenui, E. J., & Carnine, D. W. (1998). *Effective teaching strategies that accommodate diverse learners.* Upper Saddle River, NJ: Merrill.

Kean, M. H. (1992, September). Targeting education and missing the schools: A consideration of national standards. *NASSP Bulletin,* 17–22.

Kubiszyn, T., & Borich, G. (1999). *Educational testing and measurement* (6th ed.). New York: HarperCollins.

Linn, R. (1986, October). Educational testing and assessment. *American Psychologist,* 1153–1160.

Linn, R. (2000, March). Assessments and accountability. *Educational Researcher,* 4–15.

Mithaug, D. (2002, September/October). "Yes" means success: Teaching children with multiple disabilities to self-regulate during independent work. *Teaching Exceptional Children,* 22–27.

National Council of Teachers of English and International Reading Association. (1996). *Standards for the English language arts.* Urbana, IL: Author.

Office of Special Education and Rehabilitative Services. (2000). *Questions and answers about provisions in the Individuals with Disabilities Education Act amendments of 1997 related to students with disabilities and state and district wide assessments.* Washington, DC: Author.

O'Neil, J. (1992, May). Putting performance assessment to the test. *Educational Leadership,* 14–19.

O'Neill, J. (2000, February). Smart goals, smart schools. *Educational Leadership,* 46–50.

Ornstein, A. C. (1994, January). Assessing without testing. *Elementary Principal,* 16–18.

Ornstein, A. C., & Gilman, D. A. (1991, Summer). The striking contrasts between norm-reference and criterion-reference tests. *Contemporary Education,* 287–293.

Overton, T. (2003). *Assessing learners with special needs: An applied approach* (4th ed.). Upper Saddle River, NJ: Merrill/Prentice Hall.

Popham, W. J. (1992, Summer). A tale of two test-specification strategies. *Educational Measurement,* 16–17.

Popham, W. J. (1999, March). Why standardized tests don't meassure educational quality. *Educational Leadership,* 8–15.

Popham, W. J. (2000). *Modern educational measurement: Practical guidelines for educational leaders.* Boston: Allyn and Bacon.

Popham, W. J. (2001). *The truth about testing: An educator's call to action.* Alexandria, VA: Association for Supervision and Curriculum Development.

Raivetz, M. J. (1992, September). Can school districts survive the politics of state testing initiatives? *NASSP Bulletin,* 57–65.

Reutzel, D. R., & Cooter, R. Jr. (2003). *Strategies for reading assessment and instruction: Helping every child succeed* (2nd ed.). Upper Saddle River, NJ: Merrill/Prentice Hall.

Richek, M., Caldwell, J., Hennings, J., & Lerner, J. (2000). *Reading problems: Assessment and teaching strategies* (4th ed.). Boston: Allyn and Bacon.

Rothman, R. (1996, February). Taking aim at testing. *The American School Board Journal,* 27–30.

Schmoker, M., & Marzano, R. (1999, March). Realizing the promise of standards-based education. *Educational Leadership,* 17–21.

Schwartz, R. (2002, January). The status of standards. *Education Update: Conference Report,* 1, 6.

Serafini, F. (2000–2001, December/January). Three paradigms of assessment: Measurement, procedure, and inquiry. *The Reading Teacher,* 384–393.

Sikorski, M. F., Niemiec, R. P., & Walberg, H. (1994, April). Best teaching practices. *NASSP Bulletin,* 50–54.

Slavin, R. (2003, February). A reader's guide to scientifically based research. *Educational Leadership,* 12–16.

Smith, M. C., & Elish-Piper, L. (2002, October). Primary-grade educators and adult literacy: Some strategies for assisting low-literate parents. *The Reading Teacher,* 156–165.

Sperling, D. (1993, February). What's worth an "A"? Setting standards together. *Educational Leadership,* 73–75.

Spinelli, C. (2002). *Classroom assessment for students with special needs in inclusive settings.* Upper Saddle River, NJ: Merrill/Prentice Hall.

Steinberg, R. J. (1990, Summer). T & T is an explosive combination: Technology and testing. *Educational Psychologist,* 201–222.

Stiggins, R. (2002). Where is our assessment future and how can we get there from here? In R. Lissitz & W. D. Schafer (Eds.), *Assessment in educational reform* (pp. 18–48). Boston: Allyn and Bacon.

Taylor, K., & Walton, S. (1997, September). Coopting standardized testing in the service of learning. *Phi Delta Kappan,* 66–70.

Thernstom, A. (2000, September 11). Testing and its enemies. *National Review,* 38–41.

Thorndike, R. M. (1996). *Measurement and evaluation in psychology and education* (6th ed.). Upper Saddle River, NJ: Prentice Hall.

Thurlow, M., Elliott, J., & Ysseldyke, J. (1998). *Testing students with disabilities: Practical strategies for complying with district and state requirements.* Thousand Oaks, CA: Corwin Press.

Tierney, R. (1998, February). Literacy assessment reform: Shifting beliefs, principled possibilities, and emerging practices. *The Reading Teacher,* 374–390.

Tuckman, B. W. (1991, Summer). Evaluating the alternative to multiple-choice testing for teachers. *Contemporary Education,* 299–300.

U.S. Department of Education. (2000). *The use of tests when making high-stakes decisions for students: A resource guide for educators and policymakers.* Washington, DC: Author.

U.S. Office of Technology Assessment. (1992, February). *Testing in American schools: Asking the right questions.* Washington, DC: U.S. Government Printing Office.

Vandegrift, J. A., & Greene, A. L. (1992, September). Rethinking parent involvement. *Educational Leadership*, 57–59.

Venn, J. J. (2000). *Assessing students with special needs* (2nd ed.). Upper Saddle River, NJ: Merrill/Prentice Hall.

Walberg, H. J. (1985, April). Homework's powerful effects on learning. *Educational Leadership*, 75–79.

Wiggins, G. (1992, May). Creating tests worth taking. *Educational Leadership*, 26–34.

Wiggins, G., & McTighe, J. (1998). *Understanding by design*. Alexandria, VA: Association for Supervision and Curriculum Development.

Williams, J. (2002, July 11). City pupils flunk big state tests. *Daily News,* 9.

Wilson, V. L. (1991, Summer). Performance assessment, psychometric theory and cognitive learning. *Contemporary Education,* 250–254.

Wineberg, S. (1997, September). T.S. Eliot, collaboration and the quandries of assessment in a rapidly changing world. *Phi Delta Kappan,* 59–65.

Wittrock, M. C., & Baker, E. L. (1991). *Testing and cognition.* Upper Saddle River, NJ: Prentice Hall.

Wolf, D. P., & White, A. M. (2000, March). Charting the course of student growth. *Educational Leadership,* 6–11.